W9-ARE-769

DISCOVE

Reading, Writin
Thinking in t
Academic Disci

DISCOVERY

Reading, Writing, and Thinking in the Academic Disciplines

Linda R. Robertson

Hobart and William Smith Colleges
Geneva, New York

DOWNS-JONES LIBRARY
HUSTON-TILLOTSON COLLEGE

Holt, Rinehart and Winston, Inc.
New York   Chicago   San Francisco   Philadelphia
Montreal   Toronto   London   Sydney   Tokyo

PE1417
R58
1988

Editor-in-Chief   Ted Buchholz
Senior Acquisitions Editor   Charlyce Jones Owen
Senior Project Manager   Sondra Greenfield
Production Manager   Annette Mayeski
Design Supervisor   Gloria Gentile
Text Design   Nancy Sugihara
Cover Photograph   Courtesy of Erving and Joyce Wolfe

Library of Congress Cataloging-in-Publication Data

Robertson, Linda R. (Linda Raine), date
  Discovery : reading, writing, and thinking in the
academic disciplines / Linda R. Robertson.
    p.   cm.
  Includes index.
  1. College readers.   2. English language—Rhetoric.
3. Interdisciplinary approach in education.   I. Title.
PE1417.R58 1988
808′ .0427—dc19   87-32135

ISBN 0-03-007313-8

Copyright © 1988 Holt, Rinehart and Winston, Inc.
All rights reserved. No part of this publication may be
reproduced or transmitted in any form or by any means,
electronic or mechanical, including photocopy, recording,
or any information storage and retrieval system, without
permission in writing from the publisher.

Requests for permission to make copies of any part of the
work should be mailed to:
Permissions
Holt, Rinehart and Winston, Inc.
111 Fifth Avenue
New York, NY 10003

Printed in the United States of America
8 9 0 1 016 9 8 7 6 5 4 3 2 1

Holt, Rinehart and Winston, Inc.
The Dryden Press
Saunders College Publishing

Copyright acknowledgments begin on page 605.

Preface

The Attractions of Writing Across the Curriculum

Since you have this book in hand, you must have been thinking about the advantages of making clear to students that what is taught in a composition classroom is intended to help them meet the challenges of writing in their other college classes. College composition teachers have intended to teach that all along, of course, but it takes little experience to realize how unaware students often are of it. I remember once discussing with students how to prepare for an essay exam. I made what I thought was the offhanded comment that what I was saying applied generally to all of the essay exams students might take, just as what we studied about writing applied generally to college-level writing. After class a student, eyes wide with excitement, thanked me effusively for having said it. He said he had not realized it and it was something he needed to know. The semester was almost over. This book is intended to make that point clear to students from the start.

One of the special dividends realized from clearly connecting composition instruction with the curriculum in general is that the composition teacher can assume the role of a special adviser or ally to the student. As you use this book, you will find you present descriptive writing—to take one example—in the contexts of both the humanities and the observational sciences. Composition courses have traditionally encouraged students to describe the sensory world, but it is not always easy to help them understand why that is expected. I think you will discover that when this expectation is placed in the context of the various academic disciplines, explaining it is simply easier.

The Organization of the Textbook

Teaching the discourse of higher education requires integrating a number of different elements:

The writing process;
The modes of discovery;

81096

Critical reading;

The discourse conventions of the academic disciplines; and

The assumptions essential to higher learning.

The organization of *Discovery* is intended to clarify each of the elements and to illustrate that they are ultimately interrelated and inseparable.

Part I: Foundations

Chapter 1 introduces students to the basic assumptions underlying thinking and writing in the academic disciplines and introduces them to the writing process. Chapter 2 considers the reader's influence on the writer, especially the care a student must take to be sure he or she understands an assignment. Chapter 3 considers the fundamental importance of learning to question as part of the writing and thinking processes.

Part II: Modes of Discovery

Part II introduces students to the modes of discovery and the discourse conventions used by the academic disciplines. Students are introduced to these discourse conventions:

Assigning significance to experience;

Presenting findings that test a hypothesis; and

Solving a problem.

These are the modes of thinking or discovery needed to meet the demands implied by these conventions:

Drawing generalizations;

Assigning cause;

Reasoning by analogy;

Reasoning about the significance of an action, event, or behavior;

Testing a hypothesis;

Identifying a writer's arguments;

Comparing writers' arguments;

Evaluating arguments; and

Taking a position in relation to other writers' arguments.

Chapter 4 introduces students to argument and evidence. Students are introduced to the three elements characteristic of all argument:

1. *The given:* an assumption that the writer asks the reader to accept;
2. *The position or conclusion:* the position the writer takes in relation to the given; and
3. *The reasons:* the reasons the writer offers in support of the position.

The chapter also introduces students to the common forms of evidence: authoritative opinion, statistics, testimony, example, and precedent.

Chapters 5 through 11 are concerned with applying the modes of discovery to what can be observed directly. Chapters 12 through 21 turn from direct observation to the study and analysis of arguments.

Part III: The Writing Process

The chapters in Part III examine particular aspects of the writing process. Chapters 22 to 25 deal with the specifics of preliminary writing. Chapters 26 and 27 discuss aspects of drafting and revision: Chapter 26 discusses the ways in which writers transform notes into public discourse, and Chapter 27 discusses the revision process. Chapters 28 and 29 consider what editing and proofreading entail. Chapter 30 takes up something not usually considered in discussions of the writing process: the ultimate response of the reader. It discusses grading and evaluation in college.

Part IV: The Anthology

All of the readings included in the Anthology illustrate principles raised in the chapters and are directly related to the assignments. The readings are divided into four sections: The Writing Process; Assigning Significance to Experience; Presenting Observations; Testing a Hypothesis; and Summarizing, Comparing, and Evaluating Arguments. The readings include examples of student writing.

Integrating the Text: The Writing Process and the Process of Discovery

There are some obvious ways in which the readings are integrated with the text; for example, Chapter 30 discusses how grades are assigned in college and the Anthology includes essays written by two undergraduates, followed by the professors' comments on each. As another example, Chapter 26 discusses how writers move from what they have written in their notes to public discourse and the Anthology includes examples of writers' notes and the final, published works.

This text integrates reading, writing, and thinking in another way as well. Let me illustrate by suggesting one way in which you can use Chapters 6 to 10, which deal with direct observation. Chapter 6, "The Participant-Observer," illustrates the ways in which fieldworkers adapt the writing process to their process of discovery and includes comments by fieldworkers. One assignment asks students to write a proposal that tells how they will test an assumption by direct observation. They are directed to readings in the Anthology that are intended to stimulate their thinking and help them understand the challenges fieldworkers face. Some of these are reports on observations written by other undergraduates.

Chapter 7, "Learning to Observe," offers several assignments. One is directed to students who are working on testing an assumption; that is, who are working on the assignment given in Chapter 6. Chapter 7 introduces some of the special problems attendant on observation. Students are also referred to readings that illustrate how fieldworkers take notes. Chapter 8, "Describing Recollections," also includes an assignment designed for students who are testing an assumption. It discusses techniques used to present description and directs students to readings that illustrate them. It also refers students to Chapter 26, "From Journal to Public Discourse," to help them understand that part of the writing process. And, as indicated above, that chapter directs students to readings that compare a writer's notes to the final product. Chapter 9, "Presenting Your Findings: Inductive Generalizations," directs students to readings that illustrate the conventions of presenting this kind of discourse. It also directs them to Chapter 27, which discussses how a student revised a paper on observations and why. The draft and final version are included in the Anthology.

I think these examples illustrate the design of the book. The aim throughout is to:

Illustrate the connection between reading, the writing process, and the process of discovery;

Offer instruction when students can clearly understand that it is pertinent to the particular aspect of the writing and thinking processes in which they are engaged; and

Give teachers the opportunity to extend an assignment over several chapters to illustrate that writing and thinking *are* processes.

Exercises and Assignments

One other feature of this book illustrates the effort to offer instruction when students can understand the relevance and to provide clear indications of why revision is important. Most chapters begin with an exercise or assignment that is intended to alert students to the content of the chapter, to raise some questions in their minds, and to help them understand why the discussion might be of use to them. Most chapters end with an assignment that asks students to return to that preliminary assignment and to revise it in light of the discussion.

From the discussion above, you can gather that much of this textbook is integrated in a way that means that chapters and assignments refer to other chapters and assignments. This can be a liability if the interrelationship is so close that you, as the teacher, cannot shape the sequence of chapters and assignments in a way that is comfortable for you. There are separate chapters on each aspect of the writing process, so that you can choose either to follow the sequence of the textbook or put together chapters and readings in a different way. Similarly, you may not wish to extend assignments over several chapters or to tie an assignment to required readings. Each chapter includes assignments that can be completed in about a week and that do not necessarily require reading.

Your Role

One of the problems facing those of us who wish to connect composition with academic discourse is that we are not "specialists" in any field other than our own. Every effort has been made not to put the teacher in a position of pretending to a false authority or expertise. The aim has been to place what we know how to do best in the larger context of what is expected of students writing in college.

If you look at Chapter 5, "Signs," for instance, you will see that it introduces students to what we have been teaching for a long time: the essay of personal experience. But the discussion places that interest in the larger context of higher education, illustrating that much of what students read is discourse that assigns significance and that the writing of it can take many forms. The chapters that ask students to test an assumption by direct observation place "description" and "narration" in the context of the kind of thinking and writing done in the observational sciences, while the chapters on discovering, evaluating, and responding to arguments discusses another kind of discourse—argumentative—and places it in the context of a variety of academic disciplines, both in the humanities and the observational sciences.

Most teachers of composition will want to know whether this book is compatible with their own interests and with the abilities of their students. This introduction has been an effort to help you evaluate this book. Naturally, I hope that you will take the time to read the book to see how it works. I've discussed some of the connections, but you may find it useful to read the chapters on summarizing and evaluating arguments to see how they work together.

I hope you enjoy using this text, and I hope it gives you a way to help students discover the academic disciplines and the ways by which writing gives them access to the various kinds of discovering.

Acknowledgments

Whatever merit *Discovery* may have comes as a result of the considerable support and guidance I have received from others.

Let me first acknowledge the institutional support I have received. This textbook was begun at The Wichita State University, Wichita, Kansas. A grant of released time permitted me to begin writing, and the resources of the Wichita State University library were invaluable. The textbook was completed at Hobart and William Smith Colleges, Geneva, New York, which have provided me significant support in the form of outright grants-in-aid to pay for editorial and secretarial assistants. The reference librarians here have also been most helpful.

I am deeply indebted to many colleagues. I wish especially to thank those at The Wichita State University who provided intellectual guidance and emotional support during the early stages of writing: Don Blakeslee (Anthropology), Al Gossman (Engineering), Sally Kitch (Women's Studies), Carol Konek (Associate Dean and Women's Studies), Sue Nelson (English), Carole Robarchek (Anthropology), Clayton Robarchek (Anthropology), and especially Kathleen Mellor, Foreign Languages Coordinator for the Wichita Public Schools. If you are a writer, you know that the luckiest of writers is one with the sorts of friends who encourage by exaggerated compliments, cajoling, and nagging. I have been especially blessed in having such friends. Some among them have also provided me with material for this text. Carole and Clay Robarchek made an especially valuable contribution by giving me permission to use their field notes from observations undertaken in Malaysia; Don Blakeslee has permitted me to use a draft of an edited manuscript.

I have also been lucky enough to have had good writing teachers, although I have never taken a class from them, nor have they read this text. I am especially indebted in this regard to Bill Coles. He has taught me what to aim for. Donald Murray has taught me not to be afraid to aim for it. They may well be unaware of how much I think of myself as in their debt. James Reither gave me the idea for the grading "reading around" included in this text by introducing participants at the Wyoming Conference to what he calls "inkshedding," a way of reading and writing together that involves both independent expression and collaborative judgment of what has been written.

I have also been lucky enough to have worked with students who have taught me what I know about teaching writing. Students at both The Wichita State University and Hobart and William Smith Colleges have suffered through the earlier forms of this textbook, and have, by their comments, assisted me greatly in improving it. Some of their essays are included in this textbook, and I thank them for granting me permission to use them. I am also indebted to two students at Reed College, Portland, Oregon, for allowing me to reprint their essays.

Charlyce Jones Owen, Senior Acquisitions Editor, and Sondra Greenfield, Senior Project Manager, at Holt, Rinehart and Winston, Inc. have been unflagging in their attention to this textbook. I am indebted to Charlyce for her early confidence in it; to Charlyce and Sondra for the considerable patience they have shown with a first-time author struggling to wrestle a manuscript into shape. I thank them. Thanks are also due to Annette Mayeski, Production Manager, and Gloria Gentile, Design Supervisor.

For their helpful reviews of the manuscript, I would like to thank Thomas Amorose, Potsdam College of the State University of New York; Paul Connolly, Bard College; John A. R. Dick, University of Texas at El Paso; Sallyanne H. Fitzgerald, University of Missouri, St. Louis; Joan Graham, University of Washington, Seattle; Dorothy Grimes, University of Montevallo; James M. Kenkel, University of Illinois, Urbana; Nevin K. Laib, University of Houston; John S. O'Connor, George Mason University; David H. Roberts, University of Southern Mississippi.

I would have been at a considerable disadvantage without the able help of those who endeavored to secure permissions and who typed portions of this manuscript: Teresa O'Connell, Valerie O'Malley, and Celie Pigman, all of Hobart and William Smith Colleges. I was rescued from the deepest and most frantic panic when my word processor failed with a deadline pending by the calm and able assistance of Stanley Weaver and Peter Grune of the Audio-Visual Department at Hobart and William Smith.

I wish, finally, to thank various members of my family. My parents had the foresight to raise me in a house filled with books, and in a family that figured writing was worth doing. Saal and Debbie Lesser found themselves tip-toeing around a niece, seated at their dining room table for days on end in a hot August, proofreading manuscript. I appreciate their hospitality. Debora Robertson proved to be the ablest—and most ruthless—of editors. She was also most adroit at persuading permission's editors to attend to our requests, and certainly was an able research assistant. She also granted me permission to use an essay of hers, when she would, I think, have preferred me to use one she liked better. Gary Robertson has reread this textbook in its various forms innumerable times, and has endured being the companion of a writer too busy to do much else besides babble about writing or brood about not writing enough. To an extent he, like Dilsey, has endured. But beyond that, he did much to make this text possible and to keep me fed, entertained, and sane while writing it.

L.R.R

Contents

PART III

Writing Process

PART IV

The Anthology

Section One
The Writing Process

Taking Lecture Notes, Keeping a Journal, and Taking
Notes on Direct Observations

Section Three
Presenting Observations: Testing a Hypothesis

Possible Topics for Observation and Examples of Student Presentations

The Experience of Fieldworkers

Presenting Descriptions and Findings

Section Four
Summarizing, Comparing, and Evaluating Arguments

Summarizing Arguments

Comparing and Evaluating Arguments

Academic Disciplines

Literature, Language, The Personal Essay, and Writing

PART I

Foundations

Chapter 1

Writing and the Academic Disciplines

The Academic Disciplines

To write in college is to raise questions and discover answers. The best insight into what this means is provided by scholarly writers, such as your professors. A college or university is a community of scholars, a community of individuals who write for others with similar interests. Professors are students of their subjects. A student new to the academic community who wants to know what it means to write in college is really asking what it means to join a community of scholars or how the older students go about writing. One purpose of this textbook is to illustrate what it means to write in college by studying how scholars in different disciplines write.

A *discipline* is a branch of knowledge or learning; for example, anthropology is a discipline in the social sciences, English literature a discipline in the humanities, and biology a discipline in the life sciences. Professors from a variety of disciplines can be concerned with the same facts and ask the same kinds of questions about them, but each will find different evidence relevant to the answer. One way to understand what it means to write in college, then, is to understand the common questions a writer can ask and the ways in which each discipline affects the method for answering them. Naturally, that is what you will do when you take classes in different subjects. This book is intended to provide you with a general introduction to how questions are raised and answered. It examines the modes of discovery common to the disciplines.

The disciplines are grouped into two categories: the observational sciences and the humanities. The observational sciences inquire into what can be observed directly. They include the physical and life sciences as well as the social sciences. The humanities inquire into the meaning of the written word, and include literature, philosophy, history, religion, and law. You will be studying the different ways by which the observational sciences and the humanities use the modes of inquiry to discover answers relevant to their disciplines.

Same Question, Different Answers

Scholarly writing about the Irish Potato Famine illustrates how writers from different disciplines can ask the same question about the same subject and arrive at different answers. Between 1846 and 1850, about two million Irish people died of starvation and related diseases; another million to a million and a half emigrated. One of the more obvious questions to ask about the Irish famine is why it occurred. What caused it?

G. L. Carefoot and E. R. Sprott, two scientists specializing in plant disease, find the explanation in the characteristics of *Phytophthora infestans,* the parasitic fungus that infected potato plants in Ireland. In *Famine on the Wind*, (New York: Rand McNally, 1969), they state that farmers unknowingly created the conditions that allowed the fungus to survive through the winter to the spring, so that the blight returned year after year:

> The common practice has always been to sort the potato tubers in the early spring, keeping the sound ones for seed and discarding any that show signs of rot—often discarding them carelessly in cull heaps. The culled tubers sprout in the heaps and often, even before the potato fields are planted, the mounds, warmed by the spring sun, are green with young potato plants. If just one of the culls gives rise to a blighted potato, in but a few days or weeks all the plants growing from the cull heap are infected, and the heap becomes a focus of infection for the potato fields of the countryside, particularly in muggy weather, with heavy dews at night and drizzly days.
>
> In at least two of the most disastrous epidemics of late blight, the preceding year's potato crop had been phenomenally large, yielding far more potatoes than could be used as food for human beings or the livestock. The surplus was stored, but no storage system yet devised has been perfect; there never has been a year when a few blighted potatoes were not stored with the sound ones. Thus, after those record years, the rot of the late blight proceeded slowly in storage, and the infected tubers were discarded the next spring with the surplus healthy ones, dotting the land, in the springs of 1845 and 1846, with great heaps of cull potatoes. The terrible plant destroyer was ready. The spring weather in those years was warm; the summers were wet. The potatoes rotted almost overnight, it seemed, and famine, the fourth rider of the Apocalypse, rode up and down the land claiming his victims. (76-77)

The cause of the famine then, from the point of view of botanists, was the unfortunate coincidence of climate, disease, and ignorance.

Other specialists discuss the cause in different terms. Although the potato blight did destroy the potato crops in Ireland for four years, they will argue, this did not necessarily mean that two million Irish people had to starve. In *The Conquest of Famine* (London: Chatto and Windus, 1974), the social scientist W. R. Aykroyd comments on why the so-called Soup Kitchen Act, passed by Parliament in 1847 to provide free soup for the Irish, did not have the intended effect of saving them from the famine:

> Well-meaning people honestly thought that a sure way of relieving the famine had been found. But unfortunately little was known in the mid-19th century about food values and human nutritional requirements. "Soup" means hot water in which heterogeneous ingredients have been boiled, but it is mostly hot water. . . . Among the ingredients were oxheads (without the tongue), maize, carrots, turnips, cabbages, onions, peas, leeks, and other things. A bowl of such soup was no doubt warm and comforting, but it probably provided less than 200 calories to people needing up to 3000 calories daily. Famine oedema or dropsy . . . became widespread in 1847, and it is possible that the soup, by a "water-logging" effect, contributed to its occurrence. (36)

Although Carefoot and Sprott point to the characteristics of the potato blight in explaining the cause of the famine, Aykroyd points to an inadequate response on the part of the government when confronted with the needs of the malnourished. They are answering the same question— What caused the famine?—but because they are members of different academic disciplines, they adopt different perspectives, focus on different facts, and arrive at different answers.

Different yet again is the answer offered by an economic historian who studies the economic realities of nineteenth-century Ireland. The Irish tenant farmer raised wheat and other grains as cash crops, as well as livestock such as pigs, to pay rent to other tenant farmers, who in turn owed rent to the larger landowners, many of whom lived in England. The tenant farmer raised potatoes as a subsistence crop; that is, potatoes were the food on which he and his family lived. Although the potato crop was blighted, grains and livestock continued to flourish and were exported to England.

To explain why the English did not prevent the exportation of desperately needed foodstuffs from Ireland during the time of famine, the economist John Kenneth Galbraith in *The Age of Uncertainty* (Boston: Houghton Mifflin, 1977) refers to three economic theorists whose ideas, he argues, influenced government policy at the time. The first was Adam Smith, who believed that the healthiest economies are those in which each individual is allowed to follow his or her own self-interest, unimpeded by the state. The second was Robert Malthus, who argued that famine was inevitable, because populations increased geometrically—2, 4, 8, 16, 32, etc.—while the food supply increased arithmetically—2, 3, 4, 5, 6, etc. The third theorist was David Ricardo, who argued that as populations increased, more labor would be available; hence, wages would decline. At the same time, the greater demand for food would cause prices to rise. The rich would inevitably get richer, the poor would get poorer, and if the rich increased the salaries of the poor, then the problem would be compounded, because if the poor had more money, then they would only produce more children, thereby increasing the number of available workers, which would cause prices to rise.

Galbraith argues that belief in these economic theories resulted in the English failure to enact trade laws preventing the exportation of food from Ireland during the potato famine. As evidence, he cites the decisions of Charles Edward Trevelyan, assistant secretary of the treasury, or the equivalent of the U.S. treasury secretary:

> Trade, he advised, would be "paralyzed" if the government, by giving away food, interfered with the legitimate profit of private enterprise. His Chancellor, Charles Wood, assured the House of Commons at a time when the hunger was severe that every effort would be made to leave trade in grain "as much liberty as possible." . . . Trevelyan's principles were enunciated in the old Treasury offices in Whitehall. There they were impeccable; in Ireland they meant starvation and death. In the manner of men in quiet offices Trevelyan was content. The laws of classical economics had clearly justified themselves. In a reflective letter in 1846, he wrote that the problem of Ireland "being altogether beyond the powers of men, the cure has been applied by the direct stroke of an all-wise Providence in a manner as unexpected and as unthought of as it is likely to be effectual."(38)

As you can see, Galbraith argues that the Irish were left to starve because government officials clung blindly to theories of a free market, which maintained that the government should not interfere in the economy and that catastrophes such as famines were inevitable.

What caused the Irish Potato Famine? Storing blighted potatoes over the winter and carelessly discarding them during a warm, moist spring. Providing an inadequate diet to people who were starving. Adhering blindly to economic theories rather than to the impulse of human compassion. These were all causes; none of them contradict one another, but they are distinctly different. And they differ because those who addressed the question, "What caused the famine?" did so from the specialized perspectives of the botanist, the social scientist concerned with world hunger, and the economist.

Questions About Consequence

Questions about consequence are as common among the disciplines as questions about cause. Once asked, the way the question is answered depends upon the particular discipline of the questioner. In his article "Medical History of the Famine," the medical historian Sir William P.

MacArthur says the famine caused outbreaks of typhus fever, which is carried by infected lice. MacArthur describes the conditions of the tenant farmers, who were hit hardest by the blight:

> Such of their clothing as had any market value had been sold to passing ped-lars, and the rags that were left they wore night and day, huddling together for warmth. The neighbours crowded into any cabin where a fire was burning, or where some food had been obtained which might be shared or bartered. The lack of cleanliness, the unchanged clothing and the crowding together, provided conditions ideal for lice to multiply and spread rapidly. . . . In such circumstances an initial case or two of fever could serve to infect the whole district. (R. Dudley Edwards and T. Desmond Williams, eds., *The Great Famine* [NY: New York UP, 1957], 271).

Oliver MacDonagh, a historian specializing in emigration patterns, understands the Irish famine as the cause for mass emigrations to Australia and the United States. He writes that the

> universal . . . blight of July and August 1846 . . . had an instantaneous and unmistakable effect. For the first time in Irish history, there was a heavy autumn exodus. For the first time, thousands risked their lives upon a winter crossing, ready, it was said, to undergo any misery "save that of remaining in Ireland" (Edwards and Williams, 319).

Another answer to the question of the famine's effect is to consider those unfortunates who experienced it. In "The Famine in Irish Oral Tradition," Roger J. McHugh has recorded survivors' accounts of the famine, because they convey "the truth, heard from afar, of the men and women who were caught up, uncomprehending and frantic in that disaster." Some of the accounts require no comment on the harrowing visions they raise. Among these are the recollections of those who saw survivors walking long miles bearing their relatives' corpses—often without coffins—to graveyards. One informant recalls being told this story by his father: "He saw poor *Tadhg Labhrais* with a basket on his back and the corpse of his dead sister inside it. The head, he said, was drooping down over the edge of the basket and from it a twist of bright yellow hair hung down, sweeping the road" (425).

Other accounts, such as this one by an 80-year-old woman, illustrate how the famine destroyed the fabric of whole communities:

> It didn't matter who was related to you, your friend was whoever would give you a bite to put in your mouth. Sports and pastimes disappeared. Poetry, music, and dancing stopped. They lost and forgot them all and when the times improved in other respects, these things never returned as they had been. The famine killed everything.

If you reflect upon how many ways there are to study the Irish Potato Famine, you can understand that the purpose of a liberal education is to teach students to view the same ideas or events from different perspectives. The point is to provide you with a flexibility of mind so that you can learn how varied are the possible ways to answer the important questions about the human condition and the natural world. Because each discipline provides a different perspective, each uses its own conventions and specific kinds of information to answer questions. That is why in order to learn to write effectively in college, you need to become aware of the nature and purposes of the different disciplines.

The Glory of the Groves of Academe

> "I don't know what you mean by 'glory,'" said Alice.
> Humpty Dumpty smiled contemptuously. "Of course you don't—till I tell you. I meant 'there's a nice knock-down argument for you!'"
> —*Alice Through the Looking-Glass*

Within each discipline, a great deal of disagreement arises about how to assess, evaluate, or interpret the facts that everyone agrees are significant. This kind of disagreement is the heart and soul of every discipline; without it, each would be moribund and would generate no new ideas. In addition to learning to ask questions and answer them, learning to write in college means joining the debate about ideas. An example of such a debate is again provided by those who have written on the Irish famine.

Those who study the policies of the English toward Ireland during the famine disagree about how to interpret them. As we have seen, John Kenneth Galbraith believes that Treasurer Trevelyan was both callous and blinded by economic theories. Other historians might disagree, saying that the government of the nineteenth century simply lacked the expertise required to administer the newly emerging capitalist economy. This is the position taken by R. Dudley Edwards and T. Desmond Williams:

> The timidity and remoteness of the administrators in the eighteen-forties may irritate the modern observer who unhesitatingly accepts the moral responsibility of the state to intervene in economic affairs in a time of crisis. But it needs patience to realise that what is obvious and uncontroversial today was dark and confused a century ago to many persons of good will. . . . In earlier famines, men had died unnoticed by their rulers, but the new humanitarianism of the nineteenth century gradually forced upon reluctant minds a more delicate appreciation of the suffering of others. (viii-ix)

Thomas Gallagher offers a sharp rebuke to those who would excuse the actions of the English by claiming that they were well meaning but confused about the proper course of action. In his book *Paddy's Lament* (New York: Harcourt Brace Jovanovich, 1982), he includes the passage by Edwards and Williams quoted just above in order to rebut their argument:

> This kind of reasoning founders first on the issue of the *scale* of the famine affecting all of Ireland, and second in view of the humanitarianism shown by the United States in response to the same crisis. Beginning with Boston, New

York, and Philadelphia, meetings were held in cities and towns throughout the country to devise the best and speediest means of helping the starving people of Ireland. (79)

W. R. Aykroyd would also disagree with Edwards and Williams's contention that a man like Trevelyan was confused. He argues that Trevelyan was "an opinionated and obstinate bureaucrat." But he disagrees with those who see in Trevelyan's actions a malevolent conspiracy to commit genocide:

> During the famine there were indeed people in England, students of Malthus, who said that deaths from starvation and disease were to be welcomed because they reduced the surplus population of Ireland. But they said this behind closed doors. Such an idea would, I think, have shocked Trevelyan. In an article in the *Observer* of 7 February 1971, Mr. A.J.P. Taylor [a noted historian] says that the Irish famine was "actively promoted by the Treasury officials of the time," which would, of course, especially incriminate Trevelyan as administrative chief. As far as he is concerned, this is to exaggerate obstinate folly into great wickedness. (46)

Were the English blind, callous, confused, or wicked conspirators against the Irish? Were they victims of economic theories that seemed rational and that in other cases seemed to bring prosperity to the state? Were they right to argue that the government should not intervene in trade? Or should governments control the economy in order to assure equity among all citizens? As you can see, the interpretations of English motives are not only contradictory, but they ultimately raise questions of social policy that we continue to debate today.

How to Think About Right Answers

Very often, students come to college with the general notion, however vague, that if they study hard and give the right answers on tests, they will get good grades and will be graduated. But what is the right answer to the question, "What caused the famine?" And what is the right answer to the question, "How ought we to evaluate English policy toward Ireland during the famine?" Because no right answers exist for questions about cause, effect, or value, bothering with interpreting, evaluating, or judging ideas might seem a waste of time. Or we might assume that because no right answers exist, one opinion is as good as another.

To say that there is no point in addressing questions that have no right answers is tantamount to saying that we want others to make our decisions for us, to do our thinking for us. No clear right answer exists to the question of whether or not a government ought to control the economy or to what extent. Only those with closed minds assume that a correct answer exists, and they are likely to be as inflexible in the face of real and serious challenges to their doctrines as was Trevelyan. The purpose of college is to teach us how to go about testing and interpreting our assumptions, such as those we hold about an industrialized economy, and to have us study economic, political, and social history in order to evaluate the consequences of such policies.

And although no right answers exist when it comes to evaluating information, reasonable answers do exist. If you review the statements about English policy toward Ireland, you will see that each writer uses information to support the reasonableness of his point of view. One interpretation is not as good as another; the interpretation that brings to bear sound evidence and sound instincts, insight, and ethics is superior to one that lacks these qualities.

From Question to Answer: The Writing Process

Little else is more excruciating than facing a blank page with an equally blank mind and a deadline pending. All the possible instruction on grammar, punctuation, spelling, organization, and style is useless to a writer who has nothing to write about. The desire to raise questions is necessarily prior to asking the question that sets us on the path to discovering an answer. When we examine the motives of scholarly writers, we find that they are motivated by very immediate, often personal interests. John Kenneth Galbraith says in his "Foreword" that he chose for his topic "the age of uncertainty" because he felt that we lack confidence in how to solve contemporary economic problems:

> In the last century capitalists were certain of the success of capitalism, socialists of socialism, imperialists of colonialism, and the ruling classes knew they were meant to rule. Little of this certainty now survives. Given the dismaying complexity of the problems mankind now faces, it would surely be odd if it did. (7)

Galbraith, who has been a presidential adviser, wanted to explore the causes of what he interprets to be our current loss of confidence in traditional economic and political theories.

Thomas Gallagher, who is of Irish descent, felt that the Irish Potato Famine had not been properly interpreted. He believes that the Irish famine was the "historical nadir" of Anglo-Irish relations and sees in it the seeds of the current troubles in Ireland. He says of his study of the famine, "To my amazement, this famine experienced in terms of the Irish peasant had been treated superficially or at a remarkable remove. It was clear that the individual peasant was in fact the victim. But the victim of what? Who spoke for the victim?" (xiv)

W. R. Aykroyd, a specialist on world hunger, chose to write about "the conquest of famine" because he wanted both to demonstrate how famine is relieved and to sound a warning about the dangers of overpopulation:

> Without knowledge of the past history of famine it would be difficult to evaluate the present situation. But the adoption of the historical approach in much of

the book should not convey the impression that famine has simply been a disastrous episode in human history, to be relegated, like the Black Death, to the history books. At the time of writing (1973), the world food situation is precarious and causing serious anxiety. (4-5)

Galbraith, Gallagher, and Aykroyd are motivated to write by serious concerns regarding the contemporary human condition in the economic, political, and social realms. They relate these concerns directly to their areas of research. What they write about grows out of the interaction between what they know about their field or discipline and what concerns them as compassionate or concerned human beings. Perhaps you can see why some professors have trouble answering the student who asks, "What should I write about?" It depends upon the student's interests or the ideas the student is curious about and on the student's concern about the human condition, its values, or its choices.

It depends, too, on whether or not the student understands whatever disagreements or debates are current in the discipline. As we have seen, disagreement arises about how to interpret British policy toward Ireland during the famine. We have also seen that some of this debate is about the motives and character of Trevelyan. Most significant, the debate arises because one writer has read the arguments of another. It is not going too far to say that scholars decide what to write about because of what they read. Aykroyd read an article by the historian A.J.P. Taylor in the English newspaper the *Observer,* and he disagreed with it. So he set about to show, among other things, why he disagreed. Gallagher read Edwards and Williams on the same subject, and disagreed with them; so he set out, among other things, to demonstrate how additional information about the U.S. response to the famine undercut their reasoning.

Having something to write about depends upon whether or not a writer is motivated to ask questions, has read widely, and knows how to seek answers. Writing in college is inseparable from thinking, reading, and the desire to discover. Writing is really the process of discovery, and one purpose of this textbook is to help you develop useful and effective methods for discovery.

Drafting, Revising, and Collaborating

Once you have read and reflected enough to decide what questions you wish to answer for a particular assignment, you will naturally take notes to record information and to trace your responses to it. Notetaking is one step in the discovery process. At some point, you will feel that you have seen enough of a pattern in what you have learned to attempt organizing your material. You are ready to write your first draft, to see what happens when you try putting it all together. When you draft your essay, you are really seeing for the first time how your ideas connect. Rarely does such an exploratory draft result in a complete crystallizing of ideas. You may get stuck and need more information. More than likely, you may need to see whether someone else can figure out what you are trying to say. Writing can be collaborative; in other words, writing can be made easier if you work with someone else to clarify ideas, emend interpretations, and to test whether or not evidence adequately supports the conclusions.

Professional writers seek this kind of assistance because they understand themselves to be a part of a community of scholars. Many nonfiction works, including your textbooks, will include in the front a list of acknowledgments, sometimes quite a long list. The writer uses the acknowledgments pages to thank everyone who gave him or her assistance. Sometimes the writer thanks individuals or organizations for making available special sources of information; sometimes he or she thanks someone for help in preparing certain chapters; and sometimes the thanks is for help in editing.

At the time that you are trying to make your ideas connect and to present them in a clear and engaging manner, you should seek assistance from a friendly collaborator or consultant. Your professor can be such a resource; so are your peers. And if your campus has a writing center, the tutors there will be prepared to help you by discussing possible ways of organizing your ideas and of presenting them clearly and effectively.

You will find, then, that you draft and revise your essay, sometimes several times, as do all serious writers. *Revision* means *re-seeing,* and the effort to crystallize your thinking involves re-seeing the information, until you can finally see the whole forest and not just the trees.

Editing and Proofreading

Once you have organized your ideas, you will have a manuscript that you can edit. Editing involves removing redundancies, shaping paragraphs so that they are coherent and concise, rewriting sentences so that they are correct and precise, and selecting the apt word or expression. After editing, you are ready to prepare the final typescript. And after you have prepared it, you are ready for the final step, proofreading, to correct any typographical errors.

To summarize, writing involves several steps, regardless of whether you are preparing a report, an essay, or a research paper:

1. *Gathering ideas:* reading; listening; notetaking; reflecting.
2. *Shaping ideas:* deciding on a purpose; discovering the patterns that will make information, generalizations, and interpretations connect.
3. *Testing and refining:* showing your draft to a reliable consultant or adviser; reading your own work with a critical eye; re-seeing your ideas.
4. *Editing:* considering the special needs of your reader; finding the right word, the apt phrase, the coherent connections; following approved formats for margins, spacing, footnoting, and bibliography; correcting errors in grammar, punctuation, and spelling.

5. *Proofreading:* correcting errors, making sure that the appearance is neat and attractive.

How wonderful if each of these steps was easily separated from the other; if you could read and take notes, prepare an outline and a draft, show what you have written to someone else, revise the draft once, edit, retype or rewrite, and proofread. Unfortunately, although each operation is essential, one does not necessarily follow another in a neat and orderly sequence.

After we as writers have read, listened, taken notes, and reflected enough to decide on a topic, we are not necessarily ready to abandon reading, listening, and notetaking. We have more to do in the way of gathering ideas, but our focus has narrowed so that we know more precisely what to read, and what we ought to reflect upon. And even after we have seen a way to organize our information, and have arrived at a sense of purpose, we often find that as we write, we need more information and back we go to reading. Or we may find as we write that different interpretations suggest themselves to us, and back we go to organization.

So closely related are thinking and writing that one cannot be clearly distinguished from the other when you are writing. It takes time to think; thinking leads to rethinking. You will find that the paths leading to sound, reasonable, and well-expressed thoughts are rarely straight and narrow; they have switchbacks that seem to lead us back to where we began. Generally speaking, however, you will find that you can safely delay editing until the larger tasks of reading, notetaking, drafting, and revision are done. And proofreading is always the last step. You need not, then, become preoccupied with whether or not you have chosen just the right word, or be overly concerned with correcting grammar or spelling until after you have wrestled your ideas into shape.

Time: Procrastination and Police Patrols

If you approach every writing assignment as requiring you to engage in a process, you will understand why you need to leave yourself plenty of time to explore your ideas. If you have to hurry, you will find yourself "in wand'ring mazes lost," rather than walking steadily along scenic switchbacks. If you start too close to your deadline, you are likely to produce, as one student put it, "a mess of unintelligible gobbledegook." As part of this course, the particular stages of the writing process are examined in greater detail. But it won't do you much good to have the process explained unless you have a realistic sense of how much time writing will entail.

Over the years, I've asked students to compare the amount of time they spend writing an essay with the grade the essay received. I have found consistently that students who spend fewer than six to eight hours preparing an essay—even a short one—have a higher probability of receiving a below-passing grade than do students who spend at least that amount of time. Students who spend at least 10 to 12 hours have a greater probability of receiving an above-average grade, whereas students who spend 13 or more hours have the greatest possibility of receiving an A. *Writing* here means almost everything involved in the writing process: thinking, notetaking, planning, drafting, consulting, revision, editing, typing, and proofreading. We did not take into consideration how much time was spent reading in order to prepare to write. *Writing* here also means "writing for college classes," not just for composition classes. Naturally, the time spent writing varies given the length of the paper. But students who consistently receive high grades also report consistently spending at least 10 hours preparing to turn in an essay, even if it is five pages long. Nor does spending that amount of time mean that a student invested 10 or more hours *at one sitting.* Usually students who report investing 10 or more hours report that they accumulate those hours over several days.

To illustrate why this kind of time management yields good results, I'll give you an example of a student with some typical problems. One day, a student came to my office. He had been given an assignment in a history class, and it was due the next day. The student showed me what he had written; it was one paragraph long. He asked me if it was a "good introduction." The prose was nearly unintelligible. The syntax was jumbled, the sentences did not connect, and there was no clear point to what was written. The whole effect was rather like the aftermath of setting dynamite to a plate of spaghetti.

What causes this gobbledegook? This student has *begun* by trying to write the *final version* of the essay. Trying to *begin* with a finished product is simply an unrealistic goal. No professional writer would try it. Most successful student writers do not try it. Before you can write the final draft, you have to have a pretty clear notion of what you will say. And before you know what you will say, you have to know what is *possible* to say. The student who came to my office had done little or no thinking about what he might be able to say.

Discovering what you can possibly say is just that—a process of discovery. That is why we encourage students to set time aside—days and days before the assignment is due—to write about the assignment. At this point, the writer should be concerned only with self-discovery, not with what the "teacher" will think about the prose. What you write in your notebooks in preparation for a first draft will not be seen by anyone but you. It is your chance to dump onto paper everything you can think of that you might possibly say. At later stages, you can begin to consider what you will include and exclude, how you will organize it, and how you will present it in a pleasing or appealing way. But those concerns come later. The question, Is this a good introduction? should be raised near the *end* of the process, after you have drafted the piece several times.

Because so many students cripple themselves as writers by trying to write the final product first, I'm going to stay with this subject a bit longer to see whether or not I can persuade you that effectively managing your time is essential to writing successfully. Some students tell me they cannot get their ideas down on paper. Some come to me immediately after an assignment has been given and say, "How should I organize this?" When I talk to such students, they often seem paralyzed by worry, as if they have invented an imaginary Police Patrol that will arrest them and carry them to prison forever if they "make a mistake" in their writing. A student who wants to know *at the beginning* of the writing process how to organize the essay is overly concerned about how the final product will be judged, as if the Organization Police will haul them away if they do not organize properly. There is a time to be concerned about organization; but to worry about it at the beginning may inhibit you from exploring ideas because you fear they will not fit in with the organization. Plan the presentation of your ideas after you have given yourself time to discover your ideas. The watchwords here are, Plan; don't worry.

Students who say that they can't get their ideas on paper often also seem to fear an imaginary Police Patrol. I have read such students' drafts or notes for essays. I have noticed that a draft may be moving along, exploring an interesting idea, and then suddenly the passage ends, cut off. When I asked one writer about this, he told me that he was afraid it "wasn't right." But when you are exploring ideas, nothing is worse than letting the police tell you, "That's WRONG! You're under arrest!" You will find yourself *arrested* in your thinking. Your mind will stop. You will not know how to go on. There is a time to consider whether what you have written in your notes and drafts is responsive to the assignment. But the time for such consideration is not *before* you have written down your ideas or *while* you are writing them down. Discover your ideas first; then select which you want to include and exclude.

Bad Habits and Self-Esteem

Another problem that prevents some students from spending enough time on their essays has to do with a connection between some bad habits and self-esteem. Many college students developed the habit in high school of spending about an hour on an essay the night before it is due, turning it in, and getting a passing grade. They have been rewarded for procrastinating. The insidious effect of this habit goes something like this: if you are consistently given a reward for being quick, then you can associate taking time with being slow, or not too bright. I've seen this terrible, false connection between being intelligent and being quick to get work done damage many students. A student used to getting passing grades for an hour's work will probably get poor grades in college for the same amount of work. What does the student think? Too often, students come to the harmful conclusion, "I must have been really stupid all along, but now I've been found out!" Nonsense!

The reason students take more time expressing themselves in college is that they are now in a social setting that assumes that they ought to think carefully about what they say and respect what others say. In straight-forward terms, this means that your professors assume that you want your ideas to be taken seriously. No idea worth being taken seriously is dashed off in an hour. Common sense tells you that. But it is easy to ignore common sense and think the worst of yourself. Here, for instance, is a conversation I had with a first-year college student who had gotten back that FIRST PAPER with marks all over it. This student was not enrolled in one of my classes.

STUDENT: I must be the stupidest person in the world! All that time I was pretending to be stupid in high school so I would fit in I must not have been pretending!

ME: How did the other students do?

STUDENT: They must have all gotten A's.

ME: What makes you think so? Have they told you what grades they got?

STUDENT: No, no one has said anything about it.

ME: Well, I think if other students had gotten A's on their very first papers, they would have been proud enough to say so. That silence might mean that they, too, are feeling low because their first papers have bad grades. What comments are on the paper?

STUDENT: Well, the professor said I missed the point of the assignment and did not think through my ideas enough.

This student survived her first year. She also reports spending at least 10 hours on every paper. She starts assignments that are due at the end of the term about five weeks beforehand.

Before you write yourself off as stupid, think about managing your time so that you leave yourself enough time to discover those good ideas you have in your head and enough time to present them well once you have discovered them. At the early stages of an assignment, send the Police Patrol out of the room. Get down on paper those ideas that come to you. Discover what is possible to say. Then go through the process of deciding what to include and how to present it effectively. Let yourself go through the process of notetaking, drafting, revising, consulting, editing, and proofreading by managing your time so that you can attend to these over time—across several days or even over several weeks.

ASSIGNMENTS

Who you are as a scholar—that is, as a student and writer—and who you wish to be are two of the more important discoveries you can make in college. Introduce yourself as a scholar; assess yourself now and set goals for yourself.

Below are some suggestions. During the time you should set aside for writing each day until the assignment is due, you might find consulting these suggestions helpful. They are intended to give you some guidelines for completing the writing process successfully.

You might wish to read through all of the suggestions and then prepare a daily schedule that indicates how much time you will spend each day on various aspects of the writing process.

Discovering What You Might Say

Below are three possible approaches to the assignment. Read them, and choose one approach you think might work for you. Set aside time to write in response to the questions. Do not concern yourself now with whether or not what you write sounds right or is correct. Do not worry about organization. Write *all you can think to say* about each. Try writing about each more than once, leaving time between each writing session to let your ideas "brew." If you find that one approach does not work, try others until you find one that stimulates your thinking.

Suggestion I

You might try tackling this assignment by defining what you think your problems as a writer are:

1. Can you describe what your problems as a student and a writer are?

2. If you have tried to solve your problems as a student and a writer in the past, why would you say those solutions have not proven effective?

3. What would you say are the sources or causes of your problems? What in your history as a student and a writer has contributed to your problems?

4. What do you think the solutions to your problems might be? Reread Chapter 1. What possible solutions are suggested there? Which do you find most attractive?

5. Suppose somebody said, "Those solutions won't work!" What would you say to that person?

Suggestion II

You might try tackling this assignment by exploring what you assume you will learn as a student and a writer from this class:

1. Reread Chapter 1. What do you suppose will be expected of you in this class? Why do you think the class will address the issues suggested in the chapter? What is the purpose behind them?

2. Given what you assume the class will deal with, what are your thoughts and feelings about how you will do as a student and a writer? Do you think the class will suit your needs? Do you feel you have other needs that might not be addressed?

3. By the end of this class, what do you hope will characterize you as a student and a writer?

4. What do you think this class will contribute to you as a student and a writer in other classes?

Suggestion III

You might try tackling this assignment by meditating on several episodes in your history as a student and a writer that you regard as significant:

1. Think back over your history as a student and a writer. Can you think of times when you felt you were a success? Describe them in detail. Can you think of times when things did not go well? Again, describe them in detail.

2. Reread what you have written. Comment in detail on what you think the examples signify for you. What have you learned from these experiences about your strengths as a student and a writer? Your weaknesses?

3. Reread Chapter 1. Comment on what you hope this class might do to reinforce your strengths and to help you overcome your weaknesses. What will this class teach that might introduce new challenges to you? What do you make of them?

4. At the end of the class, what do you hope you will take away that will prove valuable to you as a student and a writer?

Discovering How You Might Say It

It might help you think about how to present what you have to say if you think about a possible audience. Below are some suggestions. Set aside time to write down your responses to them in your notes. Then, choose an audience you would like to address.

1. Suppose your audience is yourself. Imagine that you are writing to your future self so that you have a record of your thoughts and feelings as you embarked on the discovery of yourself as a student and a writer. How would you talk to the self you want to be?

2. Suppose your audience is someone who has a particular interest in your academic career and wants to know what you think about your education so far. How would you talk to that concerned person?

3. Suppose the audience includes others with similar interests; that is, other writers and students. Imagine your audience as the one that George Simons describes in *Keeping Your Personal Journal* (New York: Paulist Press, 1978):

> We note the stories of others, as well as those of ourselves, with awe and follow them with insatiable curiosity. Beneath it all is the suspicion that our common-

ness reveals some truth, and by sharing what we know of ourselves, we are confirmed in the validity of our humanity though each of us writes or wants to write a unique script. (21)

How would you address such an audience?

Planning and Drafting

Once you have an audience in mind, review the notes you wrote to discover what you could say. What will you include? What will you exclude? Review what you will include. In what order would you like to present it? Draft your essay. Do not worry about making it letter perfect. Concern yourself primarily with presenting what you have to say to the audience you have in mind. Set it aside for a time.

Revising and Consulting

You should regard your draft as a very preliminary effort. Be prepared to add to it and to shift around what you have said. Here are some suggestions for revising your draft. Try several of these suggestions, revising your draft each time in response to what you learn.

1. Reread the assignment. Reread your draft. Have you been responsive to the assignment? Or have you strayed too far from it?

2. After you have been away from your draft for a time, read it as if you are the audience you have chosen. Or ask someone to read it aloud to you. Often writers figure out how to improve what they have written from hearing their own words read aloud. Imagine as you listen that you are the audience you have chosen. Whether you read it or listen to it, consider whether or not your audience would like to know more. What could you add? Should you change the order? Will your audience think this sounds like you or some stranger?

3. Sometimes, reading how someone else has tackled a similar problem can help you. In Part IV, Anthology, Section Two, you will find an essay by Barbara Mellix, ''From the Outside, In.'' Read it. What do you appreciate about how she tackled this same kind of assignment? What can you learn from her that you might like to try in writing this assignment?

4. You might find consulting with others helpful. Get together with other students in the class. Read their drafts and offer your advice. What else would you like to know? What would you like to have clarified? What do you admire about the way someone else tackled the assignment that you can incorporate into your own writing? What advice can he or she offer you? You might find it helpful asking your instructor to review your draft, or a friend you trust, or someone at the writing center, if your college has one.

Editing

After you have revised your draft enough so that you are satisfied with its organization and your presentation of yourself to your audience, edit your prose. You will find some suggestions for editing in Chapter 28, "Editing." During editing, writers *eliminate* language that does not contribute to meaning and *correct* errors. Here are some of the basic elements of editing that you should consider:

1. Read your draft once, looking for grammatical errors. If you know that you have trouble recognizing your errors, seek assistance. Note the kinds of errors you make, and set yourself the goal of learning to correct them during the term.

2. Read your draft once more, looking for punctuation errors. If you know that you have trouble recognizing such errors, seek assistance. Note the kinds of errors you make, and set yourself the goal of learning to correct them during the term.

3. Read your draft once more, looking for spelling errors. If you know that you have trouble with spelling, seek assistance. Note the words that you misspell, and memorize the correct spelling.

4. Read your draft once more, looking for any words that you have included because they sound "intelligent," "erudite," or "academic," but not because they are words that you usually use or have full command over. If you have reached for a thesaurus to help you select a word, consider very carefully whether or not you fully understand the connotation of the word. You might be better off using your own vocabulary.

Appearance and Proofreading

Prepare your final draft. Then proofread it. Correct any typographical errors you find.

Chapter 2

Writer to Reader

PREPARATORY ASSIGNMENT: THE DIPLOMATIC MEMO

One of the foundations of effective writing is learning to think about the reader. Here is an exercise to help you focus on audience.

You are a Foreign Service officer in Nigeria. The Foreign Service is a branch of the State Department, which operates our embassies and consulates overseas. Foreign Service officers help arrange visas for people who want to travel to the United States, report to Washington on important developments in a country, help arrange cultural and business exchanges, and try to be of service to U.S. citizens visiting a country.

As a Foreign Service officer, you must send a memo every week reporting on current conditions to the African desk officer in Washington, D.C. A desk officer is an experienced or senior Foreign Service officer whose job it is to summarize and analyze information sent in by junior officers like you who are assigned to various U.S. embassies or consulates throughout Africa. A desk officer is responsible for making some policy recommendations based on that information.

You must send a memo that is clear and explicit and that does not offer to tell the desk officer what he or she already knows about Nigeria, because this would not only waste his or her time, but would require the desk officer to sift through the memo to find the really important information. You are not expected to analyze the information you send or to make any policy recommendations.

Select from the following list the information pertinent to this week's memo. Invent a name for your desk officer. Begin your memo with the standard memo format:

TO:
FROM:
SUBJECT:
DATE:

Place what you think is the most important information first, and provide the remaining information in descending order of importance.

1. About a month ago, the president of Nigeria was ousted in a nearly bloodless military coup.
2. Nigeria is an oil-producing nation. With declining demand for oil, Nigeria has fallen far behind its schedule for repayment of debts to the World Bank.
3. Faced with rising inflation and unemployment, the previous president had expelled thousands of foreign workers from Nigeria several months prior to the coup.
4. At the time of the coup, you were visiting a neighboring country and could not return immediately to Nigeria because the airports were closed.
5. Since the day of the coup, the constitution has been suspended and martial law imposed by the military government.
6. Since the day of the coup, U.S. businesspeople in Nigeria have been detained without warrant and held without charges or trial. Local officials are uncooperative when asked for information about these people.
7. The coup was led by senior officers in the Nigerian military.
8. Junior Army officers, jealous of having been left out, are rumored to be planning their own coup. This second coup seems imminent; it could occur any day.
9. The president of the United States has appointed a new ambassador to Nigeria. He arrived two weeks after the coup.
10. Given current circumstances, Foreign Service officers stationed in Lagos feel beleaguered and frustrated.
11. Lagos is the capital city of Nigeria.

The Diplomatic Memo and Redundant Information

The facts you included in your diplomatic memo ought to have been determined by what your desk officer—your audience—already knew about the subject.

For one thing, as a junior officer in the Foreign Service, you write to your desk officer every week. The coup in Nigeria happened four weeks before you wrote this memo. You should have told your desk officer about the coup in a previous memo. If you didn't, he or she has read about it in the newspaper and has written you a note asking you what you think your job is. The following occurrences, then, are irrelevant to this memo because they happened more than a week prior to your last memo:

Fact 1: About a month ago, the president of Nigeria was ousted in a nearly bloodless military coup.

Fact 3: Faced with rising inflation and unemployment, the previous president had expelled thousands of foreign workers from Nigeria several months prior to the coup.

Fact 4: At the time of the coup, you were visiting a neighboring country and could not return immediately to Nigeria because the airports were closed.

Fact 7: The coup was led by senior officers in the Nigerian military.

Fact 9: The president of the United States has appointed a new ambassador to Nigeria. He arrived two weeks after the coup.

You can also assume that your supervisor is familiar enough with Nigeria to know that Lagos is the capital, so Fact 11 would be an insult to his or her competence. Similarly, your supervisor is presumably aware of the economic status quo in Nigeria (Fact 2).

New and Relevant Information

The new information is:

Fact 8: Junior Army officers, jealous of having been left out, are rumored to be planning their own coup. This second coup seems imminent; it could occur any day.

Fact 10: Given current circumstances, Foreign Service officers stationed in Lagos feel beleaguered and frustrated.

Two other items are relevant because, while they refer to actions begun in the past, their consequences are still felt in an important way:

Fact 5: Since the day of the coup, the constitution has been suspended and martial law imposed by the military government.

Fact 6: Since the day of the coup, U.S. businesspeople in Nigeria have been detained without warrant and held without charges or trial. Local officials are uncooperative when asked for information about these people.

Organizing the Information

Your desk officer will probably regard Fact 8 as the most significant, so it should have been the first item in your memo. To make the information as clear as possible, you would revise the statement slightly to explain why the junior Army officers feel they have been left out of the coup. You would do this by reminding the desk officer that it was planned and executed by senior Army officers:

> Junior Army officers, jealous of having been left out of the coup by the senior officers, are rumored to be planning their own coup. This second coup seems imminent; it could occur any day.

The references to continuing concerns would come after the new information. Because getting U.S. businesspeople out of jail would be an important matter, it would naturally precede the information about martial law. It is important for your supervisor to know that martial law remains in effect, but not much can be done about it. On the other hand, the Foreign Service should certainly be doing everything it can to effect the release of the businesspeople. All you need to say is: "We continue to find local officials uncooperative when asked for information about U.S. businesspeople detained after the coup." Similarly, you need only refer briefly to the suspension of the constitution: "Martial law continues to be in effect."

Whether or not you include Fact 10 would probably depend on how you judged the character of your desk officer. If he or she understood that committed field officers need support, he or she might expect you to report regularly on morale. You would indicate that you thought the matter was very important if you placed this item second; you would indicate it was significant but not as important as other matters if you placed it last.

As illustrated by this exercise, what a reader will find informative depends very much on what the reader knows. The writer, therefore, needs to avoid unnecessary repetition of information that the reader likely knows. The writer also has to have a clear sense of purpose, or else he or she will not know what information is significant or worth including. And, finally, the writer needs some sense of the reader's character, preferences, and foibles.

Thinking About the Audience

Almost all of us have had the experience of telling the reader what the reader already knew. We have had literature papers returned to us, for instance, with the comments, "You are merely paraphrasing" or "All you do is tell me the plot again." In these cases, the messages were too redundant to inform the reader. An English teacher already knows the plot. Sometimes you may have gotten back papers marked, "This isn't what I wanted" or "You don't follow the assignment." In these cases, you have failed to meet your audience's expectations.

How can we be sure we are addressing the audience effectively? Effectiveness in writing is an art. There is no simple recipe for it. We will be discussing specific aspects of effectiveness throughout this text. But for now, just fix this firmly in mind: the audience helps shape what you say.

In general, you will find it helps to remember four factors: responsiveness, relevance, priority, and interest.

In college writing, being responsive to the assignment is especially important. This means, as the exercise on the diplomatic memo indicates, reading the assignment carefully and consulting with your professor to make sure you are on the right track. You should think of the assignment as the magnetic pole, and of your writing as the needle on the compass. Does what you say point toward the assignment? Are you being responsive to it?

As for relevance, it has to do with what the reader expects you to do. In college, this generally means that you are to be concerned less with rehearsing facts that are already known than with interpreting them—making them meaningful—by employing the rules and methods of the discipline. Whenever you include information, you should ask, "Does the reader already know this? If so, why am I including it?" You can include redundant information if you wish to remind the reader of it in order to analyze or interpret it. But if you are simply summarizing or paraphrasing for the sake of summarizing and paraphrasing, you may be offering wholly redundant information. If you ask yourself, "Is this relevant?" and can answer yes, then go on to ask, "Have I shown the reader why it is relevant?" Stopping to ask yourself a few questions as you write can help you to make sure that you are including information that the reader will find meaningful.

Assigning priorities means asking yourself whether or not the reader will be able to tell what you regard as most important, and why. Taking the time to indicate to the reader what you think your main point is and how you think other matters relate to it helps the reader follow along. Someone reading your writing is just like you when you read. No one likes to have to unscramble a text in order to figure out what the writer is trying to say.

Finally, asking yourself questions about what will interest the reader can help you give a bit of flavor to your writing. If you ask yourself what might keep the reader interested in reading from one paragraph to the next, you can sometimes think of a strong image or metaphor, a colorful example, an amusing anecdote, or maybe even a little wit. What you decide about this will depend very much on how you wish to present yourself and on what you make of the reader's taste and preferences.

Having to or Choosing to Write for a Reader

When I ask students to tell me their goals as writers, I often receive comments indicating that they feel compelled to learn to write well; for instance, students write phrases such as these:

It is *imperative* to learn to write well in order to succeed in today's world.

I want a good job and a secure future, so I *have to* learn to write well.

My parents *expect me* to do well in school, so I *must* improve my writing.

One thing professors expect is good writing, so I *have to* learn to improve my writing.

In my experience, writers who feel that they have to write because of demands placed upon them—by parents, or teachers, or even the writers' own fears and hopes about the future—often do not write well. I do not know why this is the case, really, but I might hazard a guess: most of us really do not perform well when we feel forced or compelled against our will. I think this is true of writing.

Let me give you an illustration of what I mean. In my experience, professors give C's for papers that are (1) responsive to the assignment, (2) well organized, and (3) correct (that is, generally free of errors in grammar, punctuation, and spelling). It has also been my experience that many students—I would say the majority—are not satisfied with C's on their essays. They want better grades. What this means, in effect, is that students want to write in a way that makes the reader sit up and take notice, a way that is above average or exceptional. It seems to me that the attitude "I *have to* write" is at cross purposes with the *desire* to write in a way that impresses the reader. Bear with me while I explain with what may seem a digression.

Imagine that you are part of a workshop in a composition class. The class is discussing an essay—maybe one of yours. The essay is about a personal experience; for instance, a time when a student and his or her mother went to a performance—a rock concert or a movie—that shocked the mother but pleased the student. During the workshop, the students and teacher—the audience—comment that they would like to have more details about the concert or the movie and about the mother's response. Other students say, "Well, why should the writer *have to* do that? You know about Blood, Sweat, and Tears or *The Color Purple* [or whatever performance the student has described]. You've seen people look shocked before. Why should the writer *have to* describe that?"

The point is, the writer does not *have to* do anything. And the assumption that the only reason to write is because the writer *has to* is exactly what prevents the writer from understanding that what is at issue here has nothing to do with what you have to do. At issue is whether or not the writer *chooses* to please the audience. What the audience wants is to be interested by lively, vivid detail. If the writer chooses to please the audience in that way, then the writer could revise the description to make images dance in the reader's mind. You see, as long as the assumption is, "I have to write," a writer has a difficult time thinking, "How can I please this reader? How can I invite the reader to enjoy what I want to say? How can I make this reader sit up and take notice?" When we feel someone is making us do something, one of the last things we think of is how to give to that person. Yet unless the writer *chooses* to give the reader something that is pleasurable and interesting, the writing will not make the reader sit up and take notice.

Another way to think about this is to understand that the assumption, "I have to learn to write" goes along with being a victim: somebody else or something else is in charge of making your decisions—whether it be your parents, your teachers, or your own hopes for your future. And victims, as it turns out, do not make particularly effective writers precisely because they do not feel they are in charge of anything, including their own language and how it affects others. Fortunately, it is really a very short step from the attitude of a victim to the attitude of one who is in control. Thinking, "I am choosing to please my parents just now" is so much less oppressive than "I have to learn to write to please my parents, because if I don't write well, I won't get good grades." Thinking, "I am choosing to understand this professor's expectations, and I'm going to figure out how to make him or her sit up and take notice" is a much more positive challenge than "I have to write another paper for Professor Hardheart. I don't know what he wants. He won't like whatever I say, no matter how hard I try." Thinking, "I want my future to include people understanding me and respecting me, and I want to be able to understand and respond to others. So, I'm choosing to learn how to do that through my writing" is much healthier than "I have to learn to write or I'll never get a decent job."

As you can see, thinking about an audience ultimately means thinking about yourself and what stance or attitude you choose to adopt toward your reader. Remember, if you think of writing as something you have to do, you are making a choice—you are choosing to see yourself as a victim of demands placed on you by others. Because you are going to make a choice about attitude anyway, why not make a choice that will promote your own interests? Choose to think of yourself as someone who wants to make an audience sit up and take notice. The choice alone—even without any specialized instruction—can go a long way toward helping you write in a way that you respect and for which others will respect you.

ASSIGNMENTS

Assignment I

One of the ways we characterize the relationship between the writer and the audience is by describing the writer's *tone*, which means the attitude the writer adopts toward the reader. This assignment asks you first to study the different attitudes writers adopt and then to write a report on what you learn about tone from that study.

First, complete the exercises below.

Then, write a report that explains what you as a writer have learned about the role that tone plays in effective writing. Your report should refer to what you learned from both of the exercises.

Finally, attach to your report (1) the memo you wrote as a junior Foreign Service officer and (2) the memo you will write as a senior desk officer (see below).

Exercise 1

Assume that you are the desk officer for Africa who received your original memo. Part of your job is to instruct junior Foreign Service officers in the art of sending clear, relevant, and informative memos. How do you as desk officer evaluate the memo you wrote as a junior officer? What criticism would you offer? What praise?

What tone will you adopt for addressing the junior officer? Are you kind, patient, and understanding? Patient but firm? An irritable perfectionist? How will your understanding of the junior officer's character affect the wording you choose?

Write your memo to the junior officer, using standard memo format. Bring it to class. Be prepared to read it aloud or to have it read aloud. As you listen, imagine that you are the junior officer. Jot down what you think is the attitude of the desk officer toward you and toward the reports you write. What "message" do you think the desk officer's tone conveys? How do you feel about that? Would the memo inspire you to improve your performance? Jot down a few terms that describe the desk officer's tone; for example, helpful, sympathetic, arrogant, uncaring. Share your answers with the desk officer. When a junior officer responds to your memo, note the response. Does it surprise you? Did your reader get the message you intended? As both a writer and a listener, what do you learn from this exercise about the role tone plays in effective communication?

Exercise 2

Study the tone of other memos. Included in Part IV, Anthology, Section One are:

John Kenneth Galbraith, entries of November 17, 19, and 20, 1961; letters to President Kennedy of November 28, 1961, and April 5, 1962, and Memorandum for the President, April 4, 1962, from *Ambassador's Journal;* and

H. R. Haldeman, Memorandum for Colonel Hughes, May 26, 1969.

Compare Galbraith's journal entries on Saigon and the war in Vietnam with his letter to Kennedy of November 28. What does he include in both his journal and his letter? What does he exclude? Why? As you study the letter, can you tell when Galbraith intends to inform? To entertain? What attitudes does he suppose Kennedy has?

Comment on the tone of the journal entries, the letters, and the memo. As you read them, jot down descriptive terms that apply; for example, breezy, angry, cheerful, condescending, witty, flippant. What about Galbraith's wording made you describe the tone as you did? How does the tone differ from one kind of writing to the other? How might the purpose and the audience have caused these differences?

What attitude does Haldeman have toward the subject of his memo? What makes you think so? What is his attitude toward Colonel Hughes? What makes you think so? What descriptive terms come to mind about Haldeman's character as you read his memo? Why?

Judging just from these samples of their writing, if you were president, which man would you rather have as an adviser? Why?

What did you as a writer learn about tone from your study of Galbraith and Haldeman?

Assignment II

The chapter you have just read suggests it is difficult for a writer to try and please a reader if the writer feels that he or she is being forced to write. Write an essay in which you explain what you think that part of the chapter means and tell whether you think it is true for you or not.

Here is one way to approach this assignment:

The assignment for the first chapter asked you to tell about yourself as a student and a writer and to discuss your goals. Read what you wrote. In that essay, did you use language that indicates that you feel that you *have to* learn to write? Did you use the language of a *victim?* One example of that might be that you felt that some previous teachers had not taught you properly, and that is why you are a bad writer now. Or did you use language that indicates that you *wish* to learn to write so that others will attend to what you have to say? As you reflect upon what you wrote, think about how your notions of yourself as a writer may affect your ability to write effectively. Write down these reflections in your notes.

When you write your essay in response to this assignment, tell what you think this chapter says about the relationship between a writer's attitude and effective writing. Then comment on that, using quotations from your first essay as examples to illustrate your opinion.

Chapter 3

Learning to Question

PREPARATORY ASSIGNMENT: TWO WAR POEMS

Learning to question is one of the foundations of a college education. The following exercise is intended to help you understand what questioning means, especially when you write.

Here are two poems written during World War I. The first is a complete poem; the second an excerpt from a longer poem. Can you guess the words omitted? (Hint: the second and fourth lines of each stanza rhyme.)

Poem 1

> Oh! give me the ____ of the lion,
>   The ____ of Reynard the Fox,
> And then I'll hurl troops at the Germans,
>   And give them the hardest of ____.
>
> Oh! think of the War Lord's ____ fist
>   That is ____ at England today;
> And think of the lives that our soldiers
>   Are ____ throwing away.
>
> Awake! oh you young men of England,
>   For if, when your ____'s in ____,
> You do not ____ by the thousand,
>   You truly are ____ indeed.

Poem 2

Bent double, like old ___ under sacks,
Knock-kneed, coughing like ___, we ___ through sludge,
Till on the ___ flares we turned our backs,
And toward our distant rest began to trudge.
Men marched ___. Many had lost their boots,
But ___ on, ___-shod. All went lame, all blind,
___ with fatigue; deaf even to the ___
Of gas-shells dropping softly behind.

Gas! GAS! Quick, boys! An ___ of fumbling,
Fitting the ___ helmets just in time,
But someone still was yelling out and stumbling
And flound'ring like a man in fire or ___.—
Dim through the ___ panes and ___ green light,
As under a ___ sea, I saw him ___.

First, write out both poems, guessing at the missing words. Leave blank any that you simply cannot guess. Then, explain which poem was easier to complete and why. And finally, which poet would you guess had an experience of war almost like your own? Why?

The Two War Poems Complete

Below are the two war poems; the underlined words are those that were missing in the exercise.

The first poem was written in 1914 by Eric Blair, who later wrote under the name George Orwell:

Awake! Young Men of England

Oh! give me the <u>strength</u> of the lion,
  The <u>wisdom</u> of Reynard the Fox,
And then I'll hurl troops at the Germans,
  And give them the hardest of <u>knocks</u>.

Oh! think of the War Lord's <u>mailed</u> fist
  That is <u>striking</u> at England today;
And think of the lives that our soldiers
  Are <u>fearlessly</u> throwing away.

Awake! oh you young men of England,
  For if, when your <u>Country</u>'s in <u>need</u>,
You do not <u>enlist</u> by the thousand,
  You truly are <u>cowards</u> indeed.

The second poem was written by Wilfred Owen, who died during World War I.

Dulce et Decorum Est

Bent double, like old <u>beggars</u> under sacks,
Knock-kneed, coughing like <u>hags</u>, we <u>cursed</u> through sludge,
Till on the <u>haunting</u> flares we turned our backs,
And toward our distant rest began to trudge.
Men marched <u>asleep</u>. Many had lost their boots,
But <u>limped</u> on, <u>blood</u>-shod. All went lame, all blind,
<u>Drunk</u> with fatigue; deaf even to the <u>hoots</u>
Of gas-shells dropping softly behind.

Gas! GAS! Quick, boys! An <u>ecstasy</u> of fumbling,
Fitting the <u>clumsy</u> helmets just in time,
But someone still was yelling out and stumbling
And flound'ring like a man in fire or <u>lime</u>.—
Dim through the <u>misty</u> panes and <u>thick</u> green light,
As under a <u>green</u> sea, I saw him <u>drowning</u>.

Here is the rest of this poem:

In all my dreams before my helpless sight
He plunges at me, guttering, choking, drowning.

If in some smothering dreams, you too could pace
Behind the wagon that we flung him in,
And watch the white eyes writhing in his face,
His hanging face, like a devil's sick of sin,
If you could hear, at every jolt, the blood
Come gargling from the froth-corrupted lungs
Bitten as the cud
Of vile, incurable sores on innocent tongues,—
My friend, you would not tell with such high zest
To children ardent for some desperate glory,
The old Lie: *Dulce et decorum est
Pro patria mori.*

Echoes, Questions, and Challenges

Both of these poems were written by Englishmen during World War I. Both address the same prevalent attitude toward war. English schoolboys who studied their Horace translated the Latin *dulce et decorum est pro patria mori* as "It is sweet and good to die for the nation." Such notions about war and patriotic duty inspired thousands of young men to rush to enlistment posts at the outbreak of World War I. Although Blair does not refer explicitly to Horace, the patriotic sentiment is certainly endorsed by his poem.

Despite these similarities, Blair and Owen differ sharply in their thoughts and feelings about the prevalent attitudes toward the war. Blair, who was a schoolboy when he wrote the poem, does not question them. His poem is an echo of received notions about patriotic duty, honor, and glory. So highly redundant of conventional wisdom is his thinking, the poem could almost be said to have written itself. Blair had only to turn on a kind of cultural tape recording to churn out the expected clichés. This is generic poetry, the all-purpose war poem. And like the labels on generic foods, the poem is plain vanilla. But a society at war wanted such sentiments; the poem was published in the *Henley and South Oxfordshire Standard.* Blair's poem echoes the stereotypical attitude toward war.

Owen, on the other hand, finds that his experience of the war compels him to question the stereotypes. His poem is an implicit warning to schoolboys like Blair and is a bitter criticism of people such as the publisher of the *Henley and South Oxfordshire Standard,* who encourage young men to accept unquestioningly the idea that it is sweet and good to die for the nation. For Owen, war means that young men age before their time, endure grotesque hardships, and die excruciating deaths by drowning in the fluid of their own lungs. Accepting the sentiment *dulce et decorum est pro patria mori* means we have to live with the nightmare we create by believing, and by asking young men to believe, that it is sweet and good to die for the nation. Unlike Blair, Owen does not echo a stereotype; he speaks in a voice made critical by bitter experience.

The difference between Blair and Owen is shown in their language. You can easily fill in the blanks of Blair's poem. Even if you do not guess exactly the words he uses, substituting a synonym does not really change the meaning. Blair's language is already familiar to you because you, too, know the stereotypes we use to make our wars meaningful. You may have felt that the poem was silly or naive simply because it was easy to guess what it had to say. It is obvious that Blair uses language here uncritically.

With Owen's poem, the case is quite different. There really is no way to guess what word is missing from "an ＿＿ of fumbling"; no way to anticipate that for Owen the moments between hearing the warning "Gas!" and fitting on the gas helmet were "an <u>ecstasy</u> of fumbling." To describe what he experiences, Owen has wrenched words from their usual meanings and put them into new contexts. He makes words fit his perceptions, rather than fitting his perceptions to conventional terms. Blair's poem could be made to describe any war against any enemy just by changing the name Germans. Owen's poem could not be about any war other than World War I, yet so particular is it that it seems to tell us about all wars, while Blair does not tell us about any. To substitute one word for another in Owen's poem would mean changing the meaning in a substantial way. The particular power of his language reaches us in a way that Blair's simply cannot.

What Is Interpretation?

Each of these poems offers an interpretation of war; that is, each tells us what World War I meant to an individual. The meaning of World War I for each poet lies in the thoughts and feelings each has about it. That is interpretation: making events, things, or ideas meaningful by describing what we think and feel about them. It is impossible for us to avoid assigning such meaning; we have thoughts and feelings about what we see and hear. Often we do not articulate them. The point of reading, writing, and thinking in college is to become conscious of the meaning we assign, to question the typical rules, assumptions, or stereotypes we use, and to discuss and debate our interpretations with others.

The toughest part of all this is realizing that what we think about something is distinct from what we perceive or experience. You were asked, for instance, which poem most closely resembled your experience of war. Some students answer that Owen's experience matches their own more closely than does Blair's. Yet none of these students had ever been to war. Their experiences are really much more like Blair's, who was writing from the safety of a schoolroom in England. What these students mean is that their *interpretations* of war—their thoughts and feelings about it—were closer to Owen's interpretation than to Blair's.

We frequently confuse what we think about something with what we perceive or have experienced. Let us pretend for a moment that you have been invited to the president's reception for new students. There will be professors and deans and some other students at the reception, but you are new to the campus, so you will probably not know anyone.

You go to the reception, carefully dressed and a little nervous. Soon you find yourself standing against the wall with a glass of punch in your hand, watching small knots of people around the room.

You think to yourself, "Just as I thought. Nobody here wants to talk to me. I thought there must be some mistake when they invited me. This reception is probably for really bright students. How did my name get on the list? This is so embarrassing!"

After enduring this misery for a time, you slink to the cloakroom and out the door. Later, you tell a friend, "Boy, what a dull reception that was. What a bunch of snobs."

Now, let's try it another way. You go to the reception and again find yourself standing against the wall with a glass of punch in your hand, watching other people.

You say to yourself, "Well, I guess I'm supposed to go introduce myself. They wouldn't have asked me here if they didn't want me to come, so the only way to get things going is to break the ice. I like the looks of that little group over there. I'll go introduce myself."

So you do, and soon you have met one group and are introduced to some others, and find yourself having several interesting conversations before you leave.

The next day you tell your friend, "That was a very pleasant reception. I met some very nice people."

How we understand the reception depends upon our past experiences and what we think the rules for good etiquette ought to be. If we believe, for instance, that those who are already present should come over and introduce themselves to us when we arrive, and they don't, we are likely to label them snobs. If we assume that everyone at the reception is a guest, and that guests are expected to introduce themselves, we will label others in the room guests just like us, and we will begin circulating. We would probably unthinkingly assume that what we thought about the reception was the same thing as what we perceived. What we perceive are people standing around in a room—and that is all. What we understand about them, and how we label them, are our own interpretations.

Reading, writing, and thinking in college involve testing the rules or assumptions that we use to label our perceptions and experiences. Let's return to the reception. Suppose you are standing awkwardly by the wall, and you have this dialogue with yourself:

"Nobody here wants to talk with me."

"How do you know?"

"Because nobody has come over to introduce himself, that's why."

"Maybe here you are supposed to introduce yourself. See, there's someone who came in when you did. She's just gone over to that group. It looks as if she is introducing herself. They don't seem to know each other."

"O.K. I get it. I'll give it a try."

If you test your rules or assumptions, you may well discover that what you perceive does not support them. When Owen measured the sentiment *dulce et decorum est pro patria mori* against experience, he changed his understanding of the war and the nation that had sent him and others to fight in it. Similarly, if we discover that our assumptions about manners—who should be introduced to whom—do not suit a particular occasion, we can alter our understanding of both the occasion itself and our rules about etiquette.

Confusion, Questioning, and Interpreting

Confusion is often an essential part of learning to interpret in new ways what we perceive. The sense of confusion you might have felt when you stood awkwardly waiting for people at the reception to introduce themselves could lead to a very productive questioning. First of all, it could lead to a *concentration* on the problem and to *careful observation*. Second, it could lead to a *fresh insight*, a new understanding of the rules for social behavior. We usually think of confusion as something to be avoided. But in higher education, confusion is often one of the requirements for learning. The really productive thinking begins when we are intrigued rather than repelled by evidence or ideas that seem to confound our rules, assumptions, understanding, or stereotypes.

Most of what you are asked to do as a student in college involves understanding and testing rules or assumptions. Another way to say this is that you are asked to understand and test interpretations. The best thing you can do for yourself is to become keenly aware of how often you are asked to understand someone's interpretations. It will help if you notice who wrote the textbook you are using and if you get in the habit of saying, for instance, "I'm reading John Kenneth Galbraith's interpretation of economics" rather than "I'm studying economics." Or "I'm studying Professor Schnorr's interpretation of American history" rather than "I'm taking history from Professor Schnorr." You will have a clearer idea of why you are asked to write essays if you think, "Professor Schnoor wants me to interpret some aspect of the Revolutionary War" rather than "I have to write a paper for history class."

The next step is to become aware of your own interpretations. This is easier to do if you keep the following diagram in mind.

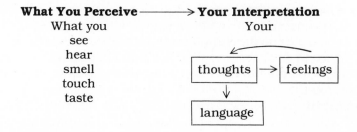

What You Perceive means whatever you are studying at the moment—the assigned readings, for instance, in any of your courses. It may be a chapter in your philosophy textbook or a lab experiment in chemistry.

Your Interpretation means your thoughts, ideas, assumptions, and feelings about what you study. Thoughts come to us in words. For each subject you study, there will be a special lexicon, a set of terms used in that field. The lexicon may contain words in common usage with highly restricted meanings or it may have terms unique to that field. There will also be rules or methods that you will use to interpret what you study. Offering your interpretation means, then, offering your thoughts within the context of the discipline; that is, using the discipline's language, rules, and assumptions.

As for feelings, they do not come to us as words, but we use words to describe them. It may seem that you are not to include your feelings in your interpretation, or that some disciplines exclude them, but that is not quite accurate. The sense of calm deliberation is, for instance, a feeling; so is the sense of being dispassionate while examining a subject. So, too, is a sense of control that comes from concentration. Even in those disciplines that seem to exclude "feeling," interpretations must convey, through the tone of the language, the sense that the writer is calm, deliberate, or dispassionate, concentrating on the central issues, and in control of the language and ideas. And these feelings are difficult to convey convincingly unless you really feel them.

Finally, interpretation requires testing rules and assumptions. You will be often tempted, especially when writing a paper, to exclude information that does not fit your interpretation. This leads to the kind of writing Blair used, in which what he was writing about—the war—was forced to fit a stereotyped set of assumptions about war.

Learning starts when we question to what extent rules, assumptions, or stereotypes really explain what we perceive or experience, and this often leads to confusion. Confusion is a state of mind; whether we make good use of it or not depends upon the feelings we attach to it. If it makes you feel inadequate or "dumb," then you will slink from the party early. If it makes you curious, then you will find yourself concentrating on it to find a way to make some sense out of it. Curiosity about confusion is really one way to define learning. It is also what leads to having a good time at a party.

When you are reading, for instance, and you say, "Plato is boring," you may mean, "I'm confused by what Plato has written. I don't see what he has to do with me. To heck with Plato!" What needs changing here is the feeling about confusion: "I'm confused by Plato, but everyone says he is so important to Western thought. That means that he is important to me in some way I don't understand yet. I'd better hit the books again!"

Similarly, you might find yourself saying, "I'm supposed to write a paper interpreting Plato. How can I do that? I can't make any sense out of him. This is awful!" Or you can say, "Suppose I start by asking what it is Plato could possibly mean in a passage I find confusing. I'll go back to the part in the *Republic* where he says the Philosopher Kings will lie to the people about religion. I think lying is always bad. Why does Plato say he thinks leaders in a perfect society will have to lie about religion? Maybe I'm wrong. Maybe he is. Maybe if I reread the passage, check my notes, and just start writing in my own words what I think he is saying, I'll come up with some ideas I can develop."

By becoming curious about confusion rather than panicked by it, you make confusion a part of the learning process, and you make writing integral to it. What this book hopes to demonstrate is just how smart that is.

A student might object by saying, "But I thought you said our essays were supposed to convey that we were calm, deliberate, and in control of our ideas. How can I do that and be confused at the same time?" Remember, confusion is a state of mind. It goes, on the diagram, under *Thoughts.* Being worried, panicked, or intimidated by it go under the heading *Feelings.* It is possible to describe a source of confusion in a calm, deliberate manner, but to do so you must study the source of confusion systematically; that is, discuss confusing matters in a way that is itself not confusing.

Summary

Questioning our interpretations is not easy. It requires, first of all, recognizing that the words we use to label our perceptions and experiences are not the perceptions and experiences themselves, but are our ways of interpreting them for ourselves. The labels and expressions we use are often stereotypes, or echoes of what is regarded as typical. Questioning such common assumptions can lead to confusion, as can encountering new information that we cannot easily accommodate into our common assumptions. Questioning is a way of testing our common assumptions. Sometimes it confirms them; other times it will lead us to alter or adjust them. Either way, without such questioning, we do not speak in our own voice as Owen does; instead, we speak as Blair did—as an echo.

ASSIGNMENTS
Assignment I

Describe an episode in which you and someone else interpreted the same thing differently or in which you were a witness to others caught in this sort of web. How does the episode you chose illustrate the discussion in this chapter?

Assignments Preliminary to Writing

1. Here is an example to help stimulate your thinking. Paul Watzlawick, in *How Real Is Real* (New York: Random House, 1977), quotes this case from Ronald D. Laing, H. Phillipson, and A. Russell Lee, in *Interpersonal Perception:*

> A husband and wife, after eight years of marriage, described one of their first fights. This occurred on the second night of their honeymoon. They were both sitting at a bar in a hotel when the wife struck up a conversation with a couple sitting next to them. To her dismay, her husband refused to join the conversation, remained aloof, gloomy, antagonistic both to her and the other couple. Perceiving his mood, she became angry at him for producing an awkward social situation and making her feel "out on a limb." Tempers rose, and they ended in a bitter fight in which each accused the other of being inconsiderate.

Eight years later, Watzlawick goes on to say, the couple finally analyzed what had happened. Each had defined *honeymoon* differently. For the wife, it "was the first opportunity to practice her newly acquired social role." As she explained it: "I had never had a conversation with another couple as a wife before. Previous to this I had always been a 'girl friend' or 'fiancee' or 'daughter' or 'sister.'" The husband, on the other hand, defined *honeymoon* as a "period of exclusive togetherness." He felt that a honeymoon was "a golden opportunity . . . to ignore the rest of the world and simply explore each other." When his wife struck up a conversation with another couple, Watzlawick says, the husband took it to mean "he was insufficient to fill her demands." (7–8)

Does this example remind you of a similar episode in your own experience? Jot down short reminders of as many of them as you can. As you review them, consider which one seems most promising for an essay.

2. Reread this chapter. Mark passages that seem relevant to this assignment. Note your responses to them.

3. Review your notes, reread the assignment, and plan how you will present your ideas.

Drafting and Revision

Draft your essay. How can you describe the episode so that your readers can easily visualize it? Will dialogue help? Will character description help? How will your readers be able to tell your attitude toward your subject? What tone do you wish to adopt toward the audience? When you explain how the episode relates to the chapter, quote or paraphrase the relevant passages to remind your audience of them.

Bring your draft to class. Be prepared to read it aloud or to have it read aloud. Offer your advice to other writers. Were you able to visualize the episode? Did you understand the point? How would you characterize the writer's tone?

Take notes on the discussion of your essay and afterward add any other ideas that you have for revising. Then, revise your essay.

Assignment II

Describe an experience that illustrates learning by questioning. How does it illustrate the discussion in this chapter?

Assignments Preliminary to First Draft

1. Here is an example to help jog your memory. A junior high school used what is called arena scheduling; that is, students enrolled for all their courses in one room, the gymnasium. On the first day of school,

each student was assigned, along with 24 others, to a classroom, where an adviser helped the students plan their schedules. Every student then filled out one card for each class he or she wanted to take. At the sound of a bell, all the students in the school—seventh, eighth, and ninth graders—took their cards to the gymnasium.

There they found long tables arranged along all four walls. Each table had a tall post with a sign indicating which department the table represented; e.g., History, English, Mathematics, Physical Education. Students dropped their class cards in appropriate boxes on the tables. If a student wanted to enroll in a Shakespeare class, for instance, he or she dropped a card in one of the boxes on the table marked *English.* After they had done this with each of their class cards, the students returned to their advising room.

Meanwhile, the clerks at the tables opened the boxes. Each course had a quota, a maximum number of students who could enroll. The clerks counted out cards up to the quota. Any additional cards were given to couriers, who took them back to the students who had not gotten the course or courses they wanted. Their advisers then helped them revise their schedules. Those students who had no cards returned to them were free to leave.

You can imagine how confusing this could become, with several hundred students scurrying about a large gymnasium to drop their cards into boxes. Seventh graders had an especially hard time. Both the building and the procedure were new to them. Moreover, seventh graders are usually a bit shorter than ninth graders, so when they came into the gym, many seventh graders saw a forest of belt buckles, not the orderly arrangements of tables, signs, and boxes.

One day, an honest and outspoken seventh grader, overwhelmed by the pandemonium of the gym, shouted at the top of his lungs, "WILL SOMEONE TELL ME WHAT'S GOING ON HERE?"

Everyone in the room froze. You could hear a pin drop. Several teachers rushed up and escorted the lad from the room. There was some nervous laughter, and then everyone in the gymnasium returned to the scurrying hubbub.

Does this remind you of a time when you felt confused because you could not understand what was going on around you, but everyone else seemed to know what the rules were? Tell what you did, or tried to do, to bring some order to your confusion. Did it work? Explain as best you can how what you went through represented learning by questioning. What steps were involved? What role did confusion play, for instance? Concentrating? Questioning? Is there a way in which this experience is like learning in general?

2. Reread this chapter, marking the relevant passages and noting your responses.

3. Review your notes, reread the assignment, and plan how you will present your ideas.

Drafting and Revision

Use the suggestions provided for Assignment I.

Assignment III

Eric Blair later wrote under the pen name George Orwell. A student who read both "Awake! Young Men of England" and Orwell's *1984* commented, "He changed more than his name." What is the change? How is it relevant to the discussion in this chapter?

Assignments Preliminary to First Draft

1. Included in Part IV, Anthology, Section Four is an excerpt from *1984*. Reread it enough to be able to state Orwell's point about the relationship between language and power. Mark the passages that illustrate this point.

2. What do you think George Orwell as an adult thought about the poem he had written as a boy? Why do you think so? What passages in *1984* would you use to illustrate your answer? Would you agree with his presumed assessment? Why?

3. Reread the chapter, marking passages relevant to this assignment. Take notes on why you think they are relevant.

4. Review your notes, reread the assignment, and plan how you will present your ideas.

Drafting and Revision

Assume that your audience is interested in the nature of language and is not very familiar with the works of George Orwell. Remember to cite and quote or paraphrase the passages to which you refer. Bring your draft to class. Be prepared to read it aloud or to have it read. Offer your suggestions to other writers. Did the essay respond to the assignment? Did you understand the main point? Did you agree or disagree with it? What suggestions would you offer? Take notes of the discussion of your essay and add any other ideas for revision that occur to you. Then revise your essay. Acknowledge those in class who helped you clarify your ideas, even if they did so by disagreeing with you.

PART I I

Modes of Discovery

Chapter 4

Overview

In the following chapters, we will study how the various disciplines ask questions and answer them. The most common questions are:

What is the significance of this?
What is the cause of a given effect?
What is a solution to this problem?
What is the value, worth, or utility of this?
How are things comparable? Distinct?
What ought we accept or reject?

A simple enough set of questions, really. And the basic way of answering them is simple enough as well. Generally, you will find four basic elements to the answers offered in the disciplines:

A *given:* This is an assumption that the writer asks the reader to accept as true from the outset.

A *position or conclusion:* This states the writer's opinion regarding some aspect of the given.

Reasons: These are the writer's statements telling why he or she has adopted the position or arrived at the conclusion.

Evidence: These are the illustrations of the writer's reasons.

The given, position, and reasons together constitute an argument. An argument is supported or illustrated by evidence. Let us examine these elements one at a time.

The Givens

We will study five kinds of givens:

A Hypothesis

A hypothesis is an educated guess about the cause of some observed effect. The notion that human behavior is shaped primarily by culture or upbringing is a hypothesis; so is the contrary notion that it is shaped primarily by genetic factors.

A Problem

As the name suggests, a problem is any condition that both the writer and the reader agree is unsatisfactory. That both the Soviet Union and the United States have too many nuclear weapons is one such problem. So is the fact that scholars cannot figure out the significance of the Old Testament prohibitions against certain foods.

The Inherent Significance of an Individual's Experience

Particularly—though not exclusively—in the humanities, it is taken as a given that even the mundane experience of an individual is significant for what it reveals about the human heart and mind.

The New or Unknown Can Be Understood by Comparison with the Known

The most available form of this kind of given is the analogy, used by poet, scientist, and inventor alike as a mode of discovery.

Evaluative Criteria

All the disciplines assume that they can assess the value, worth, or utility of what they study, according to their own critical standards.

The Position or Conclusions

These are the kinds of conclusions or positions we will study:

Findings in Relation to a Hypothesis

A researcher can find that a particular observation confirms or disconfirms a hypothesis. He or she can also find that the results are inconclusive or wholly surprising.

Positions in Relation to a Problem

A writer addressing a problem takes a position on each of the following: whether or not the problem is being properly addressed or resolved; the cause or history of the problem; a solution to the problem; and a defense of the solution against possible objections.

Conclusions About What an Experience Signifies

A writer who deals with human experience decides what the experience signifies about human nature in general.

Conclusions About Value, Worth, or Utility

The writer applies criteria for judging, choosing, or evaluating a particular subject or problem.

The Reasons

These are the kinds of reasons we will study:

Generalizations

A descriptive generalization states a typical trait or behavior that can be directly observed. An analytical generalization states what seems to be the most usual and immediate cause of a typical trait or behavior. Observers use generalizations to report what they have discovered from their direct observation.

Propositions

A proposition states the writer's understanding of what is already known. The statement, "We should reduce nuclear arms by 50 percent" is a proposition, based on what we already know about nuclear armaments and their danger.

Understanding Arguments

You will often hear that there are two basic kind of arguments: inductive and deductive. It might be convenient to have a general notion of what those terms mean. An inductive argument is one based on direct observation; a deductive argument is one based on an acknowledged principle or accepted knowledge. In practice, the distinctions between these two kinds of argument tend to blur. The scientific method, for instance, begins with a principle accepted as true—a hypothesis—which is the way a deductive argument begins. But the hypothesis is tested by direct observation; that is, by induction.

Still, it is useful to have these general distinctions in mind because they help clarify the purposes of different kinds of arguments. To understand these purposes, we have to first consider the possible kinds of statements we can make. Of the three kinds of sentences, only one can be judged true or false. An *imperative* or command, such as "While you're up, get me a cola," cannot be judged true or false. Nor can an *interrogative* or question, such as "Will he come tomorrow?" But *declarative* sentences, which make statements, can be:

Bears hibernate.
The government should not support the establishment of a religion.
All men are created equal.

Are these statements true? Well, yes, but in different ways. The statement, *Bears hibernate*, is a generalization about *all* bears based on observing some of them. As with all generalizations, we assume that what is true for those members of a class we have observed is *probably* true for all members of the same class. The less we know about a group of things that we observe, the less certain we are that our generalization is true.

What about the statements, *All men are created equal*, and *The government should not support the establishment of a religion*? True here means whether or not the statement reflects a society's consensus about values, the lessons of history, and what the society believes will contribute to its own greatest good or happiness. The question is not whether such statements might possibly be proved by direct observation; the question is whether they are morally, ethically, legally, or politically true for us. Do we assent to them? Ought we to?

An inductive argument is intended to provide persuasive reasons for accepting generalizations about what was observed directly; a deductive argument is intended to provide persuasive reasons for accepting propositions. And the disciplines, as we suggested earlier, pretty much thrive on debating the merits of various arguments. Of the questions we stated at the beginning of this chapter, perhaps the most common to all the disciplines is, What ought we accept or reject? Because this critical frame of mind is really at the heart of academic study, it is not surprising that the disciplines have certain ways of presenting their arguments. The differing natures of the disciplines are reflected in the different kinds of arguments they favor. And because you will be writing in the disciplines, we will study the ways their arguments are presented.

At issue is whether or not a writer's reasoning about information is sound. Here is a brief illustration of what that means. Suppose someone says to you, "Did you read Joe Smith's letter to the editor? He thinks we need to increase the income tax in order to reduce the national debt. He must be a Democrat."

An astute listener can transform this into an argument in the bat of an eye: *Take it as given that either* all those who favor an increase in the income tax to reduce the national debt are Democrats *or* all Democrats favor an increase in the income tax to reduce the national debt. *Then we can conclude:* Joe Smith must be a Democrat. *Because* Joe Smith favors increasing the income tax. *Evidence:* He said he wanted to increase the income tax.

Should we accept this argument? Well, you can see that you can decide even if you do not know Joe personally. Neither of the givens—both of which are possible though unstated—is true if tested against experience. When an objection can be made to the writer's given, reason, or conclusion, the argument is regarded as flawed or as an example of weak reasoning. Of course, there is another way to evaluate this argument, and that is by supplying more evidence. We could go ask Joe.

These, then, are the two ways arguments are evaluated: the quality of the reasoning and the quality of the evidence. When you write for your classes, those are the criteria that will be applied to what you say. When you are assigned a reading, those are the criteria that you are expected to apply. The disciplines have different conventions for judging different kinds of arguments (we will study them) but they have in common a critical frame of mind when it comes to assessing arguments and evidence.

Evidence

The different kinds of evidence are:

Expert or Authoritative Opinion or Commentary

In all academic disciplines, scholars comment upon what they study. Such opinion or commentary is authoritative; that is, we have good reason to believe that such writers are authorities on the subject because they have studied it for some time. Their commentary on a subject is therefore useful for supporting another writer's proposition; however, no such authority is entirely undisputed. Authorities quarrel with one another, and the arguments offered by an authority are subject to the same tests for validity and quality of information as are any others. As students, the authoritative or expert opinion available to you will usually consist of what your professors say, what your textbooks say, the wisdom of writers you are assigned to read who have exerted a profound influence on the nature of our civilization, and what the scholars say in the secondary readings you are assigned. If, for example, you are assigned to study the Declaration of Independence, you might also be asked to read George Will's commentary on it in *Inventing America*. His comments are authoritative evidence that you could draw upon to support what you have to say about the Declaration, but other authoritative commentators disagree with him, and a complete analysis would therefore involve presenting both sides of the argument and explaining which position you support.

Statistics

The results of empirical studies—such as polls—can be used as evidence to support a proposition, but they are also subject to dispute. Reliable statistics come from a qualified, unbiased source, were analyzed using approved methods, were drawn from a reliable sample, and are current; that is, the study has not been superseded by another study.

Examples

An example is a particular instance used to illustrate a proposition or generalization; it is a *for instance.*

> Mated woodpeckers are adapted so that they do not compete with one another for the same resources; for instance, the male woolly woodpecker has a long, strong beak for pecking deep into the tree in the search for bugs, while the female has a shorter, blunter beak which she uses to pry up the bark to locate bugs just under it.

The writer of the paragraph above could have cataloged every kind of woodpecker, but in the interest of economy and not boring the reader to death, she chose one illustrative example.

In the humanities, the examples a writer uses are often quotations from the reading or readings upon which the writer is commenting. Such quotations are the evidence the writer uses to support his or her interpretation—which is one kind of argument—of what the work means. For instance, here is a passage by the literary critic Gilbert Highet from *Talents and Geniuses,* (New York: Oxford UP, 1957):

> It was the best of times, it was the worst of times, it was the age of wisdom, it was the age of foolishness, it was the epoch of belief, it was the epoch of incredulity, it was the Season of Light, it was the Season of Darkness, it was the spring of hope, it was the winter of despair, we had everything before us, we had nothing before us, we were all going direct to Heaven, we were all going direct the other way—in short, the period was so far like the present period, that some of its noisiest authorities insisted on its being received, for good or for evil, in the superlative degree of comparison only.

> That is the overture to Charles Dickens's *Tale of Two Cities.* It describes the years just before the French Revolution, in the same satirical tones as Dickens used about his own period; it warns us that that was a period of confusion, it makes us feel much of its unrest, it prepares for the extremes of the French Revolution, and at the same time it shows, without announcing the fact directly, that Dickens will take no sides: he will neither oppose the French Revolution as a frightful crime, nor praise it as though it were heaven on earth. He was a skillfull writer. (225-226)

To see the importance of quoting the text as an example of the commentator's interpretation, cover up the quotation from Dickens and reread what Highet says it means, amending his first sentence to: "The opening of Dickens's *A Tale of Two Cities* describes. . . ." Even though Highet had every reason to believe his readers probably would have read *A Tale of Two Cities*, he does not tax their memories or try offering an interpretation that the reader cannot test; he quotes the passage to refresh the reader's memory and to allow the reader to judge what Highet says against the evidence itself.

Precedent

"History never repeats itself; man always does," said Voltaire. In our more egalitarian age, he would probably have said men and women always do. Precedent is used to support propositions about ethics, morality, policy decisions, and law. For instance, here is a passage from George F. Kennan's "A Proposal for International Disarmament" (see Part IV, Anthology, Section Four):

> What is it then, if not our own will, and if not the supposed wickedness of our opponents, that has brought us to this pass?
>   The answer, I think, is clear. It is primarily the inner momentum, the independent momentum, or the weapons race itself—the compulsions that arise and take charge of great powers when they enter upon a competition with each other in the building up of major armaments of any sort.
>   This is nothing new. I am a diplomatic historian. I see this same phenomenon playing its fateful part in the relations among the great European powers as much as a century ago. I see this competitive buildup of armaments conceived initially as a means to an end but soon becoming the end in itself. I see it taking possession of men's imagination and behavior, becoming a force in its own right, detaching itself from the political differences that initially inspired it, and then leading both parties, invariably and inexorably, to the war they no longer know how to avoid.

Kennan uses what has happened in the past to support his proposition that the cause of our current nuclear arms race is neither our own conscious choice nor the conscious effort of our enemy. The use of precedent as evidence simply involves the use of some event from the past to illustrate or explain the writer's position on some event in the present. Because history consists of the words written to record and explain previous events, using precedent as evidence usually means drawing upon written discourse, either quoting it directly or, as Kennan does here, summarizing a common body of knowledge.

Testimony

Testimony means simply an "eyewitness" account; for a writer, it means the evidence gathered from listening and recording what some witness to an event says about it or relating the writer's own relevant experiences.

Because personal testimony is the kind of evidence students least frequently use, often because they believe it is "illegal" to use "I," you may find it worthwhile to notice how often writers turn to their own experiences as evidence for their propositions; for example, Victor Frankl, a neurologist and psychiatrist who developed a form of therapy called logotherapy after he was released from Auschwitz, comments in *Man's Search for Meaning* (New York: Beacon Press, 1962) on what he as a doctor learned from his extreme physical deprivation about the resiliency of the human body:

> I would like to mention a few similar surprises on how much we could endure: we were unable to clean our teeth, and yet, in spite of that and a severe vitamin deficiency, we had healthier gums than ever before. We had to wear the same shirts for half a year, until they had lost all appearance of being shirts. For days we were unable to wash, even partially, because of frozen water pipes, and yet the sores and abrasions on hands which were dirty from work in the soil did not suppurate (that is, unless there was frostbite). Or for instance, a light sleeper, who used to be disturbed by the slightest noise in the next room, now found himself lying pressed against a comrade who snored loudly a few inches from his ear and yet slept quite soundly through the noise.
>
> If someone now asked of us the truth of Dostoevski's statement that flatly defines man as a being who can get used to anything, we would reply, "Yes, a man can get used to anything, but do not ask us how."(15-16)

For another example, here are the words of Charles Dodgson (who wrote fiction under the pseudonym Lewis Carroll), using his own experience as evidence that talking is a good way to resolve a problem in logic or math. He says in *Symbolic Logic and the Game of Logic* (1896; New York: Dover, 1958):

> *Talking* is a wonderful smoother-over in difficulties. When *I* come upon anything—in Logic or any other hard subject—that entirely puzzles me, I find it a capital plan to talk it over, *aloud*, even when I am all alone. One can explain things so *clearly* to oneself! And then, you know, one is so *patient* with one's self: one never gets irritated with one's own stupidity! (xvi)

Because the discourses of the humanities challenge us to ask, "Ought I to accept this?" our own experiences are often valuable sources of evidence for our decisions about whether or not a writer's propositions are warranted. In the humanities, "I" is not forbidden; in fact, it is often at center stage.

Critical Reading

Understanding and evaluating a writer's argument and evidence demand a special kind of reading. It differs from reading for simple entertainment because it requires both rereading and stopping to deliberate upon what a passage means. One of the things we have learned from comparing poor students with successful students is that poorer students keep right on reading even though they do not understand what a passage means. This is how one student describes the result:

> Many times when faced with long, complex readings, I have elected to take "the short way out" by reading endlessly through the material, disregarding the terms I did not understand. . . . Upon completion, I possessed little knowledge . . . of what had been read, only a few scattered thoughts.

Successful students stop reading when they arrive at a passage that is difficult or problematic and try to figure out what it means before going on. Understanding a writer's arguments and evidence usually requires this stop-and-go reading. It is a way of reading that is more like driving in heavy, downtown traffic than it is like cruising down a superhighway. Perhaps the best analogy is to driving daily over a regular route—to get to work, for instance—in downtown traffic. The first reading is like the first time you find your way to a new job; it familiarizes you with the route. You may get a little lost and have to go around the block once or twice. With the second reading, you become more confident of your direction; gradually, by going over the reading like a regular route, you become highly familiar with it. Critical reading means reading with pen and paper nearby, so that you can stop to formulate a writer's arguments, just as a math student has to stop to work out the problem given as an example in a discussion of some mathematical operation before moving on.

Grasping a writer's arguments places another special demand on the reader because the writer is usually responding to the arguments of another writer. To understand an assigned reading, we often have to consult secondary readings, or readings to which a writer refers, in order to understand the primary reading more completely. In *Rhetoric of Motives*, (Berkeley, CA: U of California Press, 1973) Kenneth Burke provides an illuminating analogy comparing this kind of reading to arriving late at a party:

> Imagine that you enter a parlor. You come late. When you arrive, others have long preceded you, and they are engaged in a heated discussion, a discussion too heated for them to pause and tell you exactly what it is all about. In fact, the discussion had already begun long before any of them got there, so that no one present is qualified to retrace for you all the steps that had gone before. You listen for a while, until you decide that you have caught the tenor of the argument; then you put in your oar. Someone answers; you answer him; another comes to your defense; another aligns himself against you. . . . However, the discussion is interminable. The hour grows late, you must depart. And you do depart, with the discussion still vigorously in progress. (10-11)

The issues raised by the academic disciplines have been the subject of debate since the beginning of critical discourse, for they include the imponderables of our spiritual, political, social, ethical, physical, and aesthetic natures. A writer addressing one of these subjects is implicitly engaging in a conversation with all those who have most influenced our thinking about it, so that Plato, who wrote in the fifth century B.C, may be as important a participant in the conversation as is a contemporary commentator.

Approaching a reading as if it were a conversation among the writer and those who have come before helps a reader spot the signals a writer gives that he or she is offering a counterargument or a supporting argument, and guides the reader to secondary texts that have influenced the writer. Understanding a reading as a conversation in which the reader is expected to join also helps the reader who will eventually write about what he or she has read, because all such writing—including that done by students—ultimately involves responding to the arguments presented by other writers.

Chapter 5

Signs

PREPARATORY ASSIGNMENT: THE CURIOUS INCIDENT

In Sir Arthur Conan Doyle's "The Silver Blaze," a valuable horse is stolen one night from under the noses of two sleeping stable assistants, the stable dog, and the stable boy.

The Inspector, who appreciates all the help that Holmes can provide, asks him:

"Is there any other point to which you wish to draw my attention?"
"To the curious incident of the dog in the night-time."
"The dog did nothing in the night-time."
"That was the curious incident," remarked Sherlock Holmes.

What is the significance of the dog's behavior?

Fallible and Infallible Signs

The first mode of discovery that we will study is one that you will encounter fairly frequently in the humanities. It involves finding in recollected experience a sign of some special quality of the heart of mind. In its simplest terms, a sign is an action or event that indicates that some other action or event has occurred or is about to occur. A dog's bark, for instance, is the sign that an intruder or stranger is present. That is how, in "The Silver Blaze," Sherlock Holmes solved the mystery of the theft in

55

the stable. On the evening of the theft, the dog in the stable did *not* bark, which signified—or was a sign—that the person in the stable must have been familiar to the dog. In our day-to-day lives, we regularly rely on signs, such as the dog's bark, as indicators of something that has occurred or is about to occur:

Thunder is the sign of an impending storm.

Smoke is the sign of fire.

A cock's crow is the sign of dawn.

An engagement ring is a sign of an intended marriage.

A yawn is the sign of tiredness or boredom.

A groundhog seeing his shadow on February 2 is a sign of six more weeks of winter.

A sign should not be confused with a cause; thunder does not "cause" a storm, nor does the rooster cause the sun to rise. But a sign can be an effect: the light of dawn causes the cock's crow; fire causes smoke. Circumstantial evidence in court is an example of a sign, and, as we have seen, so is a clue in a detective story.

Just as a detective in fiction or a lawyer in court uses clues as signs of what probably occurred, we sometimes use signs to inquire into the workings of the human heart and mind, prompted by the question, "Given that I did such and such, what was it a sign of?" We assign this kind of significance half-smilingly when we say, for instance, "I can't seem to ever remember where I left my glasses; it must be a sign of old age creeping up on me." In this case, we take an experience—mislaying our glasses—and assign it significance by saying the action signals something about our nature. This is one way signs are used in the humanities—in philosophy, or religion, or literature, for instance. Writers in these fields make experience significant by investigating what it signifies about the human condition. Their way of proceeding often differs a bit from the way we use common signs for such things as thunder or an engagement ring.

We already know what the signs in common usage signify. We say that such signs are either fallible or infallible indications of something else. An infallible sign is one that *invariably* and *exclusively* indicates something. As an illustration, we might choose the engagement ring. When worn on the fourth finger of a woman's left hand, it *invariably* signals an intended marriage. And it signals *only* that intention, exclusive of all others. Similarly, wood smoke *always* and *exclusively* indicates fire. But although a cock's crow invariably or always precedes the coming dawn, it does not signal it exclusively. Roosters are in the habit of crowing during broad daylight, too; hence, a cock's crow is a fallible sign of dawn. When we use signs in common usage, we know whether they are infallible—which means that they are always signs of something and only of that thing—or fallible—which means that they are not always a sign of something or are not only a sign of it.

But when a writer is assigning significance to experience, he or she cannot assume that we as readers will understand that experience as inevitably and exclusively signifying for us what it signifies for him or her. The writer cannot even be sure that we will *sometimes* assign it the same significance, as we do a fallible sign in common usage. We know, for instance, what a groundhog on Groundhog's Day is supposed to signify. But what would you say is the significance of seeing men walking along the street wearing overcoats and hats? Or of a boy stealing pears from his family's orchard? These events could mean anything. One purpose of the humanities is to assign significance to such experience and to assign it in a way that will convey that significance to the reader as if it were an infallible sign of the meaning the writer gives it.

Descartes and the Significance of Hats and Coats

Take, for instance, men walking in the street wearing overcoats and hats. In his *Meditations,* Descartes understands this as signifying something about, or as a sign of, how the human mind works:

> I remember that, when looking from a window and saying I see men who pass in the street, I really do not see them, but infer that what I see is men. . . . And yet what do I see from the window but hats and coats which may cover automatic machines? Yet I judge these to be men [see Part IV, Anthology, Section Two].

The "hats and coats" Descartes saw from the window were signs of "men who pass in the street." Yet we would not say, "I see signs of men who pass in the street;" rather, we would say, with Descartes, "I see men who pass in the street." Descartes wonders why we say so naturally and with such certainty that we "see" something, when what we see is really a sign of it. From the sign *hats and coats,* he learns something about the workings of our perception, mind, memory, imagination, and understanding. Ultimately, he is trying to discover what he can know with absolute certainty: "I shall have the right to conceive high hopes if I am happy enough to discover one thing only which is certain and indubitable." After his example of "hats and coats," among others, Descartes concludes that he has found his answer:

> But finally here I am, having insensibly reverted to the point I desired, for, since it is now manifest to me that even bodies are not properly speaking known by the senses or by the faculty of imagination, but by the understanding only, and since they are not known from the fact that they are seen or touched, but only because they are understood, I see clearly that there is nothing which is easier for me to know than my mind.

Descartes has learned that he can be certain that his existence resides in his own mind; that he does not have knowledge of the material world through his senses, but through the workings of his understanding upon what he perceives. You may be able to see how he derived from this his famous statement, "I think, therefore I am," which, in "On Method," he calls "the first principle of the Philosophy [of certainty] for which I was seeking."

What Descartes does here is an example of how writers make experiences *significant*; that is, how they make common experiences into signs that reveal human nature. He also makes it pretty clear how this is done: it is done by assuming that our lives are significant not because of what happens to us, but because of what we make of what happens to us. This is pretty much the distinction we made in Chapter 3 between what we perceive and how we interpret or understand it. Finally, Descartes illustrates that writers have to explain what significance they assign to experience. If Descartes had assumed that we understood the significance of "men who pass in the street . . . in hats and coats," then his philosophy would be harder to grasp than it already sometimes is.

St. Augustine and the Significance of Stealing Pears

Now, what about a boy stealing pears from the family orchard? St. Augustine, in his *Confessions*, tells of a time when he stole some pears, an incident that most of us would casually dismiss as a sign of youthful mischief, but that he sees as a sign revealing his—and our—moral and spiritual condition:

> A pear tree there was near our vineyard, laden with fruit, tempting neither for color nor taste. To shake and rob this, some lewd young fellows of us went, late one night, (having according to our pestilent custom prolonged our sports in the streets till then,) and took huge loads, not for our eating, but to fling to the very hogs, having only tasted them [see Part IV, Anthology, Section Two].

Augustine wants to understand what this senseless act signified about his nature. He sees a corollary in his prank to all crimes, because all are signs of "some desire of obtaining some of those which we called lower goods [sensuality, money, honor, power, or even friendship] or a fear of losing them." His theft, then, was a sign of something else. But what? Augustine decides that it indicated or signified the pleasure of sin: "Fair were those pears, but not them did my wretched soul desire; for I had store of better, and those I gathered, only that I might steal. For, when gathered, I flung them away, my only feast therein being my own sin, which I was pleased to enjoy." This leads to a consideration of what sin is a sign of; he decides that it is a sign of pride, which he defines as a perversion of the desire to imitate God. The pleasure he took in his sin was the pleasure of doing whatever he wanted, a pale and misguided imitation of God's power over nature: "What then did I love in that theft?

And wherein did I even corruptly and pervertedly imitate my Lord? Did I wish even by stealth to do contrary to Thy law, because by power I could not, so that being a prisoner, I might mimic a maimed liberty by doing with impunity things unpermitted me, a darkened likeness of Thy Omnipotency?'' For Augustine, then, the theft was an infallible sign of an adolescent desire for power. The paradox for him is that although breaking the rules even symbolically gave him a sense of freedom, power, and pleasure, he was in reality a prisoner of pointless desire, and he only mimicked ''a maimed liberty.''

Written in the third century, Augustine's *Confessions* are characteristically insightful and telling. Regarded as the first autobiography in Western literature, Augustine's introspective review of his life is made possible by his assumption that all actions—indeed, all of creation—are signs that we ought to use to comprehend our spiritual natures. His analysis of his theft is an inquiry into self, an effort to deduce something about himself and human nature generally from his implicit question, ''Given that I stole the pears, of what was it a sign?'' As with Descartes, Augustine assumes that events are meaningful only if we can assign some significance to them; that is, if we can find in them some indication of our own nature, beliefs, motives, or values. He also assumes that the significance of his experience is not self-evident, so he explains what he finds significant in a way that makes it seem to inevitably reveal our own natures as well as his own.

Martin Luther King, Jr., and the Significance of Segregation

Descartes and Augustine both illustrate that a ''significant'' experience need not be extraordinary. What they are able to do is take the commonplace and make it significant by asking what it says about human nature. One thing we might say about the humanities, then, is that they use common experience as a key that unlocks the human heart and mind. This can be true as well when the experience is one that we already understand as a sign. Martin Luther King, Jr., in ''Letter from Birmingham Jail,'' uses signs in this way with a very powerful result. He knows that we, as a culture, already know the signs of segregation. But by presenting them as recollections of his own experience, he conveys that significance in a way that no generalized discussion of segregation could:

> Perhaps it is easy for those who have never felt the stinging darts of segregation to say, ''Wait.'' But when you have seen vicious mobs lynch your mothers and fathers at will and drown your sisters and brothers at whim; when you have seen hate-filled policemen curse, kick and even kill your black brothers and sisters; when you see the vast majority of your twenty million Negro brothers smothering in an air tight cage of poverty in the midst of an affluent society;

when you suddenly find your tongue twisted and your speech stammering as you seek to explain to your six-year-old daughter why she can't go to the public amusement park that has just been advertised on television, and see tears welling up in her eyes when she is told Funtown is closed to colored children, and see ominous clouds of inferiority beginning to form in her little mental sky, and see her beginning to distort her personality by developing an unconscious bitterness toward white people; when you have to concoct an answer for a five-year-old son who is asking, "Daddy, why do white people treat colored people so mean?"; when you take a cross-country drive and find it necessary to sleep night after night in the uncomfortable corners of your automobile because no motel will accept you; when you are humiliated day in and day out by nagging signs reading "white" and "colored"; when your first name becomes "nigger," your middle name becomes "boy" (however old you are) and your last name becomes "John," and your wife and mother are never given the respected title "Mrs."; when you are harried by day and haunted by night by the fact that you are a Negro, living constantly at a tiptoe stance, never quite knowing what to expect next, and are plagued with inner fears and outer resentments; when you are forever fighting a degenerating sense of "nobodiness,"—then you will understand why we find it difficult to wait [see Part IV, Anthology, Section Four].

Before we go on to analyze how King uses signs here, we really would fail to do justice to the passage unless we notice how powerful it is. It has been said that compelling, persuasive language arises from us when our deepest convictions are aroused by a particular occasion. Beyond the skill of this passage, which is considerable, we have to say that its force on us arises from the sense it conveys of King's controlled, passionate conviction as he writes from jail to all of us in response to eight fellow clergymen who have publicly criticized him for leading peaceful demonstrations against segregation. His skill is shown in the way he blends metaphor, symbols, and personal experience into signs that inevitably and invariably indicate the presence of laws enforcing segregation and of the deeper and corrupting hatred and fear that motivated and maintained those laws. Taken together, the signs constitute a compelling argument: because of these signs, which infallibly indicate the demeaning, injurious, and life-threatening consequences of segregation to our parents, our children, and ourselves, "we find it difficult to wait" for our civil rights to be guaranteed under law.

Writing About Significance: Choosing an Experience

As writers who are interested in learning how to make our experiences significant for ourselves and for others, we naturally wonder how to go about it—how Descartes, or Augustine, or Martin Luther King managed to make their own experiences significant for us.

We began this chapter with an example of how a sign helped solve a mystery. Perhaps this suggests the answer to the question, "How can I go about making my experience significant?" At one level, the question really asks how each of us solves the mystery of our self. Perhaps more than any other of the modes of inquiry, this one can be learned, but it may be impossible to teach. Such writing obviously begins with the question, "Given what I did (or saw or thought), what does it signify about my motives, or values, or nature, or character, or understanding?" That's where the writing begins, but before that is the willingness to ask the question and to let the answer emerge as it might, unexpectedly, from our own reflections, the way the solution to a mystery does.

You have already had some experience with writing about what an experience signified. The last assignment asked you either to tell what you thought a misunderstanding signified about meaning and interpretation or to tell what you thought a confusing experience signified about learning in general. After reading essays that students have written for these assignments, I have learned that one problem writers face when trying to write about significance is that they focus very carefully on the experience but forget to assign it any significance. Or writers describe an experience and then try to tack on a little moral lesson to give it some significance.

Another problem I have noticed is that when writers are assigned to write about the significance of a person, place, thing, action, or event, they tend to focus on the general rather than the particular; for example, some writers may try discussing what music means for them in general, rather than focusing on the significance of a particular song. Instead, the best way to proceed usually is to begin with a particular experience or thing, and then write about it without worrying about what it "means." Just writing freely, without inhibition, can lead you to discover the significance of a particular episode or place or person or object in your life. This kind of writing should be done well before the assignment is due, in your own notebook, and with the Police Patrol outside, far away from your thoughts or concerns.

Conveying Significance to the Reader

Only after a writer has explored what something signifies for the writer should he or she ask, "How do I convey what I understand as the significance of an experience in a way that makes my reader feel that it inevitably signifies something similar to the reader?" When you write about the significance of experience, keep in mind that you are presenting an argument with two givens:

Given: When we write about the significance of our own experience, we assume that we write for a reader who believes that human experience ought to be explored; that is, we write for someone whom we assume is interested in knowing what we have to say about how character, motivations, values, or judgments are revealed in behavior.

Given: The immediate given is the experience the writer had: "Given that I had this experience, what did it signify about my character, values, understanding, or temperament?"

Position/Conclusion: The writer's position or conclusion is what he or she has decided the experience signified.

Reasons: The writer naturally tells why he or she felt the experience signified what the writer thinks it did; the reasons consist of the writer's reported thoughts and feelings about the various episodes included in the experience.

Evidence: The writer naturally wants to illustrate why the various episodes gave rise to his or her thoughts and feelings. The evidence, then, is the vivid and detailed description of what happened.

When you are planning to discuss the significance of an experience, it might help to consider how the givens, position, reasons, and evidence can work together to convey to your reader that the experience signified what you say it did about the workings of the human heart and mind. Writers do this in one of two ways. Which way a writer chooses usually has something to do with the nature of the sign.

The "Reporter" Style

When the sign is a matter of public knowledge, the writer may choose to use the style of a "reporter" analyzing the sign. You can find an example of this style in Susan Bordo's "Anorexia Nervosa: Psychopathology as the Crystallization of Culture" [see Part IV, Anthology, Section Two]. She begins by announcing what she takes the sign to signify. The sign in this case is anorexia nervosa, an eating disorder affecting primarily women. Bordo understands it as a sign of "some of the central ills of our culture." Her essay presents her argument in support of that conclusion. Here is how she begins:

> Psychopathology, as Jules Henry has said, "is the final outcome of all that is wrong with a culture." In no case is this more strikingly true than in the case of anorexia nervosa and bulimia, barely known a century ago, yet reaching epidemic proportions today. Far from being the result of a superficial fashion phenomenon, these disorders, I will argue, reflect and call our attention to some of the central ills of our culture—from our historical heritage of disdain for the body, to our modern fear of loss of control over our futures, to the disquieting meaning of contemporary beauty ideals in an era of greater female presence and power than ever before.

The "Participant" Style

The second style is one in which the writer is a participant in the experience, action, or event he or she presents. Often, the writer does not announce at the beginning what he or she takes the significance to be;

rather, the meaning is discovered as the writer reveals and then reflects on his or her own experience. Descartes, Augustine, and Martin Luther King all use this style. Here is an example from Loren Eiseley's "The Slit"(see Part IV, Anthology, Section Two). The reflection is italicized:

> The crack was only about body-width and, as I worked my way downward, the light turned dark and green from the overhanging grass. Above me the sky became a narrow slit of distant blue, and the sandstone was cool to my hands on either side. *The Slit was a little sinister—like an open grave, assuming the dead were enabled to take one last look—for over me the sky seemed already as far off as some future century I would never see.*

What Eiseley aims at here is to tell us what that slit signified at that moment of descent—something sinister, an open grave—and why—it made him think of himself as in his own grave. He also wants to convey to us some sense of why he had that feeling, so he gives us a vivid description of how things looked and felt.

What writers try to do when writing this kind of discourse is convey the significance of the experience cumulatively, by presenting discrete moments of the experience as Eiseley does here. You can understand what this means if you consider how he reflects upon his discovery in the slit of a prehistoric, mammalian skull:

> The skull lay tilted in such a manner that it stared, sightless, up at me as though I, too, were already caught a few feet above him in the strata and, in my turn, were staring upward at that strip of sky which the ages were carrying farther away from me beneath the tumbling debris of falling mountains. The creature had never lived to see a man, and I, what was it I was never going to see?

Now, put Eiseley's comments on these two moments together:

> [*Descent into Slit:*] The Slit was a little sinister—like an open grave, assuming the dead were enabled to take one last look—for over me the sky seemed already as far off as some future century I would never see.

> [*Reflecting on Skull:*] The skull lay tilted in such a manner that it stared, sightless, up at me as though I, too, were already caught a few feet above him in the strata and, in my turn, were staring upward at that strip of sky which the ages were carrying farther away from me beneath the tumbling debris of falling mountains. The creature had never lived to see a man, and I, what was it I was never going to see?

Eiseley clearly finds the significance of the slit as having something to do with our mortality, with the past time that shaped us and the future time we will never see.

What Eiseley does here is, I think, analogous to what you might find yourself doing if you ever work in a biology lab. Sometime or other you may find yourself taking a sample of something—like skin tissue—freezing it, and then slicing it into translucent sections, which you fix on a slide and study under a microscope, and which reveal a world you could not have known otherwise. Eiseley slices his descent into many discrete moments, examines each, comments on it, then moves to the next. The significance of his experience emerges from the accretion of his reflections. As he comments on each, meaning accumulates gradually—just as (to shift metaphors) the earth gradually laid down the strata he studies.

A writer presenting a discussion of significance can choose which style to use. Martin Luther King could have used the reporter style to comment on the significance of segregation laws; Susan Bordo could have used the participant style to discuss the significance of cultural stereotypes affecting women. A writer who wishes to comment on what an experience, action, event, person, or thing signified often chooses the participant style, probably because it allows him or her to lead the reader through the writer's own process of discovery. One of the effects of this style is that the reader becomes a participant in the discovery. This means that the writer's experience is, in a sense, universalized: the reader becomes persuaded that the event ought to signify for him or her what it signified for the writer. The purpose of this kind of writing, then, is not to present a moral lesson. Rather the purpose is for a writer to present a personal or private experience in a way that implicitly asks the reader that most human of all questions: I'm like this; you too?

ASSIGNMENTS

Write an essay in which you convey to the reader the significance for you of an experience or a relationship. You may choose any action, event, situation, or experience in which you participated, or any thing, setting, person, object, or animal with which you have had a special relationship. Your purpose is to present the experience or relationship in a way that will evoke for the reader the same significance that you assign to it.

Below are some suggestions that you might find helpful. Remember to set aside time for writing each day until the assignment is due.

Discovering What You Can Say

Your purpose is to discover what an experience or relationship signifies or signified for you. Find yourself a quiet place, away from distractions. Begin writing about an action, event, setting, person, animal, thing, object, or even a song. Do not tell yourself that what you have chosen is too silly or unimportant. Do not tell yourself that you do not know what it means. Start writing. Never mind whether or not it is well organized. Keep writing. Be as detailed as you can. If you find you are led to write about something else, then go ahead and follow your intuitions; keep writing. Write until you feel you have no more to say. Then put it aside for a day or two.

When you return to it, read what you have written. After you have read it, localize it; that is, write about precisely where and when some part of what you have already written occurred. Recollect the specific season, day, or hour. How old were you then? Write about the specific place. Where is it? Describe that place at just that moment. Be as detailed about this as you can. Now reflect on this moment and place. What were your thoughts and feelings then? What are they now as you recollect that time and place? Now, still locating what you have described in a specific time and place, what happened next? What is the next thing that occurs to you? How would you comment on it? Keep writing until you find that you have no more to say.

Write as often in this way as you wish until you feel you have accumulated enough of your own thoughts so that you are ready to try and communicate them to someone else.

Discovering Possible Ways to Say What You Wish to Say

You might find it helpful to study how other writers use the participant style to convey the significance of experience. Browse through the following in Part IV, Anthology, Section Two:

Loren Eiseley, "The Slit," from *The Immense Journey*
E. B. White, "Once More to the Lake"
N. Scott Momaday, from *The Way to Rainy Mountain*

Choose one to study. In Chapter 25, "Taking Notes from Readings," you will find a discussion of reading and taking notes from this kind of essay. Read Chapter 25 now. Then take the kind of notes suggested there using the essay you have chosen. What do you learn from this kind of close study about how this kind of essay is presented? What can you apply to your own writing for this assignment?

You might find it helpful to reread this chapter. What kinds of advice does it offer that you can use in completing this assignment?

Learning from Others: Revising

Draft and revise your essay until you feel comfortable asking for comments and advice. Bring that draft to class. Read it aloud so that others can offer their help. Share your advice with your classmates. Remember, as a reader, you are supposed to be convinced that the experience the writer describes carries the significance that the writer assigns to it. When you hear a particularly striking essay, make some notes for yourself to remind yourself of a way you might like to revise your own essay. Be sure to tell the person who wrote the essay why it struck you. After the discussion, revise your draft in light of the responses to it.

Chapter 6

The Participant-Observer

PREPARATORY ASSIGNMENT: THE STUDENT WITH THE THICK-LENSED GLASSES

The following passage from *Zen and the Art of Motorcycle Maintenance* (New York: William Morrow, 1976) by Robert M. Pirsig tells about an assignment on observation given by a composition teacher:

> He'd been having trouble with students who had nothing to say. At first he thought it was laziness but later it became apparent that it wasn't. They just couldn't think of anything to say.
>
> One of them, a girl with strong-lensed glasses, wanted to write a five-hundred word essay about the United States. He was used to the sinking feeling that comes from statements like this, and suggested without disparagement that she narrow it down to just Bozeman [Montana].
>
> When the paper came due she didn't have it and was quite upset. She had tried and tried but she just couldn't think of anything to say.
>
> He had already discussed her with her previous instructors and they'd confirmed his impressions of her. She was very serious, disciplined, and hard working, but extremely dull. Not a spark of creativity in her anywhere. Her eyes, behind the thick-lensed glasses, were the eyes of a drudge. She wasn't bluffing him, she really couldn't think of anything to say, and was upset by her inability to do as she was told.
>
> It just stumped him. Now *he* couldn't think of anything to say. A silence occurred, and then a peculiar answer: "Narrow it down to the *main street* of Bozeman." It was a stroke of insight.
>
> She nodded dutifully and went out. But just before her next class she came back in *real* distress, tears this time, distress that had obviously been there for

a long time. She couldn't think of anything to say, and couldn't see why, if she couldn't think of anything about *all* of Bozeman, she should be able to think of something about just one street.

He was furious. "You're not *looking!*" he said. A memory came back of his own dismissal from the University for having *too much* to say. For every fact there is an *infinity* of hypotheses. The more you *look* the more you *see*. She really wasn't looking and yet somehow didn't understand this.

He told her angrily, "Narrow it down to the *front* of *one* building on the main street of Bozeman. The Opera House. Start with the upper left-hand brick."

Her eyes, behind the thick-lensed glasses, opened wide.

She came in the next class with a puzzled look and handed him a five-thousand-word essay on the front of the Opera House on the main street of Bozeman, Montana. "I sat in the hamburger stand across the street," she said, "and started writing about the first brick, and the second brick, and then by the third brick it all started to come and I couldn't stop. They thought I was crazy, and they kept kidding me, but here it all is. I don't understand."

Neither did he, but on long walks through the streets of town he thought about it and concluded she was evidently stopped with the same kind of blockage that had paralyzed him on his first day of teaching. She was blocked because she was trying to repeat, in her writing, things she had already heard, just as on the first day he had tried to repeat things he had already decided to say. She couldn't think of anything to write about Bozeman because she couldn't recall anything she had heard worth repeating. She was strangely unaware that she could look and see freshly for herself, as she wrote, without primary regard for what had been said before. The narrowing down to one brick destroyed the blockage because it was so obvious she *had* to do some original and direct seeing.

1. Why do you think the composition teacher did not want the student to write an essay on the United States? Why did the teacher get a "sinking feeling" when the student suggested the topic?

2. In making the original assessments, and in narrowing the topic down until he asked the student to write about just one brick in one building, what was the teacher up to? What was he trying to prove?

3. What do you suppose happened to the student when she sat in the coffee shop looking at the brick in the building? Why was she so happy about it? How did she manage to get five thousand words out of it?

4. Do you agree with the composition teacher's assessment of what happened? Can you think of any other reasons that might explain what happened?

Discovery Through Observation

We have said that higher education challenges us to discover new ways of interpreting what we perceive and feel. *Discovery* can mean being the first to find something out, but it can also mean finding something out for yourself for the first time. In the social and natural sciences, discovery is the result of carefully observing directly what we wish to understand, or what we think we already understand because it seems so obvious that we have come to take it for granted. Although observing carefully and reporting observations vividly may at first seem like fairly simple abilities, they are in fact two of the most challenging modes of discovery in higher education to master. In this and the following chapters, we will examine how both social and natural scientists make observations and report them.

One of the hindrances to careful observation comes when we assume that the point of a writing assignment is for us to tell the audience—our professor—what we assume the professor already knows. The composition teacher of the student with the thick-lensed glasses decides that the reason his students "couldn't think of anything to say" was that they, like the student wearing the thick-lensed glasses, were trying to repeat in their writing things they had already heard. The teacher was struck by his student's unawareness "that she could look and see freshly for herself, as she wrote, without primary regard for what had been said before." Presumably, the student felt confident she could write a five-hundred-word essay about the United States because she could gum together stereotypical statements the way the young Eric Blair did in "Awake! Young Men of England" (see Chapter 3). Her teacher asked her to set aside her assumptions about what the reader wanted to know, or what everyone knows to be true about the United States, and open her senses and mind to her life in a small town. He challenged the student to discover a new way of seeing her familiar surroundings by getting her to concentrate on what she perceived and felt. It is difficult to think of anything to say about those things most familiar to us because we assume that our understanding of them is the same as what everyone else understands. This is caused by our tendency to assume that our interpretation of something is the same thing as the thing we perceive. We get mixed up and think that everyone sees things, and labels them, exactly as we do.

What the student in the thick-lensed glasses may have realized was that no one but she would describe the opera house just as she did. Nor would anyone else bring exactly the values, interests, or past associations to it. Perhaps the pleasure she felt when writing about the opera house came from realizing that what she was writing about was not "The Opera House," but her perceptions of, and thoughts on, and feelings about it. And by their very nature, our own perceptions, thoughts, and feelings cannot be known to anyone else—sometimes not even to ourselves— unless we express them. Another way to express this is that careful observation is an act of discovery, and, often, of self-discovery. One of the prerequisites for making careful observations and writing about them effectively, then, is developing a curiosity about our own perceptions and having confidence that our audience will be interested in knowing about them. This means setting aside stereotypical ways of labeling what we see and finding fresh ways to see. And because we rely on language to convey our perceptions, this means finding fresh ways to use descriptive language.

Field-Dependent Observation

Another prerequisite is having a question in mind that we wish to answer through direct observation. The absence of such a question was a real hindrance to the student with the thick-lensed glasses, and, in reality, placed a burden on her that is not felt by professional observers. Anthropologists, sociologists, natural scientists, and others who rely on direct observation not only begin their observations with a question, they also have a tentative answer in mind; that is, a kind of educated guess about what they will discover. These questions are suggested by their disciplines, which are also sometimes called "fields of study." A field limits the range of questions a student asks about a subject. You have already seen examples of this in our earlier discussion of the Irish Potato Famine, in which the question, "What was the cause of the famine?", was answered in the context of relevant fields, such as economic history or botany (see Chapter 1).

Having in mind a field-dependent question makes it possible for the observer to "see" something of interest. You can understand why this is the case if we return to the problem confronting the student asked to observe the opera house. Consider how much less frustrating her assignment would have been if she had been a student of architectural history, or of theater arts, or of cultural history of the U.S. West, or even if she had been a sociology student studying how people use public places. Each field suggests a different reason for observing the building carefully. And each suggests different questions we might ask:

Art History: What architectural styles influenced the design of this opera house?

Theatre Arts: How does the design of this building affect the staging of plays and operas?

Cultural History: What kind of statement about cultural values does the design of the opera house suggest?

Sociology: How do people use the opera house for social interaction?

It may seem somewhat peculiar when you think about it, but our ability to "see" is determined in part by what we want to learn about whatever it is we observe.

Perhaps you will understand why it is a bit futile to study observation and reporting without studying how this is done within the context of a given field. Without a field, it is difficult to formulate a question—to know, in other words, what we are looking *for*. As we said in Chapter 1, a student new to the academic community who wants to know what it means to write in college is asking how the older students—the professors—go about writing. Learning how to observe and report really requires understanding how a specialist in a field that relies on observation goes about formulating questions and seeking answers. This presents us with the practical problem of which field to choose as a model for our own study of observing and reporting. The laboratory sciences, for instance, require both, but to use them as a model we would have to undertake the very impractical plan of setting up a lab experiment. The social sciences are more promising because they observe social groups, and anthropology is perhaps most promising of all because it is the social science that relies most heavily on direct observation of societies or groups. In addition, the ways anthropologists report on their observations parallel in many striking ways how college students often describe their own experiences as learners. For the next several chapters, then, we will use the methods anthropologists use to make and report their observations as a focus for our own study of making observations. Along the way, we will also notice what we can learn from other related fields, including the natural sciences.

One of the things we will learn from anthropologists is that their method of observing and writing resembles the writing process we discussed earlier for writers in general. We might summarize the way anthropologists proceed as:

1. Defining the question the anthropologist wishes to answer: deciding what area or areas of interest he or she will focus on while living among a particular group or in the field;
2. Gathering data: while in the field, listening, watching, taking notes, including those that record the anthropologist's own thoughts and feelings;
3. Shaping ideas: discovering in the notes those typical behaviors that reveal cultural patterns or norms and testing these interpretations by behaving according to these rules of conduct to see how members of the society respond;
4. Gathering data: recording how members of the society respond to the anthropologist's efforts to "fit into" the society, using his or her observations of social norms; continuing to make observations;
5. Reshaping ideas: revising assumptions about social norms based on how members of a society respond to the anthropologist's efforts and on other cumulative observations; and
6. Presenting the interpretation: presenting information vividly, and then publishing it, so that readers can decide whether or not they agree with the anthropologist's interpretations of a society's cultural norms and values.

Formulating the Question

Because you will be given an opportunity to formulate a question and undertake observations to find an answer, let's begin with the kinds of field-dependent questions anthropologists ask. Among anthropologists, *cultural anthropologists* or *ethnographers* are most concerned with the observation and study of cultures and groups. Anthropologists must undertake *fieldwork,* an extended stay among those whom the anthropologist is studying. Often, an anthropologist travels to remote societies, but anthropologists also study aspects of U.S. culture that we might simply take for granted, such as a small rural town, the life on a single street-corner in a major city, or life in a college. Their purpose is to understand a *culture,* which in *Culture and Conduct* (Belmont, CA: Wadsworth, 1984), Richard A. Barrett defines as "the body of learned beliefs, traditions, and guides for behavior that are shared among members of any human society." (54) An anthropologist observes a culture in order to understand its rules, assumptions, and values. It is rather like trying to discover the grammatical rules of a foreign language while living among native speakers. (And many anthropologists have done just that.)

One of the reasons anthropologists study cultures is to answer the looming question; Is human behavior shaped genetically or by culture? This is often referred to as the nature versus nurture debate. The question can be crudely posed about many different human traits: Is intelligence genetically determined (nature) or the result of certain kinds of education, both in school and in the family (nurture)? Is aggression an innate characteristic (nature) or are individuals taught to be aggressive by their culture (nurture)? Is there a genetic factor in criminal behavior (nature) or is criminal behavior the result of familial abuse (nurture)? Is there a genetic factor for altruism (nature) or is altruism learned (nurture)? In practice, the questions anthropologists ask are not so starkly framed because anthropology has formulated an answer—an educated guess—to the debate, which is that culture is the significant, determining factor in how human beings behave. At issue, then, is how cultures influence behavior.

We can see how anthropologists formulate field-dependent questions by studying a portion of Margaret Mead's autobiography, *Blackberry Winter* (New York: William Morrow, 1972). In preparation for her first fieldwork, which was to be in Samoa, Mead's professor, Franz Boas, advised her on what she ought to observe in the behavior of adolescent females:

> One question that interests me very much is how the young girls react to the restraints of custom. We find very often among ourselves during the period of adolescence a strong rebellious spirit that may be expressed in sullenness or in sudden outbursts. In other individuals there is a weak submission which is accompanied, however, by a suppressed rebellion that may make itself felt in peculiar ways, perhaps in a desire for solitude which is really an expression of desire for freedom, or otherwise in forced participation in social affairs in order to drown the mental troubles. I am not at all clear in my mind in how far similar conditions may occur in primitive society and in how far the desire for independence may be simply due to our modern conditions and to a more strongly developed individualism. (138)

Boas's last sentence implicitly poses the field-dependent question that we might state as: "Is the behavior of U.S. female adolescents natural and inevitable, or is it the result of cultural influence?" Mead comments on those who thought that rebellious or sullen behavior in adolescent females was natural; that is, characteristic of all female adolescents:

> There was G. Stanley Hall, who had written a huge book on adolescence in which, equating stages of growth with stages of culture, he had discussed his belief that each growing child recapitulated the history of the human race. There were also the assumptions set forth in textbooks, mainly derived from German theory, about puberty as a period of storm and stress. (148)

In her book *Growing Up in Samoa,* Mead used her observations to argue that puberty was not necessarily "a period of storm and stress," but could be, as it was among the Samoans, a peaceful transition from childhood to adulthood. Recently, Derek Freeman, who is on the nature side of the debate, has challenged Mead's conclusion. If you are interested in understanding the nature of academic debate, you can read Mead and Freeman in Part IV, Anthology, Section Four, along with the comments of Lowell Holmes, who also did fieldwork among the Samoans.

Now, it obviously would not be reasonable to ask students to propose an observation intended to illustrate some aspect of the nature versus nurture debate. But we do want to learn from anthropologists how to observe carefully and report vividly on those observations. What we can do is to follow the example of beginning with an assumption—a given— about human behavior and proposing a question that will test it. Mead, for instance, began with the given that adolescence for all females is a time of sullen rebelliousness; she then proposed a way of discovering whether or not this was true. Because the purpose of fieldwork is to understand what typical behaviors and responses reveal about the values, assumptions, and beliefs of others, we can begin with our own assumptions about our immediate culture. Most of us could probably write fairly easily and quickly a 500-word statement about the typical U.S. family or about U.S. customs and laws associated with marriage and divorce. How difficult would it be to complete this assignment?

> Choose one of the topics below, and write a five-hundred-word essay describing typical U.S. attitudes about it:

pregnancy	birth control
children	the behavior of teenagers
the elderly	the environment
modern technology	the economy
Congress	the White House
religion	medical care

Because disagreement about what our social policies ought to be is one of our culture's characteristics, our 500 words on any of these topics would probably have to describe more than one "typical" attitude. But you would probably agree that when our eyes land on any one of these topics, we immediately start thinking of things to say about it that would explain typical U.S. attitudes toward it.

Now, consider what we know about each topic from our direct observations of people we have met or what we have ourselves experienced (as opposed to read about or seen on television). How much of what we would say is typical of our culture is based upon our having been participant-observers, the way fieldworkers are?

   We notice that although we have participated in many aspects of our own culture, we have not observed them carefully or in detail, and that there are many other aspects we have neither participated in nor observed, such as:

The environment: How many of us have observed carefully or studied. . .

   The effect of our immediate landscape, cityscape, and climate on our daily routines and moods?
   The effect we have on our homes, workplace, and natural resources?
   The designs of our dwellings and what they reflect about our needs for privacy, intimacy, and sense of status?
   How reliant we are on technology and manufactured goods for objects of everyday use?
   The roles that the decorative arts play in our homes, communities, or workplaces?

The people around us: How many. . .

   Families have we really observed carefully?
   Weddings have we seen? Or women have we known during pregnancy?
   Children have we observed during various stages of growth and development?
   Elderly, infirm, or handicapped do we know?
   Politicians or religious leaders have we met and spoken with?
   Different kinds of religious ceremonies have we attended?
   Different kinds of workers and professionals do we know?

   If you study the topics we could easily write five hundred words about, you realize that there is a good deal we know about our society from sources other than our own direct observation. One of the advantages of a literate society is that we can become informed about our own society without having to undertake face-to-face observations.

   But it takes little consideration to realize there is a problem lurking in that advantage if we simply accept or rely upon derivative information. It is the problem the composition teacher of the student with the thick-lensed glasses noticed when he found that his students could think of nothing to say unless it involved repeating the words of others. They were relying on derivative knowledge. Just as we feel we could write 500 words on what is typical in the United States about a variety of subjects, the student in the thick-lensed glasses was confident that she could write 500 meaningful words on the United States. But she was reduced to tears when she was asked to give her own statement about her hometown.

Relying heavily on derivative information can mean that we begin to think in stereotypes, which is another way of saying that we rely on what we assume is typical from what we read in newspapers or see on television or hear on radio. Such overreliance can blunt our senses, so that we observe less carefully or make our perceptions fit our limited, stereotyped assumptions.

One way to formulate a question about our own culture, then, is to begin with our own stereotypes; for instance, we might consider gender roles and the cultural stereotype that cooking is a feminine pursuit. Is it? Well, we need to have a specific time for observation and a group to observe. How about our own family during a holiday—Thanksgiving or the Fourth of July, for example. Perhaps we might formulate our question this way: During Thanksgiving, are food preparation, serving, and clearing tables gender-based roles?

In addition to posing a question, we also decide what our supposed answer will be, just as Mead supposed she would probably find that culture played a determining role in adolescent development. Our anticipated answer, like hers, is based on our prior knowledge; after all, it is our family and we know something about how it typically behaves. We might formulate our presumed answer to the question: I assume that during Thanksgiving, the female family members will take primary responsibility for food preparation, for serving the food, and for clearing away and cleaning up. The male adult relatives will be banned from the kitchen, but will have primary responsibility for serving drinks. The younger males will have no designated responsibilities.

What are the possible results of our observation? The Thanksgiving we observe could:

1. Confirm our assumption;
2. Disconfirm our assumption;
3. Neither confirm nor disconfirm it; that is, prove inconclusive; or
4. Reveal something about the behaviors of this family that we did not anticipate in our original proposal.

The method of using a question, an anticipated answer, and possible outcomes duplicates the procedures in anthropology and in the observational sciences generally. The anticipated answer is called a *hypothesis.* It is an educated guess about what the observer will discover based upon prior experience or knowledge. All the possible outcomes are equally legitimate. It is as professional for an observer to say his or her results were inconclusive or disconfirmatory as it is for an observer to find that the results confirmed the hypothesis. It is equally legitimate—and often the case—that observers discover the unexpected. Despite the effort to formulate a question before going into the field, anthropologists frequently find that they have to alter it once they arrive. As Barrett observes, "Fieldwork is first and foremost a process of discovery. The ethnographer only learns the full ramifications of the problem as he becomes involved in the research.'' Not surprisingly, one term in the anthropologists' lexicon is *serendipity,* which means pretty much what it means in general usage: ''the faculty of making fortunate and unexpected discoveries by accident.''

The Methods of Observation

With a hypothesis in mind, fieldworkers begin to observe systematically, asking the questions, Who? What? Where? When? How? How much or how many? You can see how these questions help focus attention if you consider how we might apply them just to the issue of food preparation and consumption in our proposed observation of Thanksgiving:

> Who prepares the food? Who consumes it?
> What kind of food is it? What do people prefer? What are their attitudes toward it?
> Where do people eat? What are their attitudes toward the place?
> When do they eat? Who decides?
> How is the food prepared? How do people eat? Leisurely? Hurriedly?
> How many people are we talking about?
> How much do they eat? How do they feel about the amount of food they consume?
> How do age, gender, and relative health affect what is prepared? Consumed? Attitudes toward food?

In addition to using these kinds of questions to focus our attention, we could also utilize the methods some fieldworkers use to observe social interactions. In *Argonauts of the Western Pacific* (New York: E. P. Dutton, 1960), Bronislaw Malinowski says that when he observes, he notes (1) what is routine, typical, customary, or traditional; (2) the manner in which it is carried out, and what the manner reveals about individuals' typical attitudes toward it; and (3) how individuals comment on it (89).

With these questions and methods in mind, perhaps you can understand what we might ''see'' in just one incident at Thanksgiving: for example, Aunt Hortense, who is responsible for serving the pumpkin pie, is pretty sloppy about it, and licks her fingers after she has slipped each piece onto a plate. No one else seems to notice this, except Grandpa, who stares at her with fascinated horror, his sense of fastidiousness apparently offended, and who refuses dessert, saying he is ''on a diet.''

We might conclude from this that Grandpa, at least, feels that he should not comment directly on what offends him. Another conclusion is that other members of the family do not share his beliefs about food service. What else do you think is revealed from this incident about what is routine, customary, typical, or traditional about the values, customs, or beliefs of this group at Thanksgiving?

As you might suppose, an essential part of direct observation is frequent, detailed notetaking by the fieldworker. Many carry a small note-pad and record observations while ducked into street doorways or while trying to scrape caribou skin for a winter blanket. Then they type or write more extensive notes in the evening, using their notations as reminders. They learn not to trust to memory. Hortense Powdermaker, who wrote her notes in her car immediately after her interviews with blacks in a small rural Mississippi town, says in *Strangers and Friends* (New York: Norton, 1966): "In the beginning some of the data were so vivid and interesting that I thought I could not possibly forget them. . . . But when I came to writing in my room that night or several nights later, some of the details were lost. To lose data was my idea of a cardinal sin!" (158)

A fieldworker's notes also include the fieldworker's own thoughts and feelings, because the fieldworker studies a culture as a participant-observer, which means that he or she is both involved with and detached from those observed. The overall purpose is to attempt to understand the culture so well that the observer gains a subjective understanding of it; that is, the observer gains the kind of insight that lets the observer perceive the world as a member of that culture does. Thus, a participant-observer is part of the daily drama and his or her notebook includes reflections upon how the fieldworker was treated and how he or she feels about it. This is an especially important part of participant-observation. A fieldworker is constantly testing his or her interpretations of what constitutes "typical" behaviors, characteristics, attitudes, or values. When the interpretations are wrong—that is, when the fieldworker behaves in a way unacceptable in the society—the natives will laugh or get angry, depending on how they interpret the fieldworker's behavior and the significance of the breach in custom. Even a fieldworker's mistakes, then, are important sources of information. As Dr. Don Blakeslee, a professor of anthropology, observed in a personal interview:

> All of the sciences, whether natural or social, require the practitioner to test his or her ideas in such a way that failure is possible. Thus, although anthropologists seek subjective understanding of other ways of life, they also intend for their results to be objective in that different people studying the same culture should draw similar conclusions. Participant observation is to the anthropologist what a laboratory experiment is to the physicist—a means of improving their thinking by discarding incorrect interpretations.

The obsession with notetaking is an act of faith, because at first the fieldworker cannot know which observations will prove significant. For the most part, such notetaking, like all notetaking, is a matter of dogged determination: we keep taking notes until we begin to understand the connections among the things we are studying. It also requires self-consciousness about one's own responses, questions, and feelings of confusion. A fieldworker's notebook would be as incomplete as a student's notes on lectures and readings if it did not include reflections, responses, and questions, as well as confessions of confusion and corrections of previous misinterpretations.

This brings us to the final characteristic of anthropologists, which we might consider as a model for our own study of making observations: their determined attitude toward their work. A fieldworker arrives in a strange society uncertain of what he or she will discover. The uncertainty and unfamiliar surroundings, coupled with the need to learn a new language, can be overwhelming. Sometimes students report similar attitudes of discouragement as they try to figure out what is expected of them in a new course and try to learn its lexicon. Naturally, fieldworkers sometimes want to give up. Hortense Powdermaker, for instance, remembers the first night of her first fieldwork experience, which was in the village of Lesu in New Guinea:

> I was sitting on my veranda, presumably ready to begin work, yet in a panic. I asked myself again, why am I here alone? I had to admit that no one had compelled me to come, that the expedition was not only voluntary but intensely desired. There could be only one explanation: I must have been mad. (58)

Powdermaker overcame her fear and lived in Lesu for 10 months. What seems to keep anthropologists going—despite panic, anxiety, and discouragement—is their belief that careful, prolonged observation will eventually let them see a coherent pattern. The faith that they will eventually perceive such repetition seems to carry them through the self-doubts about whether or not their study will be of interest to anyone else. As William B. Shaffir, Robert A. Stebbins, and Allan Turowetz remark in *Fieldwork Experience* (New York: St. Martin's Press, 1980):

> The requirement that one discover something only increases the anxiety of fieldwork. Nowhere does originality come easily. The field experience does offer a kaleidoscope of contrasts between the observer's routine world and that of the subjects. New patterns of behavior and thought flash before the observer's eyes. But the question is always: Are these of any importance for science? (17)

Careful observation requires a good deal of determination and care as well as preparation. In the assignments that follow, you will be asked to consider these factors in more detail.

ASSIGNMENTS

Assignment I

How does writing based on direct observation differ from writing based upon derivative, untested knowledge? How does the difference between them provide a way of defining *discovery*?

Assignments Preliminary to First Draft

1. Go back to the part in this chapter that discusses the topics about which we might write 500 words quickly and easily. Test that assumption; pick one and start writing. Two handwritten pages usually equal about 500 words.

Then write an assessment of whether this is an easy or difficult way to write. How long did it take? How do you feel about the quality? What kind of audience would be interested in reading it? If it seemed easy to write, why do you think so? Do you agree with the reasons given in the chapter? Can you think of others? If it seemed difficult, what seemed to make it so?

Use your assessment to explain why the composition teacher did not wish the student with the thick-lensed glasses to write a 500-word essay on the United States. Use your own ideas and any that seem useful from discussions in this book.

What do you learn from this study about what college-level writing is for? What might be expected of you as a writer?

2. Review your notes, reread the assignment, and plan how you will present your ideas.

Drafting and Revision

When you draft your essay, assume that your audience is yourself and others like you who want to discover what kind of writing is valued in college and why. Bring your draft to class. Be prepared to read it aloud or have it read aloud. Note the comments others make that help answer the questions of the assignment. Afterward, add any other ideas for revision that occur to you. Revise your essay.

Assignment II

Choose a group to observe in order to test a prior assumption or a stereotype that you have about the group. Study this group as a participant-observer for no less than two weeks. Write an essay in which you report on the typical customs, habits, values, and "unstated rules" of this group, showing whether they confirm or disconfirm your original assumption.

Assignments Preliminary to First Draft

1. Before a fieldworker goes into the field, he or she has a question in mind; for example: "The tribe I plan to study is reported to be very passive and nonaggressive. What specific methods of child-rearing contribute to this characteristic?" Because you will probably be studying aspects of your own culture, perhaps the easiest way for you to formulate a question is to ask which prior assumptions or stereotypes you would be interested in testing by direct observation. Bear in mind that your purpose is to *discover* something about the group you observe, which means that your aim is either (1) to confirm a prior assumption about the group; (2) to dis-

confirm a prior assumption; (3) to report that a prior assumption can be neither confirmed nor disconfirmed from observing a particular group; or (4) to report something you learned unexpectedly about a group.

If you have trouble thinking of a question you would like to answer by observing a particular group, here are a few suggestions:

a. Some of the essays in Part IV, Anthology, might stimulate your thinking.

> Francine Frank and Frank Anshen, "Talking Like a Lady: How Women Talk"
>
> Mindy Cohen, "Smoking and Socializing in the Library's Smoking Room"
>
> David McKenzie, "Poker and Pop: Collegiate Gambling Groups"
>
> Christina Mohr, "Garage Sales"

b. Another helpful exercise is to write freely for fifteen or twenty minutes without letting anything inhibit your ideas. You might try to answer the questions, "What are some of my assumptions about the people I know? What do I think typically occurs in a certain setting, like the dorm lounge? How do I suppose people behave at certain social rituals—like a football game, a college dance, in church?" When you reread what you have written, you may find the kernel for an extended observation. Some common assumptions that other students found they held are: that most teenagers who gather at malls—"mall rats"—are typically misbehaved, rebellious, drug users (an assumption that was not confirmed); that students of certain races or nationalities typically gather in specific places or territories on campus (an assumption that was confirmed); that women use the restrooms at work more frequently to socialize than do men (an assumption that was confirmed); that in lunchroom conversations between men and women, women tend to ask questions while men tend to make declarative statements (also confirmed); that in the student lounge, there is less conversation when the weather is rainy and more when the weather is pleasant (these results were inconclusive).

c. One way to get our cerebral juices flowing is called *brainstorming.* In brainstorming, a group talks together in order to come up with ideas to solve a problem. The rules for brainstorming are very simple. Everyone is free to make a suggestion, and no one can say anything *negative* about it; anyone can make a *positive* suggestion. In other words, reasons why a proposal might not work or might not be feasible are deferred so that the mind's creative and imaginative capacities are freed. A recorder writes down the ideas and suggestions so that everyone in the group can read them and comment on them (on a blackboard, for example). Here is part of a brainstorming session about a proposal for observing singles bars (the names of the students have been changed):

BUFFY: I'd kind of like to make my project observing what happens at singles bars.

HARRIET: What do you suppose you will find?

BUFFY: Well, I've been to a few, and it seems to me you could say a lot about what people expect. I mean, everyone thinks the traditional rules don't apply, but, well, for instance, I think lots of women still wait for the men to come ask them to dance. And men think that if they sit down at a table, they can stay as long as they want, even if the woman doesn't want them to.

GEORGE: What do you mean? You mean if you tell a guy to go away, he just stays?

BUFFY: Well, no, not tell him to go away. That would be rude. I mean just avoiding eye contact, not being conversational, that sort of thing.

HAROLD: I've worked in a bar, and I can tell you that for a guy that doesn't mean he should go away. It means the woman is just shy, and doesn't know how to show she's interested. (Exclamations of surprise from the females in class, who begin to clamor together that Buffy is right about what her signals mean.)

HAROLD (over the objections):   Hey, I'm telling you! If you want a guy to go away, you have to tell him, "Beat it!" Am I right? (The males all begin to talk at once, generally confirming the assumption.)

BUFFY: Well, this is great! I really could find out about the differences in the unspoken rules males and females have in singles bars.

DIANE: Yeah, like what do guys think when you ask them to dance?

CAROLE: And what eye contact means. Is it an invitation, or what?

TOM: And why people go to singles bars. Everyone thinks people go in order to, well, you know . . .

BUFFY: Yes, but most of the time I think people go there because they are lonely and want company. I think most people are really looking for a stable or meaningful relationship, not just a casual affair.

HARRIET: I wonder what kind of people go to singles bars. I mean, how old are they? Where do they come from?

MARK: And what kinds of things do they talk about? Or do they? What do they do in a singles bar?

BRIGETTE: And what about the setting? I mean most bars have flashing lights or balloons, low lights, comfortable seats. What effect does that have? Why are they designed like that?

DIANE: I was reading what we have on the blackboard so far, and thinking about what Buffy said about a man dominating a table where she was sitting. The first time I went I didn't have a very good time because that happened to me and I didn't know how to get out of it. So the next time, I didn't sit down, I circulated around the crowd that stands rather than sits, and I had a really good time—met lots of people.

BRIGETTE: So the setting and how people use it might be important.

DIANE: Yes, I think so.

BOB: And I was thinking about what Buffy said about women not asking men to dance. You know, fieldworkers are supposed to test the rules of a group, and one way to do that is to break them and see what happens. I mean, if it leads to some problem, then you know it is really important to the group. Why don't you ask some guy to dance?

BUFFY: Oh, I couldn't do that. I mean I wasn't raised that way.

DIANE: Sure you could. First of all, we're not supposed to be negative, and besides, this is supposed to be like an experiment, see? Just to see what will happen, like a scientist. I'll go with you. You'll see, it will be fun.

You might find that a brainstorming session could also help you think about the kind of observation you would like to do and some of the questions you might be able to answer.

2. Write a proposal telling what question or questions you want to answer, what you guess the answer or answers will be, and what method you will use to arrive at an answer. Be sure your proposal is feasible.

a. Drafting Your Proposal. Your proposal should fall into two parts. The first part should state the group you will study, the setting, and what assumptions you have about the group. The questions you propose to answer should be intended to test the assumptions. The first part of your proposal should answer these questions:

Who? The group or groups you will study.

What? Your assumptions about this group's typical behaviors, customs, beliefs, or unspoken rules; the specific questions to which you hope you will find answers, and the answers you anticipate finding.

Where? The setting or settings for the study.

How many? The size of the group or groups.

The second part should describe how you intend to complete the study; that is, your methodology. This section should answer the questions:

When? Exactly how much time will you give each day to observing this group? How much time will you give each day to writing your notes?

How? Do you have specific people (informants) in mind whom you will question or are you hoping you will find such informants? Will you develop a questionnaire or will you rely on overhearing conversations, participating in the group, and recording what you hear? Will you tell those you are studying that you are studying them? What ethical questions come to mind if you do not? Will you allow the group to see you taking notes?

b. Assessing Your Proposal for Feasibility. Read your proposal carefully, asking yourself whether or not you can realistically expect to answer the questions you propose in the time you have allowed yourself. Is your proposal unrealistic? One student wanted to study how the elderly are treated, but she finally realized that she had no access to any elderly people. Another wanted to study women's attitudes during pregnancy and birth, but realized that the observation could cover only two weeks, and it was unlikely that any of the pregnant women she knew would deliver during those fourteen days. She then thought about asking mothers what their attitudes had been during pregnancy and delivery, but realized that she would then be collecting oral history, rather than making direct observations. Is the proposal overly ambitious? One student wanted to study what holds families together over a long period of time. He finally realized that the question was too complex to be easily answered in fourteen days. Does the proposal meet the requirements of the assignment? The purpose of the assignment is for you to propose to learn something through direct observation by testing an assumption about a group's typical behaviors, values, beliefs, or unspoken rules. The assignment does not ask you to answer the question, "*Why* are these qualities typical of the group?"

One common pitfall is to try being an "observer" in situations in which you *must* be a participant. Some students, for instance, have tried to observe behavior where they work, but some—such as a grocery store clerk—found that they had no time to observe or take notes. Be sure that you will be able to both observe and participate.

Some of the readings included in Part IV, Anthology, Section Three by a professional fieldworker (David A. Karp) and undergraduate participant-observers might help you decide whether your proposal is feasible because they explain the demands and rigors of being a participant-observer. The undergraduate essays, written by students after they had completed this assignment and reread this chapter, recount the pitfalls they encountered. You might profit from their accounts. The essays you might find useful are:

David A. Karp, "Observing Behavior in Public Places: Problems and Strategies"
Dan Gegen, "Similarities of an Observation"
Kim Smith, "My Experience as a Fieldworker"

When you read these essays, take some notes about problems you can anticipate with your own fieldwork.

c. Redrafting Your Proposal. After you have assessed your proposal, redraft it to make it more feasible. Add a section in which you tell how you might avoid some of the problems discussed in the readings, referring to specific essays by title and author. Bring your proposal to class. Be prepared to read it aloud or to have it read aloud. When you listen to another proposal, advise the writer of whether or not you think it is fully feasible or meets the demands of the assignment. Take notes on what others say about your proposal and revise it in light of the advice you find helpful. Then, turn it in for an assessment by your instructor.

If you plan to use a questionnaire, prepare your questions. Bring them to class and be prepared to read them or to have them read aloud. If, as you listen to a classmate's questionnaire, you can think of other relevant questions for that student's questionnaire or you think some of the questions are unclear, offer your advice. Take notes on the advice others offer you about your questionnaire and revise it. Then submit it for an assessment by your instructor.

In the next several chapters, you will find other assignments preliminary to writing the first draft of your observations.

Chapter 7

Learning to Observe

PREPARATORY EXERCISE

In *Participant Observation: Theory and Practice* (Lexington, MA: Lexington Books, D. C. Heath, 1975), Jurgen Friedrichs and Harmut Ludtke include an exercise intended to sharpen the perceptions of observers. A number of participants leave the room; those remaining are given this story to read:

> A tall, lanky professor almost ran into difficulties as he went to the city last Tuesday. In his briefcase were his lecture notes and on the way home from the college, he was stopped by a small, dark, intelligent Irish policeman.
>
> "Somebody has stolen important government papers," the policeman said. "Unfortunately, I have to search your briefcase." The professor thought that the man might be an Icelandic spy, but because he had nothing to hide, he let the man search his briefcase.
>
> A very friendly, dark-haired, well-dressed man with only a badly hidden safety-razor in his pocket said, "He's not the one, you can let him go. I can assure you that he wouldn't be capable of doing such a thing."
>
> The policeman answered: "I'm not sure of that. These people are often wolves in sheep's clothing; but I'll let him go."
>
> The professor hurried home trying to recover a bit of lost time. He turned into 23rd Street and entered his own house in the middle of the block.(188)

After everyone in the room has read the story, one of those sent from the room is called back in, and one person tells him or her the story. That person then calls in another, and tells him or her the story, and so forth.

The audience listens for changes in the original story, such as additions, omissions, embellishments, analysis, explanations, and the like. Often, several different stories are used, and the process repeated, until members of the group are able to transmit information with a minimum amount of changes, omissions, or distortions.

Write a short story of the same length and kind as the example above. Make enough copies for everyone in your class or the group that will participate. Send some of your group from the room and ask the rest to read the story. Follow the procedure given above. Notice carefully the kinds of changes made by the various storytellers. Try several stories, noticing whether or not the storytellers become more accurate. See if you can tell whether or not accuracy in retelling has something to do with the way the story was written, with whether or not the reader is a careful reader, or with whether or not the listener is a careful listener.

Selective Perception

Whether we choose to write about our own experience or about our observations—as we do in the sciences and social sciences—we need to learn to observe carefully. One hindrance to careful observation is something that we all engage in: *selective perception,* which refers to our tendency to perceive and remember the same things differently. In their book *Participant Observation: Theory and Practice,* Jurgen Friedrichs and Harmut Ludtke refer to a study of the way three witnessess reported a car accident. In Fig. 7.1, the overlap of the three circles shows the portion of the witnesses' statements that agreed. As you can see, they disagreed about what they saw more often than they agreed. One of the observers was a policeman. Assuming that his perceptions were more accurate, because he has seen more car accidents than have the other two witnesses, nine percent of the statements made by the three witnesses were both similar and accurate.

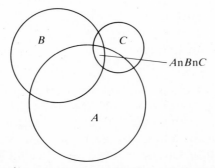

Fig. 7.1   The observation of an incident by three individuals.

If this is true of our perceptions in general, then we could say that when we witness something unusual, fewer than one out of ten of our statements about it will agree with the statements made by two other witnesses. Presumably, our statements will agree more frequently if we are describing something we typically see, rather than something as unusual as a car accident. Nonetheless, we know that each of us perceives the same things differently; we all experience selective perception. What this means for us as observers is that the sensory world—what we can see, taste, feel, smell, or hear—is a kaleidoscope of impressions, a continuous array of changing, colorful patterns. Our senses organize these impressions for us, so that we can understand them and remember them. To some extent, each of us organizes the impressions differently and understands them differently.

All of the sciences and social sciences rely upon careful, accurate observation. Learning to observe carefully involves not only becoming aware of selective perception and what it means, but also of the role language plays in both enabling and restricting observation. We use our senses to observe something, but we use language to record it, both when we take notes for ourselves and when we report what we have observed to others. In this chapter, we will consider what we can learn about the relationship between language and recording observations from anthropologists, philosophers, sociologists, and psychologists. At the end of the chapter, you will find assignments intended to help you become a keener observer by using various methods for taking notes on what you observe.

Description and Terms of Classification

Any term that names a group of things we can perceive is a term of classification; for instance, nouns such as *duck, dog, tree, woman, man,* and *chair* are terms of classification. It may not seem at first glance that these nouns name groups of things, but think about it. The word *duck,* for instance, may seem to refer to a single, specific animal, until you realize all the different kinds of ducks there are; for instance:

ring-necked	tufted	lesser scaup	greater scaup
redhead	canvasback	mallard	merganser
bufflehead	goldeneye	northern shoveler	

As a term of classification, the word *duck* blurs the distinctions among different kinds of ducks: it reminds us of what is typical of an entire class, rather than focusing on the immediate or particular. The word *duck* refers to ''ducks in general,'' rather than to a particular duck.

Terms of classification are very useful to us because they let us organize the kaleidoscopic impressions of the sensory world. They help us

shop and obtain paint samples from several different manufacturers (they are free). Take paint samples from the same color group—let's say blue—but from different manufacturers and line them up in a row. Look carefully across the rows. Do you find that none of the shades matches exactly, even though they might seem to until you look closely?

Notice the names the manufacturers give to these different hues and tones. No two names can be the same; one manufacturer cannot use the same label as another. How do they seem to come up with these names? Do they compare the color with something? Classify (group together) colors by the ways they have been named.

When A. R. Luria was in Uzbekistan he showed skeins of colored wool or silk to illiterate Uzbek peasant women. He found that the women came up with a wide variety of labels to designate differences in hue, whereas males working on collective farms or who were attending school tended to name colors by major color groups and were much less sensitive to variations in hue and shade.

The women labeled the skeins by naming things of the same color. Here are some of their color labels:

fruit-drop	iris	peach	spoiled cotton	pistachio
brown sugar	pea	lake	calf's-dung	poppy
pig's-dung	air	rubbed	cotton in bloom	
a lot of water	liver	sky		(26)

Classify these colors by the way they have been named.

Now try developing your own color labels. Repeat your observation, this time inventing color labels to show precise gradations in color. After several days, reread both sets of notes. Which seem to help you recall most vividly what you observed?

Exercise 3: Observing and Labeling People, Places, and Things

Read through one of your observations, circling all the nouns that name groups of things. Classify them under these headings: People, Places, Things. Now, do a frequency count. After each word, note the number of times you used it. What noun did you use most frequently?

Can you find more precise ways to name what you observed? Choose one of the nouns you used most frequently. Write down all the categories for that noun you can think of; for instance, let's try the word *child*.

girl	boy	tot	toddler
kid	preteen	preschooler	grandchild
schoolgirl	schoolboy	ankle-biter	tomboy
baby	infant	neonate	newborn
son	daughter	sister	brother

Now try adding some words that describe age, appearance, or behavior; for instance:

pest	angel	chubby	three-year-old
wrinkled	lively	cranky	spoiled
well-behaved	quiet	redheaded	cheerful
alert	shy	ticklish	bully

Repeat this observation, this time trying for greater precision in naming, and using more qualifiers. After several days, compare these notes. Which seem to evoke the scene or action most vividly?

Exercise 4: Observing and Labeling Textures

During one of your observations, look for what McKim calls "cubiture" (things shaped as cubes), then, "rounditure," "lumpiture," and "smoothiture." Compare these notes with the notes you made on color. How would you describe the effect on you as an observer of changing the focus from color to texture?

Exercise 5: Observing and Describing Social Interactions

Concentrate only on the social relations among the people you observe; e.g., how strangers are treated; which individuals seem to form a group; which seem to be leaders; how males and females greet and respond to one another; the degree of friendliness among individuals; typical greetings, criticism, and encouragement; and topics of conversation.

What is the action? Focus on sensory details—what you see, hear, smell, taste, or feel.

In what manner is the action carried out and what does the manner reveal about attitudes toward it? To answer this, you will have to observe body language—shrugs, winks, frowns, smiles, and the like.

What is said about it and what does it reveal about how people think and feel about it?

If you are involved, how do others react to you? Even if you are not directly involved, how do you think and feel about it?

Exercise 6: Describing Individuals

Focus on an individual, noting age, physical characteristics, clothing, gestures, language, and expressions. Take enough notes so that your description shows what makes this individual unique.

Exercise 7: Focus on Sound

During one of your observations, close your eyes and listen for a few moments. Then, record what you heard (you can open your eyes). Repeat this several times.

Now, take time just to record the words you hear spoken around you. You need not try to capture whole sentences; just listen for words as they go by.

Then, try to record a conversation, even a very brief one.

Exercise 8: Focus on Smell

Close your eyes again and take several slow, deep breaths. Now, concentrate on the odors around you. If your environment seems neutral, get closer to a few things in it, and sniff. Describe what you smell.

Chapter 8

Describing Recollections

PREPARATORY ASSIGNMENT: DESCRIBING SO OTHERS CAN VISUALIZE

Once we have observed carefully, we need to describe vividly and accurately so readers can visualize what we describe. Here is an exercise to help you understand what kinds of challenges we face when we try describing something.

Choose a common object. Write a description of it, place the object in a brown paper bag, and bring it to class along with your description. Show the description to a classmate, and ask him or her to read it, draw your object, and guess what it is.

If your partner guesses incorrectly, retire to a place where he or she cannot see what you have in your bag. Look at your object again, and see if you can tell from the drawing what you might add to your description to make it possible for your partner to identify it. Repeat this process until your partner can guess your object. When your partner finally guesses, study what you added. What kinds of descriptive details did you leave out originally?

There are three rules to this game:

1. The object you choose must be an irregular shape. It cannot be a circle, cone, square, rectangle, cylinder, pentagon, or other regular, geometric shape. Obviously, it can be a combination of these or an object of unusual design.

2. You cannot name the object in your description nor use descriptive terms that would tell how the object is used; for example, you cannot describe part of a scissors by using the word *blade*.
3. You cannot tell what the object is used for or where it is usually located.

The Demand for Verifiability

Both the humanities and the social sciences examine experience for what it reveals about the human condition; that is, both disciplines explore the significance of an experience for the individual who experienced it. But these disciplines differ in the stance each adopts toward the experience. In the humanities, the primary purpose is often to focus on what a particular experience signified for the *writer.* In the social sciences, the primary purpose is to focus on what a particular experience signifies for the *people observed.* Both disciplines use recollected experience to achieve their purposes. In the humanities, the experience is often a personal one; in the social sciences, the experiences are those recorded during direct observation.

In both disciplines, there is a special need for vivid, detailed description. When the writer's purpose is to convey what a personal experience signified for the writer, he or she has to assume that the significance will not necessarily be immediately obvious to the reader. One way to make the reader feel that the writer's experience inevitably signifies what the writer thinks it does is to describe the experience vividly and in detail. The need for vivid description in the social sciences arises for the same reason it does in all the observational sciences: because they all require that observations be verifiable. This is called *the demand for verifiability.* In the experimental or lab sciences, *verifiability* means that anyone conducting a previously performed experiment would (1) get the same results and (2) arrive at the same conclusions about what the results meant. Scientists are well aware that we can perceive the same things differently and that we can interpret the same things differently as well. For these reasons, reports on observations have to be detailed and clear.

In this chapter, we will study some of the descriptive techniques used in the humanities and the social sciences to present recollections in a way that makes it possible for the reader to visualize what is described. These methods are very similar, even though the ultimate purpose of a writer in the humanities differs from that of a scientist. All of these techniques are also used by fiction writers, as well. In other words, the ability to describe vividly is an ability relied upon at one time or another by most writers, regardless of the discipline or ultimate purpose. Common sense would tell us that if we want the reader to "see it our way," we will have to answer the questions necessary for systematic observation: Who? What? Where? When? How? How much or how many? Since presenting the answer to these questions draws attention to detail, the style of description is one that "shows" rather than "tells." As you read the examples of these various techniques, notice how often the writer describes sensory experiences—sights, sounds, tastes, smells, and textures.

Describing a Setting

Purpose: To Show What the Setting Signifies for the Writer

When the purpose of writing is to convey what an experience signified for the writer, he or she will often embed in a description of setting a statement about what the setting means for the writer. Here, for instance, is N. Scott Momaday's description of his tribal homeland in his essay "The Way to Rainy Mountain" (see Part IV, Anthology, Section Two). What does this setting signify for Momaday?

A single knoll rises out of the plain in Oklahoma, north and west of the Wichita range. For my people, the Kiowas, it is an old landmark, and they gave it the name Rainy Mountain. The hardest weather in the world is there. Winter brings blizzards, hot tornadic winds arise in the spring, and in summer, the prairie is an anvil's edge. The grass turns brittle and brown, and it cracks beneath your feet. There are green belts along the rivers and creeks, linear groves of hickory and pecan, willow and witch hazel. At a distance in July or August the steaming foliage seem almost to writhe in fire. Great green and yellow grasshoppers are everywhere in the tall grass, popping up like corn to sting the flesh, and tortoises crawl about on the red earth, going nowhere in plenty of time. Loneliness is an aspect of the land. All things in the plain are isolate; there is no confusion of objects in the eye, but *one* hill or *one* tree or *one* man. To look upon that landscape in the early morning, with the sun at your back, is to lose the sense of proportion. Your imagination comes to life, and this, you think, is where Creation was begun.

Here is another example of a writer who wants to tell us what a common experience signifies for him. What does Paul Engle want us to understand as the significance to him of the Iowa State Fair? How does he use descriptive language to make his point?

If all you saw of life was the Iowa State Fair on a brilliant August day, when you hear those incredible crops ripening out of the black dirt between the Missouri and Mississippi rivers, you would believe that this is surely the best of all possible worlds. You would have no sense of the destruction of life, only of its rich creativeness; no political disasters, no assassinations, no ideological competition, no wars, no corruption, no atom waiting in its dark secrecy to destroy us all with its exploding energy.

There is a lot of energy at the Fair in Des Moines, but it is all peaceful. The double giant Ferris wheel circles, its swaying seats more frightening than a jet plane flying through a monsoon. Eighty thousand men, women, and children walk all day and much of the night across the fairgrounds. Ponies pick up their feet in a slashing trot as if the ground burned them. Hard-rock music backgrounds the soft lowing of a Jersey cow in the cattle barn over her newborn calf, the color of a wild deer. Screaming speeches are made all around the world urging violence; here, there are plenty of voices, but they are calling for you to throw baseballs at Kewpie dolls, to pitch nickels at a dish which won't hold them, to buy cotton candy, corn dogs, a paring knife that performs every useful act save mixing a martini. (*Holiday,* March, 1975)

Purpose: To Show What the Setting Signifies for Those the Writer Observes

Frequently, the first aim of an observer is to familiarize us with the setting. Often this is done without commenting on what we might learn about the society from noticing where and how people live. Such explanations are left for later; that is, the writer delays telling us the significance of the setting for the people who live in it.

Sometimes introductory descriptions are artful and imaginative. Bronislaw Malinowski, in *Argonauts of the Western Pacific,* wants us to imagine that we are "sailing along the South coast of New Guinea towards its Eastern end" and along the adjacent archipelago for a guided tour of the areas he visited. Although he digresses occasionally to tell us something about the habits of the natives, his primary purpose is simply to introduce us to the places he visited.

Returning to our imaginary first visit ashore, the next interesting thing to do, after we have sufficiently taken in the appearance and manners of the natives, is to walk around the village. . . .

In the middle, a big circular space is surrounded by a ring of yam houses. These latter are built on piles, and present a fine, decorative front, with walls of big, round logs, laid cross-wise on one another so as to leave wide interstices through which the stored yams can be seen. Some of the store-houses strike us at once as being better built, larger, and higher than the rest, and these have also big, ornamented boards, running round the gable and across it. These are the yam houses of the chief or of persons of rank. Each yam house also has, as a rule, a small platform in front of it, on which groups of men will sit and chat in the evening, and where visitors can rest.

Concentrically with the circular row of yam houses, there runs a ring of dwelling huts, and thus a street going all round the village is formed between the two rows. The dwellings are lower than the yam houses, and instead of being on piles, are built directly on the ground. The interior is dark and very stuffy, and the only opening into it is through the door, and that is usually closed. Each hut is occupied by one family, that is, husband, wife, and small children, while adolescent and grown-up boys and girls live in separate small bachelor's houses, harbouring some two to six inmates. Chiefs and people of rank have their special, personal houses, besides those of their wives. The Chief's house often stands in the central ring of the store-houses facing the main place. (55–56)

From this brief description, we learn a good deal, in a preliminary way, about the people Malinowski studied: they cultivate yams, they are governed by chiefs, some people have higher rank than others, they live in single-family units, and chiefs at least can have more than one wife at a time. We also begin to ask questions: Why are the houses so dark and stuffy? Why do adolescents and young adults live separated from their families in communal dwellings? Is there any significance to the village being built on a plan of concentric circles? How does one become a chief? What do chiefs do?

By withholding lengthy explanations in favor of simple description, the writer puts the readers in the position of fieldworkers who have just arrived on the scene. We begin asking why things are as they are and so anticipate just those things the writer wants to explain. A skilled observer thus solves part of the problem presented by the need for verifiability by making the reader a kind of participant in observing the culture. An unskilled writer will make us ask questions the writer never answers.

Even when a fieldworker reports on a setting more familiar to us than New Guinea, he or she describes in detail what it looked like so that we will feel at home and can visualize it for ourselves. Elliot Liebow studied a group of about 20 "street corner men"—low-income black men in Washington, D.C.—who congregated in or near the New Deal Carry-out Shop. In *Tally's Corner*, Liebow first describes the neighborhood, then the restaurant. How does he hint at the significance of this setting for those whom he has observed?

> For those who hang out there, the Carry-out offers a wide array of sounds, sights, smells, tastes, and tactile experiences which titillate and sometimes assault the five senses. The air is warmed by smells from the coffee urns and grill and thickened with fat from the deep-fry basket. The jukebox offers up a wide variety of frenetic and lazy rhythms. The pinball machine is a standing challenge to one's manipulative skill or ability to will the ball into one or another hole. Flashing lights, bells and buzzers report progress or announce failure. Colorful signs exhort customers to drink Royal Crown Cola and eat Bond Bread. On the wall, above the telephone, a long legged blonde in shorts and halter smiles a fixed, wet-lipped smile of unutterable delight at her Chesterfield cigarette, her visage unmarred by a mustache or scribbled obscenities. In the background, a sleek ocean liner rides a flat blue sea to an unknown destination.
>
> In this setting, and on the broad corner sidewalk in front of it, some twenty men who live in the area regularly come together for "effortless sociability."
> (21–22)

As you can see, it makes little difference whether the purpose is for the writer to ascribe significance to the writer's experience or to the experiences of those observed. Nor does it make much difference whether the setting is "exotic" or familiar to the reader. Regardless of the purpose or context, writers craft a description of what we might see, hear, touch, taste, or smell if we were to visit the setting.

The Daily Routine: Freezing Time

Writers presenting descriptions of experience also familiarize us with what is "typical" or routine in the daily lives of those they describe. One technique used to achieve this is the descriptive summary. Such summaries are as artful and revealing as a snapshot, which artificially freezes a moment in time.

Purpose: To Show What a Typical or Routine Experience Signified for the Writer

Charles Dickens, in "The Streets—Morning," describes a typical morning in London. How does he use descriptive detail to show us why, for him, the streets signify "cold, solitary desolation"?

> The last drunken man, who shall find his way home before sunlight, has just staggered heavily along, roaring out the burden of the drinking song of the previous night: the last houseless vagrant whom penury and police have left in the streets, has coiled up his chilly limbs in some paved corner, to dream of food and warmth. The drunken, the dissipated, and the wretched have disappeared; the more sober and orderly part of the population have not yet awakened to the labours of the day, and the stillness of death is over the streets; its very hue seems to be imparted to them, cold and lifeless as they look in the grey, sombre light of daybreak. The coach-stands in the larger thoroughfares are deserted; the night houses are closed; and the chosen promenades of profligate misery are empty.

Purpose: To Show What a Typical Day or Routine Reveals about the Customs, Values, or Beliefs of Others

An anthropologist may refer to many pages of field notes, collected during the entire length of the stay, to describe a single, typical day—one that never took place in one sense, but took place every day in another. Here, for instance, is Jean Briggs's description of a "typical" evening among the Utku Eskimoe:

> With fish gutted and dogs fed and watered, people gathered around the blaze of the twig fire while Maata or Amaaqtuq boiled the remains of the morning's catch for the evening meal. Only Piuvkaq, because he was old and tired, lay on his bed, smoking his pipe as the light faded or crooning "ai ya ya's"—brief songs in which people speak their thoughts and feelings. The songs had a poignancy out of all relation to their monotonous four-or-five-note structure.
>
> The evening meal was eaten together, the steaming fish heads ladled with a caribou scapula into a single tray, around which people crowded sociably; only Piuvkaq, if he were in bed, was taken a separate bowl. The day ended as quietly as it had passed. The evening fire darted its arrows into the night and faded as a half-invisible figure carried a steaming teakettle into a tent; shadows moved

against the glowing tent wall as people drank their tea; and the camp faded into darkness.

Like Dickens, Briggs is describing a composite day, one suspended in an indefinite time, like the "once upon a time" of a story, to convey to us something of the continuity, routine, or redundancies of the lives she observed. Briggs selects and arranges details and uses tense to present what is at once a particular and a typical moment—a still life of a dynamic culture. Dickens wants to illustrate what the scene in London signified for him about the values of his own culture and to offer an implied critique of the indifference toward the poor and homeless. Briggs, on the other hand, wants to illustrate something about the values of those she is studying, such as how food preparation reveals the value of communal sharing. Here again we notice that descriptive writing, regardless of its purpose, is strongest when it sets the scene vividly before the reader's eyes, letting the reader recreate in the mind's eye what the writer saw. As you can see, such description, because it appeals to our imaginative powers, requires an artistry with language.

The Dramatis Personae: Thumbnail Sketches

Naturally, writers dealing with experience describe other individuals. Such descriptions include not only the individual's physical characteristics, but also his or her distinguishing mannerisms and characteristic behavior.

Purpose: To Describe What Another Person Signified for the Writer

How does N. Scott Momaday use a description of his grandmother to convey what she signified for him (see Part IV, Anthology, Section Two)?

Now that I can have her only in memory, I see my grandmother in the several postures that were peculiar to her: standing at the wood stove on a winter morning and turning meat in a great iron skillet; sitting at the south window bent above her beadwork, and afterwards, when her vision failed, looking down for a long time into the fold of her hands; going out upon a cane, very slowly as she did when the weight of age came upon her; praying. I remember her most often at prayer. She made long, rambling prayers out of suffering and hope, having seen many things. I was never sure that I had the right to hear, so exclusive were they of all mere custom and company. The last time I saw her she prayed standing by the side of her bed at night, naked to the waist, the light of a kerosene lamp moving upon her dark skin. Her long black hair, always drawn and braided in the day, lay upon her shoulders and against her breasts like a shawl. I do not speak Kiowa, and I never understood her prayers, but there was something inherently sad in the sound, some merest hesitation upon the syllables of sorrow. She began in a high and descending pitch, exhausting her breath to silence; then again and again—and always the same intensity of effort, of something that is, and is not, like urgency in the human voice. Transported so in the dancing light among the shadows of her room, she seemed beyond the reach of time. But that was illusion; I think I knew then that I should not see her again.

Purpose: To Describe the Traits of Another in Order to Illustrate How That Person Is Typical of a Group

In the social sciences dealing with the behaviors of groups, the purpose of writing is usually to illustrate what is typical about the groups. Sometimes this is done by describing the individuals within the group. Here, for instance, is Liebow's description of one of the street corner men he studied:

> *Sea Cat*—Sea Cat is twenty-seven years old. He was born and raised in the Carry-out neighborhood and except for his army service has lived all his life in that area. Sea Cat quit school in the tenth grade. He got married when he was twenty but he has long been separated from his wife and children. Sea Cat is of average height and weight. His large white teeth contrast sharply with his dark skin and his long, thick, processed hair. There is an air of excitement about Sea Cat. He moves with the easy grace of the athlete, and his sure, quick hands are almost always in evidence, whether he is throwing a ball or a stone around, telling a story with elaborate hand gestures or playing the pinball machine, which he dominates almost effortlessly. An excellent story-teller, Sea Cat holds his audience as much by his performance as by the content of what he has to say. If he reports that "an old man was walking down the street," his body suddenly sags with the weight of age and his hands tremble and knees almost buckle as he becomes, for that moment, an old man walking down the street. If he reports that someone shouted something, he shouts that something.
>
> Sea Cat disdains the ordinary, frequently choosing to see a special quality, talent or property in ordinary people and ordinary events. He looks at the world much like the caricaturist or the expressionist painter. By a carefully controlled distortion of reality as it is perceived by others—by hyperbole or fancy—he seeks out the individuality, the special character, of the men, women, and events around him.

Notice how Liebow's earlier careful description of the pinball machines in the Carry-out serve him well here. When we hear that Sea Cat "easily dominates" the pinball machine, we conjure the image of him playing the machine at the Carry-out, under the poster of the Chesterfield Lady. When a writer takes the time to establish setting and character, readers begin to work with the writer, because the reader begins to visualize how setting, character, and action go together.

Describing Illustrative Episodes

The descriptive techniques we have mentioned so far all use *summarizing* in some way; that is, they tell us what is typical about a setting or an individual. Naturally, writers also describe *particular* episodes that they regard as especially significant.

Purpose: To Convey Why a Particular Experience Was Significant for the Writer

E. B. White, in "Once More to the Lake" (see Part IV, Anthology, Section Two), describes what it meant to him to take his son to a fishing camp that White had often visited with his own father. How does White use one illustrative episode—a dragonfly alighting on a fishing rod while he fishes with his son—to convey what the trip meant to him?

> We went fishing the first morning. I felt the same damp moss covering the worms in the bait can, and saw the dragonfly alight on the tip of my rod as it hovered a few inches from the surface of the water. It was the arrival of this fly that convinced me beyond any doubt that everything was as it always had been, that the years were a mirage and that there had been no years. The small waves were the same, chucking the rowboat under the chin as we fished at anchor, and the boat was the same boat, the same color green and the ribs broken in the same places, and under the floorboards the same fresh-water leavings and debris—the dead helgramite, the wisps of moss, the rusty discarded fishhook, the dried blood from yesterday's catch. We stared silently at the tips of our rods, at the dragonfly that came and went. I lowered the tip of mine into the water, tentatively, pensively dislodging the fly, which darted two feet away, poised, darted two feet back, and came to rest again a little farther up the rod. There had been no years between the ducking of this dragonfly and the other one— the one that was part of my memory. I looked at the boy, who was silently watching his fly, and it was my hands that held his rod, my eyes watching. I felt dizzy and didn't know which rod I was at the end of.

Purpose: To Convey the Significance Others Attach to Their Experiences

Margaret Mead, in *Growing Up in New Guinea*, (1930; New York: William Morrow, 1962) gives the following account of a hot afternoon during which kinswomen have gathered in a hut to do various chores together. What do you gather about the values, customs, and beliefs of this group?

> One woman starts to gather up her beads: "Come, Alupwa," she says to her three year old daughter.
> "I don't want to." The fat little girl wriggles and pouts.
> "Yes, come, I must go home now. I have stayed here long enough making beadwork. Come."
> "I don't want to."
> "Yes, come, father will be home from market and hungry after fishing all night."
> "I won't." Alupwa purses her lips into ugly defiance.
> "But come, daughter of mine, we must go home now."
> "I won't."
> "If thou dost not come now, I must return for thee and what if in the meantime, my sister-in-law, the wife of my husband's brother, should take the canoe? Thou wouldst cry and who would fetch thee home?"
> "Father!" retorted the child impudently.
> "Father will scold me if thou are not home. He likes it not when thou stayest

for a long while with my kinsfolk,'' replies the mother, glancing up at the skull bowl, where the grandfather's skull hangs from the ceiling.

''Never mind!'' The child jerks away from the mother's attempt to detain her and turning, slaps her mother roundly in the face. Everyone laughs merrily.

Her mother's sister adds: ''Alupwa, thou shoulds't go home now with thy mother,'' whereupon the child slaps her also. The mother gives up the argument and begins working on her beads again. (19)

Both White and Mead select episodes illustrative of the relations between parent and child. But they do so for different purposes. White wants to tell us something about what the growth from the boy he was to the father he now is means for him. Mead wants to arouse our curiosity about what it means to grow from daughter to adult in New Guinea.

Their different purposes affect how each presents the illustrative episode. White not only describes what he saw in detail, he also describes his thoughts about it. Mead withholds any explanation of what she describes. Given typical standards of childrearing in the United States, Mead has chosen an episode clearly intended to surprise our expectations: most of us would not smile indulgently if a child struck Momma or Auntie. Since Mead withholds any explanation of what this episode tells us about this society, we are led to draw some conclusions of our own; namely, because these kinswomen seem to enjoy the girl's behavior, this society seems to find it acceptable for children to be disobedient, petulant, and abusive; and children seem to look to their fathers to do their bidding as well, because Alupwa expects her father will come get her. The mother, on the other hand, seems subservient to her husband, because she is very worried about how he will react to her having brought Alupwa to visit a kinswoman. In addition, the society seems patrilinear: the grandfather's skull hangs from the ceiling like the ''spirit'' of the household.

Mead, like Malinowski, puts us in the position of a participant-observer who has just arrived on the scene. She lets us see a social interaction that we would have difficulty interpreting given our own cultural standards for what is acceptable; we begin to infer what Manus culture must find acceptable. This serves Mead's interests. We are already asking the questions she most wants to answer. She will describe several episodes like this, one after the other, before she interprets them for us. This method familiarizes us with the society described, whets our curiosity, and makes us eager to hear how Mead interprets what she saw.

Focus on One Sensory Detail

Sometimes a writer will focus on sound, smell, color, texture, or shape. Here, for example, is how Paul Engle uses smell as a focus for his description in ''The Iowa State Fair'':

Nose has an exhausting time at the Fair. It smells the many odors rising from the grills of men competing in the Iowa Cookout King contest, grilling turkey, lamb, beef, pork, chicken, ham with backyard recipes which excite the appetite, the delicate scents of flowers in the horticulture competition, the smell of homemade foods, the crisp smell of hay. People drive hundreds of miles in air-conditioned cars which filter out smells in order to walk through heavy and hot late summer air across the manure-reeking atmosphere of the hog, cattle horse and sheep barns, to sniff again the animal odors of their childhood.

For Engle, these sensory details are included to show why for him the fair signifies a healthy awakening of the senses.

Elizabeth Warnock Fernea uses sound to describe the nightlife in *A Street in Marrakech* (New York: Doubleday, 1976):

It was true that everyone seemed awake at night, both in the houses and in the street. Except for the brief siesta time in midafternoon, the noise went on all the time. By midnight, the bustle of people passing by below our window had receded, but the radio went on and on, as did the shouting and quarreling and the crying babies in houses near us.

Order, classify, sort out, and identify the various noises, I told myself, keep our minds clear or we will all go mad. I had identified the radios easily enough, the boys playing and shouting on the street, the rustle of djellabas [the long robes worn by Moslem women in Morocco], the crying of children, the braying of donkeys, the bicycle bells, the motorcycles.

What I could not identify was a new incessant nighttime pounding, scraping, sweeping, and grinding. "Whang, rumble, rumble, rumble, *whang, whang,* rumble, rumble, rumble." From my window I could see nothing. Two a.m., 3 a.m., 4 a.m., "Whang, rumble, rumble, rumble, *whang, whang*"; it was infuriating. (44–46)

The noises Fernea describes give us a sense of the life of the street and also make us curious to know more. What is the infuriating noise? She also uses the noises to give us an insight into how she reacted to her surroundings, and, by contrast, an insight into what the natives to Marrakech accept as usual or typical.

Finding a Voice

Voice is a grammatical term that refers to the possible pronouns we can use:

	Singular	Plural
First Person	I	we
Second Person	you	you
Third Person	he, she, it	they

You might assume that the first person singular *I* would be used only by a writer describing what an experience signified for him or her, whereas the more "scientific" writers would avoid the first person. This is not the case. The writers who describe what made an experience significant for the writer sometimes choose the third person, as you can see if you reread some of the passages above. In their descriptions of setting, for instance, Paul Engle, N. Scott Momaday, and Charles Dickens do not use *I*, even though they are implicitly saying, "This is what this scene has come to mean to me." One possible effect achieved by not using *I* even though it is implied is that using a third person or "objective" voice helps the reader understand that the writer intends the significance to be universal. The writer implies, "This is what this scene has come to mean to me, and ought to mean to you, too." N. Scott Momaday makes this intention explicit when he uses the second person, you: "Your imagination comes to life, and this, you think, is where Creation was begun." Of course, writers do use the first person sometimes to tell us why a particular experience was significant, as do both Momaday in his description of his grandmother and White in his description of fishing with his son. When these writers describe in a way that summarizes what is typical, routine, or commonplace in order to make a point about what something signifies, they tend to avoid the first person. When they are describing a particular incident, they tend to prefer *I*.

The social scientists also sometimes refer to themselves and what they saw, using *I* or *we*; at other times, they will describe what they saw as if they themselves stood outside the scene. Liebow, for instance, sometimes includes himself in the picture: "We were in the Carry-out, at a time when he was looking for work." At other times, he removes himself from the scene, even though he obviously had to be present in order to observe it: "In a hallway, Stanton, Tonk, and Boley are passing a bottle around." Liebow seems to use the first person, *we*, when he is describing a conversation between himself and another. He leaves himself out of the picture when he is reporting how others were interacting among themselves.

Because anthropologists are telling us how others understand themselves, the anthropologist does not necessarily remind us constantly that he or she was present by using *I*. When evidence for a particular interpretation comes directly from an interaction between the fieldworker and one of the people he or she observed, it is often quite natural to report the incident using the first person. There are no rules governing the choice of voice. The voice a writer selects is determined simply by the immediate purpose behind what is said.

ASSIGNMENTS
Assignment I

Type your complete description of the object you chose in the Preparatory Assignment for this chapter. Underline those parts (if any) you needed to add before your partner could guess. Tell what you learned about the relationship between perception and description from this exercise.

Assignment II

Write a description using one of the descriptive techniques discussed in this chapter.

Describing a Setting
The Daily Routine: Freezing Time
The Dramatis Personae: Thumbnail Sketches
Describing Illustrative Episodes
Focus on One Sensory Detail

Options:

1. The assignments for Chapter 3, "Learning to Question," asked you to describe experiences. If you wrote an essay for one of those assignments, you might choose to revise it now, including one of the descriptive techniques asked for in this assignment.

2. The assignment for Chapter 5, "Signs," asked you to describe an experience or a relationship. If you wrote an essay in response to that assignment, you might revise it, incorporating one of the descriptive techniques asked for in this assignment.

3. The assignment for Chapter 7, "Learning to Observe," asked you to take notes on something you observed. You might want to use those notes to complete this assignment.

4. If you have been assigned to be a fieldworker, assume that the description you write for this assignment might be included in your final report.

Below you will find some exercises you might find useful as you prepare to write this assignment.

Exercises Preliminary to First Draft

Complete some or all of these exercises before you try your first draft. You might find they help you understand how to tackle it.

Exercise 1

Take some time to learn how professional writers elaborate upon or revise their journal entries to present clear and vivid descriptions. Chapter 26, "From Journal to Public Discourse," discusses how Francis Parkman elaborated on his journal entries when he wrote *The Oregon Trail*. Part IV, Anthology, Section One includes chapters from *The Oregon Trail Journal*. Compare the entries with his published work, noticing especially what kinds of information and sensory details he adds. Be especially alert to passages in *The Oregon Trail* that you enjoy or find particularly appealing. How has Parkman elaborated on his journal entry to achieve this effect? As a writer, what can you learn from him?

Part IV, Anthology, Section One also presents an article in which Clayton A. Robarchek includes his observations of 9/25/74. Compare the description in his article with his journal entry. How has he changed the entry? Why do you suppose?

Exercise 2

Compare your descriptive style with the style of a professional writer. Take an essay you have written that includes description. Select one of the descriptive passages included in this chapter. Try to choose one written with a purpose similar to the passage you have chosen from your own writing. Make the following comparisons:

Comparison 1: Choose a paragraph from one of the professional writers quoted in this chapter. Count the number of words. Circle the verbs and count them. Now, compute the following: (1) What percentage of the verbs are action verbs (the number of action verbs divided by total number of verbs equals the percentage of action verbs)?; (2) What percentage of the action verbs refer to each of the following: smelling, tasting, touching, hearing, seeing, and physical action (run, walk, jump, etc.)?

Repeat these computations for one paragraph from your essay. What conclusions do you draw from the comparison?

Comparison 2: Choose a paragraph from the professional writers. Circle all the qualifiers (adjectives and adverbs).

An *adjective* modifies the meaning of a noun. Adjectives are usually placed in front of a noun: a *single* knoll; an *old* landmark; *hot, tornadic* winds; *brilliant, August* day.

Sometimes an adjective appears in the predicate. These are called *predicate adjectives.* They modify the meaning of the subject: The grass turns *brittle* and *brown* (the adjectives describe the grass).

An *adverb* modifies the meaning of a verb, adjective, or another adverb. Many of them end in *-ly:* We have *sufficiently* taken in the appearance and manners of the natives; *better* built.

You do not need to identify whether a qualifier is an adjective or adverb. All you need do is tell whether a word qualifies or modifies a noun, verb, adverb, or adjective. Mark these words with a *Q.* Count the total number of words in the paragraph. Count the qualifiers. Compute the percentage of qualifiers (total number of qualifiers divided by total number of words).

Now, count the number of *descriptive* modifiers and the number of *empty* modifiers. A *descriptive* modifier evokes an image: green, yellow, slashing, etc. An *empty* modifier describes a quality and leaves it up to the reader to imagine what is meant: *great* grasshoppers, *a lot of* energy. What percentage of the modifiers are descriptive? What percentage are empty? Repeat these computations, using your writing. What conclusions do you draw?

Comparison 3: Using the professional writing sample, study the sentence variety. Mark the sentences, using the following codes:

Type 1 for a simple sentence (subject + predicate; e.g., The hardest weather in the world is there).

Type 2 for a compound sentence (more than one subject or predicate) of the following types:

Compound Predicate: subject + predicate + coordinating conjunction (*and, but, or*), + predicate

Compound Subject: subject + coordinating conjunction + subject + predicate

Compound Subject and Predicate: subject + conjunction + subject + predicate + conjunction + predicate.

Here is an example of a compound predicate (The air *is warmed* by smells from the coffee urns and grill and *thickened* with fat from the deep-fry basket) with a compound subject and predicate (Flashing *lights, bells,* and *buzzers report* progress or *announce* failure).

Type 3 for a complex sentence (a sentence with one or more dependent or subordinate clauses). Some of the words that signal clauses are: relative pronouns (who, which, that); possessive pronouns (whose); conjunctions (while, as, if); adverbs (only, as, now, when); gerunds (verb + *-ing*; e.g., standing); and participles (verb + *-ed*; e.g., startled).

Note that both gerunds and participles are used as different parts of speech. They function as *verbs:* He *is standing*; He *has been startled*; She *has fished* for hours on Seneca Lake.

They can also function as qualifiers: His *startled* expression told the whole story; She told me an *amusing* anecdote.

They can also introduce clauses: I see my grandmother in the several postures that were peculiar to her: *standing* at the wood stove on a winter morning and *turning* meat in a great iron skillet; The small waves were the same, *chucking* the rowboat under the chin as we fished at anchor.

Here are other examples of complex sentences: *On the wall, above the telephone,* a long legged blonde *in shorts and halter* smiles a fixed, wet-lipped smile *of unutterable delight at her Chesterfield cigarette, her visage unmarred by a mustache or scribbled obscenities.* The last drunken man, *who shall find his way home before sunlight,* has just staggered heavily along, *roaring out the burden of the drinking song of the previous night.*

Type 4 for a compound-complex sentence (more than one subject and predicate and at least one clause; e.g., The evening fire darted its arrows into the night and faded as a half-invisible figure carried a steaming tea-kettle into a tent).

Figure the following for the paragraph you are studying: (1) How many types of sentences did the writer use? (2) How many words are in the shortest sentence? How many in the longest? (3) What is the average sentence length (total number of words divided by total number of sentences equals average sentence length)?

Figure the same for one paragraph of your essay. What are your conclusions?

Comparison 4: See if you can find examples of these other stylistic techniques in the professional writer's paragraph: *onomatopoeia* (using words that sound like what they describe; e.g., *Whang, rumble, rumble, rumble*; *alliteration* (Ponies pick up their feet; Screaming speeches); *word play* (a paring knife that performs every useful act save mixing a martini); *dialogue; parallelism* (The coach-stands in the larger thoroughfares are deserted; the night houses are closed; and the chosen promenades of profligate misery are empty). Each phrase follows the same basic pattern: The + subject noun + are + descriptive term.

Can you find examples of these techniques in your paragraph? What conclusions do you draw?

Now, read again the sample of writing you chose from this chapter. What did the writer do with language that is appealing to you? What seems unappealing?

Drafting and Revision

Draft and revise your description until you feel you are ready to ask advice. Bring that draft to class.

In Part IV, Anthology, Section One, you will find an early draft of Christina Mohr's "Garage Sales" and the record of a discussion of it by her classmates. Read the original, the discussion, and the final version. What suggestions offered to Mohr could apply to your own draft? What can you learn about improving your draft from comparing her first draft with her final draft?

Ask others to comment on whether you have described in a way that will make setting, people, or actions vivid and verifiable:

Do you describe what you observed of this setting, person, action, or event, or what you heard in a conversation? Have you focused on sensory details—what you saw, heard, smelled, tasted, and felt?

If you describe a conversation or episode, do you describe in what manner it was carried out and what the manner reveals about attitudes toward it? Have you described body language? If you describe a person, have you described typical mannerisms and what they reveal about the person's personality?

If you describe an episode or setting, do you include what others said about it? If you describe a person, do you include how others comment on his or her mannerisms and behavior?

If you describe a setting, person, or episode, is it written so that it raises in the reader's mind the questions that you will presumably answer in your longer report?

Have you chosen an appropriate voice or voices?

If someone who was unfamiliar with the settings, people, or actions you describe were to read this, would he or she be able to visualize them clearly? Completely?

Chapter 9

Presenting Your Findings: Inductive Generalizations

PREPARATORY ASSIGNMENT: CHOOSING SOUPS

In this chapter, we will study inductive generalizations. To help you understand what that means, here is an exercise.

Imagine that there is a new brand of soup on the market, Heat and Eat. You are particularly fond of vegetable soup and decide to buy three cans of Heat and Eat Vegetable Soup in order to see if you like it. You find that all three cans are of inferior quality: the soup is thin, too salty, and contains very few vegetables.

Now, suppose a friend of yours asks you whether he or she should buy Heat and Eat Vegetable Soup. What would you advise? How would you explain your advice? Would you ever buy it again? Why?

Inductive Generalizations

In the previous two chapters, we have studied the similarities of writing in the humanities and social sciences when the purpose is to report on direct experience. Both call upon the writer to open the senses to experience—to become aware of color, sound, texture, taste, and smell—and to be alert to how others behave, interact, and speak to one another. Both also employ similar techniques in reporting observations by describing setting, individuals, and exemplary episodes, and in concentrating on particular sensory details. In this chapter, we will study how the *differ-*

ences in the primary purpose for reporting observations affects the way they are presented.

In Chapter 5, "Signs," we noticed that sometimes the purpose for writing in the humanities is for the writer to assign significance or meaning to an experience he or she has had. In doing so, the writer intends to universalize the experience; that is, the writer intends to invite the reader to find in the experience the same significance the writer assigns to it. Another way of saying this is that the writer wants to convince the reader that this experience inevitably signifies about human nature what the writer says it did. In Chapter 6, "The Participant-Observer," we noticed that the purpose for writing in the observational social sciences is often for the writer to report what significance or meaning a group of people typically assign to an experience. Another way of saying this is that in anthropology, for instance, the purpose of writing is to describe a culture, which was defined as "the body of learned beliefs, traditions, and guides for behavior that are shared among members of any human society" (Barrett 54).

This difference in purpose affects both the way writers in these disciplines proceed and the way they communicate their ideas. Both disciplines propose to understand a psychological reality, but they differ in whose psychological reality they wish to understand. As Hortense Powdermaker says, one purpose of anthropology is to "understand the psychological realities of a culture; that is, its meanings for the indigenous members" (*Strangers and Friends,* 9). But as you have probably gathered from reading those writers who wish to assign signficance to their own experiences, their purpose might be characterized as an effort to understand the psychological realities of an individual; that is, for the writer to understand himself or herself. It is safe to say that both the humanities and the social sciences ultimately aim at understanding what is universal about human nature, but they go at it differently. And the way they proceed affects how they communicate their discoveries.

You can see why easily enough if you ask yourself what kinds of reasons each would offer in order to make its discoveries convincing to a reader. E. B. White, for instance, says, "I would be in the middle of some simple act, I would be picking up a bait box or laying down a table fork, or I would be saying something, and suddenly it would be not I but my father who was saying the words or making the gesture. It gave me a creepy sensation" (see Part IV, Anthology, Section Two). There really is no reasonable way we could challenge the significance White assigns to his déjà vu. If he says that picking up a bait box made him feel he was his father and that this gave him a creepy sensation, then that is the significance he assigns to his experience. How can you disagree? Or argue? He is, after all, the best witness to his own psychological reality.

But when an anthropologist tells us, for instance, that Samoan adolescent females typically experience no sense of rebellion or sullenness as they move from childhood to adulthood, that is a different matter altogether because it is not a Samoan female who is telling us, nor is the claim made about just one individual—it is made about all Samoan females. In the social sciences, then, a different method has to be used in order to make the writer's discoveries convincing. This is why, as we noticed in the last chapter, the sciences impose on observers the demand for verifiability. The reader needs to be convinced that he or she would observe the same things and draw the same conclusions about them if he or she duplicated the observation. One of the ways this demand is met in the observational social sciences is through detailed and vivid reporting. The other way it is met has to do with the special requirements for presenting arguments about a hypothesis.

The Nature of the Argument

When we introduced the observational sciences in Chapter 6, "The Participant-Observer," we noticed that an observation begins with a field-dependent question and an anticipated answer. The anticipated answer, which is based on previous knowledge, is called a hypothesis. An observation is undertaken to determine whether or not the hypothesis can be supported. As you know, there can be four possible outcomes, called findings: a confirmatory instance, a disconfirmatory instance, an inconclusive result, and a serendipitous discovery. If the finding is anything other than a confirmatory instance, it can mean either that more evidence is needed—that is, more observations need to be undertaken—or that the hypothesis needs to be revised, modified, or replaced altogether with another hypothesis. Working with a hypothesis is really rather tricky business, as you can see. If your observations don't confirm the hypothesis, what should you do? Change the hypothesis? Or make some more observations?

This high degree of uncertainty about observations and what they may or may not mean is one reason why in reporting observations, the reporter follows some standard methods for presenting the findings, which is really a way of presenting an argument. If you recall the discussion in Chapter 4, "Overview," you remember that an argument has these elements:

The Given: An assumption the writer asks the reader to accept as true;
The Position or Conclusion: A position the writer takes about the given; and
The Reasons: The reasons the writer offers to explain the position.

Evidence is offered to support the argument. Evidence can include statistics, examples, testimony, precedent, or authoritative commentary.

In the sciences, a presentation of a finding includes the following:

A field-dependent question;
The given is *the hypothesis;*

The position is called the *conclusion or finding;*

The reasons are called *generalizations;* and

The evidence must include reports of *direct observations* or *statistics* or both.

To illustrate the characteristics of this kind of argument, we might return to Mead's study of Samoan adolescence:

Field-Dependent Question: Is behavior determined primarily by Nature or Nurture?

The Given is *the Hypothesis:* The behavior of female adolescents is a reflection of cultural influences.

The Position is *the Conclusion or Finding:* Observations of Samoan female adolescents provide a confirmatory instance of this.

The Reasons are *the descriptive generalizations* telling what is typical of Samoan adolescent behavior.

The Evidence is the reports of how individual adolescent females behave.

As another example, we might take the family Thanksgiving that we imagined ourselves observing. Let us assume that the observations provided a confirmatory instance of the hypothesis:

Question about Culture: What role does gender play in our culture?

The Given is *the Hypothesis:* In the United States, the chores relating to food preparation (preparing, setting the table, serving, and clearing away) are taken to be female gender roles.

The Position is *the Conclusion or Finding:* My observations of my family during this Thanksgiving provided a confirmatory instance of this.

The Reasons are *the generalizations* we would make about how females in the family typically behaved during this Thanksgiving; e.g., all the women prepared food.

The Evidence is *examples* of how individual females in the family behaved during this Thanksgiving; e.g., Grandma would not let anyone else watch over the turkey while it was cooking.

Perhaps you are wondering why we take the hypothesis as a given. We have said that a given is a statement that the writer wants the reader to accept as true, even if the writer does not provide reasons or evidence to support it. Well, that is what a hypothesis is, really. It is an assumption—a highly educated guess—that may at some point be changed or even discarded, but that the writer wants us to accept as true for now. But a confirmatory finding does not prove that the *hypothesis* is true. It is a confirmatory instance—just one. Similarly, a disconfirmatory instance does not necessarily show that the hypothesis is false. In both instances, the argument (hypothesis plus findings plus reasons for accepting the findings) and the evidence (report on the observations) may suggest to us that the hypothesis is a sound assumption or an unsound one, but it remains a kind of assumption: it might be true or it might not.

In Chapter 4, "Overview," we noted that a *deductive argument* begins with something taken as a given—a statement about accepted knowledge. We also said that the scientific method of argument blurred the distinctions between deduction and induction. That is so because a presentation of findings begins with a hypothesis, a more or less probable statement taken as "true" or "given." But the way the hypothesis is tested relies upon *inductive reasoning*, which we will discuss next.

Inductive Arguments

In arguments based on direct observations, the writer naturally gives reasons for the findings. These reasons are called *descriptive generalizations*, which are statements about what an observer has decided is typical or characteristic of the subject under observation. When you made your decision about Heat and Eat Vegetable Soup in the assignment at the beginning of this chapter, you made a generalization about *all* Heat and Eat Vegetable Soup from information about *some* samples of it. Inductive reasoning is just that: drawing conclusions about what is typical of an entire group from what we know from studying a sample. And to understand how to draw generalizations to support findings, you will need to understand how we think about induction.

For convenience, we are going to refer to "an entire group of things" with the word *class*. The class Heat and Eat Vegetable Soup includes every can of vegetable soup marketed by Heat and Eat. A descriptive generalization is a statement about what is characteristic of a class; for instance, "Heat and Eat Vegetable Soup is thin, salty, and has too few vegetables." Such generalizations answer the questions: Who usually? What generally? Where typically? When habitually? How typically? How much or many generally? After you put the findings together with generalizations about observations, you have an argument; that is, you have the conclusions and the reasons for them. It is called an inductive argument because it arises from what was observed directly. The evidence for inductive generalizations answers the questions: Who specifically? What specifically? Where exactly? When precisely? How in a given instance? How much or many in a given instance? Here, for instance, is how we might present the evidence and generalization about Heat and Eat Vegetable Soup:

Evidence

I went to the store last week and saw a new brand of soup, Heat and Eat Vegetable Soup, on the shelves. I decided to try it and bought three cans.

On Monday, I opened one can and heated it for lunch. I noticed it had only a few peas and carrots swimming around in this watery broth. When I tasted it, I found it was so salty that my mouth puckered! I was thirsty all afternoon.

On Wednesday, a couple of friends dropped by at noon. They were hungry, as usual, and I didn't have anything else in the house for lunch, so I heated the other two cans. I don't know if they'll ever come back for lunch. One of them got so few vegetables, he thought I was serving broth. Another suggested I was serving salty dishwater. We all decided to go out for hamburgers.

Generalization

Heat and Eat Vegetable Soup is thin, salty, and has too few vegetables.

The problem with presenting generalizations is figuring out how much evidence you need to adequately illustrate them because you are generalizing about an entire class from what you know about only a sample of it. In practice, you will find such generalizations based on what might seem a surprisingly small sample or length of observation or both. Here are some examples from anthropological studies:

> Elliot Liebow in *Tally's Corner* generalizes about the values and attitudes of *all* lower-income, black urban men (street corner men) from his observations of *25* of them.
>
> Richard Borshay Lee in "Eating Christmas in the Kalahari" generalizes about *Bushmen's* cultural values from the actions and behavior of *those Bushmen he observed.*
>
> Margaret Mead in *Growing Up in New Guinea* generalizes about the values typical of *Manus culture in general* from observations made in *one village* in the Admiralty Islands during a six-month stay.

How Much Evidence Is Enough?

There is no easy answer to the question, "How much evidence is sufficient to support a generalization." The question really is, "How much evidence is necessary to persuade a particular audience to accept the generalization?" This brings us back to the detail and vividness that observational reporters try to bring to their presentations. As we have said, those in the observational sciences are pretty keen on verifiability. This means that the person presenting his or her findings has to convince the reader that the generalizations are supportable. The more detailed, vivid, and elaborated is a description of what you observe, the more immediate or "realistic" is the impression on the reader. So one way to assist your audience in accepting your generalizations is to present them

How can you make it interesting? How did some of the other writers you consulted do this? What techniques of theirs can you use? Don't worry about any other part of the paper. Just concentrate on interesting the audience. Then set this section aside.

Write Down What You Think Are the Implications of This Study

Share with your readers how the lessons or conclusions might be applied, or discuss what further studies of other factors might also contribute to our understanding of the subject, or what you found most interesting, surprising, or valuable about the study, or a combination of these. Note how other writers managed this. What techniques could you try? Don't worry about any other part of the paper. Don't worry about anything except getting all your ideas about this topic onto paper. Then set this section aside.

Draft the Argument: Hypothesis + Findings + Reasons with Supportive Evidence

If you have taken good preliminary notes, as suggested above, you should be able to draft what is really the main concern of your presentation. Basically, you need to tell what you thought you would find, what you found, your reasons for saying that you found it out, and your evidence to support your reasons. Your study of other presentations should have given you a clear idea of what this entails. Draft this section.

Put It All Together

Now, take out all the sections you have drafted. Decide how you would like to put them together—in what order. Write a full draft. Be sure to signal the sections to your reader with strong transitions. You may even want to use subheadings as do many of the writers you have consulted.

Revision

Revise your full draft until you feel ready to ask for help. Show that draft to someone who matches the description of your imagined audience. What questions does he or she raise that you need to answer in order for your report to be clear and convincing? Bring your essay to class. Be prepared to read it aloud or to have it read aloud. As you listen to other essays, what suggestions can you offer about strengthening the presentation of the inductive arguments? The evidence? The appeal to the audience? The title? Is the description of methodology clear and complete? Would you like the writer to say more about the implications of the study?

Is the organization effective? Share your advice with other writers. Note the comments others make about your essay, and after the discussion, write down any further suggestions that occur to you. Then revise your report as many times as necessary to respond to these suggestions. Don't forget to edit and proofread.

Chapter 10

Assigning Cause

PREPARATORY EXERCISE

In this chapter we will discuss assigning causes. As a preparation for that discussion, consider how you would answer this question: Why do composition papers get the grades they do? How many reasons can you think of? Write them down. How many ways can you think of to prove that these are sound reasons? Write down your answers.

Answering the Question, Why?

One of the ways we use direct observation is to reason the cause from the effect. When Augustine asks himself, "Why did I steal the pears?" he takes the theft as an effect and wonders what motivated him to do it (see Part IV, Anthology, Section Two). In the observational sciences, a hypothesis can be a kind of highly educated guess about cause. Why do the females in our imagined Thanksgiving take care of the food? Because their culture has taught them that food preparation is a proper female role. The reason seems obvious. Why? What is the reason behind this effect? How do we become convinced that a cause is a good explanation for what we observe directly?

This is not a frivolous question. We have already seen that experience has no self-evident significance. The same is true of causes. Remember the questions: What is the significance of stealing pears? or What is the significance of saying, "I see men walking down the street"? or "What is the significance of a dragonfly landing on a fishing rod?" These experiences have a significance only if the person who had them tells us what the experiences signified. Now suppose we changed the question so it was clear that we were asking a question about cause; for instance, "What caused me to steal the pears?" We might say Augustine is on the nature side of the nature versus nurture debate. Augustine thinks he stole the pears because he bore the stain of Original Sin: theft is a sin, and we sin because we want to substitute our will for God's, our power for His. Would that be your explanation for a 10-year old stealing pears from the family orchard? How about stealing change from his mom's purse?

There is no certain connection between what we observe and the explanations we offer about what caused it. Consider, for instance, how you would answer the questions following these descriptions:

> Marti is a natural leader. She is the chair of several executive boards, and she can't go anywhere—even to a restaurant for dinner—without running into several acquaintances, who usually stop to ask her advice. She has a very cheerful disposition and always looks on the bright side of things. But she is also very traditional and thinks the rules ought to be followed. She is firm with her children; for instance, she sets down pretty clear rules about how much television they can watch, what chores they have to do, and what their curfews are. And she grounds them if they break the rules.

> Chris is a shy but very loving person. He worries all the time about whether he will make a mistake on his work or in his manners, but he has very close ties with many people—both male and female—and often turns to them for help. He also offers his help and support whenever one of his friends is in trouble. And everyone notices how much he enjoys going to concerts or plays.

What causes these behaviors? Nature or nurture? You might say with confidence that such traits are caused by how people are raised—by their upbringing and the kinds of behaviors each was praised for by parents, teachers, and others. Many social scientists on the nurture side of the debate would agree.

But those on the nature side would not. Since 1979, more than 350 pairs of twins have been studied by a research group at the University of Minnesota. Their recent findings are that personality traits are heritable—that is, inherited from the parents. The research group arrived at these findings from their study of 44 pairs of twins who were raised in separate families. These twins were given a questionnaire that assesses personality traits, including:

Social potency: a person high on this trait is masterful, a forceful leader who likes to be the center of attention;

Traditionalism: follows rules and authority, endorses high moral standards and strict discipline;

Stress reaction; feels vulnerable and sensitive and is given to worries and is easily upset;

Absorption: has a vivid imagination readily captured by rich experience; relinquishes sense of reality (as when a person becomes completely absorbed in listening to music);

Well being: has a cheerful disposition, feels confident and optimistic;

Social closeness: prefers emotional intimacy and close ties, turns to others for comfort and help.

According to the *New York Times* report, the study found that identical twins are very much alike in personality, even when the twins have been raised apart (see Part IV, Anthology, Section Four). The study concluded that these traits were more than 50 percent determined by inheritance: social potency, need for achievement, traditionalism, sense of well being, alienation, stress reaction, risk seeking, and absorption. The need for personal intimacy or social closeness appeared the least determined by heredity.

We learned in the last chapter that one disconfirmatory instance does not prove a hypothesis wrong, nor does one confirmatory instance prove a hypothesis correct. Another way of saying this is that the Minnesota study will not resolve the nature versus nurture debate. The responses to this study can help us understand what some of the barriers are to presenting convincing statements of cause. Objections have been raised about the *methodology.* This project used a questionnaire to assess personality traits. The questionnaire asked, for instance, whether a person agreed or disagreed with the statement, "I often keep working on a problem, even if I am very tired." If a person agreed with the statement, it was understood to signify that he or she had a strong desire for achievement. Dr. Jerome Kagan, a developmental psychologist at Harvard University, raises an objection to basing this kind of finding on such a methodology: "There is often a poor relationship between how people respond on a questionnaire and what they actually do." Seymour Epstein, a personality psychologist at the University of Massachusetts, raises questions about the *limitations imposed by what was observed:*

> The study compared people from a relatively narrow range of cultures and environments. If the range had been much greater—say Pygmies and Eskimos as well as middle-class Americans—then environment would certainly contribute more to personality. The results might have shown environment to be a far more powerful influence than heredity.

Finally, Dr. Kagan raises a more subtle issue: "Years ago, when the field was dominated by a psychodynamic [a nurture hypothesis] view, you could not publish a study like this. Now the field is shifting to a greater acceptance of genetic determinants, and there is the danger of being too uncritical of such results."

These comments indicate why it is difficult to be certain about causes. A hypothesis is an educated guess about cause. A finding is an effort to show whether or not it is reasonable to accept that cause as an explanation for what was observed. But two kinds of factors make the findings questionable. The first has to do with how an observer arrives at the findings. Perhaps the way the observer made the observations affected his or her understanding of what was observed; that is, the methods used for collecting the data may have limited the observer's range of observation. Second, what the observer chose to observe may not be the sort of sample that permits the observer ultimately to draw generalizations about the entire class.

The second kind of factor has to do not with what was observed or how, but with the hypothesis itself. Dr. Kagan's remark that up until a few years ago a finding that confirmed that personality traits were heritable would not have been published indicates this factor most clearly. In its simplest terms, the issue he raises is a feature of human nature: We tend to see what we want to see, to find what we seek to find, to understand as we believe we should understand. We have already touched on this characteristic in discussions of how we react to experience. If we go to a party assuming that people should introduce themselves to us, and they do not, then we assume they are snobs. If we go to the party assuming that we should take the initiative and introduce ourselves to others, and find that when we do so we meet some interesting people, then we would label as very friendly the same people another person might label snobs. Dr. Kagan's remark indicates that this characteristic applies to the sciences as well as to our personal lives. We also noticed this earlier when we touched on Margaret Mead's *Growing Up in Samoa,* in which she presents a confirmatory instance of the nurture hypothesis that female adolescent behavior reflects cultural values. She found that Samoan females, unlike their counterparts in the United States, make an easy transition from childhood to adulthood. Derek Freeman, however, found a confirmatory instance of his nature hypothesis from his studies of Samoan adolescent females; that is, he found that they, like their U.S. counterparts, experience adolescence as a time of stress or rebellion.

With this much in mind, we can return to the questions we asked at the beginning of the chapter: How do we become convinced that a cause is a good explanation for what we observe directly? As Dr. Kagan indicates, one interesting way to ask the same question is: How does a writer persuade a reader that there is a convincing connection between cause and effect? As he indicates, part of the answer has to do with the audience's prior predilections. An audience already favorably disposed toward a given causal explanation will be less critical of how the evidence is presented than will an audience already disposed against it. I think that all writers—and especially writers such as students, who are highly conscious of being judged for whatever they write—know this about audiences, and I think that knowing it leads to certain problems for student writers. When a professor gives an assignment, the student often knows that it is an exercise intended to prove or reveal something that the professor already knows. As one professor said, "We assign experiments in biology, even though they have been done hundreds of times before." Students know this about the experiments, too, and may come to the perfectly logical conclusion that because both the student and the audience are in agreement about the results, the writer need not take the pains to present the finding carefully. But the point of the assignment is for the audience—the professor—to review the findings *as if* the audience were a highly critical one, or one not necessarily predisposed to accept the answer. The purpose is ultimately to teach students how to present findings carefully. This feature of college-level writing applies generally. Even if the writer—the student—thinks that the audience already accepts an explanation of cause, the writer is expected to approach the assignment as if the audience were not so disposed.

Another assumption that causes writers problems occur if the writer assumes the cause is so self-evident that the writer need not take time to show the connection between the assigned cause and the evidence. By now you should see the weakness in this thinking. There is no self-evident connection. The writer has to find ways to explain the connection in a manner that is convincing to the reader.

Convincing Arguments About Cause: Analytic Generalizations

How does a writer make convincing the connection between cause and effect? The way an observer does this is similar to the techniques used to present arguments about what is typical of a class. In the last chapter, we said that a *descriptive generalization* stated what was typical of an entire class. In this chapter, we will discuss *analytic generalizations*, which are statements about what causes typical traits or behaviors.

In the last chapter, we mentioned Elliot Liebow's *Tally's Corner*, a study of "streetcorner men"—low-income black men in Washington, D.C.—who congregated in or near the New Deal Carry-out Shop. His chapter "Men and Jobs" illustrates how descriptive generalizations, analytic generalizations (statements about cause), and evidence are made to work together in order to present a persuasive explanation of what causes typical behavior. In the chapter, Liebow presents an inductive argument that the streetcorner men are chronically unemployed or underemployed. After presenting carefully detailed evidence of this, he then wants to explain *why* the streetcorner men are chronically unemployed or underemployed. One of the explanations is that they have low self-esteem.

To make his explanation convincing, he ties his first statement to generalizations that he has earlier supported with evidence from his observations:

[a] Convinced of their inadequacies, [d] not only do they not seek out those few better-paying jobs which test their resources, but they actively avoid them,

gravitating in a mass to the menial, routine jobs [a] which offer no challenge—and therefore pose no threat—to the already diminished image they have of themselves.

The statement beginning [d] is a *descriptive generalization* telling what are the characteristic traits or behaviors of this group. It answers the questions, What generally? Where typically? When habitually? How typically? The statements or phrases beginning [a] are *analytical generalizations*. They answer the question, Why is that the way these men typically behave? Notice that Liebow interweaves his analysis with descriptive generalizations that he has already tied closely to what he observed. This is one way to make causal explanations convincing: tie them to generalizations that are themselves clearly derived from what was observed.

Notice, too, how the explanation of cause suggests what Liebow will have to go on to demonstrate in order to convince us of his explanation. He argues that these men typically regard *themselves* as inadequate. He will need, then, to offer us convincing descriptive generalizations and evidence to show that this is the case. Here is some of the supporting evidence he provides:

1. Liebow describes an illustrative action or behavior:

   Thus Richard does not follow through on the real estate agent's offer. He is afraid to do on his own—minor plastering, replacing broken windows, other minor repairs and painting—exactly what he had been doing for months on a piece-work basis under someone else.

2. Liebow quotes an individual and explains what it reveals about attitudes. "Richard once offered an important clue to what may have gone on in his mind when the job offer was made. We were in the Carry-out, at a time when he was looking for work. He was talking about the kinds of jobs available to him":

   I graduated from high school [Baltimore] but I don't know anything. I'm dumb. Most of the time I don't even say I graduated, 'cause then somebody asks me a question and I can't answer it, and they think I was lying about graduating. . . . They graduated me but I didn't know anything. I had lousy grades but I guess they wanted to get rid of me.

   I was at Margaret's house the other night and her little sister asked me to help her with her homework. She showed me some fractions and I knew right away I couldn't do them. I was ashamed so I told her I had to go to the bathroom.

   "And so it must have been, surely, with the real estate agent's offer. Convinced that 'I'm dumb . . . I don't know anything,' he 'knew right away' he couldn't do it, despite the fact that he had been doing just this sort of work all along."

3. Liebow generalizes about similar behaviors in others: "Richard refuses a job, Leroy leaves one, and another man, given more

responsibility and more pay, knows he will fail and proceeds to do so, proving he was right all along.''

4. Liebow offers another illustrative incident:

> In a hallway, Stanton, Tonk, and Boley are passing a bottle around. Stanton recalls the time when he was in the service. Everything was fine until he attained the rank of corporal. He worried about everything he did then. Was he doing the right thing? Was he doing it well? When would they discover their mistake and take his stripes (and extra pay) away? When he finally lost his stripes, everything was all right again.

As Liebow illustrates, explanations of cause are made convincing in about the same way as are all other inductive arguments: the writer first draws generalizations about what was observed, then supports them with evidence. Having established what is typical of the class, the observer then raises the question of cause, which is similar to a question about signs: Given that something is typical of a class, of what is it a sign? Signs are either fallible or infallible indicators of something—such as a cause. The writer necessarily ties the evidence—what was observed—very closely to the explanation in order to persuade the reader that the typical trait is an infallible sign of the cause the writer assigns to it. To do this, the writer draws upon the arsenal of descriptive techniques also used to support generalizations about typical behavior or traits.

Concrete Terms and Concepts

This brings us to one characteristic of language that is especially important for understanding why a writer needs to be careful whenever a causal explanation is offered. Descriptive generalizations refer to what we can perceive. They use *concrete* terms because they refer to what is tangible; that is, to what we can see, hear, feel, taste, or smell. To explain cause, we use *concepts*, or *abstract terms*, that refer to what we conceive of. Liebow uses a concept to explain why the streetcorner men are underemployed or unemployed: self-esteem. It is a term that designates a state of mind. It is intangible; we cannot see it, touch it, taste it, smell it, or hear the quality it names. We can listen to what someone says about himself or herself and infer that it is a sign of low self-esteem. But although we can reason from the effect to the cause, we cannot perceive the cause with our senses. We thus take certain behaviors to be *signs* of self-esteem.

A descriptive generalization, because it describes what we can perceive, could be confirmed by other observers; for example, The black urban males Liebow studied receive low or subsistence wages. To confirm this, we could ask the 25 men he studied how much they earned and compare their earnings with either our own common sense about salaries or with

statistical information about average U.S. incomes. But an analytic explanation is less susceptible to that sort of direct verification because it
explains something by using a concept rather than a concrete term. Even
if other observers returned to the scene and heard the men say essentially
what they said to Liebow, those observers might assign different causes:
poor education, economic recession, or unambitious men. Although we
would easily agree that some people can be classified by the term *low
income*, we could well disagree about the cause.

Notice how common concepts are to the examples we have discussed in
this chapter:

Original Sin	cultural influences	social closeness
gender roles	stress reaction	risk seeking
absorption	achievement	nature versus nurture
well being	social potency	
self-esteem	traditionalism	

None of these refers to anything tangible. Some are explanations of
what we can perceive. If someone is listening to Beethoven with a rapt
expression, we can say that it is a sign that he or she is absorbed in the
music. If we see that only women cook during Thanksgiving, we can say
that it is a sign that they regard cooking as a proper gender role. But you
cannot see a gender role the way you can see a kaiser roll.

Looking for the First Cause

Sometimes concepts go one step further than naming the cause of something we can see directly. Consider the Minnesota study again. When that
study said that the way a person answered a question indicated whether
or not that person had a sense of well being, the researchers were reasoning from the effect—answers on a questionnaire—to a cause—a
sense of well being. Then the study made another move: it concluded that
a sense of well being was itself caused by heritable traits—another concept. The researchers thus use a concept—heritable traits—to explain
the cause of another concept—well being—which is itself used as a
cause to explain the way a person describes himself or herself; that is, to
label what can be observed.

In this example a cause—the sense of well being—is then treated as
an effect, and the researchers reason from that effect to yet another
cause. Perhaps you can see why when we present explanations of cause,
we have to be very cautious. For one thing, what is a cause in one context
can be studied as an effect in another. There is some terminology that
might help us talk about this. What is seen as the most immediate cause
for what we can observe directly is called a *proximate cause*, the cause
in closest proximity to the effect. What causes a proximate cause is called

a *secondary cause.* A *first cause* or *primary cause* is one that cannot itself be caused. The human mind is always looking around for a first cause; even so, we have not come up with too many of them. God is regarded as the primary, or first, cause among those who believe in Him. As we have seen in the social sciences, Nature is regarded as a primary cause by some, and nurture—genetic determinants—by others.

The point here is that the further removed is the language about cause from what can be observed directly, the less certain we can be of the explanation, and the closer we move toward belief rather than certainty. Augustine, for instance, saw the proximate cause of his theft as the desire to rebel, the secondary cause as Original Sin. The Minnesota researchers saw the proximate cause of the answers given on the test as various personality traits—such as well being—and saw the secondary cause as heritable traits. Augustine assumes that our behavior is determined ultimately by our stance toward the power of God, the first cause; the Minnesota researchers assume that our behavior is ultimately determined by how we manage our genetic programs, the first cause. Both offer explanations that are remote from what we can know with any high degree of certainty. We take it as given that God moves in mysterious ways, and as for genes determining whether or not I listen carefully to Beethoven, even the Minnesota researchers admit that we could not ever see tangible evidence for such a direct connection between genes and behavior. This uncertainty about cause is what makes reasoning about causes so interesting and problematic. But it is also why when writing about cause, we have to be very alert to the distance we may be putting between what we actually observed and our explanations for it. The more heavily we rely on concepts, the more we also have to tie our explanations to generalizations and illustrations couched in concrete language. That is how causal explanations are made persuasive to a reader.

ASSIGNMENTS

This assignment asks you to assign cause or causes to something you have observed or can observe. Here are some suggestions:

Option 1: If you did fieldwork and wrote a presentation of your findings, you might wish to explain what you think is the cause or causes of the typical traits, behaviors, customs, or beliefs you discovered.

Option 2: You might wish to do a study of grades given to essays and explain what you think is the cause or causes. If you studied the relationship between time spent writing and grade received (the assignment given in the previous chapter), you already have some data to use for this study.

Regardless of which option you choose, read how other writers present explanations of cause. What do you learn from studying them about how to present this kind of argument? Select from the following in Part IV, Anthology, Sections Three and Four:

Elliot Liebow, "Men and Jobs"
Richard Borshay Lee, "Eating Christmas in the Kalahari"
David McKenzie, "Poker and Pop: Collegiate Gambling Groups"
Margaret Mead, "The Girl in Conflict"
David L. Rosenhan, "On Being Sane in Insane Places"

Suggestions for Option 1: Assigning Cause to Typical Behavior

Reread your presentation of findings. Can you think of ways to explain the typical behavior you described? Write down all the reasons you can think of for each. Now, consider carefully how you would convince the reader that your reasons were sound. Is there evidence in your notes that you could draw from? Have you considered all the possible reasons? Or are there others? Why do you think some reasons are better than others? How would you convince the reader of it? It is probably best to choose those reasons for which you have evidence in your notes.

Suggestions for Option 2: Why Essays Receive the Grades They Do

1. Write down all the reasons you can think of to explain why essays receive the grades they do.

2. You might want to conduct a study of the correlation between time spent and grade received (see Chapter 9, "Presenting Your Findings: Inductive Generalizations").

3. If you have studied the correlation between time spent and grade received, you might ask yourself these questions: Is the amount of time spent on writing an essay the cause for the grade it receives? Is the time spent on writing a sign of some other cause that might explain the grade? Is the time spent an effect as much as a possible cause?

4. You might wish to ask yourself about other possible reasons: Suppose you studied the comments made on your essays; what would they tell you about the reasons for the grade? Suppose you interviewed other students about a specific essay; could you find out what factors affected the quality? Suppose you interviewed yourself on the same subject? Suppose you interviewed your instructor about the grade given on a specific essay; could you learn what factors led him or her to assign the grade?

When you have collected your data, ask yourself if there are multiple causes for the grades essays receive. Ask yourself whether or not you think there is a proximate cause and a secondary cause. Do you find a first cause?

When you write your essay, remember that you are making a presentation of a finding. Your hypothesis would be what you assumed the *cause* for grades to be.

Drafting and Revision

Regardless of which option you choose, bring your draft to class when you are ready to ask for help. Read it aloud. As you listen to other analyses, decide whether or not you think the analytic generalizations are well supported by the evidence. How credible are the causes? Can you think of others that the writer did not?

After the discussion, revise your draft as many times as necessary to respond to the suggestions offered. Don't forget to edit and proofread.

Chapter 11

Discovering Analogies

PREPARATORY ASSIGNMENT

In this chapter, we will discuss reasoning by analogies. In preparation for that discussion, please do the following. Describe what you think about writing by comparing it with something else; for example, "When I think of writing, I'm reminded of *x*." Here are some comments other students have made about their writing:

> For me, writing is like jumping off a high diving board into a deep pool.
> Writing for me is like a car spinning its tires in deep mud.
> When I write, I feel like a butterfly flying alone on a spring day.

Invent as many comparisons as you can. Then select one you find particularly apt and offer to explain it. Add the word *because* to your analogy and go on from there.

Analogy and Observation

A descriptive analogy drawn from what we observe compares members of one class or one category (a subgroup within a class) with members of another. We are conscious of the way poets use analogy; for example, Shakespeare in Sonnet 18 compares a woman with a summer's day:

> Shall I compare thee to a summer's day?
> Thou art more lovely and more temperate.

Analogy is also a commonly used and often powerful form of inductive argument: if we know that one class shares certain characteristics with another, we can infer that they share other characteristics as well. The experimental sciences frequently rely upon such analogies. There is little apparent similarity between any of us and a mouse, yet we belong to different categories of the same class, *mammals*. Because we know we are similar in some ways, we reason that we are similar in others. When scientists discover that certain substances cause cancer in mice, they draw an analogy between mice and men, and conclude that the same substances cause cancer in humans.

Analogies help us organize the sensory world because they indicate that there are similarities between apparently dissimilar classes or categories. We can use such analogies in three ways: (1) to *communicate* to others what we understand, but which is new or strange to them, by comparing our subject with something familiar to them; (2) to *understand* more clearly for ourselves something new by comparing it with something we already understand; and (3) to *discover* similarities among things that our perceptions might tell us are dissimilar.

In this chapter, we will examine how analogies are used to communicate, understand, and discover in the physical, natural, and social sciences. Our purpose is to help you understand how valuable analogies are when you want to understand and describe the sensory world. At the end of this chapter are assignments that ask you to use descriptive analogies.

Using Analogies to Communicate: The Trobriand (Again) and the Crown Jewels, Mites and Stowaways

An observer has to figure out how to make descriptions clear to the reader. Analogies can often solve the difficulty if the writer reminds the reader of something the reader presumably already knows and compares it with what the writer is describing. This can be a pleasant and imaginative undertaking for the writer because the most effective analogies used for this purpose are those that make comparisons between strikingly dissimilar kinds—or classes—of things.

In *Argonauts of the Western Pacific*, Malinowski faced the difficult task of making us understand the trading arrangements, called the *Kula*, practiced among the South Sea Islanders he studied. The objects they exchange are *mwali*, or bracelets made of highly polished shells, and *soulava*, or long, shell necklaces. These are exchanged among members of the Kula, which is rather like a trading club. Men of different villages, who may even live on different islands, are Kula partners and remain so for life. One Kula partner presents the other *mwali* and *soulava*, which the recipient keeps for a year or two; he then passes them on to another partner. These ornaments are worn during major festivals, and if someone—such as a member of the family, a relative, or a servant—wants to wear them on such occasions, he or she only has to ask. But the bracelets and necklaces are not prized for their ornamental value; all but 10 percent of them are too small to be worn even by a child. They are prized primarily as objects of exchange, so that one Kula partner can give them to another, who has them for a while and then passes them on.

Malinowski anticipated how incomprehensible such practices might seem to us, so he draws an analogy between the *mwali* and *soulava* and the Crown Jewels of England, which, as you may know, is one of the largest collections of jewelry in the world. He tells us of his first trip to Edinburgh Castle, where the Crown Jewels were kept at the time. One of the guards told him which jewels had been worn by which monarchs, how outraged the Scottish people were when some of the jewels were taken to England, and how pleased they were when the jewels were returned. Malinowski goes on to say:

> As I was looking at them and thinking how ugly, useless, ungainly, even tawdry they were, I had the feeling that something similar had been told to me of late, and that I had seen many other objects of this sort, which made a similar impression on me.
>
> And then arose before me the vision of a native village on coral soil, and a small, rickety platform temporarily erected under a pandanus thatch, surrounded by a number of brown, naked men, and one of them showing me long, thin red strings, and big, white, worn-out objects, clumsy to sight and greasy to touch. With reverence he also would name them, and tell their history, and by whom and when they were worn, and how they changed hands, and how their temporary possession was a great sign of the importance and glory of the village. The analogy between the European and the Trobriand *vaygu'a* (valuables) must be delimited with more precision. The Crown Jewels, in fact, any heirlooms too valuable and too cumbersome to be worn, represent the same type as *vaygu'a* in that they are merely possessed for the sake of possession itself, and the ownership of them and the ensuing renown is the main source of their value. Also both heirlooms and *vaygu'a* are cherished because of the historical sentiment which surrounds them. However ugly, useless, and—according to current standards—valueless an object may be, if it has figured in historical scenes and passed through the hands of historic persons, and is therefore an unfailing vehicle of important sentimental associations, it cannot but be precious to us. . . . Crown jewels or heirlooms are insignia of rank and symbols of wealth respectively, and in olden days with us, and in New Guinea up till a few years ago, both rank and wealth went together. The main point of difference is that the Kula goods are in possession for a time, whereas the European treasure must be permanently owned in order to have full value.(88–89)

This is an effective extended analogy for several reasons. First, it compares something unknown and strange to us with something we know about. Second, it makes the comparison *relevant* by narrowing the classification *heirlooms* to the category *heirlooms too valuable and too cumbersome to be worn*. The analogy thus excludes such heirlooms as a gold watch, which has been in a family for generations. Although we may recall fondly how many generations of relatives have owned the watch, so that it has historic and sentimental value, it is both valuable and useful. The analogy also excludes such heirlooms as the shellcasing Uncle Mort brought back from the trenches of World War I, because although it has historic and sentimental value, it is not a symbol of wealth nor is it useful. Third, it communicates clearly because Malinowski takes the time to compare *point by point* the attitudes and practices we share with the Trobriand when it comes to heirlooms. Malinowski also engages us with his dry wit, since he compares objects we generally hold in awe with "thin red strings, and big, white, worn-out objects, clumsy to sight and greasy to touch." We learn something not only about those naked men seated on a rickety porch, but something about our own values as well.

Effective analogies generally need to have the first three characteristics we noticed in Malinowski's comparison:

1. They compare something strange or unfamiliar with something familiar or known;
2. They make a precise comparison, referring to a specific category or class; and
3. They compare characteristics point by point.

Often, descriptive analogies are also playful or imaginative as well.

This is true of analogies that ask us to pretend we are something else. Robert K. Colwell, a zoologist specializing in the study of how mites fit into biologic communities, uses this technique to explain the relationshp between the mites and the hummingbirds that he studied in Costa Rica. In his article "Stowaways on the Hummingbird Express" (see Part IV, Anthology, Section Three), he asks us to pretend we are mites "just twice the size of the period at the end of this sentence." We eat the nectar and pollen of the *Hamelia* plant, which is an orange-red, inch-long blossom having no fragrance to humans. As mites, we can "smell" them using tiny hairs on our eight legs, called setae. These also take the place of eyes—which mites lack—because the setae tell us the size, gender, and age of other mites.

Imagine we are mites sitting in a *Hamelia* when we feel the vibration of a hummingbird's wings, and its bill is thrust into our flower:

> If you decide to leave, you dash up the bill of the visiting hummingbird and run into its nostril, and the odyssey begins. On board, inside the bird's nasal cavity, the accommodations are primitive. There is nothing to eat or drink. The place is crawling not only with your own kind but also with aliens of other species of hummingbird flower mites, hitching rides to their own promised land. You will know them by their smell, perhaps, and by the strange arrangement of their setae—long where yours are short, straight where yours are so beautifully curved.
>
> But the ventilation on this feathered freighter is absolutely first-class. A hundred times every minute or so, a hurricane of fresh air rushes in. More than

just a source of oxygen, the hummingbird's respiration acts as an odor pump, constantly updating information on the outside world. What you await is that familiar smell—the odor of your own host plant, *Hamelia*. . . . You have one to five seconds to disembark. With luck, if you are male, you will find females in need of a mate in your new home; if you are a mated female, you will find that a nearly empty flower . . . would be an ideal place to start your dynasty.

In making this lively point-by-point comparison, Colwell consistently uses images of a voyage or journey:

odyssey	feathered freighter	first class
on board	primitive	disembark
hitching rides	accommodations	

He is also consistent in evoking the sense of adventuresome stowaways setting out to find a new way of life:

promised land	new home	founding a dynasty
aliens		

As you can see, one way to make an analogy effective is to use the language associated with one kind of thing—stowaways voyaging to a new life—to describe another. A reader is also engaged when a writer asks him or her to shift viewpoints and pretend to be something else.

Using Analogies to Understand: Oystercatchers and Cover Girls, Gorillas and Soldiers

Before we can communicate what we have observed, we have to find ways of understanding it ourselves. One way to do this is to compare whatever we perceive as new or strange with something familiar. Such analogies yield insights because they enable us see into what would otherwise remain incomprehensible.

G. P. Baerends studied the way oystercatchers, birds resembling chubby sandpipers, identify their eggs. He placed oversize egg dummies that were painted in strongly contrasting colors alongside real oystercatchers' eggs and found that the birds sat on the dummy eggs, preferring the extra-large version. This seems a peculiar sort of trait, because it meant that the oystercatchers could make the kind of mistake that would cause them to fail to incubate their own eggs.

Konrad Lorenz, in *The Foundations of Ethology* (New York: Springer-Verlag, 1981), gains an insight into this trait by drawing an analogy to human behavior. He tells us that an

American journalist . . . having seen G. P. Baerends' film of an oystercatcher trying in vain to sit on an oversized and brightly painted egg, exclaimed, "Why that's the cover girl!"—which showed complete understanding of the phenomenon. Most measures taken by fashion to enhance female—and male—beauty function on the principle of exaggerating key stimuli. (163–164)

By comparing an oystercatcher's response to oversized eggs with human behavior, we gain insight into both the oystercatcher and ourselves. We, like the oystercatcher, respond to certain stimuli according to some sense of proportion. Drawing an analogy between oystercatchers and humans gives us an insight—or helps us understand—how both respond to certain objects.

Those who observe animals in their natural habitats regularly draw analogies between animal and human behavior to help them understand what they observe. Dian Fossey was one of the rare investigators to observe the mountain gorillas of Rwanda. To understand their behavior, she regularly drew analogies to human behavior. In *Gorilla in the Mist* (Boston: Houghton Mifflin, 1983), she describes the confrontation between the dominant male of Group 4, Uncle Bert, and the dominant male of Group 5, Beethoven. Dominant males breed exclusively with the females in their groups, and Beethoven had gained a female named Bravado from Group 4. About ten months after transferring to Group 5, Bravado began visiting again with the members of Group 4. This led to an encounter lasting several days between Beethoven and Uncle Bert. To describe it, Fossey draws an analogy to human battles. Uncle Bert began the encounter by running, beating his chest, and hooting (vocalizing) along the top of a ridge about 40 feet above Beethoven and his group.

> Nearly two hours passed before Beethoven slowly arose from his sentry position and ponderously, but silently headed toward Group 4, his females and infants left behind. Immediately Uncle Bert ceased vocalizing. He strutted up and down the ridge with such stilted and exaggerated movements that his hind legs appeared to be attached to his body by strings as they swung in arcs before hitting the ground. . . . Slowly Beethoven climbed up to meet Uncle Bert, until both stood face to face, magnifying their sizes by posing in extreme strut positions with head hair erect.
>
> After a few seconds, like mechanical soldiers the two males turned and separated, Beethoven strutting downhill and Uncle Bert up toward his silent and hushed group, which Bravado had joined. Abruptly Beethoven turned and ran up into the midst of Group 4. He was forced to retreat when the entire group surged down toward him screaming excitedly. However, Beethoven was not going to be deterred from his purpose, and charged into the midst of Group 4 again toward Bravado, who knelt submissively as he approached. He grabbed the young female's neck hair before herding her out of the group now clustered together behind her. Descending the ridge, they encountered the other three Group 5 members, and Beethoven authoritatively pig-grunted at them to accompany him. They obediently did. (68)

Fossey presents this encounter in terms associated with the military. Beethoven is described as a "sentry." Beethoven and Uncle Bert strut onto the battlefield to confront one another before hostilities commence. To Fossey, they seem "like mechanical soldiers." Beethoven "charges" and "retreats," until he gains his prize, and then he grunts orders to his underlings, who obey them.

Perhaps you noticed how easy it would be to read the passage without thinking of it as an analogy at all. This is probably because we so naturally try to connect the unfamiliar with the familiar in order to make the new comprehensible; we often draw analogies unconsciously. The analogy is also unobtrusive because Fossey does not call attention to it by saying, "Now I'm going to compare the gorillas with generals and soldiers" or "Imagine that the gorillas are human soldiers." Instead, she makes the analogy implicit by embedding the military language in the description of the encounter between Beethoven and Uncle Bert.

Comparing gorilla behavior with analogous human behavior makes it possible for Fossey to understand what she observes. Without such analogies, gorilla behavior seems enigmatic or incomprehensible, as is illustrated by Fossey's inability to understand the behavior of a five-year-old female named Tuck. When Tuck's mother, Effie, was injured on the back of her neck, head, and shoulders, Tuck nursed the wounds. What made her ministrations unusual was the little ritual she invented to go along with it:

> Tuck developed an unusual head-twirling greeting that she used only when approaching Effie for a grooming session. I could never understand what Tuck was trying to communicate. The young female would go to her mother and pivot her head around so rapidly that my own eyes could barely follow the motions. After nearly a minute of head twirling, Tuck would begin grooming the wounds intently, leaving me dizzy after having tried to follow each head movement and leaving Effie looking as puzzled as I at her daughter's strange behavior—behavior never again observed once Effie's wounds had healed. (89)

Since an immediate human analogy for Effie's behavior does not come to mind, Fossey is at a loss to explain what the head twirling meant. The ease with which we feel we understand the warfare between Uncle Bert and Beethoven, and the difficulty we have in understanding Effie's gestures, indicate how valuable analogies are as aids to understanding what we observe. We naturally try to explain the unfamiliar in terms of the familiar. This tendency is an asset to understanding what we observe, especially when we become conscious of the ways in which analogies can help us and actively try to think of them.

Using Analogies to Discover and Invent: Planets and Blood, Flounders and Roofs

Earlier we noticed how commonly scientists use analogy to draw conclusions about human physiology from laboratory experiments on animals such as mice. Even seemingly farfetched analogies often lead to discovery. William Harvey, who discovered how our blood circulates, was inspired by Copernicus. He drew an analogy between the central position of the sun in the Copernican solar system and the central position of the heart. He reasoned that the blood circulated in relation to the heart, just as the planets circulated around the sun. We are so used to using the term *circulation* to refer to our blood system that we have forgotten that it was originally an analogy with the movements of the planets.

A concise definition of scientific discovery is summed up in the comment by Albert Szent-Georgi that it "consists of seeing what everybody has seen and thinking what nobody has thought" (cited in *Discover* [Sept. 1985], 98–99). Certainly Harvey's use of analogy led to this kind of discovery. The same is often true of invention as well. W.J.J. Gordon illustrates this in his book *Synectics* (New York: Harper and Row, 1961), in which he describes how a group solved the problem of inventing a new kind of roof, one that would be more economical because it would be white in summer—to reflect the sun's rays and reduce the cost of air conditioning—and black in winter—to absorb heat and lower heating costs. The group addressed the problem by using analogies. They tried to think of what sorts of things in nature change color, and remembered that a weasel changes from white in winter to brown in summer by shedding its coat. They also thought of the chameleon, and finally, of all things, the flounder. A flounder turns white when it rests on sand; dark if it rests on mud. Here is a transcript of part of the discussion that followed. Notice how the first speaker uses an analogy to explain how flounders change color, and the second draws an analogy between flounders and the design for a roof:

B: In a flounder the color changes from dark to light and light to dark. . . . This is how the switching works: in the deepest layer of the cutis are black-pigmented chromatophores. When these are pushed toward the epidermal surface the flounder is covered with black spots so that he looks black—like an impressionistic painting where a whole bunch of little dabs of paint give the appearance of total covering. . . . When the black pigment withdraws to the bottom of the chromatophores, then the flounder appears light colored. . . .

C: You know, I've got a hell of an idea. Let's flip the flounder analogy over onto the roof problem. Let's say we make up a roofing material that's black, except buried in the black stuff are little white plastic balls. When the sun comes out and the roof gets hot the little white balls expand according to Boyle's law. They pop through the black roofing vehicle. Now the roof is white, just like the flounder. . . .(54–55)

This conversation includes a dizzying array of dissimilar things: weasels, chameleons, flounder, impressionistic painting, roofs, and plastic balls. They are all connected because the group wants to invent something by drawing on the power of analogies. By trusting that analogies will lead them somewhere, the group demonstrates that invention as well as discovery "consists of seeing what everybody has seen and thinking what nobody has thought." More precisely, they demonstrate that both invention and discovery can consist of seeing what everybody has seen in juxtapositions nobody has ever considered.

Summary

One kind of induction is reasoning by analogy, which means comparing members of one class or category with members of another. Inductive reasoning assumes that if members of two classes share some characteristics, they must share others as well. Analogies can be utilized to communicate, understand, and discover or invent. An extended analogy compares what is familiar with the new, unknown, or unfamiliar; makes clear which classes or categories are being compared; and makes a point-by-point comparison. Analogies can also show elements of playfulness or imaginativeness.

ASSIGNMENTS
Assignment I

Extend the analogy you wrote to describe how you think about writing. Then, at the end, explain whether or not you think that exploring your ideas through the use of analogy gave you an insight that you would not have had otherwise.

Assignment II

Provide the reader a fresh insight into a person, place, object, event, or action you have observed by using an analogy.

Assignments Preliminary to First Draft

1. You might ask one or several readers to mark descriptive passages in an earlier essay that seem dull, vague, or difficult to visualize. Choose one of these passages and see if you can think of an analogy that would strengthen it.

2. You can choose a comparative analogy or ask the reader to imagine that he or she is a person, object, or animal in the scene you describe.

3. You'll enjoy a greater likelihood of success with this assignment if you free your imagination to think in strong, descriptive images. Here are some exercises other writers find useful for thawing their creative juices:

Try writing freely. Begin writing about the comparison you will make; do not stop writing. Keep your pen to paper, even if you have to write, "I can't think of anything to say" several times. Be nonjudgmental. Don't discard something that comes to mind because you think it might not be a good enough idea. Decide at the outset that you will keep writing, no matter what, for a specific period—such as 20 minutes. You may find that the images and ideas begin to spring to mind very quickly, so that you have trouble writing them down.

Try meditating on the imagery you have chosen. Select a time when you can be alone and a place free from distractions where you can relax and write. Sit in a comfortable chair or lie down on a sofa. Breathe deeply, relaxing your muscles. Focus your inner eye on the images you have chosen. Concentrate on them and then allow your imagination to explore them. Be sure to allow yourself at least 15 minutes, but don't hesitate to extend the meditation. When you conclude, write down what you imagined, using the present tense. Then, later, read what you wrote to find material you can use for this assignment.

Drafting and Revision

Write the assignment. Bring your essay to class. Be prepared to read it aloud or to have it read aloud. As you listen, consider whether or not the analogy served the writer's intended purpose. Did it help you understand or appreciate what is described by analogy? Is the analogy clear, fresh, and engaging, or does it seem labored or unclear? Share your advice with other writers, and take notes on the advice you receive. After the discussion, note any other ideas that come to mind. Then, revise your essay and turn it in.

Assignment III

Write an essay on the topic, "Learning/Writing (choose one or both) is/are like being a participant-observer because. . . ."

Assignments Preliminary to First Draft

1. Reread Chapter 6, "The Participant-Observer," paying particular attention to the description of fieldworkers. Take notes on those parts that parallel your own experience.
2. Reread the essays in Part IV, Anthology, Section Three by fieldworkers describing their experiences, noting parallels between their experiences and yours:

David A. Karp, "Observing Behavior in Public Places: Problems and Strategies"
Dan Gegen, "Similarities of an Observation"
Kim Smith, "My Experience as a Fieldworker"

Drafting and Revision

Write your essay assuming that your audience includes those who have been student participant-observers but who may not have thought about how what they have learned applies to learning and writing in general. Use the first person and compare your experiences with those of other participant-observers. Bring your essay to class. Be prepared to read it aloud or to have it read. As you listen, consider whether the comparison and discussion of implications seem complete, clear, and helpful. Share your advice with other writers, and take notes on the advice they give you. After the discussion, note any other ideas that occur to you, then revise your essay and turn it in.

Assignment IV

Think of something in everyday life that bugs you. Using the technique of brainstorming by analogy, try to invent a way to fix it.

Assignments Preliminary to First Draft

First, prepare a list of what James L. Adams in *Conceptual Blockbusting* (NY: Norton, 1979) calls "small-scale needs," or a bug list:

> Take a piece of paper and pencil and construct such a list. Remember humor. If you run out of bugs before 10 minutes, you are either suffering from a perceptual or emotional block or have life unusually under control. If you cannot think of any bugs, I would like to meet you. (112)

The bugs can be anything that bothers you—no daycare for the children of students, pizza delivered cold, trying to change the time on digital wristwatches, lousy studying facilities on campus—anything that bugs you. Here are some bugs listed by students at Stanford. Is your list as specific as theirs? If not, try again. Imagine you're Andy Rooney.

TV dinners	instant breakfast	Presto logs
buying a car	buttons that must	one sock
relatives	be sewn	stamps that don't
paperless toilets	hangnails	stick
men's fashions	small, yapping dogs	chairs that won't
rotten oranges	waste of throwaway	slide on the floor
hair curlers in bed	cans	banana slugs
hypodermic needles	soft ice cream	trying to get change
for shots	crooked cue sticks	out of pockets
sweet potatoes	prize shows on TV	red tape
cleaning the oven	static charges—car,	smelly exhausts
no urinals in home	blankets, etc.	high tuition
bathrooms	ditches for pipe that	writing letters
bumper stickers	are dug too large	strip mining
that cannot be	bathtubs	dull knives
removed	cigarettes	conversion of farm-
broken shoelaces	balls that have to be	land to homes
	pumped up	

ID cards that don't do the job

pictures that don't hang straight

ice cubes that are cloudy

glary paper

swing-out garage doors

dripping faucets

doors that swell and stick in damp weather

newspaper ink that rubs off

bikes parked in the wrong place

lousy books

blunt pencils

burnt-out light bulbs

panty hose

thermodynamics

dirty aquariums

noisy clocks

plastic flowers

changing from regular to sunglasses

reading road map while driving

wobbly tables and chairs

big bunches of keys

shoe heels that wear out

campers that you can't see around

corks that break off in wine bottles

soap dishes that you can't get the soap out of

vending machines that take your money with no return

buzzing of electric shavers

pushbutton water taps

chlorine in swimming pools

polishing shoes

broken spokes

stripped threads

cold tea

X-rated movies that shouldn't be X-rated

bras

mowing lawns

locating books in the library

miniature poodles

parents' deciding a kid's career

solicitors—telephone and door-to-door

typewriter keys sticking

shock absorbers that don't work

shaving

Get together with others working on this assignment and compare lists. Narrow your attention to a few problems that seem likely to yield an interesting invention. Now, choose one and see if you can invent a solution using W.J.J. Gordon's technique of brainstorming by analogy as described in this chapter. Obviously, this is a creative kind of play, so allow your imaginations to work, offering only helpful suggestions to one another. Don't dismiss any suggestion, regardless of how outlandish. Be sure to write the ideas where everyone can see them—on a chalkboard or on big pieces of paper hung on the wall (use large felt-tip markers). See if you can imagine several different solutions for one bug, and try the technique with more than one bug. Your group should plan to meet more than once, and should plan to have uninterrupted time in a place free from distractions.

Drafting and Revision

Review the solutions, and then develop one in detail. Use drawings if you wish. Imagine that you are presenting your solution to a group you wish to interest in it. Perhaps it is a group of investors who might provide the funding for manufacturing a new product or who would purchase the patent. Or it might be those with enough authority to implement your suggestions or a citizens' action group that could help you implement them.

Tell them what the problem is in a way that shows them why the solution is a good one, and explain the solution in detail.

Give your presentation orally in class, asking your classmates to imagine that they are members of your intended audience. As you listen to the presentation, decide whether or not you would find it convincing. Would you invest in it? Would you try to implement it? What questions are unanswered? What is unclear? Raise these questions, and respond to those who question you.

Chapter 12

Discovering Others' Arguments

PREPARATORY ASSIGNMENT

To prepare for this chapter, read George F. Kennan's "A Proposal for International Disarmament" in Part IV, Anthology, Section Four.

Discovering Arguments in Written Discourse

Earlier chapters have focused on discovering what it is possible to say about our own experiences or observations. Beginning with this chapter, we are going to focus on responding to the arguments presented by others. We will be concerned with responding to what we read. In earlier chapters, you have been asked to read what others have written, but the primary intention was for you to use those readings to help you figure out how to write the same kind of discourse. Now we will turn our attention to reading for a slightly different purpose: to discover, compare, evaluate, and judge the ideas of others. It goes without saying that learning what this entails is one of the primary expectations of higher education.

This chapter is concerned with how a reader discovers the arguments of another writer. Earlier chapters have touched on this by asking you to study how other writers presented their conclusions about their own observations. Now we will turn to a kind of discourse we have not studied, which is a presentation of the writer's understanding of what is already known. Arguments of this kind do not present new information gathered from direct observation; rather, they advocate a way of understanding knowledge that is shared by the writer and the reader.

You may recall that this is called *deductive argument.* But that term is probably less important to you than understanding that an argument about what is already known functions something like discovering by analogy. An analogy combines apparently dissimilar things in order to show how they are similar. A deductive argument brings together information and presents it in a way intended to give us a new insight into it. We will study what this means by examining George F. Kennan's "A Proposal for International Disarmament."

The Nature of the Argument

A proposal is a kind of discourse in which the writer presents the solution to a problem. When the proposal is addressed to a social policy issue, it is an example of what is called *deliberative discourse.* In this case, the writer tries to persuade the reader to support a public policy because by taking action now the society as a whole will probably assure itself a secure and prosperous future.

We have said that an argument consists of the following:

A given: A statement that the writer asks the reader to accept as true;
The conclusion or position: The position the writer takes in relation to the given;
The reasons: The reasons that the writer gives for taking the position;
Evidence is offered to support the writer's reasons.

In the kind of argument Kennan presents, the reasons a writer offers in support of the positions are called *propositions* because they propose a way of understanding what we know. Sometimes they are also called *premises*, which also means "physical location." A premise is the foundation or ground of an argument because it presents the reasons for it. The evidence for this kind of argument includes some or all of the following:

authority or expert opinion   examples
testimony   precedent
statistics

The presentation of a proposal to solve a problem usually includes the following elements:

The given: A problem that the writer assumes the reader already agrees is a problem;
The positions, which consist of (1) The writer's position on the status quo: What is wrong with the way others are addressing the problem? (2) The writer's position on the cause or source of the problem: What

is the history of the unacceptable way others are addressing the problem? (3) The writer's position on the solution: What is his or her solution to the problem? (4) The writer's position on the possible objections to the solution: What are the possible objections? How can they be answered?

The reasons for the positions: Propositions; and

The evidence: Drawn from prior knowledge.

Discovering Arguments and Evidence: Taking Marginal Notes

How can we discover a writer's arguments? It requires us to read critically. To illustrate, we will study Kennan's article as if we were making marginal notes as we read. In college, *reading* means "rereading" (see Chapter 25, "Taking Notes from Readings").

It is useful to begin by finding the writer's purpose. Often the title provides a clue. Kennan's purpose is to present a proposal for nuclear disarmament. Mark on your copy of the essay *purpose* where he introduces the proposal.

In the first two paragraphs, Kennan presents the problem, which he assumes we will acknowledge as a problem as well. On your copy of the essay, number the issues he raises and mark *problem* next to the paragraphs that present them.

Beginning with the third paragraph, Kennan presents his argument on what is wrong with the status quo; that is, with the way others are addressing the problem:

> *Given that:* "For over thirty years, wise and far-seeing people have been warning us about the futility of any war fought with nuclear weapons and about the dangers involved in their cultivation."
>
> *Position:* "One has the impression that something has now been lost of the sense of urgency, the hopes, and the excitement that initially inspired [these warnings], so many years ago."
>
> *Reasons:* (1) "Over all these years the competition in the development of nuclear weaponry has proceeded steadily, relentlessly, without the faintest regard for all these warning voices." (2) "We have done this helplessly, almost involuntarily." (3) "We have achieved, we and the Russians together, in the creation of these devices and their means of delivery, levels of redundancy of such grotesque dimensions as to defy rational understanding."

You should bear in mind two characteristics of this argument as you read. The first is that the position the writer takes *refers to* a given. When you read, you need to be conscious of how a writer's position derives from what he or she has already presented. Your marginal notes should make this clear, either by drawing an arrow back to the previous statement or by an abbreviation of some sort in the margin. The second characteristic is that here the writer does not offer evidence for the reasons. These are called *unsupported propositions.* When a writer fails to support propositions, it means that he or she assumes the reader agrees with them. A good critical reader questions such propositions to decide whether or not to accept them. Your notes might say, *O.K.* or *Yes* if you agree; or *No* if you do not. Make marginal notes on this paragraph in your copy. Then see if you can state the argument in your own words.

In the following three paragraphs, Kennan continues to voice his objections to the status quo; his positions are italicized. Can you locate the reasons? What about the given or givens? (Look for the givens in his statement of the problem.)

> I say redundancy. I know of no better way to describe it. [*Position:*] *But actually, the word is too mild. It implies that there could be levels of these weapons that would not be redundant. Personally, I doubt that there could. I question whether these devices are really weapons at all.* A true weapon is at best something with which you endeavor to affect the behavior of another society by influencing the minds, the calculations, the intentions, of the men that control it; it is not something with which you destroy indiscriminately the lives, the substance, the hopes, the culture, the civilization, of another people.
>
> What a confession of intellectual poverty it would be—what a bankruptcy of intelligent statesmanship—if we had to admit that such blind, senseless acts of destruction were the best use we could make of what we have come to view as the leading elements of our military strength!
>
> [*Restatement of Position:*] *To my mind, the nuclear bomb is the most useless weapon ever invented.* It can be employed to no rational purpose. It is not even an effective defense against itself. It is only something with which, in a moment of petulance or panic, you commit such fearful acts of destruction as no sane person would ever wish to have upon his conscience.

As a reader, you can help yourself identify when a writer is presenting his or her reasons if you first notice the position a writer takes, and then ask the writer, "Why do you say so?" Kennan's position is that we have too many nuclear weapons. Why does he say so? You can very clearly identify his answer if you insert *because, for,* or *since* in the text:

> [*Position:*] Personally, I doubt that there could. I question whether these devices are really weapons at all. [*Because:*] A true weapon is at best something with which you endeavor to affect the behavior of another society by influencing the minds, the calculations, the intentions, of the men that control it; [*and because:*] it is not something with which you destroy indiscriminately the lives, the substance, the hopes, the culture, the civilization, of another people.

In written discourse, the phrase following an implied or explicit *because, for,* or *since* states the writer's reasons for adopting a certain position. Stated another way, the phrase following those terms gives the writer's premises for a conclusion:

REASON WHY	POSITION (CONCLUSION)
Since she did not study,	she will fail the exam.
Since we are Republicans,	we did not vote for Mondale.
Because I could not stop for Death,	Death kindly stopped for me.

POSITION (CONCLUSION)	REASON WHY
Blessed are the meek	*for* they shall inherit the earth.
We do not pray in public schools	*because* of the separation of church and state.

As the passage from Kennan illustrates, the words *because, for,* or *since* are sometimes implied; for example, we could write:

We are Republicans; we did not vote for Mondale.
She did not study; she will fail the exam.

Learning to read with an eye toward noticing when a writer is presenting his or her reasons—whether explicitly or implicitly—helps you understand how a writer is presenting an argument. The signal words for a writer's conclusions are *thus, therefore, so, consequently,* or *as a consequence:*

REASON WHY	POSITION (CONCLUSION)
He never listens to me;	*therefore,* it is useless to discuss anything with him.
She has apologized,	*so* peace reigns again.
The defendant has been found guilty of driving while intoxicated;	*thus,* we revoke his license.

As with the signal words introducing reasons for adopting a position, the signal words for a conclusion can also be implied:

He never listens to me; it is useless to discuss anything with him.
She has apologized; peace reigns.

One way to distinguish clearly between a reason why and a conclusion—or the writer's position on a subject—is to learn to insert the implied signal words:

We are Republicans; we did not vote for Mondale.
[Since] we are Republicans; [therefore] we did not vote for Mondale.

She has apologized; peace reigns.
[Since] she has apologized; [therefore] peace reigns.

You will discover how useful this knack is when you make notes from your reading. You can either insert the signal words or the word *reason*; i.e., the reason the writer gives for taking the position:

> [*Position:*] *I say redundancy. I know of no better way to describe it. But actually, the word is too mild. It implies that there could be levels of these weapons that would not be redundant. Personally, I doubt that there could. I question whether these devices are really weapons at all.* [*Reason:*] A true weapon is at best something with which you endeavor to affect the behavior of another society by influencing the minds, the calculations, the intentions, of the men that control it; [*reason:*] it is not something with which you destroy indiscriminately the lives, the substance, the hopes, the culture, the civilization, of another people.
>
> [*Reason:*] What a confession of intellectual poverty it would be—what a bankruptcy of intelligent statesmanship—if we had to admit that such blind, senseless acts of destruction were the best use we could make of what we have come to view as the leading elements of our military strength!
>
> [*Restatement of position:*] *To my mind, the nuclear bomb is the most useless weapon ever invented.* [*Reason:*] It can be employed to no rational purpose. It is not even an effective defense against itself. [*Reason:*] It is only something with which, in a moment of petulance or panic, you commit such fearful acts of destruction as no sane person would ever wish to have upon his conscience.

We can summarize this argument, Kennan's objection to the status quo, as:

[*Given that*] "the ultimate sanction behind the conflicting policies of these two governments is a type and volume of weaponry which could not possibly be used without utter disaster for us all" and

[*Given that*] "today we have achieved, we and the Russians together, in the creation of these devices and their means of delivery, levels of redundancy of such grotesque dimensions as to defy rational understanding."

[*Position:*] Kennan argues that any amount of nuclear weapons is "redundant"—superfluous—because "these weapons are not really weapons at all."

[*Reasons:*] (1) "A true weapon is at best something with which you endeavor to affect the behavior of another society by influencing the minds, the calculations, the intentions, of the men that control it. . ."; (2) A true weapon "is not something with which you destroy indiscriminately the lives, the substance, the hopes, the culture, the civilization, of another people"; (3) It would be "a confession of intellectual poverty" and "a bankruptcy of intelligent statesmanship" "if we had to admit that such blind, senseless acts of destruction were the best use we could make of what we have come to view as the leading elements of our military strength"; (4) The nuclear bomb "is not even an effective defense against itself"; (5) The nuclear bomb is only a weapon "with which, in a moment of petulance or panic, you commit such fearful acts of destruction as no sane person would ever wish to have upon his conscience.''

Make marginal notes for these three paragraphs on your copy of the essay; indicate the givens, the position, and the reasons.

Your marginal notes should also indicate what kind of evidence a writer uses to support the reasons. In this paragraph, Kennan continues his objections to the way others are addressing the problem. What kind of evidence does Kennan use? The evidence is underlined:

> But all right: [*Position:*] accepting for the sake of argument the profound iniquity of these adversaries, no one could deny, I think, that the present Soviet and American arsenals, presenting over a million times the destructive power of the Hiroshima bomb, are simply fantastically redundant to the purpose in question. [*Reason:*] If the same relative proportions were to be preserved, something well less than 20 percent of these stocks would surely suffice for the most sanguine concepts of deterrence, whether as between the two nuclear superpowers or with relation to any of those other governments that have been so ill-advised as to enter upon the nuclear path. [*Restatement of position:*] Whatever their suspicions of each other, there can be no excuse on the part of these two governments for holding, poised against each other and poised in a sense against the whole Northern Hemisphere, quantities of these weapons so vastly in excess of any rational and demonstrable requirements.

Kennan here uses a statistical generalization as evidence to support his reasons. Mark this paragraph in your copy of the essay to indicate the position, the reason, and the kind of evidence. Then, consider which problem, stated at the outset, Kennan here argues is not being addressed properly. Finally, write a summary of this argument, using the schema: Given the problem *x*, Kennan takes the position *y*, offering the reason *z*. As evidence he offers *a*. Be sure to explain what Kennan means when he refers to the ''purpose in question.'' To what specifically in the previous paragraph does this refer?

In addition to presenting arguments, writers also present counterarguments in response to supposed objections. In this case, Kennan is obviously presenting implicit counterarguments throughout, because he is telling us what is wrong with how the nuclear issue is currently addressed. If you figured out what ''purpose in question'' referred to, then you probably noticed as well that Kennan presents an *explicit* counterargument in the paragraph we just reviewed. What is this presumed objection? How does Kennan answer it?

Now, in your copy of the essay, reread the three paragraphs that follow, beginning with ''How have we got ourselves into this dangerous mess?'' Answer these questions:

1. Is Kennan presenting an argument or a counterargument to an implied objection?
2. What position(s) does he take?

3. What reasons does he give for the position(s)?
4. What evidence does he provide?
5. To what prior statements does this refer? What is the given?
6. We have said that discourse like this falls into the following parts: The problem, the objection to the status quo, the cause, the solution, the response to possible objections raised to the solution. Into what part would you say these paragraphs fall?

If you have difficulty answering these questions, it would help to reread this chapter.

If you are able to answer them, you have an understanding of how to discover deductive arguments. This ability should help you enormously in understanding much of what you are asked to read. And learning to discover how a writer presents arguments should also help you understand how to present your own arguments effectively when you write.

ASSIGNMENTS

Assignment I

This is a two-part assignment. In the first part, you will test your note-taking abilities. In the second, you will comment on what you learned about taking effective notes.

Part I

Complete your marginal notes on Kennan's article. Then, take notes in your notebook on the reading. Chapter 25, "Taking Notes from Readings," will give you further suggestions for taking notes on this article. Study your notes carefully. Then take the quiz on Kennan's article that your professor will give you. When your quiz is returned, consider the grade and the comments. In what way are your notes a clue that can explain why you got the grade you did?

Part II

In an essay, comment on the effectiveness of your notetaking and study skills. Assume that your audience wants to learn how to take good notes. The audience can be yourself. Use your notes and your performance on the quiz as examples. Explain the relationship among taking marginal notes, written notes, studying, and performance on a quiz.

Drafting and Revision

Draft and revise your essay until you are ready to ask for assistance with it. Bring your draft to class. Be prepared to read it aloud or to have it read aloud. As you listen, comment on what advice you find useful and what advice you would like clarified. Comment also on the tone. Is this advice offered in a tone that encourages you to accept it? Take notes on the discussion. Afterward, add any other ideas for revision that occur to you.

Assignment II

Present a solution to a problem.

Assignments Preliminary to First Draft

1. Select a problem relating to an area in which you have some expertise. You are, for instance, a greater expert on "dorm noise" if you live in a dorm than you are on the subject "nuclear disarmament." If, in the last chapter, you did the assignment that proposed a way of solving a daily bug, you might wish to take that problem as your subject.

2. Write down for yourself the following: (a) What is the problem? Who else thinks so? (b) What is wrong with the way the problem is now addressed? Write down as many reasons as you can think of. How would you illustrate them? What examples would you give? (c) What is the cause or the source of the problem? Can you think of more than one cause? What evidence can you give to support this explanation? (d) What solution would you propose? Can you give enough detail so a reader could appreciate it? (e) Why is it a good solution? What might the objections be to it? How would you answer them?

If you have trouble thinking of a solution, you might review the suggestions given in Assignment IV in the last chapter. If you have already done that assignment, you might choose to take the opportunity now to revise your presentation.

Drafting and Revision

Draft your essay. Assume that you are writing for people who agree with you on the nature of the problem, but who might not agree with you about the solution. They might even think that the way the problem is being handled is all right. Include in your essay: statement of the problem, objections to the status quo, assessment of cause, proposed solution, defense against possible objections. Bring your essay to class. Be prepared to read it aloud or to have it read aloud.

As you listen, decide whether or not you agree with the writer's position, whether or not he or she has given enough reasons for the various aspects of this kind of essay, and what objections you might raise. Take notes on the discussion. Afterward, note any other ideas that come to you for revision. Then, revise the essay. Acknowledge by name those who helped you.

Chapter 13

Reporting Arguments

PREPARATORY EXERCISE

Before you read this chapter, take careful and complete notes on George F. Kennan's "A Proposal for International Disarmament."

Reporting Arguments

In the last chapter, we began a study of how to discover, compare, evaluate, and judge the arguments we find in what we read. That chapter gave advice on how to discover arguments by taking notes. In this and the following chapters, we will discuss some of the ways you might be called upon to use notes on readings as the basis for writing a paper. In this chapter, we will discuss writing a *summary*. You will find that you use the ability to summarize in two ways. First, professors often ask students to write a summary of an assigned reading. Second, when you write essays about readings, you will find that you inevitably summarize the readings even if your larger purpose lies elsewhere, such as presenting a solution to a problem, discussing the significance of an issue, or taking a position in a debate about ideas.

A *summary* is analogous to the *report* on observations in the observational and social sciences. And like that kind of report, the summary can seem deceptively easy. If you have written an observational report, you may have discovered that you had to revise several times before your reader could visualize clearly what it was you described. It sometimes takes us a little time to realize that the way we perceive something will differ from the way others see it, even if what we are describing is something familiar to our audience. The same is true of what we read. If we are asked to summarize an assigned reading, we might suppose that what it says is obvious, and that our reader—usually the professor—already knows the content. We might suppose, then, that the assignment is intended merely to test whether or not students have done the assigned reading. This assumption can cause problems for the writer. If we assume that the reader already knows what we are going to say about a given text, we may write a superficial summary. Unfortunately, this is often interpreted to mean that the writer simply did not grasp the arguments presented in the text.

One useful way to approach writing a summary is to assume that your reader has an interest in the subject and has not read the text but might be interested in reading it after he or she learns more about it. No editorial comment is called for in this kind of summary; only your report on the writer's arguments. Usually, it is also worthwhile to convey something of the author's style, so that you are in a sense introducing the author to the reader. One way to do this is to quote the writer directly.

A summary should be an *accurate* and *complete* account of a writer's main arguments. It presents the givens, positions, reasons, and evidence. The shorter the summary, the more intense is the focus on the givens, positions, and reasons. Longer summaries not only offer more information about the arguments, but they review the evidence as well. We will use George F. Kennan's "A Proposal for International Disarmament" to illustrate how to prepare a summary.

Planning

Writing a summary without good notes is really very difficult. With good notes, you have a way to plan how you will present the summary. You can review the blocks of arguments the writer presents, and then decide in what order you would like to present them. In Kennan's essay, the blocks of arguments are:

Statement of problem;
Objections to status quo;
Cause or history;
Proposal; and
Response to possible objections.

In what order could you summarize these? You can present them in the order Kennan offers them, or you can shift the order around. Suppose you decided to begin with the argument to reduce arms on both sides by 50 percent; that is, with Kennan's proposal itself? This would have the advantage of introducing the reader immediately to the purpose of Kennan's essay. How would you present the other arguments? You might sketch a plan like this.

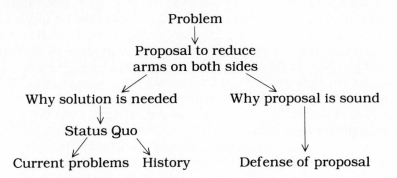

Or you might jot some notes showing the logic of your presentation:

Begin with: proposal;
Then: explain why Kennan thinks we need it—problems with status quo; history or cause;
Then: tell how Kennan defends the proposal.

Another way to think about organizing a summary is to begin with the author's purpose and the problem he or she was trying to solve. Again, using Kennan's article, preliminary notes might look like this:

Purpose
To propose an immediate arms reduction of 50 percent.
↓
Problems
To show us that the proposal is necessary and
  reasonable;
To show us that current solutions aren't working.
↓
Solutions
↓
He shows the proposal is   He shows his proposal
  necessary by: →   is reasonable by:
↓   ↓
Objections to status quo;   Defense of proposal.
History of status quo.

Or you might choose to use a topic outline:

I. Kennan proposes an immediate reduction in the aresenals of both sides by 50 percent with subsequent reductions of two-thirds

II. Kennan argues that such reductions are necessary
  A. Reviews the status quo
  B. Reviews the history or causes
III. Kennan argues that his proposal is reasonable
  A. It is better than the SALT proposal
  B. It would not interfere with negotiations on other matters related to arms control
  C. It is worth the risks

Conventions of the Summary

Once you have a plan—and you should choose a format that works for you—you should have some of the conventions of the summary in mind before you write the first draft.

Citation

The author and title should be given early in the summary. Often, it is simply written across the top, as a title:

Kennan George F. "A Proposal for International Disarmament." The Nuclear Delusion: Soviet-American Relations in the Atomic Age. New York: Pantheon, 1982. 175-182.

Openers

One of the problems facing a student preparing a summary is how it should begin. Usually, a writer tries to engage the reader's interest by beginning with a given—some principle or assumption about the subject that the writer and the reader share. Here are some examples from *The New York Times Book Review*:

> Robert T. Bakker, The Dinosaur Heresies: New Theories Unlocking the Mystery of the Dinosaurs and Their Extinction.
> Reviewed by John Noble Wilford.
>
> For several decades before the 1960s, dinosaur study was almost as fossilized as its subject. Most scientists had abandoned dinosaurs as mere curiosities of the past, unworthy of serious research; little more could be learned about them or from them that was worth knowing. So it seemed until paleontologists began making some new discoveries, particularly the Deinonychus fossils found by a Yale University expedition in 1964, which led a new generation of scientists to question all the old assumptions and theories about dinosaurs; these fossils rattled a lot of scholarly bones and imperiled the popular image of dinosaurs as nature's sluggish, overgrown failures. (Oct. 26, 1986, p. 14)
>
> Ellen Greenberger and Laurence Steinberg. When Teenagers Work: The Psychological and Social Costs of Adolescent Employment.
> Reviewed by Mickey Kaus.

For about two months in 1969, my senior year in high school, I delivered chicken and pizza for Chicken Delight in Beverly Hills, Calif. I got to wear a white shirt and bow tie with 'Chicken' running down one tassel and 'Delight' running down the other. The high point was the night I drew the run to the songwriter Burt Bacharach's house. The low point was the cole slaw, which—well, you don't want to know about the cole slaw.

I claim to have escaped this experience unscathed, but if so, I was lucky, according to Ellen Greenberger, a professor in the program in social ecology at the University of California, Irvine, and Laurence Steinberg, a professor of child and family studies at the University of Wisconsin, Madison. When Teenagers Work argues that working is bad for teen-agers—it does little to build character, interferes with education and actually encourages bad attitudes toward work and even 'deviant socialization.' (Oct. 26, 1986, p.30)

Marjorie Wallace, The Silent Twins.
Reviewed by Oliver Sacks.

We assume we are all individuals, autonomous, unique—and this assumption is suddenly tested, even shattered, when we meet twins. It is not just the biological rarity and extraordinariness of identical twins that so impress the imagination. It is the exact, the uncanny, doubling of a human being, a doubling (we may see, or imagine, or fear) which may extend to the innermost, most secret depths of the soul. There is always a shock—of interest, surprise, pleasure . . . and consternation—on encountering twins. We gaze from one to the other: identical faces, expressions, voices, movements, mannerisms—and feel a mixed sense, a double sense of both marvel and outrage (this is reflected in some cultures, which sometimes revere twins and sometimes destroy them). (Oct. 19, 1986, p. 3)

In his or her opening statement, each reviewer presents a common assumption and then introduces a book that will change our thinking about it in some way. In this sense a summary is a "news" report. It tells us the news—or what is new about the ideas the writer presents. Reread these openings. Notice the different ways the writers signal this turn; that is, notice the different ways the writers state a common assumption and then turn our attention to a different way of looking at it.

One axiom to bear in mind when drafting the opening is that the more the reader already knows about the *subject* at hand, the less the writer has to say to introduce it. This should not be confused with saying the more the writer thinks the reader already knows about the the writer's *arguments,* the less the writer needs to say. If you think that, you will assume that when your professor asks you to write a summary, you need not provide a careful review of the arguments because you will assume that your professor already knows them. In the case of Kennan's essay, the *subject* is nuclear disarmament. What the presumed reader does not know is what Kennan's proposal is and how he justifies it. For that reason, it would not be an effective opening to rehearse the nuclear dilemma, because presumably anyone old enough to have an interest in disarmament would already know the issue. This opening, for instance, would contribute little:

In our modern world, the Soviet Union and the United States have enough
nuclear weapons to destroy the world. Just one person with his finger on a
button could set off a nuclear war, because the other side would then set off
its nuclear weapons, even if the first missile was an accident.

While this introduction rehearses common knowledge, it does not lead
the reader to Kennan's proposal because nothing he says changes our
thinking about what this introduction says. It does not tell why Kennan's
proposal is news. Compare it with these two:

(a)   To those of us who often despair of either the Soviet Union or the United
States coming to some rational agreement to end the irrational race to mutual
nuclear destruction, George Kennan offers a proposal: the immediate reduction of nuclear arms on both sides by fifty percent, with subsequent reductions of two-thirds. He argues that both sides simply have too many weapons,
and that while an immediate reduction would not resolve all the issues
related to nuclear arms, it would have the advantage of simply reducing the
threat of total destruction to the Northern Hemisphere.
(b)   Confronted with thirty years of failure to control arms, and, indeed, a
steady increase in their numbers to incomprehensible volumes of destructive
power, many of us have posed the question Kennan asks: "Is it possible to
break out of this charmed and vicious circle?" Kennan hopes we can. He offers
a proposal to begin the process by immediately reducing nuclear arms on both
sides by fifty percent, with additional reductions by two-thirds. Arguing
that both sides simply have too many weapons, even for the purpose of deterrence, Kennan offers his proposal not with the assumption that it will
resolve all the issues, but that it is a beginning, and one worth the risks.

Both introductions assume that the writer and reader share common
fears about nuclear armaments and an interest in how to resolve the
threat of nuclear destruction. Both also assume that it is not necessary to
elaborate on these shared fears and hopes, but that the reader will want
an overview of what the summary will discuss.

An alternative opening simply ignores the civility of appealing directly
to the reader's interest. Here, for instance, is a review by Don Blakeslee
(see Part IV, Anthology, Section One) that appeared in an academic journal. Notice that the writer simply lists the arguments—first, second,
third:

There are three major arguments. One is that there was no single standard
unit of measure used to lay out all of the megalithic circles of the British Isles.
Instead, the mean of the units of measure used at various sites . . . and the variation of the unit from site to site . . . suggest that it was simply the human pace,
determined independently at each site. A second argument is that the builders
of the megaliths were not able to infer a minor variation in lunar motion and
hence could not have used it to predict eclipses. This argument draws from
astronomy, paleoclimatology, and anthropology. The third thesis, based on the

other two, is that the megalith builders did not have science, which is defined in terms of quantified knowledge.

Here is an introduction to Kennan's essay that adopts a similar style:

> George F. Kennan offers some interesting ideas on the subject of nuclear disarmament between the United States and the Soviet Union. This is a well-organized essay, broken down into three sections in which Kennan first presents the nuclear arms race from his point of view, then proposes his own solution for disarmament, and then defends the solution.

What kind of opening should you use? That is up to you, and it depends on the relationship you wish to establish with your reader. If you wish to appeal to the reader's interest or sense of the human condition, then do so. In general, you should assume that the opener is an invitation to read further. Which of these introductions seemed to offer that invitation most strongly to you? If you wish to present yourself as that kind of writer, then all you have to do is consider the human dimension of your reader and invite him or her to bring it to the subject you offer for discussion.

Reporting an Argument

As a reporter, you have to signal to the reader when you are referring to what the author said. Otherwise, it is hard for the reader to know whether you are offering your own commentary or reporting an argument. Here, for instance, is a weak opening because it offers an extreme example of a summary that both gives the writer's own commentary on nuclear arms and fails to signal which arguments are Kennan's, even neglecting to include quotation marks:

> Kennan presents in his essay, "A Proposal for International Disarmament" an argument involving the fear of a nuclear holocaust. According to many, a nuclear weapon is a useless weapon. Although many people know that nuclear weapons can destroy human civilization, the superpowers, the Soviet Union and the U.S., increase the development of the weapons every day. It is in one's mind that if his opponent has more power, he has to increase his, in order to not be overthrown. The U.S. and the Soviet Union have gone on piling weapon upon weapon to keep their artillery in equilibrium. When U.S. scientists come upon something new and more destructive, the Soviet Union will try to duplicate the weapon.

Which of those statements report on what Kennan says? How could you tell if you were unfamiliar with his essay? Compare this with Mickey Kaus's summary of the argument in When Teenagers Work.

Teen-age workers, the authors point out, are most often affluent, not poor. They don't work to help their families but to finance the "accoutrements of adolescence"—cars, stereos, clothes, records and drugs. Instead of teaching teen-agers the value of money, work may teach them to "value money unduly," hooking them on "'indiscretionary' spending" they may not be able to sustain once they have to pay their own rent. Intensive involvement in work may cause adolescents to "disengage" from school, extracurricular activities and family life. Work even opens up "new opportunities for deviance," as teen-agers learn to call in sick when they're not, pad their time cards and give away goods to their friends. The authors argue that teen-agers can become so cynical about their mindless jobs that they "take away from the workplace a diminished sense that work is a meaningful and satisfying human activity."

Kaus signals Greenberger and Steinberg's arguments in two ways: (1) by signal phrases—"the authors point out," "the authors argue"—and (2) by quotation marks around direct quotation.

In the previous chapter, we discussed inserting the implied terms to signal that a writer is offering reasons to support a position—*because, since, for*—or that signal a conclusion—*therefore, thus.* You should find that using these textual notes helps you summarize a writer's arguments. Here, for instance, are several passages from Kennan's essay:

> I say redundancy. I know of no better way to describe it. But actually, the word is too mild. It implies that there could be levels of these weapons that would not be redundant. Personally, I doubt that there could. I question whether these devices are really weapons at all. A true weapon is at best something with which you endeavor to affect the behavior of another society by influencing the minds, the calculations, the intentions, of the men that control it; it is not something with which you destroy indiscriminately the lives, the substance, the hopes, the culture, the civilization, of another people.
>
> What a confession of intellectual poverty it would be—what a bankruptcy of intelligent statesmanship—if we had to admit that such blind, senseless acts of destruction were the best use we could make of what we have come to view as the leading elements of our military strength!
>
> To my mind, the nuclear bomb is the most useless weapon ever invented. It can be employed to no rational purpose. It is not even an effective defense against itself. It is only something with which, in a moment of petulance or panic, you commit such fearful acts of destruction as no sane person would ever wish to have upon his conscience.

If you have taken careful notes on these passages, you are aware that they all support Kennan's contention that both the United States and the Soviet Union have too many nuclear weapons. If you have added the signal words as suggested, you can also distinguish Kennan's positions from his reasons for offering them. You can use these signal words to guide your reader through the arguments. Here is one possible summary for you to consider. The signal words are underlined to show how a writer can use them to clearly report another's argument:

```
Kennan takes the position that any amount of nuclear weapons consti-
tutes a redundancy--or an excessive amount--because nuclear weapons are not
```

really weapons. For Kennan, a "true weapon" is used "at best" to "influence
the minds, the calculations, the intentions" of those leaders who control
another society. No true weapon is something you use to destroy "the lives,
the substance, the hopes, the culture, the civilization, of another people."
Since any use of nuclear armaments would result in "such blind, senseless
acts of destruction," it would be a "confession of intellectual poverty" and
"a bankruptcy of intelligent statesmanship" to base our military strength on
nuclear weapons. No sane person of good conscience would ever wish to visit
such destruction on another society, but someone acting irrationally in a
moment of "petulance or panic" might do so. Therefore, Kennan argues, the
"nuclear bomb is the most useless weapon ever invented."

Closure

Because the summary does not call upon you to offer any editorial comment, the only thing a conclusion could do is to summarize what you have
said. That would mean that you summarized a summary. It is wiser to end
just when you have finished summarizing. Never mind a conclusion.

Revising

To decide how to revise a summary of an assigned reading, you might find
it most useful to show your drafts to two different readers, one who has
read the piece you are summarizing and one who has not. Someone familiar with the text can advise you whether or not you have omitted any
arguments and can also point out any places where you may have misunderstood an argument. In the following passage, the writer mischar-
acterizes one of Kennan's positions. Can you spot the problem?

 The solution Kennan proposes is an immediate across-the-boards reduction of nuclear arsenals by 50 percent, even though the remaining arms would
still be adequate to kill and destroy. The problem with such negotiations is
each side would still doubt the other, but the opposing governments have to
start somewhere and, to save humanity, take immediate steps toward
deterrence.

You may recall that Kennan criticizes the current policy of deterrence
as a justification for nuclear armaments. He also argues that no policy of
deterrence can justify the sheer volume of nuclear weapons in the arsenals of the United States and the Soviet Union. He certainly is not suggesting that either side rush to embrace a policy of deterrence—both do
now, and that is one reason for so many nuclear weapons.

Although a knowledgeable reader can help you revise for greater completeness and accuracy, a reader unfamiliar with the text can help you

revise for greater clarity. He or she can tell you whether or not your introduction provided a clear indication of what you intended to discuss and whether or not your summary gave a clear indication of the author's arguments and evidence.

ASSIGNMENTS
Assignment I

Drawing upon the suggestions in this chapter, write a summary of Kennan's "A Proposal for International Disarmament," making it as long as you wish.

Assignments Preliminary to First Draft

1. Reread the chapter and consider the advice it offers.
2. Be sure your summary is a complete and accurate account of Kennan's arguments.

Drafting and Revision

Show your draft to someone who has not read Kennan. Revise your summary so that you clarify any confusions you may have caused your reader. Ask your reader to comment on your introduction. Is it an invitation to read on? Then ask someone who is familiar with the essay to read your summary. Correct any inaccuracies this reader spots.

Assignment II

Write a report of your reaction to the way someone summarizes one of your essays.

Assignments Preliminary to First Draft

Photocopy one of your previous essays. Trade with someone else. Write a summary of the essay you receive. When you receive the summary of your essay, consider whether it is complete and accurate. If it is not, can you think of reasons why? Is it because you were not clear? Or because your reader was not reading carefully? If it is a complete and accurate summary, can you think why? What about your writing makes your arguments clear to others?

Drafting and Revision

Comment on what you have decided in response to the questions above. Discuss your response with the person who read your essay. Then revise your essay. Make the focus of your discussion what you have learned from this about effective writing and about writing summaries.

Chapter 14

Discovering Arguments: Comparing

PREPARATORY ASSIGNMENT

Read the Declaration of Independence of the United States of America and Ho Chi Minh's Declaration of Independence of the Democratic Republic of Viet-Nam in Part IV, Anthology, Section Four. Make marginal notes to indicate the arguments (givens + positions + reasons) and the evidence.

Introduction

The previous two chapters discussed how a reader can identify a writer's arguments and report on them. This chapter extends the discussion of those skills by considering how a reader can compare two writers' arguments. Students are often asked to compare and contrast the arguments offered by two or more writers. Sometimes students are asked to assume the stance of an observer or reporter who relates the similarities and differences expressed by two or more writers. Sometimes students are expected to become participants; that is, to tell with which arguments they agree and disagree.

To be sure you appreciate the difference, let us imagine the following: *A* is a writer who offers arguments about a subject; *B* is a writer who offers arguments about the same subject; and *C* is the subject that both writers address. When the assignment expects the student to be an observer/reporter, the question asked is: To what degree do *A* and *B* agree or disagree about *C*? In that case, the student is asked to relate those aspects of the subject upon which *A* and *B* agree and disagree with each other; the student is not expected to take sides in the argument. But when the assignment expects the student to be a participant, the question is: To what degree do you agree or disagree with *A* and *B* about *C*? In that case, the student is asked to offer an argument about the subject and to take sides in the disagreement between *A* and *B*.

In this chapter, we will discuss how you go about *reporting* what two other writers have to say about the same subject. You are not expected to take sides. But you *are* expected to take a position and give your reasons and evidence for it. This kind of assignment asks you to solve a problem: To what degree do *A* and *B* agree about *C*? You are offering a solution to a problem. Your solution is your position. You are expected to give your reasons for offering the solution and to give evidence—which means evidence from the texts you are comparing—to support your reasons.

Discovering a Solution: The Assignment

Suppose you have been given this assignment: Ho Chi Minh's Declaration of Independence of the Democratic Republic of Viet-Nam is obviously modeled on the U.S. Declaration of Independence; does that mean both Ho Chi Minh and the framers of our declaration advocated the same principles of government?

Which question does this assignment implicitly ask:

1. To what degree do *A* and *B* agree or disagree about *C*?
2. To what degree do you agree and disagree with *A* and *B* about *C*?

You should understand that this assignment implicitly asks the first question: To what degree do the (*A*) *U.S. Declaration of Independence* and (*B*) *Ho Chi Minh's Declaration of Independence of the Democratic Republic of Viet-Nam* agree and disagree about (*C*) *the principles of government?*

You may find it helpful to try to formulate an assignment that asks you to compare two or more documents in a way that will let you understand which role you are asked to adopt: the role of observer or participant. This is an important knack, especially because not all assignments ask an explicit question.

If the way an assignment presents the implied or explicit question seems boring to you, figure out how to ask the same question in a way that will engage your interest. Assume that you are given this assignment: Compare the U.S. Declaration of Independence with the Declaration of Independence of the Democratic Republic of Viet-Nam. Explain whether or not both advocate a similar theory or principle of government.

If this question does not seem particularly engaging to you, find a different way to ask yourself the same question. For example: If I tried to imagine the form of government suggested by the U.S. declaration, could I? What would it be? If I tried to imagine the form of government suggested by the Vietnamese declaration, could I? What would it be? How does what each declaration says suggest the answer to me? Here is another way of asking the question: Suppose I had lived at the time of the American Revolution, and I had to decide which side to choose. After reading the Declaration of Independence, would I have had enough confidence in the kind of government envisioned by the leaders of this revolution to join it? Why or why not? Suppose I had been Vietnamese in 1945. After reading Ho Chi Minh's declaration, would I have had enough confidence in the kind of government he envisioned to choose to follow him? Why or why not?

These quesitons aim at the same issue that the assignment raises, which is to compare the concept of government implicit in each declaration. By posing the question to yourself in a slightly different way, you might help yourself become more engaged with the assignment.

Considering Possible Solutions

Let us assume that this is the assignment you have been given: Ho Chi Minh's Declaration of Independence of the Democratic Republic of Viet-Nam is obviously modeled on the U.S. Declaration of Independence. Does that mean both advocate the same principles of government? Once you are certain that you understand the role you are expected to adopt, consider the possible answers:

Given: That Ho Chi Minh modeled the language and structure of the Declaration of Independence of the Democratic Republic of Viet-Nam (1945) on the U.S. declaration,

Question: Did he advocate the same principles of government?

Possible Answers:

Yes, Ho Chi Minh probably advocated the same principles of government.

No, Ho Chi Minh probably did not advocate the same principles of government.

In some ways Ho Chi Minh did advocate the same principles of government and in some ways he did not.

From a study of his declaration, it is not possible to tell whether Ho Chi Minh advocated any, all, or none of the concepts of government included in the U.S. Declaration of Independence.

Declaring for yourself the possible answers to an assignment based on a text is similar to positing an educated guess about what you will discover from direct observation. Listing the possible answers to an assignment is a good idea because it is useful to know where you might wind up before you embark on an expedition into unknown territory.

As you survey the possible answers, remember that you are seeking a possible solution rather than a self-evidently "right answer." Another reader may come to a different conclusion. This would not mean that he or she was wrong and you were right, nor the reverse. When a professor gives this kind of assignment, he or she will not likely judge the assignment by looking for a right answer that the professor already has in mind, as an arithmetic teacher might do. Rather, he or she will view this assignment as presenting a proposed solution. That means that the professor will assume that your solution is your *position* and that you will offer *reasons* and *evidence* to support it. This kind of assignment is given so that students can show whether or not they are able to present clear arguments (given + position + reasons) and evidence (examples from the assigned reading). Some students have difficulty grasping this purpose, so it might be useful to consider this paragraph carefully. Some students will say, "I got a bad grade on this paper because the professor did not agree with me." Sometimes—though rarely—that may be the case and, if so, then the professor is indeed unfair to grade in that way. But in the overwhelming number of cases, a bad grade is given because the student presented a position but did not offer a clear argument or sufficient evidence for it. The professor is not disagreeing with the position—or the conclusions—but with the weakness in presenting the argument. You may take a position with which the professor agrees and still receive poor marks because you presented your arguments poorly. Or you may take a position with which your professor disagrees but receive high marks because you present cogent arguments. Usually, professors who give the kinds of assignments we are discussing here—and they are as common as rain in classes that focus on texts—are not seeking "right answers" but sound reasoning.

Now, how can you decide which of the possible answers you will offer as your solution? For the rest of this discussion, we will look over the shoulder of a student, Kim, who is working on the assignment comparing the two declarations for a class in contemporary political history. After considering the assignment's question and the possible solutions, Kim begins by taking notes in outline form on the two declarations to establish their givens, arguments, and evidence. Here is a portion of Kim's notes:

```
                 The U.S. Declaration of Independence
Givens:
1. "We hold these truths to be self-evident,
   a. that all men are created equal,
   b. that they are endowed by their Creator with certain unalienable
      Rights,
      1) that among these are Life, Liberty, and the pursuit of
         Happiness.
      2) That to secure these rights, Governments are instituted among
         Men, deriving their just powers from the consent of the
         governed.
```

That whenever any Form of Government becomes destructive of these ends, it is the Right of the People to alter or to abolish it, and to institute a new Government, laying its foundation on such principles and organizing its powers in such form, as to them shall seem most likely to effect their Safety and Happiness.

2. "Prudence, indeed, will dictate that Governments long established should not be changed for light and transient causes;
   a. and accordingly all experience hath shown, that mankind are more disposed to suffer, while evils are sufferable, than to right themselves by abolishing the forms to which they are accustomed.
   b. But when a long train of abuses and usurpations, pursuing invariably the same Object evinces a design to reduce them under absolute Despotism, it is their right, it is their duty, to throw off such Government, and to provide new Guards for their future security."

Position:

"The history of the present King of Great Britain is a history of repeated injuries and usurpations, all having in direct object the establishment of an absolute Tyranny over these States."

Reasons for Taking the Position:

1. He has interfered with the colonial rights of self-governance ("He has refused his Assent to Laws, the most wholesome and necessary for the public good").

   ### Evidence:
   a. The king has demanded veto power over the laws passed in the colonies but has failed to make a decision on those laws;
   b. He has refused to pass other laws unless the constituencies they affected agreed to give up their rights to have representation in the legislative bodies that formulated the laws affecting them;
   c. He has convened colonial legislative bodies at places far from their constituencies. The inconvenience had the effect of wearing down the legislators so that they would agree to the legislation the king asked for;
   d. He has dissolved colonial legislative bodies that opposed his policies; and
   e. After he dissolved them, he called for new elections, which left individual colonies temporarily without governments to protect them from invasion and civil disturbance.

2. He has tried to prevent the colonies from growing in population.

   ### Evidence:
   a. He has interfered with laws intended to allow for the naturalization of foreigners;
   b. He has refused to approve or pass laws that would encourage migration to the colonies; and
   c. He has called for new appropriations of land by Great Britain before new immigration can occur.

3. He has interfered with the administration of justice in the colonies.

   Evidence:
   a. He appoints judges, decides how much they will be paid, pays
      their salaries, and decides how long they will serve.
      This means that judges are dependent upon the king's good graces,
      and, hence, on serving his wishes.
4. He has created a host of new offices and appointed the
   officeholders, who must be maintained by the colonists.
5. He has imposed the British Army on the colonies.

   Evidence:
   a. A standing army is maintained during times of peace;
   b. He has not asked the colonies whether or not they wanted such an
      army; and
   c. He has made the army independent of the jurisdiction of the colo-
      nies; the army reports directly to the king.
6. He has permitted Parliament to pass laws that are oppressive to the
   colonies.

   Evidence:
   Parliament has passed laws:
   a. Permitting the quartering of troops in the colonies;
   b. Protecting the king's soldiers by weak laws (which lead to mock
      trials) from prosecution for civil crimes such as murder;
   c. Cutting off colonists' trade with other parts of the world;
   d. Imposing taxes on the colonies without colonial consent;
   e. Depriving, in many cases, colonists of the right to trial by
      jury;
   f. Requiring that, for some crimes, colonists be tried in England;
   g. Suspending laws in the colonies of Canada, which sets a precedent
      for doing the same in the American colonies;
   h. Overturning the original Royal Charters that founded various
      colonies, abolishing colonial laws, and altering the fundamental
      forms of colonial government; and
   i. Suspending colonial legislatures and declaring that Parliament
      had the power to legislate laws for the colonies.
7. He has abdicated his most fundamental responsibility, which is to
   protect the colonies; instead, he has waged war against the
   colonies.

   Evidence:
   a. "He has plundered our seas, ravaged our Coasts, burnt our towns,
      and destroyed the lives of our people";
   b. He has hired mercenary soldiers to come to the colonies;
   c. He has forced colonists taken captive at sea to bear arms against
      the colonies;
   d. He has made an alliance with American Indians against the
      colonists.

The Declaration of Independence of the Democratic Republic of Viet-Nam

Givens:
1. "All men are created equal;
2. they are endowed by their Creator with certain unalienable Rights;
   among these are Life, Liberty, and the pursuit of Happiness.
       "This immortal statement was made in the Declaration of
   Independence of the United States of America in 1776. In a
   broader sense, this means: All the peoples on the earth are
   equal from birth; all the peoples have a right to live, to be
   happy and free.
       "The Declaration of the French Revolution made in 1791 on
   the Rights of Man and the Citizens also states: 'All men are
   born free and with equal rights, and must always remain free and
   have equal rights.'
       "Those are undeniable truths."

Position:
    "Nevertheless, for more than eighty years, the French imperialists,
abusing the standard of Liberty, Equality, and Fraternity, have violated our
Fatherland and oppressed our fellow citizens. They have acted contrary to
the ideals of humanity and justice."

Reasons for Taking the Position:
1. The French, "in the field of politics" have deprived the Vietnamese
   "of every democratic liberty" and "have enforced inhuman laws."

   Evidence:
   The French have
   a. Divided Vietnam into three different political regimes;
   b. "Built more prisons than schools";
   c. Slain those who opposed French colonial rule;
   d. "Fettered public opinion"; and
   e. Forced the Vietnamese to use debilitating drugs: alcohol and
      opium.
2. "In the field of economics, they have fleeced us to the backbone,
   impoverished our people and devastated our land."

   Evidence:
   The French have
   a. "Robbed" the Vietnamese of their land and natural resources;
   b. Monopolized control over their currency and trade;
   c. Imposed unfair and burdensome taxes; and
   d. Interfered with the growth of a middle class and exploited the
      working class.
3. They first accommodated the Japanese, which meant that the Vietnamese were unprotected from the Japanese and were subjugated to and
   then surrendered to them.

Evidence:
a. In 1940, the French retreated from the Japanese invaders;
b. As a result of the Japanese control of Vietnam, two million Vietnamese died from starvation in 1944;
c. In 1945, the French surrendered to the Japanese; and
d. Instead of allying with the Viet Minh--the Vietnamese resisting the Japanese--the French increased their aggression against the Viet Minh, which included massacring political prisoners.

Comparing Arguments

With just this much outline of the two declarations, we can follow Kim through part of the process of comparing the two documents. These are the questions Kim wants to answer:

1. Are the givens similar or different?
2. Are the arguments and evidence similar or different?
3. In each document, how do the arguments derive from the givens?
4. Does a comparison of the givens, arguments, and evidence indicate whether or not both documents advocate the same principles of government?

Comparing the Givens

These are Kim's notes comparing the givens:

Ho Chi Minh clearly wishes to legitimize his declaration by showing its derivation from the U.S. and French declarations. But he changes the wording when he comments on the U.S. declaration. Jefferson wrote, "All men are created equal." Ho Chi Minh interprets that to mean, "All the peoples on the earth are born free, all the peoples have a right to live, to be happy and free." Is there a significant difference in meaning between saying "All men" and "All the peoples on the earth"? What about the difference between saying that all "are created equal" and all "are born equal"? Jefferson says that all men are "endowed by their Creator with certain inalienable Rights." Jefferson says that these rights include the "pursuit of happiness." Ho Chi Minh says these rights include the right to "be happy." What about saying that "all the peoples of the earth are equal from birth" and the French statement that all are born with "equal rights"? Do they mean the same thing?

Imagine that these are your notes. How would you go on to comment on these differences? Are they inconsequential, or do they signify a difference in meaning? Commentary in your notes can be highly speculative and can raise questions that you are not yet prepared to answer. It is important to write those questions down, so that you know what you will have to explore and consider in order to decide which solution you will choose. For the same reason, stating that you cannot yet answer a question that comes to mind is also important.

This kind of comparison also considers what one writer says that another did not. Kim's notes on the givens also comment on what one document includes but the other omits:

> Ho Chi Minh omits Jefferson's givens about governments: that they "derive their just powers from the consent of the governed," that when one form of government "becomes destructive of these ends"--that is, the ends of securing the natural rights to "Life, Liberty, and the pursuit of Happiness"--then the governed have a right to "institute a new government," which will likely secure them "Safety and Happiness." What does it mean that Ho left out that part about "consent of the governed"? Was it considered too obvious to state, or did Ho Chi Minh's concepts of the purpose and legitimacy of government differ from those of the U.S. declaration?
>
> Ho Chi Minh also omits reference to the prudence advocated by the U.S. declaration and the given that revolution is justified if the government's intention is to impose an absolute despotism. Did Ho Chi Minh assume that this was too obvious to require stating as a justification? Did Jefferson mean that revolution was justified only if the aim of a colonial government was absolute despotism?

Kim adopts a sound strategy in comparing the wording carefully and in letting the comparison raise questions. As with a fieldworker taking notes on observations, we really cannot know which part of a text will eventually inspire the answer to the problem we are trying to solve. The note-taking stage should, therefore, be an especially open-minded and highly interactive exploration of the text.

Comparing Arguments and Evidence

Having compared the givens, Kim turns to comparing the arguments and evidence beginning with a summary of each:

> The U.S. declaration argues that the colonies have revolted because the king is attempting to impose an absolute despotism on the colonies. As evidence that he is attempting to do this, the declaration reports his efforts to deprive the colonies of their own legislative bodies, courts, or administration, and his interference with trade and taxation. In addition, evidence is offered that the king is taking aggressive action against the colonies.
>
> Ho Chi Minh's declaration, on the other hand, argues that the Vietnamese are justified in revolting from the French because the French have violated the human rights of the Vietnamese. He seeks to prove this by showing that the French have divided the nation into smaller political units; imprisoned or slain dissidents; censored dissident opinion; corrupted the populace; imposed exploitative monetary and trade monopolies on Vietnam; and have failed to protect Vietnam from foreign invasion or to ally with the Vietnamese in resisting it.

Imagine again that these are your notes. How would you compare these two arguments? Does a comparison suggest an answer to the question: Does Ho Chi Minh's declaration advocate the same principle of government as the U.S. declaration? Write down your comments.

Do the Arguments and Evidence Derive From the Givens?

Kim has now compared the givens, the arguments, and evidence. He goes on to ask, How do the arguments and evidence derive from the givens?

The U.S. declaration takes it as a given that all men are endowed by God with the right to life, liberty, and the pursuit of happiness. Do the argument and evidence show that these rights have been interfered with? Well, aggressive military action certainly interferes with hanging onto life. A standing army places constraints on liberty, as does external control of legislative bodies and the courts. What about the pursuit of happiness? The evidence emphasizes the king's interference with representative legislative, administrative, and legal institutions. It also includes complaints against constraints on trade and against unfair taxation. This suggests to me that the colonists wished to have the freedom to pursue their own political and economic policies and to enforce their own laws. I think that the other stated givens reinforce this. The declaration takes it as given that governments are formed by individuals so that they can guarantee to themselves life, liberty, and the pursuit of happiness. Therefore, any government "derives its just powers from the consent of the governed." The declaration suggests that as long as the government of Great Britain safeguarded these rights of the colonists, it enjoyed this consent. The list of grievances is intended to show, then, why the governed no longer give that consent.

The Vietnamese declaration takes it as given that everyone is born with the right to live, to be happy, and to be free. The argument shows that the French, by killing dissidents, corrupting the populace, and capitulating to the Japanese have certainly not protected the lives of the Vietnamese. This declaration, by declaring the right to "be free," suggests the right of one people to be free from domination by another. The argument is that the Vietnamese have the right to be free from both the Japanese and the French. It also declares that people have the right to "be happy." Because the Vietnamese are unhappy with how the French have behaved, they have the right to revolt from them.

Comparing Similarities and Differences

Kim now turns to the questions: Are there significant differences between the arguments? Similarities?

Similarities: Both declarations agree that a government ought to safe-
guard the lives of the governed, and both argue that the governments against
which they complain have not done this.

Differences: The U.S. declaration argues that the governed have a right
to liberty, which in context seems to mean the right to make their own decisions about economic, legal, and legislative policies. The Vietnamese declaration argues that people have the right to be free, which suggests, in
context, the right to be free of foreign domination.

The U.S. declaration states the relationship between human rights and
just government. This suggests to me that colonial status might have
remained acceptable, but for the king's overstepping the legitimate limits
on his power. For that reason, the evidence offered shows how the king has
overstepped those limits, emphasizing Great Britain's interference in governmental institutions. The Vietnamese declaration omits any reference to
the relationship between human rights and just government. This suggests to
me that colonial rule could never be acceptable to Ho Chi Minh because it violates the natural rights of "all peoples" to be "free." For that reason, the
evidence offered shows how the Vietnamese have suffered under foreign domination, but does not emphasize French interference in specific governmental
bodies.

What Is Not Clear: Does Ho Chi Minh mean that to be free of foreign domination also means that the governed ought to have the freedom to determine
their own economic policies or to participate in framing their own laws? It
is just not clear, because the Vietnamese declaration does not state explicitly that a government derives its powers from the consent of the governed.
It does suggest that the government ought to make sure the people are
"happy," but this seems a bit different from the principle that people consent to a form of government so long as it allows them to pursue happiness. I
mean, if I say that I want to be free to pursue my own happiness, I would mean
something different than if I said that I had a right to expect the government
to make sure I was "happy." One means I want the government to leave me alone,
to let me decide what I want to do. The other means that the government has to
provide me those things that make me happy. I wonder which Ho Chi Minh meant?

Kim's notes provide a foundation for proposing a solution to the original
question. Judging from the notes so far, which of the possible solutions
do you think Kim will choose? Why do you think so? Which parts of the
notes would be most useful in supporting the solution?

Completing the Task

What I have tried to illustrate here is how a writer uses notetaking to
move toward a solution. Because I do not want to belabor the point, I have
shown only a portion of Kim's notes. In addition, you might want to practice the same process by completing notes on the two declarations. The
U.S. declaration, for instance, includes the given that revolution should

be undertaken only if every other solution to political differences has been explored:

> Prudence, indeed, will dictate that Governments long established should not be changed for light and transient causes; and accordingly all experience hath shown, that mankind are more disposed to suffer, while evils are sufferable, than to right themselves by abolishing the forms to which they are accustomed. But when a long train of abuses and usurpations, pursuing invariably the same Object evinces a design to reduce them under absolute Despotism, it is their right, it is their duty, to throw off such Government, and to provide new Guards for their future security.

The declaration takes the position that the colonists have shown this prudence and have tried to resolve their disagreements with England in ways short of revolution. Assume that you are Kim. Take notes to answer the following questions:

1. Where does the declaration state the colonists' position on this given?
2. What reasons are offered to tell why they have taken the position?
3. Is any evidence provided to support the argument?

Ho Chi Minh's declaration does not state as a given that prudence should be exercised in revolting against a colonial government. Does this mean that he, unlike the U.S. colonists, does not feel it necessary to prove that the Vietnamese have shown by their previous actions a willingness to accommodate their European rulers? Study his declaration and take notes to get your answer. Consider, too, where his discussion is placed. Compare the placement with the placement of the comparable argument in the U.S. declaration. Does the placement suggest that Ho Chi Minh is still modeling his declaration on ours?

Then, compare what each document says about previous relations with the imperial government. Does the comparison suggest an answer to the question: Did Ho Chi Minh advocate the same principles of government as did the U.S. Declaration of Independence?

Both documents conclude by saying that the arguments presented justify revolution. Both go on to state that because revolution is justified, there are certain actions each revolutionary government will pursue, and both offer a pledge to undertake these actions. Using Kim's format, compare these two sections. Does a comparison suggest an answer to the assignment's question?

Planning: Understanding What to Include

Kim was given this assignment on a Monday. It was due the following Monday. Kim began taking notes the same evening the assignment was given and completed them on Wednesday, taking several hours each day for a total of eight. Kim was just about ready to draft the essay but was nagged by a doubt about the assignment. Kim understood this as an assignment to present a proposed solution and had in mind this model for such a paper:

Presentation of the problem;

Explanation of what is wrong with current solutions;

Explanation of the history of the problem;

Proposed solution; and

Defense of proposed solution.

Kim was fairly certain that the assignment did not call for all of these elements, but just to be sure, after Wednesday's class, he stops Professor Helphand:

KIM: I have a problem with the assignment. Could I ask you a question?

HELPHAND: Sure. Why don't we walk back to my office?

KIM: O.K.

[The two walk across the quad.]

KIM: I really don't know too much about the history of all this. I mean, I don't know much about Ho Chi Minh, except that he was the leader of the North Vietnamese during the war in Vietnam. I know he was a communist, or at least was supposed to be. I know a little bit more about our own declaration, of course. But I really don't feel I know enough about Ho to comment on his political theory without reading more sources.

HELPHAND: But you see, that is the purpose of the assignment. I don't expect students to know much about Ho Chi Minh, or even their own declaration, for that matter. Come into my office for a moment.

[They settle into chairs.]

HELPHAND: You see, what I want here is for students to learn how much can be discovered from studying historical documents by just reading them carefully and not relying on what someone else tells them the documents are supposed to mean.

KIM: [smiling] So my ignorance is a real advantage here.

HELPHAND: Yes, that's a good way of putting it. In a funny kind of way, ignorance is in fact useful to a historian. Even if we think we know what a historical document means, it is useful if we put aside our preconceptions and just read it carefully—trying to bring an open mind to it, you see.

KIM: So I should pretend I do not know anything about Ho?

HELPHAND: Well, the better way to say it is that you should separate what I call derivative knowledge from what you learn from reading the text itself.

KIM: Derivative knowledge?

HELPHAND: Well, yes, you know, the sort of things you know about Ho because of what you have picked up from what others have told you—from reading a history book, or listening to what people say about Ho or the war. It is important to be able to distinguish that kind of knowledge from what you think you learn from studying Ho's writings.

KIM: Well, I certainly was surprised to find out that he modeled his declaration on our own.

HELPHAND: Yes, most people would be, I imagine. That's what I mean about separating derivative knowledge—what you think you know— from what you learn yourself from studying things. It's those surprises that make history fun.

KIM: But, you know, I think it might be true that Ho was a communist, even if he did model his declaration on our own.

HELPHAND: But of course it might be true! The point is, can we figure that out for ourselves, without relying on what we are told is true? And if it does turn out to be true, we still have the interesting question of why he modeled his declaration on ours.

KIM: Well, I'm not certain I can talk about all that in my essay.

HELPHAND: No, no. Of course not. I've given this assignment, you see, as a sort of starting point. After you have completed it, I'll be asking for a longer paper in which you test your conclusions by reading more about Ho, and more about our own declaration.

KIM: But suppose I decide after reading some more that I was wrong?

HELPHAND: Well, so what? That's honest, isn't it? The point then would be to explain why you think now that your original conclusion was wrong.

KIM: So for this paper, I just have to say what conclusions I've come to and why.

HELPHAND: Yes, but remember, too, that conclusions are more or less probable.

KIM: Oh, yes, I see what you mean. I need to indicate how certain I am of my conclusion.

HELPHAND: Yes, exactly.

KIM: O.K. Thanks, Professor Helphand. You've really helped me out.

HELPHAND: Glad to be of help.

Planning: Preliminary Notes

Later that evening, Kim considered what the essay needed to include:

Statement of Problem: Ho Chi Minh modeled his declaration on ours. Did Ho Chi Minh advocate the same principles of government as the U.S. declaration did? Use just the two documents.

Problem with Other Proposed Solutions: I do not know how other political scientists or historians have debated this issue. Nor am I supposed to. I can just leave this out.

History of Problem: I do not know much about either the U.S. Declaration of Independence or Ho Chi Minh. I know a little from derivative knowledge. Maybe I should include some mention of this?

Proposed Solution: This is the focus of the paper.

Defense Against Other Solutions: Well, the best defense is to present my arguments clearly. I do not know how others have approached this problem, so that I really do not need to include this, either.

Then Kim made these notes to clarify the purpose of the assignment:

PURPOSE OF THE ASSIGNMENT

Expectations:

I know that the purpose of the assignment is to see what conclusions I can draw just from reading these two historical documents carefully, without consulting any other sources. To meet the expectations of the assignment, I have to show that I have read them both very carefully.

I'll have to assume that the reader starts from the same place I do-- that the two declarations are similar, which might suggest that Ho Chi Minh, even though he adopted communism, originally wanted a democratic form of government. O.K. So that will be my given--what I assume the reader and I both share. Professor Helphand said he thought most people would be surprised to learn that Ho used our declaration, so I'll stick that bit in at the beginning. That's how I'll present my givens or assumptions.

The question is, whether or not that is a reasonable assumption, judging just from these two documents. I have to assume that the reader is interested in that question and that he or she is open to a careful discussion of it.

My Solution:

I've decided that you really can't tell whether or not Ho accepted the same principle of government, but I think probably he did not. I have to indicate how certain I am of this. Well, not too. So, to complete this assignment, I need to review the problem and state my solution--which means stating my position. Then I have to give my reasons and my evidence, which means using the texts to illustrate my reasons.

LENGTH:

Five pages, typed. About 1250 words. I will have to make this concise and well organized, especially because this also has to include quotations from the text.

REASONS AND EVIDENCE:

Maybe I can just go straight through both documents as they are organized. I could start with the givens, then the arguments, then the conclusion.

At this point, Kim turns to reviewing the notes on both declarations. Kim's way of proceeding as a writer is to get a general idea in mind of what the essay will say and then to draft and revise several times. Kim calls the first draft a "dumping ground," because it includes all kinds of ideas that come to mind as Kim writes while consulting the notes taken in preparation. Kim knows that the final draft will not include many of

these but Kim always wants to see where ideas lead before honing them
in subsequent revisions. Kim's writing process is made easier by means
of a word processor; but even before using one, Kim usually took essays through several revisions, sometimes relying on cutting and
pasting.

Between Thursday and Sunday afternoon, Kim wrote three versions—
a first draft and two revisions. Sunday afternoon was set aside for preparing the final copy and proofreading. Kim spent a little over eight hours
drafting and revising in addition to the eight hours spent taking notes.
This is not unusual. Kim finds it usually takes a total of from 13 to 16
hours to prepare an essay of this sort, including notetaking.

Take a few moments for self-assessment. How does Kim's writing process compare with your own? What did you learn about writing this kind
of paper from Kim? What advice might you offer Kim?

ASSIGNMENTS

Using the suggestions given in this chapter, choose one of the following
assignments. Work on your comparison until you feel you have arrived at
a solution to the problem given in the assignment. Do not draft your solution yet. In the next chapter, we will discuss how a writer presents a comparison of this kind.

Assignment I

Ho Chi Minh's Declaration of Independence of the Democratic Republic
of Viet-Nam is obviously modeled on the U.S. declaration. Does that mean
that both Ho Chi Minh and Thomas Jefferson advocated the same principles of government?

Assignment II

The Old Testament books of Leviticus and Deuteronomy list foods that
are allowed and prohibited. Contemporary scholars have wondered why
these rules might have developed. Two scholars who have offered their
solutions are Marvin Harris, in "Riddle of the Pig" and Mary Douglas, in
"The Abominations of Leviticus," from her book *Purity and Danger*.
Read both selections in Part IV, Anthology, Section Four. On what principles do Harris and Douglas disagree? On what do they agree? Are their
solutions compatible or incompatible?

Assignment III

Anthropologists wonder which factor is more significant in determining human behavior: nature (genetic or innate traits) or nurture (cultural influences). Two anthropologists have tried answering that question by studying the relationship of Samoan adolescent females to their culture. They wanted to learn whether or not adolescence is necessarily a period of "storm and stress" as it is in our culture. Compare the reports on Samoan female adolescence written by Margaret Mead in "The Girl in Conflict" and Derek Freeman in "Adolescence" (see Part IV, Anthology, Section Four).

Assignment IV

In July 1776, Thomas Jefferson drafted the Declaration of Independence. In July 1848, the Woman's Rights Convention reminded the nation that the declaration had omitted attention to the rights of women. That convention ratified a Declaration of Sentiments and Resolutions (see Part IV, Anthology, Section Four). The declaration is modeled on the Declaration of Independence. Compare assumptions about human rights advocated in both documents. Do they differ? In all respects or in some? Are they compatible? In all respects or in some?

Assignment V

In "Letter from Birmingham Jail" (see Part IV, Anthology, Section Four), Martin Luther King, Jr., explains why he believes that nonviolent civil disobedience is justified if a law is unjust. In 399 B.C., Socrates was tried and found guilty of corrupting the minds of Athenian youth and of disbelief in the Athenian gods. He was sentenced to death or banishment, and he chose death. His friends, including Crito, arranged for his escape from prison. In the *Crito* by Plato (see Part IV, Anthology, Section Four), Socrates' friend visits him in jail and urges him to escape, but Socrates says:

> We must consider whether or not it is right for me to try to get away without an official discharge. . . . Shall we be acting rightly in paying money and showing gratitude to these people who are going to rescue me, and in escaping or arranging the escape ourselves, or shall we really be acting wrongly in doing all this?

Compare the positions of Socrates and King on the issue of obedience to the law. Explain whether Socrates and King would agree with one another or whether they would disagree, in part or in whole.

Chapter 15

Presenting Comparisons
of Arguments

PREPARATORY ASSIGNMENT

In the last chapter, we left a student, Kim, planning an essay comparing
the U.S. Declaration of Independence with the Vietnamese declaration. If
you are preparing to read this chapter, you should be working either on
that assignment, too, or preparing to compare one of the following pairs
of writings (details can be found in the assignments for Chapter
14,"Discovering Arguments: Comparing"):

The U.S. Declaration of Independence and the Woman's Rights Convention's Declaration of Sentiments and Resolutions;

Marvin Harris's "Riddle of the Pig" and Mary Douglas's "The Abominations of Leviticus";

Margaret Mead's "The Girl in Conflict" and Derek Freeman's "Adolescence"; or

Martin Luther King, Jr.,'s "Letter from Birmingham Jail" and Plato's
Crito

In this discussion, we will consider some of the conventions you might
wish to follow when you write your paper. You should read this only after
you have taken careful notes on the readings and figured out what your
solution will be. You should, in other words, be about where we left Kim
in the last chapter.

Planning Your Presentation

The kind of essay you have been assigned asks you to offer a solution to a problem. Each pair of readings addresses the same subject. The problem you are asked to address is, in its simplest terms, "To what extent do the authors agree and disagree with one another about the subject?" You are not asked to decide whether you agree or disagree with either of them. The purpose behind this kind of assignment—and you will probably get them in other classes—is to have you show that you can identify competing and similar arguments when you come upon them. Later on we'll discuss how you go about evaluating competing arguments.

Because this assignment asks you to solve a problem, you might begin planning your paper by reviewing what a presentation of a problem usually includes:

Statement of the problem;
Discussion of what is wrong with current solutions to the problem;
History or cause of the problem;
Proposed solution; and
Defense of the solution against possible objections.

As we mentioned in Chapter 14, some of these elements are irrelevant to your assignment. You cannot, for instance, discuss what is wrong with the way the issue is currently addressed; you do not know enough about the debate over any of the issues. You also cannot comment on the history of the issue or its source. You can, however, offer your solution; that is, you can tell the reader whether you think the writers disagree totally or agree in part. You can also "defend" your position. That does not mean that you must sound defensive or adopt an adversarial tone. Your defense consists of the reasons you give for your solution and the evidence you use to support those reasons. In short, the way you make your solution persuasive is by presenting arguments and evidence to support it. You do not merely present your solution; you explain why you think it is a reasonable one.

To plan your essay, then, you need to compare the arguments of both writers carefully. Are their arguments similar or different? Do they agree or disagree? Then you might want to write down your solution to the problem. How would you state it for the reader?

You should also plan how you will present your arguments in support of your solution. If you think your two writers are in disagreement on all points, then in what order will you present their arguments? If they agree on some but disagree on others, then how will you present that? Will your statement about your solution indicate to the reader how you will present your points? Your presentation should be a complete and accurate presentation of the points on which the writers agree and disagree. In Chapter 13, "Reporting Arguments," we discussed some ways to plan the order of a presentation such as this. Perhaps you will find rereading that chapter useful.

Openers

As with the summary of a single argument, the opener should be an informative introduction to the subject. The reader should learn what the essay is about, what texts you will deal with, and what you intend to say about the subject. As with the opening to a summary, you assume that the more information about the subject the reader already has, the less you need to provide. The following weak opening, a comparison of Marvin Harris's, "Riddle of the Pig" and Mary Douglas's "The Abominations of Leviticus," simply tells your reader what he or she already knows:

> In the Old Testament books of Deuteronomy and Leviticus are long lists of foods that are allowed and prohibited. If an animal has cloven hooves and chews its cud, you can eat it. But animals that do not do both you cannot eat, such as the camel, because it chews cud but is not cloven hooved. Also the hare, because it chews its cud--according to the Bible--but has claws, not hooves. The pig is forbidden because it does not do either of these things. You can eat anything that has fins and scales, but anything in the water that does not have fins and scales you cannot eat.

This tedious summary could go on through all the chapters of both Deuteronomy and Leviticus but it does not help the reader who already knows these laws to understand any more about what Harris and Douglas said about them.

A better introduction assumes that the reader is already familiar with the primary source—else why would he or she be reading your essay?—but wants some insight into it; specifically, wants to understand the insights offered by Harris and Douglas. Here is one possible introduction that addresses the reader's interest:

> In her discussion of the laws in Deuteronomy and Leviticus--"The Abominations of Leviticus"--Mary Douglas quotes Nathaniel Micklem's observation that these chapters "are perhaps the least attractive in the whole Bible. To the modern reader there is much in them that is meaningless or repulsive." Both Douglas and Marvin Harris want to make these "meaningless" laws meaningful by explaining why they were laid down. Both focus on the dietary laws-- Douglas on all of them; Harris only on the law prohibiting the eating of pork, which he calls "Riddle of the Pig." Harris argues that there were sound economic reasons for prohibiting the raising of swine, because in the ecosystem of ancient Israel, the pigs would compete directly with humans for food and resources, whereas other domesticated livestock would not. Douglas, on the other hand, rejects any explanation that treats "defilement" as "an isolated event" because "the only way in which pollution ideas make sense is in reference to a total structure of thought whose key-stone, boundaries, margins

and internal lines are held in relation by rituals of separation." She would say that the prohibitions against eating pork cannot be considered alone, but only as part of a larger, systematic set of laws that distinguished the "holy" from the "unholy," the "complete" from the "incomplete."

This introduction gives the reader a road map and explains how Douglas and Harris differ in enough detail to prepare the reader for the more elaborate explanations to follow. Notice that it opens by appealing to an attitude that the writer assumes is shared by the reader. Also notice that the introduction tells the reader both the authors and titles of the texts under discussion.

Here is how Kim decided to begin his essay comparing the two declarations:

> All men are created equal; they are endowed by their Creator with certain unalienable Rights; among these are Life, Liberty, and the pursuit of Happiness.
> This immortal statement was made in the Declaration of Independence of the United States of America in 1776. In a broader sense, this means: All the peoples on the earth are equal from birth; all the peoples have a right to live, to be happy and free.

This is the opening statement in Ho Chi Minh's Declaration of Independence of the Democratic Republic of Viet-Nam (September 2, 1945). Because Ho Chi Minh was the communist leader of North Vietnam, against which the United States sided with South Vietnam in the Vietnam War, it is surprising to learn that Ho Chi Minh consciously based his declaration on our own. The translation of it is included in Bernard B. Fall's Ho Chi Minh on Revolution: Selected Writings, 1920-1966 (New York: Frederick A. Praeger, 1967). Fall tells us: "The borrowing from the United States Declaration of Independence was open and intended. American members of the OSS mission parachuted to Ho in the summer of 1945 recall several of Ho's attempts to obtain a copy of the Declaration, or, failing this, a close approximation of its essential passages" (p. 143). Ho Chi Minh's direct quotation from the declaration, as well as the way the structure of his declaration parallels that of the U.S. declaration, indicates that he was successful in obtaining a copy.

This opening assumes that the reader will be surprised to learn that Ho based his declaration on our own. It takes the time to give the reader some additional information about how Ho obtained the document. It invites the reader to read further because it anticipates what will interest him or her and responds to that interest. Notice that this opening paragraph, unlike the opening to the essay on the dietary laws, does not tell the writer's solution; that is, it does not tell whether Ho Chi Minh advocated the same principles of government as did the U.S. declaration. An introduction does not need to be one paragraph long. It may take several paragraphs to introduce the subject and the writer's position. Kim chose to state the solution in the second paragraph.

Juggling the Sources

By now you should know that the evidence you use to support your solution comes from the texts. The problem with commenting on two texts is that you have to keep so many balls in the air: your comments and the supporting evidence from two different sources. Let's study for a moment how professional writers manage this. Here is a section from an essay by Charles W. Kegley, Jr., and Eugene R. Wittkopf. It is from a collection of essays they edited entitled *The Nuclear Reader: Strategy, Weapons, War* (New York: St. Martin's, 1985). In this essay, the authors are introducing the essays included in the first section, "Strategy." They are surveying these essays, pointing out which writers agree and disagree with one another. They are, in fact, presenting an extended version of the kind of essay you are preparing to write. In their essay, they compare two essays that adopt similar positions:

> Our first selection is an informed survey of current strategic thinking. Its author, Theodore Draper, describes what he terms *nuclear temptations:* a series of strategic proposals advocating new uses for the new generation of accurate and versatile nuclear weapons. These weapons tend to drive strategy, he argues; they make available new strategic options which in turn invite their actual use. Technological developments in weapons pose new challenges to the maintenance of deterrence, for the new temptations threaten to destroy the foundations on which peace has rested during much of the postwar era.
>
> By framing the discussion of today's strategic thinking, Draper provides the intellectual baggage necessary to evaluate strategic issues. In doing so, Draper discloses his own perspective on the temptations currently being recommended as a basis for a defense policy in the United States: he finds them troubling and deficient and rejects their acceptance (a viewpoint that has provoked a strident response from others, including Secretary of Defense Caspar Weinberger). His conclusion that "the main enemy at present is not a nuclear balance that results in mutual deterrence; it is the propaganda about the feasibility of nuclear war by way of precise and discriminating weapons allegedly capable of avoiding mass destruction," some will find reasonable, and others will see as disregarding the strategic options that such weapons make possible. But regardless of one's reaction to his conclusion, one should consider his thesis and warning that
>
>> the main reason nuclear weapons have not been used thus far is precisely the belief that they cannot be launched for any useful political purpose and that mutual mass destruction can be of no conceivable benefit to either side. But now Pied Pipers of a protracted nuclear war are trying to lure us to break through the psychological barriers to nuclear war.
>
> The temptation that Draper finds most threatening is a nuclear war-waging capability. In "MAD Versus NUTS," Spurgeon M. Keeny, Jr., and Wolfgang K. H. Panofsky further explore this proposal. Using the acronym NUTS to characterize various doctrines that seek to utilize nuclear weapons in war, and whose advocates can be described as "nuclear utilization theorists," the authors question the belief that a nuclear utilization targeting strategy can

eliminate the essentially MAD [acronym for mutual assured destruction] character of nuclear war under conditions of mutual assured destruction. Although they find the MAD doctrine inadequate, they find the dangers inherent in NUTS unacceptable. They thus find themselves in company with Draper, and the reasons on which they base their position illuminate the most fundamental issues dividing contemporary strategic theorists. How the MAD-versus-NUTS debate is resolved will affect the prospects for future strategic stability. (12–13)

Kegley and Wittkopf use many of the techniques you have already learned for presenting the summary of an argument. They paraphrase, quote directly, and use signal words to alert the reader to the argument they are reporting. What you might wish to notice most carefully is how they link their reports on the two essays. The first two sentences of the paragraph introducing the second essay are *transitional* sentences. They remind the reader of the main point of the first essay—the one that was just summarized—and tell the reader that the next essay to be discussed takes up a similar point. Notice, too, how they hammer home the point by *recapitulation.* In the paragraph summarizing the second essay, they say of the writers: "They thus find themselves in company with Draper," who wrote the first essay.

This technique of transition and recapitulation is especially useful when you are trying to tell the reader how one writer relates to another. It can be very useful when you are dealing with even more than two sources. This will be the case if you chose the essays dealing with the dietary laws in the Old Testament. In that case, you have a primary source—the Bible—two secondary sources, and your own commentary to present. If a writer is dealing with a primary text, it is especially helpful to the reader if the writer quotes the text directly as each new section of the discussion is introduced. Let us imagine, for instance, that we are writing an essay about the dietary laws and we have come to that part of the essay in which we will compare how both Harris and Douglas explain the prohibition against pork:

Harris deals only with the prohibitions against eating pork or touching swine. The relevant portions of Deuteronomy and Leviticus are:

Every animal that parts the hoof and has the hoof cloven in two, and chews the cud, among the animals you may eat. Yet of those that chew the cud or have the hoof cloven you shall not eat these: the camel, the hare and the rock badger, because they chew the cud but do not part the hoof, are unclean for you. And the swine, because it parts the hoof but does not chew the cud, is unclean for you. Their flesh you shall not eat, and their carcasses you shall not touch (Deut. 14: 6-9; New Revised Standard Translation).

Whatever parts the hoof and is cloven-footed and chews the cud, among the animals you may eat. Nevertheless among those that chew the cud or part the hoof, you shall not eat these: the camel, because it chews the cud but does not part the hoof, is unclean to you. And the hare, because it chews the cud but does not part the hoof, is unclean to you. And the swine, because it parts the hoof and is cloven-footed but does not chew the cud, is unclean to you. Of their flesh you shall not eat, and their carcasses you shall not touch; they are unclean to you (Lev. 40: 3-9; New Revised Standard Translation).

Harris argues that "the divine prohibition against pork constituted a sound ecological strategy" because "pigs were more of a threat than an asset." The ecology of the area was one of arid and "unforested plains and hills." Domesticated ruminants—cattle, sheep, and goats—are best suited to this environment. Because they are especially adapted to digesting cellulose, they can both survive in this climate and landscape and do not compete directly with humans for resources. Pigs, on the other hand, do best on nuts, fruits, tubers, and grains, which means that they compete directly with humans for food sources. They also compete for a resource precious in this region—water—because pigs need mud wallows to maintain their body temperature. Pigs cannot be herded easily, a liability for seminomadic peoples, and they do not provide the additional food source, milk, that the other domesticated animals of the region do. For these reasons, Harris argues, domesticated pigs were "an economic and ecological luxury," and the divine prohibitions were intended to warn against yielding to the temptation of this "rich, fatty meat."

Douglas, on the other hand, would argue that the laws prohibiting pork cannot be understood without considering all the dietary laws because, for reasons that we will examine below, all reflect an understanding of "holiness" as meaning both "separateness" and "wholeness." In raising livestock, the farmer helped "preserve the blessing" of the "order of creation," which included the fertility of both land and livestock. The animals they domesticated—cattle, sheep, and goats—were cloven hooved and cud-chewing. For these farmers, to eat wild beasts that were clearly like the animals they raised seemed reasonable, and therefore such animals as wild sheep, goats, and antelope would seem "complete" or "proper."

But what about animals that did not seem "complete"? Which chewed cud but were not cloven hooved? Or which were cloven hooved but did not chew cud? These "borderline cases," argues Douglas, were classed as prohibited because they did not fall into the category of "proper" or "complete" in the sense that they represented something distinct from the hooved, cud-chewing beasts of the field, beasts "set apart" from others because, by raising them, the farmer perpetuated a divine order of fertility and blessing. For that reason, the hare and the rock badger are prohibited. Douglas assumes that their rapid chewing made them appear to be cud-chewers, but they have claws, not hooves. And that brings us to the pig, which has cloven hooves but does not chew cud.

This portion of the essay introduces the discussion, quotes the relevant primary text, summarizes Harris's argument and evidence, and then Douglas's, and clearly indicates that Douglas disagrees with Harris. It would be most helpful to the reader if the writer now offered a brief recapitulation, emphasizing on what points Harris and Douglas disagree. This is easy to do in this case because Douglas offers comments that relate directly to Harris's argument. Read what she has to say in Part IV, Anthology, Section Four. Then write such a paragraph, one that would follow the paragraphs just presented.

Perhaps you will agree that in comparing two arguments about a text, you can help guide the reader if you quote any relevant text from a primary source, then summarize one writer's argument, provide a transition signaling how the next writer relates to the first, summarize the second writer's argument, and then give a recapitulation.

The summary of Douglas's argument given just above offers to clarify her definition of "holiness" later in the essay. As an exercise, you might find writing this explanation to be useful practice.

Concluding

Because we are assuming that we write a comparison for a reader who wants to understand the texts upon which we are reporting, the conclusion is our last opportunity to be certain that we have offered all the help we can. One way to do this is to bring into the sharpest focus the similarities and contrasts we have tried to explain. Just as the opening points forward to what we will discuss, the conclusion to a comparison can very usefully point back to the comparisons we have made. Some writers assume that in a conclusion they must offer an opinion. They tack on a vague sentence or two of praise or censure. Because such commentary is not integral to the whole, it seems strained or weak. When the purpose of the whole essay is evaluative—that is, when the writer is choosing up sides in the debate—then the conclusion would include the writer's judgments. We'll discuss that kind of essay later. For this kind of comparison, you more appropriately assume the role of reporter.

Another Format

What I've just described is a very conventional way of presenting a comparison of two texts. It's very utilitarian, and you should be able to use it to good purpose more than once in your life as a writer. But you might want to try presenting your report in a less conventional way, one that engages your imagination a bit more. Think about presenting it as a dialogue between the two writers you are comparing. Just imagine, for instance, Martin Luther King, Jr., in the same jail cell with Socrates. What would they say to each other? Or how about a delegation from the Woman's Rights Convention meeting with Thomas Jefferson? The delegation might include Elizabeth Cady Stanton, whose idea it was to paraphrase the Declaration of Independence; Susan B. Anthony, who was highly active in organizing the convention; and Frederick Douglass, the black abolitionist leader whose speech on woman's suffrage inspired the divided delegates to ratify the resolution calling for enfranchisement of women. Or how about Margaret Mead chatting with Derek Freeman? That would be quite a confrontation, wouldn't it, considering that by his own admission Freeman waited to publish his attack on Mead until after she was dead? How would Mary Douglas respond to Marvin Harris?

You may not know the conventions for writing a dialogue. You will find a scene from Tom Kopit's play *End of the World* in Part IV, Anthology, Section Four. As you will see, the format for presenting what your characters say is very simple really:

[*Lights up on* JIM *and* PETE]
JIM: *(while working at the meal)* So you talked with Stanley Berent!
PETE: *(also while working at the meal)* Bet *that* was fun!
TRENT: He poked a lot of holes in our deterrence strategy.

To present dialogue, type the speaker's name all the way at the left-hand margin and follow it with a colon and then whatever it is the character says. Indent every line of dialogue after the first. Then start a new line and repeat the format for another character. If you want to indicate action or attitude, put those instructions in parentheses before the character speaks. You can also provide general stage directions before the scene starts, as Kopit does for this scene. You can also use punctuation—such as underlining or exclamation points—to give clues to the way a line should be delivered.

Imagining a setting for your debaters will probably help you write a dialogue. Where are they? Are they being interviewed on television? In jail? Having a formal tea? Outside, talking under a tree somewhere? Visiting your home? Waiting for a plane? Visualize the setting and fill it in with objects that such a setting would have. Describe the setting as part of your stage directions.

Getting a "voice" and mannerisms in mind for your characters will also help. Although I have not met either of them, I can imagine Mary Douglas as Margaret Thatcher and Marvin Harris as David Letterman. I have heard Martin Luther King, Jr., speak and can hear his voice rolling through his prose. At the end of his essay "South Seas Squall," Lowell D. Holmes comments on how Mead might have responded to Freeman: "As a friend wrote in a recent letter, 'Whatever else she was, Margaret Mead was a feisty old gal and would have put up a spirited defense which would quickly have turned into a snotty offense.' I would have put my money on the plump little lady with the no nonsense attitude and the compulsion to 'get on with it'" (see Part IV, Anthology, Section Four). Perhaps you might use that much as a hint on how to present Mead.

What did Socrates sound like? Or Jefferson? You can get a feel for how a writer would sound partly by reading a text aloud. Not as you read in school when you were called on. Not that mumbly, down in the book sort of reading. But reading it so that the natural rhythm and intonation of voice come through. Paying close attention to the writer's tone also helps you to imagine the character speaking. If you read the end of Harris's essay, for instance, you will see that he is a bit playful, almost sassy. And Jefferson's prose reveals a man in love with language and ideas and someone with a real "fire in his belly."

Deciding how the character's body language might reveal him or her will also help. Are your characters seated or standing? Relaxed, downcast, erect, or alert? I can see the delegation from the Woman's Rights Convention seated on eighteenth-century chairs in a semicircle, straight backed, hands folded on their laps, while the charmingly correct Jefferson leans against the mantelpiece waiting for his servant to finish serving tea. Elizabeth Cady Stanton, Susan B. Anthony, and Frederick Douglass look on disapprovingly. What happens next?

Decide how many characters you will have. Will there be an interviewer? What kind of personality will the interviewer have? Why is he or she there? What does he or she want to know?

Although presenting your report as a dialogue calls upon your imagination, please do not fall into the foolish cultural stereotype that assumes that using the imagination means being frivolous. Play can be very hard work. Your purpose is still to show on what issues these writers agree and disagree, but you may find that if you imagine a setting, voice, mannerisms, and one speaker responding to another, you will be able to understand and present their similarities and their disagreements more clearly.

When presenting the dialogue, you will still rely on both direct quotation and paraphrase. But because the emphasis here is on *interaction,* you obviously want to juxtapose ideas as people would when they talk. Here, for instance, is one effort at presenting the differences between Marvin Harris and Mary Douglas. Imagine that they are on a Sunday morning talk show on the local public broadcasting station. The interview has gone on for some time, and the two clearly disagree. The interviewer asks Douglas what her disagreement is with Harris:

MARY: I really disagree with his assumption that the reason for one law can be distinct from the reasons for all the others. His argument might explain one prohibition in economic terms, but what about the others? What about the prohibitions against nondomesticated animals, such as the hare? What I assume is that the explanation lies in the Hebraic concept of causality, not in economics. The religious belief was that because God is the cause of all things, observing the laws "draws down prosperity, infringing them brings danger."

MARVIN: I just don't concern myself with the theology of the time. But as I suggest, obeying the prohibition against pork does "draw down prosperity," as Mary says, and disobeying it "brings danger"—economic danger. We just have different reasons for saying this.

MARY: My point is that if you take a look at the larger picture, you would see that all the laws are intended to show the difference between being holy and not being holy. They show how everything in creation, including human conduct, fits into this larger order. Really, Marvin, I don't see how you can just dismiss the beliefs of the time so cavalierly.

MARVIN: And all I might say is that I'm not sure my argument contradicts
yours.

Now, add some stage directions to bring this into focus. How old is
Mary? How old is Marvin? What difference would age make in how they
address one another? In what manner are these lines delivered? Is Harris
brash, arrogant, or gently self-defensive? What about Mary: is she impa-
tient or really engaged in a friendly way? Give the characters some character. Then take a part and ask someone else to take the other. Read it in
character. Does it help give you a better understanding of the argument
between them?

ASSIGNMENTS

Present your responses to the assignment given at the end of Chapter 14.
Use either the conventional presentation or dialogue.

Show your draft to someone familiar with the documents you have chosen to compare. Ask that reader to assess your presentation for accuracy.
Then show your draft to someone unfamiliar with the documents. Ask
that person to assess your presentation for clarity.

If you choose the dialogue, you might want to ask others in class to
assist you in presenting it orally.

Chapter 16

Evaluating Arguments

PREPARATORY ASSIGNMENT: A READ-AROUND

In this chapter, we will discuss evaluation. To help you see what evaluation involves, try this exercise.

Have a read-around. Bring one of your essays to class, choose three other students, and form a group. Those in your group should trade papers with those in another group. Each person in your group will read every essay given you by the other group.

Read each essay fairly quickly. When you come to a passage you especially like, put a vertical line in the margin beside it. Don't ask yourself why you like it; just mark it.

When everyone in your group has read and marked each essay, have a group conference on each. Discuss any passages all four of you marked with a vertical line. Why did you like the passage? Ask someone to be the group's recorder, and write down all the reasons everyone in your group agrees upon.

Encourage the recorder to take careful, complete, and well-organized notes. He or she should use separate pieces of paper to record your responses to each essay, and be sure to include the name of the person who wrote the essay on the notes; that person will want to use them.

When all the groups have finished their work, reconvene as a class. The recorder for each group should report first one quality that everyone in the group agreed upon as one that they appreciated when they read the essays. Record all of these on the blackboard or overhead. Keep rotating the reports until all groups have reported what they liked in the essays. Copy these down in your notebook.

When you have finished, ask your instructor whether he or she wants to add anything to the qualities you have decided to seek in effective writing. Naturally, you should copy down anything he or she adds.

When you have finished, the recorders should return the essays and the relevant notes to the people who wrote the essays.

Introduction

In the first chapter, we commented that debate was the life of the disciplines and that without it they would become moribund. Beginning with this chapter, we will study how debates are conducted. We also said that to study college-level writing was to study how the older students—your professors—went about their work. The evaluative exercise given as a prelude to this chapter might help you understand the implications of that comment. You are used to being evaluated by someone in a position of authority who sets certain standards for performance. The exercise asked you to join with your colleagues in defining standards for evaluating writing. The older students do something similar.

Professors in every discipline write; their work is judged or evaluated by their colleagues who apply the standards of evaluation for that discipline. A professor of philosophy, for example, might send an essay to a professional journal, such as *Philosophical Forum.* The editor of that journal might send the article to three or four readers, who are professors of philosophy at other colleges or universities. Usually these readers do not know the name of the article's author. They comment on the article, indicating whether it ought to be accepted as is, revised, or rejected. These editorial readers will also be writers who submit articles to other journals. The journal editor sends the readers' comments back to the author, indicating whether the editor thinks the article should be accepted, revised and resubmitted, or rejected. Often the author is asked to revise and resubmit, and the process starts over again. If it is accepted, the article is published in the journal, which is read by other philosophy professors, who may decide to respond to it by writing an article that criticizes it in whole or in part or praises it in whole or in part.

The process is a debate among equals, like that continuous conversation of Kenneth Burke's imagining, which we quoted in Chapter 4. As a newer student, you enter the room and find yourself hearing heated conversations that you do not at first understand; gradually, you begin to grasp them, and you join the debate. In the previous three chapters you practiced a little bit of grasping the debate. You may have found that it required a good deal of effort to simply *discover* what the arguments were and how competing arguments related to each other. Well, it is difficult.

That may be one reason students are asked to write summaries and reports. Learning to understand what is at issue is a natural prelude to joining the conversation.

To join the conversation, you need an understanding not only that a debate is going on, but also of the evaluative criteria; that is, the principles applied to respond to someone else's arguments. That is what we will be studying in this chapter and for the next several. What you should discover is that there are both general principles of evaluation and principles that are specific to a discipline, just as there are general principles for evaluating student writing and principles that emerge as specific to a group—such as your colleagues in a writing class.

In general, you will find that evaluations are made of:

1. The quality of the reasoning; that is, the writer's arguments;
2. The quality of the information; that is, the writer's evidence; and
3. The quality of the discourse; that is, the reader's response to the manner or style in which the writer presents his or her ideas.

Before we begin to take these up, let's get a sense of how these evaluations are offered. Below is a passage from Daniel Goldstine's review of Willard Gaylin's *Rediscovering Love*. Goldstine and Gaylin are colleagues in the sense of being members of the same discipline: both are psychoanalysts. Gaylin has written a book about love; so has Goldstine. This review, then, illustrates how members of the same discipline offer comments on one another's work. How would you respond if these comments were at the end of a paper you had written for a class? Is Goldstine using the same evaluative criteria your class identified?

> Dr. Gaylin's particular ideas about love form a pleasing and touching motif throughout his discussion of human behavior; however, he fails to give a rigorous argument in support of them. We are left moved by his advocacy for love but unimpressed by his evidence. However attractive and articulate his ideas, he puts them forth as if eloquence alone will carry the day.
>
> Clearly, Dr. Gaylin is a benevolent, well-read and well-intentioned person. He writes in an evocative and moving fashion. He seems to be the kind of man everybody hopes to find when they seek out a therapist (and so often don't find). But he does not, as far as I can see, have a new thesis about love, nor does he prove his case, although I am in sympathy with much if not most of what he says. (*The New York Times Book Review*, Oct. 12, 1986, p. 45)

As you may have guessed, this evaluation follows Goldstine's summary of Gaylin's central argument. In making his evaluation, he comments on the quality of the argument when he says that Gaylin does not have "a new thesis" and does not "prove his case." He also comments on the quality of the evidence, saying that he is "unimpressed" by it. He comments favorably on the quality of the discourse and what it reveals about Gaylin, but feels that Gaylin needed to offer more than "advocacy" and "eloquence."

What principles emerge from studying what Goldstine says? First, a summary of the other writer's arguments is a necessary prelude to offering an evaluation. Second, the evaluative criteria include references to both the intellectual and the affective qualities of the discourse. A third characteristic is that the respondent, Gaylin, is adopting a position and needs to go on to offer his own reasons and evidence to support it. He is now the writer being judged, in other words. A final characteristic is that in commenting on another's ideas, the commentator can notice what the writer omitted that should have been included. Goldstine indicates that he wishes that Gaylin had presented more evidence. He makes a longer comment of the same kind at the end of the review:

> Finally, while his extensive quoting from romantic literature is very pleasing, I found myself more than frustrated by his neglect of some of the darker aspects of human nature. While he has dealt with some of these issues in other books, if he going to declare love to be the *sine qua non* of human nature, rational discourse demands, at the least, that he also give more serious attention to the slaughtering in Auschwitz or Cambodia at the same time. Surely the fact that thousands of humans can systematically participate in the annihilation of millions of other humans challenges Dr. Gaylin's notion of the primacy of love. (45)

This is called a *counterargument*. Notice how it is presented. Goldstine points to Gaylin's *position*, which is that love is "the *sine qua non* of human nature." Goldstine presents evidence that suggests the contrary, evidence Gaylin did not consider but that Goldstine believes he should have. Goldstine's position is that Auschwitz and Cambodia are signs that love is not the sine qua non of human nature; that an equally significant and inherent "darker" side exists. A counterargument, then, presents someone else's position, and counters it with another argument—a position, reasons, and evidence.

Field-Specific Criteria: Evaluating Arguments in the Social Sciences

Now that you have an idea of the general criteria for evaluation, we might turn to one of the disciplines to get a notion of the specific criteria. In an earlier chapter, we mentioned a controversy in anthropology. In *Margaret Mead and Samoa; The Making and Unmaking of an Anthropological Myth* Derek Freeman challenges Margaret Mead's *Coming of Age in Samoa*. Some of you may have chosen a chapter from each of these books to compare for the assignment in Chapter 14. We'll turn now to a third party who has joined the debate. You might want to read Lowell D. Holmes's "South Seas Squall" (see Part IV, Anthology, Section IV).

If you have read Chapter 9 on inductive generalizations, you should be familiar with some of the evaluative criteria applied in the observational sciences, because you know how to present inductive arguments and evidence. The other evaluative criteria also arise from how things get done in these sciences. You will recall that a report on findings includes the following:

Field-dependent question;
Hypothesis;
Methodology;
Finding;
Descriptive and analytic generalizations;
Description of observations; and
Implications.

Each of these is subject to evaluation.

Holmes begins by setting before the reader the terms of the debate, summarizing the arguments offered by Mead and Freeman:

> Freeman argues that Mead perpetrated a hoax comparable in scope to that of the Piltdown Man when, in 1928, she described Samoa as a paradise relatively untouched by competition, sexual inhibition, or guilt. Refusing to believe that adolescents inevitably experience emotional crises because of biological changes associated with puberty (the psychological theory that then held sway), Mead set out to discover a society where passage to adulthood involves only a minimum of stress and strain. She described such a society in *Coming of Age in Samoa.*

You should be able to spot the elements Holmes puts together in this summary. Where does he state the hypothesis Mead tested? Her finding?

Holmes then summarizes Freeman's argument (when Holmes quotes Freeman's remark that Mead's finding was a "negative instance," you should understand that term as meaning Mead's was a disconfirmatory finding of the hypothesis that storm and stress during adolescence was the inevitable result of biological factors):

> In relating this "negative instance" as Freeman calls it, Mead established that nurture is more critical than nature, or heredity, in accounting for adolescent behavior. Freeman, who rejects the idea that humans are shaped primarily by culture and environment, and who believes that Boas and Mead have totally ignored the influence of genes and heredity, maintains that Mead's Samoan research has led anthropology, psychology, and education down the primrose path. He is out to rescue these disciplines, armed with the real truth about Samoa and Samoans.

Can you find the statement of the field-dependent question that generated the research of both Mead and Freeman? What about the statement of Freeman's hypothesis? And where is a reference to the implications? As you can see, Holmes, with admirable economy, summarizes the major characteristics of this kind of argument.

In countering Freeman, where does Holmes aim his arrows? Read his article again and identify his focus. Is it on the field-dependent question, the hypothesis, the methodology, the finding, the generalizations, the evidence, or the implications?

As you can see, Holmes identifies the methodology and the generalizations as the Achilles' heel. This makes sense. If the methodology is flawed, the observations derived from it will be suspect, and hence the generalizations based on the observations will be, too. In countering Freeman's generalizations about typical Samoan adolescent behavior, Holmes first argues that Freeman's observations do not meet the demand for verifiability. Holmes says, in effect, "I was there. What I observed was closer to what Mead reports than to what Freeman reports." Remember, Holmes is offering a counterargument; that means that he has to go on to present reasons and evidence to support his position. How does he do this?

First, he has to counter Freeman's argument that he himself was a biased observer. He does this by (1) stating Freeman's argument; (2) stating his own position in response; and (3) giving his reasons for the position. These are the typical characteristics of a counterargument:

> But Freeman's characterizations of Samoan personality and culture, and of Mead's work, do not jibe with what I saw. Freeman implies that, while I found much of Mead's research invalid, I was so awed by her reputation and so firmly under the thumb of Melville Herskovits, one of my professors at Northwestern, that I was afraid to reveal my true findings. The truth is that I would have loved to play the "giant killer," as Freeman now is trying to do. (What graduate student wouldn't?) But I couldn't. I had found the village and the behavior of its inhabitants to be much as Mead had described. *Coming of Age in Samoa* was like a map that represented the territory so well that I met with few surprises when I arrived. As for Herskovits's influence, all he demanded was that my criticisms of Mead's work be made with "icy objectivity," and that I deal with major issues and not trivial details.

You may need a little guidance to understand what Holmes says here. All doctoral graduate students must complete a dissertation, an extended piece of research. Graduate students in anthropology undertake fieldwork. They, as with all other graduate students, are directed in their research by graduate professors. If you fail to please the professors directing you, you may not get the Ph.D. In short, graduate professors have much influence on "their" graduate students. As his research project, Holmes went to Samoa to test Mead's findings, knowing that Mead was a pioneer in the field of anthropology, one of the "giants." Holmes says that Freeman accuses him of being a biased observer for two reasons. The first is that Holmes's graduate professor, Herskovits, would have frowned upon Holmes if he had discovered anything other than that Mead had been essentially justified in her findings. The second is that as a graduate student, Holmes would be fearful of challenging Mead. What would others in the profession think of such impudence? Who would hire a young pup of such iconoclastic audacity? Such are Freeman's implications, says Holmes.

Holmes responds by saying that he would have loved to have been a "giant killer;" that is, he would have loved to have entered the debate and trumped one of its central figures. You get some sense of how important this kind of debate is in the disciplines by Holmes's parenthetical remark: "What graduate student wouldn't?" Holmes then counters Freeman's other objection by defending his old mentor, Herskovits, saying that he simply did not engage in anything like the breach of academic integrity or standards Freeman accuses him of.

This exchange is called an *argumentem ad hominem* ("argument against the person"), which means an argument based on what one person thinks about the character of another. It is classified as a kind of fallacious reasoning; that is, reasoning that is flawed. The assumption is that attacking character rather than what a person says or does reflects more negatively on the accuser than the accused. Even so, it is often an effective form of argument. Notice that Holmes engages in it, too, when he says: "The truth is that I would have loved to play the 'giant killer,' *as Freeman now is trying to do.*" What makes *argumentem ad hominem* undesirable as a form of argument is that it is difficult to offer a counterargument because of the kind of evidence that requires. Freeman says Holmes was unduly influenced by Herskovits; Holmes says he was not. But what evidence can he provide, outside of his own testimony? None, really, so that if Freeman persists and makes the accusation again, he is calling Holmes a liar. This sort of exchange eventually creates a highly charged atmosphere, one not conducive to reasoned discourse.

Still, it reveals that a whole lot more than pure reason goes into the way the disciplines evaluate research. Now you see one of the reasons why the "conversations" are often so heated.

Having offered his defense against the charge of bias, Holmes turns to presenting the next part of his counterargument, which is that Freeman's observations do not meet the demand for verifiability. Holmes carefully details what he observed, how it agreed with and differed from what Mead found, and how she responded to his findings.

He then opens his second line of attack, which is against Freeman's methodology. Reread the article, and notice how Holmes presents his reasons and evidence for the following positions:

1. Freeman "completely disregards time, change, and locality";
2. Freeman "uses literature [here, that means other research in the field of anthropology] selectively to support his position";
3. "Every culture projects ideal behavior in its ceremonies, and real behavior in its streets and homes. Freeman shifts back and forth between these, always to the advantage of his theory."

As you can see, the attack on methodology is an attack on Freeman's reasoning. According to Holmes, Freeman mixes apples and oranges—or

tries to compare things that cannot be compared. Freeman fails to distinguish between urban and rural centers and between what a village may
have been like 40 years ago and what it is like now. He also fails to distinguish between the image a culture likes to project of itself—its ideal
self-image—and how people in fact behave on a daily basis. Holmes also
accuses Freeman of ignoring research that does not support his position.

In summary, Holmes applies the three general evaluative criteria:

1. He attacks the quality of Freeman's reasoning;
2. He attacks the quality of Freeman's information; and
3. He attacks the quality of the discourse; i.e., he defends himself
   against a personal attack, which is one way of saying that he takes
   issue with the *manner* in which Freeman presents his arguments.

Holmes applies these principles within the context of his field. He
focuses on Freeman's methodology and observations, invoking the
accepted principles of research in their discipline to criticize the methodology and the principles of verifiability to criticize the observations.

Joining the Debates

As a college student, you are invited to join the debates characteristic of
higher education. It is a special invitation in a way, because it is one you
ultimately cannot refuse. Critical thinking is simply an expectation; why
else would we have institutions of higher learning if not to question—and
that means questioning one another? Still, it can seem a bit daunting.
How is a student supposed to be able to enter a debate about ideas?

If you think about it a little bit, you will see that it is a reasonable expectation and one that in some ways you are already meeting. Consider again
the three general evaluative criteria:

1. The quality of the reasoning; that is, the writer's arguments;
2. The quality of the information; that is, the writer's evidence; and
3. The quality of the discourse; that is, the reader's response to the
   manner in which the writer presents his or her ideas.

Why shouldn't you be able to evaluate the quality of a writer's arguments? You have studied their characteristics—given, position, and
reason—and practiced them yourself. In the coming chapters, we will
consider a bit more carefully how you can decide what position to take in
response to another's arguments, but essentially you already know what
to look for. The quality of the information is a more difficult aspect of
evaluation for you to undertake, simply because you are a novice in any
of the academic disciplines and therefore do not have as much relevant
information as you will in the future. As for the quality or style of the
discourse, well, you just participated in formulating criteria for evaluating

writing. Why shouldn't you be able to apply that kind of critical awareness to whatever you read?

What the invitation to the debate calls for, then, is ultimately a willingness to apply evaluative principles to what we read and hear. Reading
with an interest in a writer's arguments is obviously necessary. So is
reading in a way that encourages you to remember the information con-
veyed. Joining the debate is a cumulative process; the more you learn, the
more able you are to assess new information. In practical terms, this
means developing a way of studying that looks beyond cramming for the
next test. Trying to stuff ideas into your head in order to perform for
someone else can mean that you do not evaluate what you learn. And you
will find that what you do not evaluate—assign value to—you soon forget. At least, that is the experience of many of us.

Finally, reading does fully engage us whether we acknowledge it consciously or not. By that I mean that we do respond to the manner or style
in which a writer writes. One of the horrors of being a teacher of writing
is to discover that students sometimes strive to sound "academic" or
"erudite." Usually, this means they are trying—albeit unwittingly sometimes—to mimic or imitate the style and manner of what they are reading
in their classes. The result is usually something like lime Jello melting in
July. One reason is that the effort is not fully conscious; students are
mimicking half-heard voices. The other reason is that the academic writing students are asked to read is often simply awful by any reasonable
standards of expression. The point is, the prose you read is going to seep
into your brain as a style whether you want it to or not, and you will find
yourself hearing its rhythms—however maimed—when you sit down
to write. It is much more beneficial to become highly conscious of how
language affects you—what you admire, what seems to confuse or
obscure the issue, what seems to reveal the writer to you—both to gain
a better understanding of what you read and so that you can make
some conscious decisions about how you wish to present yourself
when you write.

ASSIGNMENTS

Using the criteria your class developed for grading writings, evaluate an
essay. You might choose an essay from the Anthology or an essay written
by someone else in your class or one you have written.

Assume that you are a composition teacher and the essay you have chosen was written by someone who intends to enroll in this class, but who
wants to know in advance what to expect. He or she has given you the
essay and asked you to comment on it. You want to tell what the evaluative criteria are and where they originated, and you want to demonstrate
how you apply them. You will need to quote from the essay you are evaluating in order to show the writer how you are applying the criteria.

Revising

Bring your draft to class and be prepared to read it aloud or to have it read aloud. If the essay is not one included in the Anthology, make enough copies of it to distribute. As you listen to the evaluation, assume that you are the writer of the essay. If the evaluation leaves you guessing about your strengths and weaknesses, ask questions that will help clarify what the "teacher" wants. Explain also how you feel about the comments. Take notes on the discussion of your essay. Afterward, note any other ideas for revising that come to mind. Then revise your essay.

Chapter 17

Evaluating Generalizations

PREPARATORY ASSIGNMENT: SOME MORE
HEAT AND EAT VEGETABLE SOUP

In this chapter, we are going to study some more aspects of inductive reasoning. To help you get ready, here are some statements about Heat and Eat Vegetable Soup. For each situation, choose the one statement that you most agree with:

1. You purchase three cans of Heat and Eat Vegetable Soup. All three contain thin, watery, salty soup with very few vegetables. You conclude that:

   a. All Heat and Eat Soup is inferior.
   b. All Heat and Eat Vegetable Soup is probably inferior.
   c. All Heat and Eat Vegetable Soup is inferior.

2. You purchase three cans of Heat and Eat Vegetable Soup. Two of the three cans contain thin, watery, salty soup with very few vegetables; one contains a delicious soup. You conclude:

   a. A lot of Heat and Eat Vegetable Soup is inferior, but some is superior.
   b. A lot of Heat and Eat Vegetable Soup is probably inferior, but some is probably superior.
   c. Two-thirds of all Heat and Eat Vegetable Soup is probably inferior, but one-third is probably superior.
   d. Two-thirds of all Heat and Eat Vegetable Soup is inferior, but one-third is superior.

Introduction

In the last chapter, we noticed that evaluations can be made of the quality of a writer's reasoning, information, and style. We also noticed how the demands of the observational sciences shaped the manner in which such evaluations were offered in those disciplines. We examined how one writer, Lowell D. Holmes, evaluated the arguments presented by another anthropologist, Derek Freeman. In this chapter, we are going to study in more detail the criteria for evaluating inductive arguments, or arguments based on direct observation. We will focus especially on the criteria for evaluating the two kinds of generalizations: descriptive and analytic (causal). Although this discussion will help you to evaluate inductive arguments in particular, it should also help you to develop a keener critical eye for all generalizations.

Well-presented generalizations are properly qualified. *Qualified* here means having certain necessary or desirable qualities, just as we say that a person who is qualified for a job has met certain requirements. But *qualified* also means something that is modified or limited. The noun *girl* is unqualified; that is, the meaning is not modified by any other terms. But if I say "the pretty, curly-headed, four-year-old girl," I have *qualified* the noun, which means I have modified its meaning, or limited its meaning, by referring to a particular girl with a certain set of characteristics. Similarly, qualified generalizations are those that the writer has modified or limited by indicating (1) whether or not they are universally applicable; (2) how probable they are; and (3) if it is a causal explanation, what the other possible causes might be. We will consider each of these below.

Universal or Statistical Generalizations

As you learned from doing the exercise on Heat and Eat Vegetable Soup, we can decide whether or not generalizations are universally applicable:

1. A generalization about all members of a class derived from observing some of them is called a *universal generalization* because it describes what is typical of all members of a class; e.g., "Because *three* cans of Heat and Eat Vegetable Soup were inferior, *all* Heat and Eat Vegetable Soup is probably inferior."

2. A generalization about a certain percentage of a class derived from observing some members of it is called a *statistical generalization;* e.g., "Because two of the three cans of Heat and Eat Vegetable Soup were inferior, but one was marvelous, *two-thirds* of the vegetable soup marketed by Heat and Eat is probably inferior; *one-third* is probably marvelous."

Even though the generalization refers to all Heat and Eat Vegetable soup, we do not claim that all members of the class share the same characteristics. We are familiar with statistical generalizations because we are so frequently confronted with polls. A poll might ask 610 adults whether or not they knew that the United States had military advisers in Nicaragua. If 89 percent said yes, we would make the statistical generalization that 89 percent of *all* adults in the United States knew it.

When we write generalizations, we have to be careful not to *overgeneralize*. This means that we have to be careful to indicate whether or not we think that our generalization applies to all members of a class (universal) or to only a certain percentage of them (statistical). If we think that the generalization describes what is typical of all members, then we use the terms *all* or *every*. If we forget to use a term to indicate quantity, then our readers will infer either that we mean *all* members of the class or an indeterminate number.

A statement such as "Koalas are peaceful animals" usually will be read to mean "*All* koalas are peaceful animals." Statements such as the following may be read as meaning all members of the class or an indeterminate number:

> The elderly are poor in the United States.
> Teenagers in the United States are drug abusers.
> Corporations pollute the air, water, and soil.

These statements are overgeneralizations. Because they fail to indicate quantity, the reader might assume that the writer means *all* elderly are poor, *all* teenagers are drug abusers, and *all* corporations pollute the environment. Because common sense and experience tell us that such statements cannot be true of all members of the class, we would have a hard time agreeing that the writer could provide convincing evidence to support these generalizations. Or the reader might assume that the writer is referring to an indeterminate number, in which case the generalization is equally hard to substantiate. If we think that the generalization refers only to a percentage of a class, we use the terms *some, many, most, almost all, the majority,* or we can give a percentage. Because words such as *some, many, most,* and the like are indefinite, we have to be very careful not to mislead the reader or to be imprecise. Perhaps the most overused and least informative quantity term is *a lot*. It tells the reader almost nothing about number or quantity. In general, it is better to give the precise percentage when possible:

> *Acceptable:* According to a recent poll, relatively few white South Africans were happy with apartheid, whereas most expected the system to end within 10 years.
>
> *Preferable:* According to a recent poll, only 36 percent of whites were happy with apartheid, whereas 63 percent expected the system to end within 10 years. (Newsweek [Sept. 16, 1985], 31)

As you can see, one of the characteristics of a well-qualified generalization is that the writer tells the reader whether it is universal or statistical, and if it is statistical, then the writer tries to be as precise as possible in indicating how many members of a class share a certain characteristic.

Probability of Descriptive Generalizations

Generalizations about what is typical of a class are regarded as more or less probable rather than as statements of certainty. There are two reasons why this is the case:

1. Inductive generalizations draw conclusions about what is typical of all or a percentage of a class from observing only some members of the class. In our example of Heat and Eat Vegetable Soup, we drew conclusions about all Heat and Eat Soup from supposing that we had sampled three cans. This means that we would be drawing conclusions about what we did not observe directly from the conclusions we drew about the sample. All such generalizations refer to more members of a class than have actually been observed; hence, they are regarded as more or less probable rather than as true or certain.

2. Additional evidence can change or alter the generalization. Jane Godall's observations of chimpanzees in the Gombe Reserve of Tanganyika provide an illustration. Godall relates in her book *In the Shadow of Man* (New York: Dell, 1971) that until she observed chimps in the wild, it was assumed that humans were the only creatures who could make or modify tools. However, the chimps Goodall observed "used stems and sticks to capture and eat insects and, if the material picked is not suitable, then it is modified." (244) This suggests that we will need to modify our generalization about tool users, which will mean that we will have to change our explanations about human nature, as well.

   This principle explains as well why evidence is so important in supporting generalizations. A generalization that claims to be universal but is supported with insufficient evidence, or not supported at all, is sometimes called a *sweeping generalization* or a *glittering generalization;* like fool's gold, it is dazzling but worthless.

Probability of Causal Explanations

Inductive analytic generalizations—explanations of cause—are also regarded as more or less probable rather than certain for two reasons:

1. An analysis explains what has been observed. It explains the generalizations about a class. Because the generalizations describe what is probably typical of a class from observations of only a sample, the generalizations are more or less probable. It follows that explanations of what causes the typical trait will also be more or less probable.

2. An analysis uses concepts to explain what has been observed. As we noticed earlier, statements using concepts cannot be verified in the way that descriptive generalizations can be. For that reason, we recognize that there may be more than one explanation for what has been observed.

A famous case illustrates these two principles. Wilhelm Von Osten, a retired German schoolteacher, sincerely believed that he had taught his horse Clever Hans how to count. When he held up a number, Clever Hans would tap out the number with his hoof. The horse even seemed able to add and subtract. Scientists who believed that Von Osten was a fraud could not fathom how Clever Hans knew when to stop tapping his hoof. A psychologist, Oskar Pfungst, watched Von Osten carefully. If Von Osten could not see the number he held up for Clever Hans, the horse tapped out an incorrect number. Pfungst noticed that when Von Osten knew the correct number, he unconsciously signaled the horse with a slight jerk of his head. Even if the movement was as slight as one-fifth of a millimeter, Clever Hans would respond by stopping the tapping of his hoof. What Von Osten had observed was not that his horse was counting or solving problems, but that his horse was very carefully observing him. (Broad and Wade, *Betrayers of the Truth* [New York: Simon and Schuster, 1982], 110).

How can we decide whether or not a causal explanation is highly probable? If numerous observers over time make observations that seem to support a causal explanation, then the explanatory concepts are accorded a high degree of probability. The fewer the observers who have confirmed an observation and agreed on an explanation, the more speculative is the conclusion.

Evaluation: A Well-Qualified Argument

In summary, a well-qualified argument:

1. Supports the conclusions with ample evidence drawn from a variety of sources;
2. Indicates whether the conclusions are universal or statistical; and
3. Indicates the degree of probability; that is, tells whether the conclusion is probable or speculative and to what degree.

To illustrate a well-qualified argument, we can turn to Robert K. Colwell's "Stowaways on the Hummingbird Express" (Part IV, Anthology, Section Three). You might want to read it before we go on.

Colwell wonders how hummingbird mites know when to leave the bird's nose and hop onto a flower. He offers a generalization and indicates its probability: "By far the most likely source of information is odor." Colwell goes on to offer his supporting evidence, again qualifying what he says: "Our evidence is indirect but convincing." He then gives his evidence by reporting on:

1. Laboratory experiments he conducted in Trinidad, Mexico, Costa Rica, and California with several kinds of mites and several kinds of nectars;

2. The work of another scientist, Amy Heyneman, who has done bio-chemical analyses of various plant nectars; and
3. Natural observations and controlled experiments in the wild.

As you can see, Colwell supports his generalizations by drawing on observations he has made over a period of time at numerous sites, on the work of another scientist, and on experimentation. He also qualifies them by indicating how probable they are.

Colwell also offers an analysis to explain why hummingbird mites prefer only one kind of flower. Toward the end of the article, Colwell asks: "Why . . . are the mites so particular about the host plants they actually use?" He considers two possibilities: (1) that each species of mite favors certain plants because otherwise there would be too many species of mites trying to live off too few species of flowers; or (2) that by using only one kind of flower, mites of the same species are more likely to find mates.

Colwell chooses between two possible causes derived from Darwin's theory of evolution: (1) natural selection, or evolutionary changes resulting from inherited differences that improve survival rate; and (2) sexual selection, or evolutionary changes resulting from inherited differences that contribute to successful mating. Colwell explains his reasons for rejecting natural selection by referring directly to his observations: "the density of mites is quite low, relative to the nectar available, so competition between species is not a likely explanation." Notice, again, how Colwell indicates probability by saying that it is not likely; in other words, it is not a highly probable explanation, but it is not entirely ruled out. He goes on to say: "The explanation I favor for host allegiance is that hummingbird flower mites use host plants as a way of finding mates." He then goes on to give his reasons. Notice how he avoids sounding dogmatic, and how he indicates that his conclusions are tentative, by saying, "The explanation I favor."

Colwell explores more than one possible explanation, discusses why he chooses one over the other by referring directly to relevant evidence, and clearly indicates that his conclusions are more or less likely or probable. Colwell's language includes terms indicating the tentative nature of his conclusions: "if I am right," "presumably," "I favor," and "likely." Such terms concede both that observers themselves are fallible and that inductive conclusions might have to be altered later in the light of further evidence. Consider, too, that Colwell is basing his explanation on Darwin's theories, which means that he is using causal explanations that have been supported by a wide variety of observers over a fairly reasonable length of time.

Summary

When a writer is presenting generalizations, we should expect not only ample support for them but also that the writer will indicate how widely applicable they are, whether they are more or less probable, and, in the case of analysis, whether there is more than one possible explanation. When a writer fails to offer such acknowledgments and concessions, our critical radar should switch on.

Similarly, when we are writing, we have to be alert to the common human desire for certainty and the wish to appear self-confident and "right." We better serve our own integrity, as well as our reader's desire to understand, when we stop and consider:

1. Have we overgeneralized? Or have we indicated whether the generalizations are universal or statistical?
2. Are we presenting a sweeping generalization or one that we have carefully and amply supported? Have we carefully qualified it?
3. Are we presenting dogmatic conclusions? Or have we considered more than one possible explanation, applied each carefully to the evidence, and qualified our explanation by indicating its degree of probability?

ASSIGNMENTS

Assignment I

Trade at least one essay you have written for this class with another student and evaluate the generalizations by drawing upon the discussion in this chapter. The essays you trade should deal with either personal experience or direct observations. Your purpose is to help one another present more effective arguments.

To complete your evaluation, follow the instructions below. When you are done, you will have a set of notes on your colleague's essay. Revise your notes so that they will be useful to your partner. Be sure that they are neat, complete, and clear. Put your name on them.

When you receive your comments, read them carefully. Then revise your essay to reflect the suggestions that seem reasonable to you. When you turn in your revision, include the original essay that your partner marked, your partner's comments, and your revisions.

Instructions for Evaluating Generalizations

    I. Using a colored, felt-tip marker, highlight:
        A. Every descriptive generalization in one color, and number them in sequence; e.g., *Dg 1 = descriptive generalization 1;*
        B. Every analytic generalization (causal explanation) in another color, and number them in sequence; e.g., *Ag 1 = analytic generalization 1.*
    II. For each descriptive generalization:
        A. Draw a vertical line in the margin beside all the evidence used to support it. Use the same color you used to highlight the generalization;
        B. On a separate sheet of paper, evaluate each of these generaliza-

tions; for example, on your sheet of paper write *Dg 1* and your responses to each of these questions:

1. Can you tell whether the generalization is universal or statistical? If it is overgeneralized, what suggestions would you make for revising it?
2. If it is a statistical generalization, does it make a precise statement about quantity? If not, what suggestions would you make for revising? If it uses acceptable wording to indicate quantity, can you suggest preferable wording?
3. Has the writer indicated how probable the generalization is? If not, what suggestions would you make for revising?
4. Can you think of additional evidence that would change or alter the generalization? Does the writer seem to have ignored any significant and relevant evidence?
5. Can you think of any other generalizations that might be drawn from the same evidence?
6. Has the writer presented a sweeping or glittering generalization? If so, what suggestions would you make?
7. Does the writer support the generalization with ample evidence drawn from a variety of sources? If not, what suggestions would you make?

III. For each analytic generalization:
   A. Draw a vertical line in the margin beside the evidence used to support it, using the same color you used to highlight the analytic generalization, and circle in pen any words that refer to evidence given earlier.
   B. On a separate sheet of paper, assess each of the analytic generalizations: for example, on your paper, write *Ag 1* and after it your responses to the following:
      1. Has the writer indicated how probable the analysis is? If not, what suggestions would you make?
      2. Has the writer considered more than one probable cause? If he or she has, *are* they probable causes? Do they seem to be equally reasonable explanations? If he or she has considered only one probable cause, what other explanations could you suggest?
      3. Does the writer's explanation seem likely because it seems to explain the observation in a way that you have explained similar observations? Does he or she indicate that any other observers have seen the same sort of thing and have arrived at the same explanation?
      4. Does the analysis refer to descriptive generalizations or to evidence in support of the analysis? If not, what would you advise?

Assignment II

Drawing on the discussions in Chapter 16, "Evaluating Arguments," and in this chapter, write a critique of one report on observations included in the Anthology (Section Three). Your critique should include:

A summary of the argument;

An evaluation of the quality of the arguments;

An evaluation of the quality of the information (is there sufficient evidence? Varied evidence? Is it presented in sufficient detail?); and

An evaluation of the style or manner of the presentation (you might wish to use the evaluative criteria you developed with your classmates for Chapter 16).

Chapter 18

Discovering a Position: Choosing Sides

PREPARATORY ASSIGNMENT

This chapter studies formal disjunctive propositions, which are stated: Either a thing is *x* or it is not *x*. In *Summa Theologica*, St. Thomas Aquinas, a thirteenth-century philosopher and theologian, synthesized the often conflicting ideas of the classical world and Christianity. He poses a question, and then lists the contradictory arguments—which he calls "objections"—from classical and Christian thought. He then responds to the contraries, beginning with "I answer that. . . ." In this excerpt from "Question XC: On the Essence of Law," Aquinas presents the arguments of Aristotle and St. Isidore of Seville:

Second Article
Whether Law is Always Directed to the Common Good?

We proceed thus to the Second Article:—
Objection 1. It would seem that law is not always directed to the common good as to its end. For it belongs to law to command and to forbid. But commands are directed to certain individual goods. Therefore the end of law is not always the common good.

Obj. 2. Further, law directs man in his actions. But human actions are concerned with particular matters. Therefore, law is directed to some particular good.

Obj. 3. Further, Isidore [St. Isidore of Seville] says: "If law is based on reason, whatever is based on reason will be a law." But reason is the foundation not only of what is ordained to the common good, but of that which is directed to private good. Therefore law is not directed only to the good of all, but also to the private good of the individual.

On the contrary, Isidore says that laws are enacted for no private profit, but for the common benefit of the citizens.

I answer that, As we have stated above, law belongs to that which is a principle of human acts, because it is their rule and measure. Now as reason is a principle [cause] of human acts, so in reason itself there is something which is the principle in respect of all the rest. Hence to this principle chiefly and mainly law must needs be referred. Now the first principle in practical matters, which are the object of the practical reason, is the last end: and the last end of human life is happiness or beatitude. . . . Consequently, law must needs concern itself mainly with the order that is in beatitude. Moreover, since every part is ordained to the whole as the imperfect to the perfect, and since one man is a part of the perfect community, law must needs concern itself properly with the order directed to universal happiness. Therefore the Philosopher [Aristotle], in [his] definition of legal matters, mentions both happiness and the body politic, since he says that we call those legal matters *just* which are adapted to produce and preserve happiness and its parts for the body politic. For the State is a perfect community, as he says in *Politics i.*

State the contraries Aquinas addresses, using the formula: Either law is *x* or it is not *x*. Then state the arguments he summarizes in favor of each of these contraries. What is Aquinas's position? Does he choose one side over the other or does he reconcile them?

Discovering a Position: Choosing Sides

You will recall from our discussion in Chapter 14, "Discovering Arguments: Comparing," that a writer can be either an observer/reporter or a participant in a debate about ideas. In this chapter, we will study some of the choices facing writers who become participants. The preparatory exercise for this chapter illustrates the bare bones of what this kind of choice entails. As Aquinas demonstrates, one typical challenge is when we are confronted by two commentators arguing apparently contradictory points. How can we decide what position to take?

Statements that present us with such choices are called *disjunctive propositions*, which means that they offer the challenge *either/or*:

Either you're with us or against us.
Either you're part of the solution or you're part of the problem.
Either you're a liberal or a conservative.
Either we have free will or our actions are predetermined.
Either her statement is true or it is false.
Either he is guilty or he is innocent.

In the following discussion, we are going to consider three possible positions that can be taken in response to such either/or propositions. We will consider these positions one at a time.

1. Proposition: *x* is either *y* or not-*y* (example: Alf argues that the law making drinking illegal before age 21 is a just law).

Possible Positions to Take in Response: (a) agree with Alf (example: The law making drinking illegal before age 21 is just); or (b) disagree with Alf (example: The law making drinking illegal before age 21 is unjust).

2. Proposition: *a* is either *x* or *y* (example: Chris argues, ''The Surgeon General is either in favor of sex education in the schools or he is a right-wing conservative'').

Possible Positions to Take in Response: (a) argue that *a* is *x* and not *y* (example: The Surgeon General is in favor of sex education in the schools and is not a right-wing conservative); (b) argue that *a* is *y* and not *x* (example: The Surgeon General is a right-wing conservative and is not in favor of sex education in the schools); or (c) argue that *a* is both *x* and *y* (example: The Surgeon General is both in favor of sex education in the schools and a right-wing conservative).

3. Proposition: *a* is both *x* and *y* (example: Beth says that Josie is both a Republican and a liberal).

Possible Positions to Take in Response: (a) accept the proposition; or (b) argue that *a* is either *x* or *y* (example: Josie has to be either a Republican or a liberal; you can't be both at once).

x is either *y* or not-*y*: Formally Perfect Disjunctive Propositions

A *formally perfect disjunctive proposition* takes the form, *a* is either *y* or it is not-*y*, as in the statements, ''Laws are either just or they are unjust,'' or ''Human acts are either voluntary or involuntary.'' Such a statement makes it obvious that not only does one category exclude the other, but they are the only two possible choices; the proposition excludes the possibility of a third alternative. For that reason, we say: One of the alternatives must be true, and only one can be true. A writer presenting an argument about this kind of proposition has a very clear task: he or she must choose between one of the possibilities and offer reasons for the choice.

A particularly effective argument derived from a disjunctive proposition is found in Martin Luther King, Jr.'s ''Letter from Birmingham Jail'' (see Part IV, Anthology, Section Four). While jailed for leading civil rights demonstrations, King wrote that letter in response to a published statement by eight Alabama clergymen (four Catholic bishops, one rabbi, and three reverends) who deplored street demonstrations and urged all citizens of Alabama to ''observe the principles of law and order and common sense.''

To better understand how we choose positions, you might find it helpful imagining that you are Martin Luther King, Jr., at the time he reads the statement by the eight religious leaders. How can you respond? One of

King's counterarguments begins, as by now you should expect it would, by restating one of the arguments presented in the clergymen's statement. That is how counterarguments usually begin. He concedes the legitimacy of the concern, a common tactic in debate:

> You express a great deal of anxiety over our willingness to break laws. This is certainly a legitimate concern. Since we so diligently urge people to obey the Supreme Court's decision of 1954 outlawing segregation in the public schools, at first glance it may seem rather paradoxical for us to consciously break laws. One may well ask: "How can you advocate breaking some laws and obeying others?"

We could restate the argument confronting King as: You cannot advocate obeying the law while at the same time advocate breaking them. King's response is, "The answer lies in the fact that there are two types of laws: just and unjust." This can be restated as a formal disjunctive proposition: A law is either just or unjust. Now, with that proposition, King has presented a true given; it is not subject to debate or disagreement. With a formal disjunctive proposition, there is no third possibility. You cannot effectively argue that a law is both just and unjust. It is one or the other. There is no, "Yes, but . . ." possible. In other words, the given *has* to be accepted as a given. King need not offer reasons for maintaining it nor evidence to prove it.

King then states his position in relation to that given: Segregation laws are unjust. Because there is no third possibility, it must be true that either segregation laws are just or they are unjust. Now King has to give his reasons and evidence to show why he has taken that position. He begins that task by asking, "How does one determine whether a law is just or unjust?" The reasons—or propositions—he offers are italicized in the following quote. How many different kinds of evidence does King use to support his propositions? How many unsupported propositions are there? Why are they unsupported?

> *A just law is a man-made code that squares with the moral law or the law of God. An unjust law is a code that is out of harmony with the moral law.* [*Evidence:*] To put it in the terms of St. Thomas Aquinas: An unjust law is a human law that is not rooted in eternal law and natural law. Any law that uplifts human personality is just. Any law that degrades human personality is unjust. *All segregation statutes are unjust because segregation distorts the soul and damages the personality. It gives the segregator a false sense of superiority and the segregated a false sense of inferiority.* Segregation, to use the terminology of the [*evidence:*] Jewish philosopher Martin Buber, substitutes an "I-it" relationship for an "I-thou" relationship and *ends up relegating persons to the status of things. Hence segregation is not only politically, economically, and sociologically unsound, it is morally wrong and sinful.* [*Evidence:*] Paul Tillich has said that sin is separation. *Is not segregation an existential expression of man's tragic separation, his awful estrangement, his terrible sinfulness?* . . .

Let us consider a more concrete example of just and unjust laws. *An unjust law is a code that a numerical or power majority group compels a minority group to obey but does not make binding on itself. This is* difference *made legal. By the same token, a just law is a code that a majority compels a minority to follow and that it is willing to follow itself. This is* sameness *made legal.*

Let me give another explanation. *A law is unjust if it is inflicted on a minority that, as a result of being denied the right to vote, had no part in enacting or devising the law.* [*Evidence:*] Who can say that the legislature of Alabama which set up that state's segregation laws was democratically elected? Throughout Alabama all sorts of devious methods are used to prevent Negroes from becoming registered voters, and there are some counties in which, even though Negroes constitute a majority of the population, not a single Negro is registered. Can any law enacted under such circumstances be considered democratically structured?

Sometimes a law is just on its face and unjust in its application. [*Evidence:*] For instance, I have been arrested on a charge of parading without a permit. Now, there is nothing wrong in having an ordinance which requires a permit for a parade. But such an ordinance becomes unjust when it is used to maintain segregation and to deny citizens the First Amendment privilege of peaceful assembly and protest.

King uses the five common kinds of evidence to support his reasons for saying that segregation laws are unjust: (1) appeal to the *authority* of Catholic, Protestant, and Jewish philosophers (remember, he is responding to clergymen of these faiths); (2) *statistics* on the voting patterns in Alabama; (3) and (4) personal *testimony* as *example;* e.g., his arrest for holding a parade without a license; and (5) implicit and explicit references to the *precedents* of U.S. law; e.g., his explicit reference to the Constitution and his implicit reference, when he notices that segregation laws are *difference* made legal, to the principle that we are all equal in the eyes of the law.

As King indicates, the focus for the writer presenting a formal disjunctive proposition is on the reasons for the position and the evidence to support it. The writer need not spend time explaining or defending the given because it obviously excludes any alternatives or choices. King's primary task, then, is to show why he is justified in saying that segregation laws are unjust. Because the given is undebatable, the only possible refutation to a formal disjunctive argument is to attack the position, which means to counter the reasons and the evidence. As you can see, King has given his opponents a formidable problem.

Before we leave King's example, we might notice how a disjunctive argument affects the style in which the argument is presented. A disjunctive proposition is a statement about contradictories; therefore, King's argument will necessarily deal with contradictions; specifically, the contradiction between just and unjust laws.

A writer who asserts the truth of one proposition denies the truth of its contrary, whether he or she states it explicitly or not; for instance, when King says, "An unjust law is a human law that is not rooted in eternal law and natural law,'' he implies the contrary: A just law is a human law that is rooted in eternal law and natural law. But sometimes King states explicitly both contraries: ''Any law that uplifts human personality is just. Any law that degrades human personality is unjust.'' What we learn from this is that when we use a disjunctive proposition as the basis for an argument, we can assume that whatever we assert about one statement will automatically reflect on its contrary. As writers, we have to decide whether to leave that implication implicit or to make it explicit. King generally makes it explicit by stating both contraries. This suggests that stating the contraries throughout an argument derived from a formal disjunctive proposition is frequently more effective.

a is either *x* or *y:* Material Disjunctive Propositions

A *material disjunctive proposition* follows the form, *a* is either *x* or *y*, as in, He is either a teacher or a student. In *The Prince*, for example, Niccolò Machiavelli advises the rulers of Florence—the Medicis—on expedient means for remaining in power. This passage considers the subject, ''On Cruelty and Mercy, and Whether It is Better to be Loved than to be Feared or the Contrary'':

> [There] arises an argument: whether it is better to be loved than to be feared, or the contrary. I reply that one should like to be both one and the other; but since it is difficult to join them together, it is much safer to be feared than to be loved when one of the two must be lacking. For one can generally say this about men: that they are ungrateful, fickle, simulators and deceivers, avoiders of danger, greedy for gain; and while you work for their good they are completely yours, offering you their blood, their property, their lives, and their sons, as I said earlier, when danger is far away. And that prince who bases his power entirely on their words, finding himself stripped of other preparations, comes to ruin; for friendships that are acquired by a price and not by greatness and nobility of character are purchased but not owned, and at the proper moment they cannot be spent. And men are less hesitant about harming someone who makes himself loved than one who makes himself feared because love is held together by a chain of obligation which, since men are a sorry lot, is broken on every occasion in which their own self-interest is concerned; but fear is held together by a dread of punishment which will never abandon you.

State Machiavelli's argument using the formula: A prince should be either *x* or *y*. What choices does the prince have, according to Machiavelli? What evidence does Machiavelli offer in support of one contrary over the other? Suppose the term *prince* could refer to any political leader; how would you respond to Machiavelli's advice?

As you may discover from discussing this passage, material disjunctive propositions do not necessarily state mutually exclusive categories. To understand why, imagine a conversation between two state university students, Sarah and Debbi.

DEBBI: Have you met Ted? He is so good looking and intelligent, but I can't figure out whether he is a student or a teacher.

SARAH: Oh, I *know* he's cute. He must be a student, though, because once when I walked by Dr. Staples's classroom I saw him sitting there taking notes. Besides, he doesn't look old enough to be a professor, and I've seen him hanging out at the Student Union with some graduate students I know.

DEBBI: Well, he must be a student then.

We can convert this to the argument:

> *Given:* He is either a student or a teacher.
> *Position:* He is a student and not a teacher.
> *Reason:* He takes classes, he seems too young to be a professor, and his friends are students.

We saw that with formal disjunctive propositions, the given is truly a given; no other choices exist. But one problem with material disjunctive propositions is that two categories may not really be mutually exclusive, even though they appear to be; for example, *teacher* and *student* are not mutually exclusive categories at most of our state universities. A graduate student may take courses and also hold a teaching fellowship. Ted could be both a student and a teacher. In the larger sense, faculty members and students at any college or university are always both students and teachers; students learn from one another and teachers learn from students, too.

One possible response, then, to a material disjunctive proposition is to take the position that the categories are not mutually exclusive; that it is not a case of *either/or* but of *both/and*. In other words, rather than attacking the reasons and the evidence, the critic might attack the given. This is one possible position to take in response to Machiavelli's proposal—a solution he himself hints at. So, the challenge and three possible responses are:

> *Challenge:* A prince should be either feared or loved.
> *Possible Positions:* (1) A prince should be feared and not loved; (2) A prince should be loved and not feared; or (3) A prince should be both loved and feared.

The last position is called a *conjunctive proposition*, meaning it uses the conjunction *and*.

You can find an example of a writer using this solution in the excerpt "Russians" from Freeman Dyson's book *Weapons and Hope* (see Part IV, Anthology, Section Four). You might want to read it now. Dyson begins—as we would expect—by summarizing the positions held by opposing sides in the debate he has chosen to enter—the nuclear arms race:

> The two experts on whom I mostly rely for information about Soviet strategy are George Kennan and Richard Pipes. Their views of the Soviet Union are gen-

erally supposed to be sharply divergent. Kennan has a reputation for diplomatic moderation; Pipes has a reputation for belligerence.

Dyson quotes both Kennan and Pipes at length to illustrate their apparent differences. He then states his position, commenting not only on the arguments of Kennan and Pipes, but on their manner of presentation as well:

> These remarks of Pipes were intended to be frightening, whereas Kennan's remarks were intended to be soothing. And yet, if one looks at the substance of the remarks rather than at the intentions of the writers, there is no incompatibility between them. I myself have little doubt that both Kennan's and Pipes's statements are substantially true.

Dyson has to give his reasons and evidence for taking the position that despite their apparent incompatibility, both Kennan and Dyson are offering compatible interpretations of the Soviets. He begins by pointing out that each writer addresses a different sector of the Soviet power structure; hence, their views are not necessarily contradictory:

> Kennan is describing the *state of mind of political leaders* who have to deal with the day-to-day problems of managing a large and unwieldy empire. Pipes is describing the *state of mind of professional soldiers* who have accepted responsibility for defending their country against nuclear-armed enemies.

He then shows how their conclusions about Soviet attitudes toward war are compatible:

> Kennan's picture of the Soviet political power structure is quite consistent with the central conclusion of Pipes's analysis, that Soviet military doctrines are based on the assumption that the war for which the Soviet Union must be prepared is a nuclear version of World War II.

You will find it useful for understanding how to present this kind of counterargument if you study the excerpt by Dyson to see how he supports his position that far from giving incompatible versions of the Soviets, the arguments of Kennan and Pipes give a consistent picture.

Not *Both/And* But *Either/Or*

Sometimes we will be confronted with a conjunctive proposition; that is, the writer will take the position that two categories of things are compatible. We can, of course, agree. Or we can disagree; which means offering a disjunctive proposition as a counter. What this means is that we find incompatible what others find compatible. Said another way, we can attack the given.

In *Words and Values* (New York: Oxford University Press, 1983), Peggy Rosenthal offers this kind of argument. She takes issue with the Adult Development school of therapists. On the one hand, these psychologists say that we must, of necessity, follow certain developmental patterns to achieve psychological maturity. On the other hand, they say that we must *choose* to follow those same developmental patterns if we wish to become psychologically mature. The psychologists seem to say that psychological "growth" is like a natural law: just as our fingernails grow longer whether we will them to or not, so we of necessity "grow" psychologically in certain ways. But they also seem to say that psychological "growth" in those ways depends upon our conscious choice to achieve those goals. Rosenthal argues that these are mutually exclusive propositions:

> Nonconscious nature doesn't have to be encouraged or ordered to follow natural laws; it follows them by necessity, "by nature." Our own nature, though, involves consciousness, and consciousness involves choice. . . .
>
> In ordering us to follow a direction that it claims we are bound by, the developmental imperative is obviously caught in a logical difficulty. . . . If our human development is just the unfolding of natural laws, then choice can play no part in it, so to urge us to follow these laws makes no sense. Put another way, in terms of the traditional necessity/free-choice dichotomy, the difficulty is this: as soon as an element of choice (even the tiniest act of free consciousness) is brought into the operation of necessity, necessity is no longer operating in exactly the same ways; it's no longer entirely necessity. As soon, then, as laws of necessity are applied to matters involving choice, they cease being laws of necessity. Therefore the laws of nonconscious development (necessity, nature) cannot, logically, be applied to consciousness. (87–88)

Rosenthal clarifies what the Adult Development psychologists advocate by reducing their ideas to material disjunctive propositions, which we can summarize as:

Either we have conscious choice in how we develop our personality and behavior, or we are unconsciously bound by natural laws governing how we develop our personality and behavior.

Either we have free will and can choose our actions, or we are bound by the necessity of natural law, and our behavior is predetermined by it.

One way, then, for evaluating a conjunctive proposition is to accept it; the other way is to attack the given.

Discovering a Position

One knack you have to develop in order to discover what position you wish to take in an argument is learning to reformulate the arguments you read as *either*/*or* or *both*/*and* propositions. This seems difficult for some students, perhaps because they anticipate that the writer will use those actual terms. Sometimes writers do. But often they do not. What it takes is a capacity to "boil down" an argument to its essential position, to find out if the language the writer uses is *as if* the writer is offering an *either*/*or* or a *both*/*and*. It takes an alertness to when a writer is signaling a presentation of contraries or a presentation of compatibles.

Once you can fix the choices in your mind, you can then do some thinking about the possible positions to adopt. A writer who presents you with the equivalent of a formal disjunctive proposition gives you two choices: you either agree or disagree. But a writer who presents you with the equivalent of a material disjunctive proposition gives you more to think about, because what that writer takes as contraries you may see as compatible. The writer who presents you with a conjunctive proposition—*both/and*—also gives you a bit to think about because you may see as contraries what he or she sees as compatible.

ASSIGNMENTS

Assignment I

In Chapter 14, "Discovering Arguments: Comparing," you were asked to compare what two writers have to say about the same subject. In this assignment, you are asked to reconsider some of those writers, choosing one pair from the following in Part IV, Anthology, Section Four:

Marvin Harris, "Riddle of the Pig" and Mary Douglas, "The Abominations of Leviticus"
Margaret Mead, "The Girl in Conflict' and Derek Freeman, "Adolescence"

Here are the possible choices offered by the debates:

Harris and Douglas:

Choice 1: Dietary taboos are either reflective of environmental considerations or of a consistent system for distinguishing what is "pure" from what is "impure." If this is your choice, which one of the contraries do you accept? Write an essay in which you present your reasons and evidence in support of that position.

Choice 2: Dietary taboos are both reflective of environmental considerations and of a consistent system for distinguishing what is "pure" from what is "impure." If you see the apparent contraries as compatible, write an essay in which you present your reasons and evidence in support of that position.

Mead and Freeman:

Choice 1: Samoan female adolescents either experience puberty as a time relatively free of conflict with their culture or as a time of conflict with their culture. If this is your choice, which of the contraries do you accept? Write an essay in which you present your reasons and evidence in support of that position.

Choice 2: Samoan female adolescents experience puberty as both a time relatively free of conflict with the culture and a time of conflict with their culture. If you see the apparent contraries as compatible, write an essay in which you present your reasons and evidence in support of that position.

Suggestions for Presenting Your Positions

Remember, this kind of assignment asks you, To what extent do you agree and disagree with what *A* and *B* say about *C*? Take it as given that in presenting your position you will be offering evaluations of the arguments put forward by the writers you have chosen. Your presentation, then, probably should include (though not necessarily in this order):

Statement of the problem;

Your position;

Statement of the source of the problem; that is, a summary of the arguments offered by the writers you have chosen (what are they arguing about?); and

Statement of what is wrong with the status quo; that is, evaluations of the arguments offered by the writers you have chosen (who is right or wrong? Or what solution have both failed to see?).

Assignment II

Drawing upon Martin Luther King, Jr.'s ''Letter from Birmingham Jail'' and the *Crito* (see Part IV, Anthology, Section Four), give your position on the question: Should a citizen obey or disobey the law? In your presentation, you must indicate which arguments presented by each writer you accept and why, and which arguments by each writer you reject and why.

Suggestions for Completing the Assignment

Some students when asked to write this kind of paper decide that they ought to sound like movie versions of lawyers or politicians. They try to adopt a florid and defensive oratorical style.

Remember, your writing is judged as much by the manner or style of presentation as it is for the quality of arguments and the quality of information. In practice, this means that the style should fit the occasion. The purpose behind the kind of discourse called for here is to persuade others to adopt your position. Think about it: when was the last time you were persuaded by a friend of yours who was trying to sound like a Philadelphia lawyer?

Assignment III

Has it ever happened that some of the people around you took an *either/or* position that was eventually resolved when they agreed to a *both/and* position? Many quarrels or heated discussions end when the adversaries discover that they really agree with one another or when they discover a mutually acceptable compromise. Tell about a time when you either witnessed this or were a participant.

Have a point to make. Use your episode as an opportunity to teach us a little bit more about how people go about discovering the positions they wish to choose in an argument.

Chapter 19

![grey bar]

Discovering a Position: Consider the Unstated

PREPARATORY ASSIGNMENT

Before you read this chapter, reread George F. Kennan's "A Proposal for International Disarmament" (see Part IV, Anthology, Section Four) and the passage from Niccolò Machiavelli's *The Prince* that was included in Chapter 18.

Introduction

In the last chapter, we considered how to take a position in response to what a writer states. In this chapter, we will consider how to take a position in response to what a writer leaves unstated. We have already noticed that one possible response to an argument is to note omitted *evidence*. Daniel Goldstine, for instance, objects to Willard Gaylin's *Rediscovering Love* because Gaylin argues that love is the sine qua non of human nature. Goldstine points to the evidence of Auschwitz and the atrocities in Cambodia and objects that Gaylin did not consider it. Lowell Holmes attacks Derek Freeman because Freeman seems to have included only research that supported his hypothesis. He also attacks him for failing to distinguish village life from urban life in making generalizations about Samoan culture (see Chapter 16).

In this chapter, we are going to consider arguments addressed not to the *evidence* another writer omits, but to what he or she omits from the *argument* (given + position + reason).

Unstated Alternatives: Material Disjunctive Propositions

In the last chapter, we saw that one problem with material disjunctive propositions is that the categories they name as opposites may be compatible. You will recall that Debbi and Sarah wondered whether Ted was a student or a teacher. We decided that Ted could be both a student and a teacher. There is another problem with material disjunctive propositions, which we can illustrate with this example:

CORY: Josi must be either a Democrat or a Republican.
DEL: Well, I know for a fact Josi is not a Republican.
CORY: Oh, then Josi must be a Democrat.

The problem here is that the material disjunctive proposition does not exhaust all the possible choices. There are more than two political parties. To vote, you need not be a member of any party. Josi could be a Libertarian, a communist, or an independent voter. All you can conclude from knowing that Josi is not a Republican is that Josi might be a member of another party.

When confronted with material disjunctive propositions, then, we have to consider what other possibilities the writers may have excluded. As an illustration, we can return to Machiavelli's question, "Is it better for a prince to be loved or feared?" The way to lend immediacy to a reading—especially one written long ago—is to assume that the writer is your contemporary, addressing you directly, and then to think of analogous experiences that you can draw upon. To make Machiavelli our contemporary, let us substitute the word *leader* for *prince.*

Machiavelli argues that it is best if a leader is both loved and feared; however, this is hard for a leader to achieve, human nature being what it is: "For one can generally say this about men: that they are ungrateful, fickle, simulators and deceivers, avoiders of danger, greedy for gain." Is there anything in our own experience that is analogous; that is, can we point to an occasion in which a leader was rendered ineffective because he was surrounded by those who were "simulators and deceivers, avoiders of danger, greedy for gain"?

As of this writing, President Reagan is in some trouble. He has been a very popular president. People call him the Great Communicator. At least to judge from the polls and election results, Ronald Reagan is a loved leader. His advisers arranged to sell military equipment to Iran in exchange for which the Iranians would persuade other Shiite Moslems in Lebanon to release all the U.S. hostages they were holding. The Iranians got their weapons, but not all of the hostages were released. Those who arranged the deal charged the Iranians quite a bit of money for the weapons. They said that they were going to use the profit to supply arms to the Contras, who are waging guerrilla warfare against the Nicaraguan government. Congress did not want any money sent to the Contras, so Reagan's advisers did not tell Congress what they were doing because, for one thing, it may have been illegal. Investigators do not know for certain where several million dollars wound up. The Contras say they never got it. Quite a bit of money was evidently pocketed by the foreign nationals who helped broker the deal.

There certainly were "simulators and deceivers" in this case. The Iranians led on the Americans. Reagan's advisers deceived Congress and evidently also did not make clear to the president himself the exact dimensions of what they were doing. There were those who were "greedy for gain," including the Iranians who wanted the arms (and who also wanted to embarrass the United States, it would seem, because the story was originally leaked from Iran to a reporter in Lebanon), the brokers for the sale, and those in the White House who wanted money to send to the Contras. As for "avoiders of danger," well, Pat Buchanan, who was then Reagan's director of communications, published a scathing editorial in the *Washington Post* condemning Republicans for deserting the president when he needed them most. What about "fickleness"? The press and Congress have, throughout Reagan's presidency, been highly conscious of his popularity. The press has tended not to criticize him vigorously and Congress has tended to support or modify his proposals rather than reject them outright. But with a new Democratic majority in Congress and disclosure of the Iran-Contra affair, both the press and Congress have become highly critical. President Reagan will probably not be an especially effective leader after this.

Is Machiavelli right? Did Reagan become an ineffective leader because those around him did not fear him? Well, his advisers seem not to have feared the consequences for the president once this affair was disclosed, as it almost inevitably would be. Did they fear the consequences for themselves and their careers? Did they assume that the president would protect them or did they fear that he would cut them loose? Chief of Staff Donald Regan was certainly surprised and outraged when he was fired for his role in all this. The Iranians clearly did not fear Reagan. They disclosed these maneuvers to the press. And the press and Congress clearly feel that they now have nothing to fear from attacking Reagan. We might conclude, then, that Machiavelli is right. Reagan is a president loved by the people, but he is ineffective because he was not feared by his advisers or foreign heads of state and is no longer feared by the press or Congress.

But let's consider other possibilities. Are being loved or feared the only choices available to a leader? Does Machiavelli omit other qualities that are even more inherently significant? President Reagan ordered a commission to study the role of the National Security Council in the Iran-Contra affair. Headed by former Senator John Tower, the Tower Commission found that Reagan was inattentive to his own policies. He did not ask his advisers what they were doing nor did he expect them to tell him. The report also noted that Reagan's advisers knew that he was inattentive and that knowing it, they should have sought to protect him by bringing important matters to his attention. Would fearing the president have made his advisers more forthcoming? Would loving him have? Or was there some other quality needed here?

Lt. Col. Oliver North played a primary role in putting together the Iran-Contra deal. Robert "Bud" McFarlane, North's boss for a time at the National Security Council, said in a "*20/20*" interview with Barbara Walters that he thought North was motivated by what he had learned from being in the Vietnam War. He said that North felt that the United States had made a commitment to another country, had asked people to lay down their lives for that commitment, and then had betrayed those people by pulling out. North felt that the United States was repeating this betrayal by first voting funds for the Contras and then denying them money, McFarlane said. He added that North felt that he had to do whatever he could to get money to the Contras.

Assume that this is a fair assessment of North's motives. How would he have acted if he had feared the president? If he had loved him? Or should the president have sought to foster another quality in North?

Robert McFarlane attempted suicide. In the same interview he said he did so because he felt that while he was head of the National Security Council, he should have done more to convince the president to abandon the policy of selling arms to Iran. He felt he had failed the country and that the "world would be a better place without him." He said that his father had instilled in him the belief that everyone has the ability to succeed, and that to make a mistake is to fail, and that failure is a sign of weakness or vulnerability. That is why he fell into such despair when the Iran-Contra affair was disclosed.

McFarlane was a leader. Does his statement suggest that some other quality is essential to a leader besides being loved or being feared? Or is fearing failure one way of saying that a leader fears that those around him will not fear him? Or love him? We can also ask the same question we asked above. Would McFarlane have been a more effective adviser to Reagan if he had feared Reagan? If he had loved him? Or should Reagan have fostered some other quality in a man like McFarlane?

A friend of mine has offered an argument about Reagan and his advisers that I find compelling. My friend says that the men around Reagan may have loved him, but that it is difficult also not to be jealous of someone who has authority and power over you. It is rather like the complicated feelings children can have toward parents. So when they saw that Reagan was in a weakened and vulnerable position, his advisers did not move to protect him because they had ambivalent feelings toward him. This is the kind of solution that we discussed in the last chapter: it is not that the leader in this case was either loved or feared, but that he was both loved and feared. Contrary to what Machiavelli suggests, this position would argue that being both loved and feared is fraught with dangers for a leader. I find the argument compelling because, for instance, it explains some of the apparent ambivalence McFarlane expresses. Commenting on the president's visit to the hospital after McFarlane's attempted suicide, McFarlane said that Reagan was one of the "warmest" presidents in decades. But when asked why Reagan did not listen to his warnings, McFarlane said he thought that the president was more impressed by men who were "very wealthy and highly successful." His is an interesting combination of affection and envy, I think.

This little digression on the Iran-Contra affair is intended to illustrate how we can go about discovering what our position will be in regard to someone else's argument. First, we need to read in a way that makes the writer our contemporary and to try to find analogies in our own experience and knowledge. Second, we need to consider not only the choices the writer presents us, but other possible choices that are equally significant. Discovering our own thoughts on a subject, then, means adopting a certain stance toward the arguments of others, a willingness to contemplate our own experience, and an attentiveness to what is unstated.

The Enthymeme

Sometimes a writer omits some part of an argument: the given, the reason, or the position. The writer may do this because he or she assumes that the reader is familiar enough with the subject or argument that the reader can easily supply the missing statements. An argument that omits the given, reason, or position is called an *enthymeme*, which comes from the Greek and means "to have in mind." The enthymeme asks the reader "to have in mind" the unstated parts of an argument. To discover the implications of an argument, a reader tries to discover what has not been stated. How can this be done?

You can begin to understand how to do this if you remember that there are certain words that signal either a position (conclusion) or a reason (premise) for it. This sentence is an enthymeme: He must have been really hungry *because* last night he ate all his spinach.

This enthymeme states the conclusion, He must have been really hungry, and gives a reason for it, Last night, he ate all his spinach.

It may help you understand this if you refresh your memory about the signal words for conclusions and reasons. When we find a sentence using *because, since,* or *for,* the phrase that follows states one of the reasons:

REASON WHY/PREMISE	*CONCLUSION/POSITION*
Because he ate all his spinach,	he must have been really hungry.
Since she did not study,	she will fail the exam.
Because we are Republicans,	we did not vote for Mondale.

Because I could not stop for Death	Death kindly stopped for me.
Because two wrongs don't make a right	he's not going to seek revenge.

CONCLUSION/POSITION	*REASON WHY/PREMISE*
He is not going to the movie	because he dislikes violence.
We do not pray in public schools	because of the separation of church and state.
She thinks he's a boor	because he stepped on her toe.
He can't pay his bills	since he hasn't got a job.
Blessed are the meek	for they shall inherit the earth.

When a sentence uses *thus, therefore,* or *so,* the words that follow state the conclusion:

REASON WHY/PREMISE	*CONCLUSION/POSITION*
We are Democrats;	therefore, we did not vote.
They have apologized to one another	so peace reigns again.
He failed to appear;	thus, the court issues this warrant.

Testing Enthymemes for Effective Revision

When you revise, you will often find it useful to discover what you have left unstated. This can help you decide whether or not the reader will need more information to understand what you mean to say. To illustrate, we'll use the sentence: He must have been really hungry because last night he ate all his spinach. Imagine that you have said this in the draft of an essay and want to be sure that the reader does not need any additional information. First, figure out what kind of argument this is. Look at the reason: Harry ate all his spinach. What kind of reason is it? Is it a proposition or a generalization? Well, it isn't either, is it? It describes a single instance; it is an example, not a generalization. By now, you should know the characteristics of an argument about observations:

Given = Hypothesis;

Conclusion/Position = Finding;
Reasons = Generalizations about what is typically observed; and
Evidence = Report on what was observed directly.

The reason given for concluding that Harry must have been really hungry is not really a reason at all. It is evidence masquerading as a reason. What is missing is the generalization that explains the evidence:

Given/Hypothesis: ?
Conclusion/Finding: Harry must have been really hungry.
Reason/Generalization: ?
Evidence/Observation: Last night, he ate all his spinach.

One possible explanation for the evidence might be: Harry typically dislikes spinach. In that case, the argument would be:

Given/Hypothesis: ?
Conclusion/Finding: Harry must have been really hungry.
Reason/Generalization: Harry usually loathes spinach.
Evidence/Observation: Last night, he ate all his spinach.

If the unstated reason is the *only* one a reader might infer from the enthymeme, then the writer need not state it explicitly. In this case, the writer would have to be certain that the reader (1) is familiar enough with Harry's typical tastes not to have to be told what they are; and (2) would agree that Harry does not usually like spinach.

Notice, too, that there is an implied given:

Given/Hypothesis: People will eat what they do not like if they are hungry enough.
Conclusion/Finding of a confirmatory instance: Harry must have been really hungry.
Reason/Generalization: He usually loathes spinach.
Evidence/Observation: Last night, he ate all his spinach.

There is another possible given:

Given/Hypothesis: Spinach is loathsome food eaten only by the truly hungry.
Conclusion/Finding of a confirmatory instance: Harry was really hungry last night.
Reason/Generalization: Harry typically loathes spinach.
Evidence: Last night, he ate all his spinach.

The sentence, He must have been really hungry because last night he ate all his spinach, seems a straightforward enough statement until you consider what a reader could possibly infer from it. As a writer, you have to decide whether or not more information is needed to assure that the reader understands what you want to convey. One way to do this is to add an explanation:

> Harry must have been really hungry last night *because* he ate all his spinach *and* he has said many times that he hates spinach; or
> Harry must have been really hungry last night *because* he ate all his spinach *and* anyone who would touch that slime must be starved.

Reading Enthymemes: Discovering Implications

By now you should be aware that a critical reader questions the writer's givens, positions, reasons, and evidence. You are also aware that it is sometimes useful to put in the signal words indicating conclusions and reasons. Now you know that what you are doing when you insert such words is discovering implicit enthymemes. As an illustration, we can turn again to George F. Kennan's "A Proposal for International Disarmament":

> [*Position:*] I question whether these devices are really weapons at all. [*Because:*] A true weapon is at best something with which you endeavor to affect the behavior of another society by influencing the minds, the calculations, the intentions, of the men that control it; [*and because*] it is not something with which you destroy indiscriminately the lives, the substance, the hopes, the culture, the civilization, of another people.

Kennan offers two reasons for his position. Each is an implicit enthymeme:

1. I question whether these devices are really weapons at all *because* a true weapon is at best something with which you endeavor to affect the behavior of another society by influencing the minds, the calculations, the intentions, of the men that control it.
2. I question whether these devices are really weapons at all *because* a true weapon is not something with which you destroy indiscriminately the lives, the substance, the hopes, the culture, the civilization, of another people.

What is missing from both arguments is the given. Look at the second argument. Can you understand what the unstated given must be from studying the position and reason?

We could state the implied given this way:

> *Unstated Given:* Nuclear weapons are something with which you destroy indiscriminately the lives, the substance, the hopes, the culture, the civilization, of another people.
> *Conclusion/Position:* I question whether these devices are really weapons at all.

Reason/Proposition: No true weapon is something with which you destroy indiscriminately the lives,the substance, the hopes, the culture, the civilization, of another people.

Now that we can see the implicit given, we can also see that Kennan wants us to focus on the weapons we have in place for mutual deterrence and not on those nuclear weapons that might be used to "pinpoint" specific military targets or that might be used on a battlefield. What we can learn from Kennan's example is that by leaving unstated what we wish to be taken as a given, we can focus attention on the issues we wish the reader to ponder and implicitly exclude issues we wish him or her not to consider.

The first enthymeme shows another way that Kennan guides the reader's attention:

Unstated Given: A nuclear device is at best something with which you endeavor to affect the behavior of another society by influencing the minds, the calculations, the intentions, of the men that control it.

Conclusion/Position: I question whether nuclear devices are really weapons at all.

Reason/Proposition: A true weapon is at best something with which you endeavor to affect the behavior of another society by influencing the minds, the calculations, the intentions, of the men that control it.

In this case, the unstated given is not so easily accepted, is it? It apparently challenges the U.S. policy of nuclear deterrence, for isn't it true that we justify our arsenal of nuclear weapons on the grounds that we wish to convince the Soviets not to use their arsenal? Isn't that an effort to "affect the behavior of another society by influencing the minds, the calculations, the intentions, of the men that control it"?

Kennan is a good writer; he knows that his enthymeme implies this premise and that an alert reader will notice it and wonder how Kennan intends to defend it, which is just what he does:

> There are those who will agree, with a sigh, to much of what I have just said, but will point to the need for something called deterrence. This is, of course, a concept which attributes to others—to others who, like ourselves, were born of women, walk on two legs, and love their children, to human beings, in short— the most fiendish and inhuman of tendencies.
>
> But all right: accepting for the sake of argument the profound iniquity of these adversaries, no one could deny, I think, that the present Soviet and American arsenals, presenting over a million times the destructive power of the Hiroshima bomb, are simply fantastically redundant to the purpose in question. If the same relative proportions were to be preserved, something well less than 20 percent of those stocks would surely suffice for the most sanguine concepts of deterrence, whether as between the two nuclear superpowers or with relation to any of those other governments that have been so ill-advised as to enter upon the nuclear path. Whatever their suspicions of each other, there can be no excuse on the part of these two governments for holding, poised against each other and poised in a sense against the whole Northern Hemisphere, quantities

of these weapons so vastly in excess of any rational and demonstrable requirements.

What Kennan does here is carry on an argument with the reader. Knowing that his own words have raised implicitly the issue of deterrence, he first seems to offer a counterargument: The Soviets are people just like us; they would not be so inhuman as to destroy an entire civilization, anymore than we would, which suggests that nuclear devices are really useless to either of us. Having gotten in that appeal to our common humanity and to our common folly in relying on weapons that we do not intend to use, Kennan seems to concede to the other side; he accepts the proposition that we need nuclear devices as a deterrence, slyly noticing that this means we must have those "inhuman tendencies" that would let us use nuclear devices: "But all right: accepting for the sake of argument the profound iniquity of *these adversaries. . . ."* Kennan does not mean just the Soviets; he means us, too. Had he meant just the Soviets, he would have said "our adversary." The plural suggests that he refers to both the United States and the Soviet Union, that both of us claim "deterrence" as a policy, which means we would both be "fiendish and inhuman" enough to use nuclear devices if the other side did. As you can see, this is a very damning kind of concession. Once he seems to accept the policy of deterrence, he goes on to show that even if both sides pursue it, the policy does not require the enormous arsenals they now have. Kennan thus responds to the implications of deterrence by showing that we have to be fiendish and inhuman enough to suppose that we would ever use nuclear devices, but even if we are so irrational, it is clear that we do not need such a large arsenal if our only aim is deterrence.

You can see how potent the enthymeme is in the hands of a skilled writer addressing an equally skilled reader. By suppressing a proposition in one passage, Kennan raises an implicit question in the mind of an astute reader, a question he wants raised, one he anticipates and answers immediately, again with a shrewd demonstration of logical skill, by seeming to concede a point to the presumptive reader who disagrees with him. His skill lets Kennan guide the reader toward his points in the order he wishes to deal with them; his sensitivity to the expectations of a skilled reader permits him to anticipate what he will have to include in order to persuade him or her. In a very real sense, Kennan engages the reader in an implicit dialogue, one consisting of arguments and counterarguments. You should also see how helpful it is to learn to read for the implications of an argument. By discovering what is unsaid but implicit, you have a way of deciding whether you agree or disagree.

ASSIGNMENTS

Assignment I

Revise a previous essay so that you make unstated assumptions explicit.

Assignments Preliminary to First Draft

1. Read your essay carefully, looking first for sentences that include the signal words for reasons and conclusions. Then look for sentences that imply these signal words. Very often, you will find that you can link two sentences together with one signal word.

2. Study these sentences carefully. How does the wording of the conclusion and reason suggest the unstated assumption? As you study your enthymemes, ask yourself whether they could suggest more than one unstated assumption or only one.

3. Ask a friend to study your enthymemes with you. Would he or she need you to say more in order to understand precisely what you intended?

4. Try revising the sentences by adding an explanatory *and* clause; for example: He must have been really hungry *because* last night he ate all his spinach *and* he has said many times that he hates spinach.

Revising

Revise your essay, so that you make explicit any unstated assumptions that the reader needs to understand in order to easily grasp your meaning. Turn in your original and your revision.

Assignment II

Try the techniques used by Kennan to guide the reader toward the arguments you want to make.

Assignment Preliminary to First Draft

Take an essay in which you took a position or solved a problem. Read it as a critical reader would, noticing where the argument raises questions or objections. Revise such a section, so that you suppress one central assumption in the argument in such a way that you can raise it as if in answer to a reader's question.

Drafting and Revision

Bring your draft to class. Be prepared to read it aloud or to have it read aloud. As you listen, can you spot the passage the writer has revised? How would you evaluate it? What suggestions can you make? Take notes on the discussion. Afterward, add any other ideas that come to you for revision. Then, revise the essay one more time.

Assignment III

Read the excerpt from Arthur Kopit's *End of the World* (see Part IV, Anthology, Section Four). In that play, Trent, a playwright, has been commissioned to write a play about the arms race. He visits Jim and Pete, who are members of a government think tank. Pete tells Trent:

PETE: There's a curious paradox built into deterrence strategy, and no one has a *clue* how to get around it. The paradox is this: deterrence is dependent upon strength—well that's obvious; the stronger your nuclear arsenal, the more the other side's deterred. *However!* Should deterrence *fail*, for any reason, your strength *instantly* becomes your greatest liability, *inviting* attack *instead* of preventing it.

At the end of the scene, Trent says:

TRENT: Okay. Even with *my* lousy sinuses I could tell something wasn't smelling right. I figured it was *my* fault. What've I missed?

Your assignment: What do you think Trent "missed"? What considerations do Pete and Jim omit from their argument about the paradox?

Discovering What It Is Possible to Say: Some Suggestions

1. Read the scene carefully until you understand the argument Jim and Pete present. Then read it carefully again until you understand why Kopit includes certain details. How do Jim and Pete behave at work? Why is that included? What about their mannerisms? Why are they included?

2. Consider the other readings on the nuclear dilemma included in Part IV, Anthology, Section Four: George F. Kennan's, "A Proposal for International Disarmament" and Freeman Dyson's, "Russians." What clues might they provide about what is "missing" from the way Pete and Jim think about nuclear war? Draw upon any ideas you glean from reading these essays. Be sure to quote or paraphrase them if you incorporate them into your essay.

3. Consult your heart as well as your mind. Given what you know about human nature, do you think Jim and Pete overlook any inherently significant factors in their analysis?

Assignment IV

Reconsider the comparison between the U.S. Declaration of Independence and Ho Chi Minh's declaration. Remember the question: Does Ho Chi Minh advocate the same principles of government as the U.S. declaration? How does considering what Ho Chi Minh does *not* say that the U.S. declaration *does* say help answer the question?

Reconsider the comparison between the U.S. declaration and the Woman's Rights Convention declaration. How does the latter declaration's paraphrase gain its punch from the way it implies what the U.S. declaration does *not* say?

When you have considered these carefully, write an essay in which you explain to someone else how paying attention to what is unstated is an important part of reading critically. Illustrate your explanation with examples from the comparisons of the U.S. declaration with the other two declarations.

Assignment V

Accept the challenge offered in this chapter to evaluate Machiavelli's position on whether a leader should be loved or feared. Reread the passage (in Chapter 18). Reread the discussion of it in this chapter. Then adopt a position. Illustrate it with an analogous experience of your own.

Chapter 20

Discovering a Position: What Words Mean

PREPARATORY EXERCISE

What do these words mean? *stud tires* How do you know?

Introduction

One kind of critique is of the way writers define their terms. All words are signs; that is, all words signify something other than the letters used to spell them. Obviously, a written word signifies the sound we make when we wish to refer to a person, place, thing, action, or quality. But it also signifies the person, place, thing, action, or quality we wish to name. As signs, words can have fallible meanings; that is, a word may seem to the writer inevitably and invariably to signify a certain meaning, but the reader may interpret the word to signify meanings the writer never intended or overlooked.

In this chapter, we will study what is at issue when writers define their terms. First we will consider three aspects of meaning: denotation, context, and connotation. Then we will examine how these characteristics are used to present arguments about meaning in the academic disciplines. You should begin to understand that one way to evaluate another writer is through attention to how he or she uses meaning. You should also understand how attentive you as a writer need to be to your own meanings.

The *denotative* meaning of a word means simply what the word usually signifies in written discourse. Dictionaries give denotative meanings.
The *contextual* meaning refers to the particular use of a word or words
on a given occasion; for instance, *stud tires* means one thing in the context of an advertisement for snow tires, another thing in a report on
horse breeding, and yet another thing during gossip in a women's dor-
mitory. Finally *connotation* refers to the value—positive or negative—
that we assign to a term; for instance, the word *AIDS* has a highly negative connotation. To assure that language signifies what the writer
intends, he or she is attentive to the denotative, contextual, and connotative meanings that a reader is likely to assign to a term. As we shall see,
this often means that a writer presents an argument to show why a term
or phrase should be taken to signify what he or she intends.

Denotative Meaning

Although dictionaries are both useful and necessary, we rarely find
professional writers citing them in order to support an argument. Perhaps
this is because the definitions in a dictionary are generalized statements
of what a term usually signifies when it is used in written discourse; writers are very often presenting arguments that seek to show that our understanding of a term should be more precise than it generally is. For this
reason, writers will often provide the denotative meaning they wish the
reader to assign to a term. George F. Kennan, for instance, provides this
definition of weapons:

> A true weapon is at best something with which you endeavor to affect the
> behavior of another society by influencing the minds, the calculations, the
> intentions, of the men that control it; it is not something with which you destroy
> indiscriminately the lives, the substance, the hopes, the culture, the civiliza-
> tion, of another people.

Kennan's definition supports his argument that nuclear weapons are
not true weapons; he provides his own denotative definition of *weapon*
in order to direct the reader's attention to his argument.

Martin Luther King, Jr., also provides his denotative meaning. His is an
extended definition of just and unjust laws:

> A just law is a man-made code that squares with the moral law or the law of
> God. An unjust law is a code that is out of harmony with the moral law. To put
> it in the terms of St. Thomas Aquinas: An unjust law is a human law that is not
> rooted in eternal law and natural law. Any law that uplifts human personality
> is just. Any law that degrades human personality is unjust.

A writer's own denotative meanings are often propositions in the argument because he or she is making a case for a specific understanding of

what a term signifies. Presenting the argument is the way the writer controls the meaning of the term; that is, the way he or she indicates to the reader what the term inevitably and invariably signifies to the writer. A definition, then, is often a proposition.

A formal definition is a way of organizing our perceptions, thoughts, and feelings by classifying and categorizing them. A class names a group of things as similar, and a category is a subgroup within the class; for instance, *duck* is a class, whereas *mallard, teal,* and *pintail* are categories. Another way to understand this is that a class term declares how members of a group are similar, whereas a category declares how members of the class differ from one another in certain ways. Mallards, teals, and pintails are all ducks, but each kind of duck looks a bit different from other kinds. A classification collects similar things together in a group; a category divides them into subgroups.

Webster's New Twentieth Century Dictionary of the English Language (unabridged, second edition) gives these definitions of *love:*

1. A strong affection for or attachment or devotion to a person or persons;
2. A strong liking for or interest in something;
3. A strong, usually passionate, affection for a person of the opposite sex;
4. The person who is the object of such an affection;
5. Sexual passion, or its gratification;
6. (Latin) (a) Cupid or Eros, as the god of love; (b) (Rare) Venus;
7. In tennis, a score of zero; and
8. In theology, (a) God's benevolent concern for mankind; (b) man's devout attachment to God; (c) the feeling of benevolence and brotherhood that people should have for each other.

As you can see, *love* is a term that we classify and categorize in a number of ways:

CLASS	CATEGORY
Strong affection, attachment, or devotion	to a person or persons
Strong liking for or interest	in something
Strong, usually passionate, affection	for a person of the opposite sex
A person	who is the object of a strong, usually passionate affection
Sexual	passion
Sexual	gratification
A god	of love
A score [in tennis]	of zero

CLASS	CATEGORY
God's benevolent concern	for mankind
Man's devout attachment	to God
The feeling	of benevolence and brotherhood that people should have for each other

When writers present their own definitions, they often state them as formal definitions. Martin Luther King, Jr.'s definitions of just and unjust laws, for instance, state both the class and the category:

	CLASS	CATEGORY
A just law is	a man-made code	that squares with the moral law or the law of God.
An unjust law is	a man-made code	that is out of harmony with the moral order.

A writer may often present an *extended definition*, which is really an argument in support of a proposition. It consists of the given, which is the word itself; the position, which is the writer's definition of the term; the reasons for advocating that definition; and evidence to support it. In Chapter 18, we noticed that King supports his definitions of just and unjust laws by drawing upon philosophers, U.S. constitutional law, and personal experience. You might wish to review that discussion to see how a writer presents an extended definition as an argument.

Immediate Context

The immediate context consists of the parts of a sentence, paragraph, or longer unit of discourse that occur just before or after a word or phrase and that give it its precise meaning. In the following passage, you can see how the immediate context lets you know which meaning of the word *love* is intended:

At 6:00 A.M., John's dog Muffy jumped, as was its habit, onto John's bed and licked its master's nose. John opened his eyes, stretched, and being in an especially good mood, gave the dog a hug:
"Oh, you're such a good dog. I *love* you," he said.
After breakfast, John went to the stationery shop to buy a birthday card for his mother. He signed it, "With *love* from your son, John."
Then, he drove to the tennis courts to meet Glenda. John was preoccupied with the question he wanted to ask her, so he played a *love* game (a game in which his score was 0). After the match, he drove Glenda to a quiet restaurant. After they ordered, he took her hand in his and said, "Glenda, will you marry me? I *love* you."

You can see that John used *love* to refer to a variety of different kinds of feelings, and to a sport, but that we could tell which meaning to assign because of the immediate context. One thing we learn from this as writers is that unless a writer provides a clear immediate context for a term, the reader will be confused about the exact meaning he or she intends.

Larger Context

A word also derives its meaning from a larger context, which includes the history of the term and the way we normally expect it to be used. A writer often has to trust that the reader has this necessary prior knowledge. We can illustrate this with examples of words and phrases that cannot be understood simply from the immediate context. Here are some examples, along with the technical names we give to them:

Euphemism

A euphemism is an inoffensive term substituted for one considered offensively explicit. Here are two examples:

1. In the Bible, the expression "to cover one's feet" is a delicate way of referring to defecation: "And he came to the sheep-cotes by the way, where was a cave, and Saul went in *to cover his feet*."
2. In an episode of "M*A*S*H*," Hawkeye explains to Father Mulcahey that Hawkeye has treated an officer for *carnal flu*, a euphemism for venereal disease.

Irony

Irony is the use of words to convey the opposite of their denotative meaning. Here are two examples:

1. "He . . . has occasional flashes of silence that make his conversation perfectly delightful" (Sydney Smith).
2. "Armaments, universal debt and planned obsolescence—those are the three pillars of western prosperity" (Aldous Huxley).

Litotes

Litotes is understatement. For example: "It was not our finest hour" (statement made by Ambassador William Sullivan about the Iranian seizure of the U.S. Embassy in Teheran).

As these figures of speech illustrate, the meaning of a word or words is sometimes not revealed by the immediate context. We have to know the general or larger context to which the writer implicitly refers. A reader could probably understand "to cover one's feet" only if he or she had read the work of biblical scholars, who figured out what it means by studying other related texts. Similarly, the viewer of "M*A*S*H*," to understand that *carnal flu* meant "venereal disease," would have to know (1) that Hawkeye is known for his ironic wit; (2) that Hawkeye feels a genuine affection and respect for Father Mulcahey, wants to spare his feelings, likes to tease him occasionally, and regards him as somewhat naive; (3) what veneral disease is; and (4) that venereal disease is regarded by some as an unseemly topic of conversation.

To fully appreciate the irony of "He . . . has occasional flashes of silence that make his conversation perfectly delightful," the reader would have to recognize not only that "conversations" are usually deadened by silence, but that the common saying is "flashes of wit."

To understand, "Armaments, universal debt and planned obsolescence—those are the three pillars of western prosperity," the reader would have to know that much of our prosperity depends upon the manufacturing and sales of arms, on massive deficit spending, and on making products—such as cars—that wear out fairly quickly or that soon go out of style—such as clothing. To fully appreciate what Huxley is saying, the reader would have to agree that these are *not* the healthiest or most desirable foundations upon which to build an economy, and would have to know that in standard English usage, to refer to something as a *pillar* is to accord it high value; e.g., "the pillar of his community."

In order to appreciate the litotes "It was not our finest hour," the reader would have to know about the taking of hostages in Iran and the trials that the U.S. hostages endured. To fully appreciate what Sullivan says, the reader would also need to know that he is alluding to a speech by Winston Churchill, in which he said of England, "This was their finest hour." To fully appreciate Churchill's statement, the reader would have to know that he was prime minister of England during World War II. In the spring of 1940, the British were forced to retreat from the beaches of Dunkirk, their last foothold on the Continent. Even given the dark outlook for victory, Churchill, in a speech before the House of Commons on June 18, 1940, said: "Let us . . . brace ourselves to our duties, and so bear ourselves that if the British Empire and its Commonwealth last for a thousand years, men will say: 'This was their finest hour.'"

When what is said refers to what someone else has written, it is called an *allusion* or an *intertextual meaning*. As you can see, Sullivan's comment is an allusion, referring to a speech by Winston Churchill. One kind of general or larger context for written discourse, then, is other written discourse, or the intertextual meaning.

As you can see, we need to be alert to many elements that form the larger context for what a word or words mean. The larger context includes:

Expressions in common usage	Authoritative commentary
The history of terms	What is regarded as offensive

The character of the writer

When a writer lived

Current social, economic, and political conditions

Past social, economic, and political conditions

What others have written

Connotative Meaning

The connotations we assign to a term derive from the context in which the writer embeds the term. To decide whether or not we accept a writer's connotations, then, we have to decide whether or not we agree that the term signifies the larger context that he or she argues it does. This necessity is most apparent with a *loaded term,* one that arouses strong negative or positive connotations. *AIDS* is such a term, and one reason is that its connotations signify the larger context of our cultural attitudes toward homosexuality. When we think of *AIDS,* we think of homosexual intercourse as the primary vector for the disease in our country; hence, to decide whether or not we understand and agree with the connotations writers attach to the word *AIDS,* we have to decide if we understand and agree with the context in which they place homosexuality.

In 1983, for instance, in a *Newsweek* article, Jonathan Alter quotes the Reverend Jerry Falwell's description of AIDS as divine retribution on homosexuals (*Newsweek,* Sept. 23, 1985, 22). The larger context for such a remark is the belief that homosexuality violates divine law and that God is a violently retributive deity. Patrick Buchanan, before he became President Reagan's director of communications, wrote in his syndicated column: "[Homosexuals] have declared war upon nature, and now nature is exacting an awful retribution" (quoted in *Newsweek,* Sept. 23, 1985, 22). One source of the highly negative connotations of AIDS, then, is that some writers understand it in the context of a religious and moral revulsion against homosexuality.

Other contexts lead to different connotations. Although they may not approve of homosexual behavior, many argue that an open society ought to be tolerant of differences in others. Civil libertarians are concerned primarily with the social consequences of using *homosexuality* as a loaded, negative term. Their reaction has brought a new loaded term into our vocabulary, *gaybashing.* As a term of disparagement, it suggests the kind of bigoted intolerance that leads some heterosexual men to seek out and physically assault gay men. Jonathan Alter writes in *Newsweek:* "The sensitivity of gays is understandable, especially given the occasional gaybashing in the press." He gives Buchanan's comment as an example. Obviously, Alter condemns Buchanan as a brutal bigot (25).

Even so, Alter acknowledges that in their reactions against those who condemn homosexuals, reporters may have developed an opposite bias. As a society, we attach highly positive values to "tolerance" and "civil liberties.'' One of the larger contexts for understanding AIDS has come to be, then, that some people see it as a civil liberties issue because it is understood as transmitted by homosexuals, whom they regard as the victims of social intolerance. As Alter says, "Few newspapers have called editorially for the closure of the remaining gay bath houses [where casual sex is alleged to hasten transmission of the disease], implicitly accepting the dubious argument of some gay activists that the issue is more one of civil liberties than health."

Perhaps now we can see why we are having such trouble deciding what AIDS means for our culture. The debate is often couched in terms that we use frequently and to which we assign highly positive connotations: God, nature, civil liberties, and tolerance. But in the debate about AIDS, the values associated with God and nature are seen as at odds with the values associated with civil liberties and tolerance. Contexts that can be understood as compatible are, in this case, seen as mutually exclusive, which means that we assign a highly negative connotation to AIDS because we cannot yet agree in which context it ought to be understood. And we are most fearful of what we do not understand.

Denotation and Context in Academic Discourse

In academic discourse, the larger context for a term is the body of knowledge that constitutes a specific discipline. Often a discipline will use a term in common use but assign it a highly particularized meaning, a situation that presents obvious problems for the novice. A word may seem to signify the general meaning we assign to it in everyday use, when in fact the writer intends to signify a particular use within a given field. Moreover, such specific meanings are often really propositions in arguments; that is, the way one writer in a given academic discipline defines a word may be at odds with the way another writer in the same field would define it. The debate over what a term means constitutes the larger contextual meaning for the term. Sometimes, then, we are not only reading terms with new meanings, but we are confronted with an implicit argument about what the term means.

Examples of this are found in the debate in psychology over the meaning of *self* and its derivatives, such as *selfish, self-love,* and *selfless.* Because writers in this field are aware that the term *self* is controversial, they will, if they follow the best professional standards, state explicitly the larger context for the meaning of *self*, as Louis A. Zurcher does in *The Self Mutable* (Beverly Hills, CA: Sage Library, 1977).

> The assorted definitions of self in the literature [in this context, *literature* means the scholarly writing in the field of psychology] have often been divided by scholars into two types of emphasis: (1) self as process; (2) self as object. Those definitions which focus on self as process emphasize . . . the continuity of a flow of consciousness, including perceiving, thinking, planning, evaluat-

ing, choosing, willing, introspecting, intuiting, and the like. They are sometimes also taken to describe the self as knower. Those definitions which focus on self as object emphasize . . . the view a person has of himself or herself as a physical person, the sense of identity (and sources of identity) the person has, the self-esteem the person has, the sense the person has of himself or herself as an object in space, time, and interaction with others. They are sometimes also taken to describe the self as known. (25–26)

By stating clearly the terms of the debate, Zurcher makes it easier for the reader to understand that he is adopting a position in a debate.

Unfortunately, not all writers state the terms of the debate explicitly. In the absence of such clarification, we as readers should simply assume that when a scholarly or academic writer frequently uses a term that is in common usage, he or she is assigning it a special, *debatable* meaning, regardless of whether the writer acknowledges this explicitly or not. Rollo May, for instance, only implies that there is a larger debate about the meaning of "self":

> The self is thus not merely the sum of the various "roles" one plays—it is the capacity by which one *knows* he plays these roles; it is the center from which one sees and is aware of these so-called different "sides" of himself. (*The Art of Loving* [New York: Harper and Row, 1956] 58–59)

Implicit in this definition is a counterargument to some other writer. When May says, "The self is thus not merely the sum of the various 'roles' one plays," he suggests that someone has defined the "self" as "the sum of the various 'roles' one plays," but May objects to the definition as too limited. May assumes that the reader is already knowledgeable of the larger context to which he refers. How is a reader supposed to understand the debate? May provides no footnotes or references to the writers with whom he disagrees. A novice reader is therefore hampered in trying to clarify his exact contextual meaning.

A reader can raise a legitimate complaint against such omissions for the same reasons that we can object to an unsupported proposition. An example of such criticism is found in Ruth C. Wylie's *The Self Concept: A Review of Methodological Considerations and Measuring Instruments* (Lincoln, Neb.; University of Nebraska, 1974). She tells us that she examined 15 introductory psychology textbooks published between 1968 and 1972. They were intended for use in introductory, college-level psychology courses. Eleven of these introduced students to the term *self-concept*. Wylie complains that all these textbooks "made broad, unsupported, uncriticized generalizations about the self-concept," which could "seriously mislead the student and interfere with his acquiring a scientific attitude toward the topic." She finds fault with these texts for the following reasons:

> (a) No indication was given that the statements were intended to be theoretical propositions, as opposed to known relationships. The impression created is that these are obvious truths which may be validated by a reader's experiences,

when in fact they are assertions from a most complex, inadequately explored area of psychology. (b) Either no study relevant to any of the general assertions was even mentioned, or one or two were briefly cited. (c) No doubts were expressed about the methodological adequacy of the cited study or studies. (d) No inkling was given that a large volume of research has been published and that serious controversy remains, partly because of unresolved methodological problems. (xiv–xv)

Wylie points out that one of the dangers that arises from this lack of precision is that *self-concept* is a term in general usage. Because the textbooks fail to indicate that they are using the term within the more restricted context of psychology, readers are likely to rely on the generalized meanings we assign to *self-concept* in everyday use. This imprecision means that "widespread credence is lent to unsupported common-sense statements and to the idea that making such assertions in the name of scientific psychology is acceptable among experts." She also makes the astute observation: "Brighter, more discerning students will develop a disrespect for psychologists' approach to this topic."

What is the consequence for readers who read and accept the unsupported, specialized definitions of a writer? Michael and Lise Wallach are especially concerned with the effect on students of the unsupported definitions of *self* and *selfishness* in college psychology textbooks. Some of these assume that human behavior is motivated by selfishness, by the desire to seek pleasure and avoid pain or discomfort. Wallace and Wallace quote one textbook that says: "A person who has learned to accept some social values will be rewarded, or not punished, by serving them. He is still acting selfishly . . . but the selfishness will have been harnessed to some part of the collective judgment." (Wallach and Wallach, *Psychology's Sanction for Selfishness* [San Francisco, CA: W. H. Freeman, 1983] 23). The writers of this textbook—Brown and Herrnstein—explicitly deny that any motive—such as altruism or self-sacrifice—is as essential to human behavior as selfishness. They say that we should not be "so naive as to think that what a person says has anything to do with how he behaves. . . . We may act to maximize our tangible selfish rewards, and talk in a way that credits us with greater altruism" (23). In other words, if a person says that he or she acted out of a sense of charitable regard for another, the statement is hypocritical and masks the person's true, selfish motives.

Brown and Herrnstein's definitions of *selfish* and *altruistic* are the kind criticized by Wylie as "broad, unsupported, uncriticized generalizations," which create the impression that they are "obvious truths." Wallach and Wallach think it probable that students exposed to this use of language over an extended period come to accept it as true of themselves and their motives. They cite a study of "students and recent graduates who not only are familiar with psychology but also have been seriously involved in providing crisis-intervention or peer-counseling services. They have acted to help others. What do they think of their motives?"

Here is how some of the students explained why they believed they helped others:

> "Doing something for other people is gratifying needs in yourself, otherwise you wouldn't do it."

> "There is a part of me that needs to believe that altruism is alive and well, especially in me. But there's also a cynicism—something like altruism can't exist."

> "I think there's always a payoff. You always get something back. . . . Often it looks as if it's altruistic, but there's always a reason. . . . You always get things back and if you say you don't, then I think you're kidding yourself." (28)

Wallach and Wallach think these students are "confused about understanding what they do in other than cynical terms. This seems to be where the psychology they have learned has gotten them." Wallach and Wallach agree that such cynicism about human motives might be justified if it were an "obvious truth" that all human behavior is selfishly motivated. But that—as well as the definition of *selfish* as "the intention to seek pleasure and avoid pain or punishment"—is a proposition about human motives and is therefore open to debate. As Wallach and Wallach and Wylie suggest, one reason that the students may not have known a debate was going on is because the debaters fail to acknowledge that their statements are debatable or arguable; that is, they fail to state explicitly the larger context that gives the terms *selfishness* and *altruism* their meanings within the discipline of psychology.

Taking a Position: Assigning Connotative Meanings

Another kind of debate you will encounter is over the connotation a term ought to be assigned. Often, this means that the debate is about what the larger context for the term ought to be. Erich Fromm, in his book *The Art of Loving*, wants the reader to attach a positive connotation to the word *self-love:*

> Is . . . selfishness identical with self-love or is it not caused by the very lack of it?
> Before we start the discussion of the psychological aspect of selfishness and self-love, the logical fallacy in the notion that love for others and love for oneself are mutually exclusive should be stressed. If it is a virtue to love my neighbor as a human being, it must be a virtue—and not a vice—to love myself since I am a human being too. . . . The idea expressed in the Biblical "Love thy neighbor as thyself!" implies that respect for one's own integrity and uniqueness, love for and understanding of one's own self, cannot be separated from respect for and love and understanding of another individual. The love for my own self is inseparably connected with the love for any other self. (59)

Fromm wants to change the connotation of *self-love* to a positive one, and to do that, he wants to change its denotative meaning, so that it is not synonymous with *selfishness.* He therefore argues that it ought to be understood in the context of Christian ethics and virtue. We would say, then, that Fromm assigns to *self-love* the positive religious connotations of love and respect for others.

Similarly, Nathaniel Brandon says in *Honoring the Self* (New York, Bantam, 1985):

> In a world in which selflessness is commonly regarded as a synonym of virtue and selfishness a synonym of evil—and in which the presumed goal of spiritual evolution is self-transcendence—a book entitled *Honoring the Self* may sound strange, even a bit disorienting.
>
> This volume is grounded in the recognition that self-esteem and personal autonomy are indispensable conditions of human well-being. (xii–xiii)

Brandon wishes to remove the terms *self-esteem* and *personal autonomy* from the larger religious context that might lend them a negative connotation. We might say that his definitions of these terms carry the positive connotations that we associate with human well being in general.

Taking a Position: Debating Context and Connotation

Mary Midgley, in an unpublished address entitled "Head, Hearts, and Words," provides a good illustration of how an argument about connotation is couched. As you read, consider not only the terms of the argument, but the manner of its presentation. Consider the possibility that Midgely uses irony, for instance.

> Let us look . . . first at the word "rational" as it is used in economics, and more widely in such things as cost-benefit analysis. The definition given of it may vary a bit with the surrounding scenery, but essentially the word rational in these contexts is used to mean "consistently self-interested." That, at root, is the idea of economic man (it is of course no accident that the idea of economic woman is an impossible one, which no one has ever tried to use).
>
> This use of the word rational is however a very strange one. In ordinary speech, it means something quite different. It is very nearly a synonym for "sane." It certainly does not refer only to the calculation of means; choice of ends also comes into it. Somebody with a delusion system which is internally consistent is not described as rational and most of us do get considered rational in spite of many inconsistences in our thought. . . . Nor is the aim of self-interest an exception to this way of thinking. When we come across someone—say a multiple murderer—who actually has been completely consistent in putting his own interest above all other considerations, including the lives and feelings of all those around him, we are inclined to suggest that he must be a psychopath—that is, abnormal and perhaps insane. At a trial, this abnormality may even be used as part of his defence.

In their ordinary use, then, words like rational and reasonable include reference to aims as well as means. They are concepts which do their work in the central area where thought and feeling equally are engaged. Have we then got a right to complain that economists are misusing the word rational? They will object that this is naive, that the use is an accepted technical one, which everyone interested in the subject understands. It abstracts from the vulgar consideration of aims, and refers only to the consistent use of means. It speaks, in fact, only to the head and not the heart.

This defence brings me to the nub of what I want to say about language. There simply is no way in which common words can be addressed like this to only one level of the personality. If they are understood at all, they operate at all levels. Of course we can ignore or misrepresent their deeper workings, but we cannot block them out. The commoner the word used, the stronger and more obvious these resonances become. . . . Now the word rational is a thoroughly everyday word, and the most obvious fact about it is that it is a compliment. Writers on economics would have produced a very different effect if, from the start, they had described their economic man as "consistently calculating" or "radically self-centered" or "wholly out for the main chance" or simply "thoroughly selfish." Yet these are much more exact translations of what they mean. Why did they chose the word rational instead?

Choices like this are, and cannot possibly avoid being, pieces of propaganda. Anyone who uses an ordinary word with a visible cargo of value in a technical sense like this is trying to hijack the value and turn it to his own purposes. In this case, what the special usage implies is that unfailing self-interest is in fact the only sane attitude.

Both Midgley and Wylie object to certain consequences that arise when an academic discipline expropriates a term in common use for highly specialized meanings. Midgley's position on this differs from Wylie's. Wylie holds out the possibility that words like *self* can be defined in a specialized way that would distinguish them from the "common sense" use of the term. Midgley argues that shifting the context of a term cannot remove the connotations that resonate in readers who encounter it. She argues that *rational* retains its positive connotation when used in the specialized context of economics, which implies that wholly selfish means is a positive characteristic.

Midgley's argument is against those who would deny that words always have connotative meaning. Freeman Dyson, in the excerpt from *Weapons and Hope* (see Part IV, Anthology, Section Four), argues against wrenching words out of their historical context in order to give them a frightening connotation. His article analyzes George F. Kennan's and Richard Pipes's views of the Soviets. In the passage I'm about to quote, Dyson illustrates how a writer does a *close analysis* of the language used by another writer. He is commenting on Pipes. Please read the long quote from Pipes that Dyson includes in his article before you go on. Ready? Here is what Dyson says about Pipes:

> The words with which Pipes intends to scare us—"victory. . .
> superiority. . . offensive action," are precisely the goals which the Rus-

sians achieved, after immense efforts and sacrifices, at the end of World War II. If, as Pipes correctly states, Soviet strategy is still dominated by the lessons learned in World War II, it is difficult to see what other goals than these the Soviet armed forces should be expected to pursue. Pipes makes these goals sound frightening by placing them in a misleading juxtaposition with American strategic concepts taken from a different context: ''not deterrence but victory, not sufficiency in weapons but superiority, not retaliation but offensive action.'' The American strategy of deterrence, sufficiency, and retaliation is a purely nuclear strategy having nothing to do with war as it has been waged in the past. The Soviet strategy of victory, superiority, and offensive action is a continuation of the historical process by which Russia over the centuries repelled invaders from her territory. Both strategies have advantages and disadvantages. Neither is aggressive in intention. Both are to me equally frightening, because both make the survial of civilization depend on people behaving reasonably.

Dyson objects to Pipes's removing the Soviet goals of victory, superiority, and offensive action from the Russian historical context. These goals, argues Dyson, are those the Russians have used to *defend* their territories. They were the means by which the Soviets, for instance, believe that they prevailed in World War II. By removing these terms from this historical context, Dyson argues, Pipes makes the Soviets sound as if the basis for their military strategy is *offensive* rather than *defensive*. Notice how in presenting his argument, Dyson moves back and forth from Pipes's words to his own analysis. He quotes the text, comments on it, quotes the text, comments on it, and then offers his final position. This is the conventional way a writer presents an analysis of what another writer has said.

Summary

Because all words are signs, they can have fallible meanings. This means that a word does not inevitably and exclusively signify the same thing all the time. The meanings a writer attaches to words are therefore subject to debate. As a critical reader and writer, you can attend to three qualities of words:

Denotative Meaning and Context

1. You can notice when a writer supplies his or her denotative meaning to a word, regard it as a proposition in an argument, and decide whether you accept the definition or not. Evaluating a writer's own definition for a term requires the same critical skills as evaluating any other kind of argument. The given is the word itself, the position is the definition the writer assigns, the reasons are the explanations the writer offers for pro-

posing the definition, and the evidence consists of examples the writer brings forward to support the definition.

2. You can notice when a writer fails to define the denotative meaning he or she wishes a term to carry. This is especially crucial when the writer is using a common term in a specialized context. Definitions for such terms are *always* debatable, and the writer ought to provide a complete argument to support the particular meaning he or she assigns.

3. As a writer, you can learn to provide definitions whenever you are assigning a particular meaning to a term. When you are using a common term as it has been defined within a given field, you ought to tell the reader which definition you have embraced and why.

Connotative Meanings

1. You can notice when writers argue that a term ought to have a different connotation than the one it usually carries. Your task is to assess the argument the writer offers to decide whether or not you agree with that position.

2. You can notice when writers argue or imply that a term can be stripped of any connotations and take a stance on that position.

3. You can notice when writers attempt to lend words a strong connotation, especially by using them out of context. You can decide whether you agree with that effort or not.

4. As a writer, you can become alert to the connotations of words and understand the importance of indicating to readers not only the denotative meaning you intend, but the connotative meaning as well.

ASSIGNMENTS

Assignment I

Drawing upon the discussion in this chapter, write a critique of how common terms are given specialized meanings in a textbook or another reading that you have been assigned in another class. Because your reader will be unfamiliar with the work you critique, be sure to use summary and direct quotations to make your points clear.

Assignment II

Explain what Irving L. Janis in *Groupthink: Psychological Studies of Policy Decisions and Fiascos* means when he says his term *groupthink* is intended to carry an "invidious connotation" derived from George Orwell's *1984*. (see Part IV, Anthology, Section Four).

Assignments Preliminary to First Draft

Each discipline often finds it necessary to invent new terms—neologisms—either to describe something newly discovered or to describe something we have known about for some time but that is now studied from a new perspective. Discovering something new, or discovering a new way to understand what is generally known, often requires the discoverer to invent a term that describes the discovery. In coining the new term, writers seek to establish the denotative, contextual, and connotative meanings of the term. This assignment asks you to pay particular attention to the way Irving L. Janis establishes the larger context and connotations of his neologism *groupthink*, as he explains it in his book.

Janis is a psychologist who specializes in the way groups make decisions. In his book, he is especially interested in the factors that contribute to political or policy fiascoes, such as the Bay of Pigs, the escalation of the war in Vietnam, and the Watergate affair. He is also interested in decisions that led to successful policies, such as the Cuban missile crisis and the Marshall Plan, but his term *groupthink* refers to the kind of decision making that results in fiasco:

> I use the term "groupthink" as a quick and easy way to refer to a mode of thinking that people engage in when they are deeply involved in a cohesive in-group, when the members' strivings for unanimity override their motivation to realistically appraise alternative courses of action. "Groupthink" is a term of the same order as the words in the newspeak vocabulary George Orwell presents in his dismaying *1984*—a vocabulary with terms such as "doublethink" and "crimethink." By putting groupthink with those Orwellian words, I realize that groupthink takes on an invidious connotation. The invidiousness is intentional: Groupthink refers to a deterioration of mental efficiency, reality testing, and moral judgment that results from in-group pressures.

The allusion indicates both the connotation Janis wishes to attach to the term—invidious—as well as one of the contexts: George Orwell's *1984*. Your assignment is to explain how Orwell's *1984* lends itself to the invidious connotation Janis assigns to *groupthink*.

1. To gain an understanding of *groupthink*, read the excerpts from Janis's book included in the Anthology.

2. Read the excerpts from Orwell's *1984* (Part IV, Anthology, Section Four) noting especially how *groupthink* resembles the origin and purposes of words such as *doublethink* and *crimethink*, and how the purpose of the Newspeak vocabulary in *1984* illuminates what Janis means when he says *groupthink* is "invidious" because it is a "deterioration of mental efficiency, reality testing, and moral judgment that results from in-group pressures." Be sure to mark passages that help you understand what Janis means and to take notes on your ideas and insights.

3. If you think of any personal experiences or examples that illustrate what Janis means by *groupthink*, note them.

Drafting and Revision

1. Draft your response to the assignment and bring it to class. Be prepared to read it aloud. Take notes on the discussion, and afterward add any additional ideas that occur to you.

2. Revise your draft as an essay that anyone could read and understand even if he or she were unfamiliar with the assignment. Be sure to acknowledge any insights you gained from the discussion. Refer to these sources by name.

Assignment III

Explain how a newly learned definition helps us understand ourselves or our world in a new way. Here are some options you might use to complete this assignment.

Option 1

You might try inventing some new words using what you know about the conventions for writing definitions. Rich Hall has come up with a new class of terms he calls *sniglets.* You may remember these from the television show "Not Necessarily the News," or you may have seen them on cards or in bookstores. A sniglet is "any word that doesn't appear in the dictionary but should." These are words that name common objects, pleasures, or annoyances that we do not have terms for.

accordionated *adj.:* Being able to drive and refold a map at the same time.

alponium *n.* (chemical symbol: Ap): Initial blast of odor upon opening a can of dog food.

aeropalmics *n.:* The study of wind resistance conducted by holding a cupped hand out the car window.

aquadextrous *adj.:* Possessing the ability to turn the bathtub faucet on and off with your toes.

cinemuck *n.:* The combination of popcorn, soda, and melted chocolate which covers the floors of movie theatres.

erdu *n.:* The leftover accumulation of rubber particles after erasing a mistake on a test paper.

hydralation *n.:* Acclimating oneself to a cold swimming pool by bodily regions: toe-to-knee, knee-to-waist, waist-to-elbow, elbow-to-neck.

ignisecond, *n.:* The overlapping moment of time when the hand is locking the car door even as the brain is saying "my keys are in there!"

The only rule for making these up is combining elements of words we already know: *cinema + muck = cinemuck; error + do-do = erdu.*

Over several days, see what happens when you try inventing your own sniglets. Write an *extended definition* of at least one. Then add a statement in which you tell what the effect is of having a new word to name something you could not name before.

If you want some more ideas, you can purchase Hall's book at most trade bookstores: Rich Hall and Friends, *Sniglets* (New York: Macmillan, 1984).

Bring your definition to class and share it with your classmates. If you really like your sniglets, or if you think a classmate has come up with some that Hall should use, you can send them to:

SNIGLETS
P.O. Box 2350
Hollywood, CA 90078

Be sure to include your name and address. Maybe Hall will decide to use them.

Option 2

You might try discovering some new words. Open your dictionary to any page. Look for words new to you. Copy the words and the definitions of those words that are pleasing because of what they teach about human nature or the derivation of words. Here are two examples:

abligurition *n.* [Latin. *abliguritio,* feasting.]: extravagance in the preparation and serving of food. [Obs]

callow *a.:* unfledged; without feathers, as a young bird not able to fly; immature, without experience, as callow love.

Option 3

The "Almanac" feature of *Atlantic Monthly* includes a section called "Words Received." In it are "recent citations, collected and defined by the editors of *The American Heritage Dictionary* (Houghton Mifflin) for possible inclusion in a revised edition." Here are two examples:

Jingo-jangle *n.:* jingoistic rhetoric and theatrics. "The *jingo-jangle* Stallone admits is at the heart of [*Rocky IV*] is, in his eyes, not a bad thing—not after the shoving around America took in the world of the '70s" *(Newsweek).*

Quant jock *n.:* a student in a graduate school of business administration who displays expertise in quantitative course work. "*Quant jocks* (quantitative kids) who 'nail' (master) the numbers courses are the epitome of B-school success" *(Business Week).*

Consult the current or some recent back issues of *Atlantic Monthly* for possible words to use in this assignment.

Chapter 21

Discovering a Position: Evaluating Reification

PREPARATORY ASSIGNMENT: LABELING OURSELVES

Sometimes concepts can seem as descriptive as concrete terms. Test this for yourself. Here is an exercise suggested by Robert H. McKim in *Thinking Visually.*

Prepare a list of the terms that could be used to describe your self-concept. You might include roles (father, sister, sweetheart, manager, student), affiliation (Tri-Delt, Feminist, Republican, Democrat), religion, size, shape, gender, disposition, personality, values, beliefs, attitudes. You may find it helpful (and revealing) to ask a friend or relative to write down some of the labels he or she would typically apply to you. You should collect a list of about thirty labels that taken together will make up your Self-Concept List.

Live with this list for a while. Make up a large, gummed label to wear or a decorative sign to hang where you will see it often (The bathroom mirror? Over your bed? Over your desk? Hanging from the rearview mirror?).

After you have lived with it, bring it to class and destroy it. Write about this experience. What was it like to have the labels around all the time? What did it mean to destroy your labels? Which labels are you glad to be rid of, if only symbolically? Which would you regret losing?

Distinguishing Between Concepts and Concrete Terms

In the last chapter, we discussed the fallibility of words as signs. We studied three aspects of that problem: denotation, contextual meaning, and connotation. In this chapter, we are going to discuss a fourth aspect, one having to do especially with abstract terms or concepts. When we use a concept as if it described what we can perceive directly, we *reify* it. Reify is a verb that means to regard or treat an abstraction or an idea as if it had concrete or material existence. It comes from the Latin word *res*, which means "thing." To reify a concept means to use it as if it were a term that describes a thing or something tangible.

When you made your self-concept labels, you may have noticed that you used both abstract and concrete terms. A concrete term, you recall, describes what we can observe directly; for instance, that someone is blonde. An abstract term, on the other hand, names an intangible. The term *self-confident*, for instance, describes a cause for behaviors, rather than the behaviors themselves. We use concrete terms to describe our perceptions. We use abstract terms to assign cause or to evaluate and make judgments.

You may also have noticed that you responded to an abstract label just as strongly as you did to a concrete term. When someone describes us as intelligent or self-confident, it seems to reflect upon reality about as directly as if someone says we are tall or brunette. Or if someone says we are irritable or stuck-up, we might feel as self-conscious as if someone drew attention to a wart on the end of our nose or pointed out that our fingernails are always dirty. We often respond to concepts as if they were as directly descriptive of reality as concrete terms are.

In earlier chapters, we took some time to notice that concrete terms are fallible signs. We noticed, for instance, that we all are subject to selective perception, which means that the descriptions we give of an action, event, person, or thing will in all probability vary from the descriptions given by others. We also noticed how concrete terms can lead us to stereotype our perceptions, so that we fail to notice sensory details—color, shape, texture, odor, sound, and change—because common concrete terms generalize our descriptions of what we perceive.

In earlier chapters we also noticed one of the ways in which concepts or abstract terms are fallible. Because concepts do not refer directly to what we can perceive, we cannot test a statement of cause the way we can test descriptive generalizations.

Reification presents us with another problem that comes with using concepts—all concepts, not just explanations of cause. To illustrate this problem, we are going to study a particularly shabby chapter in the history of science. We will see how scientists and pseudoscientists used intelligence testing and genetic theory to confirm prior conceptions of racial superiority. Their conclusions reflect a long-standing dispute about the causes of human behavior, a dispute that continues today. It is generally referred to as the Nature versus Nurture debate. Those on the nature side argue that behavior is caused primarily by natural endowments; that is, by genetic inheritance. They are sometimes labeled biological determinists. Those on the nurture side argue that behavior is caused for the most part by environmental factors, such as family influence, the relative level of income, or the quality of education.

One purpose, then, for this chapter is to illustrate one way in which concepts are fallible signs. A second purpose is to illustrate how writers present an extended argument about the fallacy of reification.

Reifying Concepts

We have already discussed one example of reification in Chapter 3, "Learning to Question," when we imagined that we were invited to a party for new students given by the president of our college or university. We saw that the concept of etiquette we carried with us to the party affected how we explained or judged the behavior of others. If our concept of good manners is that the host and hostess ought to introduce themselves to arriving guests, we would interpret their failure to do so as a sign of rudeness, and we would label them ill-mannered, uncaring, or snobbish. If we are firmly wedded to this concept, we might fail to observe carefully what is going on around us; for instance, that other newly arrived guests begin introducing themselves. In this case, we assume that our concept of good manners is as truly descriptive of reality as the statement: Ducks have webbed feet. We cannot imagine any other way of labeling what we see. We forget that we cannot *perceive* snobbishness or rudeness. We can perceive a room full of people interacting. Calling people snobbish or rude is a way of assigning cause to behavior and of judging it. If we get mixed up and think that the label *snob* describes what we perceive, rather than how we interpret it, we have reified a concept.

The alternative is to understand that concepts are ways of explaining, evaluating, or judging what we perceive. As our awareness of what we perceive changes or develops, so might our understanding of its cause or value. If we observe that others introduce themselves when they arrive at a party, then we might change our concept of good manners, introduce ourselves to others, and hence decide that they are not rude, uncaring, or snobbish.

Most cultural stereotypes are examples of reification. People who assume that all teenagers are irresponsible hedonists, or that all young, upwardly mobile, urban professionals (Yuppies) are ambitious materialists, or that all women are inherently less capable of doing math than men use concepts of conduct, values, or intelligence as if they were concrete terms descriptive of perceived reality. And once concepts are reified, they can be so mesmerizing that we find what we unconsciously seek: we are more conscious of teenagers playing loud, obnoxious music on jamboxes at the beach than we are of them working long hours for minimum wages in order to earn money for college; we notice young corporate executives in flashy cars more than we do young people of the same age starting teaching jobs in elementary schools for pitifully low wages; we overlook the number of women teaching mathematics, using mathematics in their professional lives, or women who are single heads-of-households managing to budget relatively low incomes so that they can feed, clothe, and educate their children.

The Reification of IQ Scores

Alan Chase, who wrote *The Legacy of Malthus: The Social Costs of the New Scientific Racism* (Champaign, Ill; University of Illinois, 1980), and Stephen Jay Gould, who wrote *Mismeasure of Man* (New York: Norton, 1981, 1983), are two of the social and scientific historians who have written about the fallacious reasoning some have used to arrive at the conclusion that the ability to learn is caused solely by genetic inheritance. During the early decades of our century, psychologists reified the concepts of intelligence and rank-ordering of abilities. *Intelligence* is a concept referring to what causes our varied and varying capacities to learn to do those things we as a culture have labeled desirable. If we assume that *intelligence* is a concrete term describing a specific site that we could locate somewhere in the brain or could find residing in a single gene, then we have reified a concept. In other words, we have used an abstract term explaining cause and used it as a concrete term describing something we could perceive directly.

During the early decades of our century, the interpretation of intelligence test scores was tainted by this kind of reification. *Intelligence* was used as a concrete term describing ''a single, innate, heritable, and measurable thing,'' which allows us to rank-order individuals according to their inherent ability to learn. Intelligence testing was therefore used to support the arguments of the biological determinists. This conclusion was fostered by the coincidence of several historical factors: (1) the new science of genetics; (2) prior racial stereotypes that fostered bigotry; (3) prior economic and religious concepts that assumed poverty was a sign of sin, laziness, or degeneracy; and (4) the effort in France to develop ways of diagnosing learning disabilities.

Alfred Binet's Test for Mental Age

We can begin the story with Alfred Binet's effort to diagnose learning disabilities in French schoolchildren in 1905. Binet was director of the psychology laboratory at the Sorbonne in Paris when psychology was still a fairly new scientific discipline. He was invited by the French minister of public instruction to create a test that would identify students whom we would label today as learning disabled. Binet developed a test involving a wide variety of simple tasks intended to reveal a child's ability to order, comprehend, invent, and correct. Binet's scoring system indicated the youngest age at which a child of normal learning ability could be expected to complete the tasks given in the exam. A child began with the simplest tasks and proceeded to more difficult tasks until he or she could not complete them. A child who could complete tasks normally completed by children aged 11 was said to have a mental age of 11, regardless of his or her chronological age. In 1912, the German psychologist W. Stern divided mental age by chronological age, yielding the intelligence *quotient* or IQ.

Binet was firmly on the nurture side of the Nature versus Nurture debate. He felt that intelligence could not be quantified with a single number and stressed that his test had only a limited, pragmatic purpose. He cautioned against using the scores to reify the concept of intelligence: "The scale, properly speaking, does not permit the measure of the intelligence, because intellectual qualities . . . cannot be measured as linear surfaces are measured" (Gould, 151). Binet was especially critical of teachers who assumed that a child's intelligence or ability to learn was unaffected by teaching. He felt that teachers should intervene "actively and usefully" to help slower learners, and called it a "brutal pessimism" when biological determinists argued that "an individual's intelligence is a fixed quantity, a quantity that cannot be increased" (Gould, 153). For Binet, the intelligence of a pupil could be increased, because intelligence meant simply "the capacity to learn and assimilate instruction," a capacity clearly influenced by the kind and quality of instruction (Gould, 154).

According to Gould, Binet intended that those using his test observe three principles:

1. The scores are a practical device: they do not buttress any theory of intellect. They do not define anything innate or permanent. We may not designate what they measure as *intelligence* or any other reified entity;
2. The scale is a rough, empirical guide for identifying mildly retarded and learning-disabled children who need special help. It is not a device for ranking normal children; and
3. Whatever the cause of difficulty in children identified for help, emphasis shall be placed upon improvement through special training. Low scores shall not be used to mark children as innately incapable (Gould, 155).

When Binet's test crossed the Atlantic to the United States, all three of these principles were ignored. *Intelligence* was reified, so that instead of designating a cause for certain kinds of learning, it came to designate a single, innate, biologically determined thing.

H. G. Goddard, Immigrants, and the Kallikaks

H. G. Goddard, the director of research at the Vineland Training School for Feeble-Minded Boys and Girls, was the first person in the United

States to translate Binet's articles, to administer the tests, and to argue for their general use. Goddard was also a believer in eugenics, a particularly ugly pseudoscience that grew up in the wake of Darwin and the genetic discoveries of Mendel. Eugenicists believed that the human species could be "improved" through genetic control. This "improvement" could be accomplished by preventing "undesirables"—such as the poor, blacks, Italians, Jews, criminals, and the "feebleminded"—from breeding. Eugenicists were biological determinists who denied the effect of environment or history on behavior.

These assumptions obviously derived from deeply entrenched racial and ethnic bigotry, and from the long-standing, conscience-salving habit of assuming that the poor deserve to be or are somehow responsible for being poor. They were also based on a naive understanding of genetics that accompanied the rediscovery in 1900 of Mendel's study of the transmission of characteristics in peas. The naive assumption was that one gene existed for each characteristic. Eugenicists assumed that "intelligence" was a single unit or thing that came from a specific gene. The children of the well-to-do thus tended to fare better in life than children born to the abysmally poor not because well-to-do children enjoyed better health care, nutrition, education, and material comfort, but because they inherited a double dose of "intelligence" genes. Their parents were obviously well-off because they were intelligent. The poor were poor because they inherited "recessive" genes that made them "feebleminded" or "morons"—a term Goddard coined—and they passed these along to their children, which is why they, too, were poor. Eugenicists used similar reasoning, along with the fallacious notion that evolution "progressed" to produce the "superior" Teutonic "race," in order to "prove" that Nordic types (white Anglo-Saxon Protestants and people from Northern Europe) were genetically superior to all others.

Armed with such preconceptions and the Binet test, Goddard sent two assistants to Ellis Island (the port of entry for immigrants landing on the east coast) in 1913 to test the intelligence of immigrants. He selected two women because he felt that by using their "female intuition," they could easily spot the feebleminded or morons. These women tested 35 Jews, 22 Hungarians, 50 Italians, and 45 Russians. Goddard found that the overwhelming majority of them were "feebleminded," or below the mental age of 12. This was the result for 82 percent of the Jews, 80 percent of the Hungarians, 79 percent of the Italians, and 87 percent of the Russians.

Several factors contributed to this result. One was that Goddard, when he translated Binet, mistakenly altered the scoring system, so that people rated by Binet as "normal" were rated as "morons" by Goddard. A second factor is well stated by Gould:

> Consider a group of frightened men and women who speak no English and who have just endured an oceanic voyage in steerage. Most are poor and have never gone to school; many have never held a pencil or pen in their hand. They

march off the boat; one of Goddard's intuitive women takes them aside shortly thereafter, sits them down, hands them a pencil, and asks them to reproduce on paper a figure shown to them a moment ago, but now withdrawn from their sight. Could their failure be a result of testing conditions, of weakness, fear or confusion, rather than of innate stupidity? (166)

On the basis of these scores, Goddard decided that immigrants coming into the United States scored in the "moron" range of intelligence tests because they bore the genes that made them morons. After all, the majority of immigrants entering the country in the steerage classes during the decade 1910–1920 were not Anglo-Saxons or Northern Europeans. Not surprisingly, Goddard was delighted when deportations for mental deficiency rose 350 percent in 1913 and 570 percent in 1914 in comparision with similar deportations for the five previous years. "This was due," he said, "to the untiring efforts of the physicians who were inspired by the belief that mental tests could be used for the detection of feeble-minded aliens" (Gould, 168).

We can unravel Goddard's chain of reasoning to see how he used reification to arrive at his conclusion. First, he assumed that a test score *described* intelligence; that is, he assumed that intelligence was a trait—like blue eyes—that could be observed. Then he assumed that a single gene determined or *caused* intelligence, just as geneticists assumed that a single gene determined eye color. Then he made the *judgment* that it would be bad social policy to admit people to the United States who were genetically "inferior."

You can appreciate how different his conclusions would have been had Goddard assumed that a test score indicated how well a child born and raised in the mainstream of U.S. culture answered questions significant for our culture in comparision with how well others of the same age and background answered them. Goddard might have had the sudden insight that test scores do not describe a "thing"; they offer a way of making comparative assessments of certain abilities prized by a culture. *Intelligence* is a concept the meaning of which is culturally determined. Armed with this insight, Goddard would have had to notice that in saying that intelligence is genetically determined, he was saying that a gene could *cause* a *concept*—intelligence—which is an obviously ridiculous way to think about genes.

Just how self-blinded Goddard was by his misconceptions is further illustrated by his famous study of the Kallikak family. Goddard coined the name for the family from the Greek words *kallos*, "beauty," and *kakos*, "bad." In November 1897, an eight-year-old girl Goddard later called Deborah Kallikak was brought to his Training School for Feeble-Minded Boys and Girls in Vineland, New Jersey. She was illegitimate, illiterate, and a poor student. By the time she was 21, in 1911, she could, among other things, read and write, do arithmetic, read music and play the coronet, make dresses, and do embroidery, woodwork, and carpentry—in other words, take care of and support herself as well as any other adult. But when she was given the Goddard-Binet test, she received the score of a nine-year-old, or of someone who was too feebleminded to function as an adult (Chase, 145).

This did not suggest to Goddard that there may have been some problem in administering the test, or, as we have said, that his translation of Binet misassigned scores. Nor did he take into consideration that the environment and education that he had provided Deborah at Vineland had made her into a capable, productive young woman. He decided that if the test score was in the range labeled "feebleminded," then she must be feebleminded. This is another example of reification. Goddard assumed that the score was more descriptive of Deborah than were his direct observations of her. Not surprisingly, Goddard decided that the "cause" of Deborah's feeblemindedness was her heredity or the fact that she came from "bad stock" (Chase, 146).

Goddard dispatched his assistant, Ms. Kite, to trace the history of the Kallikak family in order to discover Deborah's "bad stock." Kite discovered that Deborah descended from one "Martin Kallikak" who, in 1776, had fathered an illegitimate child by a tavern girl. From her perspective in 1912, Kite decided that the waitress must have been "feebleminded." From this union came 480 descendants. Neither Goddard nor Kite had any way of knowing much about these descendants, but Goddard decided that 143 of them were "feebleminded." Martin Kallikak later married a Quakeress, who, Kite and Goddard concluded, must have been "respectable" or of good stock because she came from a "good family." There were 496 descendants from this union, and, not surprisingly, Goddard tells us they proved to be good citizens. Deborah Kallikak obviously must have been descended from the line of the feebleminded tavern girl.

You can undoubtedly understand how many unproven assumptions there were in Goddard's reasoning. For our purposes, we are interested in one: Goddard's research assistant, Kite, exemplifies how a concept can affect our perceptions, leading us to interpret what we see in a way that confirms our prior assumptions. Kite was one of those intuitive women Goddard later used at Ellis Island. She was not a trained biologist or psychologist. She had received a few weeks of "training" from Goddard on how to spot the "feebleminded" and was dispatched to the pine barrens of New Jersey to study Deborah's relatives. From these visits, she determined not only the mental fitness of those she actually met, but the mental fitness of their relatives and their dead progenitors (Chase, 150).

Trained to spot mental defects, she spotted them, even when environmental conditions strongly suggested that she ought to consider other causes for what she saw. Kite went to visit a boy from the "bad stock" of the Kallikaks, a boy who had lost his hearing when he contracted scarlet fever. She visited the family in their hovel on a cold day in February. This is how Goddard described what she saw and the causes she assigned:

> Used as she was to the sights of misery and degradation, she was hardly prepared for the spectacle within. The father, a strong, healthy, broad-shouldered

man, was sitting helplessly in a corner. The mother, a pretty woman still, with remnants of ragged garments drawn about her, sat in a chair, the picture of despondency. Three children, scantily clad and with shoes that would barely hold together, stood about with drooping jaws and the unmistakable look of the feeble-minded.

When Kite met the deaf child, "a glance sufficed to establish his mentality, which was low" (Chase, 151).

Neither Kite nor Goddard considered the possibility that they were observing the effects of cold, disease, malnutrition, and despair, or if they did, then they assumed that such poverty was caused by the genetic defects that led people to be so nonproductive as to be naturally poverty stricken. Just how firmly Goddard believed in biological determinism is revealed in the way he concludes this passage: "The whole family was a living demonstration of the futility of trying to make desirable citizens from defective stock through making and enforcing cumpulsory education laws" (Chase, 152).

Kite was evidently the unwitting victim of the way reified conceptions can make us discover what we expect to discover. By 1928, Goddard himself had recanted on a number of positions. For one thing, he admitted that he had set the scores for feeblemindedness too high. For another, he acknowledged that "morons" could become self-sufficient given proper education. He also acknowledged the statistical improbability that morons, if allowed to reproduce, would weaken the population by producing imbeciles or idiots—this from a man who had earlier advocated segregating "morons" or sterilizing them. Goddard may have changed his tune, but his original melody lingered on: his studies of the Kallikaks, which were widely read in general, were used by eugenicists who advocated mass sterilization of the poor and unemployed during the Depression. The Kallikaks study continued to be cited in psychology textbooks as late as 1964 (Chase, 154).

Terman and the Stanford-Binet Test

As the inclusion of the Kallikaks study in fairly recent textbooks indicates, the legacy of the eugenicists has had a pervasive effect on U.S. education. The preconceptions of the eugenicists were, from the beginning, inextricably linked with intelligence testing in the United States. Lewis M. Terman, a professor at Stanford University in 1916, was the man who revised Binet's test and gave it the name familiar today to numerous students who have taken it: the Stanford-Binet Test. It has set the standard for virtually all IQ tests that have followed.

Terman was also the first to promote the massive use of IQ testing in the public schools. He, too, believed that IQ scores revealed inherited and fixed characteristics. He discounted those foolish enough to assume that children of the well-to-do did better on the tests simply because they had better education, medical care, nutrition, and the like: "Practically all of the investigations which have been made of the influence of nature and nurture on mental performance agree in attributing far more to original endowment than to the environment" (Chase, 234).

By 1937, Terman, like Goddard, had changed his tune. He dropped his emphasis on heredity as the "cause" for differences in scores among various groups. He says of such differences that "such data do not, in themselves, offer any conclusive evidence of the relative contributions of genetic and environmental factors in determining the mean differences observed." He also acknowledged that the lower scores of rural children compared with urban children may be caused by "the relatively poorer educational facilities in rural communities" (Gould, 192).

Brigham and the Immigration Restriction Act of 1924

There were others like Goddard and Terman, such as C. C. Brigham, who became secretary of the College Entrance Examination Board and developed the Scholastic Aptitude Test. Using faulty, suspect, and now discredited results from IQ tests administered to U.S. soldiers during World War I, Brigham argued the racial superiority of Anglo-Saxons and Northern Europeans over Jews, Italians, and other immigrant groups, as well as blacks. He argued for restrictions on immigration and "the prevention of the continued propagation of defective strains on the present population" (Gould, 230). His work was influential in the passage of the Immigrant Restriction Act of 1924, which imposed harsh quota restrictions on those of "undesirable stock"; i.e., those from the same groups who had scored "low" on the bogus and faultily administered Army tests. These quotas naturally excluded Jews seeking refuge from Nazi Germany during the 1930s.

Brigham, too, changed his mind. In 1930, he put his finger on the fallacy of reification that Binet had warned against:

> Most psychologists working in the test field have been guilty of a naming fallacy which easily enables them to slide mysteriously from the score on the test to the hypothetical faculty suggested by the name given to the test. Thus, they speak of sensory discrimination, perception, memory, intelligence and the like while the reference is to a certain objective test situation (Gould, 232).

He also acknowledged the worthlessness of the Army tests as support for arguments of innate intelligence. He acknowledged that his way of figuring the scores was in error, so that the "entire hypothetical superstructure of racial differences collapses completely." And he admitted that far from measuring intelligence, the test had measured whether the draftees—many of whom were newly arrived immigrants who did not speak English—understood U.S. language and culture. He admitted that his study of racial and ethnic differences was "pretentious" and "without foundation" (Gould, 233).

Although his apology was sincerely offered, the effects of Brigham's study lived on. It is estimated that the immigration quotas of 1924 barred from immigration up to 6 million Southern, Central, and Eastern Europeans prior to the outbreak of World War II. As Gould observes, "We know what happened to many who wished to leave but had nowhere to go. The paths to destruction are often indirect, but ideas can be agents as sure as guns and bombs" (233).

Summary

One of the liabilities of using concepts is that we can get mixed up and use them or respond to them as we do to concrete terms. Concepts name causes, assign value, and express judgments. When we think that they describe what we can observe directly, we have reified a concept. This can lead us to draw erroneous conclusions and to base harmful or dangerous judgments on them. In the early decades of the twentieth century, psychologists interested in intelligence testing reified the concept of intelligence and assumed that it was caused by a single, inheritable gene. Because they failed to acknowledge that intelligence is a concept we use to explain the cause of behaviors or traits valued by our culture, they also failed to acknowledge that there might be other causes for the scores people received on intelligence tests. Although these psychologists later recanted, their studies were used to foster bigotry and to encourage eugenicists who wished to sterilize social "undesirables," and led to the exclusion of many who wished to enter our country, including those fleeing the Nazi regime. Their early mistakes have also continued to influence U.S. education. We need to use concepts when we want to explain what causes something or when we want to evaluate and judge. But we cloud our reasoning when we reify concepts or use them as terms that describe what we can perceive directly.

ASSIGNMENTS

Assignment I

Drawing upon your own experience, explain to someone else what the term *reify* means. Here are some suggestions:

1. You might use your experience labeling yourself and then destroying the list, as described in the preparatory assignment for this chapter:

Report on the list and your thoughts and feelings about it;
Answer the questions given in the assignment to make the list;
Explain why you gave the answers you did; and

Decide whether or not your response to the list illustrates the problem of reification.

2. You might choose to report on the aptitude tests you took to enter college.

Report on which test or tests you took, where and when you took them, how many people took it at the same time, how much attention or concern you gave to it, how you thought and felt about the testing and the test, what your scores were and what you thought they signified, and what others around you thought about what the test signified;

Explain why you felt and thought as you did. Decide whether or not your response to the score meant that you had reified it. Decide whether or not how others understood the score meant that they had reified it; and

Explain what you think about those test scores now and why.

Assignment II

Show how an understanding of what *reification* means can help us understand what we read. Apply your definition to David L. Rosenhan's "On Being Sane in Insane Places" (see Part IV, Anthology, Section Three) and Daniel Goleman's "Major Personality Study Finds That Traits Are Mostly Inherited" (see Part IV, Anthology, Section Four). Do both articles provide examples of how people reify terms?

PART III

Writing Process

Chapter 22

Taking Notes on Lectures

Preparing to Listen

Because a professor intends to test you on the contents of lectures or expects you to draw upon them for writing assignments, learning to listen attentively, to take effective notes, and to review them are part of the writing process. One of the things we have learned about how people listen is that their attention wanders after about ten minutes unless they concentrate. Here are some suggestions to help you concentrate:

1. Select a seat near the front of the room or hall to be sure you can hear what is said;
2. Arrive a few minutes early and review your notes for the assigned reading and the previous lecture;
3. Bring the assigned reading with you, refer to the text when your professor does, and mark the passage;
4. Pay particular attention to the professor's opening remarks; generally, they indicate what the subject will be;
5. Note anything the professor puts on the chalkboard or overhead projector. Usually, he or she regards these as particularly important;
6. Be aware of yourself as the member of an audience. Do not distract yourself, other students, or the professor by arriving late, talking, yawning, reading the newspaper, blowing bubble gum, or the like; and
7. Bring pencils, pens, and paper.

Taking Notes

Remember, no matter how inchoate the lecture may seem to you, the professor assumes that he or she is giving an organized presentation. Your job is to figure out what the underlying organization is. Another way to say this is that you need to figure out how the information, generalizations, and interpretations connect. You should also take the kinds of notes that will remind you of your reactions to the lecture and your questions about it. When you hear something that strikes you as significant, mark the note with a *****. If the professor says something you do not understand, mark the note with a **?** Whenever he or she offers an interpretation, make sure you attempt a silent dialogue. Mark that note with a **Yes!** or a **No!** or a **Is he kidding?** or a **Why does she think so?** And when your professor gives you a new inspiration, insight, or idea, mark your notes with an **Aha!** or a **!** or a **Wow!**

It is as important to review your lecture notes as it is to review your reading. Set aside time after every lecture for a course, and before the next one, to go over your notes. Again, have your pencil or pen in hand, and have a place in your notebook for this regular review. Begin by looking up any terms the professor used that you did not understand. Write them down. Review the notes until you are sure you understand how the professor was using the terms in context.

Then, spend a few minutes on each of the following:

1. Summarize, in your own words, what you took to be the main point the instructor was trying to make.
2. Write down what struck you as significant. Why?
3. What did you have trouble understanding? Write these out as questions that you will ask your professor.
4. On what points do you and the professor agree? Why? On what do you disagree? Why?
5. What insight, ideas, or inspirations did the lecture generate?
6. What do you anticipate the professor will cover in the next lecture?
7. What do you wish the professor would cover in the next lecture?

You will find that keeping this kind of notebook helps you to understand the lectures in a course. By carefully reviewing one lecture, you prepare yourself to listen to the next. And as you accumulate notes and responses, you accumulate potential ideas for essays. Taking careful notes also provides you with a basis for developing a sound relationship with your professor. If you have carefully reviewed your notes, you are prepared to ask questions in class, questions that can clarify any muddles about the subject that you find yourself in. If your professor does not allow time for discussion, he or she anticipates that you will come to the office during office hours. Professors post their office hours on their office doors, or give them to the office staff, or provide them on the syllabus.

These hours constitute a standing invitation to any student who wants to come and ask questions or discuss ideas.

In Part IV, Anthology, Section One, you will find a discussion of notetaking from Jules R. Benjamin's *A Student's Guide to History.* Study carefully his comparision of poor and effective notetaking. Then examine your own notes. Are there ways you might improve your method for taking notes on lectures?

Chapter 23

Journals

Why Writers Keep Journals

The hardest part of journal writing seems to be getting started, yet the satisfaction and benefits of keeping journals make the effort worthwhile. Because journals are above all reflections of an individual's interests and purposes, there are no rules for keeping journals, only advice.

Perhaps the most fundamental reason for keeping a journal is our own curiosity about ourselves because, as George Simons puts it in *Keeping Your Personal Journal* (New York: Paulist Press, 1978):

> We note the stories of others, as well as those of ourselves, with awe and follow them with an insatiable curiosity. Beneath it all is the suspicion that our commonness reveals some truth, and by sharing what we know of ourselves, we are confirmed in the validity of our humanity though each of us writes or wants to write a unique script. (21)

This strikes me as a succinct statement of the ultimate aim of all effective writing. Writing in a journal has the pragmatic effect of letting us rehearse what we might later wish to share with others in a more public form of discourse—such as an essay—without having to worry about whether we have said it in its best or most polished way. But even aside from such pragmatic purposes, a journal can serve as our own testament of self-discovery, a way of confirming our own humanity to ourselves simply by recording our sense of the past and the present, our hopes and fears of the future, our reflections on what we experience and learn, and our inner selves. One reason that individuals keep journals, then, is for self-discovery.

Some journals are kept with the intent of later publishing them—that is, of sharing them with a wider audience. John Kenneth Galbraith's *Ambassador's Journal: A Personal Account of the Kennedy Years* (see Part IV, Anthology, Section One) was begun because Galbraith was aware of his moment in history as ambassador to India. He began his journal to record not only for himself but for posterity the details of his experiences.

Very often, writers keep journals for a purpose halfway between a desire for a purely personal record and a desire to publish the journal itself. Francis Parkman, as a young social historian, set off to explore the Oregon Trail in 1846 with the special intention of understanding the customs of the various Indian tribes. His journals became the source for his later work, *The Oregon Trail* (see Part IV, Anthology, Section One). Professional journals are often kept for this purpose, as illustrated by the excerpts from the notebooks of anthropologists Clayton A. and Carole Robarchek, which they kept while doing fieldwork among the Semai of Malaysia (see Part IV, Anthology, Section One). Their journals naturally focus on the behaviors and customs of the Semai because they intended to publish their findings. Such journals often serve the additional purpose of providing writers with an opportunity to comment on their own writing, and on what they read, as a way of consciously improving their own self-expression. A journal in which to comment on assigned reading and critique your own writing can be a very important one for you to keep. (see Part IV, Anthology, Section One).

Assigned Journals

Students are often assigned to write journals in various classes. Usually these journals are intended to serve the purpose halfway between an entirely personal journal and a journal written with the intention of publishing the journal itself; that is, they are intended to serve a purpose similar to the journals kept by Parkman or a fieldworker. Students in a course requiring observation—such as psychology, sociology, biology, composition, anthropology, or education—may be asked to keep journals on matters relevant to the course, to be used later as a source for more extended, formal discourse. The same is often true for students enrolled in classes that emphasize reasoned opinion, meditation, introspection, or imagination—such as journalism, political science, composition, literature, religion, or creative writing. Such journals are undertaken with a specific purpose in mind, and usually the professor will provide some guidelines for entries. Often, the professor will assume that the student will maintain the journal, even if it is ungraded. In such cases, assigned journals serve the same purpose as other ungraded work, such as notes on lectures or readings. The professor assumes—usually correctly—that whether or not the student kept up the journal writing will be revealed in the quality of graded work. Sometimes, however, such assigned journals are used in class for discussion, in which case, you will be called upon to read from your journal occasionally or perhaps to turn it in for review and comment. Such journals are similar in purpose to that kept by Galbraith; that is, a journal intended to be made public at some time.

Unassigned Journals

It is worth considering keeping a journal—or journals—even when you are not asked to. We have already discussed the reasons why. Writing is a process; a journal serves the pragmatic purpose of allowing you to collect information, reflect upon it, comment on your own writing, consider what makes for effective writing, discover and change your own ideas, all prior to having to attempt a well-organized, polished expression of your ideas for a given purpose. And a journal provides you with a personal reward as well, an opportunity to express thoughts and feelings that might otherwise find no expression, as well as an opportunity to record yourself, to collect together the fragments of existence that memory alone would soon forget. You might wish to keep a separate journal for all your courses that will require writing, or you might wish to keep a single journal in which you include your personal self-account, as well as reflections upon what you study. It is up to you. The journals included in the Anthology are intended among other things to help you decide what approach might best suit you.

Chapter 24

A College Writing Class Notebook

As suggested in the last chapter, there are many possible formats for class journals or notebooks. You should choose a method for keeping notes that suits you. The suggestions offered here are just that—suggestions. You might find this format useful for keeping track of the work you do in this class.

You might wish to keep a three-ring, looseleaf notebook with divided sections, so that you can add materials to each section. You might include the following sections:

Writer's Diary

Writers are idiosyncratic. For one thing, they often have special times when their minds are ready for writing. Some find they write very easily after they have gone jogging or after a morning shower. Agatha Christie, the famous mystery writer, said—though I find it hard to believe—"The best time for planning a book is while you're doing the dishes."

Writers also have some setting especially conducive to writing. Edna Ferber said, "The ideal view for daily writing, hour on hour, is the blank brick wall of a cold-storage warehouse. Failing this, a stretch of sky will do, cloudless if possible." Obviously, Edna avoided distractions. Henry Vollam Morton, on the other hand, wrote, "The perfect place for a writer is in the hideous roar of a city, with men making a new road under his window in competition with a barrel organ, and on the mat a man waiting for the rent." The Indian Prime Minister Jawaharlal Nehru, wrote best in a unique setting: "All my major works have been written in prison. . . . I would recommend prison not only to aspiring writers, but to aspiring politicians, too."

Writers also have totems, articles with the special power to help them write. The noted author Saul Bellow has two manual Royal typewriters, one for writing fiction, one for writing nonfiction. Willam Faulkner said, "The tools I need for my work are paper, tobacco, food, and a little whiskey." One wonders how he wrote without a pen or typewriter.

The writer's diary is intended to help you discover the times and places when it is easiest for you to write. It will also help you to identify your writing totems. Each time you read or write for this class, you might record the date, time, and place using the form in Fig. 24.1. By consulting your diary at the end of each week, you should notice what conditions are best suited to you; you should, in other words, discover your idiosyncracies as a writer.

Date: **Time Started:**
                                                                 Time Ended:
Activity: **Total:**

thinking	reading	editing
drafting	revising	consulting
proofreading	typing	notetaking

Environment:
Setting:

Conducive to
writing/studying?

Helpful totems:

My Boxes: What kept me from reading, writing, or thinking effectively?

My Cheering Section: Did I get a bright idea? A good grade on an essay? Stick to my schedule? Something else related to reading, writing, or thinking?

Fig. 24.1 Writer's diary. The writer's diary is intended to help you discover the times and places when it is easiest for you to write. It will also help you identify your writing totems. Each time you work on your writing—whether you are reading, writing, or thinking—record it on a form like this one.

It is also the place for you to notice what self-induced handicaps are preventing you from writing effectively. Some students become so concerned about "not making any mistakes" or "not sounding stupid" that they freeze at the sight of a blank sheet of paper. Others delay starting an assignment so long that they write in ways that they do not respect and that do not reflect their true abilities. By becoming aware of the boxes you put yourself into, you can discover how to get out of them and stay out.

Finally, the diary is the place for you to start your own cheering section. When you have a bright idea for an essay, or get back an essay with a good grade, or stick to your schedule and get your work finished on time, record the moment. It is as important to nurture yourself as it is to notice what bad habits you need to shed.

Reading Notes

In this section, you might keep your notes on the assigned readings.

Lecture Notes

In this section, you might keep notes on any lectures your instructor gives or asks you to attend.

Think Tank

This section is for the assigned exercises. It is also the section in which you will hold all the preparatory writing you do for an assigned essay— your notes to remind yourself of ideas, your drafts, and your revisions.

Correcting Errors

In this section, you might note any common difficulties you have, such as words you frequently misspell or common errors in grammar and punctuation. You might write out the corrections your instructor indicates on your essays or include any exercises you are assigned to correct errors.

Done But Not Forgotten

This section will hold all the essays you write for this course. Some of the assignments in this textbook will ask you to refer to earlier essays and either respond to what you have written or revise previous work. You will need to save all the essays you write for this course.

Chapter 25

Taking Notes on Readings

Reading and notetaking are essential elements of the writing process. Throughout this discussion, the references to "reading" something assumes multiple readings. Grasping a writer's purpose, arguments, and evidence rarely comes with one reading or even with two. *Reading* should be understood to mean "reading and rereading." Be sure as well to circle any words new to you or familiar words used in a new way. Look these up and write the definitions in the text. We will be discussing two kinds of reading notes. *Marginal notes* are the notes a reader makes on the page itself. *Notes* are the notes a reader writes on paper. One productive way for you to take reading notes is to make marginal notes first and then take notes.

In general, what a reader looks for are the writer's purpose and how he or she achieves it. In nonfiction, the writer's purpose is to convince you of his or her position, and the way a writer achieves the purpose is through arguments and evidence. When taking notes, then, the first goal is to identify the writer's purpose, arguments, and evidence.

General Considerations

When you make marginal notes, be sure to record your responses to what you read. You might try using:

* to indicate an important or significant passage;

! to indicate surprise;

No! to indicate disagreement;

Yes! to indicate agreement; and

Huh? or **?** to indicate what you do not yet understand.

When you take notes on readings, remember to do three things. First, be sure you include the *full citation* of what you are reading. You should write down in your notebook the author, title, place of publication, publisher, and date of publication. Second, if you copy what the writer said into your notebook, be sure to put quotation marks around the words. Third, be sure to note in your notebook the pages in the original reading that offer the information or ideas you are noting.

Why should you do these three things? Most often, you will use notes to prepare yourself either for exams or for writing essays. If you want to use the notes for writing essays, you will have to do three things:

1. Provide a complete citation of all your sources. You will have to cite the author, title, place of publication, publisher, and date of publication for all the readings you use in writing your essay. If your notes do not include this information, you will have to go find it when you try to write a paper using this source. This is a waste of your time.

2. Indicate when you are quoting directly. If your notes do not indicate direct quotation, you will not indicate quotations when you write your paper. This could lead your instructor to believe that you are trying to fob off someone else's ideas as your own. This is called *plagiarism*. It is a very serious offense. Don't let it happen to you.

3. Indicate when you are drawing upon ideas gleaned from a reading, even if you don't quote them directly. This means that you will have to give the page numbers in the original reading that contain the ideas you draw upon, even if you have chosen to paraphrase them instead of quoting them directly. Failing to acknowledge the source of ideas is also considered plagiarism. If you do not indicate the page numbers in your notes, then you will have to hunt them up when you write your paper. This is frustrating and time consuming.

Identifying the General Purpose

The first time through a reading, you might want to focus on identifying what kind of discourse the writer offers. Is the writer discussing the *significance* of an action, event, person, place, thing, or text? Is the writer presenting findings on a *hypothesis?* Is the writer proposing solutions to a *problem?* Generally, you will find that the writer is aiming at one of these three purposes. You may, however, sometimes find that the writer is simply presenting a report or summary of the arguments of others. You can look for clues to the purpose in the title, the author's opening statements, the subject the writer chooses, and the closing statements. Clues are also provided in the context for assigned readings. If an anthropology professor asks you to read Margaret Mead's *Coming of Age in Samoa,* for instance, you can reasonably guess that you are being asked to read a work in which the author tests a hypothesis relevant to the social sciences. If your literature teacher asks you to read critical commentary on *Moby-Dick,* you are safe in assuming that the article will comment on the significance of something Melville offers in the novel. If your political science professor asks you to read George F. Kennan's "A Proposal for International Disarmament," you can assume that you are being asked to read a proposal to solve a problem.

The first reading, then, might be most beneficially used as an opportunity to identify what kind of discourse you are reading; that is, what the writer's overall purpose is. Subsequent readings can be used to identify what the writer's position is and how he or she goes about presenting it.

Reading a Presentation of Findings: Marginal Notes

A presentation of findings usually includes the following elements:

Field-Dependent Question: A question related to the field;

Given, Called a Hypothesis: The answer that the writer assumed he or she would find;

Methodology: How the observer set about to test the hypothesis;

Position or Conclusions, Called Findings: Whether the observations provided confirmatory, disconfirmatory, inconclusive, serendipitous results, or some combination of these;

Reasons, Called Generalizations: The writer's reasons for coming to the conclusion that he or she reaches. Descriptive generalizations tell what the writer observed as typical action or behavior; analytic generalizations assign cause;

Evidence: The presentation of what the writer observed; and

Implications: The writer's thoughts about what he or she learned and about what else might be learned from further studies.

Your goal as a reader should be to identify these parts in a writer's presentation of findings. As you read, you should use *marginal notes* to mark those elements; then you can use the marginal notes as guides for making your *notes in a notebook.*

When reading the presentation of a finding, it makes some sense to begin by seeking the field-dependent question that generates the hypothesis. You will find that writers locate this information in different places. Often, it is offered in the opening statement, but sometimes it is not. Assume, for instance, that we are reading the chapter "The Girl in Conflict'' from Margaret Mead's *Coming of Age in Samoa* (see Part IV, Anthology, Section Four). This is how she begins:

> Were there no conflicts, no temperaments which deviated so markedly from the normal that clash was inevitable? Was the diffused affection and the diffused authority of the large families, the ease of moving from one family to another, the knowledge of sex and the freedom to experiment a sufficient guarantee to all Samoan girls of a perfect adjustment? In almost all cases, yes. But I have reserved for this chapter the tales of the few girls who deviated in temperament or in conduct, although in many cases these deviations were only charged with the possibilities of conflict, and actually had no painful results.

Although this briefly summarizes the findings Mead has presented in the preceding chapters and gives a clear indication of her purpose in this chapter, it does not indicate the field-dependent question that gave rise to the study in the first place. Mead gives this earlier in the book. Her interest was in testing the assumption that adolescence—the transition from childhood to adulthood—is always a time of conflict and stress for the adolescent. Is that assumption correct? Her hypothesis was that, No, it was not, and that her observations would probably provide a disconfirmatory instance of that assumption.

To grasp what Mead intends in this chapter, then, we would necessarily have to recall the question she asked initially and her hypothesis—that is, her educated guess about what answer she would discover. You will find it helps enormously when reading a book-length presentation of findings if, at the beginning of every chapter, you write down—as a marginal note—the question and hypothesis the writer has announced earlier as the context for the study, and indicate on what page or pages in the book you could find that statement.

In shorter articles, the writer will usually present the field-dependent question that gave rise to the study. This statement is often near the beginning, as it is in David L. Rosenhan's ''On Being Sane in Insane Places'' (see Part IV, Anthology, Section Three). His first statement is the question, ''If sanity and insanity exist, how shall we know them?'' Now, an unskilled reader might mark that sentence, *field-dependent question*, and move on, confident that he or she had found all that Rosenhan had to say about it. A more skilled reader would look further. This is the fourth paragraph of his article:

> At its heart, the question of whether the sane can be distinguished from the insane (and whether degrees of insanity can be distinguished from one another) is a simple matter: do the salient characterisitics that lead to diagnoses reside in the patients themselves or in the environments and contexts in which observers find them? From Bleuler, through Kretchmer, through the formulators of the recently revised *Diagnostic and Statistical Manual* of the American Psychiatric Association, the belief has been strong that patients can be categorized, and, implicitly, that the sane are distinguishable from the insane. More

recently, however, this belief has been questioned. Based in part on theoretical and anthropological considerations, but also on philosophical, legal, and therapeutic ones, the view has grown that psychological categorization of mental illness is useless at best and downright harmful, misleading, and pejorative at worst. Psychiatric diagnoses, in this view, are in the minds of the observers and are not valid summaries of characteristics displayed by the observed.

This is Rosenhan's fully developed statement of the field-dependent question he seeks to answer. In your copy of this essay, you might want to mark it, *field-dependent question,* and run a line down the margin beside it.

We have already identified Mead's hypothesis. What about Rosenhan's? Does he state what he thought he would discover? A careful reader will have noticed the clue in his third sentence: "However much we may be personally convinced that we can tell the normal from the abnormal, the evidence is simply not compelling." You would mark this sentence and the supporting evidence he cites as *hypothesis.* Then, you should recall that a hypothesis is frequently a statement about cause. Is there more to Rosenthal's presentation than just the finding of a confirmatory instance that professionals in a psychiatric hospital cannot tell the normal from the abnormal? Is there also a hypothesis about cause? Read his article again. If you find that he assigns cause, mark it *hypothesis.* You may find more than one.

What about the methodology? Again, you may find this presented succinctly in a paragraph or two, or you may have to search the text for indications of it. In Mead's *Coming of Age in Samoa,* for instance, you would find throughout the book explanations of where the study was conducted, for how long, and how many people were observed: in the opening chapter, in the appendices, and in the chapters themselves. In the chapter "The Girl in Conflict," we are four pages into the discussion before Mead tells us that her findings on "upwardly deviant" female adolescents are based on observations of "seven girls in the household of one native pastor [and] . . . three in the household of the other," all of whom were past puberty. We are 16 pages into the study before she tells us that her findings on delinquency are based on observations of two females: one who had just achieved puberty and one who had achieved it two years earlier. Your marginal notes for this chapter, then, would include the headnote *Methodology,* followed by references to those pages in the book that tell about the observations in general. You would also want to write *methodology* in the chapter margins where Mead provides the information.

Rosenhan both gives a general explanation of the methodology near the beginning of his article and indicates throughout his discussion what observational techniques were used. Mark *all* those passages in which Rosenhan explains how he set about answering the field-dependent questions. In the margins next to the passages, write *method.*

Mead gives her *statement of findings* at the outset of her chapter, informing us that although some signs of conflict and stress were observed among the female adolescents, "in many cases these deviations were only charged with possibilities of conflict, and actually had no painful results." Rosenhan gives his statement of findings at the end of his article:

> It is clear that we cannot distinguish the sane from the insane in psychiatric hospitals. The hospital itself imposes a special environment in which the meanings of behavior can easily be misunderstood. The consequences to patients hospitalized in such an environment—the powerlessness, depersonalization, segregation, mortification, and self-labeling—seem undoubtedly counter-therapeutic.

Mark such passages *findings.* A writer is obligated to provide reasons for coming to the findings and evidence to support the reasons. What does Mead have to show? What does Rosenhan?

When we are reading the reasons and evidence provided in a statement of findings, we are reading inductive arguments. We have discussed the characteristics of such arguments in other chapters (Chapters 9 and 10). You might wish to review them now, or, if you have not yet read them, take the time to do so now.

Once a reader has identified the findings—that is, the writer's position or conclusions—then the reader necessarily has to seek out the writer's reasons for coming to those conclusions and the evidence he or she offers to support them. There are two kinds of reasons offered: descriptive generalizations and analytic generalizations. The evidence offered in a presentation of findings always includes either a description of direct observations or statistical evidence, or both. It can also include reference to other studies—that is, it can use other authorities as evidence. In your marginal notes, you might want to underline the generalizations and in the margin write *analytical generalization* or *descriptive generalization.* You might want to extend a line down the margins beside the passages presenting evidence, write *evidence* in the margin, and draw an arrow to the generalization it is intended to support.

To understand a generalization, a reader necessarily bears in mind the findings the writer is intending to support. Mead, remember, is trying to show that although there was deviation from the norm—that is, from the typical absence of conflict in the life of a female adolescent—these deviations were only potential sources of conflict and rarely resulted in a genuine clash between the female and members of her society. To support this finding, Mead will have to show potential sources of conflict and illustrate that they rarely resulted in any kind of social friction. Mead locates one source of potential conflict in the missionaries. Their religious tenets were at odds with the values of the culture because the missionaries advocated celibacy prior to marriage. Mead needs to show that when a female sought education at the missionary school, the conflicting sexual mores of the missionaries and the Samoan culture did not result in any turmoil for her. Mead offers this analytic generalization: "the attitude of the church in respect to chastity held only the germs of a conflict which was seldom realised, because of the flexibility with which it adapted itself to the nearly inevitable." She supports this generalization with descriptive generalizations and descriptions of direct observations. Reread this chapter, marking those passages that support this generalization. You will find that they appear both before and after the generalization. Draw arrows from the supporting passages to this statement so that you have a way of remembering how this argument is presented.

Rosenhan offers this descriptive generalization: "Having once been labeled schizophrenic, there is nothing the pseudopatient can do to overcome the tag. The tag profoundly colors others' perceptions of him and his behavior." Underline this and mark it *descriptive generalization.* Now draw a vertical line beside all the passages that provide the evidence to support this generalization. Mark them *evidence,* and draw arrows back to the generalization. How many different kinds of evidence does Rosenhan provide?

Do Mead and Rosenhan comment on the implications of their studies? Usually, the writer presents a discussion of implications at the end of his or her discussion, although, again, a reader needs to be alert to those instances in which a writer comments on the implications along the way. Read both again. Mark *implications* if you find the writer considering what he or she has learned from the study (not just summarizing it), suggesting other possible studies, or making recommendations based on the study results.

Taking Notes on a Presentation of Findings

Once you have made good marginal notes, you can turn to taking notes on a reading. You will use these notes when you study for exams or prepare essays, so it is a very good idea to take the time to record notes carefully. First, be sure you write across the top of the page the full citation:

EXAMPLE

Rosenhan, David L. "On Being Sane in Insane Places." <u>Science</u> 179 (1973): 250-58.

Then, leave a margin so that you can note page numbers alongside your notes:

p. 54   FIELD-DEPENDENT QUESTION:
         Rosenhan takes as his question: "do the salient characteristics
         that lead to diagnoses reside in the patients themselves or in the
         environments and contexts in which observers find them?"

Keeping account of the page numbers in the margin will let you readily notice when you have forgotten to note them. You can then correct the omission. It is very important to keep track of the page numbers.

Notice also that in the example, the notetaker has placed quotation marks around the direct quotations. Be sure you do this when you take notes.

As for the format you choose, you should choose any format that suits you, but it should be one which leads you to take substantial enough notes. Your notes should provide a complete and accurate record of the characteristics of this kind of discourse: the field-dependent question, the hypothesis, the methodology, the findings, the generalizations, the evidence, and the implications. Your notes should also remind you how the discourse hangs together—how the question generates the hypothesis, how the findings relate to the hypothesis, how the generalizations support the findings, how the generalizations are supported by evidence, and how the implications derive from the findings.

One easy way to take notes on this kind of discourse is to organize them around the elements the writer has to include. I'll start notes, and then you try finishing them:

Rosenhan, David L. "On Being Sane in Insane Places." <u>Science</u> 179 (1973): 250-58.

p. 54   FIELD-DEPENDENT QUESTION:
         Rosenhan wants to know, "If sanity and insanity exist, how shall we
         know them?" His more detailed version of the question is "do the
         salient characteristics that lead to diagnoses reside in the
         patients themselves or in the environments and contexts in which
         observers find them?"

p. 55   METHODOLOGY:
         Rosenhan conducted two different experiments.
         I. He sent eight "sane people" to 12 different hospitals. The group
         included:

p. 56   one psychology graduate student in his 20s
         three psychologists
         one pediatrician
         one psychiatrist
         one painter
         one housewife
         Females = 3
         Males = 5

         The pseudopatients used pseudonyms. Those in the health profes-
         sions gave other professions as their occupations. Except for when
         Rosenhan admitted himself, no one in the hospital knew this was an
         experiment.

A variety of hospitals were used as sites:
Five different states
Some "old and shabby"; some "new";
Some were research hospitals; some were not;
Some had sufficient staff; some did not.
One was private; the rest received public funding.

p. 57   Each pseudopatient called for an appointment, then complained of hearing voices that said things like "empty, hollow, and thud." Rosenhan says these were chosen because they are symptoms of a person who is saying, "My life is empty and hollow." But Rosenhan says he chose the symptoms because the psychological research contains no reference to psychosis with these symptoms. At least that's what I think he means.

The pseudopatients gave their "real life" history, except for the changes noted. Once admitted, they behaved "normally," which included a brief period of nervousness because they feared their fraud would be detected. The pseudopatients told staff they felt fine and that the symptoms had ceased. At first they took notes secretly, but then figured out that no one would take any particular notice of them if they took notes openly.

Each pseudopatient was told that he or she would be discharged if he or she convinced the staff that he or she was all right. They were therefore "motivated to behave sanely." Length of hospitalization ranged from 7 to 52 days; averaged 19.

p. 58   The pseudopatients observed how staff and patients interacted, including how much contact-time there was, how patients' efforts at contact were treated, how the patients were treated effectively, and nonverbal behavior, such as eye contact (referred to variously throughout the article).

p. 59   II. In a different experiment, Rosenhan told the staff of a hospital that at some time during a three-month period, "one or more pseudo-patients" would try to be admitted. But Rosenhan did not send any pseudopatients. The hospital was a research and teaching hospital.

HYPOTHESES:
I. Rosenhan assumes that even though we may be "convinced" that "we can tell the normal from the abnormal, the evidence is simply not compelling."

p. 71   FINDING:
Confirmatory instance. "It is clear that we cannot distinguish the sane from the insane in psychiatric hospitals."

p. 58   REASON FOR FINDING/GENERALIZATION:
"Despite their public 'show' of sanity, the pseudopatients were never detected by staff," but they were by other patients.

EVIDENCE:
"Admitted, except in one case, with a diagnosis of schizophrenia, each was discharged with a diagnosis of schizophrenia 'in remission.' "
"During the first three hospitalizations, when accurate counts were kept, 35 of the total of 118 patients . . . voiced their suspicions, some vigorously." Example: "You're not crazy. You're a journalist, or a professor [referring to the continual note taking]. You're checking up on the hospital."

p. 58   II. HYPOTHESIS OF CAUSE:
Rosenhan assumes there are several causes for this inability to distinguish the sane from the insane. One is that "physicians operate with a strong bias toward what statisticians call the type 2 error"; which means they are more "inclined to call a healthy person sick (a false positive, type 2) than a sick person healthy (a false negative, type 1)."

p. 59   FINDING:
Confirmatory instance of hypothesis of a bias toward finding a false positive or false negative.

REASON FOR FINDING/GENERALIZATION:
"The tendency to designate sane people as insane can be reversed when the stakes (in this case, prestige and diagnostic acumen) are high."

EVIDENCE:
When told that pseudopatients would try to be admitted during a three-month period, those involved in admitting patients gave the following diagnoses:
41 called "pseudopatients" with "high confidence" by "at least one" staff member;
23 suspected of being pseudopatients by "at least one psychiatrist";
19 suspected of being pseudopatients by "one psychiatrist and one other staff member."

With this much to get you started, complete the notes on this article. Below, I've listed the remaining hypotheses Rosenhan tested. Using them as a guide, take notes on the finding, generalizations, and evidence he offers for each. Then take notes on what Rosenhan identifies as the implications of his study. Remember—he may discuss implications throughout and not just at the end.

p. 60   III. HYPOTHESIS OF CAUSE FOR INABILITY TO DISTINGUISH SANE FROM INSANE:
A second cause has to do with effects of labeling. Rosenhan notes the Gestalt psychologists' argument that once a label is assigned, it "colors" the impression of other information about a person.

p. 63   IV. HYPOTHESIS OF CAUSE FOR INABILITY TO DISTINGUISH SANE FROM
INSANE:
A third cause Rosenhan offers as a hypothesis is that hospital workers share the general cultural bias against the mentally ill: "fear,
hostility, aloofness, suspicion, and dread." This attitude,

p. 69   balanced against the opposite--which is the desire to help or care
for the mentally ill--leads to an "ambivalence" on the part of those
who come into contact with the mentally ill.

V. HYPOTHESIS OF CAUSE OF INABILITY TO DISTINGUISH SANE FROM
INSANE:
As a fourth cause, Rosenhan offers the hypothesis that the hierarchical structure of most institutions leads to "depersonalization," which means considering others as an object, or ignoring
them, or treating them abusively. He also guesses that fiscal con-
straints--leading to stress on the part of the staff--can lead to
increased depersonalization.

Reflecting on Your Notes

When you have completed your notes on a presentation of a finding, take
the time to reflect and comment upon what you have read. This is an
important part of your notetaking. It is a way to prepare for writing
assignments that ask you to evaluate what you have read. Here are some
questions you might consider:

1. What are your thoughts on the field-dependent question? Does it
   seem a worthwhile question?
2. What are your thoughts on the hypothesis or hypotheses? Do they
   seem reasonable or too highly speculative?
3. Would you agree that the methodology was suited to testing the
   hypothesis or hypotheses? Could you think of another methodology
   that might be used that would yield similar results? Different
   results? Does the methodology present any ethical questions?
4. Does the finding seem to derive from the observations or does the
   writer have to stretch a point?
5. Are the descriptive generalizations tied closely to the description of
   observations? Are the analytic generalizations closely tied to the evidence? Might other generalizations have been made about the same
   evidence? Are there other possible explanations the writer did not
   consider? Has the writer presented well-qualified inductive arguments that clearly indicate the degree of probability we should
   attach to the generalizations?
6. Is sufficient evidence provided to support the generalizations? Is it
   presented vividly and in detail? Has the writer given the impression
   that all the evidence was included or does the writer seem to have
   excluded some relevant evidence or evidence that might not have
   supported the finding?

7. Do you agree with what the writer says are the implications of the study? Can you think of other implications that he or she did not mention?

Reading About Significance: Marginal Notes

This kind of writing has the following characteristics:

Given: The writer assumes that human experience ought to be explored; that is, the writer assumes that he or she is writing for someone interested in knowing what the writer has to say about what our responses to experience reveal about human character, motivations, values, or judgments;

Given: A second given is the experience the writer has had: "Given that I had this experience, what did it signify?" *Experience* can mean anything from stealing pears as a child to having a response to a work of art or to a text;

Position/Conclusion: The writer's position or conclusion is what he or she has decided the experience signified;

Reasons: The writer naturally tells why he or she felt the experience signified what he or she thinks it did; the reasons consist of the writer's reported thoughts and feelings about the various aspects of the experience;

Evidence: The writer naturally wants to illustrate why the various episodes gave rise to his or her thoughts and feelings. The evidence, then, is the vivid and detailed description of the experience.

It is useful first to identify what the writer takes the subject to be; that is, what is it that the writer takes as significant. Sometimes, the title tells you; for example, see the following selections in Part IV, Anthology, Section Two: "The Slit"; "The Way to Rainy Mountain"; "Once More to the Lake"; "Meditation II: Of the Nature of the Human Mind; and that it is more easily known than the Body"; and "Anorexia Nervosa: Psychopathology as the Crystallization of Culture."

Now, the question for the reader is: How does the writer get us—the readers—from contemplating the subject or the thing described to apprehending its significance as the writer does? Naturally, this question means that we have to figure out the movement of the writer's thoughts on the subject—how he or she gets us from considering the subject to considering his or her conclusions about it. Sometimes the writer simply tells us this information at the outset, as does Susan Bordo in "Anorexia Nervosa: Psychopathology as the Crystallization of Culture":

> Psychopathology, as Jules Henry has said, "is the final outcome of all that is wrong with a culture." In no case is this more strikingly true than in the case of anorexia nervosa and bulimia, barely known a century ago, yet reaching epidemic proportions today. Far from being the result of a superficial fashion phenomenon, these disorders, I will argue, reflect and call our attention to some of

the central ills of our culture—from our historical heritage of disdain for the body, to our modern fear of loss of control over our futures, to the disquieting meaning of contemporary beauty ideals in an era of greater female presence and power than ever before.

When we get a nice, straightforward statement of the writer's position at the outset, we can see what we will necessarily mark in the marginal notes.

Given that:
"Anorexia and bulimia, barely known a century ago" have reached "epidemic proportions today";
Position:
These disorders are a *sign of* some of the "central ills of our culture";
Reasons:
These disorders are signs of:

1. "our historical heritage of disdain for the body";
2. "our modern fear of loss of control over our futures"; and
3. "the disquieting meaning of contemporary beauty ideals in an era of greater female presence and power than ever before."

You need to understand that what you would look for and mark with marginal notes are those parts of the article in which Bordo offers evidence in support of those three propositions.

But not all writing about signs is presented in this style. When the "sign" is an experience unique to the writer—rather than a matter of public knowledge—he or she often adopts a reflective style; that is, the writer presents some aspect of the experience, and then comments on what he or she takes as significant about it, often also explaining why. Then the writer presents another aspect of the experience—another moment or fragment—and comments on it. This reflective commentary is cumulative, referring back to what was said and building upon it, so that through repetition and expansion the writer gradually accrues meaning to the subject.

Taking Notes

To understand how to take notes on this kind of writing, consider the question you as a reader are challenged to answer: How did the writer get the reader to share an understanding about the significance of this subject? This question is of a different order than, What is the capital of Nigeria? For that last question, there is a right answer that the questioner knows. But when in your course work you are confronted with the question we are asking here, the questioner does not know the answer. Look at the first question again; notice that the questioner wants to know something about the *reader* and his or her understanding of the *writer*. No one can know the answer to that question except the reader who reports on his or her understanding of what the writer says. Another way of asking the question, then, is: What did you learn about yourself from reading this? The "you" here is not taken as a plural; it means the singular you, you as an individual confronting a text written by someone who wants to communicate to you something about human nature by explaining how he or she understands an experience, action, event, condition, object, or text.

This suggests that the kind of notetaking called for is very much both a kind of self-reflective commentary and a dialogue with the writer. The questions that generate your notes might most productively be, Why did the writer say so? and What do I make of it? In short, you are in the position of identifying for yourself the *significance* of the text. Of what is it a sign?

How you go about taking such notes is up to you, but you should select a way that gives you the freedom to explore your responses to the text and to then test whether or not they have anything to do with what the writer conveys. This last consideration is important because sometimes readers carelessly misread the writer.

Let's consider some techniques for taking these sorts of notes. We are going to focus on taking notes from writing in the reflective style. The notetaking for the expository style used by Bardo would be similar to the style used for taking notes on a proposed solution to a problem, which we will discuss later. Your marginal notes on an essay about an experience unique to the writer will indicate the reflective commentary the writer makes and will show how one comment or passage seems to connect with another. When you take notes on this kind of reflective essay, one useful technique is to take one such passage and then seek an analogy in yourself. Here, for instance, is a reflective passage from St. Augustine (see Part IV, Anthology, Section Two):

> It was the sport, which, as it were, tickled our hearts, that we beguiled, those who little thought what we were doing, and much misliked it.

Take some time to meditate in writing upon this passage. Is it analogous with your own experience? What, for instance, would you make of Augustine's observation "[we] little thought what we were doing, and much misliked it"? He's reflecting upon a boyish prank, stealing pears from his father's orchard. Can you recall anything like that in your past? Any time you did what you were not supposed to do in the company of some pals? Any feelings you can recollect similar to Augustine's? Start writing. Don't censor yourself. This is for you alone. It's your own inquiry.

When you have written all you can think of, stop and reread. Now ask yourself, Why? Write some more, stopping only when you have written all that you can think of.

Now take another look at Augustine. How does he answer the question, Why?

> O friendship too unfriendly! thou incomprehensible inveigler of the soul, thou greediness to do mischief out of mirth and wantonness, thou thirst of others'

loss, without lust of my own gain or revenge; but when it is said, "Let's go, let's do it," we are ashamed not to be shameless.

Again, meditate in writing on this passage. Are you reflected in Augustine's commentary? Have you had any "friendship too unfriendly" that led you to do things because you were "ashamed not to be shameless"?

Now see what happens when you try connecting this passage with another. Remember, Augustine sees all the commentary connecting together to form a chain. What connection can you see between the passages you just wrote about and this one?

> What then did I love in that theft? and wherein did I even corruptly and per-vertedly imitate my Lord? Did I wish even by stealth to do contrary to Thy law, because by power I could not, so that being a prisoner, I might mimic a maimed liberty by doing with impunity things unpermitted me, a darkened likeness of Thy Omnipotency? Behold, Thy servant, fleeing from his Lord, and obtaining a shadow. O rottenness, O monstrousness of life, and depth of death! could I like what I might not, only because I might not?

With this passage, you may discover the value of thinking in analogy. Augustine's placing of his theft so firmly in the context of Christian thought may seem remote and strange to you, unrelated to your interests, values, or beliefs. You might, then, turn away, remain deaf to what it is Augustine says here about human motives. So, convert the passage to an analogy. Reread what you have already written about your own transgressions. Then consider that Augustine here asks whether he delighted in doing what he was not supposed to do only because he was not supposed to do it. Does this suggest any analogies with your own motives? Now try thinking analogously about authority here. What authority did you think would frown upon your doing whatever it is you did? Were you in any sense trying to imitate the power that authority held over you by doing what you knew was wrong? Write about that until you feel you have worked through the ideas of rebellion, authority, imitation, and freedom that Augustine suggests here.

Notetaking by analogous commentary simply means asking yourself, in response to the reflective passages you have noted in the text, how what the writer says holds a mirror up to your own nature—even if the *language* the writer uses makes him or her seem remote from you. It also means noticing how this kind of self-reflection leads you to see how the writer's reflections are linked together. Your notebook, then, would include your reference to a specific passage, your reflections upon it—including your meditations on analogous experiences, thoughts, and feelings—and then a reference to another passage, your reflection on it and on how it connects with the passages you have already commented on.

Another technique you might want to try is questioning your own responses. Your marginal notes should mark—as suggested above—those passages that elicited a special response from you. Take them and ask yourself, "Why did I have that response?" Here, for instance, is a passage that strikes me from Loren Eiseley's ''The Slit'' (see Part IV, Anthology, Section Two), in which he questions whether there is some purpose in evolution:

> Perhaps there is no meaning in it all, the thought went on inside me, save that of journey itself, so far as men can see. It has altered with the chances of life, and the chances brought us here; but it was a good journey—long, per-haps—but a good journey under a pleasant sun. Do not look for the purpose. Think of the way we came and be a little proud. Think of this hand—the utter pain of its first venture on the pebbly shore.

Imagine for the moment that you were as taken with this passage as I am. We copy this passage into our notes, and reflect upon it, asking, ''Why am I taken by it?'' You write about it for a bit, and I will, too.

When I review my notes, I find I was taken by the suggestion that this journey we have come on has no meaning except the journey, that maybe the whole enterprise has no purpose other than that, and that chance, not purpose, brought us here on that journey. And what does he mean by that word ''proud,'' that I should just be ''proud'' of the journey? I also noted that I really imagined the sensation of pebbles when I thought about my hand as the first appendage to slop out of the slime—the begin-ning of this journey that led to these hands I'm using to type.

Now, I have a set of questions that can lead me back into the text. What is this ''journey'' Eiseley talks about? What does he mean, the meaning is in the journey itself? Why use the word ''pride''? How come it works when he says that I should think of my hand as a kind of adapted fin? What does he mean by ''chance''?

Suppose I decide to take up the question of chance first. What does Eise-ley mean? Why am I so struck by it? I'm led to another passage:

> ''Whirl is king,'' said Aristophanes, and never since life began was Whirl more truly king than eighty million years ago in the dawn of the Age of Mam-mals. It would come as a shock to those who believe firmly that the scroll of the future is fixed and the roads determined in advance, to observe the teetering balance of earth's history through the age of the Paleocene.

Eiseley sets us off on a journey from the Paleocene to discovering our-selves in the prairie dogs he watches at night. We are here by chance he suggests, part of a long journey. What do I make of that? Why does it strike me so?

Taking notes in this way leads, through the questioning of your own responses, to discovering connections in the text that you might not oth-erwise make or notice. It is an open-ended kind of notetaking and highly exploratory. What prevents it from becoming divorced from the text itself is that each time you raise the question about your own response, you dive back into the text to find out what else the writer had to say about what-ever it is that evokes the response. That's what makes it like a dialogue. And the really wonderful thing about this kind of notetaking is that you do not know what you are going to discover about either the text or your-self. You discover it as you go along, as you take the notes. Some of us find it exhilarating. At the very least, you should find that it is much less a kind of drudgery than laboriously hammering out the "topic outline" sorts of reading notes.

Taking Notes on a Proposal to Solve a Problem

In Chapter 12, "Discovering Others' Arguments," we have discussed how to take marginal notes when a writer makes a presentation of deductive arguments; that is, when the writer offers general propositions and sup-ports them with evidence based upon what is already known rather than observed directly. In this section, we will discuss how to take notes on such a presentation. This discussion should be useful whenever you take notes on arguments similarly presented, even when the writer is pre-senting deductive arguments on the significance of something rather than the solution to a problem; e.g., Susan Bordo's "Anorexia Nervosa: Psychopathology as the Crystallization of Culture" (see Part IV, Anthol-ogy, Section Two).

The format you choose for taking notes on deductive arguments is up to you. It should allow you to indicate clearly to yourself how the writer supports his or her propositions. In the case of a proposal to solve a prob-lem, your notes should indicate how the writer defines the problem and how the argument against the status quo, the explanation of cause or source, the solution, and the response to objections are supported by arguments and evidence. Here is one set of notes on the paragraphs from George F. Kennan's proposal (see Part IV, Anthology, Section Four) that we discussed in Chapter 13:

Title: George F. Kennan, "A Proposal for International Disarmament," The Nuclear Delusion: Soviet-American Relations in the Atomic Age. New York: Pantheon, 1982. 175-82.

Purpose: To present a proposal for international disarmament
I. The problems Kennan will address:
    A. "We are for the moment on a collision course politically with the Soviet Union"; and
    B. "The process of rational communication between the two govern-ments seems to have broken down completely";
    C. "It is also--and even more importantly--the fact that the ulti-mate sanction behind the conflicting policies of these two gov-ernments is a type and volume of weaponry which could not possi-bly be used without utter disaster for us all";
    D. "For over thirty years, wise and far-seeing people have been

warning us about the futility of any war fought with nuclear
weapons and about the dangers involved in their cultivation";

E. "When one looks back today over the history of these warnings,
one has the impression that something has now been lost of the
sense of urgency, the hopes, and the excitement that initially
inspired them, so many years ago. One senses, even on the part of
those who today most acutely perceive the problem and are
inwardly most exercised about it, a certain discouragement,
resignation, perhaps even despair, when it comes to the question
of raising the subject again."

F. "We have achieved, we and the Russians together. . . levels of
redundancy of such grotesque dimensions as to defy rational
understanding."

II. Kennan's discussion of the nature of the problem; what is wrong
with the status quo
Problems stated at the outset that are relevant to this argument:

Given that "the ultimate sanction behind the conflicting policies
of these two governments is a type and volume of weaponry which
could not possibly be used without utter disaster for us all"; and
Given that "today we have achieved, we and the Russians together,
in the creation of these devices and their means of delivery, levels of redundancy of such grotesque dimensions as to defy rational
understanding":

Position: "I question whether these devices are really weapons at all."
Reasons:
1. "A true weapon is at best something with which you
endeavor to affect the behavior of another society by
influencing the minds, the calculations, the intentions,
of the men that control it";
2. A true weapon "is not something with which you destroy
indiscriminately the lives, the substance, the hopes, the
culture, the civilization, of another people";
3. It would be "a confession of intellectual poverty" and "a
bankruptcy of intelligent statesmanship--if we had to
admit that such blind, senseless acts of destruction were
the best use we could make of what we have come to view as
the leading elements of our military strength!"
4. The nuclear bomb "is not even an effective defense against
itself";
5. The nuclear bomb is only a weapon "with which, in a moment
of petulance or panic, you commit such fearful acts of
destruction as no sane person would ever wish to have upon
his conscience."
Position: The argument that we need to have nuclear weapons
because we have to deter the Soviets from using theirs
against us is not justification for the size of the nuclear
arsenals both sides have.

Reasons:
1. A policy of deterrence supposes that the other side is
   "fiendish and inhuman" enough to use nuclear weapons
   first;
2. Even accepting the argument of deterrence, both sides now
   have far more weapons than they need if the purpose is
   only to deter the other side from using nuclear weapons
   first.

Another form of notetaking is to summarize the arguments:

Problems: Kennan believes that we are on a "collision course" with the Soviets and that the "process of rational communication" between the countries
has "broken down." But the most important problem is that the conflict
between these two countries is dictated by their mutual reliance on nuclear
weapons, which could not be used "without utter disaster for us all." For the
past 30 years, statesmen have failed to heed the warnings of those who say
that nuclear war would be futile, and even those who have issued those warnings in the past seem in a state of despair. Instead of heeding the warnings,
both countries have "gone on piling weapon upon weapon . . . almost involuntarily" so that now both have so many nuclear weapons and means for delivering them "as to defy rational understanding."
What Is Wrong with the Status Quo: Kennan stated at the outset that the biggest problem is the policy that sanctions this buildup. He tells why he
thinks the reliance on this policy is the essential component in the nuclear
arms problem. His first argument is that nuclear weapons are not "really
weapons at all." His reasons are (1) that the best use of weapons is to
"affect the behavior of another society by influencing the minds, the calculations, the intentions, of the men that control it"; a true weapon, therefore, would not be one that destroys "indiscriminately the lives, the substance, the hopes, the culture, the civilization, of another people"; (2) it
is a sign of "intellectual poverty" and of a "bankruptcy of intelligent
statesmanship" to say that the best use we can make of our military strength
is to utterly destroy another civilization; (3) nuclear weapons cannot even
be used as defense against other nuclear weapons; and (4) only in a moment of
panic or petulance would anyone use nuclear weapons, because no sane person
would commit such "fearful acts of destruction."
    The second argument he offers is that the policy of deterrence really
does not justify the large nuclear arsenals both sides now have. For one
thing, the policy of deterrence means one side wants to deter the other from
using the weapon first. This policy on our part supposes that the Russians
are "fiendish and inhuman" enough to want to destroy our civilization, and
that if they did we would use our weapons in return. Kennan says that even if
we concede that both sides are capable of such "profound iniquities," there
still is no way to justify the size of the arsenals in terms of deterrence.
The arsenals represent "over a million times the destructive power of the
Hiroshima bomb," so that even if both sides reduced arms by 20 percent, there
would still be enough arms on both sides for the purposes of deterrence. As it

is, the amount of weapons both sides have for deterrence threatens the entire Northern Hemisphere.

Reflecting on Your Notes

When you have completed your notes, reflect upon them. You might find it useful to consider the following questions:

1. Do you agree with the problem or issue as the writer has stated it?

2. Do you agree with the writer's assessment of what is wrong with the status quo? Does the writer support the reasons for the position? Offer sufficient evidence? If there are any unsupported propositions, then do you agree or disagree with them?

3. Do you agree with the writer's characterization of the cause or history of the problem? Can you think of other causes the writer does not address? Does the writer offer sufficient reasons and evidence for the position? If there are any unsupported propositions, then do you agree or disagree with them?

4. Do you think the writer's solution to the problem is reasonable? Does the writer offer sufficient reasons and evidence for offering it as a reasonable solution? If there are any unsupported propositions, then do you agree or disagree with them?

5. Can you think of any other solutions that the writer does not consider? Can you think of any weaknesses in the proposal that the writer does not consider?

Other Kinds of Notes

Regardless of the reading, there are two kinds of notes you should be sure to take:

Glossing the Text

A gloss can be either a brief or more extended explanation of a difficult passage or phrase. Noting the meaning of words new to you is one kind of gloss. A second kind explains an allusion; for example, Kennan's reference to the Baruch Plan and the SALT Treaty. If these are new terms for you, you should find out what they are. Obviously, such allusions are not explained in a dictionary, so you will have to find other sources or reference materials. When you are confronted with this problem in a course, you might find other assigned readings helpful. You might also ask your instructor for advice. And, of course, the reference librarian's purpose is to help library patrons identify resources that can answer questions such as this.

Seeking Clarification

Even after you have read something several times, there may be passages that you do not understand. You might find it helpful writing down what you think the passage says and how you think the passage relates to the passage just preceding and just following. Then ask a classmate or your instructor to go over this passage with you, and write down in your own words what you understand your adviser to have said. If you still feel uncertain, ask again.

common criteria; that is, can you tell which factors they feel are most important, which less, and which least? Are there factors that one professor praises or criticizes that another does not?

When you have formulated some professorial criteria for judging writing, reread some of the essays you have written for this class. From the comments on your graded work, would you say that your teacher is using criteria similar to that used by other professors? How would you compare the expectations?

Suppose someone told you that a composition course is intended to help students succeed as writers in their other college courses. How would you respond?

PART IV

The Anthology

At the end of each chapter in Parts I and II of *Discovery,* you will find assignments that ask you to *respond* to readings included in this collection. Chapters in *Discovery* also *discuss* readings included here. The collection is divided into the following four sections:

The Writing Process
Assigning Significance to Experience
Presenting Observations: Testing a Hypothesis
Summarizing, Comparing, and Evaluating Arguments

At the beginning of each section, a table of contents lists the readings included in that section.

Section One

The Writing Process

This section includes selections illustrating some aspect of the writing process. An asterisk (*) before an entry indicates that the selection was written by a student or contains passages written by students.

Revising

Editing

Grading and Evaluation

How to Take Notes in Class

Jules R. Benjamin

To illustrate some of the essentials of good note taking, here are portions of two sets of class notes taken from the same lecture. The first example illustrates many of the common errors of note takers, and the second is an example of a well-written set of notes. The subject of the lecture was early European contact with Africa.

Example of Poor Note Taking

Colonization of Africa—People were afraid to sail out. Afraid of sea monsters. But they liked the stories about gold in Africa. The Portuguese King Henry sailed south to find the gold mines and he built a fort at Elmina.

England and France want to trade with Africa. They begin trading. Competing with Portugal. These countries got into wars. They wanted to control Africa.

China had spices. They traded with Cairo and Venice. The Asians wanted gold, but the Islams stopped all trade. They fought wars about religion for hundreds of years. Fought over Jerusalem. The Pope called for a crusade. This was in the Middle Ages.

Spices came from Asia. In Europe they were valuable because the kings used them to become rich. They also ate them.

The Portuguese wanted to explore Africa and make a way to India. Their boats couldn't get around until Bartholomew Diaz discovered the Cape of Good Hope in 1487.

Most of all the Portuguese wanted slaves. They shipped them back from Africa. Columbus took them after he discovered America (1492). The Pope made a line in the Atlantic Ocean so the Catholics wouldn't fight. The colonies needed slaves. They sent 15 million from 1502 to the 19th century. Slaves did the hard work. They got free later after the Civil War.

Immigrants go to Africa from Europe but they don't like the hot weather and they catch diseases. The Dutch set up their own country at the Cape. Then the English conquer them.

Example of Good Note Taking

Early European Contact with Africa   History 200
                                                     10/22/83

I. Why did Europeans come to Africa?
  A. Desire for gold
    1. Medieval legends about gold in Africa.
    2. Prince Henry (Portuguese navigator) sent men down coast of Africa to find source of gold. (Also to gain direct access to gold trade controlled by Muslims.)
    3. Portuguese built forts along the coast. Their ships carried gold and ivory back to Portugal (16th century).
    4. Then the other European states came (England, Holland, France, Spain) to set up their own trading posts.
    5. Competed with each other for African trade. (Will talk about rivalry next week.)
  B. Wanted to trade with Asia and weaken the Muslims (The Muslims had created a large empire based on the religion of Islam.)
    1. Religious conflict between Christianity and Islam. Fought a religious war in the 11th–12th centuries—the Crusades.
    2. The Muslims had expanded their empire when Europe was weak. In 15th century they controlled North Africa and they dominated trade in the Mediterranean. They controlled the spices coming from Asia, which were in great demand in Europe. In Europe they were used to preserve meat. So valuable, sometimes used as money.
    3. Portugal and Spain were ruled by Catholic monarchs. Very religious. The Catholic monarchs wanted to force the Muslims out of Europe. (They still held part of Spain.) Wanted to convert them to Christianity. [IMPORTANT]
    4. The Muslims controlled North Africa and Mediterranean trade. If the Portuguese and Spanish could sail to the Indian Ocean directly they could get goods from China and the Muslims couldn't stop them. The way to Asia was the sea route around Africa. [IMPORTANT]

C. The Europeans wanted slaves
  1. When the Portuguese explored West Africa (15th century) they sent back the first slaves (around 1480).
  2. The Spanish conquered the New World (Mexico, Peru, etc.). (Columbus had made several trips for the Queen of Spain.)
  3. In America (the name for the New World) they needed slaves. Most slaves were sent to America.
  4. Indians died from diseases of white men. They were also killed in the wars. There was nobody to run the mines (gold and silver).
  5. Sugar plantations of the Caribbean (and Brazil) needed labor. Cotton plantations in the south of U.S. also. It was hard work and nobody wanted to do it.
  6. 15 million (maybe as many as 40 million) slaves were brought to work the plantations starting in 1502 until mid-19th century.

(bracket labeled: I M P O R T A N T)

II. Colonization
  A. Immigration (why white people didn't come)
    1. They couldn't take the climate.
    2. There were a lot of tropical diseases.
    3. The Europeans didn't want to live in Africa, only run it.
    4. Only the Dutch settlers came. They set up the Boer states in South Africa. After them came British settlers.
    5. Frenchmen (some) settled in Algeria.
    6. Some English also moved to Rhodesia.
  B. Dividing Africa
    1. Whites began exploring into the interior. (Will discuss exploration next week.)

Copying notes during a lecture is difficult, and even a good set of notes can be greatly improved by being rewritten. Following is a rewriting of these notes. Note how much clearer everything becomes.

Rewritten Good Notes

Early European Contact with Africa   History 200
                                                      10/22/83

I. What Drew Europeans to Africa?
  A. Gold
     There were medieval legends that there was a lot of gold in West Africa. Access to the gold was controlled by non-Christian powers (Muslims—believers in Islamic religion). Tales of gold lured the Portuguese (led by Prince Henry) to explore the coast of

West Africa in the late 15th century. By the 16th century, the Portuguese had built several trading posts and forts along the West African coast and were bringing back gold, ivory, and pepper.

By the 17th century, English, Dutch, French, and Spanish ships challenged the Portuguese trading monopoly and set up their own trading posts. This was the beginning of rivalry between European countries over the wealth of Africa.

B. Desire to weaken the power of the Islamic Empire (Muslims), and expand trade with Asia

Conflict between Christianity and Islam was an old religious conflict (the Crusades as an example in 11th and 12th centuries). The Muslims controlled North Africa and the Mediterranean. They also controlled the spice trade from Asia. Spices were important in Europe because they were the only known way to preserve meat.

The Catholic states of Portugal and Spain wanted to fight with the Muslims. They wanted to drive them out of Spain and challenge the large Muslim empire in Africa, the Middle East, and Asia. They hoped to convert them to Christianity. *The Muslims were strong in North Africa, but if European powers could discover a way around Africa into the Indian Ocean they could outflank the Muslims and obtain direct access to the trade with India and Asia.*

C. Slaves

Portuguese trading posts in Africa had sent a small number of slaves to Europe starting in the late 15th century. With the discovery and conquest of America in the 16th century, a new and larger slave trade began to European colonies in the New World (America).

The native Indians of America died off (they were killed in war and by European diseases). There was a shortage of labor. In the 17th and 18th centuries the mines of Latin America needed workers. Large sugar plantations were set up in the Caribbean and Brazil and cotton plantations in the southern United States. *The need for laborers to do the hard agricultural work led to the importing of millions of slaves from Africa.* Somewhere between 15 and 40 million Africans were sent to America as slaves between 1502 and the mid-19th century. This slave trade made Africa valuable to the European powers.

II. The Colonization of Africa

A. Immigration

Because of the unsatisfactory climate and tropical diseases, there was no major European immigration to Africa. The only significant white colony was in South Africa by the Boers (Dutch)

and later the English. There were smaller European settlements in Rhodesia (English) and Algeria (French).
  B. Dividing up the continent
    1. Exploration

If you reread the poor notes now, you can easily see how little of the lecture material is recorded in them and how confusing and even erroneous a picture you get from them. What is there about the poor notes that makes them inferior?

First, they are not organized. They do not even record the title of the lecture, the course number, or the date. If these notes get out of order, they will be useless. In fact, they are almost useless anyway. They are nothing more than a series of sentences about gold, trade, spices, Portugal, and slaves. The sentences are not in any particular order, and they do not say anything important. Even the factual information does not cover the major points of the lecture. Instead, it is peripheral information about sea monsters, China, Jerusalem, Bartholomew Diaz, and Columbus, most of which the good note taker wisely omitted. By paying too much attention to trivial points, moreover, the poor note taker missed or did not have time to record the principal theme of the lecture—the relationship between European-Asian trade and the religious struggle between Islam and Christianity. The poor note taker also missed another major point—the connection between the enslavement of Africans and the need for plantation labor in the New World. Without these two points, this student cannot write a good exam on this subject.

The good notes, on the other hand, follow the organization of the lecture and touch upon the major points made in class. The notes make sense and can serve as the basis for reviewing the content of the lecture when studying for exams.

These notes are not crowded, but well spaced so that material and emphasis can be added later if necessary. They also have a wide margin for extra comments and the marking of important passages. (Note the emphasis on B.4 and C.5.) The instructor had emphasized these points in class, and by making special note of them, the good student will be sure to master them.

The rewritten version, which eliminates certain unimportant or repetitious phrases and smoothes the language into connected sentences, is even better as a study guide. The greatest value of rewriting, however, is that by recreating the lecture material in essay form, it becomes part of the note taker's own thinking. The mental effort that goes into revising lecture notes serves to impress the material and its meaning upon the mind. This makes it much easier to review the material at exam time.

Thoughts on Writing: A Diary

Susan Griffin

August 9, 1979

I come back to this problem of despair in writing, myself caught up in it today, feeling a dullness about all language. In the morning I am irritable. I feel as if my sleep had been disturbed, as if a dream were intruded upon, and I am not quite certain how to proceed. This is a profound disorientation. When I am not giving forth words, I am not certain any longer who I am. But it is not like the adolescent searching for an identity; no, this state of mind has an entirely different quality, because in it there is a feeling of loss, as if my old identity, which had worked so well, which seemed to be the whole structure of the universe, were now slipping away, and all my attempts to retrieve it seem graceless, or angry, or blaming. And the old voice of protection and order in me whispers like an Iago that I betray myself.

And now I remember the substance of a revelation about faith I had a few months ago. I was walking in the woods and became aware suddenly of a knowledge that enters me in that kind of silence, especially in the presence of an organic life that is not controlled by man. This is a knowledge of a deeply peaceful kinship with all that is alive, a state of mind that language struggles to render, and yet that, paradoxically, makes me want to sing. And at the same time I became aware that the whole impulse to science in western civilization must have been born of doubt. Indeed, all the great questions of science (what is the nature of matter, what is the origin of life, what is the cause of all motion in the universe, what is light) all these began as religious questions, and remained essentially religious until the nineteenth century. So one doubts the feeling of presence, the feeling of unity with all beings, in oneself; one seeks instead a proof, "scientific," quantifiable. Sense data. So perhaps this accounts for the poetic quality of many scientific truths, and yet, also, the fact that the scientific method abolishes intuition (although indeed intuition has solved many "scientific" problems).

In *Woman and Nature* I made the voice of science hostile to intuition, the voice of patriarchy, and all the time I wrote that book, the patriarchal voice was in me, whispering to me (the way the voice of order whispers to me now), that I had no proof for any of my writing, that I was wildly in error, that the vision I had of the whole work was absurd.

And what is this state of mind that the voice of order brings about in myself, and that is akin to scientific doubt, and to patriarchal disapproval? I want to draw a portrait of this creature of despair who inhabits me, capture her, name her. Write a phenomenology of her.

She is, for one thing, concerned with the question of efficiency. She would not have me "waste" any time. And so, to that end, she would have me know what I am going to write during any day's work before I write it.

And now seeing these words here, I see again how similar this creature is in every way to the patriarchal voice of science, which defends its very existence with arguments of efficiency, saving labor, use, production. But underneath this rationale, is fear of the loss of control, and fear of death.

Because each time I write, each time the authentic words break through, I am changed. The older order that I was collapses and dies. I lose control. I do not know exactly what words will appear on the page. I follow language. I follow the sound of the words, and I am surprised and transformed by what I record.

And so perhaps despair hides a refusal and perhaps in this refusal is that terror born of faithlessness, which keeps a guard over my thoughts, will not let dreams reach the surface of my mind.

When I had written the first draft of *Woman and Nature* the book had a disorganized quality. I had several small chapters, some a paragraph, some a few pages, and no final sequence for them. And so I put the little pieces all in a logical order, by topic, or chronology or whatever seemed most reasonable. But this order did not "work." It was like a well-built bench that had no grace, and so one did not want to sit on it.

So I began again putting the pieces together, but this time I simply followed the words intuitively, putting pieces next to one another where the transition seemed wonderful, and that was when the shape of the book began to seem beautiful to me.

I read this in a book on Jewish mysticism: "Language in its purest form, Hebrew, according to the Kabbalists, reflects the fundamental spiritual nature of the world."

Before I wrote *Woman and Nature* I knew I wanted a kind of symmetry and a kind of repetition built into the structure. At first I began to create these purposefully. But very soon they began to occur in the work quite unbidden. So, as more and more in the work I began to oppose science with a mystical view of the universe, my work took on a life of its own, and began to resemble the patterns of the universe that it envisioned.

From Participant Observation: Theory and Practice

Jurgen Friedrichs and Harmut Ludtke

Friedrichs and Ludtke, two German researchers, led a team of fieldworkers observing German youth centers in the early 1970s. In their book, they offer advice to other fieldworkers on effective methods for making observations.

Basic Protocols of Complex Situations

One of the methods they used was observation of general situations, such as typical club activities. This required observing club activities, interaction and communication among those observed, status symbols, the "core group and its structure," and the "informal leader."

The observations that follow are the notes of some of the students Friedrichs and Ludtke employed as fieldworkers. The observations by No. 26 offer a general picture of a typical gathering at a youth center. The observations by No. 53 record a single evening. The observations by No. 5 describe a typical day at the center, and Friedrichs and Ludtke criticize the notes. They write that No. 5's observations are "too generalized and extraordinarily lacking in information. The points are largely limited to numerical, time and place data; social indicators of the participants and their behavior are missing completely."

Compare these three descriptions. See if you can understand why Friedrichs and Ludtke think that the notes taken by No. 5 are inferior to those taken by Nos. 26 and 53.

No. 26
The boys usually sit in reversed positions on the chairs which stand in the middle of the room or are grouped around a table. Some of them sit on the floor and lean against the wall. A few (often the girls) use the tables to sit on and let their legs swing. From the loudspeaker beat-music can be heard. The volume can be regulated in each room. If a specially popular song is played (i.e., "Boots are made for walking"), then it's put on as loud as possible. Some shake their heads to the beat and hit their knees with their hands. The girls often do a few dance steps and like to show they know the song and the singer's name.

The topic of conversation is usually motor bikes, sports or last weekend. The core group in the room consists of an informal group of about 10–12 boys, of whom the large part are present every evening. Their members dress alike: black leather jackets, blue jeans, black boots—very unkempt—dirty hands and shoes. These boys sit very close together and talk amongst themselves mostly. The others, who don't belong to this clique, wear mostly grey or small-checked pants and pullovers. They appear generally better groomed. They come alone or as couples to the centre, take part in conversations and other activities in the game room; they don't get as much attention, however, when they enter as the members of the informal group do. The informal group members recognise one another right away by their walk (boots have taps and on the stone floors are especially conspicuous). "Robby's coming now," says one of them upon hearing the steps in the hall. They often are still wearing their helmets when they greet their friends. They hang them carelessly on hooks and join their friends. Almost all of those present smoke and throw the butts on the floor. The cigarettes are generously offered to one another. If someone grubs, then he'll be told to buy his own cigarettes once in a while. For a coke, they often borrow money from one another. Noticeable is the fact that the boys pay more attention to one another when they enter the room than they do to the girls.

Again and again subgroups break away from the group and go into the refreshment room, in order to play games or see what's going on there. Often it will suddenly be decided to go to a bar or get an ice-cream and the whole clubroom is empty for half an hour. By the way, the girls are not asked if they'd like to join them. They sometimes go alone to a place near the centre, because they know that some acquaintances are there.

On the inside of the door to the clubroom has been written in pencil: TBD "The bloody days." This name was given to the members of the informal group (youths with leather jackets). They call themselves "rockers" and emphasise the fact that they are not bums. It sometimes results in fights (according to reports of the youths). Girls from the centre who know hippies are laughed at. A decisive feature of this "rocker group" is their especially sloppy dress. . . .The leather jackets and a good "buck" (bike) are status symbols within the group.

The informal leader of this group wears a chain around his neck, on which a copperplate hangs with the initials TBD. This plate was made in the centre's metal workshop. Up to the end of my observation period, no one else had copied it. As far as I could see, neither he nor his friends view him as the leader of this group. However, he provides an example for their behaviour.

Example: Three boys suggest going to East Park in order to look at the queers and annoy them. The leader doesn't like the idea because it's too cold outside. He doesn't want to go and says it's a crazy idea. As a result, the three members of the group remain at the centre.

Besides, one member of this group told me that when a newcomer enters the centre and is really spruced-up, "Robby tears him to pieces."

No. 53

I have bar duty. Nine boys between 14 and 15 years old, who belong to the group of idlers, are busy with the table football. After a few minutes, a boy of about 18 years (tall, lanky, friendly, bushy hair, black leather jacket) enters the room. The youths greet him with a loud and extended "heh." The newcomer, Franz, sits without uttering a tone on a stool near the game and very indifferently looks on as they continue playing. Five minutes later another boy (the same age as Franz, also tall, lanky, but with a crew cut and wearing a suit with sailor pants) named Gert steps lackadaisically into the bar and sits down on a bar stool. Meanwhile, Franz has left his former seat and sits down next to Gert.

Franz: "Coke!," turns to Gert: "You too?" Gert shakes his head slightly, "Yeah." Franz to me: "Make that two!" While I'm busy opening the bottles Gert brings out a pack of cigarettes, which he, without a word, holds in front of Franz. Both then take out lighters from their jackets and each lights his own cigarette. I take the money for the coke which they separately had put on the counter, while they both look me over half astonished, half distrustful. Then Franz begins: "Just cut out of school; took a test in bookkeeping; Popo (the teacher) naturally thought I'd have some questions to ask about it. Of course, I said I did."—Pause.

Gert: "Erika, the one who used to go with Michael, does she now come to the club more often?"

Franz: "Yeah. The guys there (the band) are really great!"

Gert: "The girl you were with on Saturday at the Jazz Festival, is she the one from Gladbach?"

Franz: (shaking his head) "Yeah, the jerk decided she wanted to have her hair cut off recently. I told her: 'That'll be the end for us.'" Then, half to Gert half to himself but rather loud: "Damn dames, always gotta pick 'em up and bring 'em back home!"—Pause.

Miss R., one of the two fulltime workers, enters the barroom. Gert is chewing on a straw. Miss R.: "Taste good, Gert?" Gert with a slightly ironically meant move towards Miss R.: "Yeah, great! After all, it's the only free thing around this place."

After Miss R. has left the room, Brigitte (approximately 16–17 years old, wearing a bright red jacket) enters. We know one another from a lecture. After we've said hello to one another, she takes over at the bar and asks me to remain and keep her company. Both of the boys look at me curiously: bewildered that Brigitte and I should know one another. Afterwards, Gert turns to Brigitte, grins, leans his head in her direction and says: "Ha, how dandy!" Brigitte, in the same provocative manner asks, "Do you want anything?" Gert, "Yeah, but what I want, I won't get anyway." All three laugh.

Franz plays with a Red Cross button that he is wearing on his jacket lapel: "Boy, am I ever crazy about a girl with unbelievably long blond hair." Afterward, speaking rapidly, half to the others, half to himself: "Hah, but I ain't allowed to be crazy about anyone!" Brigitte, turning to Gert, in a put-on sympathetic tone: "Heh, Gert, you look really done in! Gone to bed too late?" Gert grinning: "Didn't look at the time." Brigitte: "Were probably too drunk to!"

Franz: "The Rackets (a band) really steal the show every time: it was wild!"

Brigitte: "It was really bad last time when Mecki got under the piano!"

Ecki (Franz and Gert's age, long curly hair, slightly scarred face, dressed in bell-bottoms, turtleneck sweater, black jacket) saunters into the room. He's regarded as one of the difficult cases in the centre. First, he goes to the juke box, puts some change in and then takes a seat at the bar. The three already present as well as Ecki: "Hi."—Pause.

From the juke box booms: "Sloopy." Three of the boys turned off by the selection boo, whistle and beat loudly on the counter. Ecki puts about ten straws end-to-end, then stands up and tries to stick the straws in a coke bottle. Everybody laughs. Then Brigitte, still laughing says: "Ecki, behave yourself! Otherwise, you'll get kicked out on the spot!" Franz to Brigitte: "Heh, babe, gotta ice cream for a nickel?" Brigitte: "There's no such thing." Franz shakes his head: "Here I wanted to make a big order for once and you don't have it again."

Brigitte pulls some pictures out of her handbag showing her and Angelika sunbathing and hands them to the boys. Franz says: "Oh no, Angelika! Not on your life? Not my cup of tea! She never looked good!" Gert: Brigitte, you look like a circus horse yourself in the photo." All four laugh aloud. Then Ecki gets ready to leave the barroom.

Franz calls after him: "Heh, Ecki! You driving to the club now? Can you give me a lift on the back seat (of his motor bike)?" Ecki turns around, shakes his head and says: "Make it fast! Don't dilly-dally!" Franz to Brigitte and Gert: "'Bye you guys." Franz and Ecki leave the barroom together.

No. 5

A typical "idle Tuesday": The room was, as usual, available, a record player and tape recorder installed. In the room about six people were constantly present, of whom four were members of group 63. Two played chess, I played skat with two others, those remaining listened to records. Little by little, more young people entered, who, however, on the average left the house again after five minutes. The large unfriendly room, brightly lit, plastic tablecloths on the tables, wasn't very inviting with only six people there. I really wanted to listen to a long-playing record; because the others, especially the owner of another tape recorder and several tapes, were against it, we went into the centre director's room, continued playing cards there and listened to the records. Mr S. (employee) asked us, however, to go back to the room, in order that at least a few people were sitting there. We moved again, continued playing the records there, whereupon the tape-jockey got annoyed and packed up. A group of eight boys spent about half an hour in the foyer, then disappeared again. Mr S. said most of them only came to see if there was a dance. He objects to the idle Tuesday completely, because it accomplishes nothing.

Description of Social Relations

Another procedure required observers to concentrate on subgroups, or cliques, and their apparent leaders. Friedrichs and Ludtke found that the observers tended to report on "external and behavior features" of clique leaders, but that descriptions of interactions between leaders and their groups, or between groups, were often "incomplete by comparison." The observation by No. 59, for instance, concentrates on an external feature—clothing—so that it "merely reproduce(s) symbolic attributes." The observation by No. 30 does move beyond attention solely to such externals, and describes certain typical behaviors of the person, but "the presentation remains strongly interpretative, because there is no explicit connection with concrete indicators and situations in which this behaviour and the position of persons can be observed overtly." In other words, the notes lack sensory details or examples. The observation by No. 35, on the other hand, "provides an almost optimal compromise between completeness of description and brevity of presentation" because it characterizes the leader of a clique by giving examples of how he interacted with his group, tells something about the group, indicates the kind of influence the leader had, and indicates how he sanctioned members of the group.

Compare the notes taken by these observers. See if you can understand why Friedrichs and Ludtke think the notes taken by No. 35 are superior to those of the others.

No. 59
The clothing of youth with the highest status: P always wears pants, whose broadly cut legs fall to the floor, and a blue-black jacket. Most of the time he wears black suede shoes (with buckle), which have already been the object of admiration many times.
D. often wears a pink-coloured shirt, snug-fitting or bell-bottom pants and half boots (which along with his stalking step bring cowboy boots to mind).
H. changes clothes after school and in the centre wears (intentionally) frayed snug-fitting pants, in order to adapt to the others: most of the time he, also, puts on a fashionable ski sweater, which heightens his youthful looks even more.

No. 30

The instrumental leader is 18 years old, masculine, dressed as a rocker with blue jeans and jeans jacket, sometimes with fur jacket, coloured glowing shirts, long hair, athletic build. He seeks contact with the centre staff, likes to talk to the observer, he seems to me to be unstable in character, but open to reasonable arguments and basically well-meaning, very sarcastic and ironical. Thought to be a very good billiard player. He belongs to a larger group of friends, who think a lot of him, somewhat isolated because of his often aggressive (when irritated) behaviour (threats with bodily punishment). He finds himself in a crisis to the extent that he must come to an understanding with the new director. He provoked him, opposed him until after a discussion of views the relation improved markedly and could almost be called good.

No. 35

An important clique in the centre is "the clique around Rolf." Rolf is 23 years old, wears mostly turtleneck sweaters, or white shirt and a jacket, Saturdays a blazer. He is small, athletic, has otherwise no special physical traits. At the centre he has a quasi co-worker function. He is a master mason, now a lorry driver. He decides, for example, whether his clique remains at the centre until closing time or whether they should leave earlier in order to go to another place. When he is the bar-keeper, everybody gathers at the bar. Once when he happened to be barkeeper, two girls were sitting on the bar and he said to them: "You could wash the dishes for once," which they did. When a conflict once arose between the centre direction and the clique (otherwise they have a very good relationship), Rolf was responsible for the departure of the whole clique which left without even having helped to clean up. To a large extent, he feels obliged to the centre rules, which shows itself, for example, in the fact that he expressly emphasised that all the boys must appear at the centre in a shirt and tie.

Collection of Elementary Properties of Behavior

Observers were also asked to focus on specific kinds of behavior, a method of observation that Friedrichs and Ludtke found yielded accurate observations. Observer No. 12, for instance, collected examples of "subcultural jargon," or the slang typically used by youth center habitues. Observers 34 and 59 concentrated on the "pattern of interaction between boys and girls." And No. 12 concentrated on typical expressions of pleasure, displeasure, conflict, and boredom.

Compare these observations. See if you can understand why Friedrichs and Ludtke think this method of observing is particularly effective.

No. 12 (comments on a piece of music on the radio)
"great," "swingin' beat," "he knows what he's doin'," "shaky," "groovy," "cheap imitation," "weak improvisation."
(comments about girls)
"bedroom eyes," "what a bomb," "a real doll," "a dishrag," "what a handful," "witch," "washed-out Marlene," "homesick chick," "out of this world."
(greetings)
"Well, Chick?," "Pining away?," "Just got up?," "The fire still burning?," "Got a dime to lend or is your Dad a Scot?," "Bad times," "You contaminate this whole place, two minutes ago it was fun here, but now!" "I was hoping you'd go again real soon!" "When you come, I can go," "They already let you out?," "I'd almost forgotten how gorgeous you are," "You really got a handshake there."
(parting)
"Watch out crossing the street," "Don't speak to strangers!," "Don't fall into a manhole!," "Gotta piss off?," "See you to the grave."

No. 34
Today Rainer bought two bottles of coca-cola for Ruth and himself. He placed them in front of the girl, then went back a few steps and looked around bored to tears. Ruth looked at him, without understanding. A bit later he sat down next to her. He took a large gulp from the bottle, bent over towards Ruth, kissed her and slushed the coke around in her mouth. At first she was surprised, even made a disdaining gesture, but then she wanted more, so that Rainer scarcely was able to cover her requirements. This happened openly in the clubroom. There were only a few present, a few of whom laughed about the gag, others took no notice of it whatsoever.

No. 59
The underestimation (externally) of the young ladies by boys, who hit them on their upper arms with their fists in a form of perpetual body communication between boys and girls, is apparently a ritual among them. Harry's (16 years old) and Rita's (13) greeting took the following form on several occasions:
   "Hello Rita, already here?"—Harry gives Rita a hefty punch on the arm. Rita takes hold of her arm and follows Harry making a half-smiling, half-injured face. Harry sits down on a bench, Rita next to him. Harry: "Come on, show me!" He takes the arm as if to check it over—and hits Rita hard (at the same time) on the knee. Rita begins to push. Harry hovers in the corner. During the whole thing Rita's girl friend is standing nearby and watching it all with interest. The three of them go upstairs and mix with others. The greeting lasted about ten minutes.

No. 12

The facial expression of the young people is as sloppy as possible, apparently indifferent, bored, chewing gum; avoids excitement as much as possible. This is, especially, true of the girls present. No one wants to show weaknesses; to get excited is taboo. Conflicts; verbal arguments with big words; whoever loses his cool first, has lost; the winner prominently takes his seat, which he had before—whereby, at the very most, the girls take notice or show recognition while the others pay no attention at all.

Of course, shop talk leads to rather lively discussions and standpoints are heatedly presented. Whether disinterested or involved in heated debates one has the feeling that their world view is being expressed.

One drinks soft drinks like 7-up or coke, listens to the radio, mostly rock music, waits for contact with others, new arrivals must say the first word, otherwise, they won't even be noticed. Girls are angered by being touched, messing up their hair-dos; blowing smoke in their hair; winning everyone's attention for a short time and then it's bored quiet again; chewing gum, listening to music, with half-closed eyes if possible. Cigarettes aren't offered to others, everyone smokes his own brand—unless someone asks another for one; this is guaranteed without objection.

The Oregon Trail Journal—1846

Francis Parkman

June 15th . . . Laramie Mt. [Peak], Sybil [Sabille] & Adams's deserted fort, and finally Laramie appeared, as the prospect opened among the hills. Rode past the fort, reconnoitred from the walls, and passing the highest ford of L[aramie] Fork [River], were received at the gate by Boudeau [Bordeaux], the *bourgeois* [manager]. Leading our horses into the area, we found Inds.—men, women, and children—standing around, voyageurs and trappers—the surrounding apartments occupied by the squaws and children of the traders. Fort divided into two areas—one used as a *corale*—two bastions or *clay* [*adobe*] *blockhouses*— another blockhouse over main entrance. They gave us a large apartment, where we spread our blankets on the floor. From a sort of balcony we saw our horses and carts brought in, and witnessed a picturesque frontier scene. Conversed and smoked in the windy porch. Horses made a great row in the *corale*. At night the Inds. set up their songs. At the burial place are several Inds. laid on scaffolds, and a circle of buffalo skulls below. Vaskis [Vasquez], Cimoneau, Mont[h]alon, Knight, and other traders and hunters are here.

Roubideau says that twenty Iroquois warriors, from Canada, were not many years since on the Upper Missouri, and were braver and more enterprising than any other of the Inds.

Fort Laramie, June 16th. Prices are most extortionate. Sugar, two dollars a cup—5-cent tobacco at $1.50—bullets at $.75 a pound, etc. American Fur Cmp'y. exceedingly disliked in this country—it suppresses all opposition, and keeping up these enormous prices, pays its men in necessaries on these terms.

The fort has a double gate at the main entrance under the blockhouse. When there was danger from the Inds. the inner gate was closed; the Inds., admitted to the space between, traded through an open window or orifice, opening from a large room now used as the blacksmith's shop.

Lodged in Papin's room and visited now and then by Inds., the fathers or brothers of the whitemen's squaws, who are lodged in the fort, and furnished with meat at the company's expense.

This morning, Smoke's village appeared on the opposite bank, and crossed on their wild, thin, little horses. Men and boys, naked and dashing eagerly through the water—horses with lodge poles dragging through squaws and children, and sometimes a litter of puppies—gaily attired squaws, leading the horses of their lords—dogs with their burdens attached swimming among the horses and mules—dogs barking, horses breaking loose, children laughing and shouting—squaws thrusting into the ground the lance and shield of the master of the lodge—naked and splendidly formed men passing and repassing through the swift water. . . .

A Sioux of mean family can seldom become a chief—a chief generally arises out of large families, where the number of relatives who can back him in a quarrel and support him by their influence, gives him weight and authority.

Fort Laramie from The Oregon Trail

Francis Parkman

[Entries of June 15th and 16th] Looking back, after the expiration of a year, upon Fort Laramie and its inmates, they seem less like a reality than like some fanciful picture of the olden time; so different was the scene from any which this tamer side of the world can present. Tall Indians, enveloped in their white buffalo-robes, were striding across the area or reclining at full length on the low roofs of the buildings which enclosed it. Numerous squaws, gayly bedizened, sat grouped in front of the rooms they occupied; their mongrel offspring, restless and vociferous, rambled in every direction through the fort; and the trappers, traders, and *engagés* of the establishment were busy at their labor or their amusements.

We were met at the gate, but by no means cordially welcomed. Indeed, we seemed objects of some distrust and suspicion, until Henry Chatillon explained that we were not traders, and we, in confirmation, handed to the *bourgeois* [manager] a letter of introduction from his principals. He took it, turned it upside down, and tried hard to read it; but his literary attainments not being adequate to the task, he applied for relief to the clerk, a sleek, smiling Frenchman, named Monthalon.

The letter read, Bordeaux (the *bourgeois*) seemed gradually to awaken to a sense of what was expected of him. Though not deficient in hospitable intentions, he was wholly unaccustomed to act as master of ceremonies. Discarding all formalities of reception, he did not honor us with a single word, but walked swiftly across the area, while we followed in some admiration to a railing and a flight of steps opposite the entrance. He signed to us that we had better fasten our horses to the railing; then he walked up the steps, tramped along a rude balcony, and, kicking open a door, displayed a large room, rather more elaborately furnished than a barn. For furniture it had a rough bedstead, but no bed; two chairs, a chest of drawers, a tin pail to hold water, and a board to cut tobacco upon. A brass crucifix hung on the wall, and close at hand a recent scalp, with hair full a yard long, was suspended from a nail. . . .

This apartment, the best in Fort Laramie, was that usually occupied by the legitimate *bourgeois,* Papin, in whose absence the command devolved upon Bordeaux. The latter, a stout, bluff little fellow, much inflated by a sense of his new authority, began to roar for buffalo-robes. These being brought and spread upon the floor, formed our beds; much better ones than we had of late been accustomed to.

Our arrangements made, we stepped out to the balcony to take a more leisurely survey of the long-looked-for haven at which we had arrived at last. Beneath us was the square area surrounded by little rooms, or rather cells, which opened upon it. These were devoted to various purposes, but served chiefly for the accommodation of the men employed at the fort, or of the equally numerous squaws whom they were allowed to maintain in it. Opposite to us rose the blockhouse above the gateway; it was adorned with the figure of a horse at full speed, daubed upon the boards with red paint, and exhibiting a degree of skill which might rival that displayed by the Indians in executing similar designs upon their robes and lodges. A busy scene was enacting in the area. The wagons of Vaskiss, an old trader, were about to set out for a remote post in the mountains, and the Canadians were going through their preparations with all possible bustle, while here and there an Indian stood looking on with imperturbable gravity.

Fort Laramie is one of the posts established by the "American Fur Company," which wellnigh monopolizes the Indian trade of this region. Here its officials rule with an absolute sway; the arm of the United States has little force; for when we were there, the extreme outposts of her troops were about seven hundred miles to the eastward. The little fort is built of bricks dried in the sun, and externally is of an oblong form, with bastions of clay, in the form of ordinary blockhouses, at two of the corners. The walls are about fifteen feet high, and surmounted by a slender palisade. The roofs of the apartments within, which are built close against the walls, serve the purpose of a banquette.

Within, the fort is divided by a partition: on one side is the square area, surrounded by the store-rooms, offices, and apartments of the inmates; on the other is the *corral,* a narrow place, encompassed by the high clay walls, where at night, or in presence of dangerous Indians, the horses and mules of the fort are crowded for safe keeping. The main entrance has two gates, with an arched passage intervening. A little square window, high above the ground, opens laterally from an adjoining chamber into this passage; so that when the inner gate is closed and barred, a person without may still hold communication with those within, through this narrow aperture. This obviates the necessity of admitting suspicious Indians, for purposes of trading, into the body of the fort; for when danger is apprehended, the inner gate is shut fast, and all traffic is carried on by means of the window. This precaution, though necessary at some of the company's posts, is seldom resorted to at Fort Laramie; where, though men are frequently killed in the neighborhood, no apprehensions are felt of any general designs of hostility from the Indians.

We did not long enjoy our new quarters undisturbed. The door was silently pushed open, and two eyeballs and a visage as black as night looked in upon us; then a red arm and shoulder intruded themselves, and a tall Indian, gliding in, shook us by the hand, grunted his salutation, and sat down on the floor. Others followed, with faces of the natural hue, and letting fall their heavy robes from their shoulders, took their seats, quite at ease, in a semicircle before us. The pipe was now to be lighted and passed from one to another; and this was the only entertainment that at present they expected from us. These visitors were fathers, brothers, or other relatives of the squaws in the fort, where they were permitted to remain, loitering about in perfect idleness.

All those who smoked with us were men of standing and repute. Two or three others dropped in also; young fellows who neither by their years nor their exploits were entitled to rank with the old men and war-riors, and who, abashed in the presence of their superiors, stood aloof, never withdrawing their eyes from us. Their cheeks were adorned with vermilion, their ears with pendants of shell, and their necks with beads. Never yet having signalized themselves as hunters, or per-formed the honorable exploit of killing a man, they were held in slight esteem, and were diffident and bashful in proportion. Certain formi-dable inconveniences attended this influx of visitors. They were bent on inspecting everything in the room; our equipments and our dress alike underwent their scrutiny; for though the contrary has been asserted, few beings have more curiosity than Indians in regard to sub-jects within their ordinary range of thought.

As to other matters, indeed, they seem utterly indifferent. They will not trouble themselves to inquire into what they cannot comprehend, but are quite contented to place their hands over their mouths in token of wonder, and exclaim that it is "great medicine." With this compre-hensive solution, an Indian never is at a loss. He never launches into speculation and conjecture; his reason moves in its beaten track. His soul is dormant; and no exertions of the missionaries, Jesuit or Puri-tan, of the old world or of the new, have as yet availed to arouse it.

As we were looking, at sunset, from the wall, upon the desolate plains that surround the fort, we observed a cluster of strange objects, like scaffolds, rising in the distance against the red western sky. They bore aloft some singular-looking burdens; and at their foot glimmered something white, like bones. This was the place of sepulture of some Dahcotah chiefs, whose remains their people are fond of placing in the vicinity of the fort, in the hope that they may thus be protected from violation at the hands of their enemies. Yet it has happened more than once, and quite recently, that war-parties of the Crow Indians, ranging through the country, have thrown the bodies from the scaffolds, and broken them to pieces, amid the yells of the Dahcotah, who remained pent up in the fort, too few to defend the honored relics from insult. The white objects upon the ground were buffalo skulls, arranged in the mystic circle commonly seen at Indian places of sepulture upon the prairie.

We soon discovered, in the twilight, a band of fifty or sixty horses approaching the fort. These were the animals belonging to the estab-lishment; who, having been sent out to feed, under the care of armed guards, in the meadows below, were now being driven into the *corral* for the night. A gate opened into this enclosure: by the side of it stood one of the guards, an old Canadian, with gray bushy eyebrows, and a dragoon-pistol stuck into his belt; while his comrade, mounted on horseback, his rifle laid across the saddle in front, and his long hair blowing before his swarthy face, rode at the rear of the disorderly troop, urging them up the ascent. In a moment the narrow *corral* was thronged with the half-wild horses, kicking, biting, and crowding restlessly together.

The discordant jingling of a bell, rung by a Canadian in the area, summoned us to supper. The repast was served on a rough table in one of the lower apartments of the fort, and consisted of cakes of bread and dried buffalo-meat,—an excellent thing for strengthening the teeth. At this meal were seated the *bourgeois* and superior dignitaries of the establishment, among whom Henry Chatillon was worthily included. No sooner was it finished, than the table was spread a second time (the luxury of bread being now, however, omitted), for the benefit of certain hunters and trappers of an inferior standing; while the ordinary Canadian *engagés* were regaled on dried meat in one of their lodging-rooms. By way of illustrating the domestic economy of Fort Laramie, it may not be amiss to introduce in this place a story current among the men when we were there.

There was an old man named Pierre, whose duty it was to bring the meat from the store-room for the men. Old Pierre, in the kindness of his heart, used to select the fattest and the best pieces for his companions. This did not long escape the keen-eyed *bourgeois*, who was greatly disturbed at such improvidence, and cast about for some means to stop it. At last he hit on a plan that exactly suited him. At the side of the meat-room, and separated from it by a clay partition, was another apartment, used for the storage of furs. It had no communication with the fort, except through a square hole in the partition; and of course it was perfectly dark.

One evening the *bourgeois*, watching for a moment when no one observed him, dodged into the meat-room, clambered through the hole, and ensconced himself among the furs and buffalo-robes. Soon after, old Pierre came in with his lantern, and, muttering to himself, began to pull over the bales of meat, and select the best pieces, as usual. But suddenly a hollow and sepulchral voice proceeded from the inner room: "Pierre, Pierre! Let that fat meat alone. Take nothing but lean." Pierre dropped his lantern, and bolted out into the fort, screaming, in an agony of terror, that the devil was in the store-room; but tripping on the threshold, he pitched over upon the gravel, and lay senseless, stunned by the fall. The Canadians ran out to the rescue. Some lifted the unlucky Pierre; and others, making an extempore crucifix of two sticks, were proceeding to attack the devil in his stronghold, when the *bourgeois*, with a crestfallen countenance, appeared at the door. To add to his mortification, he was obliged to explain the whole stratagem to Pierre, in order to bring him to his senses.

We were sitting, on the following morning, in the passage-way between the gates, conversing with the traders Vaskiss and May. These two men, together with our sleek friend, the clerk Monthalon, were, I believe, the only persons then in the fort who could read and write. May was telling a curious story about the traveller Catlin, when an ugly, diminutive Indian, wretchedly mounted, came up at a gallop, and rode by us into the fort. On being questioned, he said that Smoke's village was close at hand. Accordingly only a few minutes elapsed before the hills beyond the river were covered with a disorderly swarm of savages, on horseback and on foot. May finished his story; and by that time the whole array had descended to Laramie Creek, and begun to cross it in a mass.

I walked down to the bank. The stream is wide, and was then between three and four feet deep, with a very swift current. For several rods the water was alive with dogs, horses, and Indians. The long poles used in pitching the lodges are carried by the horses, fastened by the heavier end, two or three on each side, to a rude sort of pack-saddle, while the other end drags on the ground. About a foot behind the horse, a kind of large basket or pannier is suspended between the poles, and firmly lashed in its place. On the back of the horse are piled various articles of luggage; the basket also is well filled with domestic utensils, or, quite as often, with a litter of puppies, a brood of small children, or a superannuated old man. Numbers of these curious vehicles, *traineaux*, or, as the Canadians called them, *travaux*, were now splashing together through the stream. Among them swam countless dogs, often burdened with miniature *traineaux;* and dashing forward on horseback through the throng came the warriors, the slender figure of some lynx-eyed boy clinging fast behind them. The women sat perched on the pack-saddles, adding not a little to the load of the already overburdened horses.

The confusion was prodigious. The dogs yelled and howled in chorus; the puppies in the *traineaux* set up a dismal whine, as the water invaded their comfortable retreat; the little black-eyed children, from one year of age upward, clung fast with both hands to the edge of their basket, and looked over in alarm at the water rushing so near them, sputtering and making wry mouths as it splashed against their faces. Some of the dogs, encumbered by their load, were carried down by the current, yelping piteously; and the old squaws would rush into the water, seize their favorites by the neck, and drag them out. As each horse gained the bank, he scrambled up as he could. Stray horses and colts came among the rest, often breaking away at full speed through the crowd, followed by the old hags, screaming after their fashion on all occasions of excitement. Buxom young squaws, blooming in all the charms of vermilion, stood here and there on the bank, holding aloft their master's lance, as a signal to collect the scattered portions of his household.

In a few moments the crowd melted away; each family, with its horses and equipage, filing off to the plain at the rear of the fort; and here, in the space of half an hour, arose sixty or seventy of their tapering lodges. Their horses were feeding by hundreds over the surrounding prairie, and their dogs were roaming everywhere. The fort was full of warriors, and the children were whooping and yelling incessantly under the walls.

9/25/74: Observations of a Storm in a Semai (Malaysia) Village

Clayton A. Robarchek

The Semai live in the mountainous highlands of Malaysia. Their houses, of thatch and grass, are built on stilts and can be washed away in the violent rainstorms of the region. If they flee from the storms to the surrounding rain forest, they run the risk of falling trees. Because they may also be questioned by Malaysian patrols, they need to carry identity cards into the forest with them.

Clayton A. and Carole Robarchek learned that the Semai believe that during a storm, Ngku, the thunder-spirit, calls to his wife, Nangaa, a huge horned dragon, who tries to crawl from the ground to meet her husband when he calls; hence, the Semai pound the ground and tell the spirit to stay down during a storm. The Semai assume Ngku is angered when some taboo is broken, usually by children; e.g., a child laughing at a butterfly can arouse the thunder god. They try to appease the spirit by burnt offerings of incense, salt, lemon grass, tobacco, and some of the children's hair. The headsman, the shaman, and others also speak or pray to Ngku.

The Robarcheks' observations of the storm helped them to understand these customs and beliefs. What follows is a transcript of their observations of the Semai. Additional information, provided by the Robarcheks, is included in brackets.

Just before dusk, a storm came up, very fast. I closed up the house and went to the Headman's [Yeer, 45 years old] house to see what they would do. Following is a blow-by-blow account.

Heavy rain, hard wind, much thunder and lightning. Yeer, Les and Coy are out in it pounding the ground with heavy pieces of firewood, shouting, "Go down, go down"; Yeer shouts, "Hit." Comes in the house, shouting, "Burn incense, burn incense." Tells Tri' [Yeer's daughter, age 13] to get their i.d. cards and put them in the sling on her back. Gives her his magic stones. Says, "We're going to die because we don't have any incense." Bidn brings some incense from Les' house; Yeer puts it with some coals on a piece of firewood, goes out on porch and burns it; chants to Ngku. Everyone has stuff on their backs. Hwamp has a small suitcase packed. Stands holding it and waiting.

Yeer shouting his chant, "What's the good of this, doing it so hard?"; shouts at kids to cut their hair. Runs back outside, pounds the ground, shouting, "Go down!" Bedlam, people running in and out of the house screaming at each other above the storm. Ato' [the shaman; Kngledn and Sngyak's father, age 76] sits by his fire praying, too; calls for someone to give a spirit spell. Lots of people outside pounding the ground, Del, Yeer, Les. Yeer chants as he hits the ground. Wind harder, houses shaking. Everyone abandons K.W.Da's house [Yeer's sister, married, age 30] and comes here. Kngledn [headman's first wife, age 43] burns something in fire, crackles and smokes. K.W.Da says the house is going to fall. Shouting and screaming all around. Loud thunder, more shouts; Yeer still pounding ground. Rain a torrent. Front flap has blown loose on Les' house. Yeer tells everyone to get out of the house; some do, go underneath. Others stay inside. Kngledn pounding ground under house. Someone throws hot coals out of Les' house. Ato' still inside chants. Yeer has come back in, says, "Cut hair." Kngledn has her youngest on her back, is out in the rain pounding the ground. Wind less, Yeer still chants, says, "We're not guilty, we're poor people," throws salt on the fire. Kngledn pounds some twigs with a knife, throws them on the fire. Yeer tells her to cut hair of all the kids and burn it. She does, hits the hair with knife on a log, throws it in the fire. House still full of people, storm is abating. Yeer still chants, tells the storm to change. People talking about how bad it was, they couldn't stand up. Still much thunder but rain and wind are less. Yeer tells the storm to go to the lowlands, to the Malays. Says, "If Thou do keep it up, we'll die; maybe we're a little guilty, but not much." Ato' says, "Enough! listen to me!" Yeer and Kngledn say they saw the Nangga trying to claw her way out of the ground near Da's house. Yeer still chants: "Don't do this; this is no way for Thou to treat Thy grandchildren. Thou can't do this kind of thing to us." Loud thunder. "Go to another country; thou can go to the Malays. Thou knows from old times we're just poor, stupid people. If Thou kill us, we'll die; if not, we'll live. Thou can't do this. Think, Thou, we're tired, your grandchildren, think. Don't do it so hard, Thou can't. What's the good of Thy causing trouble for us?" Chanting goes on between snatches of conversation to others. "It goes back to another town"; Yeer says he saw him (Ngku?) go up; "he wasn't satisfied last night." Yeer and Ato' still chant: "We're tired, Thy grandchildren; Thou can't to this to us, Alah!"

Yeer says, "The wife [Nangaa, the dragon-spirit] was close to us." He saw her crawl beside the house; she had eyes like a person. Kids trying to think what they might have done to cause it. Hndel says, "I caught butterflies." Ato' says, "It doesn't matter if you didn't laugh at them." Yeer still chants: "Thou will ruin our houses, children completely; Thou can go to the sea." Ato' is saying a spell over some water for wife Sa (he remained sitting by the fire through it all). One of the kids shouts something; Yeer tells him to be quiet. The stuff that Kngledn burned was srai (lemon grass). Another thunderclap, Yeer tells him [Ngku, the thunder-spirit], "We're tired, don't do it any more. Thou can't do this randomly." Says, "We're not laughing or joking. We're poor, helpless people. Thou can't cause trouble for us. We're sick with the flu." Proceeds to give Ngku a reasoned argument, complete with numbered points, why he shouldn't bother us: "Our houses are flimsy. At the lowlands, they have wood and stone houses." Something about Gaji [headman's second wife; mother of Wamp] and a discussion; connected with her sending the malevolent spirit to Ngku yesterday, I wonder. Ato' says a spell over some water for Hamdadn, who has a fever. Things back to normal; Yeer still chants occasionally when a new idea occurs to him.

9/25/74: Observations of a Storm in a Semai (Malaysia) Village

Carole Robarchek

Storm

Rain and high winds started just as it was getting dark. Really hard rains come. Abi' Bah Les [father of Les, age 56] checks over his packed rattan back basket, Les [married man, age 24] and others go out in the rain and beat the ground. Women have their children tucked up in a sarong sling, children have their sarongs on with all their belongings with them, people have their knives on.

Sngyak [married man, age 54] has his pack on and six-foot long blowpipe in hand. Water is rushing down the hill in a torrent. People are continuing to pack up and stuff and stick it in their rattan back basket.

Sngyak takes off under Headman's house. Abi's Bah Les and family take off, all with belongings; Ne' [Les' wife, age 28] and Les are still pounding the ground. Ne' has kid on her back. He's asleep! Everyone is screaming all at once. Abi' Bah Les runs back in, still all loaded up with heavy pack; everyone is banging on the house posts with their knives and shouting. All little ones are strapped up in sarongs. Abi' Bah Les is burning hair. Bidn [Sngyak's son-in-law, age 36] gets his blowpipe down his pack on—all adults and children have packs on now and are milling around and screaming. Wind is really fierce. Blows the window flap half off the front of Les' compartment; fire scatters all over the floor. The hiss of water hitting the fires and the roar of the wind, the sound of the rain, the roar of the running water, the people screaming, the sound of knives banging the posts, the clubs pounding the ground, hair being pounded—the din is fierce! These people are really freaking out!

Wamp [boy, age 12] comes over with suitcase and pack and sits down to get warm by the fire. Les has halfway repaired the window flap. Incense is thrown on Les' fire by Ne'. Now the smell of burning hair is mixed with that of at least two kinds of incense, also the smell of wet dogs, cats, chicken shit, goat shit. Really wild experience. Abi' Bah Les is now sitting by fire still packed up. Les, 'iil [Abi' Bah Les' boy, age 5], Wamp sit. All rest are still standing, all loaded up. The wind has blown rain through the house; there isn't a dry spot. Jao [Abi Bah Les' wife, age 54] sits down by Les' fire. Bidn's outside trying to divert water channel from the house posts. Tama [Abi' Bah Les' son, age 6] sits down without pack, Toy [age 9] sits with pack. Sngyak sits, Kign [Abi' Bah Les' daughter, age 11] sits, wind is gone.

Ne' shouts that Bidn ran to Burudaar, another settlement. He had put Yeedn [Bidn's younger wife, age 11; daughter of Sngyak] on his back and left his child behind. Toy [Bidn's son] looks into the fire; ignores everything. She yells that the wind is gone because of the spells and the incense. Les fixes the window flap. Everyone sitting now except Alang [Sngyak's wife].

Bidn back with Yeedn, both are soaked to the skin as are most people as they had all at one time or another run out of the house.

I asked Les why they want to run. He says, "If we don't run, Ngku and the storm will tear the house out of the ground."

Everything pretty calm here; still hear Yeer yelling from his house. Can't smoke [a cigarette] now because are burning incense offering to storm. Sngyak is burning incense; "he did it first." Abi' Bah Les carries coals on a piece of bark and takes a pinch of tobacco outside. Burns the tobacco on the coals and screams, "Here's Thy tobacco, Javanese tobacco, tasty tobacco, Thy present. Don't stay here. Go back to the lowlands." Yells awhile and comes back in. Says, "Storm, you can incur rocks, little, sharpened, bamboo splinters, an iron thing." [These are placed in your body by supernatural beings and cause illness.]

From Learning to Fear: A Case Study of Emotional Conditioning

Clayton A. Robarchek

The Semai are perhaps best known in the anthropological literature for their nonaggressiveness and aversion to interpersonal violence of any sort. Dentan (1965, 1968) characterized them as nonviolent, and Alland (1972), drawing on Dentan's research, used them as an example to counter arguments that humans are innately aggressive. My own observations, obtained over a period of some fourteen months' residence in two Semai settlements, were entirely in accord with these characterizations. I found Semai social life to be almost totally free of interpersonal violence or overt hostility of any kind. Dentan (1968) stated that not a single case of murder, attempted murder, or maiming had come to the attention of the authorities since the first census of the Semai was taken in 1956. Although this may somewhat overstate the actual situation, the fact remains that the incidence of violence in Semai society is so low as to be virtually nonexistent.

This is, however, only one manifestation of what is perhaps the most fundamental feature of Semai temperament: a low level of emotionality in general. With the exception of fearful behavior (which I shall discuss at length below), emotional outbursts seldom occur. In addition to the virtual absence of strong expressions of anger, mourning is subdued, expression of joy is muted, and even laughter is restrained.

Low affective involvement is characteristic of interpersonal relationships as well. Dentan speaks of feeling as if there were a "thin glass wall" between himself and his Semai neighbors (1968:5), an experience also shared by my wife and me. This emotional reserve is, however, characteristic not only of relations with outsiders, but also of relations among the Semai themselves. One sees few overt expressions of affection, empathy, or sympathy. Dentan quotes an informant's observation on the uselessness of sympathy: "what good does it do an unhappy person," he asks, "to have another person upset?" (1968:64). My informants described to me atrocities that they had seen committed against outsiders during World War II. They viewed these as merely examples of the incomprehensible behavior of the Japanese and showed little sympathy for or empathy with the victims. Numerous other examples of low affective involvement could be cited as well: the father who, during a storm, ran away leaving his children behind; an entire household that fled when their house collapsed during a storm, leaving an elderly grandmother trapped inside; and so on.

The sole exception to this generalization of low affect is in the expression of fear. Dangers of all sorts are ubiquitous in the Semai world. They fear strangers, supernatural beings, storms, and animals; virtually everything in their culturally constituted environment is viewed as actually or potentially threatening. Even that gentlest and most harmless of nature's creatures, the butterfly, may bring disaster and death if not dealt with circumspectly. Behavior in all areas of life is rigidly circumscribed to avoid precipitating the dangers inherent in this universe (Robarchek 1977a). There are, moreover, no cultural values, no expectations of bravery to inhibit the direct expression of these fears. Men, women, and children readily admit to being afraid, and no onus is attached to such admissions (compare Dentan 1965, 1978). This allows free rein to the expression of fear, which in some cases may escalate into outright panic.

What I have tried to sketch here is the outline of a culturally determined emotional specialization, one that couples fearfulness with an overall lack of other emotionality. The following discussion addresses the problem of the ontogenetic development of this particular affective configuration: how this pattern of emotionality is generated in infants and children as a part of the process of enculturation. . . .

The Fear of Storms

The Malay Peninsula receives rainfall up to two hundred days annually. Much of this falls in relatively short but often violent and highly localized afternoon thunderstorms accompanied by intense lightning, deafening thunder, and high winds. To a non-Semai, these storms can be rather frightening; the elevated bamboo and thatch houses sway violently and threaten to collapse before the gale. In Semai, however, they can provoke abject terror.

Semai see these storms as the responses of supernatural beings to human misbehavior. This belief centers around the concept of *terlaid,* which Dentan translates "to behave in a way that will provoke disaster" (1968:23). Although such disaster may take a variety of forms, it is most commonly conceived of as a violent storm in which the houses are blown down and the hamlet is swept away by a flood or landslide, killing all the inhabitants.

Such a storm is usually caused by Ngku, a thunder "spirit," when he has been angered by human actions. A wide variety of behaviors may provoke this response, but the most frequent cause is treating or referring to some animal or insect in a frivolous or joking manner. Thus, for example, it was reported to me that one hamlet was swept away by a landslide because the children had dressed a dog in a shirt and then laughed at it. Similarly, a recent devastating flood in the lowlands was attributed to a patrol of Malay soldiers who allegedly mocked the call of a bird. Numerous folktales tell of similar occurrences.

Although frivolous treatment of any animal is *terlaid,* some creatures are inherently more dangerous in this regard than others. This is especially true of butterflies and dragonflies, who are Ngku's children. Joking about or laughing at a butterfly angers Ngku and thus is an invitation to certain disaster. The dragonfly is so dangerous that one should not even mention its name or take notice of its presence. (None of the foregoing should, however, be construed as implying worship of or reverence for animals; the Semai regularly hunt and kill animals for food, collect butterflies for sale, and kick and starve their dogs.)

This, then, is the cultural belief system that shapes the Semai response to storms. As the clouds build and the storm approaches, the elders begin chanting spells asking Ngku to spare the hamlet. Resin incense is burned as an offering to him. As the storm builds in intensity, activity becomes more and more frantic. Children are questioned about their having possibly committed some act that is *terlaid.* If a child admits to anything, a tuft of his hair is cut off, beaten against a log or stone with the blunt edge of a *parang* (machete), and cast into the fire to appease Ngku. Often, hair from all the children is burned just in case they may have unknowingly committed some *terlaid* offense. If the storm persists, people may begin to panic and run blindly into the forest, which because of the hazard of falling trees is even more dangerous than remaining in the village clearing.

The preceding paragraph does not really do justice to the climate of fear that prevails in a Semai hamlet during a severe thunderstorm; so I have excerpted the following account from my field notes in an attempt to convey more accurately the intensity of the Semai reaction to these storms:

9/25/74. Just before dusk. A storm comes up very fast; heavy rain, hard wind, much thunder and lightning. The headman, Bah Les, and Bah Coy are out in the rain, pounding the ground with heavy pieces of firewood and shouting "go down, go down!" The headman shouts to the others "hit, hit, hit!" (They are trying to keep Ngku's wife, Nanggaa', an enormous horned dragon, from bursting up out of the ground bringing with her a torrent of mud and water that would sweep away the hamlet. She is summoned by the thunder, her husband's voice.) The headman comes into his house shouting "burn *Kijai* (resin)"; someone answers that there is none. Headman shouts "We are all going to die because we don't have any incense!" Bah Bidn runs into the house bringing some incense from Bah Les's house. Headman puts it with some coals on a piece of firewood and goes outside and burns it, chanting to Ngku to go away. People are stuffing belongings into backbaskets, preparing to run. The headman is shouting his spell to Ngku: "What's the good of this, your doing it so hard?" He shouts at kids to cut their hair. Runs back outside, pounds the ground shouting "Go down!" Bedlam; people running in and out of the house screaming at each other above the storm. Many people outside pounding the ground: Bah Dol, Bah Les, the headman. Headman chanting to Ngku as he hits the ground. Wind increases; houses shaking. Everyone abandons Kning Wah Da's house and comes here (headman's house). Kning Wah Da shouts that the house is going to collapse. Kning Ledn throws salt on the fire, it crackles and smokes. Shouting and screaming all around. Loud clap of thunder, more shouts: "*wee ato'!*" (stop it, grandfather!). Loud thunder, more shouts. Headman still pounding the ground. Raining a torrent. Front flap has blown loose on Bah Les's house and rain is streaming in. Headman tells everyone to get out of the house; some do, and go underneath; others stay inside. Kning Ledn, pounding the ground under her house, has her youngest child on her back. Someone throws hot coals out of Bah Les's house (also to drive the dragon down). Kning Ledn now out in the rain, pounding the ground. Headman runs back into the house, shouts "cut hair!" Wind abates slightly; headman still chanting to Ngku: "we're not guilty; we're just poor miserable people," throws salt on the fire. Kning Ledn pounds some lemongrass with a *parang*, throws it on the fire. Headman tells her to cut hair from all the kids and burn it. She does; pounds the hair against a log with a *parang*, throws it into the fire. House still full of people. Storm is abating. Headman still chanting. Still much thunder but the wind and rain have lessened. Headman tells Ngku to take the storm to the lowlands, to the Malays: "if you keep it up, we'll die. Maybe we're a little guilty, but not much; this is no way for you to treat your grandchildren; we're just poor, ignorant people. Go down to the Malays!"

Such is the world into which Semai infants are born, a world in which storms are an almost daily occurrence. Even during the short dry seasons, seldom does a week pass without one. These storms and the beliefs and behaviors associated with them are a constant feature of the developing child's life.

Utilizing the assumptions proposed earlier, we can begin to see how this thunderstorm complex may impinge upon the development of a Semai child's emotionality, long before he is capable of understanding the beliefs themselves. I see this process as essentially one of response-mediated generalization (Dollard and Miller 1950), which may be summarized as follows:

1) The crash of the thunder (and the bedlam that surrounds the infant) are unconditioned stimuli (UCS) that elicit in him the unconditioned response (UCR) of generalized arousal and distress (the so-called innate fear of loud noises).

2) The infant is incapable at first of attaching meaning to his aroused state but, through exposure to his mother's fear (she carries him cradled in a sarong against her body) and the fear of the other members of the household, he comes to associate his internal state with the subjective emotion of fear. Thus, as the child's cognitive capacities mature, the arousal state acquires a specific meaning: threat. The child learns to *feel* afraid in the presence of the UCS (thunder) and the UCR (arousal).

3) As the child develops the capacity to perceive his own internal state of arousal, the perception of *this state itself*, from its previous association with the thunder, becomes a cue with the capacity to elicit the response of subjective fear.

4) The perception of the internal state of generalized arousal thus becomes sufficient to induce the subjective emotion of fear in contexts other than those in which it was initially learned. . . .

The Interaction of Belief and Affect

If the foregoing analysis is correct, a state of generalized arousal, regardless of the objective situation inducing it, evokes the subjective emotion of fear. The child learns to associate a particular meaning (threat) with his perception of his aroused state, and this culturally learned meaning becomes a part of *any* situation producing a state of arousal. This felt threat is a part of the information that the individual employs in his evaluation and definition of the total situation. He has, in fact, learned to fear his own emotional arousal, and any situation arousing strong affect is thus perceived as threatening.

In such a situation, fear accompanies the arousal of any emotion, and the greater the level of arousal, the more intense will be the subjective fear that accompanies it. Because fear is an unpleasant affect, it operates in a negative-feedback relationship with other subjective emotions, inhibiting emotionality of all kinds and resulting in the low level of affect that, as we have seen, is characteristic of the Semai. Moreover, it causes them to avoid situations carrying the possibility of strong affective arousal, for example, conflicts or intense interpersonal relationships, and it results in the typical Semai responses of avoidance or flight to threats or other affectively charged situations. . . .

The concept of *terlaid* is important for affective learning in later childhood as well. As children come to understand the concept of *terlaid*, the fear that it evokes is used by adults in further promoting emotional control in children. As we have seen, the blame for causing storms falls almost entirely on children; Semai adults are ordinarily assumed not to do things that are *terlaid*. Although the *terlaid* concept proscribes certain specific behaviors, especially laughing at or playing with particular creatures or objects, in practice the concept and the fear associated with it are invoked by adults whenever children's play becomes too boisterous. If their laughter becomes too loud and unrestrained, some adult is certain to shout *"terlaid,"* and thus to call up for the children the dangers of losing emotional control, even in the euphoria of play (see also Dentan 1968:60). When a severe storm occurs, it is the children who are questioned about and forced to reflect upon their actions. This interrogation, taking place in the fear-charged atmosphere of the storm, serves to impress further upon the children their responsibility for maintaining emotional control, for not to do so endangers the entire community. . . .

References Cited

[Some original footnotes have been omitted.]

Alland, Alexander, Jr.
  1972   The Human Imperative. New York: Columbia University Press.
Dentan, R. K.
  1965   Some Senoi Semai Dietary Restrictions. Unpublished Ph.D. dissertation. Yale University.
  1968   The Semai, a Nonviolent People of Malaya. New York: Holt, Rinehart and Winston.
  1978   Notes on Childhood in a Nonviolent Context: The Semai Case. *In* Learning Nonaggression. Ashley Montagu, Ed. New York: Oxford University Press. pp. 95–143.
Dollard, John, and Neal Miller
  1950   Personality and Psychotherapy. New York: McGraw-Hill.
Robarchek, Clayton A.
  1977a   Semai Nonviolence: A Systems Approach to Understanding. Unpublished Ph.D. dissertation. University of California, Riverside.

From Ambassador's Journal: A Personal Account of the Kennedy Years

John Kenneth Galbraith

[November 17, 1961]
Saigon (later)

I arrived here about noon and was met by Fritz Nolting, the Ambassador. Trimble from Cambodia was also here and we lunched at the Residence. The latter is a spacious house with pleasant rooms and high ceilings and an incredible traffic noise pounding by outside.

Saigon itself is very lively and agreeable in a French sort of way. The women are handsomely dressed in *ao dais*, these being high-waisted pajamas with flowing panels of white silk fore and aft. They are also very good-looking and especially so on a bicycle. The city shows little sign of the terror in the countryside and few soldiers are in evidence. There are reminders though. A few weeks ago, someone tossed a bomb at Nolting.

I settled down immediately to talks with Nolting and General McGarr, the head of M.A.A.G.[1] On this, more later.

November 19—Saigon

Yesterday morning I spent reading background papers at the Embassy, a shabby six-story building near the Saigon River. Then I had a long talk with members of the Embassy staff, followed by lunch with Arthur Gardiner, the head of USOM (United States Operations Mission), the AID mission here. After two or three hours, we drove for an hour or so into the country. More talks with Nolting followed, then a formal dinner at the Residence and then still more talk. Before dinner, I decided to have a few minutes' nap and nearly succeeded in sleeping through dinner.

Saigon is busy and bustling; a French provincial city, say Toulouse, comes to mind. People are clean, well-dressed and well-fed, and one is struck by the stylish-looking women in the *ao dais*, which I have mentioned.

But one learns that the city is also in a modified state of siege. The Ambassador and senior officials are followed everywhere by a car filled with gun-bearers—one went along with us into the country yesterday and was never more than a few feet behind. The members of the USOM cannot go or anyhow are not allowed out of town without an escort consisting of two or three carloads of soldiers. This makes extension work, say a visit to instruct some farmers on how to improve rice production, rather labor-intensive. In fact, to the number of about two hundred, they are all penned up in Saigon. Gardiner says they are busy; I imagine that means they are extensively advising each other.

The Vietcong has long been active on the Mekong Delta to the south of Saigon. In recent weeks, they have been attacking villages in some force in the highlands to the south, and they control countryside up to thirty miles from Saigon. Food, especially rice, no longer comes here in satisfactory quantities for the farmers are being terrorized into not selling. Rice exports have fallen to zero. This problem is not especially eased by a bad flood on the Delta.

The countryside, to the north, over which we drove yesterday on a new multi-lane highway, is green and rather sparsely populated. Rice fields alternate with stretches of low jungle. Soldiers were much in evidence although they are little to be seen in Saigon itself. I couldn't help wondering if a super-highway of this sort—it was built with American aid—was the most urgent need of the country.

I have discovered that to get to New Delhi with any promptness I must return to Hong Kong today. This is much like going to Chicago from Boston by way of Dallas.

Dinner last night was for the Economics Minister and the Health Minister, a full-dress affair. Neither seemed much perturbed by their state of siege, although if they lose, I imagine, they will either be hanged or forced into exile. The atmosphere of this city begins to leave a horrible taste in my mouth.

November 20—Bangkok—New Delhi

Yesterday morning, I had a briefing on the military situation. I can't entirely get over the fact that there are 250,000 organized forces on the government side and maybe 15,000 in opposition. Anyhow, the briefing was held in a large auditorium-like building at the M.A.A.G. headquarters. A few young officers attended and it was geared to the mentality of an idiot, or, more likely, a backwoods congressman. The presiding general became embarrassed at one point and told the officers they were telling what I already knew. Much of it bore only a limited relation to the known or demonstrable truth. One officer said that since the beginning of the year, the Vietcong had suffered 17,000 casualties at the hands of the government forces. This was the equivalent of losing their entire force and some fifty percent more in ten months for they started the year with many fewer than the 15,000 just mentioned. I asked for a figure that reflected the officer's own judgment. The general supported my request but the officer had none. One briefing officer said the jungle had no underbrush and made for easy passage. Another said it was impenetrable except on the trails. One had to remember each moment that Vietnamese divisions on the war map were not necessarily divisions in practice.

In the afternoon, I had a political discussion, much more valuable, although even the military information was so wrong as to be, in its way, a clue to the state of things.

[Letter to President Kennedy]   New Delhi, India
                                                November 28, 1961

Dear Mr. President:

You will already have had sundry more official communications from me on South Vietnam. This is by way of giving you something of the informal flavor and color of the local scene.

It is certainly a can of snakes. I am reasonably accustomed to oriental government and politics, but I was not quite prepared for Diem. As you will doubtless be warned, whenever anyone reaches an inconvenient conclusion on this country, he has been duped. My view is derived neither from the Indians nor the Saigon intellectuals but my personal capacity for error. One of the proposals which I am told was made to Max Taylor provides an interesting clue to our man.[2] It was that a helicopter be provided to pluck him out of his palace and take him directly to the airport. This is because his surface travel through Saigon requires the taking in of all laundry along the route, the closing of all windows, an order to the populace to keep their heads in, the clearing of all streets, and a vast bevy of motorcycle outriders to protect him on his dash. Every trip to the airport requires such arrangements and it is felt that a chopper would make him seem more democratic. Incidentally, if Diem leaves town for a day, all members of his cabinet are required to see him off and welcome him back although this involves less damage to efficiency than might be supposed.

The political reality is the total stasis which arises from his greater need to protect himself from a coup than to protect the country from the Vietcong. I am quite clear that the absence of intelligence, the centralization of Army control, the incredible dual role of the provincial governors as Army generals and political administrators, the subservient incompetence of the latter, are all related to his fear of being given the heave.

The desire to prolong one's days in office has a certain consistency the world around and someday somebody should explain this to the State Department with pictures. I would love to have come up with the conclusion that our man would be reformed and made into an effective military and political force. It would have given me similar hopes for . . . [some people nearer home].

Saigon has a curious aspect. It is a rather shabby version of a French provincial city—say, Toulouse, as I remember it. Life proceeds normally and it has the most stylish women in all Asia. They are tall with long legs, high breasts and wear white silk pajamas and a white silk robe, split at the sides to the armpits to give the effect of a flat panel fore and aft. On a bicycle or scooter they look very compelling and one is reminded once again that an ambassadorship is the greatest inducement to celibacy since the chastity belt. Restaurants, nightclubs and hotels flourish as they seem always to do in cities *in extremis.* Yet one moves around with an armed guard and a group of gunmen following in a car behind. The morale of the Americans seems to be rather good although I wonder a little bit about our technical assistance program. The people assigned to the country are confined almost exclusively to Saigon since travel has become too dangerous. I can't imagine that the agriculturists, for example, are of much value under these circumstances. The Ambassador there, a decent man who is trying to obey orders, has been treated abominably by the State Department. He first heard of Max's mission on the radio. He had no chance to comment on the orders resulting therefrom. I would reluctantly tell you who is responsible for this management were steps taken to overcome my natural grace and charity. . . .

[Letter to President Kennedy]

April 5, 1962

Dear Mr. President:

I have put in a lot of time the last three or four days on the scene of my well-known guerrilla activities, namely, South Vietnam. This included a long and most reassuring discussion with Bob McNamara. We are in basic agreement on most matters and for the rest I think Bob appreciated having some arguments from my side of the fence. I also had two or three long discussions with Averell and the attached memorandum, which is of no breathtaking novelty, comes close to reflecting our combined views. I think I can safely spare you another eloquent restatement of what you have already heard from me several times before. However, I do pray that in addition to reading the attached memorandum you see Governor Harriman at some early date.

I am leaving this afternoon for New York and tomorrow night for India. There are no pressing Indian issues I need to cover with you. Kashmir will continue to simmer. This is not the time for any brilliant initiatives and the best we can do is to press both sides to keep their behavior in low key and keep above the obscene politics ourselves. As I told you attitudes on the Hill toward India seem mellower than I had expected. I am coming back on a very brief private trip in early June to get an honorary degree and make a speech. I will try and give A.I.D. and India a lift before the Senate if, as Fulbright and some others believe, it may then be needed.

Last, but not least, I must tell you how much I enjoyed the other evening at Glen Ora, our survey of the problems of the nation and the world, and the chance to reflect on the unique capacity of your advisers to solve them.

April 4, 1962

MEMORANDUM FOR THE PRESIDENT
Subject: Vietnam

The following considerations influence our thinking on Vietnam:

1. We have a growing military commitment. This could expand step by step into a major, long drawn-out, indecisive military involvement.

2. We are backing a weak and, on the record, ineffectual government and a leader who as a politician may be beyond the point of no return.

3. There is consequent danger we shall replace the French as the colonial force in the area and bleed as the French did.

4. The political effects of some of the measures which pacification requires, or is believed to require, including the concentration of population, relocation of villages, and the burning of old villages, may be damaging to those and especially to Westerners associated with it.

5. We fear that at some point in the involvement there will be a major political outburst about the new Korea and the new war into which the Democrats as so often before have precipitated us.

6. It seems at least possible that the Soviets are not particularly desirous of trouble in this part of the world and that our military reaction with the need to fall back on Chinese protection may be causing concern in Hanoi.

In the light of the foregoing we urge the following:

1. That it be our policy to keep open the door for political solution. We should welcome as a solution any broadly based non-Communist government that is free from external interference. It should have the requisites for internal law and order. We should not require that it be militarily identified with the United States.

2. We shall find it useful in achieving this result if we seize any good opportunity to involve other countries and world opinion in settlement and its guarantee. This is a useful exposure and pressure on the Communist bloc countries and a useful antidote for the argument that this is a private American military adventure.

3. We should measurably reduce our commitment to the particular leadership of the government of South Vietnam.

To accomplish the foregoing, we recommend the following specific steps:

1. In the next fortnight or so the I.C.C. will present a report which we are confidentially advised will accuse North Vietnam of subversion and the Government of Vietnam in conjunction with the United States of not notifying the introduction of men and material as prescribed by the

Geneva accords. We should respond by asking the co-chairmen to initiate steps to re-establish compliance with the Geneva accords. Pending specific recommendations, which might at some stage include a conference of signatories, we should demand a suspension of Vietcong activity and agree to a standstill on an introduction of men and material.

2. Additionally, Governor Harriman should be instructed to approach the Russians to express our concern about the increasingly dangerous situation that the Vietcong is forcing in Southeast Asia. They should be told of our determination not to let the Vietcong overthrow the present government while at the same time to look without relish on the dangers that this military build-up is causing in the area. The Soviets should be asked to ascertain whether Hanoi can and will call off the Vietcong activity in return for phased American withdrawal, liberalization in the trade relations between the two parts of the country and general and non-specific agreement to talk about reunification after some period of tranquility.

3. Alternatively, the Indians should be asked to make such an approach to Hanoi under the same terms of reference.

4. It must be recognized that our long-run position cannot involve an unconditional commitment to Diem. Our support is to non-Communist and progressively democratic government not to individuals. We cannot ourselves replace Diem. But we should be clear in our mind that almost any non-Communist change would probably be beneficial and this should be the guiding rule for our diplomatic representation in the area.

In the meantime policy should *continue* to be guided by the following:

1. We should resist all steps which commit American troops to combat action and impress upon all concerned the importance of keeping American forces out of actual combat commitment.

2. We should disassociate ourselves from action, however necessary, which seems to be directed at the villagers, such as the new concentration program. If the action is one that is peculiarly identified with Americans, such as defoliation, it should not be undertaken in the absence of most compelling reasons. Americans in their various roles should be as invisible as the situation permits. . . .

Notes

1. Military Assistance Advisory Group. This designation of our military mission in other countries has the connotation of an alliance—and also, in some instances, inconvenient independence of the ambassador.
2. Meaning Diem.

Memorandum for Colonel Hughes

H. R. Haldeman

MEMORANDUM

THE WHITE HOUSE
WASHINGTON

May 26, 1969

MEMORANDUM FOR: COLONEL HUGHES

The President would like to have the bowling ball man come in and fit Mrs. Nixon and Tricia for balls as soon as possible. Could arrangements be made for this immediately, please.

H. R. Haldeman

cc:
Mr. Chapin

from "Garage Sales" [First Version]

Christina Mohr

The following description is from the first version of a report on observing buyers' behaviors during a garage sale.

```
    One of my first customers was my favorite. She was of a small frame; I
would estimate maybe 5 feet tall (in heels). She probably topped the scales
at 100 pounds (sopping wet). She was in her seventies and didn't carry her age
particularly well. A person could see the road of life had not been easy on
her by the severity of lines on her face.
    She fit my typical grandma image. Her snowy white hair had been tossed
up in an attempt to form a bun, but had not remained cooperative, as stray
hair dangled around her face. Each time she moved, she made a swiping motion
at her forehead to keep the hair out of her eyes.
    She wore hot pink double-knit slacks, a hot pink shirt, and a bulky,
loose fitting sweater. Her collar was inside out on one side but lay per-
```

fectly on the other. I found her appearance humorous. She reminded me of how a two year old would look after an unsuccessful attempt at dressing themself.

She wore a modern pair of bi-focals. They looked good on her and didn't reflect the urgent need her eyes had the them.

A quick glance at her hands revealed she suffered from crippling arthritis. The sight of them saddened me and I could nearly feel the pain she must feel with every movement. But it didn't seem to slow her down at all.

She wore false teeth. This was evident because they clattered with each word she spoke. She did not seem to mind them as she continued to talk non-stop. She started a conversation by introducing herself. Her name was Ethel; she lived around the corner.

When she wasn't speaking directly to someone in particular, she kept a continual conversation going with the infant she had pushed to the sale in a stroller. The infant was 9 months old and gurgled back to her as if he under-stood each word she spoke. He sat strapped in the seat which appeared to have limited his movement. He seemed quite content to sit, pulling his socks off. It was as if his response to her continual chattering was his continual orneriness. She would fuss at him a bit, threatening to place a price tag on him and sell him in the sale. But all the while it was apparent she was teasing.

I learned more about Grandma Ethel in the time she was at the sale than I know about alot of acquaintances. She is married to the same man she fell in love with 49 years ago. She spoke freely of her two sons and two daughters. They range in age from 45 to 34. All her children live here in Wichita. They have given her seven grandchildren, one of which was riding in the stroller.

She had been born and raised in Wichita, and had spent the majority of her life in this very neighborhood.

As she browsed around the sale something suddenly caught me as funny. Her browsing was more of a bustle in comparison with the other shoppers who had come and gone. I got the impression she was looking for something but just wasn't sure what it was. She smelled every bottle of perfume, tried on all the jewelry, and read the contents of every magazine. Nothing went untouched, nor did anything miss receiving a complete inspection.

She spent over an hour at her extensive shopping. She was a garage sale pro--a bargain hunter. When she was done and was ready to settle up for her purchase, the final bill was 15 cents. She had spent all that time shopping to purchase a key ring and a skein of black yarn. She seemed amused and apolo-gized for not being able to find anymore items she just could not live with-out. As she paid her debt and went on her merry way, I felt enriched at having met her.

"Garage Sales" [*Final Version*]

Christina Mohr

The following description is from the final version of a report on observing buyers' behaviors during a garage sale.

One of my first customers was a small woman, maybe 5 feet tall and 100 pounds. She was in her seventies and had a weather-worn look with severe lines engraved in her face. Her snowy white hair had been tossed up in an attempt to form a bun. As stray hair dangled around her face, she would make a swiping motion to keep it out of her eyes. She wore a modern pair of bifocals, which didn't magnify her eyes as glasses so often do. She wore false teeth. This was evident because they clattered with each word she spoke. A quick glance at her hands revealed she suffered from crippling arthritis. They appeared to bend in directions they were not meant to bend. As if engaged in a personal battle to fight the appearance of being an elderly crippled woman, she was dressed in hot pink slacks with matching shirt and a cream colored, bulky, loose fitting sweater.

She began a conversation by introducing herself.

"Hello, my name is Ethel." She had a pleasant, soft voice and nice smile. "Even though I just live around the corner, I don't believe we have ever met."

I replied, returning the smile, "Hi, Ethel, I'm Tina. I have lived here for several years and don't believe we have met. I'm pleased to meet you." I paused for only a moment then asked, "Are you out for a daily walk or just out for the sale?"

"Oh," she began, "I walk daily. A person must walk daily to keep their body moving. You get as old as I and it seems much easier to stay in bed. But you can't. You have to keep moving!"

Her actions provided evidence that she firmly believed this. She moved all about the garage searching each sale table. It appeared to me she was in high gear.

She was eager to share much of her life history. She had been born and raised in Wichita and had spent the majority of her life in this very neigh-borhood. It didn't take long for me to learn that she had been married for 49 years. She had two sons and two daughters from this union. They range in age from 34 to 45. All her children live in Wichita. They have given her several grandchildren, one of whom was riding in a stroller she had pushed to the sale.

When I was diverted to help another shopper, Ethel continued her conversation with the child in the stroller. The infant was 9-months old and gurgled back to her as if he understood each word she spoke. He was strapped into the stroller but this didn't limit his movement. Ethel encircled him as if she were an Indian raiding a wagon train. Each time he grabbed something, like the tablecloth, she would snap at him to keep him behaving. She fussed at him, threatening to place a price tag on him and sell him in the sale. But all the while it was apparent she was teasing.

She continued her shopping, bustling from table to table. She smelled every bottle of perfume, tried on all the jewelry and read the contents of every magazine. Nothing went untouched, nor did anything miss receiving a complete inspection. She spent over an hour at her extensive shopping. It appeared she was looking for something; she just didn't know what.

Most of my time was spent watching and talking to her. I could not believe she had been at the sale so long. Odd to me was not odd to her. She was a garage sale pro: a bargain hunter. When she was finished and was ready to settle up for her purchase, the final bill was fifteen cents. She had spent

INAPPROPRIATE   SUGGESTED ALTERNATIVES

c. Salutations for letters

Dear Sir
Gentlemen

no salutation (impersonal business letter where name of person
is unknown)
or
Dear *(Name)*
    Jane Rogers
    Ms. Leone
    Mr. Kaplan
or
Dear *(functional title)*
    Credit Manager
    Customer
    Colleague, etc.
(where individual is unknown,
but function is pertinent)

It should be noted that the alternatives suggested above involve a number of different processes. In some cases, simple substitution of a universal term such as *humanity* for an ambiguous generic such as *mankind* is sufficient. Some sentences may be recast in the plural, while in others the inappropriate pronoun is unnecessary as it carries no meaning. In still other instances, an alternative sentence structure avoids the possible ambiguity. We have given only a few examples to illustrate the process—the list of alternatives could have been much longer. One common usage not mentioned above is the use of *she or he, his or her,* and *him or her* when a pronoun seems unavoidable. Some people object to repeated use of these expressions as "clumsy," and it sometimes does represent a "lazy way out." Occasional use of *he or she,* however, is perfectly acceptable to most people. Forms such as *he/she* or *s/he* have been adopted by some writers, but they have no natural counterparts in the spoken language.

(2) Use of sex-specific terms

The use of appropriate universal terms assures that sex-specific terms will be understood unambiguously. Thus, if we state that college-educated men earn more than those with a high school education, it will be clear that we are not referring to women. Likewise, if we wish to compare women and men in the same profession, the use of such terms as *female* or *women doctors* alongside of *male* or *men doctors* is appropriate.

Questions of Evaluation

Avoiding the sexism in expressions referring to women which involve derogatory connotations, evaluation of women as inferior, and other stereotypes, is not as simple as avoiding sexist designations. Designation is often a matter of specific linguistic forms, while problems of evaluation require a recognition of the negative stereotype or attitude behind the usage. Context, both linguistic and societal, plays a more important role in questions of evaluation. There are, of course, many instances of sexist usage which involve both designation and evaluation.

(1) Asymmetrical constructions vs. parallel terms

INAPPROPRIATE	SUGGESTED ALTERNATIVES
man and wife	husband and wife (Both terms refer to a relationship.)
Mr. Jones and his family	The Jones family
Mr. Lucas and his wife Louise	Sam and Louise Lucas *or* Louise and Sam Lucas (Women and children are not viewed as possessions of men.)
Addressing or referring to male members of a group as *men* and female members as *girls*	Either *women and men or boys and girls*, according to the situation. (Many people who object to the use of the term *lady* point out that it is not parallel to *man*.)
	It is also appropriate to reverse the order of some traditional expressions so that women do sometimes precede men, e.g., *women and men, her or his*.
Referring to a woman by title (Ms. King) and to a man by last name only (McEnroe) in the same context	Ms. King and Mr. McEnroe *or* Billie Jean King and John McEnroe *or* King and McEnroe

(2) Unnecessary reference to sex in designating people

INAPPROPRIATE	SUGGESTED ALTERNATIVES
	Universal or neutral terms:
poetess	poet
sculptress	sculptor
waitress	waiter or server
male nurse	nurse
lady mayor	mayor

The suggested alternative usage for the above category of words is identical to the usage recommended for the *-man* terms in the section on designation. The problem here, however, is not one of ambiguity caused by pretending that a word like *policeman* is generic; it is the assumption that sex is a relevant characteristic when referring to a person's profession, and that there is something "different" or inferior about women who are poets or men who are nurses.

(3) Terms which belittle

These may overlap with the first category, as the belittling connotation of the term referring to women is often combined with a lack of parallel terminology.

INAPPROPRIATE	SUGGESTED ALTERNATIVES
	a. Girls vs. women
Use of girl to refer to an adult female, especially a stranger	*woman*

We recognize that some adults refer to their friends as a group as *girls* or *boys* and find nothing belittling in such usage. However, in many contexts, the use of *girl* or *girls* for adults implies immaturity and relative unimportance. And the usage is not usually paralleled in references to men. Thus, *the girls in the office* work with *men*, seldom with *boys*. Such usage reflects an evaluation of the role of women as less important than that of men. A female Vice President would probably not be referred to as a *girl*, but a female clerk would most likely be a *girl*, while her male counterpart would be a *man*. The use of *boy* might reflect the person's extreme youth, or an attitude that people in lesser positions do not merit as much respect as their superiors. We suggest that this is as inappropriate as the sexist attitudes and that everyone would gain in dignity by the use of *men* and *women*.

INAPPROPRIATE	SUGGESTED ALTERNATIVES

b. Forms of address

honey, sweetie, dear, and similar terms to address women with whom one does not have a close relationship	No address form *or* person's name (when known) *or* generic term of address like *Ma'am* or *Sir* in contexts such as service encounters

(Of course when there is a close relationship between people, there is nothing wrong with reciprocal usage of terms of endearment.)

c. Derogatory labels

chick, broad, tomato, babe, and similar terms which treat women as sex objects or objects for consumption	neutral terms which treat people with dignity and respect
Expressions such as *Miss Fidditch* to refer to the stereotypical fussy English teacher	

(4) Use of adjectives, nouns, and other forms to reflect stereotypes

INAPPROPRIATE	SUGGESTED ALTERNATIVES

a. Associating characteristics with one sex only.

masculine drive	drive
feminine wiles	wiles
feminine intuition	intuition

(The adjectives are unnecessary in the above examples.)

b. Using different adjectives to describe the same characteristic

outspoken man/bitchy woman prudent man/timid or fearful woman	When used differentially to describe the same trait, the choice of adjectives reveals the user's bias regarding the sexes. Non-discriminatory usage requires deciding on the appropriate description regardless of

INAPPROPRIATE	SUGGESTED ALTERNATIVES
	sex, and labelling both men and women as either *prudent* or *fearful*, for example.

c. Using different verbs to describe the same activity

| men shout/women scream/men guffaw/women giggle/men talk/ women chatter, gossip, etc. | The use of words often reveals attitudes regarding the sexes. As in the case of adjectives and nouns, non-discriminatory usage, as well as clarity, requires choosing the appropriate term regardless of sex. Thus, men may *giggle* and *gossip*, etc. |

d. Using stereotyped adjectives and other descriptive expressions for one sex only, such as including information regarding hair color or clothes when referring to women, regardless of context

The blond Ms. Rudnik is Chief Executive Officer of the firm.
Prime Minister Margaret Thatcher, wearing a dark blue suit, arrived for the meeting of heads of government.

The adjectives are irrelevant here and would rarely be used in references to men. This is a reflection of our stereotyped beliefs regarding the importance of looks and dress for women in all situations. It is, of course, appropriate, in certain contexts, to refer to such characteristics for both women and men. Here, as elsewhere, it is a matter of treating the sexes equally.

Finally, equal treatment of the sexes involves remembering that women constitute approximately half of humanity. Language, both spoken and written, frequently renders women all but invisible. Lists of famous people consisting only of men, references exclusively in terms of "generic" *he* and *man*, and other types of common usage may create an image of an all-male world. This is reinforced by the fact that men have dominated many spheres of activity. One cannot, of course, include women in a list of presidents of the U.S.A. until a woman has held that office. But there is no reason for making women invisible in areas where they have been present, or for assuming that people in general, including hypothetical persons, are male.

The suggestions offered above are but a few of the alternatives available to those who wish to break with the traditional clichés and stereotypes and adopt non-sexist usage. You will find that English is indeed rich in resources for creating a usage which reflects sensitivity to the social implications of language. You will also discover that the practice of non-sexist usage is fully compatible with elegance, precision, and other criteria of good style.

Radical Masculinism: Women in Book VI of the Aeneid

Ted Slupesky

```
In reading Virgil, I often cry:
"Out hyperbolical fiend! How
vexest thou this man!"

        HOUSEMAN TO MACBAIL, 1920
```
nice!

Many of the greatest and most famous women in Athenian drama are notable for their inappropriately masculine behavior, something which presumably would have been particularly threatening to the typical male audience member; nevertheless, such characters as Clytaemnestra, Antigone, and Medea were accepted in the theater and their popular stories are at the heart of Athenian drama. Such a fascinating phenomenon has been subject to many interpretations. In the article "The Conception of Women in Athenian Drama," Prof. Helene Foley argues that of all the means of analyzing the role of women in Athenian drama, the best is to apply Levi-Strauss' anthropological equation female:domestic as male:public. In other words, women in Athenian drama represent the private world of the oikos, while men represent the public world. She feels, as she said in her recent lecture, that as the distance between the public and private sphere of a society increases, women come to be seen as a threat, a destructive force in society. A similar idea is useful in understanding the role of women in the Aeneid, particularly in book VI, in which all the female characters act in sex roles normally reserved only for men. However, it is not an increasing distance between a society's domestic spheres and its public sphere which created this misalignment of the sexes; rather, Virgil is concerned with an increasing emphasis on the relationship of father and son, at the expense of the relationship between husband and wife. In order to make this argument clear, I will first analyze the images of women that Virgil uses in book VI, emphasizing first the motif of women playing masculine roles and then exploring the devaluation of the husband-wife relationship.

good

Excellent. Such clarity!

When Aeneas first beaches his ships,[1] the first thing he
sees is Daedalus' temple, the metopes of which depict Pasiphae's intercourse with a bull and the subsequent birth of the
Minotaur. A woman having sex outside of marriage is clearly
playing a masculine role in the context of classical Greek society, and a woman having sex with anything but her husband is presumably one of a Greek man's greatest fears; thus, just as the
metopes of Dido's temple, depicting the Trojan War, underscore
the Carthaginians' acceptance of Homeric virtues, so these
metopes underscore the acceptance of women in masculine roles
in Hades. Thus, with this image setting the stage for the
descent into the underworld, Aeneas meets the Sibyl of Apollo, a
strange, domineering woman who orders Aeneas around, command-
ing him to sacrifice this and to go get that; eventually, she
leads him through Hades itself. Nowhere else in the Aeneid does
Aeneas take the commands of a woman so docilely, except perhaps
those of his mother. Once in Hades, she and Aeneas gain passage
over the Styx only because they carry the Golden Bough, which is
sacred not to Pluto, but to Persepone. Indeed, not only is
Charon here submissive to Persepone, but all of Hades is run by
her. Her husband is hardly mentioned.

After entering Hades proper, Aeneas and the Sibyl meet a
series of famous and legendary Greeks and Romans. The first
women they meet are the unhappy shades "living" in the Fields of
Mourning, the very first of whom are Phaedra, Procris, Eriphyle, Evadne, Pasiphae, Laodamia, and Caeneus, all famous for
their marital problems, and all acted out of the bounds of what
is proper for women in their societies.[2] It is worth comparing
this scene to its analogue in the Odyssey, in which these same
women are mentioned among a larger group that includes many
women famous for their virtue.[3] Virgil obviously is deliberately presenting a harsh view of women, showing them only in sex
roles threatening to men and ignoring examples of virtuous
women. Indeed, the next woman Aeneas meets is Dido, who herself
functions in her society with the rights of a man. This aspect of
her personality is not brought out clearly in this passage, but
in books I-IV Virgil makes it obvious. After all, a woman running a kingdom by herself, fighting off her brother's vicious
attacks, is extremely unusual in Classical literature; the most
comparable figure is Clytaemnestra in the Agamemnon. After
leaving Dido in the Fields of Mourning, Aeneas meets no other
women in the underworld; and as shown, all the women he has met
play decidedly improper roles for women in their societies.

Now, having reviewed this point, I will explore the way
Virgil emphasizes the father-son relationship and devalues
that of the husband and wife. For one of the most notable examples in book VI, it is necessary to return to Aeneas' reunion
with Dido. Virgil has already made clear[4] that Aeneas left Dido
because of his paternal obligation to found Rome (he is, after
all, the Father of Rome). Now in book VI the reader can see more

clearly than ever the emotional price Aeneas payed by leaving
Dido in order to fulfill his destiny:

> Aeneas with such pleas tried to placate
> The burning soul, savagely glaring back,
> And tears came to his eyes. But she had turned
> With gaze fixed on the ground as he spoke on,
> Her face no more affected than if she were
> Immobile granite or Marpesian stone.
> At length she flung away from him and fled,
> His enemy still, into the shadowy grove
> Where he whose bride she once had been, Sychaeus,
> Joined in her sorrows and returned her love.
> Aeneas still gazed after her in tears,
> Shaken by her ill fate and pitying her.
> (VI.628-639)

Immediately following this is the story of Deiphobus and Helen,
in which Helen treacherously betrays her third husband Deiphobus in order to escape with Menelaus, her first. As he did previously, with Phaedra, Procris, and the other evil women, Virgil
again deliberately emphasizes the bad side of marriage; first,
he presented the famous adulteresses of mythology, and now he
presents a wife conspiring to murder her husband. Beyond this,
after leaving Deiphobus and entering the Blessed Groves, no
more examples of marriage can be found--not even any more bad
marriages; this contributes to the final part of book VI's
being, among other things, an incredible overemphasis of the
father-son relationship. As soon as Aeneas and the Sibyl enter
the Blessed Groves, where only male military heroes dwell, the
sky becomes blue and the sun shines. Very soon Aeneas meets the
ghost of his father, who proceeds to show him all their glorious
descendants and the others who make up the future glory of Rome.
Contrast this with its analogue in the Odyssey:[5] In Odysseus'
underworld journey, he does not meet his father; indeed, his
father is not even named. Rather, he sees his mother (Virgil
makes it very explicit that Anchises in the Aeneid is taking her
place[6]). Obviously this is a revision made to emphasize the role
of the father. Then, when Aeneas sees those who are to become the
major players in Roman history, he sees only men. It is hardly
conceivable that women like Cleopatra, Augusta, Agrippina, and
Livia could be left out of a work describing Roman history, but
Virgil did leave them out; compare this too with the Odyssey,
where Odysseus sees not only famous male figures from Greek
mythology, but also their wives and mothers.[7] Odysseus doesn't
see only the adulteresses of mythology! Thus it is clear that
Virgil slights the role of women as wives and mothers intentionally in order to devalue their role as wives and mothers.

Now my argument is clear. Virgil obviously portrays the
women in book VI in inappropriately masculine roles, but why he
does so is not immediately clear to the reader. However, this

pseudo-structuralist equation father:son > husband:wife provides the key insight: he characterizes them so in order to
facilitate his emphasis on the father-son relationship and to
exclude, in book VI, any notion of normal, loving husband-wife
relationship.

NOTES

[1] Aeneid, VI.1-50.

[2] Ibid., 600-605. Phaedra, wife of Theseus, fell in love with her
stepson Hippolytus; she committed suicide when he rebuffed
her. Procris was shot by her husband Cephalus when jealously
following him. Eriphyle was bribed by a necklace into allowing
her husband Amphiaraus to fight in the war against Thebes in
which he was killed. Her son Alcmaeon killed her. Evadne immo-
lated herself when her husband Capaneus, another one of the
Seven against Thebes, died. Pasiphae has already been mentioned. Laodamia, wife of Protesilaus, the first Greek killed
at Troy, also killed herself when her husband died. Caeneus'
legend is told in the text; he was born a man, became a woman,
and when he died became a man again. I believe that by including
Evadne and Laodamia among these other women Virgil is reflecting a common Roman belief, reflected also in the story of Dido,
that it is not noble for lovers to kill themselves to join the
deceased. I at least know of no examples in Homer or Virgil in
which this practice is glorified.

[handwritten marginal note: good]

[3] Odyssey, XXI, 215ff. Among others mentioned are Alkmene,
mother of Herakles; Khloris, "that most lovely lady," mother
of Nestor; Leda, mother of Castor and Pollux; and Ariadne, who
saved Theseus in the Labyrinth.

[4] Aeneid, IV.361-375:

> Is it for you
> To lay the stones for Carthage's high walls,
> Tame husband that you are, and build their city?
> Oblivious of your own world, your own kingdom!
> From bright Olympus he that rules the gods
> and turns the earth and heaven by his power--
> He and no other sent me to you, told me
> To bring this message to you on the running winds:
> What have you in mind? What hope, wasting your days
> In Libya? If future history's glories
> Do not affect you, if you will not strive
> For your own honor, think of Ascanius,
> Think of the expectations of your heir,
> Iulus, to whom the Italian realm, the land
> Of Rome, are due.

Note the slight of marriage in line 363 and the glorification
of fatherhood in 372ff.

[5] Odyssey, XXI. 153-220.

[6] Compare the lines of the Odyssey with those of the Aeneid:

> I bit my lip,
> rising perplexed, with longing to embrace her,
> and tried three times, putting my arms around her,
> but she went sifting through my hands, impalpable
> as shadows are, and wavering like a dream.
> (Odyssey, XXI.200ff)

> At this his tears brimmed over
> And down his cheeks. And there he tried three times
> To throw his arms around his father's neck,
> Three times the shade untouched slipped through his
> hands,
> Weightless as wind and fugitive as dream.
> (Aeneid, VI.938ff)

[7] Odysseus sees the heroes of Greece in lines 335-631. Among the
women mentioned are Helen, Clytaemnestra, Thetis, Gaia, and
Leto. They are not all glorious examples of women but at least
they are mentioned. Lines 400ff are instructive:

> Indulge a woman never,
> and never tell a woman all you know. Some things
> a man may tell, some he should cover up.
> Not that I see a risk for you, Odysseus,
> of death at your wife's hands. She is too wise,
> too clear-eyed. . . .

Nowhere in the Aeneid is a woman so praised as "wise" and
"clear-eyed."

[Professor Stauder's comments on "Radical Masculinism: Women in Book VI of the *Aeneid*" by Ted Slupesky, first year student:]

Ted, This paper is wonderful as far as it goes but I wish you hadn't stopped here—I know you had space and time limitations. What you do in exploring how women are portrayed here is excellent but I think you definitely need to address the question: Why does V[irgil] portray women the way he does? Why does he emphasize the father-son relationship? Yes, in some sense women are portrayed in a bad light but your structuralist equation only describes that; it doesn't penetrate into its *raison d'etre.* Let's talk about how you might go on from here.

NO-MAN ON AN ISLAND:
ODYSSEUS AND THE KYKLOPS

by

Debora Robertson

The blinding of the Kyklops in The Odyssey is an important

scene in many respects. It helps one to understand the evolution of

Odysseus as a character from a warrior to a story weaver. The scene,

additionally, helps the reader to see how and why Odysseus becomes

a nobody, creating a parallel to his actual homecoming. I think the

scene is also a useful tool to apply when trying to understand the

How can a scene be a tool?

value system of the society.

The Kyklopes are described by Odysseus as giant louts

"without a law to bless them." He paints them as lazy creatures who

neither "plow nor sow their own land," creatures who have "no mus-

ter and no meeting, no consultation or old tribal ways, but each

one dwells in his own mountain cave dealing out rough justice to

wife and child, indifferent to what others do." Because the Ky-

klopes have no tradition, no laws which they follow, they care "not

a whistle" for the gods, and therefore have no respect for the

good

guest host relationship. This ignorance and lack of respect can be

seen when Polyphemos eats Odysseus's men, his guests, as opposed

to offering them food.

The Kyklopes (cap) portrayed in this harsh light can be seen as a representation of the suitors who slob around Odysseus's house all day, slaughtering his beeves, and eating up his crops without any regard for the guest host code which dictates that a guest bring [hyphen] food to the host, or the host gives, freely, food to the guest, but not that the guest help himself to the pantry of his host. The suitors have no honor, no homes to which they return, and, for the most part, are slothful and uncaring examples of humanity. They are eating Penelope and Telemakos alive, so to speak, just as the Kyklops eats Odysseus's men.

In order for Odysseus to escape the Kyklops, he gets him drunk on wine and when the Kyklops asks Odysseus to identify himself, Odysseus says that he is called Nobody. When the Kyklops falls into a drunken sleep, Odysseus and his men blind him with a hot poker, and as the Kyklops runs out of his cave screaming for his friends, all he can say is that Nobody blinded him.

Blinding the Kyklops allows Odysseus to get on with the business of coming home, but more than that, it sets up a parallel to his actual arrival and slaughter of the suitors. Odysseus sneaks up on the Kyklops as a nobody in order to avenge the deaths of his men, just as he sneaks up on the suitors as a beggar, a nobody, in order to slaughter them and regain his family honor, as well as reestablishing his own position in the home.

Good. Notice, too, that he allows them to get drunk—in fact + metaphorically—on their own greed + vanity.

The story is placed near the beginning of the poem not only as a foreshadow to his homecoming, but as an explanation of Odysseus's character change. From this point on ⸌in the story, Odys-

seus remains a nobody ⸌in that he has no home ⸌and no more identity.

He is no longer the sacker of Troy, but is becoming a story teller.

Odysseus tells stories at each of the islands he arrives at which

make him seem more humble, and therefore assure his acceptance

into the society. He makes himself into a nobody for another rea-

son, as well. He is an unidentified stranger upon his arrival, and

until someone who lives on the island can identify him, he really

has no role in the society, no identity in that society, and is

essentially a nobody.

Odysseus is identified on these islands, each time it is by a

woman. These women act as ushers for his entry into the society.

There are several possible reasons why Odysseus is identified by

women. First, it is a woman who will eventually identify him as

Odysseus when he returns home. His nurse and Penelope identify him

by his scar, ~~therefore~~ *thereby* transforming him from a nobody to the lord

of the house. Second, women symbolize ⸌ home, and all of the good

that the home represents. Women as conduits to the wholesomeness

of the home as symbolized in The Odyssey can be seen as a contrast

to the image of women presented in The Iliad, namely Helen, who

caused the war, and therefore called the men from their homes and

now women are leading a man back to the home after the war. Another

hypothesis that can be presented on this subject is that both Odys-

seus and the women he encounters are playing games with each other

But not all women symbolize home!

with each other that are based on deceit. Odysseus weaves tales of deceit about himself to mask his identity, just as Penelope weaves a deceitful shroud for Laertes. Kirke entices the men into thinking that they are receiving a meal, and then turns them into swine, just as Penelope allows the suitors to gorge themselves so they become like fat pigs, unable to challenge Odysseus when he comes home. Nausika is also deceitful in that she tells Odysseus to walk into town behind her chariot, as if they were strangers, so as not to arouse suspicion about her virtue. All of these women are playing these deceitful games in order to protect themselves from the damage that men can cause them. Penelope fears the power the suitors can hold over her, Kirke fears that Odysseus and his men may jeopardize her way of life on the island, and Nausika fears for her reputation. Odysseus plays the game, as I have already said, in order to protect himself.

The women also reinforce Odysseus' nobody-ness as they are the dominant side in each of the relationships. Kirke, for instance, does not care that Odysseus is a warrior; that role has no place in the relationship. Odysseus is not on her island to sack it; he is there to tell her the story of his voyage, and to seek help from her. He is totally under her power in that if he wants to escape with his men in their proper form, he must prove himself to Kirke. Once she has identified him as Odysseus, he can leave and continue his voyage home. Kalypso is also dominates Odysseus,

[margin annotation, right: good]

[margin annotation, left, vertical: Overuse of verb "To be" here & on Next Page]

to say the least. His identity (is) found entirely through her. She
(is) the one who controls him, as well as his ability to get off the
island. She holds his desire to leave and go home over his head and
blackmails him with it. He serves her desires, in return she tanta-
lizes him with the idea that he might get to leave. It (is) an interesting predicament. Odysseus (is) like a concubine to Kalypso. He
takes on the role of a woman who must deceive sexually, his stories
are sexual in this case, to get what she wants. The deception and
game playing again returns as a theme.

comma splice (margin annotation)

You might credit Helen Foley for this observation. (margin annotation)

After the fall of the Kyklops and the suitors, one is left
asking what kind of values the poet was trying to reinforce. One of
the most important, certainly, would be respect for the guest host
relationship. Both the Kyklops and the suitors flaunted the guest-
host relationship, and both met their demise as a result. The fact
that the gods allowed Odysseus to blind the Kyklops and slaughter
the suitors, seems to imply that they put a good deal of emphasis on
the guest host code. Perhaps Homer is demonstrating the danger of
flaunting Zeus and his power, the danger of saying that you don't
care "a whistle" for his powers.

hyphens (margin annotation)

The effects the blinding of the Kyklops has on the poem as a
whole are many faceted. The incident seems to affect all realms of
the story, particularly Odysseus' change of role in the society.
He seems to need to experience his odyssey in order to understand
this change. Perhaps he needs to experience the role of a woman in

order to understand the trials of Penelope with the suitors, and perhaps he also experiences the role of the dominated as opposed to the dominator in order to adjust and make the change from his warrior identity to his domestic identity. It is debatable whether or not he ever actually does understand this change, or if he ever does completely make the change. One is tempted to answer that question negatively in that at the end of the poem, we see Odysseus about to go off on another journey to find a land where the inhabitants have never seen an oar. His goal in introducing the oar to this society is to not only teach them of the ocean, but also the glory of Poseidon. Still, this role, while not conducive to the role of domestic, is quite conducive to his new found role as storyteller. He is no longer leaving to sack other cities, he is leaving to exercise his new role as storyteller.

[Professor Knapp's comments on "No-Man on an Island: Odysseus and the Kyklops" by Debora Robertson, first-year student:]

A very suggestive but incompletely realized idea. What you say about the Kyclopes is sensible enough, but your discussion of the women, though at first overgeneralizing, becomes much the most interesting part of the essay. Yet you don't explicitly connect this discussion with the episode of the Kyclopes. You need to state your conceptual link more clearly—that identity requires weaving, disguise, tale-telling, arts of the female foreign to the Kyclopes—and to Odysseus—before that encounter.

Section Two

Assigning Significance to Experience

This section includes selections by writers who have discovered a significance in a particular experience. An asterisk, (*), before an entry indicates that the selection was written by a student.

From The Confessions

St. Augustine

A pear tree there was near our vineyard, laden with fruit, tempting neither for color nor taste. To shake and rob this, some lewd young fellows of us went, late one night, (having according to our pestilent custom prolonged our sports in the streets till then,) and took huge loads, not for our eating, but to fling to the very hogs, having only tasted them. And this, but to do, what we liked only, because it was misliked. Behold my heart, O God, behold my heart, which Thou hadst pity upon in the bottom of the bottomless pit. Now, behold let my heart tell Thee, what it sought there, that I should be gratuitously evil, having no temptation to ill, but the ill itself. It was foul, and I loved it; I loved to perish, I loved mine own fault, not that for which I was faulty, but my fault itself. Foul soul, falling from Thy firmament to utter destruction; not seeking aught through the shame, but the shame itself! . . .

11. When, then, we ask why a crime was done, we believe it not, unless it appear that there might have been some desire of obtaining some of those which we called lower goods, or a fear of losing them. For they are beautiful and comely; although compared with those higher and beatific goods, they be abject and low. A man hath murdered another; why? he loved his wife or his estate; or would rob for his own livelihood; or feared to lose some such thing by him; or, wronged, was on fire to be revenged. Would any commit murder upon no cause, delighted simply in murdering? Who would believe it? For as for that furious and savage man, of whom it is said that he was gratuitously evil and cruel, yet is the cause assigned; "lest" (saith he) "through idleness hand or heart should grow inactive." And to what end? That, through that practice of guilt, he might, having taken the city, attain to honors, empire, riches, and be freed from fear of the laws, and his embarrassments from domestic needs, and consciousness of villainies. . . .

[VI.] 12. What then did wretched I so love in thee, thou theft of mine, thou deed of darkness, in that sixteenth year of my age? Lovely thou wert not, because thou wert theft. But art thou any thing, that thus I speak to thee? Fair were the pears we stole, because they were Thy creation, Thou fairest of all, Creator of all, Thou good God; God, the sovereign good and my true good. Fair were those pears, but not them did my wretched soul desire; for I had store of better, and those I gathered, only that I might steal. For, when gathered, I flung them away, my only feast therein being my own sin, which I was pleased to enjoy. For if aught of those pears came within my mouth, what sweetened it was the sin. And now, O Lord my God, I enquire what in that theft delighted me; and behold it hath no loveliness; I mean no such loveliness as in justice and wisdom; nor such as is in the mind and memory, and senses, and animal life of man; nor yet as the stars are glorious and beautiful in their orbs; or the earth, or sea, full of embryo-life, replacing by its birth that which decayeth; nay, nor even that false and shadowy beauty, which belongeth to deceiving vices. . . .

What then did I love in that theft? and wherein did I even corruptly and pervertedly imitate my Lord? Did I wish even by stealth to do contrary to Thy law, because by power I could not, so that being a prisoner, I might mimic a maimed liberty by doing with impunity things unpermitted me, a darkened likeness of Thy Omnipotency? Behold, Thy servant, fleeing from his Lord, and obtaining a shadow. O rottenness, O monstrousness of life, and depth of death! could I like what I might not, only because I might not? . . .

[VIII.] 16. *What fruit had I then* (wretched man!) *in those things, of the remembrance whereof I am now ashamed?* Especially, in that theft which I loved for the theft's sake; and it too was nothing, and therefore the more miserable I, who loved it. Yet alone I had not done it: such was I then, I remember, alone I had never done it. I loved then in it also the company of the accomplices, with whom I did it? I did not then love nothing else but the theft, yea rather I did love nothing else; for that circumstance of the company was also nothing. What is, in truth? who can teach me, save He that enlighteneth my heart, and discovereth its dark corners? What is it which hath come into my mind to enquire, and discuss, and consider? For had I then loved the pears I stole, and wished to enjoy them, I might have done it alone, had the bare commission of the theft sufficed to attain my pleasure; nor needed I have inflamed the itching of my desires, by the excitement of accomplices. But since my pleasure was not in those pears, it was in the offence itself, which the company of fellow-sinners occasioned.

[IX.] 17. What then was this feeling? For of a truth it was too foul: and woe was me, who had it. But yet what was it? *Who can understand his errors?* It was the sport, which, as it were, tickled our hearts, that we beguiled, those who little thought what we were doing, and much misliked it. Why then was my delight of such sort, that I did it not alone? Because none doth ordinarily laugh alone? ordinarily no one; yet laughter sometimes masters men alone and singly when no one whatever is with them, if any thing very ludicrous presents itself to their senses or mind. Yet I had not done this alone; alone I had never never done it. Behold my God, before Thee, the vivid remembrance of my soul; alone, I had never committed that theft, wherein what I stole pleased me not, but that I stole; nor had it alone liked me to do it, nor had I done it. O friendship too unfriendly! thou incomprehensible inveigler of the soul, thou greediness to do mischief out of mirth and wantonness, thou thirst of others' loss, without lust of my own gain or revenge: but when it is said, "Let's go, let's do it," we are ashamed not to be shameless.

[X.] 18. Who can disentangle that twisted and intricate knottiness? Foul is it: I hate to think on it, to look on it. But Thee I long for, O Righteousness and Innocency, beautiful and comely to all pure eyes, and of a satisfaction unsating. With Thee is rest entire, and life imperturbable. Whoso enters into Thee, *enters into the joy of his Lord:* and shall not fear, and shall do excellently in the All-Excellent. I sank away from Thee, and I wandered, O my God, too much astray from Thee my stay, in these days of my youth, and I became to myself a barren land.

Meditation II: Of the Nature of the Human Mind; and That It is More Easily Known Than the Body

René Descartes

I shall proceed by setting aside all that in which the least doubt could be supposed to exist, just as if I had discovered that it was absolutely false; and I shall ever follow in this road until I have met with something which is certain, or at least, if I can do nothing else, until I have learned for certain that there is nothing in the world that is certain. Archimedes, in order that he might draw the terrestrial globe out of its place, and transport it elsewhere, demanded only that one point should be fixed and immoveable; in the same way I shall have the right to conceive high hopes if I am happy enough to discover one thing only which is certain and indubitable. . . .

But what then am I? A thing which thinks. What is a thing which thinks? It is a thing which doubts, understands, [conceives], affirms, denies, wills, refuses, which also imagines and feels. . . .

Let us begin by considering the commonest matters, those which we believe to be the most distinctly comprehended, to wit, the bodies which we touch and see; not indeed bodies in general, for these general ideas are usually a little more confused, but let us consider one body in particular. Let us take for example, this piece of wax: it has been taken quite freshly from the hive, and it has not yet lost the sweetness of the honey which it contains; it still retains somewhat of the odour of the flowers from which it has been culled; its colour, its figure, its size are apparent; it is hard, cold, easily handled, and if you strike it with the finger, it will emit a sound. Finally all the things which are requisite to cause us distinctly to recognise a body, are met with in it. But notice that while I speak and approach the fire what remained of the taste is exhaled, the smell evaporates, the colour alters, the figure is destroyed, the size increases, it becomes liquid, it heats, scarcely can one handle it, and when one strikes it, no sound is emitted. Does the same wax remain after this change? We must confess that it remains; none would judge otherwise. What then did I know so distinctly in this piece of wax? It could certainly be nothing of all that the senses brought to my notice, since all these things which fall under taste, smell, sight, touch, and hearing, are found to be changed, and yet the same wax remains.

Perhaps it was what I now think, viz. that this wax was not that sweetness of honey, nor that agreeable scent of flowers, nor that particular whiteness, nor that figure, nor that sound, but simply a body which a little before appeared to me as perceptible under these forms, and which is now perceptible under others. But what, precisely, is it that I imagine when I form such conceptions? Let us attentively consider this, and, abstracting from all that does not belong to the wax, let us see what remains. Certainly nothing remains excepting a certain extended thing which is flexible and movable. But what is the meaning of flexible and movable? Is it not that I imagine that this piece of wax being round is capable of becoming square and of passing from a square to a triangular figure? No, certainly it is not that, since I imagine it admits of an infinitude of similar changes, and I nevertheless do not know how to compass the infinitude by my imagination, and consequently this conception which I have of the wax is not brought about by the faculty of imagination. What now is this extension? Is it not also unknown? For it becomes greater when the wax is melted, greater when it is boiled, and greater still when the heat increases; and I should not conceive [clearly] according to truth what wax is, if I did not think that even this piece that we are considering is capable of receiving more variations in extension than I have ever imagined. We must then grant that I could not even understand through the imagination what this piece of wax is, and that it is my mind alone which perceives it. I say this piece of wax in particular, for as to wax in general it is yet clearer. But what is this piece of wax which cannot be understood excepting by the [understanding or] mind? It is certainly the same that I see, touch, imagine, and finally it is the same which I have always believed it to be from the beginning. But what must particularly be observed is that its perception is neither an act of vision, nor of touch, nor of imagination, and has never been such although it may have appeared formerly to be so, but only an intuition of the mind, which may be imperfect and confused as it was formerly, or clear and distinct as it is at present, according as my attention is more or less directed to the elements which are found in it, and of which it is composed.

Yet in the meantime I am greatly astonished when I consider [the great feebleness of mind] and its proneness to fall [insensibly] into error; for although without giving expression to my thoughts I consider all this in my own mind, words often impede me and I am almost deceived by the terms of ordinary language. For we say that we see the same wax, if it is present, and not that we simply judge that it is the same from its having the same colour and figure. From this I should conclude that I knew the wax by means of vision and not simply by the intuition of the mind; unless by chance I remember that, when looking from a window and saying I see men who pass in the street, I really do not see them, but infer that what I see is men, just as I say that I see wax. And yet what do I see from the window but hats and coats which may cover automatic machines? Yet I judge these to be men. And similarly solely by the faculty of judgment which rests in my mind, I comprehend that which I believed I saw with my eyes.

A man who makes it his aim to raise his knowledge above the common should be ashamed to derive the occasion for doubting from the forms of speech invented by the vulgar; I prefer to pass on and consider whether I had a more evident and perfect conception of what the wax was when I first perceived it, and when I believed I knew it by means of the external senses or at least by the common sense as it is called, that is to say by the imaginative faculty, or whether my present conception is clearer now that I have most carefully examined what it is, and in what way it can be known. It would certainly be absurd to doubt as to this. For what was there in this first perception which was distinct? What was there which might not as well have been perceived by any of the animals? But when I distinguish the wax from its external forms, and when, just as if I had taken from it its vestments, I consider it quite naked, it is certain that although some error may still be found in my judgment, I can nevertheless not perceive it thus without a human mind.

But finally what shall I say of this mind, that is, of myself, for up to this point I do not admit in myself anything but mind? What then, I who seem to perceive this piece of wax distinctly, do I not know myself, not only with much more truth and certainty, but also with much more distinctness and clearness? For if I judge that the wax is or exists from the fact that I see it, it certainly follows much more clearly that I am or that I exist myself from the fact that I see it. For it may be that what I see is not really wax, it may also be that I do not possess eyes with which to see anything; but it cannot be that when I see, or (for I no longer take account of the distinction) when I think I see, that I myself who think am nought. So if I judge that the wax exists from the fact that I touch it, the same thing will follow, to wit, that I am; and if I judge that my imagination, or some other cause, whatever it is, persuades me that the wax exists, I shall still conclude the same. And what I have here remarked of wax may be applied to all other things which are external to me [and which are met with outside of me]. And further, if the [notion or] perception of wax has seemed to me clearer and more distinct, not only after the sight or the touch, but also after many other causes have rendered it quite manifest to me, with how much more [evidence] and distinctness must it be said that I now know myself, since all the reasons which contribute to the knowledge of wax, or any other body whatever, are yet better proofs of the nature of my mind! And there are so many other things in the mind itself which may contribute to the elucidation of its nature, that those which depend on body such as these just mentioned, hardly merit being taken into account.

But finally here I am, having insensibly reverted to the point I desired, for, since it is now manifest to me that even bodies are not properly speaking known by the senses or by the faculty of imagination, but by the understanding only, and since they are not known from the fact that they are seen or touched, but only because they are understood, I see clearly that there is nothing which is easier for me to know than my mind. But because it is difficult to rid oneself so promptly of an opinion to which one was accustomed for so long, it will be well that I should halt a little at this point, so that by the length of my meditation I may more deeply imprint on my memory this new knowledge.

The Slit

Loren Eiseley

"Man can not afford to be a naturalist, to look at Nature directly, but only with the side of his eye. He must look through and beyond her."

HENRY DAVID THOREAU

"Unless all existence is a medium of revelation, no particular revelation is possible. . . ."

WILLIAM TEMPLE

Some lands are flat and grass-covered, and smile so evenly up at the sun that they seem forever youthful, untouched by man or time. Some are torn, ravaged and convulsed like the features of profane old age. Rocks are wrenched up and exposed to view; black pits receive the sun but give back no light.

It was to such a land I rode, but I rode to it across a sunlit, timeless prairie over which nothing passed but antelope or a wandering bird. On the verge where that prairie halted before a great wall of naked sandstone and clay, I came upon the Slit. A narrow crack worn by some descending torrent had begun secretly, far back in the prairie grass, and worked itself deeper and deeper into the fine sandstone that led by devious channels into the broken waste beyond. I rode back along the crack to a spot where I could descend into it, dismounted, and left my horse to graze.

The crack was only about body-width and, as I worked my way downward, the light turned dark and green from the overhanging grass. Above me the sky became a narrow slit of distant blue, and the sandstone was cool to my hands on either side. The Slit was a little sinister—like an open grave, assuming the dead were enabled to take one last look—for over me the sky seemed already as far off as some future century I would never see.

I ignored the sky, then, and began to concentrate on the sandstone walls that had led me into this place. It was tight and tricky work, but that cut was a perfect cross section through perhaps ten million years of time. I hoped to find at least a bone, but I was not quite prepared for the sight I finally came upon. Staring straight out at me, as I slid farther and deeper into the green twilight, was a skull embedded in the solid sandstone. I had come at just the proper moment when it was fully to be seen, the white bone gleaming there in a kind of ashen splendor, water worn, and about to be ground away in the next long torrent.

It was not, of course, human. I was deep, deep below the time of man in a remote age near the beginning of the reign of mammals. I squatted on my heels in the narrow ravine, and we stared a little blankly at each other, the skull and I. There were marks of generalized primitiveness in that low, pinched brain case and grinning jaw that marked it as lying far back along those converging roads where . . . cat and man and weasel must leap into a single shape.

It was the face of a creature who had spent his days following his nose, who was led by instinct rather than memory, and whose power of choice was very small. Though he was not a man, nor a direct human ancestor, there was yet about him, even in the bone, some trace of that low, snuffling world out of which our forebears had so recently emerged. The skull lay tilted in such a manner that it stared, sightless, up at me as though I, too, were already caught a few feet above him in the strata and, in my turn, were staring upward at that strip of sky which the ages were carrying farther away from me beneath the tumbling debris of falling mountains. The creature had never lived to see a man, and I, what was it I was never going to see?

I restrained a panicky impulse to hurry upward after that receding sky that was outlined above the Slit. Probably, I thought, as I patiently began the task of chiseling into the stone around the skull, I would never again excavate a fossil under conditions which led to so vivid an impression that I was already one myself. The truth is that we are all potential fossils still carrying within our bodies the crudities of former existences, the marks of a world in which living creatures flow with little more consistency than clouds from age to age.

As I tapped and chiseled there in the foundations of the world, I had ample time to consider the cunning manipulability of the human fingers. Experimentally I crooked one of the long slender bones. It might have been silica, I thought, or aluminum, or iron—the cells would have made it possible. But no, it is calcium, carbonate of lime. Why? Only because of its history. Elements more numerous than calcium in the earth's crust could have been used to build the skeleton. Our history is the reason—we came from the water. It was there the cells took the lime habit, and they kept it after we came ashore.

It is not a bad symbol of that long wandering, I thought again—the human hand that has been fin and scaly reptile foot and furry paw. If a stone should fall (I cocked an eye at the leaning shelf above my head and waited, fatalistically) let the bones lie here with their message, for those who might decipher it, if they come down late among us from the stars.

Above me the great crack seemed to lengthen.

Perhaps there is no meaning in it at all, the thought went on inside me, save that of journey itself, so far as men can see. It has altered with the chances of life, and the chances brought us here; but it was a good journey—long, perhaps—but a good journey under a pleasant sun. Do not look for the purpose. Think of the way we came and be a little proud. Think of this hand—the utter pain of its first venture on the pebbly shore.

Or consider its later wanderings.

I ceased my tappings around the sand-filled sockets of the skull and wedged myself into a crevice for a smoke. As I tamped a load of tobacco into my pipe, I thought of a town across the valley that I used sometimes to visit, a town whose little inhabitants never welcomed me. No sign points to it and I rarely go there any more. Few people know about it and fewer still know that in a sense we, or rather some of the creatures to whom we are related, were driven out of it once, long ago. I used to park my car on a hill and sit silently observant, listening to the talk ringing out from neighbor to neighbor, seeing the inhabitants drowsing in their doorways, taking it all in with nostalgia—the sage smell on the wind, the sunlight without time, the village without destiny. We can look, but we can never go back. It is prairie-dog town.

"Whirl is king," said Aristophanes, and never since life began was Whirl more truly king than eighty million years ago in the dawn of the Age of Mammals. It would come as a shock to those who believe firmly that the scroll of the future is fixed and the roads determined in advance, to observe the teetering balance of earth's history through the age of the Paleocene. The passing of the reptiles had left a hundred uninhabited life zones and a scrambling variety of newly radiating forms. Unheard-of species of giant ground birds threatened for a moment to dominate the earthly scene. Two separate orders of life contended at slightly different intervals for the pleasant grasslands—for the seeds and the sleepy burrows in the sun. . . .

It is this evidence of a lost chapter in the history of our kind that I used to remember on the sunny slope above prairie-dog town, and why I am able to say in a somewhat figuratively fashion that we were driven out of it once ages ago. We are not, except very remotely as mammals, related to prairie dogs. Nevertheless, through several million years of Paleocene time, the primate order, instead of being confined to trees, was experimenting to some extent with the same grassland burrowing life that the rodents later perfected. The success of these burrowers crowded the primates out of this environment and forced them back into the domain of the branches. As a result, many primates, by that time highly specialized for a ground life, became extinct. . . .

It is conceivable that except for the invasion of the rodents, the primate line might even have abandoned the trees. We might be there on the grass, you and I, barking in the high-plains sunlight. It is true we came back in fifty million years with the cunning hands and the eyes that the tree world gave us, but was it victory? Once more in memory I saw the high blue evening fall sleepily upon that village, and once more swung the car to leave, lifting, as I always did, a figurative lantern to some ambiguous crossroads sign within my brain. The pointing arms were nameless and nameless were the distances to which they pointed. One took one's choice. . . .

Perhaps the Slit, with its exposed bones and its faroff vanishing sky, has come to stand symbolically in my mind for a dimension denied to man, the dimension of time. Like the wistaria on the garden wall he is rooted in his particular century. Out of it—forward or backward—he cannot run. As he stands on his circumscribed pinpoint of time, his sight for the past is growing longer, and even the shadowy outlines of the galactic future are growing clearer, though his own fate he cannot yet see. Along the dimension of time, man, like the rooted vine in space, may never pass in person. Considering the innumerable devices by which the mindless root has evaded the limitations of its own stability, however, it may well be that man himself is slowly achieving powers over a new dimension—a dimension capable of presenting him with a wisdom he has barely begun to discern.

Through how many dimensions and how many media will life have to pass? Down how many roads among the stars must man propel himself in search of the final secret? The journey is difficult, immense, at times impossible, yet that will not deter some of us from attempting it. We cannot know all that has happened in the past, or the reason for all of these events, any more than we can with surety discern what lies ahead. We have joined the caravan, you might say, at a certain point; we will travel as far as we can, but we cannot in one lifetime see all that we would like to see or learn all that we hunger to know. . . .

Forward and backward I have gone, and for me it has been an immense journey. Those who accompany me need not look for science in the usual sense, though I have done all in my power to avoid errors in fact. I have given the record of what one man thought as he pursued research and pressed his hands against the confining walls of scientific method in his time. It is not, I must confess at the outset, an account of discovery so much as a confession of ignorance and of the final illumination that sometimes comes to a man when he is no longer careful of his pride. . . . I can at best report only from my own wilderness. The important thing is that each man possess such a wilderness and that he consider what marvels are to be observed there. . . .

From The Way to Rainy Mountain

N. Scott Momaday

A single knoll rises out of the plain in Oklahoma, north and west of the Wichita Range. For my people, the Kiowas, it is an old landmark, and they gave it the name Rainy Mountain. The hardest weather in the world is there. Winter brings blizzards, hot tornadic winds arise in the spring, and in summer the prairie is an anvil's edge. The grass turns brittle and brown, and it cracks beneath your feet. There are green belts along the rivers and creeks, linear groves of hickory and pecan, willow and witch hazel. At a distance in July or August the steaming foliage seems almost to writhe in fire. Great green and yellow grass-hoppers are everywhere in the tall grass, popping up like corn to sting the flesh, and tortoises crawl about on the red earth, going nowhere in the plenty of time. Loneliness is an aspect of the land. All things in the plain are isolate; there is no confusion of objects in the eye, but *one* hill or *one* tree or *one* man. To look upon that landscape in the early morning, with the sun at your back, is to lose the sense of proportion. Your imagination comes to life, and this, you think, is where Creation was begun.

I returned to Rainy Mountain in July. My grandmother had died in the spring, and I wanted to be at her grave. She had lived to be very old and at last infirm. Her only living daughter was with her when she died, and I was told that in death her face was that of a child.

I like to think of her as a child. When she was born, the Kiowas were living the last great moment of their history. For more than a hundred years they had controlled the open range from the Smoky Hill River to the Red, from the headwaters of the Canadian to the fork of the Arkansas and Cimarron. In alliance with the Comanches, they had ruled the whole of the southern Plains. War was their sacred business, and they were among the finest horsemen the world has ever known. But warfare for the Kiowas was preeminently a matter of disposition rather than of survival, and they never understood the grim, unrelenting advance of the U.S. Cavalry. When at last, divided and ill-provisioned, they were driven onto the Staked Plains in the cold rains of autumn, they fell into panic. In Palo Duro Canyon they abandoned their crucial stores to pillage and had nothing then but their lives. In order to save themselves, they surrendered to the soldiers at Fort Sill and were imprisoned in the old stone corral that now stands as a military museum. My grandmother was spared the humiliation of those high gray walls by eight or ten years, but she must have known from birth the affliction of defeat, the dark brooding of old warriors.

Her name was Aho and she belonged to the last culture to evolve in North America. Her forebears came down from the high country in western Montana nearly three centuries ago. They were a mountain people, a mysterious tribe of hunters whose language has never been positively classified in any major group. In the late seventeenth century they began a long migration to the south and east. It was a journey toward the dawn, and it led to a golden age. Along the way the Kiowas were befriended by the Crows, who gave them the culture and religion of the Plains. They acquired horses, and their ancient nomadic spirit was suddenly free of the ground. They acquired Tai-me, the sacred Sun Dance doll, from that moment the object and symbol of their worship, and so shared in the divinity of the sun. Not least, they acquired the sense of destiny, therefore courage and pride. When they entered upon the southern Plains they had been transformed. No longer were they slaves to the simple necessity of survival; they were a lordly and dangerous society of fighters and thieves, hunters and priests of the sun. According to their origin myth, they entered the world through a hollow log. From one point of view, their migration was the fruit of an old prophecy, for indeed they emerged from a sunless world.

Although my grandmother lived out her long life in the shadow of Rainy Mountain, the immense landscape of the continental interior lay like memory in her blood. She could tell of the Crows, whom she had never seen, and of the Black Hills, where she had never been. I wanted to see in reality what she had seen more perfectly in the mind's eye, and traveled fifteen hundred miles to begin my pilgrimage.

Yellowstone, it seemed to me, was the top of the world, a region of deep lakes and dark timber, canyons and waterfalls. But, beautiful as it is, one might have the sense of confinement there. The skyline in all directions is close at hand, the high wall of the woods and deep cleavages of shade. There is a perfect freedom in the mountains, but it belongs to the eagle and the elk, the badger and the bear. The Kiowas reckoned their stature by the distance they could see, and they were bent and blind in the wilderness.

Descending eastward, the highland meadows are a stairway to the plain. In July the inland slope of the Rockies is luxuriant with flax and buckwheat, stonecrop and larkspur. The earth unfolds and the limit of the land recedes. Clusters of trees, and animals grazing far in the distance, cause the vision to reach away and wonder to build upon the mind. The sun follows a longer course in the day, and the sky is immense beyond all comparison. The great billowing clouds that sail upon it are shadows that move upon the grain like water, dividing light. Farther down, in the land of the Crows and Blackfeet, the plain is yellow. Sweet clover takes hold of the hills and bends upon itself to cover and seal the soil. There the Kiowas paused on their way; they had come to the place where they must change their lives. The sun is at home on the plains. Precisely there does it have the certain character of a god. When the Kiowas came to the land of the Crows, they could see the dark lees of the hills at dawn across the Bighorn River, the profusion of light on the grain shelves, the oldest deity ranging after the solstices. Not yet would they veer southward to the caldron of the land that lay below; they must wean their blood from the northern winter and hold the mountains a while longer in their view. They born Tai-me in procession to the east.

A dark mist lay over the Black Hills, and the land was like iron. At the top of a ridge I caught sight of Devil's Tower up-thrust against the gray sky as if in the birth of time the core of the earth had broken through its crust and the motion of the world was begun. There are things in nature that engender an awful quiet in the heart of man; Devil's Tower is one of them. Two centuries ago, because they could not do otherwise, the Kiowas made a legend at the base of the rock. My grandmother said:

> *Eight children were there at play, seven sisters and their brother. Suddenly the boy was struck dumb; he trembled and began to run upon his hands and feet. His fingers became claws, and his body was covered with fur. Directly there was a bear where the boy had been. The sisters were terrified; they ran, and the bear after them. They came to the stump of a great tree, and the tree spoke to them. It bade them climb upon it, and as they did so it began to rise into the air. The bear came to kill them, but they were just beyond its reach. It reared against the tree and scored the bark all around with its claws. The seven sisters were borne into the sky, and they became the stars of the Big Dipper.*

From that moment, and so long as the legend lives, the Kiowas have kinsmen in the night sky. Whatever they were in the mountains, they could be no more. However tenuous their well-being, however much they had suffered and would suffer again, they had found a way out of the wilderness.

My grandmother had a reverence for the sun, a holy regard that now is all but gone out of mankind. There was a wariness in her, and an ancient awe. She was a Christian in her later years, but she had come a long way about, and she never forgot her birthright. As a child she had been to the Sun Dances; she had taken part in those annual rites, and by then she had learned the restoration of her people in the presence of Tai-me. She was about seven when the last Kiowa Sun Dance was held in 1887 on the Washita River above Rainy Mountain Creek. The buffalo were gone. In order to consummate the ancient sacrifice— to impale the head of a buffalo bull upon the medicine tree—a delegation of old men journeyed into Texas, there to beg and barter for an animal from the Goodnight herd. She was ten when the Kiowas came together for the last time as a living Sun Dance culture. They could find no buffalo; they had to hang an old hide from the sacred tree. Before the dance could begin, a company of soldiers rode out from Fort Sill under orders to disperse the tribe. Forbidden without cause the essential act of their faith, having seen the wild herds slaughtered and left to rot upon the ground, the Kiowas backed away forever from the medicine tree. That was July 20, 1890, at the great bend of the Washita. My grandmother was there. Without bitterness, and for as long as she lived, she bore a vision of deicide.

Now that I can have her only in memory, I see my grandmother in the several postures that were perculiar to her: standing at the wood stove on a winter morning and turning meat in a great iron skillet; sitting at the south window, bent above her beadwork, and afterwards, when her vision failed, looking down for a long time into the fold of her hands; going out upon a cane, very slowly as she did when the weight of age came upon her; praying. I remember her most often at prayer. She made long, rambling prayers out of suffering and hope, having seen many things. I was never sure that I had the right to hear, so exclusive were they of all mere custom and company. The last time I saw her she prayed standing by the side of her bed at night, naked to the waist, the light of a kerosene lamp moving upon her dark skin. Her long, black hair, always drawn and braided in the day, lay upon her shoulders and against her breasts like a shawl. I do not speak Kiowa, and I never understood her prayers, but there was something inherently sad in the sound, some merest hesitation upon the syllables of sorrow. She began in a high and descending pitch, exhausting her breath to silence; then again and again—and always the same intensity of effort, of something that is, and is not, like urgency in the human voice. Transported so in the dancing light among the shadows of her room, she seemed beyond the reach of time. But that was illusion; I think I knew then that I should not see her again. . . .

Once More to the Lake

E. B. White

August 1941

One summer, along about 1904, my father rented a camp on a lake in Maine and took us all there for the month of August. We all got ringworm from some kittens and had to rub Pond's Extract on our arms and legs night and morning, and my father rolled over in a canoe with all his clothes on; but outside of that the vacation was a success and from then on none of us ever thought there was any place in the world like that lake in Maine. We returned summer after summer—always on August 1 for one month. I have since become a salt-water man, but sometimes in summer there are days when the restlessness of the tides and the fearful cold of the sea water and the incessant wind that blows across the afternoon and into the evening make me wish for the placidity of a lake in the woods. A few weeks ago this feeling got so strong I bought myself a couple of bass hooks and a spinner and returned to the lake where we used to go, for a week's fishing and to revisit old haunts.

I took along my son, who had never had any fresh water up his nose and who had seen lily pads only from train windows. On the journey over to the lake I began to wonder what it would be like. I wondered how time would have marred this unique, this holy spot—the coves and streams, the hills that the sun set behind, the camps and the paths behind the camps. I was sure that the tarred road would have found it out, and I wondered in what other ways it would be desolated. It is strange how much you can remember about places like that once you allow your mind to return into the grooves that lead back. You remember one thing, and that suddenly reminds you of another thing. I guess I remembered clearest of all the early mornings, when the lake was cool and motionless, remembered how the bedroom smelled of the lumber it was made of and of the wet woods whose scent entered through the screen. The partitions in the camp were thin and did not extend clear to the top of the rooms, and as I was always the first up I would dress softly so as not to wake the others, and sneak out into the sweet outdoors and start out in the canoe, keeping close along the shore in the long shadows of the pines. I remembered being very careful never to rub my paddle against the gunwale for fear of disturbing the stillness of the cathedral.

The lake had never been what you would call a wild lake. There were cottages sprinkled around the shores, and it was in farming country although the shores of the lake were quite heavily wooded. Some of the cottages were owned by nearby farmers, and you would live at the shore and eat your meals at the farmhouse. That's what our family did. But although it wasn't wild, it was a fairly large and undisturbed lake and there were places in it that, to a child at least, seemed infinitely remote and primeval.

I was right about the tar: it led to within half a mile of the shore. But when I got back there, with my boy, and we settled into a camp near a farmhouse and into the kind of summertime I had known, I could tell that it was going to be pretty much the same as it had been before—I knew it, lying in bed the first morning, smelling the bedroom and hearing the boy sneak quietly out and go off along the shore in a boat. I began to sustain the illusion that he was I, and therefore, by simple transposition, that I was my father. This sensation persisted, kept cropping up all the time we were there. It was not an entirely new feeling, but in this setting it grew much stronger. I seemed to be living a dual existence. I would be in the middle of some simple act, I would be picking up a bait box or laying down a table fork, or I would be saying something, and suddenly it would be not I but my father who was saying the words or making the gesture. It gave me a creepy sensation.

We went fishing the first morning. I felt the same damp moss covering the worms in the bait can, and saw the dragonfly alight on the tip of my rod as it hovered a few inches from the surface of the water. It was the arrival of this fly that convinced me beyond any doubt that everything was as it always had been, that the years were a mirage and that there had been no years. The small waves were the same, chucking the rowboat under the chin as we fished at anchor, and the boat was the same boat, the same color green and the ribs broken in the same places, and under the floorboards the same fresh-water leavings and débris—the dead helgramite, the wisps of moss, the rusty discarded fishhook, the dried blood from yesterday's catch. We stared silently at the tips of our rods, at the dragonflies that came and went. I lowered the tip of mine into the water, tentatively, pensively dislodging the fly, which darted two feet away, poised, darted two feet back, and came to rest again a little father up the rod. There had been no years between the ducking of this dragonfly and the other one—the one that was part of memory. I looked at the boy, who was silently watching his fly, and it was my hands that held his rod, my eyes watching. I felt dizzy and didn't know which rod I was at the end of.

We caught two bass, hauling them in briskly as though they were mackerel, pulling them over the side of the boat in a businesslike manner without any landing net, and stunning them with a blow on the back of the head. When we got back for a swim before lunch, the lake was exactly where we had left it, the same number of inches from the dock, and there was only the merest suggestion of a breeze. This seemed an utterly enchanted sea, this lake you could leave to its own devices for a few hours and come back to, and find that it had not stirred, this constant and trustworthy body of water. In the shallows, the dark, water-soaked sticks and twigs, smooth and old, were undulating in clusters on the bottom against the clean ribbed sand, and the track of the mussel was plain. A school of minnows swam by, each minnow with its small individual shadow, doubling the attendance, so clear and sharp in the sunlight. Some of the other campers were in swimming, along the shore, one of them with a cake of soap, and the water felt thin and clear and unsubstantial. Over the years there had been this person with the cake of soap, this cultist, and here he was. There had been no years. . . .

We had a good week at the camp. The bass were biting well and the sun shone endlessly, day after day. We would be tired at night and lie down in the accumulated heat of the little bedrooms after the long hot day and the breeze would stir almost imperceptibly outside and the smell of the swamp drift in through the rusty screens. Sleep would come easily and in the morning the red squirrel would be on the roof, tapping out his gay routine. I kept remembering everything, lying in bed in the mornings—the small steamboat that had a long rounded stern like the lip of a Ubangi, and how quietly she ran on the moonlight sails, when the older boys played their mandolins and the girls sang and we ate doughnuts dipped in sugar, and how sweet the music was on the water in the shining night, and what it had felt like to think about girls then. After breakfast we would go up to the store and the things were in the same place—the minnows in a bottle, the plugs and spinners disarranged and pawed over by the youngsters from the boys' camp, the Fig Newtons and the Beeman's gum. Outside, the road was tarred and cars stood in front of the store. Inside, all was just as it had always been, except there was more Coca-Cola and not so much Moxie and root beer and birch beer and sarsaparilla. We would walk out with the bottle of pop apiece and sometimes the pop would backfire up our noses and hurt. We explored the streams, quietly, where the turtles slid off the sunny logs and dug their way into the soft bottom; and we lay on the town wharf and fed worms to the tame bass. Everywhere we went I had trouble making out which was I, the one walking at my side, the one walking in my pants.

One afternoon while we were there at that lake a thunderstorm came up. It was like the revival of an old melodrama that I had seen long ago with childish awe. The second-act climax of the drama of the electrical disturbance over a lake in America had not changed in any important respect. This was the big scene, still the big scene. The whole thing was so familiar, the first feeling of oppression and heat and a general air around camp of not wanting to go very far away. In mid-afternoon (it was all the same) a curious darkening of the sky, and a lull in every-thing that had made life tick; and then the way the boats suddenly swung the other way at their moorings with the coming of a breeze out of the new quarter, and the premonitory rumble. Then the kettle drum, then the snare, then the bass drum and cymbals, then crackling light against the dark, and the gods grinning and licking their chops in the hills. Afterward the calm, the rain steadily rustling in the calm lake, the return of light and hope and spirits, and the campers running out in joy and relief to go swimming in the rain, their bright cries perpetu-ating the deathless joke about how they were getting simply drenched, and the children screaming with delight at the new sensation of bath-ing in the rain, and the joke about getting drenched linking the gener-ations in a strong indestructible chain. And the comedian who waded in carrying an umbrella.

When the others went swimming, my son said he was going in, too. He pulled his dripping trunks from the line where they had hung all through the shower and wrung them out. Languidly, and with no thought of going in, I watched him, his hard little body, skinny and bare, saw him wince slightly as he pulled up around his vitals the small, soggy, icy garment. As he buckled the swollen belt, suddenly my groin felt the chill of death.

from Anorexia Nervosa: Psychopathology as the Crystallization of Culture

Susan Bordo

Historians long ago began to write the history of the body. They have studied the body in the field of historical demography or pathology; they have consid-ered it as the seat of needs and appetites, as the locus of physiological processes and metabolisms, as a target for the attacks of germs or viruses; they have shown to what extent historical processes were involved in what might seem to be the purely biological base of existence; and what place should be given in the history of society to biological "events" such as the circulation of bacilli, or the extension of the lifespan. But the body is also directly involved in a political field; power relations have an immediate hold upon it; they invest it, mark it, train it, torture it, force it to carry out tasks, to perform ceremonies, to emit signs.

(Michel Foucault, *Discipline and Punish*)

I believe in being the best I can be,
I believe in watching every calorie . . .

("Crystal Light" commercial)

I. Statement of Problem and Theoretical Framework

Psychopathology, as Jules Henry has said, "is the final outcome of all that is wrong with a culture."[1] In no case is this more strikingly true than in the case of anorexia nervosa and bulimia, barely known a century ago, yet reaching epidemic proportions today. Far from being the result of a superficial fashion phenomenon, these disorders, I will argue, reflect and call our attention to some of the central ills of our culture—from our historical heritage of disdain for the body, to our modern fear of loss of control over our futures, to the disquieting meaning of contemporary beauty ideals in an era of greater female presence and power than ever before.

Changes in the incidence of anorexia[2] have been dramatic. In 1945, when Ludwig Binswanger chronicled the now famous case of Ellen West, he was able to say that "from a psychiatric point of view we are dealing here with something new, with a symptom."[3] In 1973, Hilde Bruch, one of the pioneers in understanding and treating eating disorders, could still say that anorexia was "rare indeed."[4] Today, in 1984, it is estimated that as many as one in every 200–250 women between the ages of 13 and 22 suffer from anorexia,[5] and that anywhere from 12–33% of college women control their weight through vomiting, diuretics, and laxatives.[6] The New York Center for the Study of Anorexia and Bulimia reports that in the first five months of 1984, it received 252 requests for treatment, as compared to the 30 requests received in all of 1980.[7] Even discounting for increased social awareness of eating disorders, and a greater willingness of sufferers to report their illness, these statistics are startling and provocative. So, too, is the fact that 90% of all anorexics are women, and that of the 5,000 people each year who have their intestines removed to lose weight 80% are women.[8] . . .

What we need to ask is *why* our culture is so obsessed with keeping our bodies slim, tight, and young that when 500 people were asked, in a recent poll, what they feared most in the world, 190 replied "getting fat.''[9] In an age when our children regularly have nightmares of nuclear holocaust, that as adults we should give *this* answer—that we most fear "getting fat"—is far more bizarre than the anorexic's mis-perceptions of her body image, or the bulimic's compulsive vomiting. The nightmares of nuclear holocaust and our desperate fixation on our bodies as arenas of control—perhaps one of the few available arenas of control we have left in the twentieth-century—are not unconnected, of course. The connection, if explored, could be significant, de-mysti-fying, instructive.

So, too, do we need to explore the fact that it is women who are most oppressed by what Kim Chernin calls "the tyranny of slenderness,"[10] and that this particular oppression is a post-nineteen-sixties, post-fem-inist phenomenon. In the fifties, by contrast, with women once again out of the factories and safely immured in the home, the dominant ideal of female beauty was exemplified by Marilyn Monroe—hardly your androgynous, athletic, adolescent body type. At the peak of her popularity, Monroe was often described as "femininity incarnate," "femaleness embodied"; last term, a student of mine described her as "a cow." Is this merely a change in what size hips, breasts, and waist are considered attractive, or has the very idea of incarnate femaleness come to have a different meaning, different associations, the capacity to stir up different fantasies and images, for the culture of the eighties? These are the sorts of questions that need to be addressed if we are to achieve a deep understanding of the current epidemic of eating disorders.

The central point of intellectual orientation for this paper is expressed in its subtitle. I take the psychopathologies that develop within a culture, far from being anomalies or aberrations, as charac-teristic expressions of that culture, as the crystallization, indeed, of much that is wrong with it. For that reason they are important to exam-ine, as keys to cultural self-diagnosis and self-scrutiny. "Every age," says Christopher Lasch, "develops its own peculiar forms of pathology, which express in exaggerated form its underlying character struc-ture."[11] The only thing with which I would disagree in this formulation, with respect to anorexia, is the idea of the expression of an underlying, unitary cultural character structure. Anorexia appears less as the extreme expression of a character structure than as a remarkably over-determined *symptom* of some of the multi-faceted and heterogeneous distresses of our age. Just as it functions in a variety of ways in the psychic economy of the anorexic individual, so a variety of cultural cur-rents or streams converge in anorexia, find their perfect, precise expression in it.

I will call those streams or currents "axes of continuity": *axes* because they meet or converge in the anorexic syndrome; *continuity* refers to the fact that when we place or locate anorexia on these axes, its family resemblances and connections with other phenomena emerge. Some of these axes represent anorexia's *synchronicity* with other contemporary cultural practices and forms—such as body-building and jogging, for example. Other axes will bring to light *historical* connections: for example, between anorexia and earlier examples of extreme manipulation of the female body, such as corsetting, or between anorexia and long-standing traditions and ideologies in Western culture, such as our Greco-Christian traditions of dualism. The three axes that I will discuss in this paper (although they by no means exhaust the possibilities for cultural understanding of anorexia) are *the dualist axis, the control axis, and the gender/power axis.*[12] . . .

II. The Dualist Axis

I will begin with the most general and attenuated axis of continuity—the one that begins with Plato, winds its way to its most lurid expression in Augustine, and finally becomes metaphysically solidified and "scientized" by Descartes. I am referring, of course, to our dualistic heritage: the view that human existence is bifurcated into two realms or substances—the bodily or material, on the one hand, and the mental or spiritual, on the other. Despite some fascinating historical variations, which I will not go into here, the basic imagery of dualism has remained fairly constant. Let me briefly describe its central features; they will turn out, as we will see, to comprise the basic body imagery of the anorexic.

First, the body is experienced as alien, as the not-self, the not-me. *It* is "fastened and glued" to me, "nailed" and "riveted" to me, as Plato describes it in the *Phaedo.*[13] For Descartes, it is the brute material envelope for the inner and essential self, the thinking thing—ontologically distinct from it, as mechanical in its operations as a machine, comparable to animal existence. *Second,* the body is experienced as *confinement* and *limitation:* a "prison," a "swamp," a "cage," a "fog"—all images which occur in Plato, Descartes, and Augustine—from which the soul, will, or mind struggle to escape. "The enemy ['the madness of lust'] held my will in his power and from it he made a chain and shackled me," says Augustine.[14] In all three, images of the soul being "dragged" by the body are prominent. The body is "heavy, ponderous," as Plato describes it;[15] it exerts a downward pull. *Third,* the body is the *enemy,* as Augustine explicitly describes it time and again, and as Plato and Descartes strongly suggest in their diatribes against the body as the source of obscurity and confusion in our thinking. "A source of countless distractions by reason of the mere requirement of food," says Plato, "liable also to diseases which overtake and impede us in the pursuit of truth: it fill[s] us full of loves, and lusts, and fears, and fancies of all kinds, and endless foolery, and in very truth, as men say, takes away from us the power of thinking at all. Whence come wars, and fightings, and factions? Whence but from the body and the lusts of the body."[16]

Finally, whether as an impediment to reason, or as the home of the "slimy desires of the flesh" (as Augustine calls them), the body is the locus of all that which threatens our attempts at *control.* It overtakes, it overwhelms, it erupts and disrupts. This situation, for the dualist, becomes an incitement to battle the unruly forces of the body, to show it who is boss. For, as Plato says, "Nature orders the soul to rule and govern and the body to obey and serve."[17] All three, Plato, Augustine, and, most explicitly, Descartes provide instructions, rules or models of how to gain control over the body, with the ultimate aim—for this is what it finally boils down to—of learning to live without it. That is: to achieve intellectual independence from the lure of its illusions, to become impervious to its distractions, and most importantly, to kill off its desires and hungers. Once control has become the central issue for the soul, these are the only possible terms of victory, as Alan Watts makes clear:

> Willed control brings about a sense of duality in the organism, of conscious-
> ness in conflict with appetite. . . . But this mode of control is a peculiar exam-
> ple of the proverb that nothing fails like success. For the more consciousness
> is individualized by the success of the will, the more everything outside the
> individual seems to be a threat—including . . . the uncontrolled spontaneity
> of one's own body. . . . Every success in control therefore demands a further
> success, so that the process cannot stop short of omnipotence.[18]

Dualism here appears as the offspring, the by-product, of the identification of the self with control, an identification that Watts sees as
lying at the center of Christianity's ethic of anti-sexuality. The attempt
to subdue the spontaneities of the body in the interests of control only
succeeds in constituting them as more alien, and more powerful, and
thus, more needful of control. The only way to win this no-win game is
to go beyond control, is to kill off the body's spontaneities entirely. That
is: to cease to *experience* our hungers and desires.

This is what many anorexics describe as their ultimate goal. "[I want]
to reach the point," as one put it, "when I don't need to eat at all."[19]
Kim Chernin recalls her surprise when after fasting, her hunger
returned: "I realized [then] that my secret goal in dieting must have
been the intention to kill off my appetite completely."[20]

It is not usually noted, in the popular literature on the subject, that
anorexic women are as obsessed with *hunger* as they are with being
slim. Far from losing her appetite, the typical anorexic is haunted by
her appetite, in much the same way as Augustine describes being
haunted by sexual desire, and is in constant dread of being overwhelmed by it. Many describe the dread of hunger—"of not having
control, of giving in to biological urge," to "the craving, never satisfied
thing"[21] as the "original fear" (as one puts it),[22] or, as Ellen West
describes it, "the real obsession." "I don't think the dread of becoming
fat is the real . . . neurosis," she writes, "but the constant desire for
food. . . . [H]unger, or the dread of hunger, pursues me all morning. . . .

Even when I am full, I am afraid of the coming hour in which hunger will start again." Dread of becoming fat, she interprets, rather than being originary, served as a "brake" to her horror of her own unregulatable, runaway desire for food.[23] Bruch reports that her patients are often terrified by the prospect of taking just one bite of food, lest they never be able to stop.[24] (Bulimic anorexics, who binge on enormous quantities of food—sometimes consuming up to 15,000 calories a day[25]—indeed *cannot* stop.)

For these women, hunger is experienced as an alien invader, marching to the tune of its own seemingly arbitrary whims, disconnected from any normal self-regulating mechanisms. How could it be so connected? For, it is experienced as coming from an area *outside* the self. One patient of Bruch's says she ate breakfast because "my stomach wanted it,"[26] expressing here the same sense of alienation from her hungers (and her physical self) that Augustine expresses when he speaks of his "captor," "the law of sin that was in my member."[27] Bruch notes that this "basic delusion," as she calls it, "of not owning the body and its sensations" is a typical symptom of all eating disorders. "These patients act," she says, "as if for them the regulation of food intake was outside [the self]."[28] This experience of bodily sensation as foreign, strikingly, is not limited to the experience of hunger. Patients with eating disorders have similar problems in identifying cold, heat, emotions, and anxiety as originating in the self.[29]

While the body is experienced as alien and outside, the soul or will is described as being trapped or confined in this alien "jail," as one woman describes it.[30] "I feel caught in my body," "I'm a prisoner in my body"[31] is the theme that is repeated again and again. A typical fantasy, as it is for Plato, is of total liberation from the bodily prison: "I wish I could get out of my body entirely and fly!"[32] "Please dear God, help me. . . . I want to get out of my body, I want to get out!"[33] Ellen West, astute as always, sees a central meaning of her self-starvation in this "ideal of being too thin, of being *without a body*" (emphasis added).[34]

Anorexia is not a philosophical attitude; it is a debilitating affliction. Yet quite often a highly conscious and articulate scheme of images and associations—one could go as far as to call it a metaphysics—is presented by these women. The scheme is strikingly Augustinian, with evocations of Plato. This is not to say, of course, that anorexics are followers of Plato or Augustine, but that in the anorexic's "metaphysics" elements are made explicit, historically grounded in Plato and Augustine, that run deep in our culture. As Augustine often speaks of the "two wills" within him, "one the servant of the flesh, the other of the spirit," who "between them tore my soul apart,"[35] so the anorexic describes a "spiritual struggle," a "contest between good and evil,"[36] often conceived explicitly as a battle between mind or will and appetite or body. "I feel myself, quite passively," says West, "the stage on which two hostile forces are mangling each other."[37] Sometimes there is a more aggressive alliance with mind against body: "When I fail to exercise as often as I prefer, I become guilty that I have let my body 'win' another day from my mind. I can't wait 'til this semester is over. . . . My body is going to pay the price for the lack of work it is currently getting. I can't wait!"[38]

In this battle, thinness represents a triumph of the will over body, and the thin body (i.e., the non-body) is associated with "absolute purity, hyperintellectuality and transcendence of the flesh. My soul seemed to grow as my body waned; I felt like one of those early Christian saints who starved themselves in the desert sun. I felt invulnerable, clean and hard as the bones etched into my silhouette."[39] Fat (i.e., becoming *all* body) is associated with the "taint" of matter and flesh, "wantonness,"[40] mental stupor and mental decay.[41] One woman describes how after eating sugar she felt "polluted, disgusting, sticky through the arms, as if something bad had gotten inside."[42] Very often, sexuality is brought into this scheme of associations, and hunger and sexuality are psychically connected. Cherry Boone O'Neill describes a late night binge, eating scraps of left-overs from the dog's dish:

> I started slowly, relishing the flavor and texture of each marvelous bite. Soon I was ripping the meager remains from the bones, stuffing the meat into my mouth as fast as I could detach it. [Her boyfriend surprises her, with a look of "total disgust" on his face.] I had been caught red-handed . . . in an animalistic orgy on the floor, in the dark, alone. Here was the horrid truth for Dan to see. I felt so evil, tainted, pagan. . . . In Dan's mind that day, I had been whoring after food.[43]

A hundred pages earlier, she had described her first romantic involvement in much the same terms: "I felt secretive, deceptive, and . . . tainted by the ongoing relationship" (which never went beyond kisses).[44] Sexuality, similarly is "an abominable business" to Aimée Liu; for her, staying reed-thin is seen as a way of avoiding sexuality, by becoming "androgynous," as she puts it.[45] In the same way, Sarah, a patient of Levenkron's, connects her dread of gaining weight with "not wanting to be a 'temptation' to men."[46] In Aimée Liu's case, and in Sarah's, the desire to appear unattractive to men is connected to anxiety and guilt over earlier sexual abuse. Whether or not such episodes are common to many cases of anorexia,[47] "the avoidance of any sexual encounter, a shrinking from all bodily contact," according to Bruch, is characteristic.[48]

III. The Control Axis

Having pointed to the axis of continuity from Plato to anorexia, we should feel cautioned against the impulse to regard anorexia as expressing entirely modern attitudes and fears. Disdain for the body, the conception of it as an alien force and impediment to the soul, is very old in our Greco-Christian traditions (although it has usually been expressed most forcefully by male philosophers and theologians rather than adolescent women!).

But although dualism is as old as Plato, in many ways contemporary culture appears *more* obsessed than previous eras with the control of the unruly body. Looking now at contemporary American life, a second axis of continuity emerges on which to locate anorexia. I will call it the *control axis.*

The anorexic, typically, experiences her life as well as her hungers as being out of control. She is a perfectionist, and can never fulfill the tasks she sets to her own rigorous standards. She is torn by conflicting and contradictory expectations and demands, wanting to shine in all areas of student life, confused about where to place most of her energies, what to focus on, as she develops into an adult. Characteristically, her parents expect a great deal of her in the way of individual achievement (as well as physical appearance, particularly her father), yet have made most important decisions for her. Usually, the anorexic syndrome emerges, *not* as a conscious decision to get as thin as possible, but as the result of her having begun a diet fairly casually, often at the suggestions of a parent, having succeeded splendidly in taking off five or ten pounds, and then gotten *hooked* on the intoxicating feeling of accomplishment and control.

Recalling her anorexic days, Aimée Liu recreates her feelings:

> The sense of accomplishment exhilarates me, spurs me to continue on and on. It provides a sense of purpose and shapes my life with distractions from insecurity. . . . I shall become an expert [at losing weight]. . . . The constant downward trend [of the scale] somehow comforts me, gives me visible proof that I can exert control.[49]

The diet, she realizes ''is the one sector of my life over which I and I alone wield total control.''[50]

The frustrations of starvation, the rigors of the constant exercise and physical activity in which anorexics engage, the pain of the numerous physical complications of anorexia do not trouble the anorexic; indeed, her ability to ignore them is further proof to her of her mastery of her body. ''This was something I could control,'' says one of Bruch's patients, ''I still don't know what I look like or what size I am, but I know my body can take anything.''[51] ''Energy, discipline, my own power will keep me going,'' says Liu. ''Psychic fuel. I need nothing and no one else, and I will prove it. . . . Dropping to the floor, I roll. My tailbone crunches on the hard floor. . . . I feel no pain. I will be master of my own body, if nothing else, I vow.''[52] And finally, from one of Bruch's patients: *''You make of your own body your very own kingdom where you are the tyrant, the absolute dictator.''*[53]

Surely we must recognize in this last honest and explicit statement a central *modus operandi* for the control of contemporary bourgeois anxiety. Consider: compulsive jogging and marathon-running, often despite shin-splints and other painful injuries, with intense agitation over missed days, or not meeting goals for particular runs. Consider the increasing popularity of triathlon events like the "Iron Man," which appear to have no other purpose than to allow people to find out how far they can push their bodies before collapsing. Consider lawyer Mike Frankfurt, who runs ten miles every morning: ". . . *To run with pain is the essence of life.*"[54] Or the following excerpts from student journals:

> . . . [T]he best times I like to run are under the most unbearable conditions. I love to run in the hottest, most humid and steepest terrain I can find. . . . For me running and the pain associated with it aren't enough to make me stop. I am always trying to overcome it and the biggest failure I can make is to stop running because of pain. Once I ran five of a ten-mile run with a severe leg cramp but wouldn't stop—it would have meant failure.[55]

> When I run I am free. . . . The pleasure is closing off my body—as if the incessant pounding of my legs is so total that the pain ceases to exist. There is no grace, no beauty in the running—there is the jarring reality of sneaker and pavement. Bright pain that shivers and splinters sending its white hot arrows into my stomach, my lung, but it cannot pierce my mind. I am on automatic pilot—there is no remembrance of pain, there is freedom—I am losing myself, peeling out of this heavy flesh. . . . Power surges through me.[56]

None of this is to dispute that the contemporary concern with fitness has non-pathological, non-dualist dimensions as well. Particularly for women, who have historically suffered from the ubiquity of rape and abuse, from the culturally instilled conviction of our own helplessness, and from lack of access to facilities and programs for rigorous physical training, the cultivation of strength, agility, and confidence has a clearly positive dimension. Nor are the objective benefits of daily exercise and concern for nutrition in question here. My focus, rather, is on a subjective stance, increasingly more prominent over the last five years, which, although preoccupied with the body and deriving narcissistic enjoyment from its appearance, takes little pleasure in the *experience* of embodiment. Rather, the fundamental identification is with mind (or will), ideals of spiritual perfection, fantasies of absolute control. . . .

The sense of security derived from the attainment of this goal appears, first of all, as the pleasure of control and independence. "Nowadays," says Michael Sacks, associate professor of psychiatry at Cornell Medical College, "people no longer feel they can control events outside themselves—how well they do in their jobs or in their personal relationships, for example—but they can control the food they eat and how far they can run. Abstinence, tests of endurance, are ways of proving their self-sufficiency."[57] In a culture, moreover, in which our continued survival is often at the mercy of "specialists," machines, and sophisticated technology, the body takes on a special sort of vulnerability and dependency. We may live longer than ever before, but the circumstances surrounding illness and death may often be perceived as more alien, inscrutable, and arbitrary than ever before.

Our contemporary body-fetishism, however, expresses more than a fantasy of self-mastery in an increasingly unmanageable culture. It also reflects our alliance *with* culture against all reminders of the inevitable decay and death of the body. "Everybody wants to live forever" is the refrain from the theme song of *Pumping Iron*. The most youth-worshipping of popular television shows, *Fame*, opens with a song that begins, "I want to live forever." And it is striking that although the anorexic may come very close to death (and 15% do indeed die), the dominant experience throughout the illness is of *invulnerability*.

The dream of immortality is, of course, nothing new. But what is unique to modernity is that the defeat of death has become a scientific fantasy rather than a philosophical or religious mythology. We no longer dream of eternal union with the gods; we build devices that can keep us alive indefinitely, and we work on keeping our bodies as smooth and muscular and elastic at 40 as they were at 18. We even entertain dreams of halting the aging process completely: "Old age," according to Durk Pearson and Sandy Shaw, authors of the popular *Life Extension*, "is an unpleasant and unattractive affliction."[58] The mega-vitamin regime they prescribe is able, they claim, to prevent and even to *reverse* the mechanisms of aging.

Finally, it may be that in cultures characterized by gross excesses in consumption, the "will to conquer and subdue the body" (as Chernin calls it)[59] expresses an aesthetic or moral rebellion. Anorexics initially came from affluent families, and the current craze for long distance running and fasting is largely a phenomenon of young, upwardly-mobile professionals (Dinitia Smith calls it "Deprivation Chic"). To those who are starving *against* their wills, of course, starvation cannot function as an expression of the power of the will. At the same time, we should caution against viewing anorexia as a trendy illness of the elite and privileged. Rather, powerlessness is its most outstanding feature.

IV. The Gender/Power Axis

Ninety percent of all anorexics are women. We do not need, of course, to know that particular statistic to realize that the contemporary "tyranny of slenderness" is far from gender neutral. Women are more obsessed with their bodies than men, less satisfied with them,[60] and permitted less latitude with them by themselves, by men, and by the culture. In a recent *Glamour* magazine poll of 33,000 women, 75% said that they thought they were "too fat." Yet by Metropolitan Life Insurance Tables—although they are themselves notoriously affected by cultural standards—only 25% of these women were heavier than the specified standards, and a full 30% were *below*.[61] The anorexic's distorted image of her body—her inability to see it as anything but "too fat," while more extreme, is not radically discontinuous, then, from fairly common female misperceptions.

Consider, too, actors like Nick Nolte and William Hurt, who are permitted a certain amount of softening, of thickening about the waist, while still retaining romantic lead status. Individual style, wit, the projection of intelligence, experience, and effectiveness still go a long way for men, even in our fitness-obsessed culture. But no female can achieve the status of romantic or sexual ideal without the appropriate *body*. That body, if we use television commercials as a gauge, has gotten steadily leaner over the past ten years.[62] What used to be acknowledged as extremes required of high fashion models only is now the dominant image that beckons to high school and college women. Over and over, extremely slender women students complain of hating their thighs, or their stomachs (the anorexic's most dreaded danger spot); often, they express concern and anger over frequent teasing by their boyfriends; Janey, a former student, is 5'10" and weighs 132 pounds. Yet her boyfriend calls her "Fatso" and "Big Butt" and insists she should be 100 pounds because "that's what Brooke Shields weighs." He calls this "constructive criticism," and seems to experience extreme anxiety over the possibility of her gaining any weight: "I can tell it bothers her yet I still continue to badger her about it. I guess that I think that if I continue to remind her things will change faster. . . ."[63] This sort of relationship—within which the woman's weight has become a focal issue—is not at all atypical, as I've discovered from student journals and papers.

Hilde Bruch reports that many anorexics talk of having a "ghost" inside them or surrounding them, "a dictator who dominates me," as one woman describes it; "a little man who objects when I eat" is the description given by another.[64] The little ghost, the dictator, the "other self" (as he is often described), is always male, reports Bruch. The anorexic's *other* self—the self of the uncontrollable appetites, the impurities and taints, the flabby will and tendency to mental torpor—is the body, as we have seen. But it is also (and here the anorexic's associations are surely in the mainstream of Western culture) the *female* self. These two selves are perceived as at constant war. But it is clear that it is the male side—with its associated values of greater spirituality, higher intellectuality, strength of will—which is being expressed and developed in the anorexic syndrome.

What is the meaning of these gender associations in the anorexic? I propose that there are two levels of meaning. One has to do with fear and disdain for traditional female *roles* and social limitations. The other has to do, more profoundly, with a deep fear of "The Female," with all its more nightmarish archetypal associations: voracious hungers and sexual insatiability. Let us examine each of these levels in turn.

Adolescent anorexics express characteristic fears about growing up to be mature, sexually developed, and potentially reproductive women. "I have a deep fear," says one, "of having a womanly body, round and fully developed. I want to be tight and muscular and thin."[65] Cherry Boone O'Neill speaks explicitly of her "fear of womanhood."[66] If only she could stay thin, says yet another, "I would never have to deal with having a woman's body; like Peter Pan I could stay a child forever."[67] The choice of Peter Pan is telling here—what she means is, stay a *boy* forever. And indeed, as Bruch reports, many anorexics, when children, dreamt and fantasized about growing up to be boys.[68] Some are quite conscious of playing out this fantasy through their anorexia: Adrienne, one of Levenkron's patients, was extremely proud of the growth of facial and body hair that often accompanies anorexia, and especially proud of her "skinny, hairy arms."[69] Many patients report, too, that their fathers had wanted a boy,[70] were disappointed to get "less than" that,[71] or had emotionally rebuffed their daughters when they began to develop sexually.[72]

In a characteristic scenario, anorexia will develop just at the outset of puberty. Normal body changes are experienced by the anorexic, not surprisingly, as the take-over of the body by disgusting, womanish fat. "I grab my breasts," says Aimée Liu, "pinching them until they hurt. If only I could eliminate them, cut them off if need be, to become as flat-chested as a child again."[73] She is exultant when her periods stop (as they do in *all* cases of anorexia).[74] The disgust with menstruation is typical: "I saw a picture at a feminist art gallery," says another woman, "there was a woman with long red yarn coming out of her, like she was menstruating. . . . I got that *feeling*—in that part of my body that I have trouble with . . . my stomach, my thighs, my pelvis. That revolted feeling."[75]

Some authors interpret these symptoms as a species of unconscious feminist protest, involving anger at the limitations of the traditional female role, rejection of values associated with it, and fierce rebellion against allowing their futures to develop in the same direction as their mothers' lives.[76] In her portrait of the typical anorexic family configuration, Bruch describes nearly all of the mothers as submissive to their husbands, while very controlling of their children.[77] Practically all had had promising careers which they gave up to care for their husbands and families full-time, a task they take very seriously, although often expressing frustration and dissatisfaction.

Certainly, many anorexics appear to experience anxiety over falling into the lifestyle they associate with their mothers. It is a prominent theme in Aimée Liu's *Solitaire.* Another woman describes her feeling that she is "full of my mother . . . she is in me even if she isn't there" in nearly the same breath as she complains of her continuous fear of being "not human . . . of ceasing to exist."[78] And Ellen West, nearly a century earlier, had quite explicitly equated becoming fat with the inevitable (for a woman of her time) confinements of domestic life and the domestic stupor she associates with it:

> Dread is driving me mad . . . the consciousness that ultimately I will lose everything; all courage, all rebelliousness, all drive for doing; that it—my little world—will make me flabby and fainthearted and beggarly. . . . [79]

Several of my students with eating disorders reported that their anorexia had developed after their families had dissuaded or forbidden them from embarking on a traditionally male career. . . .

But we must recognize that the anorexic's "protest," like that of the classical hysterical symptom, is written on the bodies of anorexic women, and *not* embraced as a conscious politics, nor, indeed, does it reflect any social or political understanding at all. Moreover, the symptoms themselves function to preclude the emergence of such an understanding: The *idée fixe*—staying thin—becomes at its farthest extreme so powerful as to render any other ideas or life-projects meaningless. Liu describes it as "all-encompassing."[80] West writes that "I felt all inner development was ceasing, that all becoming and growing were being choked, because a single idea was filling my entire soul."[81]

Paradoxically—and often tragically—these pathologies of female "protest" . . . actually function as if in collusion with the cultural conditions which produced them. The same is true for more moderate expressions of the contemporary female obsession with slenderness. Women may feel themselves deeply attracted by the aura of freedom and independence suggested by the boyish body ideal of today. Yet, each hour, each minute that is spent in anxious pursuit of that ideal (for it does not come "naturally" to most mature women) is *in fact* time and energy deprived of inner development and social achievement. As a feminist protest, the obsession with slenderness is hopelessly counter-productive.

It is important to recognize, too, that the anorexic is terrified and repelled, not only by the traditional female domestic role—which she associates with mental lassitude and weakness—but by a certain archetypal image of the female: as hungering, voracious, all-needing, and all-wanting. It is this image that shapes and permeates her experience of her own hunger for food as insatiable and out-of-control, which makes her feel that if she takes just one bite, she won't be able to stop.

Let's explore this image. Let's break the tie with food and look at the metaphor: Hungering. Voracious. Extravagantly and excessively needful. Without restraint. Always wanting. Always wanting too much affection, reassurance, emotional and sexual contact and attention. This is how many women frequently experience themselves, and, indeed, how many men experience women. "Please, please God, keep me from telephoning him," prays the heroine in Dorothy Parker's classic "The Telephone Call," experiencing her need for reassurance and contact as being as out-of-control and degrading as the anorexic experiences her desire for food. The male counterpart to this is found in someone like Paul Morel in Lawrence's *Sons and Lovers:* "Can you never like things without clutching them as if you wanted to pull the heart out of them?" he accuses Miriam as she fondles a flower, "Why don't you have a bit more restraint, or reserve, or something. . . . You're always begging things to love you, as if you were a beggar for love. Even the flowers, you have to fawn on them."[82] How much psychic authenticity do these images carry in 1980s America? One woman in my class provided a stunning insight into the connection between her perception of herself and the anxiety of the compulsive dieter: "You know," she said, "the anorexic is always convinced she is taking up too much space, eating too much, wanting food too much. I've never felt that way, but I've often felt that I was *too much*—too much emotion, too much need, too loud and demanding, too much *there,* if you know what I mean."

The most extreme cultural expressions of the fear of woman-as-too-much—which almost always revolve around her sexuality—are strikingly full of eating and hungering metaphors. "Of woman's unnatural, *insatiable* lust, what country, what village doth not complain?" queries Burton in *The Anatomy of Melancholy.*[83] "You are the true hiennas," says Walter Charleton, "that allure us with the fairness of your skins, and when folly hath brought us within your reach, you leap upon us and *devour* us."[84]

The mythology/ideology of the devouring, insatiable female (which, as we have seen, is the internalized image the anorexic has of her female self) tends historically to wax and wane. But not without rhyme or reason. In periods of gross environmental and social crisis, such as characterized the period of the witch-hunts in the fifteenth and sixteenth centuries, it appears to flourish.[85] "All witchcraft comes from carnal lust, which is in women *insatiable,*" say Kramer and Sprenger, authors of the official witch-hunters handbook, *Malleus Malificarum.*[86] For the sake of fulfilling the "*mouth* of the womb . . . [women] consort even with the devil."[87]

Anxiety over women's uncontrollable hungers appears to peak, as well, during periods when women are becoming independent, and asserting themselves politically and socially. The second half of the nineteenth century, concurrent with the first feminist wave discussed earlier, saw a virtual "flood" (as Peter Gay calls it) of artistic and literary images of the dark, dangerous, and evil female: "sharp-teethed, devouring" Sphinxes, Salomés and Delilahs, "biting, tearing, murderous women."[88] "No century," claims Gay, "depicted woman as vampire, as castrator, as killer, so consistently, so programmatically, and so nakedly as the nineteenth."[89] No century, too, was as obsessed with female sexuality and its medical control. Treatment for excessive "sexual excitement" and masturbation included placing leeches on the womb,[90] clitoridectomy, and removing of the ovaries (also recommended for "troublesomeness, eating like a ploughman, erotic tendencies, persecution mania, and simple 'cussedness'").[91] The importance of female masturbation in the etiology of the "actual neurosis" was a topic in which the young Freud and his friend and colleague Wilhelm Fliess were especially interested. Fliess believed that the secret to controlling such "sexual abuse" lay in the treatment of nasal "genital spots"; in an operation that was sanctioned by Freud, he attempted to "correct" the "bad sexual habits" of Freud's patient Emma Eckstein by removal of the turbinate bone of her nose.[92]

It is in the second half of the nineteenth century, too, despite a flurry of efforts by feminists and health reformers,[93] that the stylized "S-curve," which required a tighter corset than ever before, comes into fashion.[94] "While the suffragettes were forcefully propelling all women toward legal and political emancipation," says Amaury deRiencourt, "fashion and custom imprisoned her physically as she had never been before."[95] Described by Thorsten Veblen as a "mutilation, undergone for the purpose of lowering the subject's vitality and rendering her permanently and obviously unfit for work,"[96] the corset indeed did just that. In it, a woman could barely sit or stoop, was unable to move her feet more than six inches at a time, and had difficulty keeping herself from regular fainting fits. (In 1904, a researcher reported that "monkeys laced up in these corsets moped, became excessively irritable and within weeks sickened and died"!)[97] The connection was often drawn in popular magazines between enduring the tight corset and the exercise of self-restraint and control. The corset is "an ever present monitor," says one 1878 advertisement, "of a well-disciplined mind and well-regulated feelings."[98] Today, of course, we diet to achieve such control. . . .

On the gender/power axis the female body appears, then, as the unknowing medium of the historical ebbs and flows of the fear of woman-as-too-much. That, as we have seen, is how the anorexic experiences her female, bodily self: as voracious, wanton, needful of forceful control by her male will. Living in the tide of cultural backlash against the second major feminist wave, she is not alone in these images. Christopher Lasch, in *The Culture of Narcissism*, speaks of what he describes as "the apparently aggressive overtures of sexually liberated women" which "convey to many males the same message— that women are *voracious, insatiable*," and call up "early fantasies of a possessive, suffocating, *devouring* and castrating mother."[99] (emphasis added)

Our contemporary beauty ideals, on the other hand, seemed purged, as Kim Chernin puts it, "of the power to conjure up memories of the past, of all that could remind us of a woman's mysterious power."[100] The ideal, rather, is an "image of a woman in which she is not yet a woman": Darryl Hannah as the lanky, new-born mermaid in *Splash;* Lori Singer (appearing virtually anorexic) as the reckless, hyper-kinetic heroine of *Footloose;* The Charlie Girl; "Cheryl Tiegs in shorts, Margaux Hemingway with her hair wet, Brooke Shields naked on an island. . . ."[101] The dozens of teen-age women who appear in coke commercials, in jeans commercials, in chewing gum commercials.

The images suggest amused detachment, casual playfulness, flirtatiousness without demand, and lightness of touch. A refusal to take sex, death, or politics too deadly seriously. A delightfully unconscious relationship to her body. The twentieth century has seen this sort of feminine ideal before, of course: When, in the 1920s, young women began to flatten their breasts, suck in their stomachs, bob their hair, and show off long colt-like legs, they believed they were pursuing a new freedom and daring that demanded a carefree, boyish style.[102] If the traditional female hour glass suggested anything, it was confinement and immobility. Yet the flapper's freedom, as Mary McCarthy's and Dorothy Parker's short stories brilliantly reveal, was largely an illusion—as any obsessively cultivated sexual style must inevitably be. Although today's images may suggest androgynous independence, we need only consider who is on the receiving end of the imagery in order to confront the pitiful paradox involved.

Watching the commercials are thousands of anxiety-ridden women and adolescents (some of whom are likely the very ones appearing in the commercials) with anything *but* an unconscious relation to their bodies. They are involved in an absolutely contradictory state of affairs, a totally no-win game: caring desperately, passionately, obsessively about attaining an ideal of coolness, effortless confidence, and casual freedom. Watching the commercials is a little girl, perhaps ten years old, who I saw in Central Park, gazing raptly at her father, bursting with pride: "Daddy, guess what? I lost two pounds!" And watching the commercials is the anorexic, who associates her relentless pursuit of thinness with power and control, but who in fact destroys her health and imprisons her imagination. She is surely the most startling and stark illustration of how cavalier power relations are with respect to the motivations and goals of individuals, yet how deeply they are etched on our bodies, and how well our bodies serve them.

Le Moyne College

Footnotes

[Editor's note: Some original footnotes have been omitted.]

This paper, like all intellectual projects, has been a collaborative enterprise. All of the many students, friends, and colleagues who have discussed its ideas with me, suggested articles and resources, commented on earlier versions, shared personal experiences, or allowed me to glimpse their own fears and angers, have collaborated with me on this project, have made its development possible. In particular, I owe a large debt to the students of my metaphysics and "Gender, Culture, and Experience" classes, whose articulate and honest journals I have drawn on in these pages, and whose own work often pushed forward my own. Here, I would single out Christy Ferguson, Vivian Conger, and Nancy Monaghan, whose research on Victorian and early twentieth century ideals of femininity contributed insights and information that proved significant to this paper. Although many people have commented on earlier drafts, Lynne Arnault, Mario Moussa, and Nancy Fraser were especially helpful in providing systematic and penetrating criticisms and editorial suggestions for the final version. Finally, Edward Lee and Mario Moussa have been constant sources of insight and support, from beginning to end of this project.

1. Jules Henry, *Culture Against Man* (New York: Knopf, 1963).

2. Throughout this paper, the term "anorexia" will be used as it is used by most clinicians: to designate a general class of eating disorders within which intake-restricting (or abstinent) anorexia and bulimia/anorexia (characterized by alternating bouts of gorging and starving and/or gorging and vomiting) are distinct sub-types (See Hilde Bruch, *The Golden Cage: The Enigma of Anorexia Nervosa* [New York: Vintage, 1979], p. 10; Steven Levenkron, *Treating and Overcoming Anorexia Nervosa* [New York: Warner Books, 1982], p. 6; R. L. Palmer, *Anorexia Nervosa* [Middlesex, England: Penguin, 1980], p. 14, 23–24; Paul Garfinkel and David Garner, *Anorexia Nervosa: A Multidimensional Perspective* [New York: Brunner/Mazel, 1982], p. 4). . . .

3. Ludwig Binswanger, "The Case of Ellen West," in *Existence*, ed. Rollo May (New York: Simon and Schuster, 1958), p. 288.

4. Hilde Bruch, *Eating Disorders* (New York: Basic Books, 1973), p. 4.

5. Levenkron, p. 1.

6. Susan Squire, "Is the Binge-Purge Cycle Catching?", *Ms.*, October, 1983; *Anorexia/Bulimia Support*, Syracuse, New York.

7. Dinitia Smith, "The New Puritans," *New York* magazine, June 11, 1984, p. 28.

8. Kim Chernin, *The Obsession: Reflections on the Tyranny of Slenderness* (New York: Harper and Row, 1981), pp. 63, 62.

9. Chernin, pp. 36–37. My use of the term "our culture" may seem overly homogenizing here, disrespectful of differences among ethnic groups, socioeconomic groups, subcultures within American society, etc. It must be stressed here that I am discussing ideology and images whose power is *precisely* the power to homogenize culture. . . .

10. Until very recently, this dimension was largely ignored or underemphasized, with a very few notable exceptions. Kim Chernin and Susie Ohrbach (*Fat Is a Feminist Issue*) were groundbreakers in exploring the connections between eating disorders and images and ideals of femininity. . . .

11. Christopher Lasch, *The Culture of Narcissism* (New York: Warner Books, 1979), p. 88.

12. I choose these three primarily because they are where my exploration of the imagery, language, and metaphor produced by anorexic women led me. Delivering earlier versions of this paper at colleges and conferences, I dis-

covered that one of the commonest responses of members of the audiences was the proferring of further axes; the paper presented itself less as a statement about the ultimate "meaning" or causes of a phenomenon than as an invitation to continue my "unpacking" of anorexia as a crystallizing formation. Yet the particular axes chosen have more than a purely auto-biographical rationale. The dualist axes serves to identify and articulate the basic body imagery of anorexia. The control axis is an exploration of the question "Why Now?" The gender/power axis continues this explora-tion, but focuses on the question "Why Women?" The sequence of axes takes us from the most general, most historically diffuse structure of con-tinuity—the dualist experience of self—to ever narrower, more specified "arenas" of comparison and connection. At first, the connections are made without regard to historical context, drawing on diverse historical sources to exploit their familiar coherence in an effort to sculpt the "shape" of the anorexic experience. In this section, too, I want to suggest that the Greco-Christian tradition provides a particularly fertile soil for the development of anorexia. Then, I turn to the much more specific context of American fads and fantasies in the nineteen-eighties, considering the contemporary scene largely in terms of popular culture (and therefore through the "fic-tion" of homogeneity), without regard for gender difference. In this section, the connections drawn point to a historical experience of self common to both men and women. Finally, my focus shifts to consider, not what con-nects anorexia to other general cultural phenomena, but what presents itself as a rupture from them, and what forces us to confront how ulti-mately opaque the current epidemic of eating disorders remains unless it is linked to the particular situation of women.

The reader will notice that the axes are linked thematically as well as through their convergence in anorexia: e.g., the obsession with control is linked with dualism, and the gender/power dynamics discussed implicitly deal with the issue of control (of the feminine) as well. Obviously the notion of a "crystallizing formation" requires further spelling out: e.g., more pre-cise articulation of the relation of cultural axes to each other and elabora-tion of general principles for the study of culture suggested by this sort of analysis. I have chosen not to undertake this project within this paper, however, but to reserve it for a more extended treatment of the relationship between psychopathology and culture. The inevitable complexity of such a theoretical discussion would divert from the concrete analysis which is the focus of the paper.

13. Plato, *Phaedo*, in *The Dialogues of Plato*, trans. Benjamin Jowett, 4th ed. rev. (Oxford: The Clarendon Press, 1953), 83d.

14. St. Augustine, *The Confessions*, trans. R. S. Pine-Coffin (Middlesex, England: Penguin Books, 1961), p. 164.

15. *Phaedo*, 81d.

16. *Phaedo*, 66c. For Descartes on the body as a hindrance to knowledge, see *Conversations with Burman* (Oxford: Clarendon, 1976), p. 8 and *Passions of the Soul* in *Philosophical Works of Descartes*, trans. Elizabeth Haldane and G.R.T. Ross (Cambridge: Cambridge Univ. Press, 1969), Vol. 1, p. 353.

17. *Phaedo*, 80a.

18. Alan Watts, *Nature, Man and Woman* (New York: Vintage, 1970), p. 145.

19. Bruch, *Eating Disorders*, p. 84.

20. Chernin, p. 8.

21. Entry in student journal, 1984.

22. Bruch, *The Golden Cage*, p. 4.

23. Binswanger, "The Case of Ellen West," p. 253.

24. Bruch, *Eating Disorders*, p. 253.

25. Steven Levenkron, *Treating and Overcoming Anorexia Nervosa*, p. 6.

26. Bruch, *Eating Disorders*, p. 270.

27. Augustine, *Confessions*, p. 164.

28. Bruch, *Eating Disorders*, p. 50.

29. Bruch, *Eating Disorders*, p. 254.

30. Entry in student journal, 1984.

31. Bruch, *Eating Disorders*, p. 279.

32. Aimée Liu, *Solitaire* (New York: Harper, 1979), p. 141.

33. Jennifer Woods, "I Was Starving Myself to Death," *Mademoiselle*, May, 1981, p. 200.

34. Binswanger, "The Case of Ellen West," p. 251.

35. Augustine, *Confessions*, p. 165.

36. Liu, p. 109.

37. Binswanger, "The Case of Ellen West," p. 343.

38. Entry in student journal, 1983.

39. Woods, p. 242.

40. Liu, p. 109.

41. "I equated gaining weight with happiness, contentment, then slothfulness, then atrophy, then death." (From case notes of Binnie Klein, MSW, to whom I am grateful for having provided parts of a transcript of her work with an anorexic patient.) See also, Binswanger, "The Case of Ellen West," p. 343.

42. Klein, case notes.

43. Cherry Boone O'Neill, *Starving for Attention* (New York: Dell, 1982), p. 131.

44. O'Neill, p. 49.

45. Liu, p. 101.

46. Levenkron, p. 122.

47. In a Minnesota study of high school students, it was determined that one in every ten anorexics were victims of sexual abuse. Comments by and informal discussion with therapists at the Third Annual Conference for the Study of Anorexia and Bulimia bear these findings out; therapist after therapist remarked on the high incidence of early sexual violence and incest in their anorexic patients.

48. Bruch, *The Golden Cage*, p. 73. The same is not true of bulimic anorex-

ics, who tend to be sexually active (Garfinkel and Garner, p. 41). Bulimic anorexics, as seems symbolized by the binge/purge cycle itself, stand in a somewhat more ambivalent relationship to their hungers than do abstinent anorexics.

49. Liu, p. 36.

50. Liu, p. 46.

51. Bruch, *Eating Disorders*, p. 95.

52. Liu, p. 123.

53. Bruch, *The Golden Cage*, p. 65.

54. Smith, p. 24.

55. Entry in student journal, 1984.

56. Entry in student journal, 1984.

57. Smith, p. 29.

58. Durk Pearson and Sandy Shaw, *Life Extension* (New York: Warner, 1982), p. 15.

59. Chernin, p. 47.

60. Sidney Journard and Paul Secord, "Body Cathexis and the Ideal Female Figure," *Journal of Abnormal and Social Psychology* 50: pp. 243–46; Orland Wooley, Susan Wooley and Sue Dyrenforth, "Obesity and Women—A Neglected Feminist Topic," *Women's Studies Institute Quarterly,* 1979, 2: pp. 81–92. Student journals and informal conversations with women students certainly have borne this out. See also Garfinkel and Garner, pp. 110–15.

61. "Feeling Fat in a Thin Society," *Glamour,* February, 1984, p. 198.

62. The same trend is obvious when the measurements of Miss America winners are compared over the last fifty years (See Garfinkel and Garner, p. 107). Recently, there is some evidence that this tide is turning, and that a solider, more muscular, athletic style is emerging as the latest fashion tyranny.

63. Entry in student journal, 1984.

64. Bruch, *The Golden Cage*, p. 58.

65. Entry in student journal, 1983.

66. O'Neill, p. 53.

67. Entry in student journal, 1983.

68. Bruch, *The Golden Cage,* p. 72; Bruch, *Eating Disorders,* p. 277. Others have fantasies of androgyny: "I want to go to a party and for everyone to look at me and for no one to know whether I was the most beautiful slender woman or handsome young man" (as reported by therapist April Benson, panel discussion, "New Perspectives on Female Development," Third Annual Conference of the Center for the Study of Anorexia and Bulimia, New York, 1984.)

69. Levenkron, p. 82.

70. See, for example, Levenkron's case studies; O'Neill, p. 107; Susie Ohrbach, *Fat is a Feminist Issue* (New York: Berkley, 1978), pp. 174–75.

71. Levenkron, p. 103.

72. Levenkron, p. 45.

73. Liu, p. 79.

74. Bruch, *The Golden Cage*, p. 65.

75. Klein, case study.

76. Chernin, pp. 102–03; Robert Seidenberg and Karen DeCrow, *Women Who Marry Houses: Panic and Protest in Agoraphobia*, pp. 88–97; Bruch, *The Golden Cage*, p. 58; Ohrbach, pp. 169–70.

77. Bruch, *The Golden Cage*, pp. 27–28.

78. Bruch, *The Golden Cage*, p. 12.

79. Binswanger, ''The Case of Ellen West,'' p. 243.

80. Liu, p. 141.

81. Binswanger, ''The Case of Ellen West,'' p. 257.

82. D. H. Lawrence, *Sons and Lovers* (New York: Viking, 1958), p. 257.

83. Quoted in Brian Easlea, *Witch-Hunting, Magic and the New Philosophy* (Great Britain: Humanities Press, 1980), p. 242.

84. Easlea, p. 242.

85. See Peggy Reeve Sanday, *Female Power and Male Dominance* (Cambridge: Cambridge Univ. Press, 1981), pp. 172–84.

86. Easlea, p. 8.

87. Easlea, p. 8.

88. Peter Gay, *The Bourgeois Experience*, vol. one, *Education of the Senses* (New York: Oxford Univ. Press, 1984), pp. 197–201.

89. Gay, p. 207.

90. Chernin, p. 38.

91. Barbara Ehrenreich and Dierdre English, *For Her Own Good* (Garden City: Doubleday, 1979), p. 124.

92. See Jeffrey Masson's controversial *The Assault of Truth: Freud's Suppression of the Seduction Theory* (Toronto: Farrar Straus Giroux, 1984) for a fascinating discussion of how this operation (which, due to Fliess' failure to remove a half a meter of gauze from the patient's nasal cavity, nearly resulted in her death) may have figured in the development of Freud's ideas on hysteria. Whether or not one agrees fully with Masson's interpretation of the events, his account casts light on important dimensions of the nineteenth century treatment of female disorders, and raises questions about the origins and fundamental assumptions of psychoanalytic theory which go beyond any debate about Freud's motivations. The quotations cited in this paper can be found on p. 76; Masson's discussion of the Eckstein case is on pp. 55–106.

93. Lois Banner, *American Beauty* (Chicago: University of Chicago Press, 1983) pp. 86–105.

94. Banner, pp. 149–50.

95. Amaury deRiencourt, *Sex and Power in History* (New York: David McKay, 1974), p. 319.

96. Quoted in deRiencourt, p. 319.

97. Kathryn Weibel, *Mirror, Mirror: Images of Women Reflected in Popular Culture* (New York: Anchor, 1977), p. 194.

98. Christy Ferguson, "Images of the Body: Victorian England," philosophy research project, LeMoyne College, 1983.

99. Lasch, *The Culture of Narcissism*, p. 343.

100. Chernin, p. 148.

101. Charles Gaines and George Butler, "Iron Sisters," *Psychology Today*, November, 1983, p. 67.

102. Some disquieting connections can be drawn, as well, between the anorexic and the flapper, who, according to Banner, expressed her sensuality "not through eroticism but through constant vibrant movement." The quality that marked the sex appeal of the nineteen twenties—the "It" made famous by Clara Bow—was characterized by "vivacity, fearlessness and a basic indifference to men" (p. 279), qualities high on the list of anorexic values.

From the Outside, In

Barbara Mellix

Two years ago, when I started writing this paper, trying to bring order out of chaos, my ten-year-old daughter was suffering from an acute attack of boredom. She drifted in and out of the room complaining that she had nothing to do, no one to "be with" because none of her friends were at home. Patiently I explained that I was working on something special and needed peace and quiet, and I suggested that she paint, read, or work with her computer. None of these interested her. Finally, she pulled up a chair to my desk and watched me, now and then heaving long, loud sighs. After two or three minutes (nine or ten sighs), I lost my patience. "Looka here, Allie," I said, "you too old for this kinda carryin' on. I done told you this is important. You wronger than dirt to be in her haggin' me like this and you know it. Now git on outta here and leave me off before I put my foot all the way down."

I was at home, alone with my family, and my daughter understood that this way of speaking was appropriate in that context. She knew, as a matter of fact, that it was almost inevitable; when I get angry at home, I speak some of my finest, most cherished black English. Had I been speaking to my daughter in this manner in certain other environments, she would have been shocked and probably worried that I had taken leave of my sense of propriety.

Like my children, I grew up speaking what I considered two distinctly different languages—black English and standard English (or as I

thought of them then, the ordinary everyday speech of "country" col-
oreds and "proper" English)—and in the process of acquiring these
languages, I developed an understanding of when, where, and how to
use them. But unlike my children, I grew up in a world that was primarily black. My friends, neighbors, minister, teachers—almost
everybody I associated with every day—were black. And we spoke to
one another in our own special language: *That sho is a pretty dress
you got on. If she don' soon leave me off I'm gon tell her head a
mess. I was so mad I could'a pissed a blue nail. He all the time
trying to low-rate somebody. Ain't that just about the nastiest thing
you ever set ears on?*

Then there were the "others," the "proper" blacks, transplanted
relatives and one-time friends who came home from the city for weddings, funerals, and vacations. And the whites. To these we spoke
standard English. "Ain't?" my mother would yell at me when I used
the term in the presence of "others." "You *know* better than that."
And I would hang my head in shame and say the "proper" word.

I remember one summer sitting in my grandmother's house in Greeleyville, South Carolina, when it was full of the chatter of city relatives
who were home on vacation. My parents sat quietly, only now and then
volunteering a comment or answering a question. My mother's face
took on a strained expression when she spoke. I could see that she was
being careful to say just the right words in just the right way. Her voice
sounded thick, muffled. And when she finished speaking, she would
lapse into silence, her proper smile on her face. My father was more
articulate, more aggressive. He spoke quickly, his words sharp and
clear. But he held his proud head higher, a signal that he, too, was
uncomfortable. My sisters and brothers and I stared at our aunts,
uncles, and cousins, speaking only when prompted. Even then, we hesitated, formed our sentences in our minds, then spoke softly, shyly.

My parents looked small and anxious during those occasions, and I
waited impatiently for our leave-taking when we would mock our relatives the moment we were out of their hearing. "Reeely," we would say
to one another, flexing our wrists and rolling our eyes, "how dooo you
stan' this heat? Chile, it just too hy*ooo*-mid for words." Our relatives
had made us feel "country," and this was our way of regaining pride
in ourselves while getting a little revenge in the bargain. The words
bubbled in our throats and rolled across our tongues, a balming.

As a child I felt this same doubleness in uptown Greeleyville where
the whites lived. "Ain't that a pretty dress you're wearing!" Toby, the
town policeman, said to me one day when I was fifteen. "Thank you
very much," I replied, my voice barely audible in my own ears. The
words felt wrong in my mouth, rigid, foreign. It was not that I had never
spoken that phrase before—it was common in black English, too—but
I was extremely conscious that this was an occasion for proper English.
I had taken out my English and put it on as I did my church clothes,

and I felt as if I were wearing my Sunday best in the middle of the week. It did not matter that Toby had not spoken grammatically correct English. He was white and could speak as he wished. I had something to prove. Toby did not.

Speaking standard English to whites was our way of demonstrating that we knew their language and could use it. Speaking it to standard-English-speaking blacks was our way of showing them that we, as well as they, could "put on airs." But when we spoke standard English, we acknowledged (to ourselves and to others—but primarily to ourselves) that our customary way of speaking was inferior. We felt foolish, embarrassed, somehow diminished because we were ashamed to be our real selves. We were reserved, shy in the presence of those who owned and/or spoke *the* language.

My parents never set aside time to drill us in standard English. Their forms of instruction were less formal. When my father was feeling particularly expansive, he would regale us with tales of his exploits in the outside world. In almost flawless English, complete with dialogue and flavored with gestures and embellishment, he told us about his attempt to get a haircut at a white barbershop; his refusal to acknowledge one of the town merchants until the man addressed him as "Mister"; the time he refused to step off the sidewalk uptown to let some whites pass; his airplane trip to New York City (to visit a sick relative) during which the stewardesses and porters—recognizing that he was a "gentleman"—addressed him as "Sir." I did not realize then—nor, I think, did my father—that he was teaching us, among other things, standard English and the relationship between language and power.

My mother's approach was different. Often, when one of us said, "I'm gon wash off my feet," she would say, "And what will you walk on if you wash them off?" Everyone would laugh at the victim of my mother's "proper" mood. But it was different when one of us children was in a proper mood. "You think you are so superior," I said to my oldest sister one day when we were arguing and she was winning. "Superior!" my sister mocked. "You mean I'm acting 'biggidy'?" My sisters and brothers sniggered, then joined in teasing me. Finally, my mother said, "Leave your sister alone. There's nothing wrong with using proper English." There was a half-smile on her face. I had gotten "uppity," had "put on airs" for no good reason. I was at home, alone with the family, and I hadn't been prompted by one of my mother's proper moods. But there was also a proud light in my mother's eyes; her children were learning English very well.

Not until years later, as a college student, did I begin to understand our ambivalence toward English, our scorn of it, our need to master it, to own and be owned by it—an ambivalence that extended to the public-school classroom. In our school, where there were no whites, my teachers taught standard English but used black English to do it. When my grammar-school teachers wanted us to write, for example, they usually said something like, "I want y'all to write five sentences that make a statement. Anybody git done before the rest can color." It was probably almost those exact words that led me to write these sentences in 1953 when I was in the second grade:

> The white clouds are pretty.
> There are only 15 people in our room.
> We will go to gym.
> We have a new poster.
> We may go out doors.

Second grade came after "Little First" and "Big First," so by then I knew the implied rules that accompanied all writing assignments. Writing was an occasion for proper English. I was not to write in the way we spoke to one another: The white clouds pretty; There ain't but 15 people in our room; We going to gym; We got a new poster; We can go out in the yard. Rather I was to use the language of "other": clouds *are*, there *are*, we *will*, we *have*, we *may*.

My sentences were short, rigid, perfunctory, like the letters my mother wrote to relatives:

> Dear Papa,
> How are you? How is Mattie? Fine I hope. We are fine. We will come to see you Sunday. Cousin Ned will give us a ride.
>
> > Love,
> > Daughter

The language was not ours. It was something from outside us, something we used for special occasions.

But my coloring on the other side of that second-grade paper is different. I drew three hearts and a sun. The sun has a smiling face that radiates and envelops everything it touches. And although the sun and its world are enclosed in a circle, the colors I used—red, blue, green, purple, orange, yellow, black—indicate that I was less restricted with drawing and coloring than I was with writing standard English. My valentines were not just red. My sun was not just a yellow ball in the sky.

By the time I reached the twelfth grade, speaking and writing standard English had taken on new importance. Each year, about half of the newly graduated seniors of our school moved to large cities—particularly in the North—to live with relatives and find work. Our English teacher constantly corrected our grammar: "Not 'ain't,' but 'isn't.'" We seldom wrote papers, and even those few were usually plot summaries of short stories. When our teacher returned the papers, she usually lectured on the importance of using standard English: "I *am;* you *are;* he, she or it *is*," she would say, writing on the chalkboard as she spoke. "How you gon git a job talking about 'I is,' or 'I isn't' or 'I ain't'?"

In Pittsburgh, where I moved after graduation, I watched my aunt and uncle—who had always spoken standard English when in Greeleyville—switch from black English to standard English to a mixture of the two, according to where they were or who they were with. At home and with certain close relatives, friends, and neighbors, they spoke black English. With those less close, they spoke a mixture. In public and with strangers, they generally spoke standard English.

In time, I learned to speak standard English with ease and to switch smoothly from black to standard or a mixture, and back again. But no matter where I was, no matter what the situation or occasion, I continued to write as I had in school:

> Dear Mommie,
> How are you? How is everybody else? Fine I hope. I am fine. So are Aunt and Uncle. Tell everyone I said hello. I will write again soon.
>
> > Love,
> > Barbara

At work, at a health insurance company, I learned to write letters to customers. I studied form letters and letters written by co-workers, memorizing the phrases and the ways in which they were used. I dictated:

> Thank you for your letter of January 5. We have made the changes in your coverage you requested. Your new premium will be $150 every three months. We are pleased to have been of service to you.

In a sense, I was proud of the letters I wrote for the company: they were proof of my ability to survive in the city, the outside world—an indication of my growing mastery of English. But they also indicate that writing was still mechanical for me, something that didn't require much thought.

Reading also became a more significant part of my life during those early years in Pittsburgh. I had always liked reading, but now I devoted more and more of my spare time to it. I read romances, mysteries, popular novels. Looking back, I realize that the books I liked best were simple, unambiguous: good versus bad and right versus wrong with right rewarded and wrong punished, mysteries unraveled and all set right in the end. It was how I remembered life in Greeleyville.

Of course I was romanticizing. Life in Greeleyville had not been so very uncomplicated. Back there I had been—first as a child, then as a young woman with limited experience in the outside world—living in a relatively closed-in society. But there were implicit and explicit principles that guided our way of life and shaped our relationships with one another and the people outside—principles that a newcomer would find elusive and baffling. In Pittsburgh, I had matured, become more experienced: I had worked at three different jobs, associated with a wider range of people, married, had children. This new environment with different prescripts for living required that I speak standard

English much of the time and slowly, imperceptibly, I had ceased seeing a sharp distinction between myself and "others." Reading romances and mysteries, characterized by dichotomy, was a way of shying away from change, from the person I was becoming.

But that other part of me—that part which took great pride in my ability to hold a job writing business letters—was increasingly drawn to the new developments in my life and the attending possibilities, opportunities for even greater change. If I could write letters for a nationally known business, could I not also do something better, more challenging, more important? Could I not, perhaps, go to college and become a school teacher? For years, afraid and a little embarrassed, I did no more than imagine this different me, this possible me. But sixteen years after coming north, when my youngest daughter entered kindergarten, I found myself unable—or unwilling—to resist the lure of possibility. I enrolled in my first college course: Basic Writing, at the University of Pittsburgh.

For the first time in my life, I was required to write extensively about myself. Using the most formal English at my command, I wrote these sentences near the beginning of the term:

> One of my duties as a homemaker is simply picking up after others. A day seldom passes that I don't search for a mislaid toy, book, or gym shoe, etc. I change the Ty-D-Bol, fight "ring around the collar," and keep our laundry smelling "April fresh." Occasionally, I settle arguments between my children and suggest things to do when they're bored. Taking telephone messages for my oldest daughter is my newest (and sometimes most aggravating) chore. Hanging the toilet paper roll is my most insignificant.

My concern was to use "appropriate" language, to sound as if I belonged in a college classroom. But I felt separate from the language— as if it did not and could not belong to me. I couldn't think and feel genuinely in that language, couldn't make it express what I thought and felt about being a housewife. A part of me resented, among other things, being judged by such things as the appearance of my family's laundry and toilet bowl, but in that language I could only imagine and write about a conventional housewife.

For the most part, the remainder of the term was a period of adjustment, a time of trying to find my bearings as a student in a college composition class, to learn to shut out my black English whenever I composed, and to prevent it from creeping into my formulations; a time for trying to grasp the language of the classroom and reproduce it in my prose; for trying to talk about myself in that language, reach others through it. Each experience of writing was like standing naked and revealing my imperfection, my "otherness." And each new assignment was another chance to make myself over in language, reshape myself, make myself "better" in my rapidly changing image of a student in a college composition class.

But writing became increasingly unmanageable as the term progressed, and by the end of the semester, my sentences sounded like this:

> My excitement was soon dampened, however, by what seemed like a small voice in the back of my head saying that I should be careful with my long awaited opportunity. I felt frustrated and this seemed to make it difficult to concentrate.

There is a poverty of language in these sentences. By this point, I knew that the clichéd language of my Housewife essay was unacceptable, and I generally recognized trite expressions. At the same time, I hadn't yet mastered the language of the classroom, hadn't yet come to see it as belonging to me. Most notable is the lifelessness of the prose, the apparent absence of a person behind the words. I wanted those sentences—and the rest of the essay—to convey the anguish of yearning to, at once, become something more and yet remain the same. I had the sensation of being split in two, part of me going into a future the other part didn't believe possible. As that person, the student writer at that moment, I was essentially mute. I could not—in the process of composing—use the language of the old me, yet I couldn't image myself in the language of "others."

I found this particularly discouraging because at midsemester I had been writing in a much different way. Note the language of this introduction to an essay I had written then, near the middle of the term:

> Pain is a constant companion to the people in "Footwork." Their jobs are physically damaging. Employers are insensitive to their feelings and in many cases add to their problems. The general public wounds them further by treating them with disgrace because of what they do for a living. Although the workers are as diverse as they are similar, there is a definite link between them. They suffer a great deal of abuse.

The voice here is stronger, more confident, appropriating terms like "physically damaging," "wounds them further," "insensitive," "diverse"—terms I couldn't have imagined using when writing about my own experience—and shaping them into sentences like, "Although the workers are as diverse as they are similar, there is a definite link between them." And there is the sense of a personality behind the prose, someone who sympathizes with the workers: "The general public wounds them further by treating them with disgrace because of what they do for a living."

What caused these differences? I was, I believed, explaining other people's thoughts and feelings, and I was free to move about in the language of "others" so long as I was speaking *of* others. I was unaware that I was transforming into my best classroom language my own thoughts and feelings about people whose experiences and ways of speaking were in many ways similar to mine.

The following year, unable to turn back or to let go of what had become something of an obsession with language (and hoping to catch and hold the sense of control that had eluded me in Basic Writing), I enrolled in a research writing course. I spent most of the term learning how to prepare for and write a research paper. I chose sex education as my subject and spent hours in libraries, searching for information, reading, taking notes. Then (not without messiness and often-demoralizing frustration) I organized my information into categories, wrote a thesis statement, and composed my paper—a series of paraphrases and quotations spaced between carefully constructed transitions. The process and results felt artificial, but as I would later come to realize I was passing through a necessary stage. My sentences sounded like this:

> This reserve becomes understandable with examination of who the abusers are. In an overwhelming number of cases, they are people the victims know and trust. Family members, relatives, neighbors and close family friends commit seventy-five percent of all reported sex crimes against children, and parents, parent substitutes and relatives are the offenders in thirty to eighty percent of all reported cases.[12] While assault by strangers does occur, it is less common, and is usually a single episode.[13] But abuse by family members, relatives, and acquaintances may continue for an extended period of time. In cases of incest, for example, children are abused repeatedly for an average of eight years.[14] In such cases, "the use of physical force is rarely necessary because of the child's trusting, dependent relationship with the offender. The child's cooperation is often facilitated by the adult's position of dominance, an offer of material goods, a threat of physical violence, or a misrepresentation of moral standards."[15]

The completed paper gave me a sense of profound satisfaction, and I read it often after my professor returned it. I know now that what I was pleased with was the language I used and the professional voice it helped me maintain. "Use better words," my teacher had snapped at me one day after reading the notes I'd begun accumulating from my research, and slowly I began taking on the language of my sources. In my next set of notes, I used the word "vacillating"; my professor applauded. And by the time I composed the final draft, I felt at ease with terms like "overwhelming number of cases," "single episode," and "reserve," and I shaped them into sentences similar to those of my "expert" sources.

If I were writing the paper today, I would of course do some things differently. Rather than open with an anecdote—as my teacher suggested—I would begin simply with a quotation that caught my interest as I was researching my paper (and which I scribbled, without its source, in the margin of my notebook): "Truth does not do so much good in the world as the semblance of truth does evil." The quotation felt right because it captured what was for me the central idea of my essay—an idea that emerged gradually during the making of my

paper—and expressed it in a way I would like to have said it. The anecdote, a hypothetical situation I invented to conform to the information
in the paper, felt forced and insincere because it represented—to a
great degree—my teacher's understanding of the essay, *her* idea of
what in it was most significant. Improving upon my previous experiences with writing, I was beginning to think and feel in the language I
used, to find my own voices in it, to sense that how one speaks influences how one means. But I was not yet secure enough, comfortable
enough with the language to trust my intuition.

Now that I know that to seek knowledge, freedom, and autonomy
means always to be in the concentrated process of becoming—always
to be venturing into new territory, feeling one's way at first, then getting one's balance, negotiating, accommodating, discovering one's self
in ways that previously defined "others"—I sometimes get tired. And
I ask myself why I keep on participating in this highbrow form of violence, this slamming against perplexity. But there is no real futility in
the question, no hint of that part of the old me who stood outside standard English, hugging to herself a disabling mistrust of a language she
thought could not represent a person with her history and experience.
Rather, the question represents a person who feels the consequence of
her education, the weight of her possibilities as a teacher and writer
and human being, a voice in society. And I would not change that person, would not give back the good burden that accompanies my growing expertise, my increasing power to shape myself in language and
share that self with "others."

"To speak," says Frantz Fanon, "means to be in a position to use a
certain syntax, to grasp the morphology of this or that language, but it
means above all to assume a culture, to support the weight of a civilization."* To write means to do the same, but in a more profound sense.
However, Fanon also says that to achieve mastery means to "get" in a
position of power, to "grasp," to "assume." This, I have learned—both
as a student and subsequently as a teacher—can involve tremendous
emotional and psychological conflict for those attempting to master
academic discourse. Although as a beginning student writer I had a
fairly good grasp of ordinary spoken English and was proficient at what
Labov calls "code-switching" (and what John Baugh in *Black Street
Speech* terms "style shifting"), when I came face to face with the
demands of academic writing, I grew increasingly self-conscious, constantly aware of my status as a black and a speaker of one of the many
black English vernaculars—a traditional outsider. For the first time, I
experienced my sense of doubleness as something menacing, a built-in
enemy. Whenever I turned inward for salvation, the balm so available
during my childhood, I found instead this new fragmentation which
spoke to me in many voices. It was the voice of my desire to prosper,

* *Black Skin, White Masks* (1952; rpt. New York: Grove Press, 1967), pp. 17–18.

but at the same time it spoke of what I had relinquished and could not regain: a safe way of being, a state of powerlessness which exempted me from responsibility for who I was and might be. And it accused me of betrayal, of turning away from blackness. To recover balance, I had to take on the language of the academy, the language of "others." And to do that, I had to learn to imagine myself a part of the culture of that language, and therefore someone free to manage that language, to take liberties with it. Writing and rewriting, practicing, experimenting, I came to comprehend more fully the generative power of language. I discovered—with the help of some especially sensitive teachers—that through writing one can continually bring new selves into being, each with new responsibilities and difficulties, but also with new possibilities. Remarkable power, indeed. I write and continually give birth to myself.

Section Three

Presenting Observations: Testing a Hypothesis

This section includes selections intended to help you complete the process of formulating a question and testing your assumed answer by direct observation. An asterisk (*) before an essay indicates that the selection was written by a student.

Presenting Descriptions and Findings

Talking Like a Lady: How Women Talk

Francine Frank and Frank Anshen

Are there systematic differences in pronunciation, vocabulary, and grammar between females and males that we can call "genderlects"? In this chapter, we will examine some of the common beliefs on this subject and attempt to determine whether they correspond to reality. . . .

Perhaps the most common stereotype about women's speech is that women talk a lot. If we take "a lot" to mean more than men, we are faced with the surprising fact that there seems to be no study which supports this belief, while there are several which show just the opposite. One such study, by Otto Sonder, Jr., is particularly interesting. Sonder organized discussion groups which included women and men and assigned them specific topics. The discussions were recorded and transcribed, but in the transcripts, the participants were identified only by letters, as A, B, etc. Panels of judges who tried to identify the sex of each speaker from these transcripts were correct about fifty-five percent of the time, a result which is better than chance, but not overwhelmingly so. Closer examination of the data, however, reveals some interesting facts. A word count of the recorded discussions showed a clear tendency for the men who participated in the study to utter more words than the women. In other words, men, on the average, actually talked more than did women. Even more interesting is the fact that individuals of either sex who talked a lot were more likely to be judged as males, while taciturn individuals of either sex were more likely to be identified as females. Not only does this study suggest that men are more talkative, it also suggests that the judges "knew" this fact and used it to make judgments about the sexual identity of unknown speakers. Although, consciously, they would probably subscribe to the cultural stereotype of the talkative woman, their judgments show that they knew that the real situation is the direct opposite of the stereotype. . . .

There are many other common stereotypes about women's speech. Have you ever heard the one about the woman who told her husband to stop talking while she was interrupting? This sexist joke reflects a widely held stereotype that women interrupt in conversations more than do men. But it doesn't seem to reflect the facts. When Candace West and Don Zimmerman studied conversations, they found that ten of the eleven conversations between men and women contained interruptions but that, oddly enough, of the total of forty-eight interruptions, forty-six were by men. In other words, men interrupted women twenty-three times as often as women interrupted men. In contrast, only three of the twenty same-sex conversations showed any interruptions at all. What is going on here? Perhaps these results are not really so odd when we consider that interrupting is a violation of an individual's right to speak and is therefore often the privilege of the more powerful, while being interrupted is the fate of the less powerful. Perhaps, as it is news when woman bites dog, it is just this rarity of occurrence of women interrupting men which makes it so noticeable when it does happen. Then again, we may just be indulging our penchant for believing evil of women. Have you heard the one about the man who told his wife not to talk while he was interrupting?

Some interesting facts about how men exercise the prerogatives of male power in conversations between couples are revealed in a study by Pamela Fishman. She points out that conversation is "a process of ongoing negotiated activity between people." In order to have a conversation, the participants must interact on a number of levels and so we might well expect conversations between men and women to reflect the relative power of the sexes in our society. Firstly, to note the obvious, conversations must be about something, they must have a topic. Fishman analyzes how topics are initiated and controlled. In some twelve hours of recordings of spontaneous talk, seventy-six topics were raised, forty-seven by women and twenty-nine by men. But more than half, twenty-eight to be exact, of the women's topics failed; that is, although women brought up the topics, they did not become the subject of conversation. In contrast, all but one of the men's topics were successful, even though several of these were identical to a woman's topic which had failed. As a result of all this, of the forty-five successful topics, twenty-eight were proposed by men and only seventeen were proposed by women.

Topic failure in Fishman's study was caused by the failure of the men to respond. Many women who work or live with men have had the experience of raising a topic or making a suggestion to a group composed mainly of men and receiving absolutely no response, only to find some time later, that when one of the men raises the same idea, it is greeted with interest and respect. How is one to react to such a situation? In the face of the failure of their conversation topics, women in Fishman's study resorted to a number of strategies, including the use of questions—women asked three times as many questions as men. Some people have claimed that women's frequent use of questions reflects a lack of assertiveness and self-confidence. Fishman points out that women may often use question forms because questions demand a response from the other person, thus assuring that the topic will continue at least a little while longer, even if it turns out to be just long enough to permit the male conversational partner to utter a grunt.

Other strategies employed by the women in Fishman's study included the expressions *D'y know what?* and *This is really interesting.* The first functions as an attention-getter and is often used by children to claim a right to speak. The natural response—*what?*—is an invitation to continue the conversational exchange. The second strategy *(this is really interesting)*, used as an introductory remark, represents an attempt by the woman to establish interest in the topic on her own, as she cannot assume male cooperation. Finally, women used the expression *You know* ten times more frequently than did the men. Use of this form increased as men's responses decreased. Obviously, such expressions are not exclusive to women; men use them too, although they seem to need them much less, as women tend to support men's conversational topics. Women, then, are found to do much of the work in developing and sustaining these conversations, while men exercise veto power, picking and choosing among the topics offered by women for their approval. Women consistently help develop topics introduced by men, but much of the time, men respond to women's topics by silence or by minimal responses such as *uhm, hmh, mm,* etc. And this seems to be the way men want things, as who wouldn't, if they could get away with it? In *The New Seventeen Book of Etiquette and Young Living,* published in 1970, we find a ''survey of opinions'' of boys, who are reported to have said ''I hate girls who can't stop talking,'' and ''I like girls who listen to me without interrupting.'' Apparently, such boys live in a world they enjoy. . . .

Men get to talk more, at times of their own choosing, about topics which interest them. Conversations, then, seem to represent in microcosm the distribution of power in other areas of our lives. It is tempting to speculate that the superior scores which women, as a group, exhibit on standardized tests of verbal ability, represent the results of Darwinian evolution. Women need superior verbal skills just to get a word in edgewise!

A number of other studies have found the same general tendency of women to use more ''proper'' language than men. Frank Anshen, for example, found that adult Black women in a North Carolina town were more likely to use standard pronunciation of words like *running, this,* and *mouth,* while men in the same town were more likely to pronounce these words *runnin', dis,* and *mouf.* One possible explanation for this ''correctness'' of women's speech is that they tend to be more status conscious than men in our society. Women are often judged on the basis of their social status and their adherence to prescriptive social norms; accordingly, they are socialized to exhibit "better" social behavior than men.

Peter Trudgill reports that women in Great Britain exhibit similar behavior to their American sisters. In Norwich, England, women used more "proper" language than did men. As for the men, they not only used more non-standard forms than did the women, but seemed to be unconsciously proud of the fact, reporting their speech to be even more non-standard than it was. The men were aware of the more standard forms and often stated that women speak "better," but they made no attempt to change their own speech to these better varieties. How do we explain this? Trudgill concludes that male speakers in general seem, subconsciously, to favor non-standard, low-status speech forms associated with the working class. Such speech has connotations of "toughness" and "masculinity" which gives it a sort of covert prestige. Similarly, William Labov found that New Yorkers' ratings of how well a male speaker would do in a fight went up as his use of standard forms declined. . . .

An example of speech which has traditionally been considered more "masculine" and less proper is the use of obscenities. In a study among Long Island college students, Anshen found that male students were twice as likely as female students to use obscenities, although there was little difference in the strength of the obscenities that were used by the two sexes. Interestingly, though, while men made a clear effort to "clean up" their speech in the presence of women, no similar effect was noticed for women in mixed company. Although they still used obscenities less often than did men, their usage did not seem at all inhibited by the presence of men. . . .

[Editor's note: Citations have been omitted.]

Poker and Pop: Collegiate Gambling Groups

David McKenzie

The university educates people, and the student union "develops" them. It might indeed be claimed that education is not life, but something added to life. Childhood, adolescent, and adult peer groups are life to their members. Like other intimate groups, they are the measures through which we try to understand the larger world, including that of education. Students of large organizations have long been aware that the rational visible organizational layout often belies the influential presence of informal groups of personnel, which play a major role in the functioning of that organization as "enlightened man-

agement" has finally come to realize. Too often, we take the official definition of reality to be fact, and ignore the part played by these groups
in shaping the development of institutions.

Among groups of this kind are the numerous student cliques inhab-
iting college campuses. Prominent among these are the Greek letter
fraternities and sororities, but they are only a few of the varied and
shifting groupings. Any visitor to the student unions, lounges, or any
hangouts on campuses would soon discover that these places form natural environments for the proliferation of student cliques of various
interests and orientations: some mirror student involvements with recognized campus organizations; others reflect the informal configura-
tions of the various "crowds." The visitor to any midwestern university
student union, for example, would see knots of "kibitzers" gathered
around the makeshift gaming tables where the campus card players
hold sway. These clusters are often foci of action even within a room
filled with cigarette smoke, a booming jukebox, and animated conversations. But while there is action at the card table, it is not mayhem.
The players are in various attitudes and poses: now one is pensive, tug-
ging at his ear, tweaking his chin, wrinkling his nose, slyly smiling,
and finally shrieking with joy or angered disappointment as the hand
is called. Another seems businesslike, with no emotion crossing his
face as he glances at his hand and scans the table, watching the cards
fall. At one moment tension fills the air, and at the next it is gone as a
hand ends and the group lapses into easy conversation, joking, and the
relating of anecdotes while the next hand is dealt.

This type of setting is not necessarily typical of all university unions,
but reflects particularly the character of a midwestern university
branch campus as a two-year feeder extension to a large state university. The student population is small—the majority living in the surrounding community—and shows only slight participation in extracurricular events. In this respect, the formal organization has some
apparent influence on the structure and operations of the card-playing
groups, for the relative lack of involvement in extracurricular activities
more or less leaves the students to their own devices. Radical political
activity is almost absent due to the lack of upper classmen and other
cultural influences. Hence, the environmental "press" lends to the
card players the use of university facilities for unofficial activities. This
expropriation of public space is quite visible and sets the card players
off from the rest of the student population; they thus are defined by the
latter and the institution's officials as mildly deviant.

At the midwestern university campus union under study, the geog-
raphy of the setting reflects its ecology and the activities that take place
in it. In various sections there are a pool table, a television viewing
area, a canteen service and cafeteria, a jukebox and radio, and recreation tables. The card-playing area is unofficially marked off from the
eating and recreation tables by a partition with pop coolers and vend-

ing machines; it forms a geographic barrier, although occasionally a player or two could be found on the other side of the "fence," as it is commonly called.

As has been intimated, card-playing serves purposes other than simple recreation. The card-playing peer group becomes for many a universe where they can gain status and recognition, hung on the skeleton of gaming techniques and social skills. . . .

Hoyle Notwithstanding: The Role of Argot and Folklore

During the course of a game there is much conversation about group concerns other than cards: argot, folklore, jokes, conversation about "what's happening" regarding the dating scene, the local bands playing at the beer bars, exams, and so on. These conversations function to bring the group together as morale-building devices. The whole conglomeration of group-specific knowledge establishes in-group boundaries and conveys an air of group exclusiveness which puts off strangers and keeps newcomers hanging. If there is a new player in the group, he is almost always left out of the conversation and ongoing banter. The only conversational foothold he has is confined to the topic of cards; the argot includes terms which enable the players readily to distinguish insiders from outsiders. As one student of pool-playing groups put it: "The argot itself is not protected, but an open secret; that is, its meanings are easily learned by any outsider who wishes to learn them and is an alert listener and questioner. Argots develop partly to provide a shorthand way of referring to technicalities, but also as an elaborately inventive, ritualistic, often rather playful way of reinforcing group identity or 'we feeling.'" Thus, the argot of the poker and bridge groups sets it off not for the purposes of secrecy but rather to enhance the sense of colleagueship.

The following are examples of poker and bridge argot and the contexts in which they appear: "Christ, did I get zilched" (meaning "Did I ever get slammed!"); "I shot him the moon" (meaning to give someone a rotten card, which connotes a dirty trick. "Mooning" is an adolescent prank whereby the person pulls his pants down and contemptuously flaunts his buttocks); "How many did you eat?" (meaning "He took the queen of spades in the game of hearts"). Other less game-specific argot includes: "Ain't that a kick in the groin!" "You hairy whimp, butterball," and so on. Slang in everyday life has often originated from the argot of card-playing: expressions such as *passing the buck, blue chips, ace-in-the hole, trump his ace, ante up, four flusher, poker faced, stand pat,* and *showdown* are typical examples. There are also gestures, used illegally in bridge, such as hand signals between partners, and certain significant facial expressions—wincing, showing one's teeth, a nod of the head, and a deep smile.

The degree to which traditional folklore promotes stability in the card group depends on the degree to which these popular conceptions have been internalized. The myth that gamblers as a rule have no consciences—hence, no feelings—is certainly reflected in the "poker face" assumed by many in the peer group.

Informal conversation usually revolves around girls and dating and takes place while shuffling between games. Jokes and wisecracks also reflect these focal concerns and function to ease the complexion of the situation from seriousness to casual laughter. Representative of the typical repartee and banter encountered during a game are the following:

> "The gas tank is falling off of my car."
> "Well, I'll follow you out to the junkyard, Lois."

> "Were you out to Mountview last night?"
> "No, why?"
> "You're lucky—about fifty boys to one girl, and they were all skags."

> "Hey, see that girl over there? Well, if you want a nice piece of ass the first time, she's gotta be it. I guess she screws the first time."
> "You mean the skinny blond over there?"
> "Yeh, pretty nice, huh?"
> "Yeh, where'd you ever find that out?"
> "One of my friends took her out and . . . "
> "Um, I'll have to take her out."

> "Hey, you got a lighter I can use?"
> "Yeh." (He pulls out a cigarette lighter)
> "Christ, where'd you get that?"
> "For Christmas."

> "Hold out your finger and I'll snap it off!"
> "No dice."
> "That's no finger-snapper-offer—that's a killer!"

Conversation is rarely about school or grades. In addition, players often sing or hum along with songs on the radio or jukebox, a constant noisy accompaniment to all student-union activities.

The repetition of argot and topics of conversation borders on and serves the same purpose as a folklore—the development of interaction ritual, drawing of group boundaries, and strengthening of group solidarity. Repetition is the basis of habit and customs which resist modifying pressures from changes in the surrounding milieu, and hence limit the possibilities of variation of activity. In this way, folklore and rituals in the card group are analogous to the myths of all societies. They reinforce group beliefs and practices and legitimatize the group's values. This explains the monotonous character of the endlessly repeated conversations about girls, the local bars, and weekend events. . . .

The Communication of Status

The criteria one can use to determine status within the group seem at first obvious, but as one becomes assimilated into the actual trade, he finds this can be very tricky. Likewise, upon first observation, a stranger can easily be deceived as to who really holds high status. One is often led to believe that the loud, boisterous players are the possessors of high status, but upon further observation, the calm players usually score highest and are the real leaders. Of course, leader in this context suggests more than the unidimensional leader-follower prototype. There are several dimensions of leadership, important among them being who has the greatest playing skill and, behaviorally, who is the object of address by most members. However, other members who are mediocre players are often well integrated into the group. Status, therefore, has its horizontal as well as its vertical dimensions, which is to say that playing skill as an index of status is crosscut by other qualities, such as sociability and adeptness at handling group-specific "knowledge"—argot, repartee, folklore, mythology, and so on. In some cases the two dimensions intersect, and in others they do not.

Skilled players often present an aura of invincibility through the demonstration of intricate and daring moves. In poker, for example, a leader remains aloof and rarely engages in conversation extraneous to cards; nevertheless he determines the tone of the betting. High status players give one the impression of an "I-don't-give-a-damn" attitude. The players of less importance are usually the ones who get loud and slam their fists on the table, groan audibly from time to time, and show their displeasure through overt actions like kicking chairs. Rarely do the high status players lose their "cool." They appear less nervous and take advice willingly because they claim to want to learn new things about the game, and laugh their losses off as bad luck or something; this is their way of kicking chairs. . . .

It should be made clear, however, that the winners, the enterprising players, are not simply liked or trusted. While the steady winners always display good sportsmanship and pay their debts immediately, these can be considered mere tactics used to "cool the mark out," that is, to keep the interaction of the situation running smoothly and to prevent the hostility of losers from expressing itself in anything but obsequious admiration. The performances of all the individuals taken together help to maintain a definition of the game situation as an affable gathering of friends rather than a showdown game of cutthroat competition. A disgruntled loser is a threat to this ambiance. The appearance of the individual card player suggests one in which informal recreation and work are combined, and is directly reflected in the "poker face" of the most experienced card players. As an extreme example, the irate mother of a daughter made pregnant by one of the players burst into the student union and came after him with a butcher

pretty quiet. At night, the room seems more active. Since I always thought of
the smoking room as a place to talk, I was interested to find out whether more
people went there to study or socialize. Right after dinner and before the
partying begins seems to be the most convenient time for students to study,
so I thought I would find my best observations between the hours of seven and
ten in the evening. I planned to observe the study habits of people in the
smoking room, and expected to find that most of the people inside do not get
much accomplished while they are there. My findings were partly confirmatory. Approximately half of the students that I observed working in the smoking room actually accomplished some of their work. The other half rambled on
and on, and usually left the library with just a slightly lighter work load
than when they entered.

   The first night of my observation, I went to the smoking room, plopped
into a comfortable chair, took out my notebook and pen, and began noticing my
surroundings. Staring out the windows, I thought to myself, "Wow, this chair
is comfortable." I had not had much sleep the night before, so I was really
tired. I took a few notes about the loud noise level of the room, then, unfortunately, I fell asleep. A friend woke me up as she was leaving. It was useless to try to take any more notes that evening, so I decided that I would
start observing the next night.

   Well rested, I came back the next night at 7:15. The smoke-filled room
was beginning to fill up rapidly with the after-dinner crowd. Groups of people formed at the rectangular study tables and in the rows of comfortable,
cushiony chairs. The smoking room is located in the back of the library on the
second and third floors. You can enter the room from either floor, and move
from floor to floor within the room. A black and orange modern staircase
leads up to the top level. The third floor looks down upon the second floor
like a balcony in a theater. Seven-by-five-feet sheets of glass divide the
noise in the smoking room from the sounds of silence in the rest of the
library.

   My friends and I call this room "the airport" because we always get the
feeling that we are waiting in an airport lobby for a plane to arrive. Looking
through the wall of windows, made up of sixty-six sheets of glass, I see a
string of lights along the road to the women's dorms that resembles a runway.
The comfortable chairs, upholstered with a brightly colored plaid, face the
windows, and when you sit in them, your head tilts back and you just stare
into the sky. The cushions on the chairs reek of smoke and so do some of the
people in them. The hum of the air conditioning system soothes the mind, so it
is easier to think. The lights that are set in the ceiling have a bluish-green
tint that remind me of the transporter room on Star Trek. If only I could be
"beamed" up to my dorm room, instead of having to walk.

   Conversations among students of both sexes can be heard from a few
places around the room. A burst of laughter from some really giddy girls is
not uncommon. Since it is the middle of winter, coughs, sneezes, and sniffles
are often heard. The big black doors squeak every time someone enters or
exits the room. Some people have a habit of looking up from their book whenever they hear the door open. It is as if they are waiting for a certain person
to come walking into the room.

   The scene seems to be different every evening. One night that I was in
"the airport," there was not much action going on. Three girls at one table
were chatting about old love affairs, and three guys and two girls were

laughing about their weekend at a cabin in Vermont. Four study tables were
completely filled with hard-working students and nine people were scattered
in the rows of chairs. Clouds of smoke could be seen drifting over two
tables and three chairs. Tin ashtrays were overflowing with butts on most of
the tables. The only sounds to be heard were pages turning and the two
groups chatting quietly. I concluded that Thursday nights did not seem
to be very busy for "the airport." Most everyone was working really hard
that night.

When I went to "the airport" on Sunday night, the social scene was quite
different. The noise level was much louder, people were laughing hysterically, and some were even shouting across the room. Many tables had a rowdy
conversation going on and groups of people were forming in the lounge chairs.
One freshman girl, who obviously had her face made up perfectly, wandered
around the room, and stopped at every table that a guy was sitting at. Her
bracelets jingled every time she pulled her hair out of her face and fixed her
collar. If she was trying to be noticed, she sure did a good job at it because
four people were giving her some really strange looks.

All sorts of people come to the smoking room to study. I have noticed
that students from each class work in the smoking room. Smokers, nonsmokers,
males, and females are all found there. There is one group of girls that can
be considered "locals" in the smoking room. I have seen them there about
three or four nights a week. They wear heavy coats of purple eye shadow and
bright pink lipstick. Some nights they gossip about guys, stare at them as
they walk by, and have constant laugh attacks. Other times they work diligently at a table and just make small talk once in a while. They seem to have a
lot of male friends because guys are always stopping at their table to flirt
with them. When the guy leaves, the girls will remain quiet for about thirty
seconds, then look each other in the eyes and discuss the guy that had just
stopped by. Sometimes, facial expressions of love are shown, but most of the
time the guy is rated "Blah." They gave me the impression that they were
very snobby.

One evening at 8:45, a sophomore guy walked in with his coat, hat, and
gloves on, but was not carrying any books. He walked from table to table,
talked for about thirty seconds at each one, and then, left the library.
Overhearing his conversation at the tables closest to me, I found out that
there was an after-hours party at Sigma Chi. Apparently, he was the informer.
Three girls at a table nearby me debated whether or not they should "blow off"
their psychology test. They decided that if they stay in to study, then they
would probably just stay up talking all night. They might as well go to the
party and have fun if they are not going to get anything done by staying in.
Five minutes after the informer left, the three girls packed up their books,
put their coats on, and went to the party. I noted before that they had
arrived at 8:00, but the time was now 9:00. During the hour that they were
there, they talked half of it away. Obviously, they did not get much work
done. They did not seem bothered by the fact that they might fail their test.
They were more "psyched" to go out and get sloshed. One of them said, "I know
I'll get hammered tonight. I can't wait!"

I did not go to the party that night because I had the same psychology
test the next day. When we received our grades three days later, I found out
that I only beat them by a few points. I could not understand it. I stayed up
until 3:00 a.m. studying, while they talked in the library, went to a party,

the sign flashing the news from the Times Tower like a scoreboard. . . . Along this street I see young masculine men milling idly. Sometimes they walk up to older men and stand talking in soft tones . . . going off together, or if not, moving to talk to someone else. . . . From the thundering underground . . . the maze of New York subways . . . the world pours into Times Square. Like lost souls emerging from the purgatory of the trains, the New York faces push into the air: spilling into 42nd Street and Broadway . . . a scattered defeated army. And the world of that street bursts like a rocket into a shattered phosphorescent world. Giant signs . . . Bigger . . . Than . . . Life . . . blink off and on. And a great hungry sign groping luridly as the darkness screams

F*A*S*C*I*N*A*T*I*O*N

Times Square is buildings and businesses of nearly every shape and variety. There are fleabag hotels on nearly every street, catering to prostitutes and those down on their luck. There are theaters showing the latest movies, both of the Hollywood and pornographic variety. There are theaters where for ninety-nine cents you can spend the afternoon sleeping in air-conditioned comfort, legs draped over two or three seats. There are numerous small shops selling novelty items to tourists. Here you can buy a variety of items, ranging from postcards to garish ties, to plastic replicas of the Statue of Liberty, to glasses that will drip their contents on the lap of the unsuspecting victim of a practical joke. There are "Playlands" where for a quarter you can get pictures of yourself in six different poses and test your skills at a variety of games. There are bookstores where persons satisfy their taste for every imaginable kind of erotic literature. There are "peepshow" places where for a quarter customers view a "XXX" movie, in full color and sound and in the privacy of a separate booth. There are cheap restaurants and numerous bars, some with a cover of three dollars and nude dancers and others badly run down, frequented mostly by local alcoholics.

But Times Square is not a static place. Its flavor, its motif, its tenor change at different times of the day. By 9 A.M. the streets are bustling with persons on their way to work, entering the various office buildings in the area. By 10:30 A.M. some "regulars" have already appeared and are lounging especially near the subway stop at Forty-second Stree and Seventh Avenue. By now, also, the movies have all opened, an here and there a few persons enter, perhaps to kill a couple of hours to sleep off the events of the previous night. By this time one is li to be accosted by someone needing a quarter, or someone secret displaying "an expensive diamond-studded watch" for a "terrifi gain." A quotation from field notes illustrates my general imp of Times Square at this time of day:

Times Square gets real active early—by 10:30 there are lots of t pening around me. A young boy (18 or 19) walks up beside me more to himself than to me says "I'd better watch out or I'll get

---

and got "hammered," and their grades were similar to mine. When did they get their work done? Obviously, not in the smoking room.

My next observation was of a male and female sitting at a study table. The female was a cute freshman with a sparkling personality, who was trying hard to concentrate on her sociology book. The male was a tall, good-looking sophomore with a buzz cut. The guy asked the girl many obnoxious and sarcastic questions such as, "Where did you sleep Saturday night?" and "Who gave you that beautiful hickie on your neck?" His tone of voice made it obvious that he was just joking around and teasing her. The girl laughed a little, but kept looking down at her book. I got the feeling that she was getting really annoyed with this guy. He kept throwing little comments at her and moving closer and closer to her face. Finally, when he was practically resting his head on her shoulder, she turned her head, looked him directly in the eyes, and said, "Get away!" Her voice was almost too loud for the smoking room. A few heads turned and the room became quieter. Whispers went back and forth and many people waited to see what would happen next. The guy moved his chair away from her very slowly and chuckled a little. He sat quietly in his chair, and doodled on the table for about five minutes, then he put his coat on and left the library. He stormed out of the library without even saying goodbye to the girl. She turned around to talk to her friend behind her. "Mission accomplished." Her friend replied, "Wow, you really blew him off big time!" She responded, "I know. I couldn't stand his bad breath any longer."

I decided to take part in the socialization scene, so I leaned over the edge of the balcony, and threw a paper airplane down so that it hit a guy named Josh. Josh is a friend of mine that I have had a crush on for a while. I tried to hide before he could look up and see who shot the plane, but it did not do any good. He saw me planning the whole thing in the reflection of the windows. I was so embarrassed. What a fool I had been to think that he would not see me. Just then, I noticed Josh was walking up the stairs and was looking at me with a cute smile on his face. He walked over to where I was sitting and sat down next to me. We talked about our weekends and how much work we had to catch up on. I found out that he had just broke up with his girlfriend over the weekend. He suggested that we go to the café later on to get something to eat. I accepted the offer, and then he went down to finish his work. I was so excited. I could not work anymore. My heart was beating a million times a minute, and I was sure that my face was as red as a cherry. I decided that even after my observation was over, I was going to spend more time in the smoking room. I was beginning to understand why so many girls "hung out" there all the time.

One evening, a handsome freshman guy walked into the top floor of the smoking room at 8:10, looked at his buddies, and blatantly said, "I'm in the mood to bother people." He began scribbling over his friends' notebooks and antagonizing them with comments about their drunken weekend. I found out that one guy shaved his head while he was intoxicated, one guy threw up on a girl, and another guy ate a large pizza all by himself. The three guys at the table were getting really annoyed with their obnoxious friend. Soon, a pen war developed. The kid with the shaved head had a red magic marker, and put a big, fat line across the obnoxious kid's face. A few swear words came out of their mouths, and he finally left the room. The whole incident was all in fun because the three guys at the table laughed hysterically for about ten minutes afterwards.

Some students seem perfectly content sitting in a comfortable chair, by themselves, with a book in their hands. They are not really into the social scene. Enjoying a cigarette, thinking alone, or just sitting in front of the window are their reasons for choosing the smoking room to study in. One guy that I talked to had long, straggly, blond hair, a long face, and an extremely thin body. He was wearing faded red pants and a brown and purple sweater. He was a very different-looking person. I sat down next to him, introduced myself, and told him about my study of the smoking room. I asked him what he thought of the room, and why he chose to study there. He looked away from me, thought for a minute, looked around the room, and then, gave me an answer. "More than half the people in this room come here only to be noticed. Making a good appearance, and socializing with the 'in' people is very important to many of the people in this room. Personally, I think of this room as the only place in the library where I can smoke and relax in front of the beautiful picture window." I asked him if the noise level bothered him at all and he replied that he gets too involved in his work to be distracted by the people talking around him. He cannot work in complete silence. Each night, there are usually a few serious students in the smoking room, like the guy I talked to. They enjoy the casual atmosphere, the big comfortable chairs, and the fact that they can smoke while they study.

The smoking room is excellent for scoping. The wall of windows, facing outside, are set up perfectly so you can see the reflection of everything in the room. Two freshmen girls were sitting in the lounge chairs with books open on their laps. They talked sometimes and giggled about private jokes. I studied them for a while and figured out their plan of scoping. Whenever the squeaky black doors would open, they would raise their eyes just enough to be able to look at the windows to see who was walking in. If it was one of their crushes, they would casually turn themselves around, as if they were stretching, and say, "Hi." If a close friend walked in the room, they would catch them as they walked by to talk for a while.

I've found that most students spend about two to three hours per evening in the smoking room. People sitting at study tables seem to be working only half of the time though. Those sitting in lounge chairs are usually more into their studies, and seem to be working about two-thirds of the time. The rest of the time is spent goofing off. The clock ticks away at a rapid rate. People wonder where the time goes without realizing that they talk the time away. I have overheard many people say that they had been in the smoking room for a certain number of hours and only accomplished a small fraction of their work. A very talkative sophomore girl announced to her friends that she had been there for three hours and had read eight-and-a-half pages. Then she commented that even though she did not get much work done in the smoking room, she got caught up on all the weekend gossip.

At around ten, the crowd in the smoking room gets smaller and the noise level decreases. Most people leave to study in their rooms or to get ready for an after-hours party. The last few true gossipers are left. They could ramble for hours. The really hard-working students remain also. Two guys in the corner are cramming for a big midterm that is the next day. Books, papers, cigarettes, and coffee are all sprawled out on the table. When I talked to them, they said that they were not leaving until the library closed.

The smoking room can hold about forty-five people on the second floor

and thirty people on the third floor. The average number of peopl is usually thirty for the bottom floor and twenty for the top. Ma wander in and out of the room during the evening, so there are alw ent groups of people mingling with one another.

After my two weeks of observation, I have learned that my as were not totally correct. I thought that no one ever got any work smoking room, but I discovered that this idea was partly wrong. I that many people talk, goof off, and accomplish a small amount of some people actually do get work done. The room is used for socia well as studying and smoking. To some people, it is a place to be the "in" people, and to others it is just the most convenient plac and study in a comfortable atmosphere. Even though I did not get n done for my other classes over the two weeks in "the airport," I d lot of juicy gossip and had a lot of laughs observing some of the p

Observing Behavior in Public Places: Prob and Strategies

David A. Karp

The central goal of this selection is to describe the access experienced while spending nearly two years (between Febr and September 1970) trying to learn about the public sexu the Times Square area of New York City. During this period, persons' behaviors primarily in pornographic bookstores theaters. In such contexts persons engage in activities that a at the least, as unconventional. Given the general social va on their behaviors, I was initially interested in how book movie patrons managed their personal identities, fostered a and controlled information about themselves. Persons er deviant or stigmatized behaviors will normally seek to mir costs and risks of such behaviors. Through ethnographic a regularities in bookstore and theater behavior, I hoped to bet stand the meaning of these settings to the participants and, the quality of their experiences. . . .

Times Square: The Research Setting

One novelist, John Rechy, in his book *City of Night* (1963:2 describes Times Square in the following way:

Times Square, New York is an electric island floating on a large lonesome parks and lonesome apartment houses and knifepointe stretching up. . . . Times Square is the magnet for all the lones jammed into this city. . . . I stand on 42nd Street and Broadway

mouth.'' (His mouth is all cut up and lots of blood spots are on his shirt); a young Negro boy is in business selling tokens at the subway entrance; an older man walks up to a group of young boys and begins to joke with them. Abruptly he lifts up the shirt of one and rubs his stomach. They all laugh. He walks off with one of the boys. The crowd builds up and rushes by. A very effeminate looking man makes a telephone call. Shortly thereafter he is met by a badly dressed, gaunt, unshaven man. They talk with one another as if making plans. The second man guardedly shows the first a new watch in its case. They walk off together. An older man talks with a young boy in the middle of the sidewalk. They laugh and joke. The boy walks off. The man seems bewildered. He stands for a few minutes in place as if deciding what to do now. He disappears into the subway. These are the kinds of things one can see in a short time and in a limited space. The same kinds of things, however, are happening all along the street.

By noon, the business offices have begun to expel their workers for lunch, and again the streets around Forty-second teem with activity. Remarkably, as if guided by radar, hundreds of persons pass each other without colliding. A kind of controlled chaos describes the flow of sidewalk traffic. On Eighth Avenue there are a surprisingly large number of prostitutes casually strolling the street. The streets remain relatively quiet during the afternoon. Between five and six, as the workers leave the area, the street traffic seems especially chaotic. By 7 P.M. the Times Square nightlife is underway. Most of the men and women who work in the area during the day have gone, and the pace has lessened. Persons appear in no particular hurry as they casually walk down the street, taking in the store windows and bright lights. Tourists, cameras around their necks, talk animatedly. They are also identified by the presence of their children and by their clothes. Tourists are much more conservatively dressed than the habitués of the area.

Early in the evening, groups of young men begin to stand around, some obviously homosexual, holding hands and whispering intimately. The ''queens'' are in ''high drag,'' wearing carefully done hairdos, tight multicolored slacks, and high-heeled shoes. The regulars constantly cruise up and down Forty-second Street to bump into friends, to find out ''what's up,'' and to make plans for the evening. Periodically, however, a bargain is struck. The encounter is generally brief and straightforward:

> Right near me I saw a well dressed man about 40-years old. After a short time, a young black man stands beside him along a store-front. The older man initiates the conversation with a simple ''Hi.'' They talk for some time (I could not hear). . . . Intermittently the man looks at his watch. Finally I see him nod his head and the men leave together. . . .

On Eighth Avenue, between Forty-fourth and Forty-ninth Streets, and on Broadway in the vicinity of Forty-sixth Street, prostitutes have begun work by 8:30 or 9 P.M. As the night wears on, they must periodically get off the streets as the police go by either on foot or in cars. By 11:00 the movie theaters have released hundreds of persons onto the street. At this time the streets appear more crowded than at any time during the day. Now Forty-second Street is populated by large numbers of men and women holding hands as they slowly amble along, absorbing the street's excitement.

As the night wears on, the number of moviegoers, tourists, and passersby begins to diminish, and by 2 A.M. the streets take on a different tone altogether—a sinister tone. As the tourists depart, only the denizens of the area remain. On Forty-fourth and Forty-fifth Streets, between Broadway and Sixth Avenue, the prostitutes appear in large numbers, hanging together in groups of three or four all along the street, much more overtly propositioning men than earlier in the evening. In contrast to the incessant activity earlier, the streets seem silent and forbidding.

Early Research Strategies and Problems

During the early stages of my work, I tried to become as well acquainted with the Times Square area as I could and self-consciously remained as flexible as possible in the accumulation of data. Generally speaking, my days and nights in the field were spent observing a variety of behaviors. At this point my strategy was to record everything that was even vaguely interesting or relevant since I did not know whether it might be useful later on as my problem developed and my focus narrowed. A "liberal," detailed recording of events is necessary especially during the early stages of an observational study. As my study became more focused later in its development, there proved to be considerable data the use of which I could not have readily foreseen during the initial stages of the study.

I carried a small pocket-sized notebook and tried to record my observations or conversations with persons as soon as possible after they occurred. This often necessitated moving off to a "private" or "semiprivate" place (doorways, coffee shops) where I could unobtrusively make notes. Whenever possible, I transcribed these brief notes in detail the same day or night that they were made. I found it helpful at times to dictate my notes and descriptions into a tape recorder before trying to put them down on paper.

Although I considered a number of alternative methods, I soon came to believe that observation was the most feasible means of data collection given the deviant nature of the context that I was studying. Even if I knew exactly what I was after, it would have been impossible to question systematically a sample of persons. At first I saw my inability to talk with customers as a critical problem. My notes at the time expressed this concern.

There is the problem of being unable to use techniques other than pure observation. It would seem extemely doubtful that I could talk to customers in either a structured or a nonstructured way. The inability to interact in any way with customers in the bookstores or theaters may be a crucial flaw in the study of behavior in this context. . . .

Related to restrictions in data-gathering techniques, I soon realized a variety of additional problems. Questions of the following sort began to appear in my field notes:

How long can I stand outside the bookstores in the cold weather? What is the best way to record my observations? Should I start out with preconceived categories? . . . The problems of observation inside the bookstore seem especially difficult. . . . How can I stand around the bookstores for any length of time without getting kicked out?

Shortly after beginning the study, I had these thoughts:

Clearly the study of deviant behavior poses special problems. Perhaps the biggest problem is the problem of access. Given the fact that I would like to observe what must be considered deviant behavior, by at least some involved, I may not be welcome in the stores by owners to observe for any length of time. Given the type of business I might be considered a threat. Am I really a member of the police department, Better Business Bureau, local civic association or whatever? So, how do I present myself to owners? How do you explain the nature of the study especially when you are far from sure yourself? How am I to convince them that I am not a spy, that I am morally neutral?

Plainly, there is no logical progression of events that uniformly occurs in participant observation. The choice of behaviors for observation is particularly arbitrary at the beginning of the research, although even then researchers are necessarily curious about certain behaviors or events and may have some a priori and vaguely formulated hypotheses which they will want to verify or discard in a loose way. As the research progresses, however, and researchers begin to accumulate more detailed information, hypotheses begin to present themselves more systematically and the choice of events and persons for observation becomes increasingly focused. From an early period, though, I began to appreciate the problems of access existing for even the researcher studying public places.

Problems of Access

Although the context of my own work was a public one and I could freely enter bookstores or theaters, there were still difficult problems of access. A few examples will illustrate just how tricky the problem of access can be. My field notes describe first attempts to gain entry to bookstores.

I tried to gain access to a couple of bookstores today. I got up the guts to tell the managers in two places that, in essence, I would like to hang around and observe behavior for a few hours. I say it took guts because I had absolutely no idea of what their reactions might be. I began to feel, though, that were I flatly refused or thrown out that it could mean the end of the study.

In the first place that I went, I sought out the manager and told him, by way of legitimizing myself, that I was a professor at Queens College [I was actually an instructor, but that didn't sound as good as professor]. I told him that all I wanted was permission to stay in the store for a few hours and that I simply wanted to watch the people and nothing more. I told him that I was interested in how people behaved in the Times Square Area and stores like his own were natural places to watch people. I assured him that neither he nor his store would in any way be identified in anything that might eventually be written. During all this time he smiled broadly, almost suppressing a laugh as if there were something funny about me and my observing behavior there. He seemed to think about it for a few seconds and then told me that he didn't "think it was practical." I assured him that I would in no way jeopardize his business, but for the time being his mind seemed made up. I did not persist. I thanked him and left.

Several times I had similar experiences in stores as I told my story. Although I did finally obtain access to several of the stores, I was puzzled by my early failures. I was particularly puzzled, however, by the grin that covered the faces of the managers and workers, puzzled by the suppressed laughter that I kept getting from these men as I delivered my opening remarks. These early attempts at access were frustrating and may have been much easier had I realized what I was doing wrong. My initial attempt at access provides a useful example to show how researchers make mistakes that cannot be anticipated prior to entering the field.

When I discussed the access problem with colleagues, they pointed out where the mistake in my opening approach might have been. The clue was the suppressed laughter itself. They suggested that the mistake was in introducing myself as a professor at Queens College. The store managers had probably not heard of Queens College, which is part of the New York City University system. Rather, they understood the word "queen" in its slang form, meaning "effeminate homosexual." My colleagues suggested that I was introducing myself as a kind of "super queer" or "super freak," and the combination of "queen" with "professor"—"a professor of queens"—was more humorous still. Quite unwittingly, therefore, an attempt to legitimate myself had exactly the opposite effect.

Later, I found that in certain instances the explanation "I am writing a book about Times Square" proved quite enough. In other cases, persons required a much more detailed explanation. In still other cases, potential informants refused to be bothered with me at all. I was always trying to make contact with useful informants. To that end, I frequently tried to strike up conversations with persons on the street, bookstore personnel, and so on. The norm against speaking to customers in bookstores was so strong, however, that I could never bring myself to break it. . . .

Attempts to establish relationships with prostitutes in the Times Square area proved especially difficult. On several occasions, I tried to get a picture of the typical working day of a prostitute. I wanted to observe the women just as an occupational sociologist might want to observe workers on, say, an assembly line. I wanted to know, for example, when they started work, when they took their breaks, how much territory they covered, how many "tricks" they "turned" during their working hours. I wanted to stand around and record their behaviors all day, if possible. However, this plan was continually frustrated when the women became aware that I was standing around for a longer period of time than they deemed normal. They no doubt thought I was a plainclothes policeman, many of whom, like me, dress casually and have beards. Consequently, I could not obtain the kind of detailed information on the behavior of prostitutes that I wanted.

I was able to have short conversations with some women but did not normally identify myself as a researcher. I had a few extended interviews which proved uninformative and cost me ten to twenty dollars. My zeal to talk to some of these women created potentially dangerous situations for me. For example, I had this confrontation:

> About halfway down 47th Street between 6th and 7th Avenues I spotted five women working. I decided to try to strike up a deal; to talk to one of the women. All the women were white.
>
> As I leaned up against a car one woman came up and said to me, "Do you want to go out?" I said, "Look, I'll level with you. I'm doing a study of the Times Square Area. I'm not interested in sex but I am interested in information. I'll pay you for it. How much will it cost me?" She asked, "How long?" . . . "A half hour" . . . "Twenty five." . . . "That's a little bit too steep." She walked away from me but I continued to lean against the car. At that point a new woman came and was greeted by the others. One of them said, "Here's the girl in white." This woman was very tall and wore an all white pants suit. Then the woman that I first talked to made a general announcement to all of the others. She said, "He's making a survey. Do you want to go with him? He'll pay." The new arrival, the "girl in white," turned to me and said, "I won't talk to you, you'll bring me in." I replied, "No, I'm straight." Finally, she did walk over to me and said, "What are you doing?" . . . "I'm interested in prostitution. I'd like to talk to you." . . . "How much?" . . . "Ten dollars." . . . Then she said something like "Are you kidding? The best way to find out is to go out with me." I said, "No." She then said, "Then get the hell out of here. Get the hell off the street. I'll call a cop. You better believe it. Get the fuck out of here. Fuck, bastard, go write that I said fuck in your fucking survey. . . ."

In the last few pages, I have tried to convey some of the access difficulties likely to arise in studies of public contexts, especially those in which persons have reason to conceal their activities. We would do well, however, not to overstate these access problems. Field researchers who are flexible in the research roles and methods they adopt can collect the data necessary for rendering a valid picture of the public settings they study. . . .

Getting the Data

Reliance on pure observation is not as much a limitation as it might first appear. Researchers who develop an eye for detail in observing settings can collect an enormous wealth of data. Close, careful observation allows the discovery of important aspects of behavior and social structure in any setting. Using only observation, I was able to collect data on a wide range of activities occurring in the Times Square area. Without talking to anyone, I could learn such things as the way persons enter and leave bookstores and theaters, space rules governing behavior in bookstores, the way persons browse at pornographic magazines, the purchasing techniques of customers, the manner of choosing seats in pornographic movies, how bargains are struck between prostitutes and clients, conflict between prostitutes and the police, and rules of territoriality established by prostitutes (particularly along racial lines) on the street.

Sometimes researchers studying public places will want to adopt a more active stance. To test the operation of norms, they may intervene in a situation; they may purposely break a presumed norm, predicting in advance persons' responses. I did attempt such strategies as sitting next to persons in movie theaters when I believed that behavior was improper. Persons indicated their discomfort by screwing up their faces, sighing loudly, shifting their bodies away from me, and the like. In nearly all cases, those whose space I invaded eventually moved to a more isolated seat.

Researchers should also consider as data their own feelings and behaviors. Because personal introspection is unavoidable, researchers' own experiences will significantly shape their ideas and hypotheses, and so the course of future data collection. Data of the following sort informed my own research activity:

> I can on the basis of my own experience substantiate, at least in part, the reality of impression-management problems for persons involved in the Times Square sexual scene. I have been frequenting pornographic bookstores and movie theaters for some nine months. Despite my relatively long experience I have not been able to overcome my uneasiness during activity in these contexts. I feel, for example, nervous at the prospect of entering a theater. This nervousness expresses itself in increased heartbeat. I consciously wait until few people are in the vicinity before entering; I take my money out well in advance of entering; I feel reticent to engage the female ticket seller in even the briefest eye contact.

Of course, whenever the opportunity arises, researchers will have casual conversations with persons in the setting. These conversations, however brief, can serve to validate earlier observations and to open up new and sometimes unexpected areas for inquiry. Once I became familiar to bookstore personnel as a "regular" (which took some time), I could engage them in brief conversations, and in some cases we became friendly enough to have more extended conversations. These conversations provided valuable data on various aspects of bookstore behavior. In one case, for example, I discovered a category used by store clerks in typing customers:

> There's an interesting type. There's a little humor here. We call them the "moochers." These are the guys that browse aimlessly. There's no buying potential here. This guy uses a lot of gimmicks. Generally, he picks up a magazine, looks through it, but then doesn't put it down again. He holds the magazine in his hands trying to give the impression that he is going to buy it. He keeps collecting magazines this way. Finally, on his way out he puts each magazine back in place. There are others too. Instead of piling books up in his hand, he keeps the money out in his hand. These must feel that you will believe the money; that you won't believe his just piling up books in his hand.

As I began to collect substantial data from casual conversations, I was able to check on the validity of information provided by one clerk by asking questions of others. In one case a store clerk described some of his customers as "weirdoes" [sic]. Because I was interested in how store personnel thought about and evaluated their customers, this description of customers became a standard part of my conversation with the several clerks I had come to know.

> I once heard someone in another store describe some of their customers as "weirdoes." What does that mean to you?
>
> Well, maybe forty percent of the people who come into the store are straight, the others all have some kind of hangup.
>
> How can you tell the "weirdoes?"
>
> I don't know. After a while you can tell just by looking at them. You know, by the way they walk, by the way they talk, the look in their eyes. . . . Well, what do you have to think when a guy buys a book on teenage lesbianism. You've got to think there is something wrong with the guy. He's got to have some interest in the subject matter and must at least fantasize about it. Same thing with the sado-masochism stuff. I mean, that's not normal.

With the foregoing examples, I have tried to describe the kinds of data it is possible to collect in those public situations in which norms governing interaction between strangers prohibit extensive conversation. Data of the sort I collected enabled me to analyze the structure of urban anonymity and the social organization of everyday city life. Before concluding, however, I should mention the kinds of data that I was never able to collect, data that might have produced a quite different line of analysis from the one I took.

Every researcher finds that he or she must make personal decisions concerning aspects of the studied situation to be left untouched. My data were limited primarily to the interactions of persons in the public places I observed. Although I did participate in both movie and bookstore behaviors, there were certain areas of the sexual scene that I never learned much about. Although interested in the relations of prostitutes and clients, I never became a total participant in this aspect of sexual activity. In another instance, I considered trying to learn about the more private world of pimps and prostitutes. This meant hanging around the bars where the pimps congregated (see Milner and Milner, *Black Players: The Secret World of Black Players* 1972). Feeling thoroughly out of place in these bars and concerned with personal safety, I eliminated this area of data collection. As a last example, I note that my data do not illuminate how the pornography industry is structured and organized. I was never able to find out who owned the stores and theaters, their possible links to organized crime, and so on. The collection of these data would no doubt have changed the overall direction of my research. . . .

[Editor's note: Citations have been omitted.]

My Experience as a Fieldworker

Kim Smith

It is difficult for me to use the fieldworker's experience as an extended analogy because I didn't do the assignment correctly the first time. I guess you could say I had too much confusion. Mentally, I drifted in and out of understanding the assignment. As I finished my essay I thought I understood what I was supposed to be doing, but I did not.

As with the student in Zen and the Art of Motorcycle Maintenance I found that the setting and the people I was observing were so familiar to me, I was less able to interpret what I saw and heard. I just saw the same things that I see every week and I ran into trouble trying to see anything else. Now I know that instead of trying to see something else, I should have been working on describing what I was observing. Unlike the student, I didn't overcome my block. I described my church easily because of its familiarity but since I wasn't clear on what the assignment was asking me to do I didn't give my true thoughts, perceptions, and feelings about the church or its members.

I feel my observation failed because I didn't discover anything new, and after all, that is what anthropologists set out to do. The reason I didn't discover anything new was because I didn't set out to discover anything. Somehow that part of the assignment escaped me.

The six steps in the preferred mode of inquiry also escaped me.

(1) Defining the question the anthropologist wishes to answer: my questions were not well defined.

a woman in labour. The village is dazzling and dead; any sound seems oddly loud and out of place. Words have to cut through the solid heat slowly. And then the sun gradually sinks over the sea.

A second time, the sleeping people stir, roused perhaps by the cry of "a boat," resounding through the village. The fishermen beach their canoes, weary and spent from the heat, in spite of the slaked lime on their heads, with which they have sought to cool their brains and redden their hair. The brightly coloured fishes are spread out on the floor, or piled in front of the houses until the women pour water over them to free them from taboo. Regretfully, the young fishermen separate out the "Taboo fish," which must be sent to the chief, or proudly they pack the little palm leaf baskets with offerings of fish to take to their sweethearts. Men come home from the bush, grimy and heavy laden, shouting as they come, greeted in a sonorous rising cadence by those who have remained at home. They gather in the guest house for their evening kava drinking. The soft clapping of hands, the high-pitched intoning of the talking chief who serves the kava echoes through the village. Girls gather flowers to weave into necklaces; children, lusty from their naps and bound to no particular task, play circular games in the half shade of the late afternoon. Finally the sun sets, in a flame which stretches from the mountain behind to the horizon on the sea, the last bather comes up from the beach, children straggle home, dark little figures etched against the sky; lights shine in the houses, and each household gathers for its evening meal. The suitor humbly presents his offering, the children have been summoned from their noisy play, perhaps there is an honoured guest who must be served first, after the soft, barbaric singing of Christian hymns and the brief and graceful evening prayer. In front of a house at the end of the village, a father cries out the birth of a son. In some family circles a face is missing, in others little runaways have found a haven! Again quiet settles upon the village, as first the head of the household, then the women and children, and last of all the patient boys, eat their supper.

After supper the old people and the little children are bundled off to bed. If the young people have guests the front of the house is yielded to them. For day is the time for the councils of old men and the labours of youth, and night is the time for lighter things. Two kinsmen, or a chief and his councillor, sit and gossip over the day's events or make plans for the morrow. Outside a crier goes through the village announcing that the communal breadfruit pit will be opened in the morning, or that the village will make a great fish trap. If it is moonlight, groups of young men, women by twos and threes, wander through the village, and crowds of children hunt for land crabs or chase each other among the breadfruit trees. Half the village may go fishing by torchlight and the curving reef will gleam with wavering lights and echo with shouts of triumph or disappointment, teasing words or smothered cries of outraged modesty. Or a group of youths may dance for the pleasure of some visiting maiden. Many of those who have retired to sleep, drawn by the merry music, will wrap their sheets about them and set out to find the dancing. A white-clad ghostly throng will gather in a circle about the gaily lit house, a circle from which every now and then a few will detach themselves and wander away among the trees. Sometimes sleep will not descend upon the village until long past midnight; then at last there is only the mellow thunder of the reef and the whisper of lovers, as the village rests until dawn.

Men and Jobs

Elliot Liebow

A pickup truck drives slowly down the street. The truck stops as it comes abreast of a man sitting on a cast-iron porch and the white driver calls out, asking if the man wants a day's work. The man shakes his head and the truck moves on up the block, stopping again whenever idling men come within calling distance of the driver. At the Carry-out corner, five men debate the question briefly and shake their heads no to the truck. The truck turns the corner and repeats the same performance up the next street. In the distance, one can see one man, then another, climb into the back of the truck and sit down. In starts and stops, the truck finally disappears.

What is it we have witnessed here? A labor scavenger rebuffed by his would-be prey? Lazy, irresponsible men turning down an honest day's pay for an honest day's work? Or a more complex phenomenon marking the intersection of economic forces, social values and individual states of mind and body?

Let us look again at the driver of the truck. He has been able to recruit only two or three men from each twenty or fifty he contacts. To him, it is clear that the others simply do not choose to work. Singly or in groups, belly-empty or belly-full, sullen or gregarious, drunk or sober, they confirm what he has read, heard and knows from his own experience: these men wouldn't take a job if it were handed to them on a platter.

Quite apart from the question of whether or not this is true of some of the men he sees on the street, it is clearly not true of all of them. If it were, he would not have come here in the first place; or having come, he would have left with an empty truck. It is not even true of most of them, for most of the men he sees on the street this weekday morning do, in fact, have jobs. But since, at the moment, they are neither working nor sleeping, and since they hate the depressing room or apartment they live in, or because there is nothing to do there,[1] or because they want to get away from their wives or anyone else living there, they are out on the street, indistinguishable from those who do not have jobs or do not want them. Some, like Boley, a member of a trash-collection crew in a suburban housing development work Saturdays and are off on this weekday. Some, like Sweets, work nights cleaning up middle-class trash, dirt, dishes and garbage, and mopping the floors of the office buildings, hotels, restaurants, toilets and other public places dirtied during the day. Some men work for retail businesses such as liquor stores which do not begin the day until ten o'clock. Some laborers, like Tally, have already come back from the job because the ground was too wet for pick and shovel or because the weather was too cold for pouring concrete. Other employed men stayed off the job today for personal reasons: Clarence to go to a funeral at eleven this morning and Sea Cat to answer a subpoena as a witness in a criminal proceeding.

Also on the street, unwitting contributors to the impression taken away by the truck driver, are the halt and the lame. The man on the cast-iron steps strokes one gnarled arthritic hand with the other and says he doesn't know whether or not he'll live long enough to be eligible for Social Security. He pauses, then adds matter-of-factly, "Most times, I don't care whether I do or don't." Stoopy's left leg was polio-withered in childhood. Raymond, who looks as if he could tear out a fire hydrant, coughs up blood if he bends or moves suddenly. The quiet man who hangs out in front of the Saratoga apartments has a steel hook strapped onto his left elbow. And had the man in the truck been able to look into the wine-clouded eyes of the man in the green cap, he would have realized that the man did not even understand he was being offered a day's work.

Others, having had jobs and been laid off, are drawing unemployment compensation (up to $44 per week) and have nothing to gain by accepting work which pays little more than this and frequently less.

Still others, like Bumdoodle the numbers man, are working hard at illegal ways of making money, hustlers who are on the street to turn a dollar any way they can: buying and selling sex, liquor, narcotics, stolen goods, or anything else that turns up.

Only a handful remains unaccounted for. There is Tonk, who cannot bring himself to take a job away from the corner, because, according to the other men, he suspects his wife will be unfaithful if given the opportunity. There is Stanton, who has not reported to work for four days now, not since Bernice disappeared. He bought a brand new knife against her return. She had done this twice before, he said, but not for so long and not without warning, and he had forgiven her. But this time, "I ain't got it in me to forgive her again." His rage and shame are there for all to see as he paces the Carry-out and the corner, day and night, hoping to catch a glimpse of her.

And finally, there are those like Arthur, able-bodied men who have no visible means of support, legal or illegal, who neither have jobs nor want them. The truck driver, among others, believes the Arthurs to be representative of all the men he sees idling on the street during his own working hours. They are not, but they cannot be dismissed simply because they are a small minority. It is not enough to explain them away as being lazy or irresponsible or both because an able-bodied man with responsibilties who refuses work is, by the truck driver's definition, lazy and irresponsible. Such an answer begs the question. It is descriptive of the facts; it does not explain them. . . .

Objective economic considerations are frequently a controlling factor in a man's refusal to take a job. How much the job pays is a crucial question but seldom asked. He knows how much it pays. Working as a stock clerk, a delivery boy, or even behind the counter of liquor stores, drug stores and other retail businesses pays one dollar an hour. So, too, do most busboy, car-wash, janitorial and other jobs available to him. Some jobs, such as dishwasher, may dip as low as eighty cents an hour and others, such as elevator operator or work in a junk yard, may offer $1.15 or $1.25. Take-home pay for jobs such as these ranges from $35 to $50 a week, but a take-home pay of over $45 for a five-day week is the exception rather than the rule.

One of the principal advantages of these kinds of job is that they offer fairly regular work. Most of them involve essential services and are therefore somewhat less responsive to business conditions than are some higher paying, less menial jobs. Most of them are also inside jobs not dependent on the weather, as are construction jobs and other higher-paying outside work.

Another seemingly important advantage of working in hotels, restaurants, office and apartment buildings and retail establishments is that they frequently offer an opportunity for stealing on the job. But stealing can be a two-edged sword. Apart from increasing the cost of the goods or services to the general public, a less obvious result is that the practice usually acts as a depressant on the employee's own wage level. Owners of small retail establishments and other employers frequently anticipate employee stealing and adjust the wage rate accordingly. Tonk's employer explained why he was paying Tonk $35 for a 55–60 hour workweek. These men will all steal, he said. Although he keeps close watch on Tonk, he estimates that Tonk steals from $35 to $40 a week.[2] What he steals, when added to his regular earnings, brings his take-home pay to $70 to $75 per week. The employer said he did not mind this because Tonk is worth that much to the business. But if he were to pay Tonk outright the full value of his labor, Tonk would still be stealing $35–$40 per week and this, he said, the business simply would not support. . . .

With or without stealing, and quite apart from any interior processes going on in the man who refuses such a job or quits it casually and without apparent reason, the objective fact is that menial jobs in retailing or in the service trades simply do not pay enough to support a man and his family. This is not to say that the worker is underpaid; this may or may not be true. Whether he is or not, the plain fact is that, in such a job, he cannot make a living. Nor can he take much comfort in the fact that these jobs tend to offer more regular, steadier work. If he cannot live on the $45 or $50 he makes in one week, the longer he works, the longer he cannot live on what he makes.[3]

Construction work, even for unskilled laborers, usually pays better, with the hourly rate ranging from $1.50 to $2.60 an hour.[4] Importantly, too, good references, a good driving record, a tenth grade (or any high school) education, previous experience, the ability to "bring police clearance with you" are not normally required of laborers as they frequently are for some of the jobs in retailing or in the service trades.

Construction work, however, has its own objective disadvantages. It is, first of all, seasonal work for the great bulk of the laborers, beginning early in the spring and tapering off as winter weather sets in. And even during the season the work is frequently irregular. Early or late in the season, snow or temperatures too low for concrete frequently sends the laborers back home, and during late spring or summer, a heavy rain on Tuesday or Wednesday, leaving a lot of water and mud behind it, can mean a two or three day workweek for the pick-and-shovel men and other unskilled laborers.

The elements are not the only hazard. As the project moves from one construction stage to another, laborers—usually without warning—are laid off, sometimes permanently or sometimes for weeks at a time. The more fortunate or the better workers are told periodically to "take a walk for two, three days,"

Both getting the construction job and getting to it are also relatively more difficult than is the case for the menial jobs in retailing and the service trades. Job competition is always fierce. In the city, the large construction projects are unionized. One has to have ready cash to get into the union to become eligible to work on these projects and, being eligible, one has to find an opening. Unless one "knows somebody," say a foreman or a laborer who knows the day before that they are going to take on new men in the morning, this can be a difficult and disheartening search.

Many of the nonunion jobs are in suburban Maryland or Virginia. The newspaper ads say, "Report ready to work to the trailer at the intersection of Rte. 11 and Old Bridge Rd., Bunston, Virginia (or Maryland)," but this location may be ten, fifteen, or even twenty-five miles from the Carry-out. Public transportation would require two or more hours to get there, if it services the area at all. Without access to a car or to a car-pool arrangement, it is not worthwhile reading the ad. So the men do not. Jobs such as these are usually filled by word of mouth information, beginning with someone who knows someone or who is himself working there and looking for a paying rider. Furthermore, nonunion jobs in outlying areas tend to be smaller projects of relatively short duration and to pay somewhat less than scale.

Still another objective factor is the work itself. For some men, whether the job be digging, mixing mortar, pushing a wheelbarrow, unloading materials, carrying and placing steel rods for reinforcing concrete, or building or laying concrete forms, the work is simply too hard. Men such as Tally and Wee Tom can make such work look like child's play; some of the older work-hardened men, such as Budder and Stanton, can do it too, although not without showing unmistakable signs of strain and weariness at the end of the workday. But those who lack the robustness of a Tally or the time-inured immunity of a Budder must either forego jobs such as these or pay a heavy toll to keep them. For Leroy, in his early twenties, almost six feet tall but weighing under 140 pounds, it would be as difficult to push a loaded wheelbarrow, or to unload and stack 96-pound bags of cement all day long, as it would be for Stoopy with his withered leg. . . .

Sea Cat was "healthy, sturdy, active and of good intelligence." When a judge gave him six weeks in which to pay his wife $200 in back child-support payments, he left his grocery-store job in order to take a higher-paying job as a laborer, arranged for him by a foreman friend. During the first week the weather was bad and he worked only Wednesday and Friday, cursing the elements all the while for cheating him out of the money he could have made. The second week, the weather was fair but he quit at the end of the fourth day, saying frankly that the work was too hard for him. He went back to his job at the grocery store and took a second job working nights as a dishwasher in a restaurant, earning little if any more at the two jobs than he would have earned as a laborer, and keeping at both of them until he had paid off his debts.

Tonk did not last as long as Sea Cat. No one made any predictions when he got a job in a parking lot, but when the men on the corner learned he was to start on a road construction job, estimates of how long he would last ranged from one to three weeks. Wednesday was his first day. He spent that evening and night at home. He did the same on Thursday. He worked Friday and spent Friday evening and part of Saturday draped over the mailbox on the corner. Sunday afternoon, Tonk decided he was not going to report on the job the next morning. He explained that after working three days, he knew enough about the job to know that it was too hard for him. He knew he wouldn't be able to keep up and he'd just as soon quit now as get fired later.

Logan was a tall, two-hundred-pound man in his late twenties. His back used to hurt him only on the job, he said, but now he can't straighten up for increasingly longer periods of time. He said he had traced this to the awkward walk he was forced to adopt by the loaded wheelbarrows which pull him down into a half-stoop. He's going to quit, he said, as soon as he can find another job. If he can't find one real soon, he guesses he'll quit anyway. It's not worth it, having to walk bent over and leaning to one side.

Sometimes, the strain and effort is greater than the man is willing to admit, even to himself. In the early summer of 1963, Richard was rooming at Nancy's place. His wife and children were ''in the country'' (his grandmother's home in Carolina), waiting for him to save up enough money so that he could bring them back to Washington and start over again after a disastrous attempt to ''make it'' in Philadelphia. Richard had gotten a job with a fence company in Virginia. It paid $1.60 an hour. The first few evenings, when he came home from work, he looked ill from exhaustion and the heat. Stanton said Richard would have to quit, ''he's too small [thin] for that kind of work.'' Richard said he was doing O.K. and would stick with the job.

At Nancy's one night, when Richard had been working about two weeks, Nancy and three or four others were sitting around talking, drinking, and listening to music. Someone asked Nancy when was Richard going to bring his wife and children up from the country. Nancy said she didn't know, but it probably depended on how long it would take him to save up enough money. She said she didn't think he could stay with the fence job much longer. This morning, she said, the man Richard rode to work with knocked on the door and Richard didn't answer. She looked in his room. Richard was still asleep. Nancy tried to shake him awake. ''No more digging!'' Richard cried out. ''No more digging! I can't do no more God-damn digging!'' When Nancy finally managed to wake him, he dressed quickly and went to work.

Richard stayed on the job two more weeks, then suddenly quit, ostensibly because his pay check was three dollars less than what he thought it should have been.

In summary of objective job considerations, then, the most important fact is that a man who is able and willing to work cannot earn enough money to support himself, his wife, and one or more children. A man's chances for working regularly are good only if he is willing to work for less than he can live on, and sometimes not even then. On some jobs, the wage rate is deceptively higher than on others, but the higher the wage rate, the more difficult it is to get the job, and the less the job security. Higher-paying construction work tends to be seasonal and, during the season, the amount of work available is highly sensitive to business and weather conditions and to the changing requirements of individual projects. Moreover, high-paying construction jobs are frequently beyond the physical capacity of some of the men, and some of the low-paying jobs are scaled down even lower in accordance with the self-fulfilling assumption that the man will steal part of his wages on the job.

Bernard assesses the objective job situation dispassionately over a cup of coffee, sometimes poking at the coffee with his spoon, sometimes staring at it as if, like a crystal ball, it holds tomorrow's secrets. He is twenty-seven years old. He and the woman with whom he lives have a baby son, and she has another child by another man. Bernard does odd jobs—mostly painting—but here it is the end of January, and his last job was with the Post Office during the Christmas mail rush. He would like postal work as a steady job, he says. It pays well (about $2.00 an hour) but he has twice failed the Post Office examination (he graduated from a Washington high school) and has given up the idea as an impractical one. He is supposed to see a man tonight about a job as a parking attendant for a large apartment house. The man told him to bring his birth certificate and driver's license, but his license was suspended because of a backlog of unpaid traffic fines. A friend promised to lend him some money this evening. If he gets it, he will pay the fines tomorrow morning and have his license reinstated. He hopes the man with the job will wait till tomorrow night.

A "security job" is what he really wants, he said. He would like to save up money for a taxi-cab. (But having twice failed the postal examination and having a bad driving record as well, it is highly doubtful that he could meet the qualifications or pass the written test.) That would be a "good life." He can always get a job in a restaurant or as a clerk in a drugstore but they don't pay enough, he said. He needs to take home at least $50 to $55 a week. He thinks he can get that much driving a truck somewhere . . . Sometimes he wishes he had stayed in the army . . . A security job, that's what he wants most of all, a real security job . . .

Notes

1. The comparison of sitting at home alone with being in jail is commonplace.

2. Exactly the same estimate as the one made by Tonk himself. On the basis of personal knowledge of the stealing routine employed by Tonk, however, I suspect the actual amount is considerably smaller.

3. It might be profitable to compare, as Howard S. Becker suggests, gross aspects of income and housing costs in this particular area with those reported by Herbert Gans for the low-income working class in Boston's West End. In 1958, Gans reports, median income for the West Enders was just under $70 a week, a level considerably higher than that enjoyed by the people in the Carry-out neighborhood five years later. Gans himself rented a six-room apartment in the West End for $46 a month, about $10 more than the going rate for long-time residents. In the Carry-out neighborhood, rooms that could accommodate more than a cot and a miniature dresser—that is, rooms that qualified for family living—rented for $12 to $22 a week. Ignoring differences that really can't be ignored—the privacy and self-contained efficiency of the multi-room apartment as against the fragmented, public living of the rooming-house "apartment," with a public toilet on a floor always different from the one your room is

on (no matter, it probably doesn't work, anyway)—and assuming comparable states of disrepair, the West Enders were paying $6 or $7 a month for a room that cost the Carry-outers at least $50 a month, and frequently more. Looking at housing costs as a percentage of income—and again ignoring what cannot be ignored: that what goes by the name of "housing" in the two areas is not at all the same thing—the median income West Ender could get a six-room apartment for about 12 percent of his income, while his 1963 Carry-out counterpart, with a weekly income of $60 (to choose a figure from the upper end of the income range), often paid 20–33 percent of his income for one room. See Herbert J. Gans, *The Urban Villagers*, pp.10–13.

4. The higher amount is 1962 union scale for building laborers. According to the Wage Agreement Contract for Heavy Construction Laborers (Washington, D.C., and vicinity) covering the period from May 1, 1963 to April 30, 1966, minimum hourly wage for heavy construction laborers was to go from $2.75 (May 1963) by annual increments to $2.92, effective November 1, 1965.

On Being Sane in Insane Places

David L. Rosenhan

If sanity and insanity exist, how shall we know them?

The question is neither capricious nor itself insane. However much we may be personally convinced that we can tell the normal from the abnormal, the evidence is simply not compelling. It is commonplace, for example, to read about murder trials in which eminent psychiatrists for the defense are contradicted by equally eminent psychiatrists for the prosecution on the matter of the defendant's sanity. More generally, there is a great deal of conflicting data on the reliability, utility, and meaning of such terms as "sanity," "insanity," "mental illness," and "schizophrenia."

Finally, as early as 1934 Benedict suggested that normality and abnormality are not universal. What is viewed as normal in one culture may be seen as quite aberrant in another. Thus, notions of normality and abnormality may not be quite as accurate as people believe they are.

To raise questions regarding normality and abnormality is in no way to question the fact that some behaviors are deviant or odd. Murder is deviant. So, too, are hallucinations. Nor does raising such questions deny the existence of the personal anguish that is often associated with "mental illness." Anxiety and depression exist. Psychological suffering exists. But normality and abnormality, sanity and insanity, and the diagnoses that flow from them may be less substantive than many believe them to be.

At its heart, the question of whether the sane can be distinguished from the insane (and whether degrees of insanity can be distinguished from one another) is a simple matter: do the salient characteristics that lead to diagnoses reside in the patients themselves or in the environments and contexts in which observers find them? From Bleuler, through Kretchmer, through the formulators of the recently revised *Diagnostic and Statistical Manual* of the American Psychiatric Association, the belief has been strong that patients present symptoms, that those symptoms can be categorized, and, implicitly, that the sane are distinguishable from the insane. More recently, however, this belief has been questioned. Based in part on theoretical and anthropological considerations, but also on philosophical, legal, and therapeutic ones, the view has grown that psychological categorization of mental illness is useless at best and downright harmful, misleading, and pejorative at worst. Psychiatric diagnoses, in this view, are in the minds of the observers and are not valid summaries of characteristics displayed by the observed.

Gains can be made in deciding which of these is more nearly accurate by getting normal people (that is, people who do not have, and have never suffered, symptoms of serious psychiatric disorders) admitted to psychiatric hospitals and then determining whether they were discovered to be sane and, if so, how. If the sanity of such pseudopatients were always detected, there would be prima facie evidence that a sane individual can be distinguished from the insane context in which he is found. Normality (and presumably abnormality) is distinct enough that it can be recognized wherever it occurs, for it is carried within the person. If, on the other hand, the sanity of the pseudopatients were never discovered, serious difficulties would arise for those who support traditional modes of psychiatric diagnosis. Given that the hospital staff was not incompetent, that the pseudopatient had been behaving as sanely as he had been outside of the hospital, and that it had never been previously suggested that he belonged in a psychiatric hospital, such an unlikely outcome would support the view that psychiatric diagnosis betrays little about the patient but much about the environment in which an observer finds him.

This article describes such an experiment. Eight sane people gained secret admission to twelve different hospitals. Their diagnostic experiences constitute the data of the first part of this article; the remainder describes their experiences in psychiatric institutions. . . .

Pseudopatients and Their Settings

The eight pseudopatients were a varied group. One was a psychology graduate student in his twenties. The remaining seven were older and "established"; among them were three psychologists, a pediatrician, a psychiatrist, a painter, and a housewife. Three pseudopatients were women, five were men. All of them used pseudonyms, lest their alleged diagnoses embarrass them later. Those who were in mental health professions alleged another occupation in order to avoid the special attentions that might be accorded by staff, as a matter of courtesy or caution, to ailing colleagues. With the exception of myself (I was the first pseudopatient, and my presence was known to the hospital administrator and chief psychologist and, as far as I can tell, to them alone), the presence of pseudopatients and the nature of the research program was not known to the hospital staffs.

The settings were similarly varied. In order to generalize the findings, admission into a variety of hospitals was sought. The twelve hospitals in the sample were located in five different states on the East and West coasts. Some were old and shabby, some were quite new. Some were research oriented, others were not. Some had good staff-patient ratios, others were quite understaffed. Only one was a strictly private hospital. All of the others were supported by state or federal funds or, in one instance, by university funds.

After calling the hospital for an appointment, the pseudopatient arrived at the admissions office complaining that he had been hearing voices. Asked what the voices said, he replied that they were often unclear, but as far as he could tell they said "empty," "hollow," and "thud." The voices were unfamiliar and were of the same sex as the pseudopatient. The choice of these symptoms was occasioned by their apparent similarity to existential symptoms. Such symptoms are alleged to arise from painful concerns about the perceived meaninglessness of one's life. It is as if the hallucinating person were saying, "My life is empty and hollow." The choice of these symptoms was also determined by the *absence* of a single report of existential psychoses in the literature.

Beyond alleging the symptoms and falsifying name, vocation, and employment, no further alterations of person, history, or circumstances were made. The significant events of the pseudopatient's life history were presented as they had actually occurred. Relationships with parents and siblings, with spouse and children, and with people at work and in school were described as they were or had been, consistent with the aforementioned exceptions. Frustrations and upsets were described along with joys and satisfactions. These facts are important to remember. If anything, they strongly biased the subsequent results in favor of detecting sanity, for none of their histories or current behaviors were seriously pathological in any way.

Immediately upon admission to the psychiatric ward, the pseudopatient ceased simulating *any* sumptoms of abnormality. In some cases, there was a brief period of mild nervousness and anxiety, for none of the pseudopatients really believed that they would be admitted so easily. Indeed, their shared fear was that they would be immediately exposed as frauds and greatly embarrassed. Moreover, many of them had never visited a psychiatric ward; even those who had, nevertheless had some genuine fears about what might happen to them. Their nervousness, then, was quite appropriate to the novelty of the hospital setting, and it abated rapidly.

Apart from that short-lived nervousness, the pseudopatient behaved on the ward as he behaved "normally." The pseudopatient spoke to patients and staff as he might ordinarily. Because there is uncommonly little to do on a psychiatric ward, he attempted to engage others in conversation. When asked by staff how he was feeling, he indicated that he was fine, that he no longer experienced symptoms. He responded to instructions from attendants, to calls for medication (which was not swallowed), and to dining-hall instructions. Beyond such activities as were available to him on the admissions ward, he spent his time writing down his observations about the ward, its patients, and the staff. Initially, these notes were written "secretly," but as it soon became clear that no one much cared, they were subsequently written on standard tablets of paper in such public places as the dayroom. No secret was made of these activities.

The pseudopatient, very much as a true psychiatric patient, entered a hospital with no foreknowledge of when he would be discharged. Each was told that he would have to get out by his own devices, essentially by convincing the staff that he was sane. The psychological stresses associated with hospitalization were considerable, and all but one of the pseudopatients desired to be discharged almost immediately after being admitted. They were, therefore, motivated not only to behave sanely, but to be paragons of cooperation. That their behavior was in no way disruptive is confirmed by nursing reports, which have been obtained on most of the patients. These reports uniformly indicate that the patients were "friendly," "cooperative," and "exhibited no abnormal indications."

The Normal Are Not Detectably Sane

Despite their public "show" of sanity, the pseudopatients were never detected. Admitted, except in one case, with a diagnosis of schizophrenia, each was discharged with a diagnosis of schizophrenia "in remission." The label "in remission" should in no way be dismissed as a formality, for at no time during any hospitalization had any question been raised about any pseudopatient's simulation. Nor are there any indications in the hospital records that the pseudopatient's status was suspect. Rather, the evidence is strong that once labeled schizophrenic, the pseudopatient was stuck with that label. If the pseudopatient was to be discharged, he must naturally be "in remission"; but he was not sane, nor, in the institution's view, had he ever been sane.

The uniform failure to recognize sanity cannot be attributed to the quality of the hospitals, for although there were considerable variations among them, several are considered excellent. Nor can it be alleged that there was simply not enough time to observe the pseudo-patients. Length of hospitalization ranged from 7 to 52 days, with an average of 19 days. The pseudopatients were not, in fact, carefully observed, but this failure clearly speaks more to traditions within psychiatric hospitals than to lack of opportunity.

Finally, it cannot be said that the failure to recognize the pseudopatients' sanity was due to the fact that they were not behaving sanely. Though there was clearly some tension present in all of them, their daily visitors could detect no serious behavioral consequences—nor, indeed, could other patients. It was quite common for the patients to "detect" the pseudopatients' sanity. During the first three hospitalizations, when accurate counts were kept, 35 of a total of 118 patients on the admissions ward voiced their suspicions, some vigorously. "You're not crazy. You're a journalist, or a professor [referring to the continual note taking]. You're checking up on the hospital." While most of the patients were reassured by the pseudopatient's insistence that he had been sick before he came in but was fine now, some continued to believe that the pseudopatient was sane throughout his hospitalization. The fact that the patients often recognized normality when staff did not raises important questions.

Failure to detect sanity during the course of hospitalization may be due to the fact that physicians operate with a strong bias toward what statisticians call the type 2 error. That is, physicians are more inclined to call a healthy person sick (a false positive, type 2) than a sick person healthy (a false negative, type 1). The reasons for this are not hard to find: it is clearly more dangerous to misdiagnose illness than health. Better to err on the side of caution, to suspect illness even among the healthy.

But what holds for medicine does not hold equally well for psychiatry. Medical illnesses, though unfortunate, are not commonly pejorative. Psychiatric diagnoses, on the contrary, carry with them personal, legal, and social stigmas. It was therefore important to see whether the tendency toward diagnosing the sane insane could be reversed. The following experiment was arranged at a research and teaching hospital whose staff had heard these findings but doubted that such an error could occur in their hospital. The staff was informed that at some time during the following three months, one or more pseudopatients would attempt to be admitted into the psychiatric hospital. Each staff member was asked to rate each patient who presented himself at admissions or on the ward according to the likelihood that the patient was a pseudopatient. A 10-point scale was used, with a 1 and 2 reflecting high confidence that the patient was a pseudopatient.

Judgments were obtained on 193 patients who were admitted for psychiatric treatment. All staff who had had sustained contact with or primary responsibility for the patient—attendants, nurses, psychiatrists, physicians, and psychologists—were asked to make judgments. Forty-one patients were alleged, with high confidence, to be pseudopatients by at least one member of the staff. Twenty-three were considered suspect by at least one psychiatrist. Nineteen were suspected by one psychiatrist *and* one other staff member. Actually, no genuine pseudopatient (at least from my group) presented himself during this period.

The experiment is instructive. It indicates that the tendency to designate sane people as insane can be reversed when the stakes (in this case, prestige and diagnostic acumen) are high. But what can be said of the 19 persons who were suspected of being "sane" by one psychiatrist and another staff member? Were these people truly "sane," or was it rather the case that in the course of avoiding the type 2 error the staff tended to make more errors of the first sort—calling the crazy "sane"? There is no way of knowing. But one thing is certain: any diagnostic process that lends itself so readily to massive errors of this sort cannot be a very reliable one.

The Stickiness of Psychodiagnostic Labels

Beyond the tendency to call the healthy sick—a tendency that accounts better for diagnostic behavior on admission than it does for such behavior after a lengthy period of exposure—the data speak to the massive role of labeling in psychiatric assessment. Having once been labeled schizophrenic, there is nothing the pseudopatient can do to overcome the tag. The tag profoundly colors others' perceptions of him and his behavior. . . .

As far as I can determine, diagnoses were in no way affected by the relative health of the circumstances of a pseudopatient's life. Rather, the reverse occurred: the perception of his circumstances was shaped entirely by the diagnosis. A clear example of such translation is found in the case of a pseudopatient who had had a close relationship with his mother but was rather remote from his father during his early childhood. During adolescence and beyond, however, his father became a close friend, while his relationship with his mother cooled. His present relationship with his wife was characteristically close and warm. Apart from occasional angry exchanges, friction was minimal. The children had rarely been spanked. Surely there is nothing especially pathological about such a history. Indeed, many readers may see a similar pattern in their own experiences, with no markedly deleterious consequences. Observe, however, how such a history was translated in the psychopathological context, this from the case summary prepared after the patient was discharged.

> This white 39-year-old male . . . manifests a long history of considerable ambivalence in close relationships, which begins in early chidhood. A warm

relationship with his mother cools during his adolescence. A distant relationship to his father is described as becoming very intense. Affective stability is absent. His attempts to control emotionality with his wife and children are punctuated by angry outbursts and, in the case of the children, spankings. And while he says that he has several good friends, one senses considerable ambivalence embedded in those relationships also. . . .

The facts of the case were unintentionally distorted by the staff to achieve consistency with a popular theory of the dynamics of a schizophrenic reaction. . . .

All pseudopatients took extensive notes publicly. Under ordinary circumstances, such behavior would have raised questions in the minds of observers, as, in fact, it did among patients. Indeed, it seemed so certain that the notes would elicit suspicion that elaborate precautions were taken to remove them from the ward each day. But the precautions proved needless. The closest any staff member came to questioning these notes occurred when one pseudopatient asked his physician what kind of medication he was receiving and began to write down the response. "You needn't write it," he was told gently. "If you have trouble remembering, just ask me again."

If no questions were asked of the pseudopatients, how was their writing interpreted? Nursing records for three patients indicate that the writing was seen as an aspect of their pathological behavior. "Patient engages in writing behavior" was the daily nursing comment on one of the pseudopatients who was never questioned about his writing. Given that the patient is in the hospital, he must be psychologically disturbed. And given that he is disturbed, continual writing must be a behavioral manifestation of that disturbance, perhaps a subset of the compulsive behaviors that are sometimes correlated with schizophrenia. . . .

It is not known why powerful impressions of personality traits such as "crazy" or "insane," arise. Conceivably, when the origins of and stimuli that give rise to a behavior are remote or unknown, or when the behavior strikes us as immutable, trait labels regarding the *behaver* arise. When, on the other hand, the origins and stimuli are known and available, discourse is limited to the behavior itself. Thus, I may hallucinate because I am sleeping, or I may hallucinate because I have ingested a peculiar drug. These are termed sleep-induced hallucinations, or dreams, and drug-induced hallucinations, respectively. But when the stimuli to my hallucinations are unknown, that is called craziness, or schizophrenia—as if that inference were somehow as illuminating as the others.

The Experience of Psychiatric Hospitalization

The term "mental illness" is of recent origin. It was coined by persons who were humane in their inclinations and who wanted very much to raise the station of (and the public's sympathies toward) the psychologically disturbed from that of witches and "crazies" to one that was akin to the physically ill. And they were at least partially successful, for the treatment of the mentally ill *has* improved considerably over the years. But although treatment has improved, it is doubtful that people really regard the mentally ill in the same way that they view the physically ill. A broken leg is something one recovers from, but mental illness allegedly endures forever. A broken leg does not threaten the observer, but a crazy schizophrenic? There is by now a host of evidence that attitudes toward the mentally ill are characterized by fear, hostility, aloofness, suspicion, and dread. The mentally ill are society's lepers.

That such attitudes infect the general population is perhaps not surprising, only upsetting. But that they affect the professionals—attendants, nurses, physicians, psychologists, and social workers—who treat and deal with the mentally ill is more disconcerting, both because such attitudes are self-evidently pernicious and because they are unwitting. Most mental health professionals would insist that they are sympathetic toward the mentally ill, that they are neither avoidant nor hostile. But it is more likely that an exquisite ambivalence characterizes their relations with psychiatric patients, such that their avowed impulses are only part of their entire attitude. Negative attitudes are there too and can easily be detected. Such attitudes should not surprise us. They are the natural offspring of the labels patients wear and the places in which they are found.

Consider the structure of the typical psychiatric hospital. Staff and patients are strictly segregated. Staff have their own living space, including their dining facilities, bathrooms, and assembly places. The glassed quarters that contain the professional staff, which the pseudopatients came to call "the cage," sit out on every dayroom. The staff emerge primarily for caretaking purposes—to give medication, to conduct a therapy or group meeting, to instruct or reprimand a patient. Otherwise, staff keep to themselves, almost as if the disorder that afflicts their charges is somehow catching.

So much is patient-staff segregation the rule that in four public hospitals in which an attempt was made to measure the degree to which staff and patients mingle, it was necessary to use "time out of the staff cage" as the operational measure. . . . On the average, daytime nurses emerged from the cage 11.5 times per shift, including instances when they left the ward entirely (range, 4 to 39 times). Late afternoon and night nurses were even less available, emerging on the average 9.4 times per shift (range, 4 to 41 times). Data on early morning nurses, who arrived usually after midnight and departed at 8 A.M., are not available because patients were asleep during most of this period.

Physicians, especially psychiatrists, were even less available. They were rarely seen on the wards. Quite commonly, they would be seen only when they arrived and departed, with the remaining time being spent in their offices or in the cage. On the average, physicians emerged on the ward 6.7 times per day (range, 1 to 17 times). It proved difficult to make an accurate estimate in this regard, because physicians often maintained hours that allowed them to come and go at different times.

The hierarchical organization of the psychiatric hospital has been commented on before, but the latent meaning of that kind of organization is worth noting again. Those with the most power have the least to do with patients, and those with the least power are most involved with them. Recall, however, that the acquisition of role-appropriate behaviors occurs mainly through the observation of others, with the most powerful having the most influence. Consequently, it is understandable that attendants not only spend more time with patients than do any other members of the staff—that is required by their station in the hierarchy—but also, insofar as they learn from their superiors' behavior, spend as little time with patients as they can. Attendants are seen mainly in the cage, which is where the models, the action, and the power are.

I turn now to a different set of studies, these dealing with staff response to patient-initiated contact. It has long been known that the amount of time a person spends with you can be an index of your significance to him. If he initiates and maintains eye contact, there is reason to believe that he is considering your requests and needs. If he pauses to chat or actually stops and talk, there is added reason to infer that he is individuating you. In four hospitals, the pseudopatient approached the staff member with a request that took the following form: "Pardon me, Mr. [or Dr. or Mrs.] X, could you tell me when I will be eligible for grounds privileges?" (or ". . . when I will be presented at the staff meeting?" or ". . . when I am likely to be discharged?"). Though the content of the question varied according to the appropriateness of the target and the pseudopatient's (apparent) current needs, the form was always a courteous and relevant request for information. Care was taken never to approach a particular member of the staff more than once a day, lest the staff member become suspicious or irritated. In examining these data, remember that the behavior of the pseudopatients was neither bizarre nor disruptive. One could indeed engage in good conversation with them. . . .

Minor differences among these four institutions were overwhelmed by the degree to which staff avoided continuing contacts that patients had initiated. By far, their most common response consisted of either a brief response to the question, offered while they were "on the move" and with head averted, or no response at all.

The encounter frequently took the following bizarre form. Pseudopatient: "Pardon me, Dr. X. Could you tell me when I am eligible for grounds privileges?" Physician: "Good morning, Dave. How are you today?" (Moves off without waiting for a response.) . . .

It is instructive to compare these data with data recently obtained at Stanford University. It has been alleged that large and eminent universities are characterized by faculty who are so busy that they have no time for students. For this comparison, a young lady approached individual faculty members who seemed to be walking purposefully to some meeting or teaching engagement and asked them to the following six questions.

1. "Pardon me, could you direct me to Encina Hall?" (At the medical school: " . . . to the Clinical Research Center?")
2. "Do you know where Fish Annex is?" (There is no Fish Annex at Stanford.)
3. "Do you teach here?"
4. "How does one apply for admission to the college?" (At the medical school: " . . . to the medical school?")
5. "Is it difficult to get in?"
6. "Is there financial aid?"

Without exception, . . . all of the questions were answered. No matter how rushed they were, all respondents not only maintained eye contact but also stopped to talk. Indeed, many of the respondents went out of their way to direct or take the questioner to the office she was seeking, to try to locate "Fish Annex," or to discuss with her the possibilities of being admitted to the university.

Powerlessness and Depersonalization

Eye contact and verbal contact reflect concern and individuation; their absence, avoidance and depersonalization. The data I have presented do not do justice to the rich daily encounters that grew up around matters of depersonalization and avoidance. I have records of patients who were beaten by staff for the sin of having initiated verbal contact. During my own experience, for example, one patient was beaten in the presence of other patients for having approached an attendant and told him, "I like you." Occasionally, punishment meted out to patients for misdemeanors seemed so excessive that it could not be justified by the most radical interpretations of psychiatric canon. Nevertheless, they appeared to go unquestioned. Tempers were often short. A patient who had not heard a call for medication would be roundly excoriated, and the morning attendants would often wake patients with, "Come on, you m——f——s, out of bed!"

Neither anecdotal nor "hard" data can convey the overwhelming sense of powerlessness that invades the individual as he is continually exposed to the depersonalization of the psychiatric hospital. It hardly matters *which* psychiatric hospital—the excellent public ones and the very plush private hospital were better than the rural and shabby ones in this regard, but, again, the features that psychiatric hospitals had in common overwhelmed by far their apparent differences.

Powerlessness was evident everywhere. The patient is deprived of many of his legal rights by dint of his psychiatric commitment. He is shorn of credibility by virtue of his psychiatric label. His freedom of movement is restricted. He cannot initiate contact with the staff, but may only respond to such overtures as they make. Personal privacy is minimal. Patient quarters and possessions can be entered and examined by any staff member, for whatever reason. His personal history and anguish is available to any staff member (often including the "grey lady" and "candy striper" volunteer) who chooses to read his folder, regardless of their therapeutic relationship to him. His personal hygiene and waste evacuation are often monitored. The water closets may have no doors.

At times, depersonalization reached such proportions that pseudopatients had the sense that they were invisible, or at least unworthy of account. Upon being admitted, I and other pseudopatients took the initial physical examinations in a semipublic room, where staff members went about their own business as if we were not there.

On the ward, attendants delivered verbal and occasionally serious physical abuse to patients in the presence of other observing patients, some of whom (the pseudopatients) were writing it all down. Abusive behavior, on the other hand, terminated quite abruptly when other staff members were known to be coming. Staff are credible witnesses. Patients are not.

A nurse unbuttoned her uniform to adjust her brassiere in the presence of an entire ward of viewing men. One did not have the sense that she was being seductive. Rather, she didn't notice us. A group of staff persons might point to a patient in the dayroom and discuss him animatedly, as if he were not there.

One illuminating instance of depersonalization and invisibility occurred with regard to medications. All told, the pseudopatients were administered nearly 2100 pills, including Elavil, Stelazine, Compazine, and Thorazine, to name but a few. (That such a variety of medications should have been administered to patients presenting identical symptoms is itself worthy of note.) Only two were swallowed. The rest were either pocketed or deposited in the toilet. The pseudopatients were not alone in this. Although I have no precise records of how many patients rejected their medications, the pseudopatients frequently found the medications of other patients in the toilet before they deposited their own. As long as they were cooperative, their behavior and the pseudopatients' own in this matter, as in other important matters, went unnoticed throughout.

Reactions to such depersonalization among pseudopatients were intense. Although they had come to the hospital as participant observers and were fully aware that they did not "belong," they nevertheless found themselves caught up in and fighting the process of depersonalization. Some examples: a graduate student in psychology asked his wife to bring his textbooks to the hospital so he could "catch up on his homework"—this despite the elaborate precautions taken to conceal his professional association. The same student, who had trained for quite some time to get into the hospital, and who had looked forward to the experience, "remembered" some drag races that he had wanted to see on the weekend and insisted that he be discharged by that time. Another pseudopatient attempted a romance with a nurse. Subsequently, he informed the staff that he was applying for admission to graduate school in psychology and was very likely to be admitted, since a graduate professor was one of his regular hospital visitors. The same person began to engage in psychotherapy with other patients—all of this as a way of becoming a person in an impersonal environment.

The Sources of Depersonalization

What are the origins of depersonalization? I have already mentioned two. The first are attitudes held by all of us toward the mentally ill—including those who treat them—attitudes characterized by fear, distrust, and horrible expectations on one hand, and benevolent intentions on the other. Our ambivalence leads, in this instance as in others, to avoidance.

Second, and not entirely separate from the first, the hierarchical structure of the psychiatric hospital facilitates depersonalization. Those who are at the top have the least to do with patients, and their behavior inspires the rest of the staff. Average daily contact with psychiatrists, psychologists, residents, and physicians—combined—ranged from 3.9 to 25.1 minutes, with an overall mean of 6.8 (six pseudopatients over a total of 129 days of hospitalization). Included in this average are time spent in the admissions interview, ward meetings in the presence of a senior staff member, group and individual psychotherapy contacts, case presentation conferences, and discharge meetings. Clearly, patients do not spend much time in interpersonal contact with doctoral staff. And doctoral staff serve as models for nurses and attendants.

There are probably other sources. Psychiatric installations are presently in serious financial straits. Staff shortages are pervasive, staff time at a premium. Something has to give, and that something is patient contact. Yet, although financial stresses are realities, too much can be made of them. I have the impression that the psychological forces that result in depersonalization are much stronger than the fiscal ones and that the addition of more staff would not correspondingly improve patient care in this regard. The incidence of staff meetings and the enormous amount of record keeping on patients, for example, have not been reduced as substantially as has patient contact. Priorities exist, even during hard times. Patient contact is not a significant priority in the traditional psychiatric hospital, and fiscal pressures do not account for this. Avoidance and depersonalization may.

Heavy reliance upon psychotropic medication tacitly contributes to depersonalization by convincing staff that treatment is indeed being conducted and that further patient contact may not be necessary. Even here, however, caution needs to be exercised in understanding the role of psychotropic drugs. If patients were powerful rather than powerless, if they were viewed as interesting individuals rather than as diagnostic entities, if they were socially significant rather than social lepers, if their anguish truly and wholly compelled our sympathies and concerns, would we not *seek* contact with them, despite the availability of medications? Perhaps for the pleasure of it all?

The Consequences of Labeling and Depersonalization

Whenever the ratio of what is known to what needs to be known approaches zero, we tend to invent "knowledge" and assume that we understand more than we actually do. We seem unable to acknowledge that we simply don't know. The needs for diagnosis and remediation of behavioral and emotional problems are enormous. But rather than acknowledge that we are just embarking on understanding, we continue to label patients "schizophrenic," "manic-depressive," and "insane," as if in those words we had captured the essence of understanding. The facts of the matter are that we have known for a long time that diagnoses are often not useful or reliable, but we have nevertheless continued to use them. We now know that we cannot distinguish insanity from sanity. It is depressing to consider how that information will be used.

Not merely depressing, but frightening. How many people, one wonders, are sane but not recognized as such in our psychiatric institutions? How many have been needlessly stripped of their privileges of citizenship, from the rights to vote, to drive, and to handle their own accounts? How many have feigned insanity in order to avoid the criminal consequences of their behavior, and, conversely, how many would rather stand trial than live interminably in a psychiatric hospital—but are wrongly thought to be mentally ill? How many have been stigmatized by well-intentioned but nevertheless erroneous diagnoses? On the last point, recall again that a "type 2 error" in psychiatric diagnosis does not have the same consequences it does in medical diagnosis. A diagnosis of cancer that has been found to be in error is cause for celebration. But psychiatric diagnoses are rarely found to be in error. The label sticks, a mark of inadequacy forever.

496 The Anthology

Finally, how many patients might be "sane" outside the psychiatric hospital but seem insane in it—not because craziness resides in them, as it were, but because they are responding to a bizarre setting, one that may be unique to institutions that harbor nether people? Goffman calls the process of socialization to such institutions "mortification"— an apt metaphor that includes the processes of depersonalization that have been described here. And though it is impossible to know whether the pseudopatients' responses to these processes are characteristic of all inmates—they were, after all, not real patients—it is difficult to believe that these processes of socialization to a psychiatric hospital provide useful attitudes or habits of response for living in the "real world."

Summary and Conclusions

It is clear that we cannot distinguish the sane from the insane in psychiatric hospitals. The hospital itself imposes a special environment in which the meanings of behavior can easily be misunderstood. The consequences to patients hospitalized in such an environment—the powerlessness, depersonalization, segregation, mortification, and self-labeling—seem undoubtedly countertherapeutic.

I do not, even now, understand this problem well enough to perceive solutions. But two matters seem to offer some promise. The first concerns the proliferation of community mental health facilities, of crisis intervention centers, of the human potential movement, and of behavior therapies that, for all of their own problems, tend to avoid psychiatric labels, to focus on specific problems and behaviors, and to retain the individual in a relatively nonpejorative environment. Clearly, to the extent that we refrain from sending the distressed to insane places, our impressions of them are less likely to be distorted. (The risk of distorted perceptions, it seems to me, is always present, because we are much more sensitive to an individual's behaviors and verbalizations than we are to the subtle contextual stimuli that often promote them. At issue here is a matter of magnitude. And, as I have shown, the magnitude of distortion is exceedingly high in the extreme context of a psychiatric hospital.)

The second matter that might prove promising speaks to the need to increase the sensitivity of mental health workers and researchers to the Catch-22 position of psychiatric patients. Simply reading materials in this area will help some such workers and researchers. For others, directly experiencing the impact of psychiatric hospitalization will be of enormous use. Clearly, further research into the social psychology of such total institutions will both facilitate treatment and deepen understanding.

[Editor's note: Citations have been omitted.]

Eating Christmas in the Kalahari

Richard Borshay Lee

[NOTE: *The !Kung and other Bushmen speak click languages. In the story, three different clicks are used:*

1. The dental click (/), as in /ai/ai, /ontah, and /gaugo. The click is sometimes written in English as tsk-tsk.

2. The alveopalatal click (!), as in Ben!a and !Kung.

3. The lateral click (//), as in //gom. Clicks function as consonants; a word may have more than one, as in /n!nu.]

The !Kung Bushmen's knowledge of Christmas is thirdhand. The London Missionary Society brought the holiday to the southern Tswana tribes in the early nineteenth century. Later, native catechists spread the idea far and wide among the Bantu-speaking pastoralists, even in the remotest corners of the Kalahari Desert. The Bushmen's idea of the Christmas story, stripped to its essentials, is "praise the birth of white man's god-chief"; what keeps their interest in the holiday high is the Tswana-Herero custom of slaughtering an ox for his Bushmen neighbors as an annual goodwill gesture. Since the 1930's, part of the Bushmen's annual round of activities has included a December congregation at the cattle posts for trading, marriage brokering, and several days of trance-dance feasting at which the local Tswana headman is host.

As a social anthropologist working with !Kung Bushmen, I found that the Christmas ox custom suited my purposes. I had come to the Kalahari to study the hunting and gathering subsistence economy of the !Kung, and to accomplish this it was essential not to provide them with food, share my own food, or interfere in any way with their food-gathering activities. While liberal handouts of tobacco and medical supplies were appreciated, they were scarcely adequate to erase the glaring disparity in wealth between the anthropologist, who maintained a two-month inventory of canned goods, and the Bushmen, who rarely had a day's supply of food on hand. My approach, while paying off in terms of data, left me open to frequent accusations of stinginess and hardheartedness. By their lights, I was a miser.

The Christmas ox was to be my way of saying thank you for the cooperation of the past year; and since it was to be our last Christmas in the field, I determined to slaughter the largest, meatiest ox that money could buy, insuring that the feast and trance dance would be a success.

Through December I kept my eyes open at the wells as the cattle were brought down for watering. Several animals were offered, but none had quite the grossness that I had in mind. Then, ten days before the holiday, a Herero friend led an ox of astonishing size and mass up to our camp. It was solid black, stood five feet high at the shoulder, had a five-foot span of horns, and must have weighed 1,200 pounds on the hoof. Food consumption calculations are my specialty, and I quickly figured that bones and viscera aside, there was enough meat—at least four pounds—for every man, woman, and child of the 150 Bushmen in the vicinity of /ai/ai who were expected at the feast.

Having found the right animal at last, I paid the Herero £20 ($56) and asked him to keep the beast with his herd until Christmas day. The next morning word spread among the people that the big solid black one was the ox chosen by /ontah (my Bushman name; it means, roughly, "whitey") for the Christmas feast. That afternoon I received the first delegation. Ben!a, an outspoken sixty-year-old mother of five, came to the point slowly.

"Where were you planning to eat Christmas?"

"Right here at /ai/ai," I replied.

"Alone or with others?"

"I expect to invite all the people to eat Christmas with me."

"Eat what?"

"I have purchased Yehave's black ox, and I am going to slaughter and cook it."

"That's what we were told at the well but refused to believe it until we heard it from yourself."

"Well, it's the black one," I replied expansively, although wondering what she was driving at.

"Oh, no!" Ben!a groaned, turning to her group. "They were right." Turning back to me she asked, "Do you expect us to eat that bag of bones?"

"Bag of bones! It's the biggest ox at /ai/ai."

"Big, yes, but old. And thin. Everybody knows there's no meat on that old ox. What did you expect us to eat off it, the horns?"

Everybody chuckled at Ben!a's one-liner as they walked away, but all I could manage was a weak grin.

That evening it was the turn of the young men. They came to sit at our evening fire. /gaugo, about my age, spoke to me man-to-man.

"/ontah, you have always been square with us," he lied. "What has happened to change your heart? That sack of guts and bones of Yehave's will hardly feed one camp, let alone all the Bushmen around /ai/ai." And he proceeded to enumerate the seven camps in the /ai/ai vicinity, family by family. "Perhaps you have forgotten that we are not few, but many. Or are you too blind to tell the difference between a proper cow and an old wreck? That ox is thin to the point of death."

"Look, you guys," I retorted, "that is a beautiful animal, and I'm sure you will eat it with pleasure at Christmas."

"Of course we will eat it; it's food. But it won't fill us up to the point where we will have enough strength to dance. We will eat and go home to bed with stomachs rumbling.''

That night as we turned in, I asked my wife, Nancy: ''What did you think of the black ox?''

''It looked enormous to me. Why?''

''Well, about eight different people have told me I got gypped; that the ox is nothing but bones.''

''What's the angle?'' Nancy asked. ''Did they have a better one to sell?''

''No, they just said that it was going to be a grim Christmas because there won't be enough meat to go around. Maybe I'll get an independent judge to look at the beast in the morning.''

Bright and early, Halingisi, a Tswana cattle owner, appeared at our camp. But before I could ask him to give me his opinion on Yehave's black ox, he gave me the eye signal that indicated a confidential chat. We left the camp and sat down.

''/ontah, I'm surprised at you; you've lived here for three years and still haven't learned anything about cattle.''

''But what else can a person do but choose the biggest, strongest animal one can find?'' I retorted.

''Look, just because an animal is big doesn't mean that it has plenty of meat on it. The black one was a beauty when it was younger, but now it is thin to the point of death.''

''Well I've already bought it. What can I do at this stage?''

''Bought it already? I thought you were just considering it. Well, you'll have to kill it and serve it, I suppose. But don't expect much of a dance to follow.''

My spirits dropped rapidly. I could believe that Ben!a and /gaugo just might be putting me on about the black ox, but Halingisi seemed to be an impartial critic. I went around that day feeling as though I had bought a lemon of a used car.

In the afternoon it was Tomazo's turn. Tomazo is a fine hunter, a top trance performer, . . . and one of my most reliable informants. He approached the subject of the Christmas cow as part of my continuing Bushmen education.

''My friend, the way it is with us Bushmen,'' he began, ''is that we love meat. And even more than that, we love fat. When we hunt we always search for the fat ones, the ones dripping with layers of white fat: fat that turns into a clear, thick oil in the cooking pot, fat that slides down your gullet, fills your stomach and gives you a roaring diarrhea,'' he rhapsodized.

''So, feeling as we do,'' he continued, ''it gives us pain to be served such a scrawny thing as Yehave's black ox. It is big, yes, and no doubt its giant bones are good for soup, but fat is what we really crave and so we will eat Christmas this year with a heavy heart.''

The prospect of a gloomy Christmas now had me worried, so I asked Tomazo what I could do about it.

"Look for a fat one, a young one . . . smaller, but fat. Fat enough to make us //*gom* ('evacuate the bowels'), then we will be happy."

My suspicions were aroused when Tomazo said that he happened to know of a young, fat, barren cow that the owner was willing to part with. Was Tomazo working on commission, I wondered? But I dispelled this unworthy thought when we approached the Herero owner of the cow in question and found that he had decided not to sell.

The scrawny wreck of a Christmas ox now became the talk of the /ai/ai water hole and was the first news told to the outlying groups as they began to come in from the bush for the feast. What finally convinced me that real trouble might be brewing was the visit from u!au, an old conservative with a reputation for fierceness. His nickname meant spear and referred to an incident thirty years ago in which he had speared a man to death. He had an intense manner; fixing me with his eyes, he said in clipped tones:

"I have only just heard about the black ox today, or else I would have come here earlier. /ontah, do you honestly think you can serve meat like that to people and avoid a fight?" He paused, letting the implications sink in. "I don't mean fight you, /ontah; you are a white man. I mean a fight between Bushmen. There are many fierce ones here, and with such a small quantity of meat to distribute, how can you give everybody a fair share? Someone is sure to accuse another of taking too much or hogging all the choice pieces. Then you will see what happens when some go hungry while others eat."

The possibility of at least a serious argument struck me as all too real. I had witnessed the tension that surrounds the distribution of meat from a kudu or gemsbok kill, and had documented many arguments that sprang up from a real or imagined slight in meat distribution. The owners of a kill may spend up to two hours arranging and rearranging the piles of meat under the gaze of a circle of recipients before handing them out. And I also knew that the Christmas feast at /ai/ai would be bringing together groups that had feuded in the past.

Convinced now of the gravity of the situation, I went in earnest to search for a second cow; but all my inquiries failed to turn one up.

The Christmas feast was evidently going to be a disaster, and the incessant complaints about the meagerness of the ox had already taken the fun out of it for me. Moreover, I was getting bored with the wisecracks, and after losing my temper a few times, I resolved to serve the beast anyway. If the meat fell short, the hell with it. In the Bushmen idiom, I announced to all who would listen:

"I am a poor man and blind. If I have chosen one that is too old and too thin, we will eat it anyway and see if there is enough meat there to quiet the rumbling of our stomachs."

On hearing this speech, Ben!a offered me a rare word of comfort. "It's thin," she said philosophically, "but the bones will make a good soup."

At dawn Christmas morning, instinct told me to turn over the butchering and cooking to a friend and take off with Nancy to spend Christmas alone in the bush. But curiosity kept me from retreating. I wanted to see what such a scrawny ox looked like on butchering, and if there *was* going to be a fight, I wanted to catch every word of it. Anthropologists are incurable that way.

The great beast was driven up to our dancing ground, and a shot in the forehead dropped it in its tracks. Then, freshly cut branches were heaped around the fallen carcass to receive the meat. Ten men volunteered to help with the cutting. I asked /gaugo to make the breast bone cut. This cut, which begins the butchering process for most large game, offers easy access for removal of the viscera. But it also allows the hunter to spot-check the amount of fat on the animal. A fat game animal carries a white layer up to an inch thick on the chest, while in a thin one, the knife will quickly cut to bone. All eyes fixed on his hand as /gaugo, dwarfed by the great carcass, knelt to the breast. The first cut opened a pool of solid white in the black skin. The second and third cut widened and deepened the creamy white. Still no bone. It was pure fat; it must have been two inches thick.

"Hey /gau," I burst out, "that ox is loaded with fat. What's this about the ox being too thin to bother eating? Are you out of your mind?"

"Fat?" /gau shot back, "You call that fat? This wreck is thin, sick, dead!" And he broke out laughing. So did everyone else. They rolled on the ground, paralyzed with laughter. Everybody laughed except me; I was thinking.

I ran back to the tent and burst in just as Nancy was getting up. "Hey, the black ox. It's fat as hell! They were kidding about it being too thin to eat. It was a joke or something. A put-on. Everyone is really delighted with it!"

"Some joke," my wife replied. "It was so funny that you were ready to pack up and leave /ai/ai."

If it had indeed been a joke, it had been an extraordinarily convincing one, and tinged, I thought, with more than a touch of malice as many jokes are. Nevertheless, that it was a joke lifted my spirits considerably, and I returned to the butchering site where the shape of the ox was rapidly disappearing under the axes and knives of the butchers. The atmosphere had become festive. Grinning broadly, their arms covered with blood well past the elbow, men packed chunks of meat into the big cast-iron cooking pots, fifty pounds to the load, and muttered and chuckled all the while about the thinness and worthlessness of the animal and /ontah's poor judgment.

We danced and ate that ox two days and two nights; we cooked and distributed fourteen potfuls of meat and no one went home hungry and no fights broke out.

But the "joke" stayed in my mind. I had a growing feeling that something important had happened in my relationship with the Bushmen and that the clue lay in the meaning of the joke. Several days later, when most of the people had dispersed back to the bush camps, I raised the question with Hakekgose, a Tswana man who had grown up among the !Kung, married a !Kung girl, and who probably knew their culture better than any other non-Bushman.

"With us whites," I began, "Christmas is supposed to be the day of friendship and brotherly love. What I can't figure out is why the Bushmen went to such lengths to criticize and belittle the ox I had bought for the feast. The animal was perfectly good and their jokes and wisecracks practically ruined the holiday for me."

"So it really did bother you," said Hakekgose. "Well, that's the way they always talk. When I take my rifle and go hunting with them, if I miss, they laugh at me for the rest of the day. But even if I hit and bring one down, it's no better. To them, the kill is always too small or too old or too thin; and as we sit down on the kill site to cook and eat the liver, they keep grumbling, even with their mouths full of meat. They say things like, 'Oh this is awful! What a worthless animal! Whatever made me think that this Tswana rascal could hunt!'"

"Is this the way outsiders are treated?" I asked.

"No, it is their custom; they talk that way to each other too. Go and ask them."

/gaugo had been one of the most enthusiastic in making me feel bad about the merit of the Christmas ox. I sought him out first.

"Why did you tell me the black ox was worthless, when you could see that it was loaded with fat and meat?"

"It is our way," he said smiling. "We always like to fool people about that. Say there is a Bushman who has been hunting. He must not come home and announce like a braggard, 'I have killed a big one in the bush!' He must first sit down in silence until I or someone else comes up to his fire and asks, 'What did you see today?' He replies quietly, 'Ah, I'm no good for hunting. I saw nothing at all [pause] just a little tiny one.' Then I smile to myself," /gaugo continued, "because I know he has killed something big.

"In the morning we make up a party of four or five people to cut up and carry the meat back to the camp. When we arrive at the kill we examine it and cry out, 'You mean to say you have dragged us all the way out here in order to make us cart home your pile of bones? Oh, if I had known it was this thin I wouldn't have come.' Another one pipes up, 'People, to think I gave up a nice day in the shade for this. At home we may be hungry but at least we have nice cool water to drink.' If the horns are big, someone says, 'Did you think that somehow you were going to boil down the horns for soup?'

"To all this you must respond in kind. 'I agree,' you say, 'this one is not worth the effort; let's just cook the liver for strength and leave the rest for the hyenas. It is not too late to hunt today and even a duiker or a steenbok would be better than this mess.'

"Then you set to work nevertheless; butcher the animal, carry the meat back to the camp and everyone eats," /gaugo concluded.

Things were beginning to make sense. Next, I went to Tomazo. He corroborated /gaugo's story of the obligatory insults over a kill and added a few details of his own.

"But," I asked, "why insult a man after he has gone to all that trouble to track and kill an animal and when he is going to share the meat with you so that your children will have something to eat?"

"Arrogance," was his cryptic answer.

"Arrogance?"

"Yes, when a young man kills much meat he comes to think of himself as a chief or a big man, and he thinks of the rest of us as his servants or inferiors. We can't accept this. We refuse one who boasts, for someday his pride will make him kill somebody. So we always speak of his meat as worthless. This way we cool his heart and make him gentle."

"But why didn't you tell me this before?" I asked Tomazo with some heat.

"Because you never asked me," said Tomazo, echoing the refrain that has come to haunt every field ethnographer.

The pieces now fell into place. I had known for a long time that in situations of social conflict with Bushmen I held all the cards. I was the only source of tobacco in a thousand square miles, and I was not incapable of cutting an individual off for noncooperation. Though my boycott never lasted longer than a few days, it was an indication of my strength. People resented my presence at the water hole, yet simultaneously dreaded my leaving. In short I was a perfect target for the charge of arrogance and for the Bushmen tactic of enforcing humility.

I had been taught an object lesson by the Bushmen; it had come from an unexpected corner and had hurt me in a vulnerable area. For the big black ox was to be the one totally generous, unstinting act of my year at /ai/ai, and I was quite unprepared for the reaction I received.

As I read it, their message was this: There are no totally generous acts. All "acts" have an element of calculation. One black ox slaughtered at Christmas does not wipe out a year of careful manipulation of gifts given to serve your own ends. After all, to kill an animal and share the meat with people is really no more than Bushmen do for each other every day and with far less fanfare.

In the end, I had to admire how the Bushmen had played out the farce—collectively straight-faced to the end. Curiously, the episode reminded me of the *Good Soldier Schweik* and his marvelous encounters with authority. Like Schweik, the Bushmen had retained a thoroughgoing skepticism of good intentions. Was it this independence of spirit, I wondered, that had kept them culturally viable in the face of generations of contact with more powerful societies, both black and white? The thought that the Bushmen were alive and well in the Kalahari was strangely comforting. Perhaps, armed with that independence and with their superb knowledge of their environment, they might yet survive the future.

The Hard Part Was the Hard Parts

Pat Shipman

Place of Thieves, that's what they called it. In Masai, the name is Lainyamok. Apparently the site had been used as a hideout by cattle rustlers years before. At the time, Rick Potts, my collaborator on the project, and I passed it off as one of those charming ethnographic anecdotes. We knew that the Masai, the tall, handsome, cattle-herding people of East Africa, had a history of stock theft rivaling that of the Wild West. Maybe the name of the fossil site should have served as a warning. But we never imagined we'd be robbed there, since we owned no goats, sheep, or cows. The theft was of a still dearer possession: a fond (and entirely reasonable) hypothesis. . . .

Magadi is an alkaline soda lake, the most extreme of the many soda lakes that dot the floor of the Rift Valley in Kenya. Each time we drove to Lainyamok, Rick and I were struck anew with its surreal quality. From a distance, the lake shows up as a bizarre pinkish-white expanse; the image gets more unearthly as you approach. At close range, you can see that two to three feet of dead-white solidified soda floats on the water. The water itself is an unappealing, murky, brownish-black where it's deep. In the shallows it's thick with a peculiar alga that colors it New Wave fuschia and pink. An unmistakable sulphurous odor pervades the area. Only this special alga and one species of fish can survive in the lake. And Magadi township, on its shore, is said to be the hottest place on earth that's inhabited year-round by humans. . . .

I first saw Lainyamok some years ago, when Bill Bishop took me and several other colleagues to see the site. I was impressed by the litter of stone tools and by the extraordinarily good preservation of bones. Unfortunately, Bill died before he could complete his work there. In 1982, haunted by what I'd seen, I invited Rick to collaborate in studying the site. That year we did some prospecting of the area and examined and identified the few hundred bones and artifacts from Lainyamok picked up by various scientists over the years. . . .

With Bill's map in hand, Rick and I began to see fascinating features of the site. First, all the bones were derived from a single layer, a reworked tuff, or volcanic ash, of a distinctive khaki color, that had been deposited along the margins of the ancient lake. Because a volcanic layer was involved, the site could probably be dated; because the bones all came from a single geological bed, they might be a realistic sample of the local fauna at a single point in time. Further, if more hominid bones were found, we might be able to determine whether the species was *Homo erectus* or archaic *Homo sapiens.* Because the transition between the two is still poorly documented, it would be of tremendous importance to have a dated site and a good record of fauna associated with either species. Thus, working the site systematically would be likely to reveal a great deal about the evolution of our ancestors.

The second and third points involved the arrangement and identity of the fossils visible on the surface. The bones were distributed in small clumps or patches, a meter or two in diameter, and separated by wide barren areas. Neither of us had seen or read of such a distribution at any other fossil site. Even more interesting was the fact that each patch appeared to contain the partial skeleton of one or two animals. This pattern of distribution reminded us strongly of what had been called single-animal scatters at modern hunter-gatherer sites where animals had been killed or butchered. It was an almost irresistible hypothesis that we were looking at places where similar events had occurred perhaps half a million years ago. This tentative interpretation was strengthened by the fact that artifacts were often near these bone patches, although there was undoubtedly a general scatter of artifacts across the entire surface. . . .

In 1984 the Lainyamok Research Project got under way. An important member of our team was Joseph Mutaba, on loan from the National Museums of Kenya, where he is Chief Preparator, who supervised our Kenyan crew. Rick and I had also invited Ellery Ingall, a graduate student in geology, now at Yale, to revise and extend Bill's work on the geological setting. Because the Kenyans found "Ellery" a difficult and unfamiliar name, he quickly became known as Duke (his middle name), which lent an additional Wild West air to the project. Another member of our team was my niece Karen Walker, who's now in graduate school in archaeology at Yale.

Our first task was to revise Bill's map, since significant erosion had occurred in the years since he had been at the site, and to use that map to collect all fossils and artifacts on the surface. We laid out a grid of 20-meter squares, each designated by a number and letter. The specimens on the surface of each square were then collected systematically. In this way, we were able to map densities of specimens in different areas and thus target likely areas for excavation. Some squares yielded hundreds of stone tools, bones, and bone fragments, each of which was numbered and bagged separately. Others yielded only stone tools, and still others were nearly barren.

The Masai herds had crossed and re-crossed the site for years, and it took some weeks for us to persuade the elders to divert the cattle so they didn't come straight through our excavations (and our tents) twice daily. It was hard to assess how much the herds had disrupted the site, but we found that most bones that were originally part of one animal were still within a 20-meter square. Of course, the herds had broken fossils, too. But the fragments weren't widely dispersed, and many splinters could be refitted into whole bones. The surface collecting and re-mapping greatly increased the number of specimens as well as showing us where fossils had been exposed by erosion of the sediment.

In the next phase, Duke measured sections, took notes on geological structures, and sampled different beds for dating and quantitative chemical analysis in the U.S. He was often trailed by one or two boys who watched everything he did. Karen and I had our own audience of women who liked to watch us excavate. They found us fascinating, partly because we were wearing shorts and tank tops, partly because Masai women never dig in the earth, and partly because of my straight blonde hair.

Later, Duke joined the rest of us in excavating the bone patches and recording the spatial position and association of all *in situ* material. We also recorded the compass orientation and dip, or degree of declination, of each bone as it lay in the rock, since both are strongly influenced by water currents. Although we didn't think the bones had been sorted or moved by water, we wanted to gather the data to test this alternative, unlikely, hypothesis. After weeks of such work, several points were clear.

First, the bone patches were real, a genuine reflection of what had gone on in the past, not just a recent accident. One of them even yielded a partial hominid femur, or thigh bone, that more closely resembled *Homo sapiens* than *Homo erectus* in anatomical details. Although we excavated the obvious bone patches, we also sank several long trenches into the hard khaki layer in areas between the patches. This made it excruciatingly apparent that if there were no bones protruding from the rock, there were none beneath it either. The barren areas between patches were truly barren.

Second, each patch contained bones of many more animals than we'd thought. The richest yielded the remains—often including whole limbs—of at least 16, yet the patch was only two meters long and a meter deep! This was a much denser concentration than we'd expected.

Third, carnivores were even more abundant than the initial study showed. They made up 16 of 53 taxa at the site and approximately 15 to 20 per cent of the individual animals in the fauna. This finding stopped us cold, since carnivores constitute only five to ten per cent of living faunas. Quite simply, carnivores have to be rare in any animal community or they quickly run out of prey to eat. It seemed impossible that carnivores were two to three times as abundant in the Middle Pleistocene fauna as in any modern fauna we knew of. Therefore, we reasoned that whatever or whoever concentrated the bones into patches at Lainyamok selected carnivore remains way out of proportion to their abundance in the then-living community. Could this have been the action of hominids trying to eliminate competitors? If so, we'd expect to find tools consistently associated with the bone patches and lots of cut marks on the bones.

At this juncture, the hypothesis disintegrated. For all that the surface collection yielded several thousand stone tools, we found only twelve in the rock, and most of those weren't associated with bone patches. As for cut marks, we found only a few dozen, of which just two show some of the microscopic features we expect to see in marks made by stone tools. In short, except for the fact that at least one left a leg in one of these patches, there was almost no evidence that hominids had anything to do with forming them.

There were still the thousands of stone tools to be explained, but that was all too simple. Stone tools never die. Bones or fossils can be destroyed in any number of ways, but stone tools are almost impossible to get rid of. They sit quietly on land surfaces nearly eternally, surviving weathering, water transport, sedimentary abrasion, trampling hooves, root action, and time with stony calm. There's no telling where ours came from. Of course, they might have been derived from several small archaeological sites destroyed by the erosion of the khaki layer. It would be bad luck if erosion had preferentially destroyed the areas where the stone tools lay, but odder things have happened. Equally plausibly, the tools may have been eroded from higher beds laid down later than the fossils. Or they may have come from archaeological sites some unknown distance away, only to be swept up and transported to the site with the tuffs, and later concentrated by erosion on the remaining surface. There's little evidence on which to choose among these alternatives.

The other question we're pursuing as analysis continues is: What concentrated the bones into such dense, discrete patches? Water action is a hypothesis we can probably eliminate. If the remains had been transported very far, the high frequency of articulated and associated bones would be most unlikely—especially considering that large animals like zebras and elands are common at Lainyamok. However, the bones in the three biggest patches do show preferred orientations, a feature of bones deposited by a current. The problem is that the orientation of two of the patches is at right angles to the third. This fact could be explained as the effect of a meandering channel, but the patches are very close together for this to be true, and the sediments show none of the features of channel deposits.

Our best guess—I hesitate to label this an "interpretation" or "hypothesis," having been spectacularly wrong about this site before—is that *carnivores*, not hominids, were primarily responsible for forming the Lainyamok bone patches. Modern carnivores often take bones back to their lairs, presumably for leisurely snacks. Over time, some build up huge concentrations of bones within the confines of their lairs. To test this guess further, we're comparing the representation of different skeletal elements, the patterns of damage, and the abundance of different species in these patches and in modern carnivore lair assemblages. One comforting fact is that bones collected by modern brown hyenas show high frequencies of carnivores, probably as a result of competition between carnivores over kills. However, I'd feel a lot better about the carnivore lair idea if there were any sedimentary evidence for lairs—which there isn't. Were lairs dug into the fine, soft, lake margin sediments in the wet season, only to collapse without a trace in the dry season? Would bones in a long, narrow carnivore lair develop a preferred orientation as the carnivores moved in and out? Maybe. Or maybe not. We don't know yet.

Why write about the Place of Thieves then, when the only clear answer is that it has nothing to do with human evolution? Because in an odd sort of way, Lainyamok has everything to do with human evolution. At worst, human evolution is a just-so story. What makes the study of Lainyamok a tale I can recount without blushing is that, at best, paleoanthropology is *science*. We didn't sit back after the preliminary analysis and stroke our favorite interpretation like a lap cat. To tell the truth, that would have been easier, and I wouldn't now be nursing my sense of loss. But we stuck our necks out, formulated tests of our hypothesis, and went to Kenya to collect the data. Along the way, we got ambushed by some pretty tough facts that we're struggling to subdue with a substitute hypothesis.

Stories of good ideas that got shot down are more common in science than many will admit. No one likes to tell of his "failures," and they rarely make their way into textbooks. But the failures in science demonstrate how it works, teaching us fundamental lessons that are more enduring than the particulars of any theory.

One of the great truths about science is that if you never test your hypothesis, you might as well go home, because you aren't doing science. All the clever explanations in the world aren't worth a plugged nickel if you can't tell whether they're right or wrong. In this context, right means only not yet proved wrong. Most theories that have been extensively tested and not yet proved wrong are accepted as fact—or as close enough to fact to be treated as such. We don't, after all, worry too much about whether or not the sun will come up tomorrow, which is only a manifestation of the theory that the earth revolves around the sun.

Another great truth is that this continual testing isn't done in the calm, dispassionate, and downright noble way that old movies would have you believe. Indeed no. There are few more passionate attachments than that between a scientist and a pet theory, the one lovingly nurtured since its birth as a vague, itchy intuition. Part of the passion arises from the sheer fun of pitting your wits against a recalcitrant world that refuses to reveal its ways until you outsmart it. And then, if you succeed, there is that lovely elation of suddenly glimpsing what you believe is the truth of the matter. The other side of the coin is that there are few crueler moments than the one in which you watch your own splendid idea drop like a bad guy with a belly full of bullets.

What follows the bitter disappointment is a rekindling of hope. Maybe you did the experiment wrong; maybe your predictions were flawed at the outset; maybe just a tiny little modification in the theory will stretch it enough to incorporate the new findings. So you rework your ideas, review the data, think it all out again with renewed energy, all the while fighting the notion that you were fundamentally wrong and hoping that you were only wrong in some minor way. In time, your theory is either improved and renewed or stretched so thin that you see through the fabric and reluctantly give it up.

In the experimental sciences, like chemistry or cell biology, the tests of the theories are literally tests performed in the laboratory. Paleoanthropology and other historical sciences involve a different sort of testing and experimentation. The question here is not what *will* happen when the experiment is performed but what *did* happen when the experiment *was* performed. Another way of expressing this is to say that experimental sciences deal in predictions, whereas historical sciences deal in retrodictions. In effect, the experiment has already been conducted, by someone else, and the trick is to discover what the experiment was and thus what the results mean. The tests of paleontological hypotheses lie in the features of new fossils or of new sites, or sometimes in innovative analyses that reveal new facts about known material.

The take-home message here is twofold. First, the testing itself is a crucial component of any type of science—what effectively distinguishes the sciences from both the humanities and such chimera as creation science. Second, the remarkable and even admirable thing is that this testing proceeds despite the emotional investment of the scientists in particular theories. In short, the failures of science are often its greatest successes.

Stowaways on the Hummingbird Express

Robert K. Colwell

To our eyes, the red and orange flowers of hummingbird-pollinated plants stand out in the deep shade of the rain forest like rubies on green velvet. To hummingbirds—whose range of color vision is even greater than ours—the contrast must be just as striking. But the rich world of odors is closed to hummingbirds, and our own poor olfactory equipment is little better.

The perennial human daydream to fly like a bird surely has its roots, in part, in the similarity of our sensory worlds. Who would not welcome the chance to be a tropical hummingbird for a day, given proper training? The exhilaration of fast and agile flight, the high-calorie diet, the beauty of the forest—all this we can envy and imagine.

But now enter the same world on a different scale. Imagine yourself a mite just twice the size of the period at the end of this sentence. You are having a breakfast of nectar and pollen with your family and neighbors inside the orange-red, inch-long flower of a *Hamelia* plant at the edge of a rain forest clearing. You have no eyes and need none, because your four pairs of legs and your body are equipped with precisely arranged, minute hairs, called setae, that provide exact information about your special world. When you meet another mite in your flower, a quick touch with your foreleg tells you its sex and age, and the rate of encounter tells you how many other mites share your flower. You can even ''smell'' with some very special setae on the tips of your forelegs. Although neither hummingbirds nor humans can smell your flower, it has a distinct and very important fragrance for you. It smells like home, and home means safety, your own kind, mates, and food.

Suddenly you sense the vibrant approach of a hummingbird outside the flower. A half second later a bill sixty times the length of your body is thrust deep into your home and you must dodge the rapidly licking tongue that is draining your larder. In the one to five seconds before the hummingbird leaves for the next flower, you must make a decision that will affect the rest of your life. What are the future prospects for food, mates, and the welfare of your offspring on this branch of this *Hamelia* plant, compared with the chance that a risky journey will turn up better prospects elsewhere?

If you decide to leave, you dash up the bill of the visiting hummingbird and run into its nostril, and the odyssey begins. On board, inside the bird's nasal cavity, the accommodations are primitive. There is nothing to eat or drink. The place is crawling not only with your own kind but also with aliens of other species of hummingbird flower mites, hitching rides to their own promised land. You will know them by their smell, perhaps, and by the strange arrangement of their setae—long where yours are short, straight where yours are so beautifully curved.

But the ventilaiton on this feathered freighter is absolutely first-class. A hundred times every minute or so, a hurricane of fresh air rushes in. More than just a source of oxygen, the hummingbird's respiration acts as an odor pump, constantly updating information on the outside world. What you await is that familiar smell—the odor of your own host plant, *Hamelia.* The hummingbird may visit the flowers of half a dozen other plant species, and the aliens on board may come and go, but you wait until the scent of *Hamelia* tells you the bird has its bill in the flower. You have one to five seconds to disembark. With luck, if you are a male, you will find females in need of a mate in your new home; if you are a mated female, you will find that a nearly empty flower, with a male or two present to replenish your supply of sperm, would be an ideal place to start your own dynasty.

A primary research journal would probably scorn the shamelessly dramatic account you have just read. Yet every good naturalist learns to "see into the life of things," as Darwin put it, in part by identifying with the organisms studied. Even botanists do it. The danger, of course (and the reason for the taboo on exposing such musings in scientific print), is that we may unwittingly and inappropriately impose human capabilities, limitations, or even values on nonhuman organisms. For example, a mite certainly makes a "decision" in a very different sense than we do.

Fortunately, our understanding of the biology of hummingbird flower mites rests on more than daydreams. I first stumbled on the existence of these mites and guessed their relationship with flowers and hummingbirds in 1969 in the Costa Rican highlands. In succeeding years, the project that began at that time broadened geographically and scientifically as my colleagues and I developed new techniques of study and a deeper understanding of the daily lives of hummingbird flower mites. Peter Feinsinger, of the University of Florida, an authority on tropical hummingbirds, has collaborated generously, and my doctoral students, David Dobkin, Amy Heyneman, and Shahid Naeem, have poked their own noses into the flowers of *Hamelia* and other hummingbird plants in intensive field research in California, Mexico, Costa Rica, and Trinidad. Barry O'Connor, of the University of Michigan, has scientifically described and named many of the new mite species we have found.

Hummingbird flower mites are freeloaders. As far as we can tell, they do nothing of note for their host plants or for hummingbirds. Yet their survival depends on the interdependence of birds and flowers, which are mutually linked by the exchange of nectar for pollination service. A closer look at hummingbirds and plants reveals the way this network operates. . . .

Hummingbird flower mites are very discriminating in regard to their host plants. In the lowland tropics, each species typically occupies only a single host plant species, which blooms all year. By contrast, mite species at high elevations and high latitudes, where flowering is more seasonal and less reliable, usually have a choice of two or more host species that they often use sequentially. In most cases there is only one species of hummingbird flower mite per plant species, but in a few cases there are two—always a *Rhinoseius* species and a *Proctolaelaps* species, never two species of the same mite genus. . . .

Hitching a ride on a hummingbird requires timing and agility. Taking the length of the mite as two-hundredths of an inch (some species are smaller), the bill length of the bird as about one and a quarter inches (some are longer), and allowing a generous five-second feeding visit by the bird, the mite must run as fast as a cheetah, for its size, to make it into the nostril before the bird moves on. (In other words, both hummingbird flower mites and cheetahs can run about twelve body lengths per second. We have actually clocked the mites at this speed in wind sprints around the lip of a test tube.)

"Deplaning" presents new difficulties. Before racing down the bill into a flower, the mites must first determine whether or not the flower is of their own host species. Our records for many thousands of mites show that no more than one in two hundred has disembarked in the wrong flower. Yet many hummingbirds visit several species of plants in an hour's time, and often each plant has its own species of hummingbird flower mite. How do they know when to get off?

By far the most likely source of information is odor. With the bird's bill in a flower, mites in the bird's nostrils could quickly determine the species of the flower and act accordingly, based on odors provided by the bird's rapid respiration. Our evidence is indirect but convincing.

Given a choice of nectars in a T chamber, hummingbird flower mites choose nectar from their own host plant species. In Trinidad, for example, we offered the mite *Proctolaelaps kirmsii*, which lives in the flowers of *Hamelia patens*, a choice between nectar from uninhabited flowers of *Hamelia* and equally "virgin" nectar from flowers of *Centropogon cornutus*, the home of another mite. We put a drop of *Hamelia* nectar in the tip of a tiny glass capillary tube and a drop of *Centropogon* nectar in another. The open ends of the two tubes lead into an enclosed three-way "intersection" in a small block of acrylic. The third entrance to the intersection (the leg of the T) is another capillary tube with a mite from *Hamelia* in it. Twenty identical chambers were simultaneously set up. We kept track of the location of each mite in its chamber over a period of hours.

The mites in this experiment strongly preferred the nectar of their natural host plant—nearly all of them ended up in the tubes with *Hamelia* nectar, rather than in the tubes with "alien" *Centropogon* nectar. But when we put mites from *Centropogon* (another species, *Proctolaelaps glaucis*) in the same setup, they preferred *Centropogon* to *Hamelia* nectar. The mites are even more consistent in nature, where they are presented with one host plant odor at a time in a moving stream of air rather than two odors in still air.

Many species of hummingbird flower mites from Trinidad, Mexico, Costa Rica, and California have participated in our T-chamber experiments. A consistent pattern emerges. Each species prefers its own host nectar to the nectar of other species of mite plants. The mites also choose their own host nectar over sugar water of the same concentration and over nectar from miteless plants, that is, hummingbird-visited species that never support hummingbird flower mites. Amy Heyneman, who has analyzed dozens of nectars from both kinds of plants, has found biochemical differences between the two groups of nectars. Our field experiments, however, show that, within broad limits, the host nectar of one mite species is nutritionally acceptable to other mite species in the same habitat. We forced mites to live in newly opened, unoccupied host flowers of a plant normally inhabited by another mite species. A nylon mesh bag excluded hummingbirds and thereby prevented escape of the mites, many of which survived to reproduce successfully.

Why, then, are the mites so particular about the host plants they actually use? If every flower were densely populated with mites, competition among mite species for nectar might explain the adherence of each mite species to certain host plant species. However, the density of mites is quite low, relative to the nectar available, so competition between mite species is not a likely explanation for the very rigid plant-mite affiliation. Another possible explanation is that each mite species aggressively excludes "aliens" from its host plant. But most pairs of mite species get along quite amicably in laboratory tests. Moreover, certain pairs of species share the same host plant on a regular basis.

The explanation I favor for host allegiance is that hummingbird flower mites use host plants as a way of finding mates. Once a particular host plant species becomes the most popular jumping-off place for a given mite species, the mating success of mites that get off elsewhere will suffer, on average. Because in these species both males and females must mate many times to achieve their maximum reproductive potential, mites of either sex that disembark at the correct host plant will leave more descendants.

If I am right in thinking that plant affiliation evolved among hummingbird flower mites in large part through differences in mating success, then host affiliation can be viewed as the product of sexual selection. Darwin first drew the important distinction between evolutionary changes based on inherited differences in survival rate and in the potential for reproduction, the process he called natural selection, and evolutionary changes based on differences in mating success in itself, a phenomenon he termed sexual selection.

Darwin believed that natural selection and sexual selection could, at times, conflict. Some physical and behavioral traits of animals are thought to have evolved largely through their role in courtship and mating, perhaps even at the cost of decreased survival. Well-known examples include the beautiful but cumbersome peacock's tail, the elaborate and seemingly arbitrary bowers constructed by male bowerbirds, and the magnificent songs of thrushes, which can attract predators as well as mates.

Just as more elaborate peacock tails presumably increased their owners' success in attracting peahens, strong allegiance to a particular host plant species boosted the mating success of hummingbird flower mites. Like other sexually selected characters, host affiliation involves a degree of arbitrariness and probably carries an element of risk as well. For a mite that has specialized on a single host species, even a brief flowering failure in the plant could mean the mite's extinction.

My co-workers and I suspect such extinctions must be rather common, on the scale of mere thousands of years. However, unless the flowering of all host species were to fail simultaneously from California to Chile and throughout the New World tropics—a most unlikely event—the future of hummingbird flower mites as a group seems assured. Their dynamic evolution all but guarantees that newly evolved species will eventually replace extinct ones, even in the same host plants. Some species even thrive harmlessly on the nectar of garden plants (including African aloes in California) along with the hummingbird visitors that delight the gardener. Despite the risks that they face daily, stowaway mites are well suited to life on the run.

Section Four

Summarizing,
Comparing, and
Evaluating Arguments

This section includes readings that you may use to report, compare, and evaluate arguments.

A Proposal for International Disarmament

George F. Kennan

Adequate words are lacking to express the full seriousness of our present situation. It is not just that we are for the moment on a collision course politically with the Soviet Union, and that the process of rational communication between the two governments seems to have broken down completely; it is also—and even more importantly—the fact that the ultimate sanction behind the conflicting policies of these two governments is a type and volume of weaponry which could not possibly be used without utter disaster for us all.

For over thirty years, wise and far-seeing people have been warning us about the futility of any war fought with nuclear weapons and about the dangers involved in their cultivation. Some of the first of these voices to be raised were those of great scientists, including outstandingly that of Albert Einstein himself. But there has been no lack of others. Every president of this country, from Dwight Eisenhower to Jimmy Carter, has tried to remind us that there could be no such thing as victory in a war fought with such weapons. So have a great many other eminent persons.

When one looks back today over the history of these warnings, one has the impression that something has now been lost of the sense of urgency, the hopes, and the excitement that initially inspired them, so many years ago. One senses, even on the part of those who today most acutely perceive the problem and are inwardly most exercised about it, a certain discouragement, resignation, perhaps even despair, when it comes to the question of raising the subject again. The danger is so obvious. So much has already been said. What is to be gained by reiteration? What good would it now do?

Look at the record. Over all these years the competition in the development of nuclear weaponry has proceeded steadily, relentlessly, without the faintest regard for all these warning voices. We have gone on piling weapon upon weapon, missile upon missile, new levels of destructiveness upon old ones. We have done this helplessly, almost involuntarily: like the victims of some sort of hypnotism, like men in a dream, like lemmings heading for the sea, like the children of Hamlin marching blindly along behind their Pied Piper. And the result is that today we have achieved, we and the Russians together, in the creation of these devices and their means of delivery, levels of redundancy of such grotesque dimensions as to defy rational understanding.

I say redundancy. I know of no better way to describe it. But actually, the word is too mild. It implies that there could be levels of these weapons that would not be redundant. Personally, I doubt that there could. I question whether these devices are really weapons at all. A true weapon is at best something with which you endeavor to affect the behavior of another society by influencing the minds, the calculations, the intentions, of the men that control it; it is not something with which you destroy indiscriminately the lives, the substance, the hopes, the culture, the civilization, of another people.

What a confession of intellectual poverty it would be—what a bankruptcy of intelligent statesmanship—if we had to admit that such blind, senseless acts of destruction were the best use we could make of what we have come to view as the leading elements of our military strength!

To my mind, the nuclear bomb is the most useless weapon ever invented. It can be employed to no rational purpose. It is not even an effective defense against itself. It is only something with which, in a moment of petulance or panic, you commit such fearful acts of destruction as no sane person would ever wish to have upon his conscience.

There are those who will agree, with a sigh, to much of what I have just said, but will point to the need for something called deterrence. This is, of course, a concept which attributes to others—to others who, like ourselves, were born of women, walk on two legs, and love their children, to human beings, in short—the most fiendish and inhuman of tendencies.

But all right: accepting for the sake of argument the profound iniquity of these adversaries, no one could deny, I think, that the present Soviet and American arsenals, presenting over a million times the destructive power of the Hiroshima bomb, are simply fantastically redundant to the purpose in question. If the same relative proportions were to be preserved, something well less than 20 percent of those stocks would surely suffice for the most sanguine concepts of deterrence, whether as between the two nuclear superpowers or with relation to any of those other governments that have been so ill-advised as to enter upon the nuclear path. Whatever their suspicions of each other, there can be no excuse on the part of these two governments for holding, poised against each other and poised in a sense against the whole Northern Hemisphere, quantities of these weapons so vastly in excess of any rational and demonstrable requirements.

How have we got ourselves into this dangerous mess?

Let us not confuse the question by blaming it all on our Soviet adversaries. They have, of course, their share of the blame, and not least in their cavalier dismissal of the Baruch Plan so many years ago. They too have made their mistakes; and I should be the last to deny it.

But we must remember that it has been we Americans who, at almost every step of the road, have taken the lead in the development of this sort of weaponry. It was we who first produced and tested such a device; we who were the first to raise its destructiveness to a new level with the hydrogen bomb; we who introduced the multiple warhead; we who have declined every proposal for the renunciation of the principle of "first use"; and we alone, so help us God, who have used the weapon in anger against others, and against tens of thousands of helpless non-combatants at that.

I know that reasons were offered for some of these things. I know that others might have taken this sort of a lead, had we not done so. But let us not, in the face of this record, so lose ourselves in self-righteousness and hypocrisy as to forget our own measure of complicity in creating the situation we face today.

What is it then, if not our own will, and if not the supposed wickedness of our opponents, that has brought us to this pass?

The answer, I think, is clear. It is primarily the inner momentum, the independent momentum, of the weapons race itself—the compulsions that arise and take charge of great powers when they enter upon a competition with each other in the building up of major armaments of any sort.

This is nothing new. I am a diplomatic historian. I see this same phenomenon playing its fateful part in the relations among the great European powers as much as a century ago. I see this competitive buildup of armaments conceived initially as a means to an end but soon becoming the end itself. I see it taking possession of men's imagination and behavior, becoming a force in its own right, detaching itself from the political differences that initially inspired it, and then leading both parties, invariably and inexorably, to the war they no longer know how to avoid.

This is a species of fixation, brewed out of many components. There are fears, resentments, national pride, personal pride. There are misreadings of the adversary's intentions—sometimes even the refusal to consider them at all. There is the tendency of national communities to idealize themselves and to dehumanize the opponent. There is the blinkered, narrow vision of the professional military planner, and his tendency to make war inevitable by assuming its inevitability.

Tossed together, these components form a powerful brew. They guide the fears and the ambitions of men. They seize the policies of governments and whip them around like trees before the tempest.

Is it possible to break out of this charmed and vicious circle? It is sobering to recognize that no one, at least to my knowledge, has yet done so. But no one, for that matter, has ever been faced with such great catastrophe, such inalterable catastrophe, at the end of the line. Others, in earlier decades, could befuddle themselves with dreams of something called "victory." We, perhaps fortunately, are denied this seductive prospect. We have to break out of the circle. We have no other choice.

How are we to do it?

I must confess that I see no possibility of doing this by means of discussions along the lines of the negotiations that have been in progress, off and on, over this past decade, under the acronym of SALT. I regret, to be sure, that the most recent SALT agreement has not been ratified. I regret it, because if the benefits to be expected from that agreement were slight, its disadvantages were even slighter; and it had a symbolic value which should not have been so lightly sacrificed.

But I have, I repeat, no illusion that negotiations on the SALT pattern—negotiations, that is, in which each side is obsessed with the chimera of relative advantage and strives only to retain a maximum of the weaponry for itself while putting its opponent to the maximum disadvantage—I have no illusion that such negotiations could ever be adequate to get us out of this hole. They are not a way of escape from the weapons race; they are an integral part of it.

Whoever does not understand that when it comes to nuclear weapons the whole concept of relative advantage is illusory—whoever does not understand that when you are talking about absurd and preposterous quantities of overkill the relative sizes of arsenals have no serious meaning—whoever does not understand that the danger lies, not in the possibility that someone else might have more missiles and warheads than we do, but in the very existence of these unconscionable quantities of highly poisonous explosives, and their existence, above all, in hands as weak and shaky and undependable as those of ourselves or our adversaries or any other mere human beings: whoever does not understand these things is never going to guide us out of this increasingly dark and menacing forest of bewilderments into which we have all wandered.

I can see no way out of this dilemma other than by a bold and sweeping departure, a departure that would cut surgically through the exaggerated anxieties, the self-engendered nightmares, and the sophisticated mathematics of destruction in which we have all been entangled over these recent years, and would permit us to move, with courage and decision, to the heart of the problem.

President Reagan recently said, and I think very wisely, that he would "negotiate as long as necessary to reduce the numbers of nuclear weapons to a point where neither side threatens the survival of the other."

Now that is, of course, precisely the thought to which these present observations of mine are addressed. But I wonder whether the negotiations would really have to be at such great length. What I would like to see the president do, after due consultation with the Congress, would be to propose to the Soviet government an immediate across-the-boards reduction by 50 percent of the nuclear arsenals now being maintained by the two superpowers; a reduction affecting in equal measure all forms of the weapon, strategic, medium-range, and tactical, as well as all means of their delivery: all this to be implemented at once and without further wrangling among the experts, and to be subject to such national means of verification as now lie at the disposal of the two powers.

Whether the balance of reduction would be precisely even—whether it could be construed to favor statistically one side or the other—would not be the question. Once we start thinking that way, we would be back on the same old fateful track that has brought us where we are today. Whatever the precise results of such a reduction, there would still be plenty of overkill left—so much so that if this first operation were successful, I would then like to see a second one put in hand to rid us of at least two-thirds of what would be left.

Now I have, of course, no idea of the scientific aspects of such an operation; but I can imagine that serious problems might be presented by the task of removing, and disposing safely of, the radioactive contents of the many thousands of warheads that would have to be dismantled. Should this be the case, I would like to see the president couple his appeal for a 50 percent reduction with the proposal that there be established a joint Soviet-American scientific committee, under the chairmanship of a distinguished neutral figure, to study jointly and in all humility the problem not only of the safe disposal of these wastes but also of how they could be utilized in such a way as to make a positive contribution to human life, either in the two countries themselves or—perhaps preferably—elsewhere. In such a joint scientific venture we might both atone for some of our past follies and lay the foundation for a more constructive relationship.

It will be said this proposal, whatever its merits, deals with only a part of the problem. This is perfectly true. Behind it there would still lurk the serious political differences that now divide us from the Soviet government. Behind it would still lie the problems recently treated, and still to be treated, in the SALT forum. Behind it would still lie the great question of the acceptability of war itself, any war, even a conventional one, as a means of solving problems among great industrial powers in this age of high technology.

What has been suggested here would not prejudice the continued treatment of these questions just as they might be treated today, in whatever forums and under whatever safeguards the two powers find necessary. The conflicts and arguments over these questions could all still proceed to the heart's content of all those who view them with such passionate commitment. The stakes would simply be smaller; and that would be a great relief to all of us.

What I have suggested is, of course, only a beginning. But a beginning has to be made somewhere; and if it has to be made, is it not best that it should be made where the dangers are the greatest, and their necessity the least? If a step of this nature could be successfully taken, people might find the heart to tackle with greater confidence and determination the many problems that would still remain.

It will also be argued that there would be risks involved. Possibly so. I do not see them. I do not deny the possibility. But if there are, so what? Is it possible to conceive of any dangers greater than those that lie at the end of the collision course on which we are now embarked? And if not, why choose the greater—why choose, in fact, the greatest—of all risks, in the hopes of avoiding the lesser ones?

We are confronted here, my friends, with two courses. At the end of the one lies hope—faint hope, if you will, uncertain hope, hope surrounded with dangers, if you insist. At the end of the other lies, so far as I am able to see, no hope at all.

Can there be—in the light of our duty not just to ourselves (for we are all going to die sooner or later) but of our duty to our own kind, our duty to the continuity of the generations, our duty to the great experiment of civilized life on this rare and rich and marvelous planet—can there be, in the light of these claims on our loyalty, any question as to which course we should adopt?

In the final week of his life, Albert Einstein signed the last of the collective appeals against the development of nuclear weapons that he was ever to sign. He was dead before it appeared. It was an appeal drafted, I gather, by Bertrand Russell. I had my differences with Russell at the time as I do now in retrospect; but I would like to quote one sentence from the final paragraph of that statement, not only because it was the last one Einstein ever signed, but because it sums up, I think, all that I have to say on the subject. It reads as follows:

> We appeal, as human beings to human beings: Remember your humanity, and forget the rest.

The Declaration of Independence

Thomas Jefferson

In Congress, July 4, 1776

The Unanimous Declaration of the Thirteen
United States of America

When in the Course of human events, it becomes necessary for one people to dissolve the political bands which have connected them with another, and to assume among the Powers of the earth, the separate and equal station to which the Laws of Nature and of Nature's God entitle them, a decent respect to the opinions of mankind requires that they should declare the causes which impel them to the separation.

We hold these truths to be self-evident, that all men are created equal, that they are endowed by their Creator with certain unalienable Rights, that among these are Life, Liberty and the pursuit of Happiness. That to secure these rights, Governments are instituted among Men, deriving their just powers from the consent of the governed. That whenever any Form of Government becomes destructive of these ends, it is the Right of the People to alter or to abolish it, and to institute a new Government, laying its foundation on such principles and organizing its powers in such form, as to them shall seem most likely to effect their Safety and Happiness. Prudence, indeed, will dictate that Governments long established should not be changed for light and transient causes; and accordingly all experience hath shown, that mankind are more disposed to suffer, while evils are sufferable, than to right themselves by abolishing the forms to which they are accustomed. But when a long train of abuses and usurpations, pursuing invariably the same Object evinces a design to reduce them under absolute Despotism, it is their right, it is their duty, to throw off such Government, and to provide new Guards for their future security.—Such has been the patient sufferance of these Colonies; and such is now the necessity which constrains them to alter their former Systems of Government. The history of the present King of Great Britain is a history of repeated injuries and usurpations, all having in direct object the establishment of an absolute Tyranny over these States. To prove this, let Facts be submitted to a candid world.

He has refused his Assent to Laws, the most wholesome and necessary for the public good.

He has forbidden his Governors to pass Laws of immediate and pressing importance, unless suspended in their operation till his Assent should be obtained; and when so suspended, he has utterly neglected to attend to them.

He has refused to pass other laws for the accommodation of large districts of people, unless those people would relinquish the right of Representation in the Legislature, a right inestimable to them and formidable to tyrants only.

He has called together legislative bodies at places unusual, uncomfortable, and distant from the depository of their Public Records, for the sole purpose of fatiguing them into compliance with his measures.

He has dissolved Representative Houses repeatedly, for opposing with manly firmness his invasions on the rights of the people.

He has refused for a long time, after such dissolutions, to cause others to be elected; whereby the Legislative Powers, incapable of Annihilation, have returned to the People at large for their exercise; the State remaining in the mean time exposed to all the dangers of invasion from without, and convulsions within.

Declaration of Sentiments and Resolutions

Woman's Rights Convention of July 1848

When, in the course of human events, it becomes necessary for one portion of the family of man to assume among the people of the earth a position different from that which they have hitherto occupied, but one to which the laws of nature and of nature's God entitle them, a decent respect to the opinions of mankind requires that they should declare the causes that impel them to such a course.

We hold these truths to be self-evident: that all men and women are created equal; that they are endowed by their Creator with certain inalienable rights; that among these are life, liberty, and the pursuit of happiness; that to secure these rights governments are instituted, deriving their just powers from the consent of the governed. Whenever any form of government becomes destructive of these ends, it is the right of those who suffer from it to refuse allegiance to it, and to insist upon the institution of a new government, laying its foundation on such principles, and organizing its powers in such form, as to them shall seem most likely to effect their safety and happiness. Prudence, indeed, will dictate that governments long established should not be changed for light and transient causes; and accordingly all experience hath shown that mankind are more disposed to suffer, while evils are sufferable, than to right themselves by abolishing the forms to which they were accustomed. But when a long train of abuses and usurpations, pursuing invariably the same object evinces a design to reduce them under absolute despotism, it is their duty to throw off such government, and to provide new guards for their future security. Such has been the patient sufferance of the women under this government, and such is now the necessity which constrains them to demand the equal station to which they are entitled.

The history of mankind is a history of repeated injuries and usurpations on the part of man toward woman, having in direct object the establishment of an absolute tyranny over her. To prove this, let facts be submitted to a candid world.

He has never permitted her to exercise her inalienable right to the elective franchise.

He has compelled her to submit to laws, in the formation of which she had no voice.

He has withheld from her rights which are given to the most ignorant and degraded men—both natives and foreigners.

Having deprived her of this first right of a citizen, the elective franchise, thereby leaving her without representation in the halls of legislation, he has oppressed her on all sides.

He has made her, if married, in the eye of the law, civilly dead.

He has taken from her all right in property, even to the wages she earns.

He has made her, morally, an irresponsible being, as she can commit many crimes with impunity, provided they be done in the presence of her husband. In the covenant of marriage, she is compelled to promise obedience to her husband, he becoming, to all intents and purposes, her master—the law giving him power to deprive her of her liberty, and to administer chastisement.

He has so framed the laws of divorce, as to what shall be the proper causes, and in case of separation, to whom the guardianship of the children shall be given, as to be wholly regardless of the happiness of women—the law, in all cases, going upon a false supposition of the supremacy of man, and giving all power into his hands.

After depriving her of all rights as a married woman, if single, and the owner of property, he has taxed her to support a government which recognizes her only when her property can be made profitable to it.

He has monopolized nearly all the profitable employments, and from those she is permitted to follow, she receives but a scanty remuneration. He closes against her all the avenues to wealth and distinction which he considers most honorable to himself. As a teacher of theology, medicine, or law, she is not known.

He has denied her the facilities for obtaining a thorough education, all colleges being closed against her.

He allows her in Church, as well as State, but a subordinate position, claiming Apostolic authority for her exclusion from the ministry, and, with some exceptions, from any public participation in the affairs of the Church.

He has created a false public sentiment by giving to the world a different code of morals for men and women, by which moral delinquencies which exclude women from society, are not only tolerated, but deemed of little account in man.

He has usurped the prerogative of Jehovah himself, claiming it as his right to assign for her a sphere of action, when that belongs to her conscience and to her God.

He has endeavored, in every way that he could, to destroy her confidence in her own powers, to lessen her self-respect, and to make her willing to lead a dependent and abject life.

Now, in view of this entire disfranchisement of one-half the people of this country, their social and religious degradation—in view of the unjust laws above mentioned, and because women do feel themselves aggrieved, oppressed, and fraudulently deprived of their most sacred rights, we insist that they have immediate admission to all the rights and privileges which belong to them as citizens of the United States.

In entering upon the great work before us, we anticipate no small amount of misconception, misrepresentation, and ridicule; but we shall use every instrumentality within our power to effect our object.

We shall employ agents, circulate tracts, petition the State and National legislatures, and endeavor to enlist the pulpit and the press in our behalf. We hope this Convention will be followed by a series of Conventions embracing every part of the country.

Resolutions

WHEREAS, The great precept of nature is conceded to be, that "man shall pursue his own true and substantial happiness." Blackstone in his Commentaries remarks, that this law of Nature being coeval with mankind, and dictated by God himself, is of course superior in obligation to any other. It is binding over all the globe, in all countries and at all times; no human laws are of any validity if contrary to this, and such of them as are valid, derive all their force, and all their validity, and all their authority, mediately and immediately, from this original; therefore,

Resolved, That such laws as conflict, in any way, with the true and substantial happiness of woman, are contrary to the great precept of nature and of no validity, for this is "superior in obligation to any other."

Resolved, That all laws which prevent woman from occupying such a station in society as her conscience shall dictate, or which place her in a position inferior to that of man, are contrary to the great precept of nature, and therefore of no force or authority.

Resolved, That woman is man's equal—was intended to be so by the Creator, and the highest good of the race demands that she should be recognized as such.

Resolved, That the women of this country ought to be enlightened in regard to the laws under which they live, that they may no longer publish their degradation by declaring themselves satisfied with their present position, nor their ignorance, by asserting that they have all the rights they want.

Resolved, That inasmuch as man, while claiming for himself intellectual superiority, does accord to woman moral superiority, it is preeminently his duty to encourage her to speak and teach, as she has an opportunity, in all religious assemblies.

Resolved, That the same amount of virtue, delicacy, and refinement of behavior that is required of woman in the social state, should also be required of man, and the same transgressions should be visited with equal severity on both man and woman.

Resolved, That the objection of indelicacy and impropriety, which is so often brought against woman when she addresses a public audience, comes with a very ill-grace from those who encourage, by their attendance, her appearance on the stage, in the concert, or in feats of the circus.

Resolved, That woman has too long rested satisfied in the circumscribed limits which corrupt customs and a perverted application of the Scriptures have marked out for her, and that it is time she should move in the enlarged sphere which her great Creator has assigned her.

Resolved, That it is the duty of the women of this country to secure to themselves their sacred right to the elective franchise.

Resolved, That the equality of human rights results necessarily from the fact of the identity of the race in capabilities and responsibilities.

Resolved, therefore, That, being invested by the Creator with the same capabilities, and the same consciousness of responsibility for their exercise, it is demonstrably the right and duty of woman, equally with man, to promote every righteous cause by every righteous means; and especially in regard to the great subjects of morals and religion, it is self-evidently her right to participate with her brother in teaching them, both in private and in public, by writing and by speaking, by any instrumentalities proper to be used, and in any assemblies proper to be held; and this being a self-evident truth growing out of the divinely implanted principles of human nature, any custom or authority adverse to it, whether modern or wearing the hoary sanction of antiquity, is to be regarded as a self-evident falsehood, and at war with mankind.

From Crito

Plato

SOCRATES: Here already, Crito? Surely it is still early?

CRITO: Indeed it is.

SOCRATES: About what time?

CRITO: Just before dawn.

SOCRATES: I wonder that the warder paid any attention to you.

CRITO: He is used to me now, Socrates, because I come here so often. Besides, he is under some small obligation to me.

SOCRATES: Have you only just come, or have you been here for long?

CRITO: Fairly long.

SOCRATES: Then why didn't you wake me at once, instead of sitting by my bed so quietly?

CRITO: I wouldn't dream of such a thing, Socrates. I only wish I were not so sleepless and depressed myself. I have been wondering at you, because I saw how comfortably you were sleeping, and I deliberately didn't wake you because I wanted you to go on being as comfortable as you could. I have often felt before in the course of my life how fortunate you are in your disposition, but I feel it more than ever now in your present misfortune when I see how easily and placidly you put up with it.

SOCRATES: Well, really, Crito, it would be hardly suitable for a man of my age to resent having to die.

CRITO: Other people just as old as you are get involved in these misfortunes, Socrates, but their age doesn't keep them from resenting it when they find themselves in your position.

SOCRATES: Quite true. But tell me, why have you come so early?

CRITO: Because I bring bad news, Socrates—not so bad from your point of view, I suppose, but it will be very hard to bear for me and your other friends, and I think that I shall find it hardest of all.

SOCRATES: Why, what is this news? Has the boat come in from Delos—the boat which ends my reprieve when it arrives?

CRITO: It hasn't actually come in yet, but I expect that it will be here today, judging from the report of some people who have just arrived from Sunium and left it there. It's quite clear from their account that it will be here today, and so by tomorrow, Socrates, you will have to . . . to end your life.

SOCRATES: Well, Crito, I hope that it may be for the best. . . .

CRITO: I know some people who are willing to rescue you from here and get you out of the country for quite a moderate sum. And then surely you realize how cheap these informers are to buy off; we shan't need much money to settle them, and I think you've got enough of my money for yourself already. And then even supposing that in your anxiety for my safety you feel that you oughtn't to spend my money, there are these foreign gentlemen staying in Athens who are quite willing to spend theirs. One of them, Simmias of Thebes, has actually brought the money with him for this very purpose, and Cebes and a number of others are quite ready to do the same. So, as I say, you mustn't let any fears on these grounds make you slacken your efforts to escape, and you mustn't feel any misgivings about what you said at your trial—that you wouldn't know what to do with yourself if you left this country. Wherever you go, there are plenty of places where you will find a welcome, and if you choose to go to Thessaly, I have friends there who will make much of you and give you complete protection, so that no one in Thessaly can interfere with you.

Besides, Socrates, I don't even feel that it is right for you to try to do what you are doing, throwing away your life when you might save it. You are doing your best to treat yourself in exactly the same way as your enemies would, or rather did, when they wanted to ruin you. What is more, it seems to me that you are letting your sons down too. You have it in your power to finish their bringing-up and education, and instead of that you are proposing to go off and desert them, and so far as you are concerned they will have to take their chance. And what sort of chance are they likely to get?

The sort of thing that usually happens to orphans when they lose their parents. Either one ought not to have children at all, or one ought to see their upbringing and education through to the end. It strikes me that you are taking the line of least resistance, whereas you ought to make the choice of a good man and a brave one, considering that you profess to have made goodness your object all through life. Really, I am ashamed, both on your account and on ours, your friends'. It will look as though we had played something like a coward's part all through this affair of yours. First there was the way you came into court when it was quite unnecessary—that was the first act. Then there was the conduct of the defense—that was the second. And finally, to complete the farce, we get this situation, which makes it appear that we have let you slip out of our hands through some lack of courage and enterprise on our part, because we didn't save you, and you didn't save yourself, when it would have been quite possible and practicable, if we had been any use at all.

There, Socrates, if you aren't careful, besides the suffering there will be all this disgrace for you and us to bear. Come, make up your mind. Really it's too late for that now; you ought to have it made up already. There is no alternative; the whole thing must be carried through during this coming night. If we lose any more time, it can't be done; it will be too late. I appeal to you, Socrates, on every ground; take my advice and please don't be unreasonable! . . .

SOCRATES: . . . [W]e must consider whether or not it is right for me to try to get away without an official discharge. If it turns out to be right, we must make the attempt; if not, we must let it drop. As for the considerations you raise about expense and reputation and bringing up children, I am afraid, Crito, that they represent the reflections of the ordinary public, who put people to death, and would bring them back to life if they could, with equal indifference to reason. Our real duty, I fancy, since the argument leads that way, is to consider one question only, the one which we raised just now. Shall we be acting rightly in paying money and showing gratitude to these people who are going to rescue me, and in escaping or arranging the escape ourselves, or shall we really be acting wrongly in doing all this? If it becomes clear that such conduct is wrong, I cannot help thinking that the question whether we are sure to die, or to suffer any other ill effect for that matter, if we stand our ground and take no action, ought not to weigh with us at all in comparison with the risk of doing what is wrong.

CRITO: I agree with what you say, Socrates, but I wish you would consider what we ought to *do*.

SOCRATES: Let us look at it together, my dear fellow; and if you can challenge any of my arguments, do so and I will listen to you; but if you can't, be a good fellow and stop telling me over and over again that I ought to leave this place without official permission. I am very anxious to obtain your approval before I adopt the course which I have in mind. I don't want to act against your convictions. Now give your attention to the starting point of this inquiry—I hope that you will be satisfied with my way of stating it—and try to answer my questions to the best of your judgment.

CRITO: Well, I will try.

SOCRATES: Do we say that one must never willingly do wrong, or does it depend upon circumstances? Is it true, as we have often agreed before, that there is no sense in which wrongdoing is good or honorable? Or have we jettisoned all our former convictions in these last few days? Can you and I at our age, Crito, have spent all these years in serious discussions without realizing that we were no better than a pair of children? Surely the truth is just what we have always said. Whatever the popular view is, and whether the alternative is pleasanter than the present one or even harder to bear, the fact remains that to do wrong is in every sense bad and dishonorable for the person who does it. Is that our view, or not?

CRITO: Yes, it is.

SOCRATES: Then in no circumstances must one do wrong.

CRITO: No.

SOCRATES: In that case one must not even do wrong when one is wronged, which most people regard as the natural course.

CRITO: Apparently not.

SOCRATES: Tell me another thing, Crito. Ought one to do injuries or not?

CRITO: Surely not, Socrates.

SOCRATES: And tell me, is it right to do an injury in retaliation, as most people believe, or not?

CRITO: No, never.

SOCRATES: Because, I suppose, there is no difference between injuring people and wronging them.

CRITO: Exactly.

SOCRATES: So one ought not to return a wrong or an injury to any person, whatever the provocation is. Now be careful, Crito, that in making these single admissions you do not end by admitting something contrary to your real beliefs. I know that there are and always will be few people who think like this, and consequently between those who do think so and those who do not there can be no agreement on principle; they must always feel contempt when they observe one another's decisions. I want even you to consider very carefully whether you share my views and agree with me, and whether we can proceed with our discussion from the established hypothesis that it is never right to do a wrong or return a wrong or defend oneself against injury by retaliation, or whether you disso-

ciate yourself from any share in this view as a basis for discussion.
I have held it for a long time, and still hold it, but if you have formed
any other opinion, say so and tell me what it is. If, on the other
hand, you stand by what we have said, listen to my next point.

CRITO: Yes, I stand by it and agree with you. Go on.

SOCRATES: Well, here is my next point, or rather question. Ought one
to fulfill all one's agreements, provided that they are right, or break
them?

CRITO: One ought to fulfill them.

SOCRATES: Then consider the logical consequence. If we leave this
place without first persuading the state to let us go, are we or are
we not doing an injury, and doing it in a quarter where it is least
justifiable? Are we or are we not abiding by our just agreements?

CRITO: I can't answer your question, Socrates. I am not clear in my
mind.

SOCRATES: Look at it in this way. Suppose that while we were preparing to run away from here—or however one should describe it—
the laws and constitution of Athens were to come and confront us
and ask this question. Now, Socrates, what are you proposing to
do? Can you deny that by this act which you are contemplating you
intend, so far as you have the power, to destroy us, the laws, and
the whole state as well? Do you imagine that a city can continue to
exist and not be turned upside down, if the legal judgments which
are pronounced in it have no force but are nullified and destroyed
by private persons?

How shall we answer this question, Crito, and others of the same
kind? There is much that could be said, especially by a professional
advocate, to protest against the invalidation of this law which
enacts that judgments once pronounced shall be binding. Shall we
say, Yes, I do intend to destroy the laws, because the state wronged
me by passing a faulty judgment at my trial? Is this to be our
answer, or what?

CRITO: What you have just said, by all means, Socrates.

SOCRATES: Then what supposing the laws say, Was there provision for
this in the agreement between you and us, Socrates? Or did you
undertake to abide by whatever judgments the state pronounced?

If we expressed surprise at such language, they would probably
say, Never mind our language, Socrates, but answer our questions;
after all, you are accustomed to the method of question and
answer. Come now, what charge do you bring against us and the
state, that you are trying to destroy us? Did we not give you life in
the first place? Was it not through us that your father married your
mother and begot you? Tell us, have you any complaint against
those of us laws that deal with marriage?

No, none, I should say.

Well, have you any against the laws which deal with children's upbringing and education, such as you had yourself? Are you not grateful to those of us laws which were instituted for this end, for requiring your father to give you a cultural and physical education?

Yes, I should say.

Very good. Then since you have been born and brought up and educated, can you deny, in the first place, that you were our child and servant, both you and your ancestors? And if this is so, do you imagine that what is right for us is equally right for you, and that whatever we try to do to you, you are justified in retaliating? You did not have equality of rights with your father, or your employer— supposing that you had had one—to enable you to retaliate. You were not allowed to answer back when you were scolded or to hit back when you were beaten, or to do a great many other things of the same kind. Do you expect to have such license against your country and its laws that if we try to put you to death in the belief that it is right to do so, you on your part will try your hardest to destroy your country and us its laws in return? And will you, the true devotee of goodness, claim that you are justified in doing so? Are you so wise as to have forgotten that compared with your mother and father and all the rest of your ancestors your country is something far more precious, more venerable, more sacred, and held in greater honor both among gods and among all reasonable men? Do you not realize that you are even more bound to respect and placate the anger of your country than your father's anger? That if you cannot persuade your country you must do whatever it orders, and patiently submit to any punishment that it imposes, whether it be flogging or imprisonment? And if it leads you out to war, to be wounded or killed, you must comply, and it is right that you should do so. You must not give way or retreat or abandon your position. Both in war and in the law courts and everywhere else you must do whatever your city and your country command, or else persuade them in accordance with universal justice, but violence is a sin even against your parents, and it is a far greater sin against your country.

What shall we say to this, Crito—that what the laws say is true, or not?

CRITO: Yes, I think so.

SOCRATES: Consider, then, Socrates, the laws would probably continue, whether it is also true for us to say that what you are now trying to do to us is not right. Although we have brought you into the world and reared you and educated you, and given you and all your fellow citizens a share in all the good things at our disposal, nevertheless by the very fact of granting our permission we openly proclaim this principle, that any Athenian, on attaining to manhood and seeing for himself the political organization of the state and us its laws, is permitted, if he is not satisfied with us, to take his property and go away wherever he likes. If any of you chooses to go to one of our colonies, supposing that he should not be satisfied with us and the state, or to emigrate to any other country, not one of us laws hinders or prevents him from going away wherever he likes, without any loss of property. On the other hand, if any one of you stands his ground when he can see how we administer justice and the rest of our public organization, we hold that by so doing he has in fact undertaken to do anything that we tell him. And we maintain that anyone who disobeys is guilty of doing wrong on three separate counts: first because we are his parents, and secondly because we are his guardians, and thirdly because, after promising obedience, he is neither obeying us nor persuading us to change our decision if we are at fault in any way. And although all our orders are in the form of proposals, not of savage commands, and we give him the choice of either persuading us or doing what we say, he is actually doing neither. These are the charges, Socrates, to which we say that you will be liable if you do what you are contemplating, and you will not be the least culpable of your fellow countrymen, but one of the most guilty.

If I asked why, they would no doubt pounce upon me with perfect justice and point out that there are very few people in Athens who have entered into this agreement with them as explicitly as I have. They would say, Socrates, we have substantial evidence that you are satisfied with us and with the state. You would not have been so exceptionally reluctant to cross the borders of your country if you had not been exceptionally attached to it. You have never left the city to attend a festival or for any other purpose, except on some military expedition. You have never traveled abroad as other people do, and you have never felt the impulse to acquaint yourself with another country or constitution. You have been content with us and with our city. You have definitely chosen us, and undertaken to observe us in all your activities as a citizen, and as the crowning proof that you are satisfied with our city, you have begotten children in it. Furthermore, even at the time of your trial you could have proposed the penalty of banishment, if you had chosen to do so—that is, you could have done then with the sanction of the state what you are now trying to do without it. But whereas at that time you made a noble show of indifference if you had to die, and in fact preferred death, as you said, to banishment, now you show no respect for your earlier professions, and no regard for us, the laws, whom you are trying to destroy. You are behaving like the lowest type of menial, trying to run away in spite of the contracts and undertakings by which you agreed to live as a member of our state. Now first answer this question. Are we or are we not speaking the truth when we say that you have undertaken, in deed if not in word, to live your life as a citizen in obedience to us?

What are we to say to that, Crito? Are we not bound to admit it?

CRITO: We cannot help it, Socrates.

SOCRATES: It is a fact, then, they would say, that you are breaking covenants and undertakings made with us, although you made them under no compulsion or misunderstanding, and were not compelled to decide in a limited time. You had seventy years in which you could have left the country, if you were not satisfied with us or felt that the agreements were unfair. You did not choose Sparta or Crete—your favorite models of good government—or any other Greek or foreign state. You could not have absented yourself from the city less if you had been lame or blind or decrepit in some other way. It is quite obvious that you stand by yourself above all other Athenians in your affection for this city and for us its laws. Who would care for a city without laws? And now, after all this, are you not going to stand by your agreement? Yes, you are, Socrates, if you will take our advice, and then you will at least escape being laughed at for leaving the city.

We invite you to consider what good you will do to yourself or your friends if you commit this breach of faith and stain your conscience. It is fairly obvious that the risk of being banished and either losing their citizenship or having their property confiscated will extend to your friends as well. As for yourself, if you go to one of the neighboring states, such as Thebes or Megara, which are both well governed, you will enter them as an enemy to their constitution, and all good patriots will eye you with suspicion as a destroyer of law and order. Incidentally you will confirm the opinion of the jurors who tried you that they gave a correct verdict; a destroyer of laws might very well be supposed to have a destructive influence upon young and foolish human beings. Do you intend, then, to avoid well-governed states and the higher forms of human society? And if you do, will life be worth living? Or will you approach these people and have the impudence to converse with them? What arguments will you use, Socrates? The same which you used here, that goodness and integrity, institutions and laws, are the most precious possessions of mankind? Do you not think that Socrates and everything about him will appear in a disreputable light? You certainly ought to think so.

But perhaps you will retire from this part of the world and go to Crito's friends in Thessaly? That is the home of indiscipline and laxity, and no doubt they would enjoy hearing the amusing story of how you managed to run away from prison by arraying yourself in some costume or putting on a shepherd's smock or some other conventional runaway's disguise, and altering your personal appearance. And will no one comment on the fact that an old man of your age, probably with only a short time left to live, should dare to cling so greedily to life, at the price of violating the most stringent laws?

Perhaps not, if you avoid irritating anyone. Otherwise, Socrates, you will hear a good many humiliating comments. So you will live as the toady and slave of all the populace, literally 'roistering in Thessaly,' as though you had left this country for Thessaly to attend a banquet there. And where will your discussions about goodness and uprightness be then, we should like to know? But of course you want to live for your children's sake, so that you may be able to bring them up and educate them. Indeed! By first taking them off to Thessaly and making foreigners of them, so that they may have that additional enjoyment? Or if that is not your intention, supposing that they are brought up here with you still alive, will they be better cared for and educated without you, because of course your friends will look after them? Will they look after your children if you go away to Thessaly, and not if you go away to the next world? Surely if those who profess to be your friends are worth anything, you must believe that they would care for them.

No, Socrates, be advised by us your guardians, and do not think more of your children or of your life or of anything else than you think of what is right, so that when you enter the next world you may have all this to plead in your defense before the authorities there. It seems clear that if you do this thing, neither you nor any of your friends will be the better for it or be more upright or have a cleaner conscience here in this world, nor will it be better for you when you reach the next. As it is, you will leave this place, when you do, as the victim of a wrong done not by us, the laws, but by your fellow men. But if you leave in that dishonorable way, returning wrong for wrong and evil for evil, breaking your agreements and covenants with us and injuring those whom you least ought to injure—yourself, your friends, your country, and us—then you will have to face our anger in your lifetime, and in that place beyond when the laws of the other world know that you have tried, so far as you could, to destroy even us their brothers, they will not receive you with a kindly welcome. Do not take Crito's advice, but follow ours.

That, my dear friend Crito, I do assure you, is what I seem to hear them saying, just as a mystic seems to hear the strains of music, and the sound of their arguments rings so loudly in my head that I cannot hear the other side. I warn you that, as my opinion stands at present, it will be useless to urge a different view. However, if you think that you will do any good by it, say what you like.

CRITO: No, Socrates, I have nothing to say.

SOCRATES: Then give it up, Crito, and let us follow this course, since God points out the way.

Letter from Birmingham Jail*

Martin Luther King, Jr.

April 16, 1963

MY DEAR FELLOW CLERGYMEN:

While confined here in the Birmingham city jail, I came across your recent statement calling my present activities "unwise and untimely." . . .

You deplore the demonstrations taking place in Birmingham. But your statement, I am sorry to say, fails to express a similar concern for the conditions that brought about the demonstrations. I am sure that none of you would want to rest content with the superficial kind of social analysis that deals merely with effects and does not grapple with underlying causes. It is unfortunate that demonstrations are taking place in Birmingham, but it is even more unfortunate that the city's white power structure left the Negro community with no alternative.

In any nonviolent campaign there are four basic steps: collection of the facts to determine whether injustices exist; negotiation; self-purification; and direct action. We have gone through all these steps in Birmingham. There can be no gainsaying the fact that racial injustice engulfs this community. Birmingham is probably the most thoroughly segregated city in the United States. Its ugly record of brutality is widely known. Negroes have experienced grossly unjust treatment in the courts. There have been more unsolved bombings of Negro homes and churches in Birmingham than in any other city in the nation. These are the hard brutal facts of the case. On the basis of these conditions, Negro leaders sought to negotiate with the city fathers. But the latter consistently refused to engage in good-faith negotiation.

Then, last September, came the opportunity to talk with leaders of Birmingham's economic community. In the course of the negotiations, certain promises were made by the merchants—for example, to remove the stores' humiliating racial signs. On the basis of these promises, the Reverend Fred Shuttlesworth and the leaders of the Alabama Christian Movement for Human Rights agreed to a moratorium on all demonstrations. As the weeks and months went by, we realized that

---

* This response to a published statement by eight fellow clergymen from Alabama (Bishop C.C.J. Carpenter, Bishop Joseph A. Durick, Rabbi Hilton L. Grafman, Bishop Paul Hardin, Bishop Holan B. Harmon, the Reverend George M. Murray, the Reverend Edward V. Ramage and the Reverend Earl Stallings) was composed under somewhat constricting circumstances. Begun on the margins of the newspaper in which the statement appeared while I was in jail, the letter was continued on scraps of writing paper supplied by a friendly Negro trusty, and concluded on a pad my attorneys were eventually permitted to leave me. Although the text remains in substance unaltered, I have indulged in the author's prerogative of polishing it for publication. [King's note]

we were the victims of a broken promise. A few signs, briefly removed, returned; the others remained.

As in so many past experiences, our hopes had been blasted, and the shadow of deep disappointment settled upon us. We had no alternative except to prepare for direct action, whereby we would present our very bodies as a means of laying our case before the conscience of the local and the national community. Mindful of the difficulties involved, we decided to undertake a process of self-purification. We began a series of workshops on nonviolence, and we repeatedly asked ourselves: "Are you able to accept blows without retaliating?" "Are you able to endure the ordeal of jail?" . . .

You may well ask, "Why direct action? Why sit-ins, marches, and so forth? Isn't negotiation a better path?" You are quite right in calling for negotiation. Indeed, this is the very purpose of direct action. Nonviolent direct action seeks to create such a crisis and foster such a tension that a community which has constantly refused to negotiate is forced to confront the issue. It seeks so to dramatize the issue that it can no longer be ignored. My citing the creation of tension as part of the work of the nonviolent resister may sound rather shocking. But I must confess that I am not afraid of the word "tension." I have earnestly opposed violent tension, but there is a type of constructive, nonviolent tension which is necessary for growth. Just as Socrates felt that it was necessary to create a tension in the mind so that individuals could rise from the bondage of myths and half truths to the unfettered realm of creative analysis and objective appraisal, so must we see the need for nonviolent gadflies to create the kind of tension in society that will help men rise from the dark depths of prejudice and racism to the majestic heights of understanding and brotherhood.

The purpose of our direct-action program is to create a situation so crisis-packed that it will inevitably open the door to negotiation. I therefore concur with you in your call for negotiation. Too long has our beloved Southland been bogged down in a tragic effort to live in monologue rather than dialogue.

One of the basic points in your statement is that the action that I and my associates have taken in Birmingham is untimely. . . .

We know through painful experience that freedom is never voluntarily given by the oppressor; it must be demanded by the oppressed. Frankly, I have yet to engage in a direct-action campaign that was "well timed" in the view of those who have not suffered unduly from the disease of segregation. For years now I have heard the word "Wait!" It rings in the ear of every Negro with piercing familiarity. This "Wait" has almost always meant "Never." We must come to see, with one of our distinguished jurists, that "justice too long delayed is justice denied."

We have waited for more than 340 years for our constitutional and God-given rights. The nations of Asia and Africa are moving with jet-like speed toward gaining political independence, but we still creep at horse-and-buggy pace toward gaining a cup of coffee at a lunch counter. Perhaps it is easy for those who have never felt the stinging darts of segregation to say, "Wait." But when you have seen vicious mobs lynch your mothers and fathers at will and drown your sisters and brothers at whim; when you have seen hate-filled policemen curse, kick, and even kill your black brothers and sisters; when you see the vast majority of your twenty million Negro brothers smothering in an airtight cage of poverty in the midst of an affluent society; when you suddenly find your tongue twisted and your speech stammering as you seek to explain to your six-year-old daughter why she can't go to the public amusement park that has just been advertised on television, and see tears welling up in her eyes when she is told that Funtown is closed to colored children, and see ominous clouds of inferiority beginning to form in her little mental sky, and see her beginning to distort her personality by developing an unconscious bitterness toward white people; when you have to concoct an answer for a five-year-old son who is asking, "Daddy, why do white people treat colored people so mean?"; when you take a cross-country drive and find it necessary to sleep night after night in the uncomfortable corners of your automobile because no motel will accept you; when you are humiliated day in and day out by nagging signs reading "white" and "colored"; when your first name becomes "nigger," your middle name becomes "boy" (however old you are) and your last name becomes "John," and your wife and mother are never given the respected title "Mrs."; when you are harried by day and haunted by night by the fact that you are a Negro, living constantly at tiptoe stance, never quite knowing what to expect next, and are plagued with inner fears and outer resentments; when you are forever fighting a degenerating sense of "nobodiness"—then you will understand why we find it difficult to wait. There comes a time when the cup of endurance runs over, and men are no longer willing to be plunged into the abyss of despair. I hope, sirs, you can understand our legitimate and unavoidable impatience.

You express a great deal of anxiety over our willingness to break laws. This is certainly a legitimate concern. Since we so diligently urge people to obey the Supreme Court's decision of 1954 outlawing segregation in the public schools, at first glance it may seem rather paradoxical for us consciously to break laws. One may well ask: "How can you advocate breaking some laws and obeying others?" The answer lies in the fact that there are two types of laws: just and unjust. I would be the first to advocate obeying just laws. One has not only a legal but a moral responsibility to obey just laws. Conversely, one has a moral responsibility to disobey unjust laws. I would agree with St. Augustine that "an unjust law is no law at all."

Now, what is the difference between the two? How does one determine whether a law is just or unjust? A just law is a man-made code that squares with the moral law or the law of God. An unjust law is a code that is out of harmony with the moral law. To put it in the terms of St. Thomas Aquinas: An unjust law is a human law that is not rooted in eternal law and natural law. Any law that uplifts human personality is just. Any law that degrades human personality is unjust. All segregation statutes are unjust because segregation distorts the soul and damages the personality. It gives the segregator a false sense of superiority and the segregated a false sense of inferiority. Segregation, to use the terminology of the Jewish philosopher Martin Buber, substitutes an "I-it" relationship for an "I-thou" relationship and ends up relegating persons to the status of things. Hence segregation is not only politically, economically, and sociologically unsound, it is morally wrong and sinful. Paul Tillich has said that sin is separation. Is not segregation an existential expression of man's tragic separation, his awful estrangement, his terrible sinfulness? Thus it is that I can urge men to obey the 1954 decision of the Supreme Court, for it is morally right, and I can urge them to disobey segregation ordinances, for they are morally wrong.

Let us consider a more concrete example of just and unjust laws. An unjust law is a code that a numerical or power majority group compels a minority group to obey but does not make binding on itself. This is *difference* made legal. By the same token, a just law is a code that a majority compels a minority to follow and that it is willing to follow itself. This is *sameness* made legal.

Let me give another explanation. A law is unjust if it is inflicted on a minority that, as a result of being denied the right to vote, had no part in enacting or devising the law. Who can say that the legislature of Alabama which set up that state's segregation laws was democratically elected? Throughout Alabama all sorts of devious methods are used to prevent Negroes from becoming registered voters, and there are some counties in which, even though Negroes constitute a majority of the population, not a single Negro is registered. Can any law enacted under such circumstances be considered democratically structured?

Sometimes a law is just on its face and unjust in its application. For instance, I have been arrested on a charge of parading without a permit. Now, there is nothing wrong in having an ordinance which requires a permit for a parade. But such an ordinance becomes unjust when it is used to maintain segregation and to deny citizens the First Amendment privilege of peaceful assembly and protest.

I hope you are able to see the distinction I am trying to point out. In no sense do I advocate evading or defying the law, as would the rabid segregationist. That would lead to anarchy. One who breaks an unjust law must do so openly, lovingly, and with a willingness to accept the penalty. I submit that an individual who breaks a law that conscience tells him is unjust, and who willingly accepts the penalty of imprisonment in order to arouse the conscience of the community over its injustice, is in reality expressing the highest respect for law.

Of course, there is nothing new about this kind of civil disobedience. It was evidenced sublimely in the refusal of Shadrach, Meshach, and Abednego to obey the laws of Nebuchadnezzar, on the ground that a higher moral law was at stake. It was practiced superbly by the early Christians, who were willing to face hungry lions and the excruciating pain of chopping blocks rather than submit to certain unjust laws of the Roman Empire. To a degree, academic freedom is a reality today because Socrates practiced civil disobedience. In our own nation, the Boston Tea Party represented a massive act of civil disobedience.

We should never forget that everything Adolf Hitler did in Germany was "legal" and everything the Hungarian freedom fighters did in Hungary was "illegal." It was "illegal" to aid and comfort a Jew in Hitler's Germany. Even so, I am sure that, had I lived in Germany at the time, I would have aided and comforted my Jewish brothers. If today I lived in a Communist country where certain principles dear to the Christian faith are suppressed, I would openly advocate disobeying that country's antireligious laws.

I must make two honest confessions to you, my Christian and Jewish brothers. First, I must confess that over the past few years I have been gravely disappointed with the white moderate. I have almost reached the regrettable conclusion that the Negro's great stumbling block in his stride toward freedom is not the White Citizen's Counciler or the Ku Klux Klanner, but the white moderate, who is more devoted to "order" than to justice; who prefers a negative peace which is the absence of tension to a positive peace which is the presence of justice; who constantly says, "I agree with you in the goal you seek, but I cannot agree with your methods of direct action"; who paternalistically believes he can set the timetable for another man's freedom; who lives by a mythical concept of time and who constantly advises the Negro to wait for a "more convenient season." Shallow understanding from people of good will is more frustrating than absolute misunderstanding from people of ill will. Lukewarm acceptance is much more bewildering than outright rejection.

I had hoped that the white moderate would understand that law and order exist for the purpose of establishing justice and that when they fail in this purpose they become the dangerously structured dams that block the flow of social progress. I had hoped that the white moderate would understand that the present tension in the South is a necessary phase of the transition from an obnoxious negative peace, in which the Negro passively accepted his unjust plight, to a substantive and positive peace, in which all men will respect the dignity and worth of human personality. Actually, we who engage in nonviolent direct action are not the creators of tension. We merely bring to the surface the hidden tension that is already alive. We bring it out in the open, where it can be seen and dealt with. Like a boil that can never be cured so long as it is covered up but must be opened with all its ugliness to the natural medicines of air and light, injustice must be exposed, with all the tension its exposure creates, to the light of human conscience and the air of national opinion, before it can be cured.

In your statement you assert that our actions, even though peaceful, must be condemned because they precipitate violence. But is this a logical assertion? Isn't this like condemning a robbed man because his possession of money precipitated the evil act of robbery? Isn't this like condemning Socrates because his unswerving commitment to truth and his philosophical inquiries precipitated the act by the misguided populace in which they made him drink hemlock? Isn't this like condemning Jesus because his unique God-consciousness and never-ceasing devotion to God's will precipitated the evil act of crucifixion? We must come to see that, as the federal courts have consistently affirmed, it is wrong to urge an individual to cease his efforts to gain his basic constitutional rights because the quest may precipitate violence. Society must protect the robbed and punish the robber.

I had also hoped that the white moderate would reject the myth concerning time in relation to the struggle for freedom. I have just received a letter from a white brother in Texas. He writes: "All Christians know that the colored people will receive equal rights eventually, but it is possible that you are in too great a religious hurry. It has taken Christianity almost two thousand years to accomplish what it has. The teachings of Christ take time to come to earth." Such an attitude stems from a tragic misconception of time, from the strangely irrational notion that there is something in the very flow of time that will inevitably cure all ills. Actually, time itself is neutral; it can be used either destructively or constructively. More and more I feel that the people of ill will have used time much more effectively than have the people of good will. We will have to repent in this generation not merely for the hateful words and actions of the bad people, but for the appalling silence of the good people. Human progress never rolls in on wheels of inevitability; it comes through the tireless efforts of men willing to be co-workers with God, and without this hard work, time itself becomes an ally of the forces of social stagnation. We must use time creatively, in the knowledge that the time is always ripe to do right. Now is the time to make real the promise of democracy and transform our pending national elegy into a creative psalm of brotherhood. Now is the time to lift our national policy from the quicksand of racial injustice to the solid rock of human dignity. . . .

But though I was initially disappointed at being categorized as an extremist, as I continued to think about the matter I gradually gained a measure of satisfaction from the label. Was not Jesus an extremist for love: "Love your enemies, bless them that curse you, do good to them that hate you, and pray for them which despitefully use you, and persecute you." Was not Amos an extremist for justice; "Let justice roll down like waters and righteousness like an ever-flowing stream." Was not Paul an extremist for the Christian gospel: "I bear in my body the marks of the Lord Jesus." Was not Martin Luther an extremist: "Here

I stand; I cannot do otherwise, so help me God.'' And John Bunyan: ''I will stay in jail to the end of my days before I make a butchery of my conscience.'' And Abraham Lincoln: ''This nation cannot survive half slave and half free.'' And Thomas Jefferson: ''We hold these truths to be self-evident, that all men are created equal. . . .'' So the question is not whether we will be extremists, but what kind of extremists we will be. Will we be extremists for hate or for love? Will we be extremists for the preservation of injustice or for the extension of justice? In that dramatic scene on Calvary's hill three men were crucified. We must never forget that all three were crucified for the same crime—the crime of extremism. Two were extremists for immorality, and thus fell below their environment. The other, Jesus Christ, was an extremist for love, truth, and goodness, and thereby rose above his environment. Perhaps the South, the nation, and the world are in dire need of creative extremists. . . .

Never before have I written so long a letter. I'm afraid it is much too long to take your precious time. I can assure you that it would have been much shorter if I had been writing from a comfortable desk, but what else can one do when he is alone in a narrow jail cell, other than write long letters, think long thoughts, and pray long prayers?

If I have said anything in this letter that overstates the truth and indicates an unreasonable impatience, I beg you to forgive me. If I have said anything that understates the truth and indicates my having a patience that allows me to settle for anything less than brotherhood, I beg God to forgive me.

I hope this letter finds you strong in the faith. I also hope that circumstances will soon make it possible for me to meet each of you, not as an integrationist or a civil rights leader but as a fellow clergyman and a Christian brother. Let us all hope that the dark clouds of racial prejudice will soon pass away and the deep fog of misunderstanding will be lifted from our fear-drenched communities, and in some not too distant tomorrow the radiant stars of love and brotherhood will shine over our great nation with all their scintillating beauty.

> Yours in the cause of
> Peace and Brotherhood,
> MARTIN LUTHER KING, JR.

Riddle of the Pig

Marvin Harris

When the God of the ancient Hebrews told them not to eat pork, He must have realized that generations of scholars were going to try to figure out why. From my ecological perspective, I would like to offer an explanation that relates Jewish and Muslim attitudes toward the pig to the cultural and natural ecosystems of the Middle East.

Naturalistic explanations for the taboo on pork go back to Maimonides, who lived in the twelfth century. Maimonides said that God had intended the ban on pork as a public health measure since swine's flesh "had a bad and damaging effect upon the body." This explanation gained favor in the mid-nineteenth century when it was discovered that there was a parasite present in undercooked pork that caused trichinosis.

Impressed by this rational answer to the ancient riddle, American Jews who belonged to the reformed congregations proceeded forthwith to revoke the scriptural taboo on the grounds that if properly cooked, pork no longer menaced the community's health. But Maimonides's explanation has a big hole in it: the flesh of all undercooked domestic animals can serve as a vector for human diseases. Cattle, sheep, and goats, for example, transmit brucellosis and anthrax, both of which have fatality rates as high as that of trichinosis.

Although Maimonides's explanation must be rejected, I think he was closer to the truth than modern anthropologists, including Sir James Frazer, renowned author of *The Golden Bough.* Frazer declared that pigs, like "all so-called unclean animals were originally sacred; the reason for not eating them was that many were originally divine." This doesn't help us very much since the sheep, goat, and cow were also once worshiped in the Middle East, and yet their meat is much enjoyed by all ethnic and religious groups in the area.

Other scholars have suggested that pigs, along with the rest of the foods prohibited in the Bible, were the original totem animals of the Hebrew clans. But why interdict the consumption of a valuable food resource? After all, eagles, ravens, spiders, and other animals that are of only limited significance as a source of human food are also used as clan totems.

Maimonides at least tried to place the taboo in a natural context in which definite, intelligible forces were at work. His mistake was that he conceived of public health much too narrowly. What he lacked was an understanding of the threat that the pig posed to the integrity of the broad cultural and natural ecosystem of the ancient Hebrew habitat.

I think we have to take into account that the protohistoric Hebrews—the children of Abraham—were adapted to life in the rugged, sparsely inhabited arid lands between Mesopotamia and Egypt. Until their conquest of the Jordan Valley in Palestine, which began in the thirteenth century B.C., they were primarily nomadic pastoralists, living almost entirely on their sheep, goats, and cattle. But like all pastoral peoples they maintained close relationships with sedentary agriculturalists who held the oasis and fertile river valley.

From time to time certain Hebrew lineages adopted a more sedentary, agriculturally oriented mode of existence, as appears to have been the case with the Abrahamites in Mesopotamia, the Josephites in Egypt, and the Isaacites in the western Negev. But even during the climax of urban and village life under David and Solomon, the herding of sheep, goats, and cattle continued to play a vital, if not predominant, economic role everywhere except in the irrigated portions of the Jordan Valley.

Within the over-all pattern of this mixed farming and pastoral complex, the divine prohibition against pork constituted a sound ecological strategy. During periods of maximum nomadism, it was impossible for the Israelites to raise pigs, while during the semi-sedentary and even fully village farming phases, pigs were more of a threat than an asset. The basic reason for this is that the world zones of pastoral nomadism correspond to unforested plains and hills that are too arid for rainfall agriculture and that cannot easily be irrigated. The domestic animals best adapted to these zones are the ruminants—cattle, sheep, and goats. Because ruminants have sacks anterior to their stomachs, they are able to digest grass, leaves, and other foods consisting mainly of cellulose more efficiently than any other mammals.

The pig, however, is primarily a creature of forests and shaded river banks. Although it is omnivorous, its best weight gain is from food low in cellulose—nuts, fruits, tubers, and especially grains, making it a direct competitor of man. It cannot subsist on grass alone and nowhere in the world do fully nomadic pastoralists raise significant numbers of pigs. The pig has the further disadvantage of not being a practical source of milk and of being difficult to herd over long distances.

Above all, the pig is ill-adapted to the heat of the Negev, the Jordan Valley, and the other biblical lands. Compared to cattle, goats, and sheep, the pig is markedly incapable of maintaining a constant body temperature when the temperature rises.

In spite of the expression "to sweat like a pig," it has now become clear that pigs can't sweat through their relatively hairless skins. Human beings, the sweatiest of all mammals, cool themselves by evaporating as much as three ounces of body liquid per hour from each square foot of body surface. The best a pig can manage is one-tenth ounce per square foot, and none of this is sweat. Even sheep evaporate twice as much body liquid through their skins as pigs. And sheep have the advantage of thick white wool, which both reflects the sun's rays and provides insulation when the ambient temperature rises above body temperature. According to L. E. Mount of the Agricultural Research Council Institute of Animal Physiology in Cambridge, England, adult pigs will die if exposed to direct sunlight and air temperatures over 97 degrees F. In the Jordan Valley, air temperatures of 110 degrees occur almost every summer and there is intense sunshine throughout the year.

To compensate for its lack of protective hair and its inability to sweat, the pig must dampen its skin with external moisture. It usually does this by wallowing in fresh, clean mud, but if nothing else is available, it will cover its skin with its own urine and feces. Mount reports that below 84 degrees F. pigs kept in pens deposit their excreta away from their sleeping and feeding areas, while above 84 degrees they excrete throughout the pen.

Sheep and goats were the first animals to be domesticated in the Middle East, possibly as early as 9000 B.C. Pigs were domesticated in the same general region about 2,000 years later. Bone counts conducted by archeologists at early prehistoric village farming sites show that sheep and goats were in the majority while the domesticated pig was almost always a relatively minor part—about 5 percent—of the village fauna. This is what one would expect of a creature that ate the same food as man, couldn't be milked, and had to be provided with shade and mudholes. Domesticated pigs were from the beginning an economical and ecological luxury, especially since goats, sheep, and cattle provided milk, cheese, meat, hides, dung, fiber, and traction for plowing. But the pig, with its rich, fatty meat, was a delectable temptation—the kind, like incest and adultery, that mankind finds difficult to resist. And so God was heard to say that swine were unclean, not only as food, but to the touch as well. This message was repeated by Mohammed for the same reason: it was ecologically more adaptive for the people of the Middle East to cater to their goats, sheep, and cattle. Pigs tasted good but they ate you out of house and home and, if you gave them a chance, used up your water as well. Well, that's my answer to the riddle of why God told the Jews and the Muslims not to eat pork. Anyone have a better idea?

The Abominations of Leviticus

Mary Douglas

Defilement is never an isolated event. It cannot occur except in view of a systematic ordering of ideas. Hence any piecemeal interpretation of the pollution rules of another culture is bound to fail. For the only way in which pollution ideas make sense is in reference to a total structure of thought whose key-stone, boundaries, margins and internal lines are held in relation by rituals of separation.

To illustrate this I take a hoary old puzzle from biblical scholarship, the abominations of Leviticus, and particularly the dietary rules. Why should the camel, the hare and the rock badger be unclean? Why should some locusts, but not all, be unclean? Why should the frog be clean and the mouse and the hippopotamus unclean? What have chameleons, moles and crocodiles got in common that they should be listed together (Leviticus xi, 27)?

To help follow the argument I first quote the relevant versions of Leviticus and Deuteronomy using the text of the New Revised Standard Translation.

3. You shall not eat any abominable things. *4.* These are the animals you may eat: the ox, the sheep, the goat, *5.* the hart, the gazelle, the roe-buck, the wild goat, the ibex, the antelope and the mountain-sheep. *6.* Every animal that parts the hoof and has the hoof cloven in two, and chews the cud, among the animals you may eat. *7.* Yet of those that chew the cud or have the hoof cloven you shall not eat these: The camel, the hare and the rock badger, because they chew the cud but do not part the hoof, are unclean for you. *8.* And the swine, because it parts the hoof but does not chew the cud, is unclean for you. Their flesh you shall not eat, and their carcasses you shall not touch. *9.* Of all that are in the waters you may eat these: whatever has fins and scales you may eat. *10.* And whatever does not have fins and scales you shall not eat; it is unclean for you. *11.* You may eat all clean birds. *12.* But these are the ones which you shall not eat: the eagle, the vulture, the osprey. *13.* the buzzard, the kite, after their kinds; *14.* every raven after its kind; *15.* the ostrich, the night-hawk, the sea gull, the hawk, after their kinds; *16.* the little owl and the great owl, the water hen, *17.* and the pelican, the carrion vulture and the cormorant, *18.* the stork, the heron, after their kinds; the hoopoe and the bat. *19.* And all winged insects are unclean for you; they shall not be eaten. *20.* All clean winged things you may eat. (Deuteronomy xiv)

2. These are the living things which you may eat among all the beasts that are on the earth. *3.* Whatever parts the hoof and is cloven-footed and chews the cud, among the animals you may eat. *4.* Nevertheless among those that chew the cud or part the hoof, you shall not eat these: The camel, because it chews the cud but does not part the hoof, is unclean to you. *5.* And the rock badger, because it chews the cud but does not part the hoof, is unclean to you. *6.* And the hare, because it chews the cud but does not part the hoof, is unclean to you. *7.* And the swine, because it parts the hoof and is cloven-footed but does not chew the cud, is unclean to you. *8.* Of their flesh you shall not eat, and their carcasses you shall not touch; they are unclean to you. *9.* These you may eat of all that are in the waters. Everything in the waters that has fins and scales, whether in the seas or in the rivers, you may eat. *10.* But anything in the seas or the rivers that has not fins and scales, of the swarming creatures in the waters and of the living creatures that are in the waters, is an abomination to you. *11.* They shall remain an abomination to you; of their flesh you shall not eat, and their carcasses you shall have in abomination. *12.* Everything in the waters that has not fins and scales is an abomination to you. *13.* And these you shall have in abomination among the birds, they shall not be eaten, they are an abomination: the eagle, the ossifrage, the osprey, *14.* the kite, the falcon according to its kind, *15.* every raven according to its kind, *16.* the ostrich and the nighthawk, the sea gull, the hawk according to its kind, *17.* the owl, the cormorant, the ibis, *18.* the water hen, the pelican, the vulture, *19.* the stork, the heron according to its kind, the hoopoe and the bat. *20.* All winged insects that go upon all fours are an abomination to you. *21.* Yet among the winged insects that go on all fours you may eat those which have legs above their feet, with which to leap upon the earth. *22.* Of them you may eat: the locust according to its kind, the bald locust according to its kind, the cricket according to its kind, and the grasshopper according to its kind. *23.* But all other winged insects which have four feet are an abomination to you. *24.* And by these you shall become unclean; whoever touches their carcass shall be unclean until the evening, *25.* and whoever carries any part of their carcass shall wash his clothes and be unclean until the evening. *26.* Every animal which parts the hoof but is not cloven-footed or does not chew the cud is unclean to you: everyone who touches them shall be unclean. *27.* And all that go on their paws, among the animals that go on all fours, are unclean to you; whoever touches their carcass shall be unclean until the evening, *28.* and he who carries their carcass shall wash his clothes and be unclean until the evening; they are unclean to you. *29.* And these are unclean to you among the swarming things that swarm upon the earth; the weasel, the mouse, the great lizard according to its kind, *30.* the gecko, the land crocodile, the lizard, the sand lizard and the chameleon. *31.* These are unclean to you among all that swarm; whoever touches them when they are dead shall be unclean until the evening. *32.* And anything upon which any of them falls when they are dead shall be unclean.

41. Every swarming thing that swarms upon the earth is an abomination; it shall not be eaten. *42.* Whatever goes on its belly, and whatever goes on all fours, or whatever has many feet, all the swarming things that swarm upon the earth, you shall not eat; for they are an abomination. (Leviticus xi) . . .

Any interpretations will fail which take the Do-nots of the Old Testament in piecemeal fashion. The only sound approach is to forget hygiene, aesthetics, morals and instinctive revulsion . . . and start with the texts. Since each of the injunctions is prefaced by the command to be holy, so they must be explained by that command. There must be contrariness between holiness and abominations which will make over-all sense of all the particular restrictions.

Holiness is the attribute of Godhead. Its root means 'set apart'. What else does it mean? We should start any cosmological inquiry by seeking the principles of power and danger. In the Old Testament we find blessing as the source of all good things, and the withdrawal of blessing as the source of all dangers. The blessing of God makes the land possible for men to live in.

God's work through the blessing is essentially to create order, through which men's affairs prosper. Fertility of women, livestock and fields is promised as a result of the blessing and this is to be obtained by keeping covenant with God and observing all his precepts and ceremonies (Deuteronomy xxviii, 1–14). Where the blessing is withdrawn and the power of the curse unleashed, there is barrenness, pestilence, confusion. . . .

From this it is clear that the positive and negative precepts are held to be efficacious and not merely expressive: observing them draws down prosperity, infringing them brings danger. We are thus entitled to treat them in the same way as we treat primitive ritual avoidances whose breach unleashes danger to men. The precepts and ceremonies alike are focused on the idea of the holiness of God which men must create in their own lives. So this is a universe in which men prosper by conforming to holiness and perish when they deviate from it. . . .

Granted that its root means separateness, the next idea that emerges is of the Holy as wholeness and completeness. Much of Leviticus is taken up with stating the physical perfection that is required of things presented in the temple and of persons approaching it. The animals offered in sacrifice must be without blemish, women must be purified after childbirth, lepers should be separated and ritually cleansed before being allowed to approach it once they are cured. All bodily discharges are defiling and disqualify from approach to the temple. Priests may only come into contact with death when their own close kin die. But the high priest must never have contact with death.

> *17.* Say to Aaron, None of your descendants throughout their generations who has a blemish may approach to offer the bread of his God. *18.* For no one who has a blemish shall draw near, a man blind or lame, or one who has a mutilated face or a limb too long. *19.* or a man who has an injured foot or an injured hand, *20.* or a hunch-back, or a dwarf, or a man with a defect in his sight or an itching disease or scabs, or crushed testicles; *21.* no man of the descendants of Aaron the priest who has a blemish shall come near to offer the Lord's offerings by fire; . . . (Leviticus xxi)

In other words, he must be perfect as a man, if he is to be a priest. . . .

Wholeness is also extended to signify completeness in a social context. An important enterprise, once begun, must not be left incomplete. This way of lacking wholeness also disqualifies a man from fighting. Before a battle the captains shall proclaim:

> *5.* What man is there that has built a new house and has not dedicated it? Let him go back to his house, lest he die in the battle and another man dedicate it. *6.* What man is there that has planted a vineyard and has not enjoyed its fruit? Let him go back to his house, lest he die in the battle and another man enjoy its fruit. *7.* And what man is there that hath betrothed a wife and has not taken her? Let him go back to his house, lest he die in the battle and another man take her. (Deuteronomy xx) . . .

Other precepts develop the idea of wholeness in another direction. The metaphors of the physical body and of the new undertaking relate to the perfection and completeness of the individual and his work. Other precepts extend holiness to species and categories. Hybrids and other confusions are abominated.

23. And you shall not lie with any beast and defile yourself with it, neither shall any woman give herself to a beast to lie with it: it is perversion. (Leviticus xviii)

The word perversion is a significant mistranslation of the rare Hebrew word *tebhel*, which has as its meaning mixing or confusion. The same theme is taken up in Leviticus xix, 19.

You shall keep my statutes. You shall not let your cattle breed with a different kind; you shall not sow your field with two kinds of seed; nor shall there come upon you a garment of cloth made of two kinds of stuff.

All these injunctions are prefaced by the general command: 'Be holy, for I am holy.' We can conclude that holiness is exemplified by completeness. Holiness requires that individuals shall conform to the class to which they belong. And holiness requires that different classes of things shall not be confused.

Another set of precepts refines on this last point. Holiness means keeping distinct the categories of creation. It therefore involves correct definition, discrimination and order. Under this head all the rules of sexual morality exemplify the holy. Incest and adultery (Leviticus xviii, 6–20) are against holiness, in the simple sense of right order. Morality does not conflict with holiness, but holiness is more a matter of separating that which should be separated than of protecting the rights of husbands and brothers. . . .

We have now laid a good basis for approaching the laws about clean and unclean meats. To be holy is to be whole, to be one; holiness is unity, integrity, perfection of the individual and of the kind. The dietary rules merely develop the metaphor of holiness on the same lines.

First we should start with livestock, the herds of cattle, camels, sheep and goats which were the livelihood of the Israelites. These animals were clean inasmuch as contact with them did not require purification before approaching the Temple. Livestock, like the inhabited land, received the blessing of God. Both land and livestock were fertile by the blessing, both were drawn into the divine order. The farmer's duty was to preserve the blessing. For one thing, he had to preserve the order of creation. So no hybrids, as we have seen, either in the fields or in the herds or in the clothes made from wool or flax. . . . Cloven hoofed, cud-chewing ungulates are the model of the proper kind of food for a pastoralist. If they must eat wild game, they can eat wild game that shares these distinctive characters and is therefore of the same general species. This is a kind of casuistry which permits scope for hunting antelope and wild goats and wild sheep. Everything would be quite straightforward were it not that the legal mind has seen fit to give ruling on some borderline cases. Some animals seem to be ruminant, such as the hare and the hyrax (or rock badger), whose constant grinding of their teeth was held to be cud-chewing. But they are definitely not cloven-hoofed and so are excluded by name. Similarly for animals which are cloven-hoofed but are not ruminant, the pig and the camel. Note that this failure to conform to the two necessary criteria for defining cattle is the only reason given in the Old Testament for avoiding the pig; nothing whatever is said about its dirty scavenging habits. As the pig does not yield milk, hide nor wool, there is no other reason for keeping it except for its flesh. And if the Israelites did not keep pig they would not be familiar with its habits. I suggest that originally the sole reason for its being counted as unclean is its failure as a wild boar to get into the antelope class, and that in this it is on the same footing as the camel and the hyrax, exactly as is stated in the book.

After these borderline cases have been dismissed, the law goes on to deal with creatures according to how they live in the three elements, the water, the air and the earth. The principles here applied are rather different from those covering the camel, the pig, the hare and the hyrax. For the latter are excepted from clean food in having one but not both of the defining characters of livestock. Birds I can say nothing about, because, as I have said, they are named and not described and the translation of the name is open to doubt. But in general the underlying principle of cleanness in animals is that they shall conform fully to their class. Those species are unclean which are imperfect members of their class, or whose class itself confounds the general scheme of the world.

To grasp this scheme we need to go back to Genesis and the creation. Here a three-fold classification unfolds, divided between the earth, the waters and the firmament. Leviticus takes up this scheme and allots to each element its proper kind of animal life. In the firmament two-legged fowls fly with wings. In the water scaly fish swim with fins. On the earth four-legged animals hop, jump or walk. Any class of creatures which is not equipped for the right kind of locomotion in its element is contrary to holiness. Contact with it disqualifies a person from approaching the Temple. Thus anything in the water which has not fins and scales is unclean (xi, 10–12). Nothing is said about predatory habits or of scavenging. The only sure test for cleanness in a fish is its scales and its propulsion by means of fins.

Four-footed creatures which fly (xi, 20–26) are unclean. Any creature which has two legs and two hands and which goes on all fours like a quadruped is unclean (xi, 27). Then follows (v, 29) a much disputed list. On some translations, it would appear to consist precisely of creatures endowed with hands instead of front feet, which perversely use their hands for walking: the weasel, the mouse, the crocodile, the shrew, various kinds of lizards, the chameleon and mole (Danby, 1933), whose forefeet are uncannily hand-like. This feature of this list is lost in the New Revised Standard Translation which uses the word 'paws' instead of hands.

The last kind of unclean animal is that which creeps, crawls or swarms upon the earth. This form of movement is explicitly contrary to holiness (Leviticus xi, 41–4). Driver and White use 'swarming' to translate the Hebrew *shérec*, which is applied to both those which teem in the waters and those which swarm on the ground. Whether we call it teeming, trailing, creeping, crawling or swarming, it is an indeterminate form of movement. Since the main animal categories are defined by their typical movement, 'swarming', which is not a mode of propulsion proper to any particular element, cuts across the basic classification. Swarming things are neither fish, flesh nor fowl. Eels and worms inhabit water, though not as fish; reptiles go on dry land, though not as quadrupeds; some insects fly, though not as birds. . . .

If the proposed interpretation of the forbidden animals is correct, the dietary laws would have been like signs which at every turn inspired meditation on the oneness, purity and completeness of God. By rules of avoidance holiness was given a physical expression in every encounter with the animal kingdom and at every meal. Observance of the dietary rules would thus have been a meaningful part of the great liturgical act of recognition and worship which culminated in the sacrifice in the Temple.

[Citations Omitted]

The Girl in Conflict

Margaret Mead

Were there no conflicts, no temperaments which deviated so markedly from the normal that clash was inevitable? Was the diffused affection and the diffused authority of the large families, the ease of moving from one family to another, the knowledge of sex and the freedom to experiment a sufficient guarantee to all Samoan girls of a perfect adjustment? In almost all cases, yes. But I have reserved for this chapter the tales of the few girls who deviated in temperament or in conduct, although in many cases these deviations were only charged with possibilities of conflict, and actually had no painful results. . . .

In the girl's religious life the attitude of the missionaries was the decisive one. The missionaries require chastity for church membership and discouraged church membership before marriage, except for the young people in the missionary boarding schools who could be continually supervised. This passive acceptance by the religious authorities themselves of pre-marital irregularities went a long way towards minimising the girls' sense of guilt. Continence became not a passport to heaven but a passport to the missionary schools which in turn were regarded as a social rather than a religious adventure. The girl who indulged in sex experiments was expelled from the local pastor's

pretty stranger who was a year younger than herself, but whose rank as visiting *taupo* gave her precedence. Lola again became troublesome. She quarrelled with the younger girls, was impertinent to the older ones, shirked her work, talked spitefully against the stranger. Perhaps all of this might have been only temporary and had no more far-reaching results than a temporary lack of favour in her new household, had it not been for a still more unfortunate event. The Don Juan of the village was a sleek, discreet man of about forty, a widower . . . a man of circumspect manner and winning ways. He was looking for a second wife and turned his attention toward the visitor who was lodged in the guest house of the next village. But Fuativa was a cautious and calculating lover. He wished to look over his future bride carefully and so he visited her house casually, without any declaration of his intention. And he noticed that Lola had reached a robust girlhood and stopped to pluck this ready fruit by the way, while he was still undecided about the more serious business of matrimony.

With all her capacity for violence, Lola possessed also a strong capacity for affection. Fuativa was a skilled and considerate lover. Few girls were quite so fortunate in their first lovers, and so few felt such unmixed regret when the first love affair was broken off. Fuativa won her easily and after three weeks which were casual to him, and very important to her, he proposed for the hand of the visitor. . . . The rage of Lola was unbounded and she took an immediate revenge, publicly accusing her rival of being a thief and setting the whole village by the ears. The women of the host household drove her out with many imprecations and she fled home to her mother, thus completing the residence cycle begun four years ago. She was now in the position of the delinquent in our society. She had continuously violated the group standards and she had exhausted all the solutions open to her. No other family group would open its doors to a girl whose record branded her as a liar, a trouble maker, a fighter, and a thief, for her misdeeds included continual petty thievery. Had she quarrelled with a father or been outraged by a brother-in-law, a refuge would have been easy to find. But her personality was essentially unfortunate. In her mother's household she made her sisters miserable, but she did not lord it over them as she had done before. She was sullen, bitter, vituperative. The young people of the village branded her as the possessor of a *lotu le aga*, ("a bad heart") and she had no companions. Her young rival left the island to prepare for her wedding, or the next chapter might have been Lola's doing her actual physical violence. When I left, she was living, idle, sullen, and defiant in her long-suffering mother's house.

Mala's sins were slightly otherwise. Where Lola was violent, Mala was treacherous; where Lola was antagonistic, Mala was insinuating. Mala was younger, having just reached puberty in January, the middle of my stay on the island. She was a scrawny, ill-favoured little girl, always untidily dressed. Her parents were dead and she lived with her uncle, a sour, disgruntled man of small position. His wife came from another village and disliked her present home. The marriage was childless. The only other member of the house group was another niece who had divorced her husband. She also was childless. None showed Mala any affection, and they worked her unmercifully. The life of the only young girl or boy in a Samoan house, in the very rare cases when it occurs, is always very difficult. . . . From her early childhood she had been branded as a thief, a dangerous charge in a country where there are no doors or locks, and houses are left empty for a day at a time. Her first offence had been to steal a foreign toy which belonged to the chief's little son. The irate mother had soundly berated the child, on boat day, on the beach where all the people were gathered. When her name was mentioned, the information that she was a thief and a liar was tacked on as casually as was the remark that another was cross-eyed or deaf. Other children avoided her. Next door lived Tino, a dull good child, a few months younger than Mala. Ordinarily these two would have been companions and Mala always insisted that Tino was her friend, but Tino indignantly disclaimed all association with her. And as if her reputation for thievery were not sufficient, she added a further misdemeanour. She played with boys, preferred boys' games, tied her *lavalava* like a boy. This behaviour was displayed to the whole village who were vociferous in their condemnation. "She really was a very bad girl. She stole; she lied; and she played with boys." As in other parts of the world, the whole odium fell on the girl, so the boys did not fight shy of her. They teased her, bullied her, used her as general errand boy and fag. Some of the more precocious boys of her own age were already beginning to look to her for possibilities of other forms of amusement. Probably she will end by giving her favours to whoever asks for them, and sink lower and lower in the village esteem and especially in the opinion of her own sex from whom she so passionately desires recognition and affection.

Lola and Mala both seemed to be the victims of lack of affection. They both had unusual capacity for devotion and were abnormally liable to become jealous. Both responded with pathetic swiftness to any manifestations of affection. At one end of the scale in their need for affection, they were unfortunately placed at the other end in their chance of receiving it. Lola had a double handicap in her unfortunate temperament and the greater amiability of her three sisters. Her temperamental defects were further aggravated by the absence of any strong authority in her immediate household. Sami, the docile sister, had been saddled with the care of the younger children; Lola, harder to control, was given no such saving responsibility. These conditions were all as unusual as her demand and capacity for affection. And, similarly, seldom were children as desolate as Mala, marooned in a household of unsympathetic adults. So it would appear that their delinquency was produced by the combination of two sets of casual factors, unusual emotional needs and unusual home conditions. Less affection-ate children in the same environments, or the same children in more favourable surroundings, probably would never have become as defi-nitely outcast as these. . . .

And here ends the tale of serious conflict or serious deviation from group standards. The other girls varied as to whether they were sub-jected to the superior supervision of the pastor's household or not, as to whether they came from households of rank or families of small prestige, and most of all as to whether they lived in a biological family or a large heterogeneous household.

Adolescence

Derek Freeman

In Samoa . . . according to Mead the "disruptive concomitants" inher-ent in adolescence had, because of the mild and easy social environ-ment, been "successfully muted." Adolescence among the Samoans, she claimed, being "peculiarly free of all those characteristics which make it a period dreaded by adults and perilous for young people in more complex—and often also, in more primitive—societies," was "the age of maximum ease." Thus human nature, within the "differ-ent social form" of Samoa, lacked "the conflicts which are so often characteristic of adolescence." On the basis of this claim . . . Mead unequivocally asserted the sovereignty of culture over biology.

Is it in fact true, as Mead claimed, that the behavior of Samoan ado-lescents is untroubled and unstressed and lacks the conflicts that are so often characteristic of this period of development? As Herant Kat-chadourian notes, "research on ordinary adolescents has generally failed to substantiate claims of the inevitability and universality of ado-lescent stress." Nonetheless, the findings of W. A. Lunden, M. R. Has-kell and L. Yablonsky, and others have clearly shown that the years of adolescence are hazardous for many, with delinquency in the United States and elsewhere reaching a peak at about age 16. To what extent, then, is adolescent delinquency present in Samoa? In particular, what can be concluded about delinquency among Samoan female adoles-cents from the information Mead herself has provided?

Mead discusses delinquency in *Coming of Age in Samoa* in the gen-eral context of deviance. For Benedict and Mead deviance was a con-cept derived directly from their theory of cultural determinism, the basic notion of which was of the "undifferentiated" raw material of human nature being "moulded into shape by its society." One of the corollaries of this notion was that this molding process was sometimes ineffective, with the individual who "failed to receive the cultural imprint" becoming a "cultural misfit," or deviant. These deviants from the cultural pattern of their society Benedict and Mead then relegated to a special category, as in the chapter of *Coming of Age in Samoa* entitled "The Girl in Conflict." In this chapter, which is crucially important for her whole argument, Mead distinguishes between what she calls "deviants upwards" from the pattern of Samoan culture, and deviants "in a downward direction." Upward deviants, she writes, are those who demand "a different or improved environment," and reject "the traditional choices." In this category she puts . . . girls . . . whom she lists as having had "no heterosexual experience." Lita, two months past menarche, who "wished to go to Tutuila and become a nurse or teacher"; [and] Sona, three years past menarche, who was "overbearing in manner, arbitrary and tyrannous towards younger people, impudently deferential towards her elders," and who blatantly proclaimed "her pursuit of ends different from those approved by her fellows." . . . All . . . of these girls, according to Mead, might, at any time, have come into real conflict with their society, but at the time of her inquiries they had not, and so remained deviants upwards, rather than deviants in a downward direction, or delinquents.

A delinquent, Mead defined as an individual who is "maladjusted to the demands of her civilization, and who comes definitely into conflict with her group, not because she adheres to a different standard, but because she violates the group standards which are also her own." Of her sample of twenty-five adolescent girls, says Mead, two girls, Lola and Mala, had been delinquents for several years. Lola, aged 17, of Si'ufaga, was a quarrelsome, insubordinate, vituperative, and spiteful girl who had "continuously violated" the standards of her group. She "contested every point, objected to every request, shirked her work, fought her sisters, mocked her mother," had been expelled from residence in the pastor's house after a fight with another delinquent, and in a jealous rage had publicly accused a female rival of being a thief, so "setting the whole village by the ears." Mala, aged about 16, also of Si'ufaga, was insinuating and treacherous, as well as being a liar and a thief.

In addition to these two girls of Si'ufaga, Mead also mentions under her "conception of delinquency" a girl of Faleasao, called Sala. Sala, three years past menarche, was a "stupid, underhand, deceitful" girl who had been expelled from residence in the pastor's house for "sex offences." This expulsion, which is a serious matter in Samoan eyes, shows that Sala had also violated group standards, and that she too, in terms of Mead's definition, was a delinquent. Another girl of Faleasao whom Mead discusses was Moana, 16 and a half, who, having begun her "amours" at 15, allowed her uncle, who had been asked by her parents "to adopt her and attempt to curb her waywardness," to avail himself "of her complacency." This sexual liaison, as Mead notes, was "in direct violation of the brother and sister taboo," Moana's uncle being young enough for her to call him brother. It was thus an instance of incest, a heinous offense, the perpetrators of which, according to Samoans, are liable to supernatural punishment. Thus Schultz recounts that when Mata'utia had sexual intercourse with his cousin Levalasi, he was attacked by a loathsome disease, while Levalasi gave birth to a clot of blood. Moana's incestuous liaison with her uncle resulted, Mead states, in a family feud. Moana's violation of one of the strictest prohibitions of Samoan society was thus unquestionably a delinquent act in terms of Mead's definition, although Mead inexplicably did not even class her as a deviant.

It is evident, then, from Mead's own account that four of her twenty-five adolescent girls were delinquents. Further, from her descriptions of the actions of these four girls, it is apparent that instances of delinquent behavior by Lola and Moana occurred during Mead's brief sojourn in Manu'a from November 1925 to May 1926. If we assume, conservatively, on the basis of Mead's reports, that among the twenty-five adolescents she studied there was *one* delinquent act per annum, this is equivalent to a rate of forty such acts per thousand.

How does this rate compare with delinquency rates in other societies? Mead, as we have seen, defines a delinquent as one who violates the standards of her group. The examples she gives of delinquent behavior plainly caused considerable social disruption, setting a whole village by the ears in the case of Lola and resulting in a family feud in the case of Moana. They were, in other words, of a kind that would warrant their being considered by a juridical fono [tribal court]. It thus is possible, though Mead did not attempt this, to compare the incidence of delinquent behavior in Samoa with that of Western countries, where delinquency, as Sandhu notes, is defined as "any act . . . which might be brought before court and adjudicated." Mead's twenty-five female adolescents, as she notes, ranged in age from 14 or 15 to 19 or 20. If we assume an age range of 14 to 19, it becomes possible to make a comparison, on the basis of the rates given by D. J. West in *The Young Offender*, for indictable offenses by females per thousand of population of the same age, in England and Wales in 1965. In the age-group 14–19 the average rate per thousand was 4.00. In other words, the delinquency rate which seems likely to have been characteristic of Mead's Samoan female delinquents in 1925, was about ten times higher than that which existed among female adolescents in England and Wales in 1965.

This comparison is obviously only approximate. It does, however, indicate that among the girls studied by Mead in 1925–1926 delinquency was in fact at quite a high level. Further, Mead's relegating of delinquents to a separate population of deviants, or "cultural misfits," to which her generalizations about Samoan adolescence supposedly do not apply, is revealed as a decidedly unscientific maneuver, for her four delinquents and three ''upwards deviants,'' who, together, make up 28 percent of her sample of twenty-five female adolescents, are obviously every bit as much the product of the Samoan social environment as are the eighteen other adolescent girls who were, Mead tells us, untroubled and unstressed.

The conclusions about adolescence in Samoa to which Mead came in 1929 were based, as we have seen, on a few months' study of twenty-five girls. She had no compunction, however, in extending these conclusions, in later years, to male adolescents. Thus, in 1937 her statement that adolescence in Samoa was ''the age of maximum ease'' was applied to both males and females, and in 1950 she asserted that ''the boy who would flee from too much pressure on his young manhood hardly exists in Samoa.'' These statements were made without specific investigation by Mead of Samoan male adolescents. As we have seen, the delinquency rate among Samoan female adolescents is, in comparative terms, high. It has long been known that delinquency in male adolescents is commonly four to five times higher than in females. In this respect Samoa is no different from other countries; the ratio of males to females among 932 adolescent first offenders in Western Samoa was five to one. Mead's statements about Samoan male adolescents are, then, entirely unwarranted. As I shall presently show, Samoan delinquency rates for male adolescents are closely comparable to those of other countries. . . .

A sample of first offenders drawn at random from the police records of Western Samoa yielded 528 cases of acts of violence by males and 218 by females in the age range of 12 to 22 years. . . . [There] is a rapid rise in the incidence of acts of violence from about age 14 onward, with this incidence reaching a peak at age 16. . . . [From] early adolescence onward both males and females tend to join in affrays.

There is also a peak at age 16 in offenses against authority, particularly by males. From early adolescence onward Samoan youths may be observed grimacing and making threatening gestures at their elders, including chiefs, behind their backs, especially after having been punished or reprimanded; with the attainment of puberty, youths will occasionally lose control and openly attack those in authority over them. For example, in April 1965 a 31-year-old chief, patroling a village in Savai'i to enforce the ten P.M. curfew, came upon a group of five male adolescents who were breaking this curfew by playing a guitar and singing, and he at once set about chastising them with a board. Instead of scattering, as would children, at this show of chiefly authority, one of these youths hurled a stone at the chief with such force as to expose the bone of his forehead and put him in hospital for a fortnight with concussion.

Another measure of the involvement of adolescents in aggressive activity is obtained from a sample of forty cases, drawn at random from police records, of convictions for using insulting or indecent words. In this sample sixteen, or 40 percent, of those convicted were aged between 14 and 19, with thirteen of these sixteen adolescents being girls. As these figures indicate, verbal aggression is very common among adolescent girls in Samoa, and gives rise to much fighting between them.

Samoan adolescents from about 14 years of age onward begin to become involved in stressful situations that are sexual in origin. In a sample of 2,180 male first offenders there were no convictions for sexual offenses by individuals younger than 14. There was, however, one case of indecent assault by a 14-year-old youth, and of the total of forty-five convictions for indecent assault, rape, and attempted rape, nineteen, or 42 percent, of the offenders were males aged between 14 and 19, an incidence comparable to that existing in the United States. Menachem Amir, for example, records that in the United States 40.3 percent of forcible rape offenders are aged between 15 and 19. In the case of victims of rape, however, there is an appreciable difference between the United States and Samoa. Whereas according to Amir only 24.9 percent of rape victims in the United States are in the age-group 15–19, in a sample of thirty-two cases of rape and attempted rape from Western Samoa, 62 percent of the victims were in this age-group. A statistic available from Australia suggests that the incidence of virgins among rape victims is appreciably higher in Samoa than in other cultures: while according to J. P. Bush 30.5 percent of rape victims in Victoria, Australia were virgins before they were assaulted, the incidence of virgins in my Samoan sample of rape victims was 60 percent.

As these incidences indicate, the traditional sexual mores of their society subject Samoan girls, from puberty onward, to formidable stresses. Within their families, and as members of the *Ekalesia* [the Church] (as the great majority of them are), they are subjected to a searching discipline aimed at safeguarding their virginity until a respectable marriage can be arranged—while during this same time they are exposed to the risk of both surreptitious and forcible rape. Thus, it is commonplace in Samoan villages for pubescent girls to be warned that they must sleep in the company of other girls of their family, so lessening the likelihood of becoming the victim of a moetotolo [rapist], and in particular that they must not walk alone beyond the precincts of a village for fear of being raped. Again, when a girl does finally elope from her family, as most do, from about 19 years of age onward, this occasion is commonly fraught with uncertainty and tension. These ordeals that the sexual mores of Samoa present to girls at puberty can generate very appreciable stresses, culminating from time to time in acts of suicide, as in the cases of Tupe and Malu . . . and of the 22-year-old girl . . . who took her own life after having lost her virginity to a moetotolo.

Now to return to the general discussion of delinquency among Samoan adolescents: as we have already seen, an analysis of the information that Mead herself provides on the behavior of Samoan girls aged 14–19 in Manu'a in the mid-1920s reveals what appears to have been a comparatively high rate of adolescent delinquency. In order to test further Mead's assertion that the adolescent period in Samoa in both males and females is untroubled and lacks the conflicts that tend to exist elsewhere, I decided, in 1967, to make a more detailed inquiry into the incidence of delinquency among adolescents in Western Samoa. At that time the only statistics available in Western Samoa on the incidence of criminal offenses were contained in the annual reports of the Police and Prisons Department, and these did not include information on the ages of offenders. A method that was open to me, however, was to compile, from police records, a *random* sample of convicted offenders, noting in each case the age and sex of the offender, the nature of the offense, and the date of conviction. The sample I compiled in this way totaled 2,717 convicted offenders. The offenses covered in this random sample included assault and various other crimes of violence; the "provoking of a breach of the peace"; theft and other offenses against property; trespass; rape and indecent assault; abduction; obstructing the police; uttering threatening, insulting, or indecent words; drunkenness; and perjury. In the great majority of cases they were offenses committed during the early 1960s, predominantly by inhabitants of the island of Upolu.

When this sample was tabulated in terms of age at first conviction the total range was from 9 to 80 years of age, and of the 2,717 offenders, 2,180 were males and 537 females, yielding a ratio of approximately four males to one female. However, of the 932 individuals whose age at first conviction was between 15 and 19, 777 were males and 155 females, a ratio of approximately five to one.

South Seas Squall

Lowell D. Holmes

"New Samoa Book Challenges Margaret Mead's Conclusions" ran the front-page headline in *The New York Times* last January. "Two months before its official publication date," the article reported, "a book maintaining that the late Margaret Mead seriously misrepresented the culture and character of Samoa has ignited heated discussion within the behavioral sciences."

The book that stirred this advance notice and notoriety was *Margaret Mead and Samoa: The Making and Unmaking of An Anthro-*

pological Myth, by Derek Freeman, an emeritus professor of anthropology at the Australian National University, in Canberra. It attacks the conclusions of Mead's first research project, which she began when she was only twenty-three, and which she documented in *Coming of Age in Samoa.* "The entire academic establishment and all the encyclopedias and all the textbooks accepted the conclusions in her book, and these conclusions are fundamentally in error," Freeman told the *Times* reporter. "There isn't another example of such wholesale deception in the history of the behavioral sciences."

The *Times* article had special meaning for me, because, in 1954, I lived in Ta'u, where Mead had worked twenty-nine years earlier, talked to many of her informants, and analyzed every word she had written about life in that Samoan village. In that year I was conducting what is known as a methodological restudy. I retraced Mead's steps with the express purpose of testing the reliability and validity of her investigation and establishing the kinds of errors of interpretation that she might have made. Margaret Mead was a woman in a male-dominated society; she was young in a culture that venerates age; she was on her first field trip at a time when research methods were crude; and she was a student of the influential anthropologist Franz Boas, and so went armed with a particular theoretical frame of reference. Not only was I to analyze how my findings differed from hers (if they did), I was also to speculate how our differences in age, status, personality, and outlook might have accounted for differences in our collecting and interpreting of data.

As of 1954, a number of anthropologists favored restudies as a way of understanding the anthropologist's role in fieldwork. But Mead thought restudies a wasteful use of limited research funds, though she had written that "there is no such thing as an unbiased report on any social situation," and at one point had even suggested that, in order to control personal bias, a fieldworker ought to be psychoanalyzed before going into the field.

On the day the *Times* story appeared, my phone began to ring. News people who had been directed to me by anthropologists familiar with my 1954 restudy wanted comment on the controversy. While many of these reporters had received advance copies of Freeman's book in the form of bound page proofs, I had not been among the privileged. So, although I had some idea of Freeman's viewpoint from correspondence I had had with him in 1966 and 1967, I was not ready to comment. A phone call to Harvard University Press, Freeman's publisher, brought a copy of the page proofs, which I read with considerable interest. Now I am ready to respond.

In his book, Freeman argues that Mead perpetrated a hoax comparable in scope to that of the Piltdown Man when, in 1928, she described Samoa as a paradise relatively untouched by competition, sexual inhibition, or guilt. Refusing to believe that adolescents inevitably experience emotional crises because of biological changes associated with puberty (the psychological theory that then held sway), Mead had set out to discover a society where passage to adulthood involves only a minimum of stress and strain. She described such a society in *Coming of Age in Samoa.*

In relating this "negative instance," as Freeman calls it, Mead established that nurture is more critical than nature, or heredity, in accounting for adolescent behavior. Freeman, who rejects the idea that humans are shaped primarily by culture and environment, and who believes that Boas and Mead have totally ignored the influence of genes and heredity, maintains that Mead's Samoan research has led anthropology, psychology, and education down the primrose path. He is out to rescue these disciplines, armed with the real truth about Samoa and Samoans.

In Freeman's view, Samoans are sexually inhibited (even puritanical), aggressive and highly competitive, prone to jealousy, and subject to psychological disturbances because of the rigid authority system under which they live. Not only is it more difficult to come of age in Samoa than in the United States, but Samoans also exhibit an unnatural range of pathological behavior; they assault, rape, and commit suicide and murder. Freeman claims that he could not publish these findings during Mead's lifetime because, until recently, he did not have access to government statistics that, he says, show rates of criminal behavior in Samoa many times higher than those found in the United States.

But Freeman's characterizations of Samoan personality and culture, and of Mead's work, do not jibe with what I saw. Freeman implies that, while I found much of Mead's research invalid, I was so awed by her reputation and so firmly under the thumb of Melville Herskovits, one of my professors at Northwestern, that I was afraid to reveal my true findings. The truth is that I would have loved to play the "giant killer," as Freeman now is trying to do. (What graduate student wouldn't?) But I couldn't. I had found the village and the behavior of its inhabitants to be much as Mead had described. *Coming of Age in Samoa* was like a map that represented the territory so well that I met with few surprises when I arrived. As for Herskovits's influence, all he demanded was that my criticisms of Mead's work be made with "icy objectivity," and that I deal with major issues and not trivial details.

After exhaustively reviewing Mead's writings on Samoa, I did find that the culture was not quite as simple as she had claimed, nor was Ta'u village quite the paradise that she would have us believe. For instance, Mead took some literary license in her chapter "A Day in Samoa"; she crowded typical activities into a "typical" day, and thus sketched a more bustling, vibrant scene than I ever encountered in any single twenty-four-hour period. I also could not agree with Mead on the degree of sexual freedom supposedly enjoyed by her informants, but then I am sure that she had greater rapport with teenagers than I (and probably Freeman). In fact, I found it extremely difficult to investigate anything of a sexual nature. There was considerable family and even village pressure for young people to maintain at least the outward appearance of chaste behavior. Yet the number of illegitimate children in the village, and the fact that grounds for divorce frequently involved adultery, gave the impression that more was going on than met the eye.

I also saw Samoan culture as considerably more competitive than Mead did, though I never saw it as inflexible or aggressive as Freeman does. I sensed a great preoccupation with status, power, and prestige, and on more than one occasion I observed fierce verbal duels between talking chiefs trying to enhance their own prestige or that of their village. The best fisherman, housebuilder, dancer, or orator was often pointed out to me. But I also learned that one was respected more for modesty than conceit, that it was better to have someone else laud your abilities than to do it yourself. And in matters of the heart, it seemed that Samoans often played for higher stakes than Mead had indicated. I sensed that there was a concept of romantic love—in folklore and in contemporary life—and there were even cases of unrequited love ending unhappily in suicide. These were rare, but they did exist.

I communicated my criticisms concerning life in Ta'u village to Mead, and she discussed them, in a chapter titled "Conclusion 1969," in a reissue of *Social Organization of Manua*, published by the Bishop Museum. We differed on a number of matters. But despite her tender age, her inexperience, and the great possibilities for error in a seminal scientific study, I found Mead's Samoan research remarkably reliable. The differences between our findings that could not be attributed to change were relatively minor and, in most cases, involved not discrepancies in data but differences in interpretation. In short, I confirmed Mead's conclusion that in 1925 it was undoubtedly easier to come of age in Samoa than in the United States.

The line between the child's world and the adult's world is effectively erased in Ta'u village, making for a more tranquil passage through adolescence. Since each household has a number of adults, any of whom may discipline children and respond to their needs, both authority and affection are diffused, easing the intensity of individual parent-child relationships. And if tensions do arise, flexible patterns of residence permit young people to flee to households of kinsmen. (While Freeman maintains that this does not happen in Samoa, I know of several such cases in Ta'u village; one informant revealed that when he was growing up he moved from house to house to avoid onerous work assignments.)

In Samoan homes, children are exposed to the facts of life—to sex, death, childbirth, and family leadership responsibilities—before they assume these responsibilities themselves. Coming of age is thus not a jolting experience; whenever the child is physically and mentally able, he simply assumes family chores and responsibilities. A child may begin caring for siblings as early as five or six years of age, and many adolescents take on plantation work, fishing chores, or household tasks long before such weighty responsibilities would be thrust upon an American child. While some observers have emphasized the oppressive work load forced upon teenagers, in this relatively bountiful environment no one puts in a forty-hour week or is required to work beyond his or her capacity.

Provided they stay out of serious trouble, teenage and young adult males are given a great deal of personal freedom. Members of *Aumaga* (a society of untitled men), some of whom are teenagers, often sleep together in the home of one of the village families, and frequently sit up until wee hours strumming guitars, joking, and playing cards. If these young people are repressed, they are also adept at hiding it. Young women are perhaps more restricted and given more household responsibility than men. But even they seem relaxed in family interactions.

By adolescence, Samoans have learned to regulate their own personal conduct, and there is practically no testing of the limits of sanctioned behavior. While young children are punished for misbehaving—mostly for making noise or standing up in the house when chiefs are seated— no Samoan child was ever forced to finish dinner, go to bed at a particular time, or stop fighting with siblings. Nor have I ever seen an adolescent struck by a parent, or even severely lectured for misbehavior. And when limits are violated, punishment is expected, not resented.

Indeed, Samoans seemed to go to extremes to avoid conflict and to arrive at compromises. Village council decisions always had to be unanimous, and council meetings often dragged on for days while the assembled chiefs made minor concessions until everyone was satisfied with the collective decision. Breaches of acceptable conduct or the moral code often involved elaborate ceremonies of apology, called *ifoga*, during which persons, families, or even entire villages publicly humbled themselves, sitting cross-legged with mats over their bowed heads, until forgiven by the offended party. Even murder and manslaughter were handled this way if government authorities permitted it.

All in all, life in Samoa was simpler and encumbered by fewer decision-making dilemmas than in the United States. In 1954 (and certainly in 1925), there were fewer career choices, fewer alternative lifestyles, and fewer conflicting moral and ethical codes to choose from. In Mead's Samoa, young people grew up knowing that they would spend their lifetimes as farmers or famers' wives; most men knew that if they worked hard for their family and their village they would someday acquire a chief's title and responsibility for a household unit. In Ta'u, there was but one sanctioned denomination—the London Missionary Society—and church membership and attendance were compulsory.

Other traits that the study concludes were more than 50 percent determined by heredity included a sense of well-being and zest for life; alienation; vulnerability or resistance to stress, and fearfulness or risk-seeking. Another highly inherited trait, though one not commonly thought of as part of personality, was the capacity for becoming rapt in an aesthetic experience, such as a concert.

Vulnerability to stress, as measured on the Tellegen test, reflects what is commonly thought of as "neuroticism," according to Dr. Lykken. "People high in this trait are nervous and jumpy, easily irritated, highly sensitive to stimuli, and generally dissatisfied with themselves, while those low on the trait are resilient and see themselves in a positive light," he said. "Therapy may help vulnerable people to some extent, but they seem to have a built-in susceptibility that may mean, in general, they would be more content with a life low in stress."

The need to achieve, including ambition and an inclination to work hard toward goals, also was found to be genetically influenced, but more than half of this trait seemed determined by life experience. The same lower degree of hereditary influence was found for impulsiveness and its opposite, caution.

The need for personal intimacy appeared the least determined by heredity among the traits tested; about two-thirds of that tendency was found to depend on experience. People high in this trait have a strong desire for emotionally intense relationships; those low in the trait tend to be loners who keep their troubles to themselves.

"This is one trait that can be greatly strengthened by the quality of interactions in a family," Dr. Lykken said. "The more physical and emotional intimacy, the more likely this trait will be developed in children, and those children with the strongest inherited tendency will have the greatest need for social closeness as adults."

No single gene is believed responsible for any one of these traits. Instead, each trait, the Minnesota researchers propose, is determined by a great number of genes in combination, so that the pattern of inheritance is complex and indirect.

No one believes, for instance, that there is a single gene for timidity but rather a host of genetic influences. That may explain, they say, why previous studies have found little connection between the personality traits of parents and their children. Whereas identical twins would share with each other the whole constellation of genes that might be responsible for a particular trait, children might share only some part of that constellation with each parent.

That is why, just as a short parent may have a tall child, an achievement-oriented parent might have a child with little ambition.

The Minnesota findings are sure to stir debate. Though most social scientists accept the careful study of twins, particularly when it includes identical twins reared apart, as the best method of assessing the degree to which a trait is inherited, some object to using these methods for assessing the genetic component of complex behavior patterns or question the conclusions that are drawn from it.

Further, some researchers consider paper-and-pencil tests of personality less reliable than observations of how people act, since people's own reports of their behavior can be biased. "The level of heritability they found is surprisingly high, considering that questionnaires are not the most sensitive index of personality," said Dr. Kagan. "There is often a poor relationship between how people respond on a questionnaire and what they actually do."

"Years ago, when the field was dominated by a psychodynamic view, you could not publish a study like this," Dr. Kagan added. "Now the field is shifting to a greater acceptance of genetic determinants, and there is the danger of being too uncritical of such results."

Seymour Epstein, a personality psychologist at the University of Massachusetts, said he was skeptical of precise estimates of heritability. "The study compared people from a relatively narrow range of cultures and environments," he said. "If the range had been much greater—say Pygmies and Eskimos as well as middle-class Americans—then environment would certainly contribute more to personality. The results might have shown environment to be a far more powerful influence than heredity," he said.

Dr. Tellegen himself said: "Even though the differences between families do not account for much of the unique attributes of their children, a family still exercises important influence. In cases of extreme deprivation or abuse, for instance, the family would have a much larger impact—though a negative one—than any found in the study. Although the twins studied came from widely different environments, there were no extremely deprived families."

Gardner Lindzey, director of the Center for Advanced Studies in the Behavioral Sciences in Palo Alto, Calif., said the Minnesota findings would "no doubt produce empassioned rejoinders."

"They do not in and of themselves say what makes a given character trait emerge," he said, "and they can be disputed and argued about, as have similar studies of intelligence."

For parents, the study points to the importance of treating each child in accord with his innate temperament.

"The message for parents is not that it does not matter how they treat their children, but that it is a big mistake to treat all kids the same," said Dr. Lykken. "To guide and shape a child you have to respect his individuality, adapt to it and cultivate those qualities that will help him in life.

"If there are two brothers in the same family, one fearless and the other timid, a good parent will help the timid one become less so by giving him experiences of doing well at risk-taking, and let the other develop his fearlessness tempered with some intelligent caution. But if the parent shelters the one who is naturally timid, he will likely become more so.''

The Minnesota results lend weight and precision to earlier work that pointed to the importance of a child's temperament in development. For instance, the New York Longitudinal Study, conducted by Alexander Thomas and Stella Chess, psychiatrists at New York University Medical Center, identified three basic temperaments in children, each of which could lead to behavioral problems if not handled well.

''Good parenting now must be seen in terms of meeting the special needs of a child's temperament, including dealing with whatever conflicts it creates,'' said Stanley Grossman, a staff member of the medical center's Psychoanalytic Institute.

From 1984

George Orwell

In the low-ceilinged canteen, deep under ground, the lunch queue jerked slowly forward. The room was already very full and deafeningly noisy. From the grille at the counter the steam of stew came pouring forth, with a sour metallic smell which did not quite overcome the fumes of Victory Gin. On the far side of the room there was a small bar, a mere hole in the wall, where gin could be bought at ten cents the large nip.

''Just the man I was looking for,'' said a voice at Winston's back.

He turned round. It was his friend Syme, who worked in the Research Department. Perhaps ''friend'' was not exactly the right word. You did not have friends nowadays, you had comrades; but there were some comrades whose society was pleasanter than that of others. Syme was a philologist, a specialist in Newspeak. Indeed, he was one of the enormous team of experts now engaged in compiling the Eleventh Edition of the Newspeak dictionary. He was a tiny creature, smaller than Winston, with dark hair and large, protuberant eyes, at once mournful and derisive, which seemed to search your face closely while he was speaking to you.

''I wanted to ask you whether you'd got any razor blades,'' he said.

''Not one!'' said Winston with a sort of guilty haste. ''I've tried all over the place. They don't exist any longer.''

Everyone kept asking you for razor blades. Actually he had two unused ones which he was hoarding up. There had been a famine of them for months past. At any given moment there was some necessary article which the Party shops were unable to supply. Sometimes it was buttons, sometimes it was darning wool, sometimes it was shoelaces; at present it was razor blades. You could only get hold of them, if at all, by scrounging more or less furtively on the "free" market.

"I've been using the same blade for six weeks," he added untruthfully.

The queue gave another jerk forward. As they halted he turned and faced Syme again. Each of them took a greasy metal tray from a pile at the edge of the counter.

"Did you go and see the prisoners hanged yesterday?" said Syme.

"I was working," said Winston indifferently. "I shall see it on the flicks, I suppose."

"A very inadequate substitute," said Syme.

His mocking eyes roved over Winston's face. "I know you," the eyes seemed to say, "I see through you, I know very well why you didn't go to see those prisoners hanged." In an intellectual way, Syme was venomously orthodox. He would talk with a disagreeable gloating satisfaction of helicopter raids on enemy villages, the trial and confessions of thought-criminals, the executions in the cellars of the Ministry of Love. Talking to him was largely a matter of getting him away from such subjects and entangling him, if possible, in the technicalities of Newspeak, on which he was authoritative and interesting. Winston turned his head a little aside to avoid the scrutiny of the large dark eyes. . . .

They threaded their way across the crowded room and unpacked their trays onto the metal-topped table, on one corner of which someone had left a pool of stew, a filthy liquid mess that had the appearance of vomit. Winston took up his mug of gin, paused for an instant to collect his nerve, and gulped the oily-tasting stuff down. When he had winked the tears out of his eyes he suddenly discovered that he was hungry. He began swallowing spoonfuls of the stew, which, in among its general sloppiness, had cubes of spongy pinkish stuff which was probably a preparation of meat. Neither of them spoke again till they had emptied their pannikins. From the table at Winston's left, a little behind his back, someone was talking rapidly and continuously, a harsh gabble almost like the quacking of a duck, which pierced the general uproar of the room.

"How is the dictionary getting on?" said Winston, raising his voice to overcome the noise.

"Slowly," said Syme. "I'm on the adjectives. It's fascinating."

He had brightened up immediately at the mention of Newspeak. He pushed his pannikin aside, took up his hunk of bread in one delicate hand and his cheese in the other, and leaned across the table so as to be able to speak without shouting.

"The Eleventh Edition is the definitive edition," he said. "We're getting the language into its final shape—the shape it's going to have when nobody speaks anything else. When we've finished with it, people like you will have to learn it all over again. You think, I dare say, that our chief job is inventing new words. But not a bit of it! We're destroying words—scores of them, hundreds of them, every day. We're cutting the language down to the bone. The Eleventh Edition won't contain a single word that will become obsolete before the year 2050.''

He bit hungrily into his bread and swallowed a couple of mouthfuls, then continued speaking, with a sort of pedant's passion. His thin dark face had become animated, his eyes had lost their mocking expression and grown almost dreamy.

''It's a beautiful thing, the destruction of words. Of course the great wastage is in the verbs and adjectives, but there are hundreds of nouns that can be got rid of as well. It isn't only the synonyms; there are also the antonyms. After all, what justification is there for a word which is simply the opposite of some other words? A word contains its opposite in itself. Take 'good,' for instance. If you have a word like 'good,' what need is there for a word like 'bad'? 'Ungood' will do just as well—better, because it's an exact opposite, which the other is not. Or again, if you want a stronger version of 'good,' what sense is there in having a whole string of vague useless words like 'excellent' and 'splendid' and all the rest of them? 'Plusgood' covers the meaning, or 'doubleplusgood' if you want something stronger still. Of course we use those forms already, but in the final version of Newspeak there'll be nothing else. In the end the whole notion of goodness and badness will be covered by only six words—in reality, only one word. Don't you see the beauty of that, Winston? It was B.B.'s idea originally, of course,'' he added as an afterthought.

A sort of vapid eagerness flitted across Winston's face at the mention of Big Brother. Nevertheless Syme immediately detected a certain lack of enthusiasm.

''You haven't a real appreciation of Newspeak, Winston,'' he said almost sadly. ''Even when you write it you're still thinking in Oldspeak. I've read some of those pieces that you write in the *Times* occasionally. They're good enough, but they're translations. In your heart you'd prefer to stick to Oldspeak, with all its vagueness and its useless shades of meaning. You don't grasp the beauty of the destruction of words. Do you know that Newspeak is the only language in the world whose vocabulary gets smaller every year?''

Winston did know that, of course. He smiled sympathetically he hoped, not trusting himself to speak. Syme bit off another fragment of the dark-colored bread, chewed it briefly, and went on:

''Don't you see that the whole aim of Newspeak is to narrow the range of thought? In the end we shall make thoughtcrime literally impossible, because there will be no words in which to express it. Every concept that can ever be needed will be expressed by exactly *one* word, with its meaning rigidly defined and all its subsidiary meanings rubbed out and forgotten. Already, in the Eleventh Edition, we're not far from that point. But the process will still be continuing long after you and I are dead. Every year fewer and fewer words, and the range of consciousness always a little smaller. Even now, of course, there's no reason or excuse for committing thoughtcrime. It's merely a question of self-discipline, reality-control. But in the end there won't be any need even for that. The Revolution will be complete when the language is perfect. . . .

"By 2050—earlier, probably—all real knowledge of Oldspeak will have disappeared. The whole literature of the past will have been destroyed. Chaucer, Shakespeare, Milton, Byron—they'll exist only in Newspeak versions, not merely changed into something different, but actually changed into something contradictory of what they used to be. Even the literature of the Party will change. Even the slogans will change. How could you have a slogan like 'freedom is slavery' when the concept of freedom has been abolished? The whole climate of thought will be different. In fact there will *be* no thought, as we understand it now. Orthodoxy means not thinking—not needing to think. Orthodoxy is unconsciousness."

One of these days, thought Winston with sudden deep conviction, Syme will be vaporized. He is too intelligent. He sees too clearly and speaks too plainly. The Party does not like such people. One day he will disappear. It is written in his face.

Appendix: The Principles of Newspeak, from 1984

George Orwell

Newspeak was the official language of Oceania and had been devised to meet the ideological needs of Ingsoc, or English Socialism. . . .

The purpose of Newspeak was not only to provide a medium of expression for the world-view and mental habits proper to the devotees of Ingsoc, but to make all other modes of thought impossible. It was intended that when Newspeak had been adopted once and for all and Oldspeak forgotten, a heretical thought—that is, a thought diverging from the principles of Ingsoc—should be literally unthinkable, at least so far as thought is dependent on words. Its vocabulary was so constructed as to give exact and often very subtle expression to every meaning that a Party member could properly wish to express, while excluding all other meanings and also the possibility of arriving at them by indirect methods. This was done partly by the invention of new words, but chiefly by eliminating undesirable words and by stripping such words as remained of unorthodox meanings, and so far as possible of all secondary meanings whatever. To give a single example. The word *free* still existed in Newspeak, but it could only be used in such statements as "This dog is free from lice" or "This field is free from weeds." It could not be used in its old sense of "politically free" or "intellectually free," since political and intellectual freedom no longer existed even as concepts, and were therefore of necessity nameless. Quite apart from the suppression of definitely heretical words, reduction of vocabulary was regarded as an end in itself, and no word that could be dispensed with was allowed to survive. Newspeak was designed not to extend but to *diminish* the range of thought, and this purpose was indirectly assisted by cutting the choice of words down to a minimum. . . .

The B vocabulary. The B vocabulary consisted of words which had been deliberately constructed for political purposes: words, that is to say, which not only had in every case a political implication, but were intended to impose a desirable mental attitude upon the person using them. Without a full understanding of the principles of Ingsoc it was difficult to use these words correctly. In some cases they could be translated into Oldspeak . . . but this usually demanded a long paraphrase and always involved the loss of certain overtones. The B words were a sort of verbal shorthand, often packing whole ranges of ideas into a few syllables, and at the same time more accurate and forcible than ordinary language.

The B words were in all cases compound words. They consisted of two or more words, or portions of words, welded together in an easily pronounceable form. The resulting amalgam was always a noun-verb, and inflected according to the ordinary rules. To take a single example: the word *goodthink,* meaning, very roughly, "orthodoxy," or, if one chose to regard it as a verb, "to think in an orthodox manner." This inflected as follows: noun-verb, *goodthink;* past tense and past participle, *goodthinked;* present participle, *goodthinking;* adjective, *goodthinkful;* adverb, *goodthinkwise;* verbal noun, *goodthinker.* . . .

Some of the B words had highly subtilized meanings, barely intelligible to anyone who had not mastered the language as a whole. Consider, for example, such a typical sentence from a *Times* leading article as *Oldthinkers unbellyfeel Ingsoc.* The shortest rendering that one could make of this in Oldspeak would be: "Those whose ideas were formed before the Revolution cannot have a full emotional understanding of the principles of English Socialism." But this is not an adequate translation. To begin with, in order to grasp the full meaning of the Newspeak sentence quoted above, one would have to have a clear idea of what is meant by Ingsoc. And, in addition, only a person thoroughly grounded in Ingsoc could appreciate the full force of the word *bellyfeel,* which implied a blind, enthusiastic acceptance difficult to imagine today; or of the word *oldthink,* which was inextricably mixed up with the idea of wickedness and decadence. But the special function of certain Newspeak words, of which *oldthink* was one, was not so much to express meanings as to destroy them. These words, necessarily few in number, had had their meanings extended until they contained within themselves whole batteries of words which, as they were sufficiently covered by a single comprehensive term, could now be scrapped and forgotten. The greatest difficulty facing the compilers of the Newspeak dictionary was not to invent new words, but, having invented them, to make sure what they meant: to make sure, that is to say, what ranges of words they canceled by their existence.

As we have already seen in the case of the word *free,* words which had once borne a heretical meaning were sometimes retained for the sake of convenience, but only with the undesirable meanings purged out of them. Countless other words such as *honor, justice, morality, internationalism, democracy, science,* and *religion* had simply ceased to exist. A few blanket words covered them, and, in covering them, abolished them. All words grouping themselves round the concepts of liberty and equality, for instance, were contained in the single word *crimethink,* while all words grouping themselves round the concepts of objectivity and rationalism were contained in the single word *oldthink.* Greater precision would have been dangerous. What was required in a Party member was an outlook similar to that of the ancient Hebrew who knew, without knowing much else, that all nations other than his own worshipped "false gods." He did not need to know that these gods were called Baal, Osiris, Moloch, Ashtaroth, and the like; probably the less he knew about them the better for his orthodoxy. He knew Jehovah and the commandments of Jehovah; he knew, therefore, that all gods with other names or other attributes were false gods. In somewhat the same way, the Party member knew what constituted right conduct, and in exceedingly vague, generalized terms he knew what kinds of departure from it were possible. His sexual life, for example, was entirely regulated by the two Newspeak words *sexcrime* (sexual immorality) and *goodsex* (chastity). *Sexcrime* covered all sexual misdeeds whatever. It covered fornication, adultery, homosexuality, and other perversions, and, in addition, normal intercourse practiced for its own sake. There was no need to enumerate them separately, since they were all equally culpable, and in principle, all punishable by death. . . .

No word in the B vocabulary was ideologically neutral. A great many were euphemisms. Such words, for instance, as *joycamp* (forced-labor camp) or *Minipax* (Ministry of Peace, i.e., Ministry of War) meant almost the exact opposite of what they appeared to mean. Some words, on the other hand, displayed a frank and contemptuous understanding of the real nature of Oceanic society. An example was *prolefeed,* meaning the rubbishy entertainment and spurious news which the

Party handed out to the masses. Other words, again, were ambivalent, having the connotation "good" when applied to the Party and "bad" when applied to its enemies. But in addition there were great numbers of words which at first sight appeared to be mere abbreviations and which derived their ideological color not from their meaning but from their structure.

So far as it could be contrived, everything that had or might have political significance of any kind was fitted into the B vocabulary. The name of every organization, or body of people, or doctrine, or country, or institution, or public building, was invariably cut down into the familiar shape; that is, a single easily pronounced word with the smallest number of syllables that would preserve the original derivation. In the Ministry of Truth, for example, the Records Department, in which Winston Smith worked, was called *Recdep,* the Fiction Department was called *Ficdep,* the Teleprograms Department was called *Teledep,* and so on. This was not done solely with the object of saving time. Even in the early decades of the twentieth century, telescoped words and phrases had been one of the characteristic features of political language; and it had been noticed that the tendency to use abbreviations of this kind was most marked in totalitarian countries and totalitarian organizations. Examples were such words as *Nazi, Gestapo, Comintern, Inprecorr, Agitprop.* In the beginning the practice had been adopted as it were instinctively, but in Newspeak it was used with a conscious purpose. It was perceived that in thus abbreviating a name one narrowed and subtly altered its meaning, by cutting out most of the associations that would otherwise cling to it. The words *Communist International,* for instance, call up a composite picture of universal human brotherhood, red flags, barricades, Karl Marx, and the Paris Commune. The word Comintern, on the other hand, suggests merely a tightly knit organization and a well-defined body of doctrine. It refers to something almost as easily recognized, and as limited in purpose, as a chair or a table. *Comintern* is a word that can be uttered almost without taking thought, whereas *Communist International* is a phrase over which one is obliged to linger at least momentarily. In the same way, the associations called up by a word like *Minitrue* are fewer and more controllable than those called up by *Ministry of Truth.* This accounted not only for the habit of abbreviating whenever possible, but also for the almost exaggerated care that was taken to make every word easily pronounceable.

In Newspeak, euphony outweighed every consideration other than exactitude of meaning. Regularity of grammar was always sacrificed to it when it seemed necessary. And rightly so, since what was required, above all for political purposes, were short clipped words of unmistakable meaning which could be uttered rapidly and which roused the minimum of echoes in the speaker's mind. The words of the B vocabulary even gained in force from the fact that nearly all of them were very much alike. Almost invariably these words—*goodthink, Minipax, prolefeed, sexcrime, joycamp, Ingsoc, bellyfeel, thinkpol,* and countless others—were words of two or three syllables, with the stress distributed equally between the first syllable and the last. The use of them encouraged a gabbling style of speech, at once staccato and monotonous. And this was exactly what was aimed at. The intention was to make speech, and especially speech on any subject not ideologically neutral, as nearly as possible independent of consciousness. For the purposes of everyday life it was no doubt necessary, or sometimes necessary, to reflect before speaking, but a Party member called upon to make a political or ethical judgment should be able to spray forth the correct opinions as automatically as a machine gun spraying forth bullets. His training fitted him to do this, the language gave him an almost foolproof instrument, and the texture of the words, with their harsh sound and a certain willful ugliness which was in accord with the spirit of Ingsoc, assisted the process still further.

So did the fact of having very few words to choose from. Relative to our own, the Newspeak vocabulary was tiny, and new ways of reducing it were constantly being devised. Newspeak, indeed, differed from almost all other languages in that its vocabulary grew smaller instead of larger every year. Each reduction was a gain, since the smaller the area of choice, the smaller the temptation to take thought. Ultimately it was hoped to make articulate speech issue from the larynx without involving the higher brain centers at all. This aim was frankly admitted in the Newspeak word *duckspeak,* meaning "to quack like a duck." Like various other words in the B vocabulary, *duckspeak* was ambivalent in meaning. Provided that the opinions which were quacked out were orthodox ones, it implied nothing but praise, and when the *Times* referred to one of the orators of the Party as a *doubleplusgood duckspeaker* it was paying a warm and valued complement.

Preface, from Groupthink: Psychological Studies of Policy Decisions and Fiascoes

Irving L. Janis

The main theme of this book occurred to me while reading Arthur M. Schlesinger's chapters on the Bay of Pigs in *A Thousand Days*. At first, I was puzzled: How could bright, shrewd men like John F. Kennedy and his advisers be taken in by the CIA's stupid, patchwork plan?

I began to wonder whether some kind of psychological contagion, similar to social conformity phenomena observed in studies of small groups, had interfered with their mental alertness. I kept thinking about the implications of this notion until one day I found myself talking about it, in a seminar of mine on group psychology at Yale University. I suggested that the poor decision-making performance of the men at those White House meetings might be akin to the lapses in judgment of ordinary citizens who become more concerned with retaining the approval of the fellow members of their work group than with coming up with good solutions to the tasks at hand.

Shortly after that, when I reread Schlesinger's account, I was struck by some observations that earlier had escaped my notice. These observations began to fit a specific pattern of concurrence-seeking behavior that had impressed me time and again in my research on other kinds of face-to-face groups, particularly when a "we-feeling" of solidarity is running high. Additional accounts of the Bay of Pigs yielded more such observations, leading me to conclude that group processes had been subtly at work, preventing the members of Kennedy's team from debating the real issues posed by the CIA's plan and from carefully appraising its serious risks.

Then in Joseph de Rivera's *The Psychological Dimension of Foreign Policy*, I found an impressive example of excluding a deviant from Truman's group of advisers during the period of the ill-fated Korean War decisions. De Rivera's comments about the group's behavior prompted me to look further into that series of decisions and soon I encountered evidence of other manifestations of group processes, like those apparently operating in the Bay of Pigs decision.

By this time, I was sufficiently fascinated by what I began to call the groupthink hypothesis to start looking into a fairly large number of historical parallels. I selected for intensive analysis two additional United States foreign-policy decisions and again found consistent indications of the same kind of detrimental group processes. Later I added a case study of a president's criminal conspiracy to obstruct justice, which I now regard as the most impressive example of groupthink.

This book presents five case studies of major fiascoes, resulting from poor decisions made during the administrations of five American presidents—Franklin D. Roosevelt (failure to be prepared for the attack on Pearl Harbor), Harry S Truman (the invasion of North Korea), John F. Kennedy (the Bay of Pigs invasion), Lyndon B. Johnson (escalation of the Vietnam War), and Richard M. Nixon (the Watergate cover-up). Each of these decisions was a *group* product, issuing from a series of meetings of a small body of government officials and advisers who constituted a cohesive group. And in each instance, the members of the policy-making group made incredibly gross miscalculations about both the practical and moral consequences of their decisions.

Introduction: *Why So Many Miscalculations?*, *from* Groupthink: Psychological Studies of Policy Decisions and Fiascoes

Irving L. Janis

What Is Groupthink?

The group dynamics approach is based on the working assumption that the members of policy-making groups, no matter how mindful they may be of their exalted national status and of their heavy responsibilities, are subjected to the pressures widely observed in groups of ordinary citizens. In my earlier research on group dynamics, I was impressed by repeated manifestations of the effects—both unfavorable and favorable—of the social pressures that typically develop in cohesive groups—in infantry platoons, air crews, therapy groups, seminars, and self-study or encounter groups of executives receiving leadership training. In all these groups, just as in the industrial work groups described by other investigators, members tend to evolve informal norms to preserve friendly intragroup relations and these become part of the hidden agenda at their meetings. When conducting research on groups of heavy smokers at a clinic set up to help people stop smoking, I noticed a seemingly irrational tendency for the members to exert pressure on each other to increase their smoking as the time for the final meeting approached. This appeared to be a collusive effort to display mutual dependence and resistance to the termination of the group sessions.

Sometimes, even long before members become concerned about the final separation, clear-cut signs of pressures toward uniformity subvert the fundamental purpose of group meetings. At the second meeting of one group of smokers, consisting of twelve middle-class American men and women, two of the most dominant members took the position that heavy smoking was an almost incurable addiction. The majority of the others soon agreed that no one could be expected to cut down drastically. One heavy smoker, a middle-aged business executive, took issue with this consensus, arguing that by using will power he had stopped smoking since joining the group and that everyone else could do the same. His declaration was followed by a heated discussion, which continued in the halls of the building after the formal meeting adjourned. Most of the others ganged up against the man who was deviating from the group consensus. Then, at the beginning of the next meeting, the deviant announced that he had made an important decision. "When I joined," he said, "I agreed to follow the two main rules required by the clinic—to make a conscientious effort to stop smoking and to attend every meeting. But I have learned from experience in this group that you can only follow one of the rules, you can't follow both. And so, I have decided that I will continue to attend every meeting but I have gone back to smoking two packs a day and I will not make any effort to stop smoking again until after the last meeting." Whereupon, the other members beamed at him and applauded enthusiastically, welcoming him back to the fold. No one commented on the fact that the whole point of the meetings was to help each individual to cut down on smoking as rapidly as possible. As a psychological consultant to the group, I tried to call this to the members' attention, and so did my collaborator, Dr. Michael Kahn. But during that meeting the members managed to ignore our comments and reiterated their consensus that heavy smoking was an addiction from which no one would be cured except by cutting down very gradually over a long period of time.

This episode—an extreme form of groupthink—was only one manifestation of a general pattern that the group displayed. At every meeting, the members were amiable, reasserted their warm feelings of solidarity, and sought complete concurrence on every important topic, with no reappearance of the unpleasant bickering that would spoil the cozy atmosphere. The concurrence-seeking tendency could be maintained, however, only at the expense of ignoring realistic challenges (like those posed by the psychological consultants) and distorting members' observations of individual differences that would call into question the shared assumption that everyone in the group had the same type of addiction problem. It seemed that in this smoking group I was observing another instance of the groupthink pattern I had encountered in observations of widely contrasting groups whose members came from diverse sectors of society and were meeting together for social, educational, vocational, or other purposes. Just like the group in the smoking clinic, all these different types of groups had shown signs of high cohesiveness and of an accompanying concurrence-seeking tendency that interfered with critical thinking—the central features of groupthink.

I use the term "groupthink" as a quick and easy way to refer to a mode of thinking that people engage in when they are deeply involved in a cohesive ingroup, when the members' strivings for unanimity override their motivation to realistically appraise alternative courses of action. "Groupthink" is a term of the same order as the words in the newspeak vocabulary George Orwell presents in his dismaying *1984*— a vocabulary with terms such as "doublethink" and "crimethink." By putting groupthink with those Orwellian words, I realize that groupthink takes on an invidious connotation. The invidiousness is intentional: Groupthink refers to a deterioration of mental efficiency, reality testing, and moral judgment that results from in-group pressures. . . .

Selection of the Fiascoes

At least seven major defects in decision-making contribute to failures to solve problems adequately. First, the group's discussions are limited to a few alternative courses of action (often only two) without a survey of the full range of alternatives. Second, the group does not survey the objectives to be fulfilled and the values implicated by the choice. Third, the group fails to reexamine the course of action initially preferred by the majority of members from the standpoint of nonobvious risks and drawbacks that had not been considered when it was originally evaluated. Fourth, the members neglect courses of action initially evaluated as unsatisfactory by the majority of the group: They spend little or no time discussing whether they have overlooked nonobvious gains or whether there are ways of reducing the seemingly prohibitive costs that had made the alternatives seem undesirable. Fifth, the members make little or no attempt to obtain information from experts who can supply sound estimates of losses and gains to be expected from alternative courses of actions. Sixth, selective bias is shown in the way the group reacts to factual information and relevant judgments from experts, the mass media, and outside critics. The members show interest in facts and opinions that support their initially preferred policy and take up time in their meetings to discuss them, but they tend to ignore facts and opinions that do not support their initially preferred policy. Seventh, the members spend little time deliberating about how the chosen policy might be hindered by bureaucratic inertia, sabotaged by political opponents, or temporarily derailed by the common accidents that happen to the best of well-laid plans. Consequently, they fail to work out contingency plans to cope with foreseeable setbacks that could endanger the overall success of the chosen course of action.

I assume that these seven defects and some related features of inadequate decision-making result from groupthink. But, of course, each of the seven can arise from other common causes of human stupidity as well—erroneous intelligence, information overload, fatigue, blinding prejudice, and ignorance. Whether produced by groupthink or by other causes, a decision suffering from most of these defects has relatively little chance of success.

The five major policy fiascoes I have selected for intensive case studies are the ones of greatest historical importance among the defective decisions by the United States government I have examined. Each clearly meets two important criteria for classifying a decision as a candidate for psychological analysis in terms of group dynamics: Each presents numerous indications that (1) the decision-making group was cohesive and that (2) decision-making was extremely defective. . . .

When the conditions specified by these two criteria are met, according to the groupthink hypothesis there is a better-than-chance likelihood that one of the causes of the defective decision was a strong concurrence-seeking tendency, which is the motivation that gives rise to all the symptoms of groupthink. . . .

Hardhearted Actions by Softheaded Groups

At first I was surprised by the extent to which the groups in the fiascoes I have examined adhered to group norms and pressures toward uniformity. Just as in groups of ordinary citizens, a dominant characteristic appears to be remaining loyal to the group by sticking with the decisions to which the group has committed itself, even when the policy is working badly and has unintended consequences that disturb the conscience of the members. In a sense, members consider loyalty to the group the highest form of morality. That loyalty requires each member to avoid raising controversial issues, questioning weak arguments, or calling a halt to softheaded thinking.

Paradoxically, softheaded groups are likely to be extremely hardhearted toward out-groups and enemies. In dealing with a rival nation, policy-makers comprising an amiable group find it relatively easy to authorize dehumanizing solutions such as large-scale bombings. An affable group of government officials is unlikely to pursue the difficult and controversial issues that arise when alternatives to a harsh military solution come up for discussion. Nor are the members inclined to raise ethical issues that imply that this "fine group of ours, with its humanitarianism and its high-minded principles, might be capable of adopting a course of action that is inhumane and immoral."

Many other sources of human error can prevent government leaders from arriving at well worked out decisions, resulting in failures to achieve their practical objectives and violations of their own standards of ethical conduct. But, unlike groupthink, these other sources of error do not typically entail increases in hardheartedness along with softheadedness. Some errors involve blind spots that stem from the personality of the decision-makers. Special circumstances produce unusual fatigue and emotional stresses that interfere with efficient decision-making. Numerous institutional features of the social structure in which the group is located may also cause inefficiency and prevent adequate communication with experts. In addition, well-known interferences with sound thinking arise when the decision-makers comprise a noncohesive group. For example, when the members have no sense of loyalty to the group and regard themselves merely as representatives of different departments, with clashing interests, the meetings may become bitter power struggles, at the expense of effective decision-making.

The concept of groupthink pinpoints an entirely different source of trouble, residing neither in the individual nor in the organizational setting. Over and beyond all the familiar sources of human error is a powerful source of defective judgment that arises in cohesive groups—the concurrence-seeking tendency, which fosters overoptimism, lack of vigilance, and sloganistic thinking about the weakness and immorality of out-groups. This tendency can take its toll even when the decision-makers are conscientious statesmen trying to make the best possible decisions for their country and for all mankind.

I do not mean to imply that all cohesive groups suffer from group-think, though all may display its symptoms from time to time. Nor should we infer from the term "groupthink" that group decisions are typically inefficient or harmful. On the contrary, a group whose members have properly defined roles, with traditions and standard operating procedures that facilitate critical inquiry, is probably capable of making better decisions than any individual in the group who works on the problem alone. And yet the advantages of having decisions made by groups are often lost because of psychological pressures that arise when the members work closely together, share the same values, and above all face a crisis situation in which everyone is subjected to stresses that generate a strong need for affiliation. In these circumstances, as conformity pressures begin to dominate, groupthink and the attendant deterioration of decision-making set in.

The central theme of my analysis can be summarized in this generalization, which I offer in the spirit of Parkinson's laws: *The more amiability and esprit de corps among the members of a policy-making in-group, the greater is the danger that independent critical thinking will be replaced by groupthink, which is likely to result in irrational and dehumanizing actions directed against out-groups.*

Russians

Freeman Dyson

Iosip Shklovsky is a Soviet astronomer of unusual brilliance, with several major discoveries to his credit. He is known to the Soviet public as a writer of books and magazine articles describing the astronomical universe in a lively popular style. At scientific meetings he spices his technical arguments with jokes and paradoxes. He has wide interests outside astronomy and can talk amusingly on almost any subject. He enjoys unorthodox ideas, and he took a leading part in encouraging international efforts to listen for radio signals which might reveal the existence of intelligence in remote parts of the universe. In his professional life he projects an image of a happy, active, and successful man of the world. In private, like many Soviet intellectuals, he is melancholic. He told me once that he has lived with a feeling of inner loneliness since he discovered, at the end of World War II, that he was the only one of his high school graduating class to have survived. He was the scientist in the class, and the authorities kept him out of the army to work on technical projects. The others went to the front and died. Soviet citizens of Shklovsky's generation still bear the scars of war. Those who are younger grew up hearing tales of war told by their parents and grandparents. All alike carry deep in their consciousness a collective memory of suffering and irreparable loss. This is the central fact conditioning the Soviet view of war. Russians, when they think of war, think of themselves not as warriors but as victims.

Another vignette of Soviet life illustrates the same theme. It was a cold Sunday in late November, and I had the day free after a week of astronomical meetings in Moscow. The radio astronomer Nikolai Kardashev took me on a sightseeing trip to the ancient cities of Vladimir and Suzdal, halfway between Moscow and Gorky. We started before dawn and drove two hundred kilometers in darkness in order to arrive before the crowds. As we approached Suzdal we saw old monasteries shining golden in the light of the rising sun. Vladimir and Suzdal were places of refuge for monks and artists during the bitter centuries when Mongols and Tartars ruled in Russia. Both cities were taken and destroyed by the Mongols in 1238. They lay directly in the path of the army of Subutai, which swept across half of Europe in a merciless campaign of conquest. The inhabitants later rebuilt the cities, raised churches and filled them with religious paintings. Vladimir and Suzdal lie far enough to the North-East so that they escaped the invasions which ravaged Kiev and Moscow in later centuries. Andrei Rublov, the greatest painter of old Russia, worked at Vladimir in the fifteenth century. Buildings and paintings survive from the thirteenth century onward. Kardashev and I spent the day wandering from church to church among busloads of schoolchildren from Moscow and Gorky. The last stop on our tour was the city museum of Vladimir. Here we found the densest concentration of schoolchildren. The museum is in a tower over one of the ancient gates of the city. Its emphasis is historical rather than artistic. The main exhibit is an enormous diorama of the city as it was at the moment of its destruction in 1238, with every detail faithfully modeled in wood and clay. Across the plains come riding endless lines of Mongol horsemen, slashing arms, legs, and heads off defenseless Russians whom they meet outside the city walls. The armed defenders of the city are on top of the walls, but the flaming arrows of the Mongols have set fire to the buildings behind them. Already a party of horsemen has broken into the city through a side gate and is beginning a general slaughter of the inhabitants. Blood is running in the streets and flames are rising from the churches. On the wall above this scene of horror there is a large notice for schoolchildren and other visitors to read. It says: "The heroic people of Vladimir chose to die rather than submit to the invader. By their self-sacrifice they saved Western Europe from suffering the same fate, and saved European civilization from extinction.''

The diorama of Vladimir gives visible form to the dreams and fears which have molded the Russian people's perception of themselves and their place in history. Central to their dreams is the Mongol horde slicing through their country, swift and implacable. It is difficult for English-speaking people to share such dreams. The Russian experience of the Mongol invasions is so foreign to us that we gave the word ''horde'' a new and inappropriate meaning when we borrowed it into our language. English-speaking people came to Asia as traders and conquerors protected by a superior technology. Our view of Asia is mirrored in the image which the word ''horde'' conveys to an English-speaking mind. A horde in our language is a sprawling, undisciplined mob. In Russian and in the original Turkish, a horde is a camp or a tribe organized for war. The organization of the Mongol horde in the thirteenth century was technically far in advance of any other military system in the world. The Mongols could travel and maintain communications over vast distances; they could maneuver their armies with a speed and precision which no other power could match. It took the Russians a hundred and fifty years to learn to fight them on equal terms, and three hundred years to defeat them decisively. The horde in the folk memory of Russia means an alien presence moving through the homeland, ravaging and consuming the substance of the people, subverting the loyalty of their leaders with blackmail and bribes. This is the image of Asia which three centuries of suffering implanted in the Russian mind. It is easy for us in the strategically inviolate West to dismiss Russian fears of China as ''paranoid.'' If we had lived for three centuries at the mercy of the alien horsemen, we would be paranoid too.

British prime ministers, soon after they come into office, customarily visit Washington and Moscow to get acquainted with American and Soviet leaders. When Prime Minister Thatcher made her state visit to Moscow she had two amicable meetings with Chairman Brezhnev. At the end of the second day she remarked (this was before the Afghanistan invasion and the Polish crisis) that she was happy to discover that there were no urgent problems threatening to bring the United Kingdom and the Soviet Union into conflict. Brezhnev then replied with some emphatic words in Russian. Thatcher's interpreter hesitated, and instead of translating Brezhnev's remark asked him to repeat it. Brezhnev repeated it and the interpreter translated: ''Madam, there is only one important question facing us, and that is the question whether the white race will survive.'' Thatcher was so taken aback that she did not venture either to agree or to disagree with this sentiment. She made her exit without further comment. What she had heard was a distant echo of the Mongol hoofbeat still reverberating in Russian memory.

After the Mongols, invaders came to Russia from the West—from Poland, from Sweden, from France, and from Germany. Each of the invading armies was a horde in the Russian sense of the word, a disciplined force of warriors superior to the Russians in technology, in mobility, and in generalship. Especially the German horde invading Russia in 1941 conformed to the ancient pattern. But the Russians had made some progress in military organization between 1238 and 1941. It took them three hundred years to drive out the Mongols but only four years to drive out the Germans. During the intervening centuries the Russians, while still thinking of themselves as victims, had become in fact a nation of warriors. In order to survive in a territory perennially exposed to invasion, they maintained great armies and gave serious study to the art of war. They imposed upon themselves a regime of rigid political unity and military discipline. They gave high honor and prestige to their soldiers, and devoted a large fraction of their resources to the production of weapons. Within a few years after 1941, the Russians who survived the German invasion had organized themselves into the most formidable army on earth. The more they think of themselves as victims, the more formidable they become.

The Russian warriors are now armed with nuclear weapons on a massive scale. The strategic rocket forces of the Soviet Union are comparable in size and quality with those of the United States. The Soviet rocket commanders could, if they were ordered to do so, obliterate within thirty minutes the cities of the United States. It therefore becomes a matter of some importance for us to understand what may be in the Soviet commanders' minds. If we can read their intentions correctly, we may improve our chances of avoiding fatal misunderstanding at moments of crisis. Nobody outside the Soviet government can know with certainty the purposes of Soviet deployments. The American experts who study Soviet armed forces and analyze the Soviet literature devoted to military questions have reached diverse conclusions concerning Soviet strategy. Some say that Soviet intentions are predominantly defensive, others that they are aggressive. But the disagreements among the experts concern words more than substance. To a large extent, the disagreements arise from attempts to define Soviet policies in a language derived from American experience. The language of American strategic analysis is alien and inappropriate to the Russian experience of war. If we make the intellectual effort to understand Russian strategy in their terms rather than ours, as a product of Russian history and military tradition, we shall find that it is usually possible to reconcile the conflicting conclusions of the experts. An awareness of Russian historical experience leads us to a consistent picture of Soviet policies, stripped of the distorting jargon of American strategic theory.

The two experts on whom I mostly rely for information about Soviet strategy are George Kennan and Richard Pipes. Their views of the

Soviet Union are generally supposed to be sharply divergent. Kennan has a reputation for diplomatic moderation; Pipes has a reputation for belligerence. Kennan recently summarized his impressions of the Soviet leadership as follows:

> This is an aging, highly experienced, and very steady leadership, itself not given to rash or adventuristic policies. It commands, and is deeply involved with, a structure of power, and particularly a higher bureaucracy, that would not easily lend itself to policies of that nature. It faces serious internal problems, which constitute its main preoccupation. As this leadership looks abroad, it sees more dangers than inviting opportunities. Its reactions and purposes are therefore much more defensive than aggressive. It has no desire for any major war, least of all for a nuclear one. It fears and respects American military power even as it tries to match it, and hopes to avoid a conflict with it. Plotting an attack on Western Europe would be, in the circumstances, the last thing that would come into its head.

Pipes is a Harvard professor who has been on the staff of the National Security Council in the Reagan administration in Washington. He stated his view of Soviet strategy in a recent article with a provocative title: "Why the Soviet Union Thinks It Could Fight and Win a Nuclear War." Here are a couple of salient passages:

> The classic dictum of Clausewitz, that war is politics pursued by other means, is widely believed in the United States to have lost its validity after Hiroshima and Nagasaki. Soviet doctrine, by contrast, emphatically asserts that while an all-out nuclear war would indeed prove extremely destructive to both parties, its outcome would not be mutual suicide: the country better prepared for it and in possession of a superior strategy could win and emerge a viable society. . . . Clausewitz, buried in the United States, seems to be alive and prospering in the Soviet Union. . . .
>
> For Soviet generals the decisive influence in the formulation of nuclear doctrine were the lessons of World War 2, with which, for understandable reasons, they are virtually obsessed. This experience they seem to have supplemented with knowledge gained from professional scrutiny of the record of Nazi and Japanese offensive operations, as well as the balance-sheet of British and American strategic-bombing campaigns. More recently, the lessons of the Israeli-Arab wars of 1967 and 1973 in which they indirectly participated seem also to have impressed Soviet strategists, reinforcing previously held convictions. They also follow the Western literature, tending to side with the critics of mutual deterrence. The result of all these diverse influences is a nuclear doctrine which assimilates into the main body of the Soviet military tradition the technical implications of nuclear warfare without surrendering any of the fundamentals of this tradition. The strategic doctrine adopted by the USSR over the past two decades calls for a policy diametrically opposite to that adopted in the United States by the predominant community of civilian strategists: not deterrence but victory, not sufficiency in weapons but superiority, not retaliation but offensive action.

These remarks of Pipes were intended to be frightening, whereas Kennan's remarks were intended to be soothing. And yet, if one looks at the substance of the remarks rather than at the intentions of the writers, there is no incompatibility between them. I have myself little doubt that both Kennan's and Pipes's statements are substantially true. Kennan is describing the state of mind of political leaders who have to deal with the day-to-day problems of managing a large and unwieldy empire. Pipes is describing the state of mind of professional soldiers who have accepted responsibility for defending their country against nuclear-armed enemies. It is perhaps a virtue of the Soviet system that the problems of everyday politics and the problems of preparation for a supreme military crisis are kept apart and are handled by separate groups of specialists. The Soviet military authorities themselves insist vehemently on the necessity of this separation of powers. They know that Stalin's mingling of the two powers in 1941, when for political reasons he forbade his generals to mobilize the army in preparation for Hitler's attack, caused enormous and unnecessary Soviet losses and almost resulted in total defeat. Kennan's picture of the Soviet political power structure is quite consistent with the central conclusion of Pipes's analysis, that Soviet military doctrines are based on the assumption that the war for which the Soviet Union must be prepared is a nuclear version of World War II. We should be relieved rather than frightened when we hear that Soviet generals are still obsessed with World War II. World War II was from the Soviet point of view no lighthearted adventure. One thing of which we can be quite sure is that nobody in the Soviet Union looks forward with enthusiasm to fighting World War II over again, with or without nuclear weapons.

The words with which Pipes intends to scare us, "victory . . . superiority . . . offensive action," are precisely the goals which the Russians achieved, after immense efforts and sacrifices, at the end of World War II. If, as Pipes correctly states, Soviet strategy is still dominated by the lessons learned in World War II, it is difficult to see what other goals than these the Soviet armed forces should be expected to pursue. Pipes makes these goals sound frightening by placing them in a misleading juxtaposition with American strategic concepts taken from a different context: "not deterrence but victory, not sufficiency in weapons but superiority, not retaliation but offensive action." The American strategy of deterrence, sufficiency, and retaliation is a purely nuclear strategy having nothing to do with war as it has been waged in the past. The Soviet strategy of victory, superiority, and offensive action is a continuation of the historical process by which Russia over the centuries repelled invaders from her territory. Both strategies have advantages and disadvantages. Neither is aggressive in intention. Both are to me equally frightening, because both make the survival of civilization depend on people behaving reasonably.

The central problem for the Soviet military leadership is to preserve the heritage of World War II against oblivion, to transmit that heritage intact to future generations of soldiers who never saw the invader's boot tramping over Russian soil. Soviet strategists know well what nuclear weapons can do. They are familiar with the American style of nuclear strategic calculus, which treats nuclear war as a mathematical exercise with the result depending only on the numbers and capabilities of weapons on each side. Soviet generals can do such calculations as well as we can. But they do not believe the answers. The heritage of World War II tells them that wars are fought by people, not by weapons, that morale is in the end more important than equipment, that it is easy to calculate how a war will begin but impossible to calculate how it will end. The primary concern of all Soviet strategic writing that I have seen is to make sure that the lessons of World War II are well learned and never forgotten by the rising generation of Soviet citizens. These lessons which the agonies of World War II stamped indelibly into Russian minds were confirmed by the later experience of the United States in Vietnam. A Russian acquaintance once asked me how it happened that American nuclear strategists appeared to have learned nothing from the lessons of Vietnam. I had to reply that the reason they learned nothing was probably because they did not fight in Vietnam themselves. If they had fought in Vietnam, they would have learned to distrust any strategic theory which counts only weapons and discounts human courage and tenacity.

Tolstoy's *War and Peace* is the classic statement of the Russian view of war. Tolstoy understood, perhaps more deeply than anyone else, the nature of war as Russia experienced it. He fought with the Russian army at Sevastopol. He spent some of his happiest years as an artillery cadet on garrison duty in the Caucasus. In *War and Peace* he honored the courage and steadfastness of the ordinary Russian soldiers who defeated Napoleon in spite of the squabbles and blunders of their commanders. He drew from the campaign of 1812 the same lessons which a later generation of soldiers drew from the campaigns of World War II. He saw war as a desperate improvisation, in which nothing goes according to plan and the historical causes of victory and defeat remain incalculable.

Tolstoy's thoughts about war and victory are expressed by his hero Prince Andrei on the eve of the battle of Borodino. Andrei is talking to his friend Pierre.

> "To my mind what is before us to-morrow is this: a hundred thousand Russian and a hundred thousand French troops have met to fight, and the fact is that these two hundred thousand men will fight, and the side that fights most desperately and spares itself least will conquer. And if you like, I'll tell you that whatever happens, and whatever mess they make up yonder, we shall win the battle to-morrow; whatever happens we shall win the victory."
> "So you think the battle to-morrow will be a victory," said Pierre. "Yes, yes," said Prince Andrei absently. "There's one thing I would do, if I were in power," he began again, "I wouldn't take prisoners. What sense is there in taking prisoners? That's chivalry. The French have destroyed my home and are coming to destroy Moscow; they have outraged and are outraging me at

every second. They are my enemies, they are all criminals to my way of
thinking. . . . They must be put to death. . . . War is not a polite recreation,
but the vilest thing in life, and we ought to understand that and not play at
war. We ought to accept it sternly and solemnly as a fearful necessity.''

The battle was duly fought, and Prince Andrei was mortally
wounded. The Russians lost, according to the generally accepted meaning of the word ''lose'': half of the Russian army was destroyed; after
the battle the Russians retreated and the French advanced. And yet, in
the long view, Prince Andrei was right. Russia's defeat at Borodino was
a strategic victory. Napoleon's army was so mauled that it had no stomach for another such battle. Napoleon advanced to Moscow, stayed
there for five weeks waiting for the Czar to sue for peace, and then fled
with his disintegrating army in its disastrous stampede to the West.
''Napoleon,'' concludes Tolstoy, ''is represented to us as the leader in
all this movement, just as the figurehead in the prow of a ship to the
savage seems the force that guides the ship on its course. Napoleon in
his activity all this time was like a child, sitting in a carriage, pulling
the straps within it, and fancying he is moving it along.''

The fundamental divergence between American and Soviet strategic
concepts lies in the fact that American strategy demands certainty
while Soviet strategy accepts uncertainty as inherent in the nature of
war. The American objectives—deterrence, sufficiency, and retaliation—are supposed to be guaranteed by the deployment of a suitable
variety of invulnerable weapons. The name of the American nuclear
strategy is ''assured destruction,'' with emphasis upon the word
''assured.'' Any hint of doubt concerning the assurance of retaliation
creates consternation in the minds of American strategists and even in
the minds of ordinary American citizens. This demand for absolute
assurance of retaliation is the main driving force on the American side
of the nuclear arms race. Soviet strategists, on the other hand, consider
the quest for certainty in war to be a childish delusion. The Soviet strategic objectives—victory, superiority, and offensive action—are goals
to be striven for, not conditions to be guaranteed. These objectives cannot be assured by any fixed quantity of weapons, and they remain valid
even when they are not assured. Soviet strategy sees war as essentially
unpredictable, and the objectives as dimly visible through chaos and
fog.

Richard Pipes's statement, ''The Soviet Union thinks it could fight
and win a nuclear war,'' while literally true, does not have the dire
implications which Americans are inclined to impute to it. It does not
mean that the Soviet high command has a plan for attacking the
United States with a calculable assurance of victory. It means that the
Soviet leaders have an intuitive confidence, based on their historical
experience, in the ability of the Soviet armed forces and population to
withstand whatever devastation may be inflicted upon them and ulti-

mately to defeat and destroy whoever attacks them. This confidence of the Soviet leaders in the superior endurance and discipline of their own people is not based upon calculation. It is not a threat to American security. Hard as it may be for Americans to accept, the confidence of the Russian people in their ability to survive the worst that we can do to them is a stabilizing influence which it is to our advantage to preserve. The demand for survival is the main driving force on the Soviet side of the arms race. Insofar as we undermine the confidence of the Soviet leaders in the ability of their people to endure and survive, we are forcing them to drive their side of the arms race harder.

Because of the divergent views of American and Soviet strategists concerning the nature of nuclear war and the possibility of technical assurance, American and Soviet strategic objectives are strictly incommensurable. It is natural for Americans to believe that the American objective of deterrence is more reasonable or more modest than the Soviet objective of victory. But the objective of deterrence comes with a demand for absolute assurance, while the objective of victory comes, if at all, only at the end of a long road of incalculable chances and immense suffering. From a Soviet viewpoint, the objective of victory may be considered the more modest, since it is based only on hope and faith while the objective of deterrence is based on calculated threats. It is futile to expect that we can convert the Soviet military leaders to our way of thinking or that they can convert us to theirs. Our different ways of thinking are deeply rooted in our different historical experiences. We do not need to think alike in order to survive together on this planet. We need only to understand that it is possible to think differently and to respect each other's points of view.

Act II, from End of the World

Arthur Kopit

(Lights up on JIM and PETE)

TRENT.   I will call them Jim and Pete. *(We are in JIM's kitchen.)* Both were connected with the Harley Corporation, a government think tank in nearby Virginia. *(PETE and JIM are preparing a meal—tiny birds stuffed, seasoned, wrapped in gauze, cooked in a microwave.)* But the place was off-limits to plain ol' folk like me, so they very graciously invited me to Jim's house, though perhaps it was Pete's, I was never altogether sure—*one* of theirs. For a meal in my honor. Why had they gone to all this trouble for me? Something was very odd.

JIM.   *(while working at the meal)* So you talked with Stanley Berent!

PETE.   *(also, while working at the meal)* Bet *that* was fun!

TRENT.   He poked a lot of holes in our deterrence strategy.

JIM.   I'm sure he was right, it's not hard to do. *(They work in tandem on the meal; lots of coordinated teamwork.)*

PETE.   There's a curious paradox built into deterrence strategy, and no one has a *clue* how to get around it. The paradox is this: deterrence is dependent upon strength—well that's obvious; the stronger your nuclear arsenal, the more the other side's deterred. *However!* Should deterrence *fail,* for any reason, your strength *instantly* becomes your greatest liability, *inviting* attack *instead* of preventing it.

JIM.   HOIST on your own petard!

PETE.   And *that* is where all these crazy scenarios come in, in which war breaks out PRECISELY because *no one* WANTS it to! Really! I'm not kidding. This business is *filled* with paradox! Here, I'll run one by you.

JIM.   I think, before you do, we should point out, it isn't *easy starting* a nuclear war.

PETE.   Right! Sorry. Getting carried away.

JIM.   In fact, we can run scenario after scenario—the Persian Gulf is the most popular. That's the hot spot!

PETE.   People just will not go nuclear.

JIM.   Right! And at first, it absolutely drove us up the wall! Here we had all these tests designed to see what happens when people go nuclear?

PETE.   And no one would do it!

JIM.   To the man, they just refused to believe there wasn't some other way to resolve the crisis!

PETE.   Well, the military started freaking out.

JIM.   They figured all those guys down in the silos—maybe they won't push the button when they're told.

PETE.   Real freak-out scene.

JIM.   The whole Pentagon—

PETE.   They just went bananas! *Total* banana scene.

JIM.   Some general called me up. He said, "You incompetent jackass, what the hell kind of scenario are you *giving* these guys?" I said, "We're giving 'em every scenario we can think of, SIR! No one'll push the button, SIR!" You know what he said?

PETE.   Get this!—"Don't tell 'em it's the button!"

JIM.   "Really!" we said, "Then what good's the test?"

PETE.   Anyway, happy ending.

JIM.   Finally, we solved it.

PETE.   *You* solved it.

JIM.   *I* solved it, *you* solved it, what's it matter? We *solved* the thing!

PETE.   What a bitch!

JIM.   People think it's *easy* starting a nuclear war?

PETE.   Hey! Let 'em try!

TRENT.   Okay, I'll bite: how *do* you start a nuclear war?

JIM.   Well *first*, you have to assume that a nuclear war is the *last* thing either side wants.

PETE.   Right! That's the key! Who would've thought it! Jim?

JIM.   Okay. Let's say we're in a confrontation situation where we and the Soviets are facing down in the Middle East: let's say Iran. Big Soviet pour-down. Let's further say we're losing conventionally on the ground—

PETE.   Not hard to believe—

JIM.   —and the President decides he wants the option of using nuclear weapons in the area, so he moves them in.

PETE.   Mind you, he doesn't want to *use* them now.

JIM.   Right! Absolutely not! Last thing he wants!

PETE.   He's just hoping by showing strength, the Soviets will re-think their position and pull back.

JIM.   In other words, it's a *bluff*.

PETE.   Right, good ol' poker bluff!

JIM.   And by the way, probably the proper move to make.

PETE.   Now, at the *same* time, we ask our NATO allies to join us in raising the military alert level in Europe. Why? We want to tie the Soviet forces down that are in Eastern Europe.

JIM.   Again, absolutely the right move.

PETE.   So far, the President's batting a thousand. No appeasement here. Yet, not too strong, nothing precipitous.

JIM.   Okay. The Soviets now go to a higher level of readiness them-selves. Why? They want to tie *our* forces down so *we* don't shift 'em to the Middle East.

PETE.   Now we start to move nuclear weapons out of storage! *(He mimics the sound of a trumpet.)*

JIM.   Okay, now, let's suppose the Soviets, in the heat of this crisis, *misinterpret* the moves we've made, and believe that in fact we're about to *launch* these weapons! Not a farfetched supposition!

PETE.   Particularly, given their tendency to paranoia!

JIM.   Right!

PETE.   Okay. Now at *this* point, the issue for them is *not* do they want to be *in* a war.

JIM.   They're already *in* a war in the Middle East!

PETE.   Right. The issue isn't even, do they want to launch a nuclear attack against the West.

JIM.   That's because they know they'll HAVE to if the West attacks *them!*

PETE.   You see?

JIM.   *The only issue—*

PETE.   Absolutely ONLY issue—!

JIM.   —is: do they want to go *first*, and *pre-empt* this attack?

PETE.   Or wait it out—

JIM.   —and go second.

PETE.   Now, they recognize, just as much as we . . .

JIM.   That going *first*—?

PETE.   —is going *best*.

JIM.   Right!

PETE.   And by a shocking margin, too. No scenario *ever* shows ANY-THING else! I mean, these notions of us riding out a nuclear attack and then launching again, without substantial loss of capability, well it's nonsense.

JIM.   By the way, you have to posit here that events are moving rapidly. A short time-frame is crucial to this scenario. No time to sit back and say, "Hey! wait, why would he want to shoot at me? I know he's in trouble, but he isn't crazy!" No. He doesn't have *time* to think things out. He's got to make a move! Okay. What's he do? *(PETE makes the gesture and sound of a missile taking off.)* He shoots. Now, are we saying it's a likely thing? No. But, from the Soviet perspective, they HAVE to shoot. Under these conditions, holding back is clearly wrong, politically and militarily.

PETE.   And *that*—!

JIM.   —is how a nuclear war begins.

PETE.   Not out of anger.

JIM.   Or greed.

PETE.   But *fear!*

JIM.   With neither side *wanting* to.

PETE.   Yet, each side *having* to.

JIM.   'Cause the other guy thinks they're *going* to.

PETE.   So they'd better.

PETE and JIM.   *(together, a la W. C. Fields)* HOIST ON OUR OWN PETARD!

JIM.   By the way, where *is* the petard?

PETE.   *(tossing a jar of mustard)* Petard!

JIM.   *(catching it)* Petard!

PETE and JIM.   *(together, a la W. C. Fields)* Ahhh yes!

TRENT.   You guys are a scream.

JIM.   Actually,—should we tell him?

PETE.   Sure.

JIM.   Actually, over at the center, we all try to scream at least once a day.

PETE.   Usually it happens in the cafeteria.

JIM.   Someone on the staff will stand up and shout "SCREAMIN' TIME!" And everyone just, you know . . . *(JIM gives a choked comic scream.)*

PETE.   It's a ritual we only do when no one from the Pentagon's around.

JIM.   We did it once when some honcho military brass were there?

PETE.   *Freaked them out!*

JIM.   Within minutes we had lost, I don't know *how* many grants! *(He laughs.)*

PETE.   So, anyway, now we're pretty choosey 'bout who we scream in front of.

JIM.   I'll tell you, . . . I sometimes think, if it really happens, and we all, you know . . . *(He makes the sound and gesture of a giant explosion.)* . . . and by the way, the whole thing *could* be over! No matter what anybody says, no one knows *what* happens to the ozone layer in a nuclear war. Really! No idea! *(He laughs.)* Okay, so I sometimes think, now it's all over, and we're all up there in the big de-briefing space in the sky, and the good Lord decides to hold a symposium 'cause he's curious: how did this thing happen? And everybody says, "Hey, don't look at me, I didn't wanna do it!" The end result being that everyone realizes *no* one wanted to do it! But there was suddenly no choice. Or no choice they could *see.* And the symposium gets nowhere.

TRENT.   How do we get out of this?

PETE.   Well, you try like hell to not get *into* these kinds of conflicts!

JIM.   Obviously, sometimes it can't be helped.

TRENT.   This is not pleasant news.

PETE.   *(putting the birds into the microwave)* On the other hand, let's not exaggerate. Things are not that bad, maybe we *shouldn't* get out of it. *(with a laugh, to JIM)* Would you not love to have a snapshot of this man's expression? *(JIM mimes taking a snapshot of TRENT.)*

TRENT.   So you mean we're just supposed to sit around, twiddle our thumbs, and WAIT?

PETE.   Well, . . .

JIM.   Sometimes, . . . there's really not an awful lot you *can* do.

PETE.   Except *hold on.*

JIM.   And hope for some kind of discontinuity.

PETE.   Right.

TRENT.   Ah! Discontinuity! What the hell is that?

PETE.   It's an event . . . by definition unpredictable, which causes a sudden and radical shift in the general mode of thinking.

JIM.   Sadat's going to Jeruselum is the prime example.

PETE.   Sadat looked down the road and saw nuclear weapons in Cairo and Alexandria in maybe five, ten years, and he just didn't like what he saw.

JIM.   So he decided he was gonna do something about it.

PETE.   And what he decided to do no one, I mean *no* one anticipated.

JIM.   And it changed the whole ball game.

PETE.   *Just like that!*

JIM.   And THAT—!

PETE.   —is a discontinuity.

TRENT.   Okay! all right! . . . any candidates?

PETE.   Well, I'd say the best we've come up with so *far* is . . . *(He looks to JIM for help.)*

JIM.   *(to PETE)* Extraterrestrial?

PETE.   Ya. *(to TRENT)* Extraterrestrial.

TRENT.   *(stunned)* You mean, like E.T. comes down?

PETE.   You got it!

TRENT.   Jesus Christ!

JIM.   That's another!

TRENT.   You guys are a riot!

JIM.   Hey! In this business? Important to keep smiling.

TRENT.   No, I can see that. Listen, have you guys given any real thoughts to, you know, touring the country? Night clubs, things like that?

PETE.   Oh sure, it's occurred to us.

TRENT.   I'm sure it has.

JIM.   People are very interested in this nuclear issue.

PETE.   And we're right there at the dirty heart of it!

TRENT.   Good. Listen, while we're on the subject of humor, what's your attitude towards doom?

PETE.   . . . "Doom?" *(PETE looks at JIM. JIM looks at PETE.)*

JIM.   It's just no solution.

PETE.   No. No solution.

TRENT.   I'm being serious!

PETE and JIM.   *(together)* So are we! *(They smile at TRENT.)*

(Blackout on JIM and PETE. TRENT turns to the audience. Music: "Trent's Theme.")

TRENT.   Okay. Even with *my* lousy sinuses I could tell something wasn't smelling right. I figured it was *my* fault. What've I missed? I decided to retrace my steps.

Copyright Acknowledgments

p. 4   G.L. Carefoot and E.R. Sprott. *Famine on the Wind.* Pp. 76–77. Copyright © New York: Rand McNally & Co., 1967. Reprinted with permission.

p. 5   W.R. Aykroyd, C.B.E., late Director of the Nutrition Division of the Food and Agriculture Organization of the United Nations. *The Conquest of Famine.* 1974. P. 36. Reprinted with permission of F.K. Aykroyd, Woodstock, Oxford. England

p. 6   John Kenneth Galbraith. *Age of Uncertainty.* P. 38. Copyright © 1977 by John Kenneth Galbraith. Reprinted by permission of Houghton Mifflin Company.

p. 30   George Orwell. "Awake! Young Men of England." Reprinted by permission of the Estate of the late Sonia Brownell Orwell.

p. 30   Wilfred Owen. "Dulce et Decorum Est." From *War Poems and Others* by permission of the estate of Wilfred Owen and Chatto & Windus.

p. 38   Paul Waztlawick. *How Real Is Real?* Copyright © New York: Random House, 1977. Pp. 7–8. Reprinted by permission.

p. 50 Gilbert Highet. *Talents and Geniuses.* Pp. 225–226. Reprinted with permission of Curtis Brown, Ltd. Copyright © 1957.

p. 52   Viktor E. Frankl. *Man's Search for Meaning.* Pp. 26–27. Copyright © 1959, 1962, 1984 by Viktor E. Frankl. Reprinted by permission of Beacon Press.

p. 53   Kenneth Burke. *Rhetoric of Motives.* Berkeley, CA: University of California Press, 1973. Pp. 10–11. Copyright © 1950 Prentice Hall, 1969, Kenneth Burke. Reprinted with permission of University of California Press.

p. 66   From Robert M. Pirsig. *Zen and the Art of Motorcycle Maintenance.* Pp. 191–192. Copyright © 1974 by Robert Pirsig. Reprinted by permission of William Morrow & Company.

p. 85   Jurgen Friedrichs and Harmut Ludtke. "The observation of an incident by three individuals" (figure). Reprinted by permission of the publisher, from *Participant Observation: Theory and Practice.* Lexington, MA: Lexington Books, D.C. Heath & Company, copyright © 1975, D.C. Heath and Company.

p. 91   A.R. Luria. *Cognitive Development.* Pp. 55–56. Harvard University Press. 1978. Reprinted by permission.

p. 91   A.R. Luria. "Geometrical figures presented to subjects" (figure). *Cognitive Development.* Harvard University Press, 1978. Reprinted by permission.

p. 103   Bronislaw Malinowski. From *Argonauts of the Western Pacific.* First published, 1961, by E.P. Dutton. All rights reserved. Reprinted by permission of the publisher, E.P. Dutton, a division of NAL Penguin. Pp. 55–56.

p. 105   Jean Briggs. *Never in Anger: Portrait of an Eskimo Family.* Harvard University Press. Pp. 25–26. Copyright © 1970 by The President and Fellows of Harvard College. Reprinted by permission.

p. 108   Margaret Mead. *Growing Up in New Guinea.* P. 19. Copyright © 1930, 1958, 1962 by Margaret Mead. Reprinted by permission of William Morrow & Company.

p. 109   Paul Engle. "Iowa State Fair." *Holiday.* (March, 1975). Reprinted by permission of *Travel/Holiday Magazine.*

p. 125 Odis E. Bigus. "The Milkman and His Customer." *Urban Life and Culture.* Vol. 1. No. 2 (July, 1972), pp. 131–132. Copyright © 1972. Reprinted by permission of Sage Publications, Inc.

p. 137 Elliot Liebow. *Tally's Corner: A Study of Negro Streetcorner Men.* Pp. 21–22; 24–25; 31–32; 54–55. Copyright © 1967 by Little, Brown, and Company (Inc.). By permission of Little, Brown, and Company.

p. 146 From Bronislaw Malinowski. *Argonauts of the Western Pacific.* First published, 1961, by E.P. Dutton. All rights reserved. Reprinted by permission of the publisher, E.P. Dutton, a division of NAL Penguin. Pp. 88–89.

p. 149 Dian Fossey. *Gorillas in the Mist.* Pp. 68 and 69. Copyright © 1983 by Dian Fossey. Reprinted with permission by Houghton Mifflin Company.

p. 151 W.J.J. Gordon. *Synectics.* 1961. Pp. 54–56. Reprinted by permission of W.J.J. Gordon, SES Associates, 121 Brattle, Cambridge, MA. 02138.

p. 155 James Adams. *Conceptual Blockbusting*, p. 113. Copyright 1974, 1976, 1979. Reading, Massachusetts: Addison-Wesley Publishing Co. Reprinted with permission.

p. 169 Mickey Kaus. Review of Greenberger and Steinberg, *When Teenagers Work* in *New York Times Book Review.* October 26, 1986, p. 30. Copyright © 1986 by The New York Times Company. Reprinted by permission.

p. 169 John Noble Wilford. Review of Bakker, *Dinosaur Heresies* in *New York Times Book Review.* October 26, 1986, p. 14. Copyright © 1986 by The New York Times Company. Reprinted by permission.

p. 170 Oliver Sacks. Review of Wallace, *Silent Twins* in *New York Times Book Review.* October 19, 1986, p. 3. Copyright © 1986 by The New York Times Company. Reprinted by permission.

p. 198 Charles W. Kegley and Eugene R. Wittkopf, eds., *The Nuclear Reader: Strategy, Weapons, War.* Pp. 12–13. Copyright © 1985 by St. Martin's Press and used with publisher's permission.

p. 207 Daniel Goldstine. "Better than Pleasure." Book review of Willard Gaylin's *Rediscovering Love*, in *New York Times Book Review*, October 12, 1986, p. 45. Copyright © 1986 by The New York Times Company. Reprinted by permission.

p. 256 Louis A. Zurcher. *The Mutable Self.* Pp. 25–26. Copyright © 1977 by Sage Publications, Inc. Reprinted by permission of Sage Publications.

p. 257 Ruth C. Wylie. *The Self Concept: A Review of Methodological Considerations and Measuring Instruments.* Published by University of Nebraska Press, 1974.

p. 259 Erich Fromm. *The Art of Loving.* P. 59. Copyright © 1956, Harper and Row Publishers, Inc. Reprinted by permission.

p. 260 Mary Midgley, formerly Senior Lecturer in Philosophy, University of Newcastle-on-Tyne; author of *Beast and Man.* "Head, Hearts and Words." Unpublished address delivered at the Pacific Northwest Writing Consortium Conference, 1982. Reprinted by permission.

p. 265 Rich Hall and Friends. *Sniglets.* Reprinted with permission of Macmillan Publishing Company from *Sniglets* by Rich Hall and Friends. Copyright © 1984 Not the Network Company.

p. 273 Stephen Jay Gould. *Mismeasure of Man.* P. 166. Reprinted by permission of W.W. Norton and Company, Inc. Copyright © 1981 by Stephen Jay Gould.

p. 338 From Jules R. Benjamin. *A Student's Guide to History.* Third edition. Pp. 33–39. Copyright 1983. New York: St. Martin's Press. Reprinted with permission.

p. 343 From Susan Griffin. "Thoughts on Writing: A Diary." Reprinted from *The Writer on Her Work.* Pp. 111–113. Edited by Janet Sternburg, by permission of W.W. Norton & Company, Inc. Copyright © 1980 by Janet Sternburg.

p. 345   From Jurgen Friedrichs and Harmut Ludkte. *Participant Observation: Theory and Practice.* Pp. 113–116; 120–126. Reprinted by permission of the publisher, from *Participant Observation: Theory and Practice.* Lexington, MA: Lexington Books, D.C. Heath & Company, copyright © 1975, D.C. Heath and Company.

p. 352   From Francis Parkman. *The Oregon Trail Journal—1846.* Ed. Mason Wade, *The Journals of Francis Parkman.* Vol. II. Pp. 439–443. Copyright © 1947 Harper & Brothers Publishers.

p. 359   Clayton A. Robarchek. Department of Anthropology. Wichita State University, Wichita, Kansas. "9/25/74: Observations of a Storm in a Semai (Malaysia) Village." Unpublished journal. Reprinted by permission.

p. 361   Carole Robarchek. "9/25/74: Observations of a Storm in a Semai (Malaysia) Village." Unpublished journal. Reprinted by permission.

p. 362   From Clayton A. Robarchek. "Learning to Fear: A Case Study of Emotional Conditioning." Reproduced by permission of the American Anthropological Association from *American Ethnologist* 6:3, 1979. Not for further reproduction.

p. 368   From John Kenneth Galbraith. *Ambassador's Journal: A Personal Account of the Kennedy Years.* Pp. 225–299. Copyright © 1969 by John Kenneth Galbraith. Reprinted by permission of Houghton Mifflin Company.

p. 374   "May 26 1969 memo from H.R. Haldeman re: bowling balls." *The Hazards of Walking and Other Memos from Your Bureaucrats.* P. 3. Edited by Carol Trueblood and Donna Fenn. Copyright © 1982 by the Washington Monthly Company. Reprinted by permission of Houghton Mifflin Company.

p. 374   Christina Mohr. Student, Wichita State University, Wichita, Kansas. "Garage Sales." Reprinted by permission.

p. 377   Donald Blakeslee. Department of Anthropology. The Wichita State University, Wichita, Kansas. "Comment on Schwartz." The publication in which this comment originally appeared asked that we omit the name of the author who wrote the article upon which Dr. Blakeslee comments. The name "Schwartz" is a pseudonym.

p. 379   From Francine Frank and Frank Anshen. "Guidelines for Non-Discriminatory Language Use." *Language and the Sexes.* Pp. 107–114. Reprinted from *Language and the Sexes* by Francine Frank and Frank Anshen by permission of the State Unviersity of New York Press. Copyright © SUNY, 1983.

p. 386   Ted Slupesky. Student, Reed College, Portland, Oregon. "Radical Masculinism: Women in Book VI of the Aeneid." Reprinted by permission.

p. 390   Dr. Ellen K. Stauder, Reed College, Portland Oregon. Comment on "Radical Masculinism." Reprinted by permission.

p. 391   Debora B. Robertson. Student, Reed College, Portland, Oregon. "No-Man on an Island: Odysseus and the Kyklops." Reprinted by permission.

p. 396   Dr. Robert Knapp, Reed College, Portland Oregon. Comment on "No Man on an Island." Reprinted by permission.

p. 397   From *The Confessions of St. Augustine.* Book II, pp. 26–30. Copyright © 1968. New York, New York: Airmont Publishing Co., Inc. Reprinted with permission.

p. 400   From René Descartes. "Meditation II: Of the Nature of the Human Mind; and That It Is More Easily Known Than the Body." *Descartes: Selections.* Ed. and trans., Ralph M. Eaton. Pp. 95–105. Copyright © Charles Scribner's Sons, 1927; copyright © renewed 1955, Charles Scribner's Sons, an imprint of Macmillan Publishing Company.

608 *Copyright Acknowledgments*

p. 403 From Loren Eiseley, "The Slit." *The Immense Journey.* Pp. 2–14. Copyright © 1957 by Loren Eiseley. Reprinted from *The Immense Journey* by Loren Eiseley, by permission of Random House, Inc.

p. 406 From N. Scott Momaday, *The Way to Rainy Mountain.* First published in *The Reporter,* 26 January, 1967. Reprinted form *The Way to Rainy Mountain.* Copyright © 1969, The University of New Mexico Press.

p. 410 From E.B. White. "Once More to the Lake." *Essays of E.B. White* Pp. 197–202. Harper & Row. Copyright © 1977 by E.B. White.

p. 413 From Susan Bordo. "Anorexia Nervosa: Psychopathology as the Crystallization of Culture." *The Philosophical Forum.* Volume 17. No. 2 (Winter, 1985–86). Pp. 73–104. Reprinted with permission.

p. 434 Barbara Mellix. "From the Outside, In." Originally appeared in *The Georgia Review,* Volume XLI. No. 2 (Summer, 1987). Reprinted by permission of Barbara Mellix and *The Georgia Review.*

p. 445 From Francine Frank and Frank Anshen. "Talking Like a Lady: How Women Talk." *Language and the Sexes.* Pp. 25–50. Reprinted from *Language and the Sexes* by Francine Frank and Frank Anshen by permission of the State University of New York Press. Copyright © SUNY, 1983.

p. 448 From David McKenzie. "Poker and Pop: Collegiate Gambling Groups." Reprinted from *The Participant Observer* by Glen Jacobs, ed. by permission of George Braziller, Inc. New York. Copyright © 1970, George Braziller, Inc. Pp. 161–178.

p. 456 Mindy Cohen. Student, Hobart and William Smith Colleges, Geneva, New York. "Socializing and Studying in the Library's Smoking Room." Reprinted by permission.

p. 461 From David A. Karp. "Observing Behavior in Public Places: Problems and Strategies." From *Fieldwork Experience: Qualitative Approaches to Social Research* by William Shaffir, Robert A. Stebbins, and Allan Turowetz, copyright © 1980 by St. Martin's Press and used with permission. Pp. 82–97.

p. 470 Kim Smith. Student, Wichita State University, Wichita, Kansas. "My Experience as a Fieldworker." Reprinted by permission.

p. 471 Dan Gegen. Student, Wichita State University, Wichita, Kansas. "Similarities of an Observation."

p. 473 From Margaret Mead. *Coming of Age in Samoa.* Pp. 14–19. Copyright © 1928, 1955, 1961 by Margaret Mead. Reprinted by permission of William Morrow & Company.

p. 476 Adapted from *Tally's Corner: A Study of Negro Streetcorner Men* by Elliot Liebow. Copyright © 1967 by Little, Brown, and Company (Inc.). By permission of Little, Brown, and Company. Pp. 28–53.

p. 483 Excerpted from David L. Rosenhan. "On Being Sane in Insane Places." *Science.* Vol. 179, pp. 250–(8), 19 January, 1973. Copyright © 1973 by the AAAS. Reprinted by permission by the publisher and the author.

p. 497 Richard Borshay Lee. "Eating Christmas in the Kalahari." With permission from *Natural History.* Vol. 78. No. 10. Copyright © 1969 The American Museum of Natural History.

p. 504 From Pat Shipman. "The Hard Part Was the Hard Parts." Copyright © *Discover Magazine,* 2/86. Reprinted by permission.

p. 509 From Robert K. Colwell. "Stowaways on the Hummingbird Express." Pp. 57–62. With permission from *Natural History.* Vol. 84. No. 7; Copyright © the American Museum of Natural History, 1985.

p. 516 George F. Kennan. "A Proposal for International Disarmament." *The Nuclear Delusion: Soviet-American Relations in the Atomic Age.* Pantheon Books, 1976. Pp. 175–182.

p. 524 Ho Chi Minh, "Declaration of Independence of the Democratic Republic of Viet-Nam, September 2, 1945." *Ho Chi Minh on Revolution: Selected Writings, 1920–66.* Pp. 143–145. Edited by Bernard B. Fall. 1967. Reprinted by permission of Dorothy Fall, Washington, D.C.

p. 530 From *Crito* from *The Last Days of Socrates* by Plato, translated by Hugh Tredennick (Penguin Classics, 1954, 1959), copyright © Hugh Tredennick, 1954, 1959, pp. 79–96. Reprinted by permission.

p. 539 From Martin Luther King, Jr., "Letter from Birmingham Jail." *Why We Can't Wait.* Harper & Row Co.

p. 545 Marvin Harris. "Riddle of the Pig." Pp. 208–209. With permission from *Natural History* Vol. 81. No. 8. Copyright © The American Museum of Natural History, 1972.

p. 548 From Mary Douglas. "The Abominations of Leviticus" from *Purity and Danger: An Analysis of Concepts of Pollution and Taboo.* Pp. 54–72. 1966. Reprinted by permission of Routledge & Kegan Paul Plc.

p. 554 From Margaret Mead. *Coming of Age in Samoa.* Pp. 158–84. Copyright © 1928, 1955, 1961 by Margaret Mead. Reprinted by permission of William Morrow & Company.

p. 561 From Derek Freeman. "Adolescence." *Margaret Mead and Samoa.* Pp. 254–267. Reprinted by permission from *Margaret Mead and Samoa: The Making & Unmaking of an Anthropological Myth,* by Derek Freeman, Cambridge, Mass: Harvard University Press, Copyright © 1983 by Derek Freeman.

p. 566 Lowell D. Holmes. "South Sea Squall." This article is reprinted by permission of *The Sciences* and is from the July/August 1983 issue (pp. 224–227).

p. 573 Daniel Goleman. "Major Personality Study Finds That Traits Are Mostly Inherited." *New York Times,* December 12, 1986. Copyright © 1986 by The New York Times Company. Reprinted by permission.

pp. 577; 580 From George Orwell. *Nineteen Eighty-Four.* Copyright © 1949 by Harcourt, Brace, Jovanovich, Inc.; renewed 1977 by Sonia Brownell Orwell. Reprinted by permission of the publisher.

pp. 584; 586 From Irving L. Janis. *Groupthink: Psychological Studies of Policy Decisions and Fiascoes.* 2nd Edition. Pp. vii; 7–9. Copyright © 1982 by Houghton Mifflin Company. Used by permission.

p. 590 From Freeman Dyson. *Weapons and Hope.* Pp. 181–191. Copyright © 1984 by Freeman Dyson. Reprinted by permission of Harper & Row, Publishers, Inc.

p. 598 From Arthur Kopit. *End of the World.* Copyright © 1984 by Arthur Kopit. Reprinted by permission of Hill and Wang, a division of Farrar, Straus, and Giroux, Inc.

Name Index

Adams, James L., 154
Anshen, Frank, 79, 327, 379–386, 445–448
Aquinas, Saint Thomas, 224–225, 227
Aristotle, 224–225
Augustine, Saint, 58–59, 133–134, 141, 303–304, 397–399
Aykroyd, W. R., 5, 9–11

Baerends, G. P., 148
Bakker, Robert T., 169
Barrett, Richard A., 71, 74
Benjamin, Jules R., 283, 338–342
Bigus, Odis, 125–126
Binet, Alfred, 270–276
Blair, Eric (pseud. George Orwell), 31–35, 41, 68, 263–264, 577–580, 580–584
Blakeslee, Donald J., 76, 171, 323, 377–379
Bordo, Susan, 62, 64, 301–303, 306, 413–434
Brandon, Nathaniel, 260
Briggs, Jean, 105–106
Brigham, C. C., 276–277
Bruner, Jerome, 87
Burke, Kenneth, 53

Carefoot, G. L., 4
Carroll, Lewis. *See* Dodgson, Charles
Chase, Alan, 270
Clairbourne, Robert, 94
Cohen, Mindy, 79, 456–461
Colwell, Robert K., 147–148, 219–220, 509–514

Copernicus, Nicholas, 150
Crito, 193

Descartes, René, 57–59, 89–90, 400–403
Dickens, Charles, 50–51, 106, 111
Dodgson, Charles (pseud. Lewis Carroll), 52
Douglas, Mary, 192–204, 233, 548–554
Draper, Theodore, 198–199
Dyson, Freeman, 230–231, 247, 261–262, 590–598

Edwards, R. Dudley, 8, 11
Eiseley, Loren, 63–65, 305, 403–406
Engle, Paul, 102–103, 109–111
Epstein, Seymour, 135

Fernea, Elizabeth Warnock, 110
Fossey, Dian, 149–150
Frank, Francine, 79, 327, 379–386, 445–448
Frankl, Victor, 52
Freeman, Derek, 72, 136, 193–194, 201–202, 208–212, 216, 233, 236, 561–566
Friedrichs, Jurgen, 84–85, 96, 345–352
Fromm, Erich, 259–260

Galbraith, John Kenneth, 5–6, 8, 10, 28–29, 285–286, 313, 368–373
Gallagher, Thomas, 8, 10–11
Gaylin, Willard, 207–208, 236
Gegen, Dan, 82, 153, 471–473

Subject Index